JOSEPH ELLICOTT.

PIONEER HISTORY

OF THE

HOLLAND PURCHASE

OF

WESTERN NEW YORK:

EMBRACING

SOME ACCOUNT OF THE ANCIENT REMAINS;

A BRIEF HISTORY OF

OUR IMMEDIATE PREDECESSORS, THE CONFEDERATED IROQUOIS, THEIR SYSTEM OF GOVERNMENT, WARS, ETC.— A SYNOPSIS OF COLONIAL HISTORY: SOME NOTICES OF THE BORDER WARS OF THE REVOLUTION:

AND A HISTORY OF

PIONEER SETTLEMENT

UNDER THE AUSPICES OF THE HOLLAND COMPANY;

INCLUDING

REMINISCENCES OF THE WAR OF 1812;

THE ORIGIN, PROGRESS AND COMPLETION OF THE

ERIE CANAL,

ETC. ETC. ETC.

BY O. TURNER.

BUFFALO:
PUBLISHED BY JEWETT, THOMAS & CO.:
GEO. H. DERBY & CO.

1850.

Land of Promise Edition, 2007
Printed in the United States of America
ISBN 1-60135-500-9

Entered according to act of Congress, in the year 1849, by O. TURNER, in the Clerk's Office of the District Court of the Northern District of New York.

JEWETT, THOMAS & CO.
STEREOTYPERS AND PRINTERS,
Buffalo, N. Y.

TO THE

SURVIVING PIONEERS

AND

DESCENDANTS OF PIONEERS,

OF THE

HOLLAND PURCHASE,

THIS WORK IS RESPECTFULLY INSCRIBED, BY

THE AUTHOR.

PREFACE.

READ THE PREFACE! A command that may be regarded as too imperative, and yet one that an author has some right to make, in consideration of the deep interest which he may be supposed to have in its observance. Having prepared an entertainment, as he is about to open the door to his guests, it is quite natural he should wish to pass them in with his own introduction.

First, as to the general plan of the work:—There may be readers of it who have anticipated a history more strictly local in its character, than they will find this. It was the original intention of the author to have commenced with the close of the Revolution, and traced settlement and its progress westward, very much as has been done, with the exception of a more extended detail. Upon proceeding to his task, however, after materials for it had been collected, the important consideration presented itself, that, although there existed, in detached forms, sketches of the earliest approaches of civilization to this region — of early colonization tending in this direction — of the French and Indian and French and English wars; the long contest for supremacy and dominion; the occupancy of that extraordinary race of men, the Jesuit Missionaries; the Border Wars of the Revolution; still, there was no history extant that connected all this, and furnished an unbroken chain of events allied to the region of Western New York, and especially the Holland Purchase. The distinguished historian, Mr. BANCROFT, was the first to draw from French sources any considerable amount of the history of French occupancy of the valley of the St. Lawrence, and the borders of our lakes and rivers; of the advents of Jesuit Missionaries, and their cotemporaries, the fur traders; and embellish his country's history with a long series of interesting events, before almost unnoticed. But little could be gathered by an humble local historian, after such a gleaner had passed over the ground; but his work is of a magnitude to preclude access to it, by the great mass of readers;

and that portion of it having reference to this region, but incidental to the general history of the United States. Aside from this, the early history of our region, embracing the periods and events alluded to, was to be found only in detached forms — much of it in old newspaper files and magazines — in conditions to make it generally inaccessible.

Having adopted the title, *Pioneer* History of the Holland Purchase, early events, the first glimpses that our own race had of this region, was indicated as the starting point; and taking position there, the necessity of going even still farther back, seemed involved. The ancient remains, the mysterious, rude fortifications upon the bluffs, ridges, and banks of streams, throughout our local region, form an interesting feature, and one that claimed a place in our local annals. Some account of our immediate predecessors, the Seneca Iroquois, was suggested as coming within the immediate range of local history; and especially as they were to be mingled in almost our entire narrative. All that relates to them possesses a peculiar interest; that which relates to the system of government of the confederacy to which they belong, is a branch of their history but recently investigated to any considerable extent; is far less generally understood than most things appertaining to them, and has therefore been made to occupy a prominent position in that portion of the work.*

As civilization approached this region, from that direction, colonization upon the St. Lawrence has necessarily been the main feature of that portion of the work having reference to European Pioneer advents. Enough, however, of early colonization elsewhere has been embraced, to afford a glimpse of cotemporary events; and especially such as finally had a bearing upon events in this quarter. Starting principally with the advent of CHAMPLAIN, a connected chain of events has been attempted, extending through long and eventful years, down to the extinguishing of the Indian title, the advent of the Holland Company, Pioneer settlement under their auspices, and the two prominent events, the war of 1812, and the construction of the Erie Canal, belonging to a later period. The title of the work, of itself, indicates its general character, and the intention of the author not to embrace events, generally, beyond early settlement,— *pioneer* advents. Another volume would have been necessary, had it been concluded to extend the work to a later period; and besides, as a

---

* The credit of a thorough investigation of this admirable specimen of Indian legislation — of unschooled forest statesmanship — and wisdom, if we regard its practical workings — belongs to LEWIS H. MORGAN, Esq. of Rochester, who communicated the result of his labors, in numbers, to the North American Review. In reading his essays, it is difficult to determine which most to admire, the careful and industrious researches of the author, in a matter so difficult to comprehend, with no records, and little beyond obscure tradition for his guides; or the zealous and lively feelings he manifests, in every thing that concerns the character and welfare of the unfortunate race whose interesting traditions he has aided in rescuing from oblivion.

general rule, public events should not assume the form of history, until time has ripened them for it; and especially such as have involved controversy, many of the prominent actors in which may survive — the asperities it engendered, unobliterated. A political history of the Holland Purchase, has formed no part of the plan of work; on the contrary, even allusions to partisan contentions have been mostly avoided. That should form a distinct branch of history; its appropriate alliance is with the general history of the state; and those who may desire to study it, have the means furnished them in the candid and impartial work of Judge HAMMOND.

The range of the work thus extended, its magnitude has been increased far beyond the original design. In adopting the general plan, there was a purpose to be subserved, in addition to those that have been named. Had the work been merely a history of settlement and local events upon the Holland Purchase, it must necessarily have been one of considerable magnitude — attended with an expense that any prospective local sale would not have warranted. It has therefore been the aim of the author, to impart to it both a local and general interest; how far he has been successful, time, and the ordeal to which he submits his labors, must determine. From the moment the general plan of the work was adopted, and its expense to the purchaser enhanced beyond the mark originally indicated, it has been the constant aim of the author to give it a corresponding value. It will be seen that little expense has been spared in its mechanical execution; and the author flatters himself that the twenty-two illustrations will be adequately appreciated by those who possess themselves of a copy of the work. The Maps of the eight Counties have been prepared by a competent hand, carefully adapted to localities as they now exist, and may be considered of themselves as having an intrinsic value, equal to any addition that has been made to the price of the work, from the lowest sum that has been named in connection with the enterprize; while the number of excellent Portraits of distinguished Pioneers, have been extended far beyond what was originally contemplated. The careful legal deduction of title in the Appendix, in addition to the historical deduction in the body of the work, will be found a valuable accession to law libraries, while it will aid the general reader in a better understanding of that subject, than can be obtained from any facilities hitherto furnished in a form of general access.

It is hardly necessary to inform the intelligent reader, that Mr. BANCROFT's History of the United States has been the basis of all that relates to French and English occupancy; though the author has been materially aided by LANMAN's History of Michigan, and BROWN's History of Illinois, both of which had traced events from the mouth of the St. Lawrence to their local regions; and he regards himself as somewhat fortunate, in having been enabled to add, from various sources, no inconsiderable amount of materials that have hitherto had no place in history, other than in the form of manuscript records, neglected newspaper files, or among the collections of Historical Societies.* If, as most historians are obliged to do, he has been under the necessity of culling his materials, in many instances, from fields already explored, he may, perhaps, without incurring the charge of egotism, assume that he has occasionally been enabled to bring fresh contributions to the common stock of historical knowledge.

There are those to whom the author is indebted for local statistics, who will miss a portion of their contributions. The omissions have been reluctantly made. To have carried out the plan of giving in detail, all that related to early county and town organizations, would have been to exclude large portions of the work that were deemed more essential, and it is hoped, will prove in the end quite as acceptable. It was intended, however, to have given sketches of the first organization of all the Counties; but that intention has been but imperfectly consummated, owing principally, to the absence of the necessary materials. The records of the primitive organization of the Courts, etc. of *old* Niagara, were inaccessible, owing to the condition in which the large mass of records were in, preparatory to a new arrangement of them, in the Clerk's office of Erie. The author unexpectedly failed in procuring the primitive records of Chautauque and Allegany.

It was a paramount object in giving sketches of the Pioneer settlement of the Holland Purchase, to embrace as many of the names, and as much of personal reminiscences, as practicable. To this end, the general plan was adopted, of giving a list of all who took contracts previous to January 1st, 1807; and of the first five or six, and sometimes more, of those who took contracts in all the townships upon the Purchase that were not broken into previous to that date. These lists have been made with a great deal of care and labor, and yet, there are undoubtedly many errors in them. Contracts in many instances, were in the name of those who never became settlers, and in numerous other instances perhaps, there were transfers of contracts, the name of the actual settler not appearing upon the contract books. Although there are in these tabular lists, and in various other forms, the names of four or five thousand of the Pioneers upon the Holland Purchase, the author has sincerely to regret, in many instances, the omission of the names of early, prominent Pioneers. These omissions are principally of those who became settlers after January 1st, 1807, and were

---

* A principal one, having been that of the State of Maryland, as indicated in some portions of the work.

not the earliest in their respective townships. The Table in the Appendix, containing a list of the townships, with reference to towns as they now exist, will be found useful, in designating the localities of early settlement.

Errors in dates, names, and events, in reference to Pioneer settlement, will undoubtedly be found; in some instances they were unavoidable. They have depended, of course, mainly, upon the memory of the aged and infirm. None but those who have been engaged in gathering reminiscences from such sources, can know their liability to errror and discrepancies. Any two or three will seldom agree in their recollections. In many instances interesting reminiscences have been omitted, where it was impossible to reconcile conflicting statements. It is presumed, upon a consciousness of having exercised great care in this respect, that but few material errors will be found; where such exist, and the author is referred to them, they will be corrected in a second edition.

Much as perhaps the necessity of apologies may be indicated throughout the work, they will be indulged in but sparingly. Intelligent narrative has been the highest mark aimed at in its literary execution. Long accustomed, as the author has been, to writing for the newspaper press — a branch of composition where a careful weighing of words and sentences is generally precluded by exigencies allied to it — he may have brought to his new task something of habit thus acquired, and incurred the just criticism of those who apply to the work no more than fair tests, or subject it to no more than a liberal ordeal. Reared amid the most rugged scenes of Pioneer life upon the Holland Purchase, with little of early opportunities for education, beyond those afforded in the primitive log school house, he can prefer no claim to any considerable attainments in scholarship; and submits a work to the public, of the character and pretensions of this, not in the absence of an anxiety, and a distrust, which may be supposed to arise from a consciousness of what he has thus frankly acknowledged. "Literary leisure," so essential to the faultless execution of such a task as this has been, he has not enjoyed. It is about eighteen months since the collection of materials was commenced; during the fore part of that period, a connection with a newspaper necessarily divided the time and attention of the Author; and since the preparation of the work for the press commenced, his own ill health, consequent upon a phyical constitution much impaired, and ill health in his family, have been the cause of frequent interruptions. Much the largest portion of the work has been prepared since the printing commenced. All this is not intended to disarm any just and fair criticism; but may perhaps, with some propriety, be preferred to break the force of technical cavilling, or the asperities of faultfinding, if they are encountered.

It only remains to make personal acknowledgments of the kind offices and essential aids of those who have coöperated in the enterprise:— To the Hon. WASHINGTON HUNT, of Niagara, for early encouragement to embark in it, and generous assistance, whenever needed, in its progress; and to the Hon. HIRAM GARDNER, of Lockport, and the Hon. WM. BUEL, of Rochester, the Author is under like obligations. To his brother, C. P. TURNER, Esq. of Black Rock, who, in various ways, has lent his zealous coöperation and assistance.

To LYMAN C. DRAPER, Esq. a resident of Philadelphia, but a native of the Holland Purchase, for essential aid in procuring valuable and rare materials for the work. Leaving this region an ambitious boy, in search of an education; that acquired, he engaged in historical researches, and now enjoys a well earned fame for valuable contributions to American history. Apprised of the Author's intention to commence this work, prompted by private friendship, and a laudable zeal to aid in the history of the region in which his parents were Pioneers, he has volunteered to search the archives of historical societies, and give to the work the benefit of his discoveries. He is now engaged in Philadelphia, in preparing for the press "The Life and Times of Gen. GEORGE ROGERS CLARK, of Kentucky," and intends to follow it up with histories of others of the prominent pioneers of the Valley of the Mississippi.

To O. H. MARSHALL, Esq. of Buffalo, for free access to a library, in which he has gratified a highly cultivated literary taste, by the accumulation of rare works, in various departments of American history. Meeting him as a stranger, the Author has found in him a friend, patiently and generously, from time to time, coöperating in his enterprise, and giving him the benefit of his more than ordinary familiarity with early Colonial history, and all that relates to our immediate predecessors, the Seneca Iroquois.

To EBENEZER MIX, Esq. of Batavia, for the benefit of his long familiar acquaintance with the Holland Purchase, and the details of the Land Office, in the preparation of the Maps, the Topographical Sketch, and the deduction of title in the Appendix. To Gov. CASS, of Michigan, and the Hon. HENRY C. MURPHY, of Long Island, for the possession of books and pamphlets, essential to the work. To JAMES D. BEMIS, Esq. of Canandaigua, the respected Father of the Press of Western New York, for early coöperation in the enterprize; and to Judge OLIVER PHELPS, of the same place, for free access to the papers of his grandfather, the patroon of settlement, whose brief biography is given in the body of the work. To the Members of the Buffalo Young Men's Association, for the benefit of free access to their extensive Library, and all the facilities their praiseworthy institution afforded. To HENRY O'RIELLY, Esq. for the possession of valuable papers that he had accumulated with reference to an historical enterprise that it is hoped he will yet find leisure to consummate. To the young friend of the author, DANIEL W. BALLOU, JR. of Lockport, whom he transferred from his place as compositor in a printing office, to assist him as a copyist; for aid in historical researches he had so well qualified himself to render, by early studious habits, and an employment of his leisure hours in the laudable pursuit of knowledge. To all, who are identified in the body of the work, as having lent their coöperation and assistance; and especially to such surviving Pioneers as have cheerfully given the author the benefit of their recollections.

The Author closes with an acknowledgement of his obligations to the enterprising Printers and Publishers, Messrs. JEWETT, THOMAS, & Co. prompted as well by a sense of gratitude for their uniform personal courtesy and kindness, as by the gratification which is derived from seeing his work go out from their hands so good a specimen of the progress of the art of typography upon the Holland Purchase; and so creditable to a craft with which he has himself been so long identified.

NOTE.— The Portraits in the work are mostly daguerreotype transfers from oil paintings, made at the Gallery of Messrs. EVANS & POWELSON, Buffalo. To the correctness of the transfers, their excellence is in a great measure to be attributed; though their after execution is regarded as a creditable specimen of the progress of the art of Lithography in the United States. The artists employed upon the illustrations are indicated by their names.

INDEX.

	Page.		Page.
Ancient Pre-occupants of Western N. York,	17	Blackman, Mrs.	386
Ancient Relics,	19	Barton, Benj.	392
Ancient Battle Field,	30	Brisbane, James.	416
Aurora, remains and implements found	30	Buffalo,	418, 498
An aged Indian,	31	Burr, Aaron	419
Ancient works at Lancaster and Shelby	35	Busti, Paul	426
Antiquity of the Iroquois,	48	Batavia,	464, 545
Arrangement of Tribes at the Council Fires,	59	Bush, Wm. H.	471
Allouez,	111, 113	Blacksnake, Gov.	509
Aix La Chappelle, treaty of 1748,	177	Brief reminiscences of the war of 1812	584
Amherst, General	205, 217	Burning of Buffalo,	597
Account of a French Colony, 1655,	243	Buffalo Gazette,	601
Arnold, Benedict	272	Brown, Major General,	608
Alden, Col.	275	Bouck, Wm. C.	631
Allan, Ebenezer.	296	Changes of time,	19
Autrechy, Alex'r.	414	Clinton, De Witt.	20, 623
Alexander,	531	Cuisick's History, (note)	29
Allegany County,	579	Captives of the Iroquois,	45
Attica,	532	Council of the League,	50
		Civil and Military Relations of the Iroquois,	52
Brebeuf's journey to the Neuter Nation	65	Consanguinity of the Iroquois,	56
Biart, Father.	99	Cabot, John and Sebastian.	71
Barre, De La	137	Cortereal, Gaspar.	72
Blacksmith's Tradition,	150	Cartier, James	77, 79
Burnet, Gov. William.	175	Champlain, Samuel.	84, 109
Barnwell,	179	Company of New France,	108
Bradstreet, Col.	204, 233, 234	Colonists of New France, (note)	109
Brief notices of events under English dominion,	226	Colbert,	112
Battle near Buffalo,	231	Charlevoix's Description of Niagara Falls,	194
Burnt Ship Bay,	233	Crown Point,	216
Border Wars of the Revolution,	253	Church at Lewiston,	265
Brant — Thayendanega,	259	Campbell, Mrs. (note)	276
Brant, John	263	Clinton, General James	277
Butler, Col. Zebulon	274	Chamberlin, Hinds.	321
Butler, Col. John	274, 278	Cornplanter's Speech,	335
Boyd, Lieut.	279	Culver, Oliver.	387
Butler, Walter	282	Cazenove, Theophilus	425
Brief Biographical Sketches,	286	Commencement of settlement and its Progress to 1812,	445
Butler, Thomas	317	Chapin, Cyrenius	452, 598
Bruff, Capt.	348	Clinton, Gov. George	466, 620
Butler, Richard	349	Chipman, Lemuel.	481
Boughton, Jared.	378		

INDEX.   xiii

	Page.		Page.
Cook, Lemuel	496	First settlers on the Holland Purchase, from the commencement of land sales to 1807,	454
Crouse, Peter R.	510		
Cuba,	538		
Coon, Alexander	552	First settlers in townships, from 1808 to 1821,	526
Carpenter, Rev. James	553		
Carey, Ebenezer	568	Farmersville,	540
Chautauque County,	576	Fillmore, Rev. Gleason	546
Cattaraugus County,	578	Fort Niagara	183, 206, 590
Cook, Lothrop and Bates	592		
Cass's visit to Niagara Frontier,	604	Geographical position of the Iroquois,	42
Commerce of the Upper Lakes,	638	Goshnold,	80
Colles, Christopher	619	Griffin, the	121, 126, 133
		Garangula,	138, 142
Dominion of the Iroquois,	41	Graffenried,	178
Decay of the Iroquois,	43	Greenhalph, Wentworth	236
Discoveries by Europeans, accidental	90	Gansevoort, Col.	269, 272
De Laet's Description of New Netherlands,	91	Glimpses of Western New York after the Revolution,	310
Dutch trade with the Natives,	91	Gould, John	313
Duhaut,	131	Gorham, Nathaniel,	329
Dulbut,	137	Green, John	508
Dongan, Gov.	138, 158, 162	Garnsey, Hon. D. G.	511, 642
De Nonville's Expedition,	143	Griffith, Eli	516
Dallion, Joseph De La Roche	192	Griffin, John	538
Dieskau,	200	Genesee County	574
Du Quesne, Fort	205		
Devil's Hole,	227	Human bones excavated,	27
Dorchester's, Lord, Indian Speech,	342	Ho-de-no-sau-nee	42
Dunham, Gideon	467	Henry VII,	71
Dunn, Jeptha	497	Hochelaga,	78
Doolittle, Ormus and Reuben	533	Hunt, Capt.	81
Douglass' description of Buffalo	606	Hudson, Henry	82, 87
		Hennepin's account of La Salle's boat,	119
Equality of the Iroquois Confederacy,	59	Hennepin,	129
Early European Voyages and Discoveries,	71	Hennepin's account of the Falls,	193
		Hudson Bay Company,	222
Exports of Fur,	91	Herkimer, General,	268
Early Notices of Niagara Falls,	192	Hopkins, Silas	310
Early glimpses of Western New York,	236	Hosmer, Timothy	376
Ellicott, Joseph	404, 412, 430	Historical Deduction of Holland Company Title,	401
Ellicott, Benjamin	408, 432		
Ellicott, Andrew	432	Haudecour	414
Evans, David E.	442	Howell, Hon. Nathaniel W.	417
Egleston, George	414	Hamilton, Alexander	418
Eddy, David	475	Hopkins, Gen'l Timothy S.	421
Erie County,	575	Holland Co's. West Geneseo Lands,	424
Erie Canal.	617	Hurd, Reuben	497
Eddy, Thomas	624	Hoops, Maj. Adam	504
		Hart, Joseph	554
Fort Hill,	31, 152	Hall, General	594
Franciscans,	93	Hawley, Jesse	621, 629
First vessels upon the Upper Lakes,	116	Holley, Myron	626
Frontenac, Count.	137, 162, 170, 172		
Frontenac, Fort	161	Indications of preceding Races,	18
Fur Trade,	223	Indian Burial Grounds,	26
Farmers Brother,	230, 291	Indian Remains on Genesee River,	36
Fairbanks, Joshua	319	Iroquois or Five Nations,	40
Frontier Posts after peace of 1783,	338	Independence of each Indian Nation,	51
First assault and battery case in Buffalo	414	Iroquois Laws of Descent,	56
First crops raised on the Holland Purchase,	420	Indian Treatment of Children,	64
		Indian Trade,	175
Foster, Mrs. Anna	470	Indian Treaties for Lands,	304

INDEX.

	Page.
Joliet,	114, 117
Joutel,	132
Joncaire,	184, 186
Journal of the Seige of Fort Niagara,	209
Johnson, Sir William.	217, 228, 233, 247
Johnson, Guy	255
Johnson, Sir John	265, 267
Jones, Horatio	286
Jemison, Mary	293
Jemison, John	295
Johnston, Capt. Wm.	411, 498
Kienuka,	26
Kah-Kwahs	30
Kirkland's Visit to Genesee,	36
Kirkland's Observations on Indian Remains,	37
Kirkland, Rev. Samuel	238
Kelsey, Jehiel	383
Kemp, Burgoyne	387
L'Allemant,	65
Letters Patent,	81
Leon, Ponce De	90
Loyola, Ignatius	95
La Salle,	116
L'Archiveque	131
La Hontan's Account of De Nonville's Expedition,	147
La Hontan's Account of Niagara Falls,	157
La Force, (note)	210
Lindsay,	246
Laincourt, La Rochefoucauld	318
Land Titles,	325
Lessee Company's Claims, (note)	337
Lewiston,	420
Loomis, Chauncey	485
Lost Boy,	486
Le Couteulx,	501
Lockport, Prominent Settlers	551
Lovejoy, Mrs.	599
Mountain Ridge,	26
Missions among the Iroquois,	41
Marriage Regulations,	54
Marquette,	112
Mercer, Col.	201
Montcalm,	202, 214
Murray, Gen'l.	217
Massacre of Wyoming,	274
Mountpleasant, John	314
Morris, Robert	349
Morris Purchase.	396
Morris's Reserve,	397
McKay, John.	381
Mile Strip,	409
McKain, James	487
Morrison, Major John	494
Molyneux, William.	496
Mather, David	498
Marshall, Mrs.	510
McMahan, Col. James	511

	Page.
Maxon, Joseph	534
Methodist Church,	547
McCall, James	536
Mathews, James	555
Mix, Ebenezer	567
McClure, Gen	589
Names of the Iroquois Confederacy,	40
Naming of children,	58
Neuter Nation,	65
Number of Jesuit Missionaries,	103
North West Company,	223
Noble, Russell	468
New Amsterdam,	500
Niagara County,	582
Newark,	589
Original Nations of the Iroquois,	40
Order of the Jesuits,	95
Oswego,	175, 202
Oglethrop, Gen.	176
Onondagas, destruction of.	281
Otto, Jacob S.	441
O'Fling, Patrick	467
Olean Point,	506
Organization of Courts,	521
Oil Springs,	539
Oak Orchard,	558
Orleans County,	581
Poem,	28
Power and bravery of the Iroquois,	43
Periods of holding Council Fires,	60
Plymouth Company,	81
Protestant Missionaries of New England,	99
Pallisades of Fort Niagara,	134
Pitt, William.	203
Prideaux, Gen.	206
Pontiac,	218, 235
Palatines,	245
Palatine Committee,	254
Parrish, Jasper	292
Pickering, Timothy	307
Progress of settlement westward after the Revolution,	304
Pemberton, James	316
Phelps and Gorham's purchase,	325
Pultney, Sir William.	327
Phelps, Oliver.	328
Porter, Augustus.	358, 489
Porter's Narrative,	361
Pitts, Capt. Peter.	385
Pine Grove,	446
Palmer, James R.	454
Palmer, Joseph	466
Peters, T. C.	547
Pioneer Settler upon the Holland Purchase and his progress,	562
Phelps and Chipman's purchase,	481
Peacock, William	569
Porter, Peter B.	611

INDEX. xv

	Page.		Page.
Ring Fort,	29	Trails,	62
Romans of the West,	47	Tonti,	118
Representatives of the Iroquois,	49	Tuscaroras,	177
Roche, Francis De La	79	Treaty of 1763,	219
Raleigh, Sir Walter	80, 90	Treaty of Fort Stanwix, 1784,	304
Ralle, Father	105	Tax Roll,	390
Reminiscences of Fort Niagara,	188	Turner, Roswell	481
Rogers, Major	218	Turner, Otis	557
Red Jacket and Lafayette, (note)	305	Topography of the Holland Purchase,	570
Ransom, Asa and Elias	453		
Rhea, Alexander	467	Unanimity of the Iroquois Council,	61
Ridge Road,	497	Utrecht, treaty of	174
Rushford,	535		
Rawson, Solomon	537	Verrazana,	72
Riddle, Lieut.	598	Victor,	145
		Vaudreuil,	170, 216
Structure of the Iroquois Confederacy,	48	Van Schaick,	281
Senecas and Eries,	69	Van Campen,	288
Smith, John	81	Variation of the Magnetic Needle,	
Slowness of Colonization,	89	(note,)	407
Schenectady,	164	Vander Kemp, John J.	429
Shirley, Gov.	201	Van Horn, Judge	551
Seige of Fort Niagara,	206		
Stanwix, Gen'l	205	Washington, (note,)	200, 619
Schlosser, Fort (note)	227	Williams, Col. Ephraim	200
Stedman, John	229	Wolfe, Gen. James	205, 213
St. Leger, Gen'l	269	Walpole,	177
Schuyler, Gen'l	267	West, Dr. Joseph	188
Schuyler, Han Yost	272	Womp,	240
Sullivan's Expedition,	277	Willett, Col.	271, 282
Steuben, Baron	338	Williamson, Charles	329, 417
Simcoe, Governor	341	Wayne, Gen.	344
Scotch Colony	380	Wilkenson, Gen. James	446
Surveys,	404	Winne,	418
Stevens, James	474	Walthers, Frederick	420
Sheldon,	482	Warren, Gen. William	473
Slayton, Joshua	495	Warren, Mrs.	488
Salt Works,	558	Wilder, John	479
State of the frontier at the beginning of the War,	585	Walsworth, James	517
		Wilson, Reuben	548, 593
St. John, Mrs.	599	Whitney, Gen.	559
Sortie of Fort Erie,	606	Wyoming County,	580
		Wadsworth, Gen.	587
Tonawanda Island,	34	Walden, Judge	598
Territory of the Iroquois,	41	Watson, Elkanah	620
Treatment of Prisoners among the Indians,	45	Wilkeson, Samuel	643
Tradition of the Senecas,	46	Yonnondio,	152
Ta-do-da-hoh,	50	Young, John	469
Tribes of the Iroquois,	53		

INDEX TO APPENDIX AND NOTES.

	Page.		Page.
Albion,	658	Canal Villages,	653
Ancient Remains,	663	Clerks in Land Office,	663
Black Rock,	653	Deduction of Title from Robert Morris to Holland Company,	646
Brant's Birthplace,	664		
Brace, Orange	665		
Battle of Buffalo,	665	Ellicott's Monument,	659

INDEX.

	Page.		Page.
Expeditions of Gen. Sullivan and Col. Brodhead—Cotemporary Records in possession of D. W. Ballou, Jr.	660	Marshall's Communications to the Historical Society,	664
Ellicott's Ancestors,	665	Ogden Pre-emption,	662
Fort Porter,	666	Pioneer Printers upon the Holland Purchase,	663
German Emigrants,	662		
Islands in Niagara River,	663	Sequel of Holland Company's Investment,	661
Indian Burial at Black Rock,	664	Smith, Richard	662
		Sainted Seneca Maiden,	664
Joncaire's Sons,	664	Sources of Morris's Biography,	665
Joncaire and the Oil Springs,	666		
		Townships of the Holland Purchase,	651
Lockport,	654	Tonawanda,	653
Middleport,	657	Williamson, Charles	665
Medina,	658	Warren, Gen.	665
Middlebury Academy,	664		

PART FIRST.

CHAPTER I.

THE ANCIENT PRE-OCCUPANTS OF THE REGION OF WESTERN NEW-YORK.

THE local historian of almost our entire continent, finds at the threshold of the task he enters upon, difficulties and embarrassments. If for a starting point the first advent of civilization is chosen, a summary disposition is made of all that preceded it, unsatisfactory to author and reader. Our own race was the successor of others. Here in our own region, when the waters of the Niagara were first disturbed by a craft of European architecture —when the adventurous Frenchman would first pitch a tent upon its banks, there were "lords of the Forests and the Lakes" to be consulted.—Where stood that humble primitive "pallisade," its site grudgingly and suspiciously granted, in process of time arose strong walls—ramparts, from behind which the armies of successive nations have been arranged to repel assailants. The dense forests that for more than a century enshrouded them, unbroken by the woodman's axe, have now disappeared, or but skirt a peaceful and beautiful cultivated landscape. Civilization, improvement and industry, have made an Empire of the region that for a long period was tributary to this nucleus of early events. Cities have been founded—the Arts, Sciences taught;—Learning has its temples and its votaries; History its enlightened and earnest enquirers. And yet, with the pre-occupant lingering until even now in our midst, we have but the unsatisfactory knowledge of him and his race, which is gathered from dim and obscure tradition. That which is suited to the pages of fiction and romance, but can be incorporated in the pages of history, only with suspicion and distrust. The learned and the curious have from time to time enquired of their old men; they have set down in their wigwams and listened to their recitals; the pages of history have been searched and compared with their imperfect revelations, to discover some faint coincidence or analogy; and yet we know nothing of the origin, and have but unsatisfactory traditions of the people we found here, and have almost dispossessed.

If their own history is obscure; if their relations of themselves, after they have gone back but little more than a century beyond the period of the first European emigration, degenerates to fable and obscure tradition; they are but poor revelators of a still greater mystery. We are surrounded by evidences that a race preceded them, farther advanced in civilization and the arts, and far more numerous. Here and there upon the brows of our hills, at the head of our ravines, are their fortifications; their locations selected with skill, adapted to refuge, subsistence and defence. The uprooted trees of our forest, that are the growth of centuries, expose their mouldering remains; the uncovered mounds masses of their skeletons promiscuously heaped one upon the other, as if they were the gathered and hurriedly entombed of well contested fields. In our vallies, upon our hill sides, the plough and the spade discover their rude implements, adapted to war, the chase, and domestic use. All these are dumb yet eloquent chronicles of by-gone ages. We ask the red man to tell us from whence they came and whither they went? and he either amuses us with wild and extravagant traditionary legends, or acknowledges himself as ignorant as his interrogators. He and his progenitors have gazed upon these ancient relics for centuries, as we do now,—wondered and consulted their wise men, and yet he is unable to aid our inquiries. We invoke the aid of revelation, turn over the pages of history, trace the origin and dispersion of the races of mankind from the earliest period of the world's existence, and yet we gather only enough to form the basis of vague surmise and conjecture. The crumbling walls—the "Ruins," overgrown by the gigantic forests of Central America, are not involved in more impenetrable obscurity, than are the more humble, but equally interesting mounds and relics that abound in our own region.

We are prone to speak of ourselves as the inhabitants of a *new* world; and yet we are confronted with such evidences of antiquity! We clear away the forests and speak familiarly of subduing a "virgin soil;"—and yet the plough up-turns the skulls of those whose history is lost! We say that Columbus discovered a *new* world. Why not that he helped to make two *old* ones acquainted with each other?

Our advent here is but one of the changes of TIME. We are consulting dumb signs, inanimate and unintelligible witnesses, gleaning but unsatisfactory knowledge of races that have preceded us. Who in view of earth's revolutions; the developments that the young but rapidly progressive science of Geology has made; the organic remains that are found in the alluvial deposits in our vallies, deeply embedded under successive strata of rock in our mountain ranges; the impressions in our coal formations; history's emphatic teachings; fails to reflect that our own race may not be exempt from the operations of what may be regarded as general laws? Who shall say that the scholar, the antiquarian, of another far off century, may not be a Champollion deciphering the inscriptions upon our monuments,—or a Stevens, wandering among the ruins of our cities, to gather relics to identify our existence?

> " Since the first sun-light spread itself o'er earth ;
> Since Chaos gave a thousand systems birth ;
> Since first the morning stars together sung ;
> Since first this globe was on its axis hung ;
> Untiring CHANGE, with ever moving hand,
> Has waved o'er earth its more than magic wand."*

Although not peculiar to this region, there is perhaps no portion of the United States where ancient relics are more numerous. Commencing principally near the Oswego River, they extend westwardly over all the western counties of our State, Canada West, the western Lake Region, the vallies of the Ohio and the Mississippi. Either as now, the western portion of our State had attractions and inducements to make it a favorite residence; or these people, assailed from the north and the east, made this a refuge in a war of extermination, fortified the commanding eminences, met the shock of a final issue; were subject to its adverse results. Were their habits and pursuits mixed ones, their residence was well chosen. The Forest invited to the chase; the Lakes and Rivers to local commerce,—to the use of the net and the angling rod; the soil, to agriculture. The evidences that this was one at least, of their final battlegrounds, predominate. They are the fortifications, entrenchments, and warlike instruments. That here was a war of extermination, we may conclude, from the masses

---

* " Changes of Time," a Poem by B. B. French.

of human skeletons we find indiscriminately thrown together, indicating a common and simultaneous sepulture; from which age, infancy, sex, no condition, was exempt.

In assuming that these are the remains of a people other than the Indian race we found here, the author has the authority of DE WITT CLINTON,—a name scarcely less identified with our literature, than with our achievements in internal improvements. In a discourse delivered before the New-York Historical Society in 1811, Mr. Clinton says:—"Previous to the occupation of this country by the progenitors of the present race of Indians, it was inhabited by a race of men much more populous, and much farther advanced in civilization." Indeed the abstract position may be regarded as conceded. Who they were, whence they came, and whither they went, have been themes of speculation with learned antiquarians, who have failed to arrive at any satisfactory conclusions. In a field, or historical department, so ably and thoroughly explored, the author would not venture opinions or theories of his own, even were it not a subject of enquiry in the main, distinct from the objects of his work. It is a topic prolific enough, of reflection, enquiry and speculation, for volumes, rather than an incidental historical chapter. And yet, it is a subject of too much local interest, to be wholly passed over. A liberal extract from the historical discourse of Mr. CLINTON, presents the matter in a concise form, and while it will serve as a valuable memento of a venerated Scholar, Statesman, and Public Benefactor; the theories and conclusions are far more consistent and reasonable than any others that have fallen under the author's observation:—

"I have seen several of these works in the western part of this state. There is a large one in the town of Onondaga, one in Pompey, and another in Manlius; one in Camillus, eight miles from Auburn; one in Scipio, six miles, another one mile, and one about half a mile from that village. Between the Seneca and Cayuga Lakes there are several—three within a few miles of each other. Near the village of Canandaigua there are three. In a word, they are scattered all over that country.

"These forts were, generally speaking, erected on the most commanding ground. The walls or breastworks were earthen. The ditches were on the exterior of works. On some of the parapets, oak trees were to be seen, which, from the number of concentric circles, must have been standing 150, 260, and 300 years; and there were evident indications, not only that they had sprung up since the creation of those works, but that they were at least a second growth. The trenches were in some cases deep and wide, and in others shallow and narrow; and the breastworks varied in altitude from three to eight feet. They sometimes had one, and sometimes two entrances, as was to be inferred from there being no ditch at those places. When the works were protected by a deep ravine or a large stream of water no ditch was to be seen. The areas of these forts varied from two to six acres; and the form was generally an irregular elipsis; and in some of them fragments of earthenware and pulverized substances, supposed to have been originally human bones, were to be found.

"These fortifications, thus diffused over the interior of our country, have been generally considered as surpassing the skill, patience, and industry of the Indian race, and various hypotheses have been advanced to prove them of European origin.

"An American writer of no inconsiderable repute pronounced some years ago that the two forts at the confluence of the Muskingum and Ohio Rivers, one covering forty and the other twenty acres, were erected by Ferdinand de Soto, who landed with 1000 men in Florida in 1539, and penetrated a considerable distance into the interior of the country. He allotted the large fort for the use of the Spanish army; and after being extremely puzzled how to dispose of the small one in its vicinity, he at last assigned it to the swine that generally, as he says, attended the Spaniards in those days — being in his opinion very necessary, in order to prevent them from becoming estrays, and to protect them from the depredations of the Indians.

"When two ancient forts, one containing six and the other three acres, were found in Lexington in Kentucky, another theory was propounded; and it was supposed that they were erected by the descendants of the Welsh colonists who are said to have migrated under the auspices of Madoc to this country, in the twelfth century; that they formerly inhabited Kentucky; but, being attacked by the Indians, were forced to take refuge near the sources of the Missouri.

"Another suggestion has been made, that the French, in their expeditions from Canada to the Mississippi, were the authors of these works; but the most numerous are to be found in *the territory of the Senecas*, whose hostility to the French was such, that they were not allowed for a long time to have any footing among them.* The fort at Niagara was obtained from them by the intrigues and eloquence of Joncaire, an adopted child of the nation.†

"Lewis Dennie, a Frenchman, aged upward of seventy, and who had been settled and married among the Confederates for more than half a century, told me (1810)that, according to the traditions of the ancient Indians, these forts were erected by an army of Spaniards, who were the first Europeans ever seen by them — the

---

* 1 Colden, p. 61.   † 3 Charlevoix, letter 15, p. 227.

French the next — then the Dutch — and, finally, the English; that this army first appeared at Oswego in great force; and penetrated through the interior of the country, searching for the precious metals; that they continued there two years, and went down the Ohio.

"Some of the Senecas told Mr. Kirkland, the missionary, that those in their territory were raised by their ancestors in their wars with the western Indians, three, four, or five hundred years ago. All the cantons have traditions that their ancestors came originally from the west; and the Senecas say that theirs first settled in the country of the Creeks. The early histories mention that the Iroquois first inhabited on the north side of the great lakes; that they were driven to their present territory in a war with the Algonkins or Adirondacks, from whence they expelled the Satanas. If these accounts are correct, the ancestors of the Senecas did not, in all probability, occupy their present territory at the time they allege.

"I believe we may confidently pronounce that all the hypotheses which attribute those works to Europeans are incorrect and fanciful — first, on account of the present number of the works; secondly, on account of their antiquity; having from every appearance, been erected a long time before the discovery of America; and, finally, their form and manner are totally variant from European fortifications, either in ancient or modern times.

"It is equally clear that they were not the work of the Indians. Until the Senecas, who are renowned for their national vanity, had seen the attention of the Americans attracted to these erections, and had invented the fabulous account of which I have spoken, the Indians of the present day did not pretend to know anything about their origin. They were beyond the reach of all their traditions, and were lost in the abyss of unexplored antiquity.

"The erection of such prodigious works must have been the result of labor far beyond the patience and perseverance of our Indians; and the form and materials are entirely different from those which they are known to make. These earthen walls, it is supposed, will retain their original form much longer than those constructed with brick and stone. They have undoubtedly been greatly diminished by the washing away of the earth, the filling up of the interior, and the accumulation of fresh soil: yet their firmness and solidity indicate them to be the work of some remote age. Add to this, that the Indians have never practiced the mode of fortifying by intrenchments. Their villages or castles were protected by palisades, which afford a sufficient defence aginst Indian weapons. When Cartier went to Hochelaga, now Montreal, in 1535, he discovered a town of the Iroquois, or Hurons, containing about fifty huts. It was encompassed with three lines of palisadoes, through which was one entrance, well secured with stakes and bars. On the inside was a rampart of timber, to which were ascents by ladders; and heaps of stones were laid in proper places to cast at an enemy. Charlevoix and other writers agree in representing the Indian fortresses as fabricated with wood. Such, also, were the forts of Sassacus, the great chief of the Pequots; and the principal fortress of the Narragansets was on an island in a swamp, of five or six acres of rising land: the sides were made with palisades set upright, encompassed with a hedge of a rod in thickness.*

"I have already alluded to the argument for the great antiquity of those ancient forts to be derived from the number of concentric circles. On the ramparts of one of the Muskingum forts, 463 were ascertained on a tree decayed at the centre; and there are likewise the strongest marks of a former growth of a similar size. This would make those works near a thousand years old.

"But there is another consideration which has never before been urged, and which appears to me to be not unworthy of attention. It is certainly novel, and I believe it to be founded on a basis which cannot easily be subverted.

"From the Genesee near Rochester to Lewiston on the Niagara, there is a remarkable ridge or elevation of land running almost the whole distance, which is seventy-eight miles, and in a direction from east to west. Its general altitude above the neighbouring land is thirty feet, and its width varies considerably; in some places it is not more than forty yards. Its elevation above the level of Lake Ontario is perhaps 160 feet, to which it decends with a gradual slope; and its distance from that water is between six and ten miles. This remarkable strip of land would appear as if intended by nature for the purpose of an easy communication. It is, in fact, a stupendous natural turnpike, descending gently on each side, and covered with gravel; and but little labour is requisite to make it the best road in the United States. When the forests between it and the lake are cleared, the prospect and scenery which will be afforded from a tour on this route to the Cataract of Niagara will surpass all competition for sublimity and beauty, variety and number.

"There is every reason to believe that this remarkable ridge was the ancient boundary of this great lake. The gravel with which it is covered was deposited there by the waters; and the stones everywhere indicate by their shape the abrasion and agitation produced by that element. All along the borders of the western rivers and lakes there are small mounds or heaps of gravel of a conical form, erected by the fish for the protection of their spawn; these fishbanks are found in a state that cannot be mistaken, at the foot of the ridge, on the side towards the lake; on the opposite side none have been discovered. All rivers and streams which enter the lake from the south have their mouths effected with sand in a peculiar way, from the prevalence and power of the northwesterly winds. The points of the creeks which pass through this ridge correspond exactly in appearance with the entrance of the streams into the lakes. These

---

* Mather's Magnalia, p. 693.

facts evince beyond doubt that Lake Ontario has, perhaps, one or two thousand years ago, receded from this elevated ground. And the cause of this retreat must be ascribed to its having enlarged its former outlet, or to its imprisoned waters (aided, probably, by an earthquake) forcing a passage down the present bed of the St. Lawrence, as the Hudson did at the Highlands, and the Mohawk at Little Falls. On the south side of this great ridge, in its vicinity, and in all directions through this country, the remains of numerous forts are to be seen; but on the north side, that is, on the side towards the lake, not a single one has been discovered, although the whole ground has been carefully explored. Considering the distance to be, say seventy miles in length, and eight in breadth, and that the border of the lake is the very place that would be selected for habitation, and consequently for works of defence, on account of the facilities it would afford for subsistence, for safety, and all domestic accommodations and military purposes; and that on the south shores of Lake Erie these ancient fortresses exist in great number, there can be no doubt that these works were erected when this ridge was the southern boundary of Lake Ontario, and, consequently, that their origin must be sought in a very remote age.

"A great part of North America was then inhabited by populous nations, who had made considerable advances in civilization. These numerous works could never have been supplied with provisions without the aid of agriculture. Nor could they have been constructed without the use of iron or copper, and without a perseverance, labour, and design which demonstrate considerable progress in the arts of civilized life. A learned writer has said, "I perceive no reason why the Asiatic North might not be an officina virorum, as well as the European. The overteeming country to the east of the Riphæan Mountains must find it necessary to discharge its inhabitants. The first great wave of people was forced forward by the next to it, more tumid and more powerful than itself: successive and new impulses continually arriving, short rest was given to that which spread over a more eastern tract: disturbed again and again, it covered fresh regions. At length, reaching the farthest limits of the old world, it found a new one, with ample space to occupy, unmolested for ages."* After the north of Asia had thus exhausted its exuberant population by such a great migration, it would require a very long period of time to produce a co-operation of causes sufficient to effect another. The first mighty stream of people that flowed into America must have remained free from external pressure for ages. Availing themselves of this period of tranquility, they would devote themselves to the arts of peace, make rapid progress in civilization, and acquire an immense population. In course of time discord and war would rage among them, and compel the establishment of places of security. At last, they became alarmed by the

---

* 1 Pennant's Arctic Zoology, 260.

irruption of a horde of barbarians, who rushed like an overwhelming flood from the north of Asia—

> "A Multitude, like which the populous North
> Poured from her frozen loins to pass
> Rhene or the Danaw, when her barbarous sons
> Came like a deluge on the South, and spread
> Beneath Gibraltar to the Lybian sands."*

"The great law of self-preservation compelled them to stand on their defence, to resist these ruthless invaders, and to construct numerous and extensive works for protection. And for a long series of time the scale of victory was suspended in doubt, and they firmly withstood the torrent; but, like the Romans in the decline of their empire, they were finally worn down and destroyed by successive inroads and renewed attacks. And the fortifications of which we have treated are the only remaining monuments of these ancient and exterminated nations. This is perhaps, the airy nothing of imagination, and may be reckoned the extravagant dream of a visionary mind: but may we not, considering the wonderful events of the past and present times, and the inscrutable dispensations of an overruling Providence, may we not look forward into futurity, and without departing from the rigid laws of probability, predict the occurrence of similar scenes at some remote period of time? And, perhaps, in the decrepitude of our empire, some transcendant genius, whose powers of mind shall only be bounded by that impenetrable circle which prescribes the limits of human nature,† may rally the barbarous nations of Asia under the standard of a mighty empire. Following the track of the Russian colonies and commerce towards the northwest coast, and availing himself of the navigation, arms, and military skill of civilized nations, he may, after subverting the neighbouring despotisms of the Old World, bend his course towards European America. The destinies of our country may then be decided on the waters of the Missouri or on the banks of Lake Superior. And if Asia shall then revenge upon our posterity the injuries we have inflicted upon her sons, a new, a long, and a gloomy night of Gothic darkness will set in upon mankind. And when, after the efflux of ages, the returning effulgence of intellectual light shall again gladden the nations, then the widespread ruins of our cloud-capped towers, of our solemn temples, and of our magnificent cities, will, like the works of which we have treated, become the subject of curious research and elaborate investigation."

At the early period at which Mr. Clinton advanced the theory that the Ridge Road was once the southern shore of Lake Ontario—1811 —when settlement was but just begun, and a dense forest precluded a close observation, he was quite liable to fall into the error, that

---

* Milton's Paradise Lost. † Roscoe's Lorenzo de Medicis, 241.

time and better opportunities for investigation have corrected. The formation, composition, alluvial deposits, &c., of the Ridge Road, with reference to its two sides, present almost an entire uniformity. There is at least, not the distinction that would be apparent if there had been the action of water, depositing its materials only upon its nothern side. By supposing the Mountain Ridge to have once been the southern shore of Lake Ontario, it would follow that the Ridge Road may have been a *Sand bar.* The nature of both, their relative positions, would render this a far more reasonable hypothesis than the other; and when we add the fact that the immediate slope, or falling off, is almost as much generally, upon the south as the north side of the Ridge Road, we are under the necessity of abandoning the precedent theory. There is from the Niagara to the Genesee River, upon the *Mountain* Ridge, a line, or cordon, of these ancient fortifications — none, as the author concludes, from observation and enquiry, between the Ridge and Lake.*

But a few of the most prominent of these ancient fortifications, will be noticed, enough only to give the reader who has not had an opportunity of seeing them, a general idea of their structure, and relics which almost uniformly may be found in and about them.

Upon a slope or offset of the Mountain Ridge three and a half miles from the village of Lewiston, is a marked spot, that the Tuscarora Indians call *Kienuka*.† There is a burial ground, and two eliptic mounds or barrows that have a diameter of 20 feet, and an elevation of from 4 to 5 feet. A mass of detached works, with spaces intervening, seem to have been chosen as a rock citadel; and well chosen, — for the mountain fastnesses of Switzerland are but little better adapted to the purposes of a look-out and defence. The sites of habitations are marked by remains of pottery, pipes, and other evidences.

Eight miles east of this, upon one of the most elevated points of the mountain ridge in the town of Cambria, upon the farm until recently owned by Eliakim Hammond, now owned by John Gould,

---

* Upon an elevation, on the shore of Lake Ontario near the Eighteen-mile-Creek, there is a mound similar in appearance to some of those that have been termed *ancient*; though it is unquestionably incident to the early French and Indian wars of this region. And the same conclusion may be formed in reference to other similar ones along the shore of the lake.

†Meaning a fort, or strong hold, that has a commanding position, or from which there is a fine view.

is an ancient fortification and burial place, possessing perhaps as great a degree of interest, and as distinct characteristics as any that have been discovered in Western New York. The author having been one of a party that made a thorough examination of the spot soon after its first discovery in 1823, he is enabled from memory and some published accounts of his at the time, to state the extent and character of the relics.

The location commands a view of Lake Ontario and the surrounding country. An area of about six acres of level ground appears to have been occupied; fronting which upon a circular verge of the mountain, were distinct remains of a wall. Nearly in the centre of the area was a depository of the dead. It was a pit excavated to the depth of four or five feet, filled with human bones, over which were slabs of sand stone. Hundreds seem to have been thrown in promiscuously, of both sexes and all ages. Extreme old age was distinctly identified by toothless jaws, and the complete absorption of the aveola processes; and extreme infancy, by the small skulls and incomplete ossification. Numerous barbs or arrow points were found among the bones, and in the vicinity. One skull retained the arrow that had pierced it, the aperture it had made on entering being distinctly visible. In the position of the skeletons, there was none of the signs of ordinary Indian burial; but evidences that the bodies were thrown in promiscuously, and at the same time. The conjecture might well be indulged that it had been the theatre of a sanguinary battle, terminating in favor of the assailants, and a general massacre. A thigh bone of unusual length, was preserved for a considerable period by a physician of Lockport, and excited much curiosity. It had been fractured obliquely. In the absence of any surgical skill, or at least any application of it, the bone had strongly re-united, though evidently so as to have left the foot turned out at nearly a right angle. Of course, the natural surfaces of the bone were in contact, and not the fractured surfaces; and yet spurs, or ligaments were thrown out by nature, in its healing process, and so firmly knit and interwoven, as to form, if not a perfect, a firm re-union! It was by no means a finished piece of surgery, but to all appearances had answered a very good purpose. The medical student will think the patient must have possessed all the fortitude and stoicism of his race, to have kept his fractured limb in a necessary fixed position, during the long months that the healing process must have been going on, in the absence of splints and gum elastic bands. A tree had been cut down growing directly over the mound, upon the stump of which could be counted 230 concentric circles. Remains of rude specimens of earthen ware, pieces of copper, and iron instruments of rude workmanship were ploughed up within the area; also, charred wood, corn and cobs.

Soon after these ancient relics had begun to excite public attention, the author received the following poetic contribution which he inserted in the columns of a newspaper of which he was the editor. Upon a review of it, he regards it as not unworthy to be preserved with the other reminiscences, in a more durable form. From a note made at the time, it would seem to have been anonymous:—

THE ARGUMENT.

The author's imagination, kindled by a description of the mouldering relics, the evidences of a sanguinary conflict of arms, aided by the then recently published traditions of DAVID CUSICK, supposes the spirit of an Erie Chieftain, (whose skeleton is one of the congregated mass) to rise and address the gazing and enquiring antiquarian:— He reminds him of their common origin and common destiny, notwithstanding the lapse of intervening ages; that his ancestors are the races which slumber in the vallies of the Caucassus, the Alps, and plains of Britain; the relator assuming that this was the forest home of his fathers. He sketches the last battle, fatal to his nation and himself; from the shouts of the victors echoing amid his native scenery, he adverts to the disembodied repose of his fathers;— and concludes with the pleasing anticipation of again meeting the disturber of his sleep of ages, in "happier regions undefined," when he too shall have finished the pilgrimage of mortality.

"Mortal of other age and clime,
  Pilgrim not having reach'd the bourne,
Know thou that kindred soul with thine,
  Once tenanted this mould'ring form.

Here once the warm blood freely flow'd,
  By the heart's active impulse press'd,
And all the varied passions glow'd,
  That struggle in thy throbbing breast.

Though o'er this crumbling dust of mine,
  Full many a summer's sun has roll'd ;
Yet equal destiny is thine,
  Though fairer cast of kindred mould.

E'en though afar thy sires may sleep,
  Beyond the Atlantic's rolling waves
Where Caucassus' stupendous steep,
  O'er hangs the shores, the Caspian laves.

Or where the Alpine glaciers pile,
  High o'er thy Gothic fathers' graves,
Or where Brittania's verdant isle
  Smiles in the bosom of the waves.

Deep in Columbia's wilds, afar
  Upon lake Erie's forest shores,
Where, glimm'ring 'neath the ev'ning star,
  Niagara's awful torrent roars.

Where the broad plain abrupt descends,
  To where Ontario's billows lave,
Whence the delighted view extends
  Far o'er the blue and boundless wave;

There brightly blaz'd my country's fires,
  While oft succeeding ages roll'd,
And there the ashes of my sires
  Lie mingled with the forest mould.

There on the heights refulgent play'd
  Aurora's brightest, earliest ray ;
And vesper's milder beams delay'd
  To lengthen the departing day.

There brightening with the shades of even,
  The hunter's scatter'd watch fires beam'd
Respondent to the stars of Heaven,
  That o'er my native forests gleamed.

Gladly would memory restore
  That scenery from oblivion's night,
Ere from those happy scenes of yore,
  My deathless spirit took its flight.

The vapours o'er the lake that lour,
  How bright the setting sun display'd,
When mid those scenes in childhood's hour,
  The boyhood of the village stray'd.

Or listen'd as our fathers taught
To recognize the 'Manitou,'
Eternal Power with wisdom fraught
Throughout Creation's boundless view.

Or as some hoary chieftain told
The wampum legend of his band,
Chivalric scenery of old,
On limpid lake or shaded land.

When youthful vigor nerv'd my prime,
How oft I chas'd the bounding deer,
Or o'er the mountain's height sublime,
Or through the ravine dark and drear.

How the melodious echoes rang,
Responsive through those awful groves,
When the returning hunter sang
The ardor of his youthful loves.

Such were the happy scenes of yore,
Ere from another world afar,
Thy fathers sought this western shore,
Where ocean hides the morning star.

Those happy scenes, alas! are o'er,
Extinguished are my country's fires,
Where on lake Erie's forest shore,
Crumble the ashes of my sires.

The foreign ploughshare rudely drives
Where sunk in peace my fathers rest,
And a sad remnant scarce survives
In the dark forests of the west.

Bid me not further to pursue
The sad'ning theme that mercy stores,
And all the murd'rous scenes renew
That slumber on lake Erie's shores.

When from toward the morning light,
Along the ocean's sounding strand,
The 'Menque' poured their banded might
Relentless o'er my native land :

Then proudly waved my Eagle plume,
Amid the foeman's fiercest yell,
Where, on my struggling country's tomb
The War Club's bloodiest effort fell.

Till slowly forced at last to yield
Unconquer'd in the arms of death,
Where sunk upon the leaf strown field,
Her bravest sons resign'd their breath.

As rising from Ontario's waves,
Amid the tumult of the fight,
Pale on the fainting warrior's grave
The moon beams shed a glim'ring light.

And loudly broke the victor's yell
Upon the distant torrent's roar,
And my devoted country's knell
Re-echoed from the sounding shore.

Calmly my buoyant spirit rose
High o'er the echoing scenery,
To join my father's long repose
In undisturb'd eternity.

In happier regions undefin'd,
Where, stranger! happy we may greet
In the great Haven of mankind,
Where mingling generations meet.

Then we'll the broken tale renew,
When we shall meet to part no more,
Our mortal pilgrimage review
And tell of joys and sorrows o'er."

At the head of a deep gorge, a mile west of Lockport, (similar to the one that forms the natural canal basin, from which the combined Locks ascend,) in the early settlement of the country, a circular raised work, or ring-fort, could be distinctly traced. Leading from the enclosed area, there had been a covered way to a spring of pure cold water that issues from a fissure in the rock, some 50 or 60 feet

---

NOTE.—The following passage appears in "Cusick's History of the Six Nations," the extraordinary production of a native Tuscarora, that it will be necessary to notice in another part of the work.

About this time the King of the Five Nations had ordered the Great War chief, Shorihawne, (a Mohawk,) to march directly with an army of five thousand warriors to aid the Governor of Canandaigua against the Erians, to attack the Fort Kayquatkay and endeavor to extinguish the council fire of the enemy, which was becoming dangerous to the neighboring nations ; but unfortunately during the siege, a shower of arrows was flying from the fort, the great war chief Shorihawne was killed, and his body was conveyed back to the woods and was buried in a solemn manner ; but however, the siege continued for several days ; the Erians sued for peace ; the army immediately ceased from hostilities, and left the Erians in entire possession of the country.

down the declivity. Such covered paths, or rather the remains of them, lead from many of these ancient fortifications. Mr. Schoolcraft concludes that they were intended for the emergency of a prolonged siege. They would seem now, to have been but a poor defence for the water carriers, against the weapons of modern warfare; yet probably sufficient to protect them from arrows, and a foe that had no sappers or miners in their ranks.

There is an ancient battle field upon the Buffalo creek, six miles from Buffalo, near the Mission station. There are appearances of an enclosed area, a mound where human bones have been excavated, remains of pottery ware, &c. The Senecas have a tradition that here was a last decisive battle between their people and their inveterate enemies the Kah-Kwahs; though there would seem to be no reason why the fortification should not be classed among those that existed long before the Senecas are supposed to have inhabited this region.

A mile north of Aurora village, in Erie county, there are several small lakes or ponds, around and between which, there are knobs or elevations, thickly covered with a tall growth of pine; upon them, are several mounds, where many human bones have been excavated. In fact, Aurora and its vicinity, seems to have been a favorite resort not only for the ancient people whose works and remains we are noticing, but for the other races that succeeded them. Relics abound there perhaps to a greater extent than in any other locality in Western New York. An area of from three to four miles in extent, embracing the village, the ponds, the fine springs of water at the foot of the bluffs to the north, and the level plain to the south, would seem to have been thickly populated. There are in the village and vicinity few gardens and fields where ancient and Indian relics are not found at each successive ploughing. Few cellars are excavated without discovering them. In digging a cellar a few years since upon the farm of Chas. P. Pierson, a skeleton was exhumed, the thigh bones of which would indicate great height; exceeding by several inches, that of the tallest of our own race. In digging another cellar, a large number of skeletons, or detached bones, were thrown out. Upon the farm of M. B. Crooks, two miles from the village, where a tree had been turned up, several hundred pounds of axes were found; a blacksmith who was working up some axes that were found in Aurora, told the author that most of them were without any steel, but that the iron was of a superior quality. He had one that was *entirely of steel,* out of which he was manufacturing some edge tools.

Near the village, principally upon the farm of the late HORACE S. TURNER, was an extensive Beaver Dam. It is but a few years since an aged Seneca strolled away from the road, visited the ponds, the springs, and coming to a field once overflowed by the dam, but then reclaimed and cultivated, said these were the haunts of his youth — upon the hills he had chased the deer, at the springs he had slaked his thirst, and in the field he had trapped the beaver.

The ancient works at Fort Hill, Le Roy, are especially worthy of observation in connection with this interesting branch of history, or rather enquiry. The author is principally indebted for an account of them to MR. SCHOOLCRAFT's "Notes on the Iroquois," for which it was communicated by F. FOLLETT, of Batavia. They are three miles north of Le Roy, on an elevated point of land, formed by the junction of a small stream called Fordham's Brook, with Allan's Creek. The better view of Fort Hill, is had to the north of it, about a quarter of a mile on the road leading from Bergen to Le Roy. From this point of observation it needs little aid of the imagination to conceive that it was erected as a fortification by a large and powerful army, looking for a permanent and inaccessible bulwark of defence. From the center of the hill, in a northwesterly course, the country lies quite flat ; more immediately north, and inclining to the east, the land is also level for one hundred rods, where it rises nearly as high as the hill, and continues for several miles quite elevated. In approaching the hill from the north it stands very prominently before you, rising rather abruptly but not perpendicularly, to the height of eighty or ninety feet, extending about forty rods on a line east and west, the corners being round or truncated, and continuing to the south on the west side for some fifty or sixty rods, and on the east side for about half a mile, maintaining about the same elevation on the sides as in front; beyond which distance the line of the hill is that of the land around. There are undoubted evidences of its having been resorted to as a fortification, and of its having constituted a valuable point of defence to a rude and half civilized people. Forty years ago an entrenchment ten feet deep, and some twelve or fifteen feet wide, extended from the west to the east end, along the north or front part, and continued up each side about twenty rods, where it crossed over, and joining, made the circuit of entrenchment complete. At this day a portion of the entrenchment is easily perceived, for fifteen rods along the extreme western half of the north or front part, the cultivation of the soil and other causes having nearly obliterated all other portions. It would seem that this fortification was arranged more for protection against invasion from the north, this direction being evidently its most commanding position. Near the northwest corner, piles of rounded stones, have, at different times, been collected of hard consistence, which are supposed to have been used as weapons of defence by the besieged against the besiegers. Such skeletons as have been found in and about this locality, indicate a race of men averaging one third larger than the present race; so adjudged by anatomists. From the fortification, a trench leads to a spring of water. Arrow heads, pipes, beads, gouges, pestles, stone hatchets, have been found upon the ground, and excavated, in and about these fortifications. The pipes were of both stone and earthen ware ; there was one of baked clay, the bowl of which was in the form of a man's head and face, the nose, eyes, and other features being depicted in a style resembling some of the figures in Mr. STEVEN's plate of the ruins of Central America. Forest trees were standing in the trench and on its sides, in size and age not differing from those in the neighboring forests ; and upon the ground, the heart-woods of black-cherry trees of large size, the remains undoubtedly of a growth of timber that preceded the present growth. They were in such a state of soundness as to be used for timber by the first settlers. This last circumstance would establish greater antiquity for these works, than has been generally claimed from other evidences. The black-cherry of this region, attains usually the age of two hundred and seventy-five, and three hundred years ; the beech and maple groves of Western New York, bear evidences of having existed at least two hundred and forty or fifty years. These aggregates would shew that these works were over five hundred years old. But this, like other timber growth testimony that has been adduced — that seems to have been relied upon somewhat by Mr. CLINTON and others — is far from being satisfactory. We can only determine by this species of evidence that timber has been growing upon these mounds and fortifications at least a certain length of time ;— have no warrant for saying how much longer. Take for instance the case under immediate consideration :— How is it to be determined that there were not more than the two growths, of cherry, and beech and maple ; that other growths did not precede or intervene. These relics are found in our dense and heaviest timbered wood lands, below a deep vegetable mould interspersed with evidences of a long succession of timber growths and decays. We can in truth, form but a vague conception of the length of time since these works were constructed,—while we are authorized in saying they are of great antiquity, we are not authorized in limiting the period.

The following are among some reflections of Professor DEWEY of Rochester, who has reviewed Fort Hill at Le Roy, and furnished Mr. SCHOOLCRAFT with his observations. They may aid the reader, who is an antiquarian, in his speculations:—

"The forest has been removed. Not a tree remains on the quadrangle, and only a few on the edge of the ravine on the west. By cultivating the land, the trench is nearly filled in some places, though the line of it is clearly seen. On the north side the trench is considerable, and where the bridge crosses it, is three or four feet deep at the sides of the road. It will take only a few years more to obliterate it entirely, as not even a stump remains to mark out its line.

From this view it may be seen, or inferred,

1. That a real trench bounded three sides of the quadrangle. On the south side there was not found any trace of trench, palisadoes, blocks, &c.

2. It was formed long before the whites came into the country. The large trees on the ground and in the trench, carry us back to an early era.

3. The workers must have had some convenient tools for excavation.

4. The direction of the sides may have had some reference to the four cardinal points, though the situation of the ravines naturally marked out the lines.

5. It cannot have been designed merely to catch wild animals, to be driven into it from the south. The oblique line down to the spring is opposed to this supposition, as well as the insufficiency of such a trench to confine the animals of the forest.

6. The same reasons render it improbable that the quadrangle was designed to confine and protect domestic animals.

7. It was probably a sort of fortified place. There might have been a defence on the south side by a stockade, or some similar means which might have entirely disappeared.

By what people was this work done?

The articles found in the burying ground here, offer no certain reply. The axes, chisels, &c. found on tne Indian grounds in this part of the state, were evidently made of the green stone or trap of New England, like those found on the Connecticut river in Massachusetts. The pipe of limestone might be from that part of the country. The pipes seem to belong to different eras.

1. The limestone pipe indicates the work of the savage or aborigines.

2. The third indicates the age of French influence over the Indians. An intelligent French gentleman says such clay pipes are frequent among the town population in parts of France.

3. The second, and most curious, seems to indicate an earlier age and people.

The beads found at Fort Hill are long and coarse, made of baked clay, and may have had the same origin as the third pipe.

Fort Hill cannot have been formed by the French as one of their posts to aid in the destruction of the English colony of New-York; if the French had made Fort Hill a post as early as 1660 or 185 years ago, and then deserted it, the trees could not have grown to the size of the forest generally in 1810, or in 150 years afterwards. The white settlements had extended only twelve miles west of Avon in 1798, and some years after, (1800,) Fort Hill was covered with a dense forest. A chestnut tree, cut down in 1842, at Rochester, showed 254 concentric circles of wood, and must have been more than 200 years old in 1800. So opposed is the notion that this was a deserted French post.

Must we not refer Fort Hill to that race which peopled this country before the Indians who raised so many monuments greatly exceeding the power of the Indians, and who lived at a remote era."

Upon the upper end of Tonawanda Island, in the Niagara River, near the dwelling house of the late STEPHEN WHITE, in full view of the village of Tonawanda, and the Buffalo and Niagara Falls Rail Road, is an ancient mound, the elevation of which within the recollection of the early settlers, was at least ten feet. It is now from six to eight feet,—circular—twenty-five feet diameter at the base. In the centre, a deep excavation has been made, at different periods, in search of relics. A large number of human bones have been taken from it,—arrows, beads, hatchets, &c. The mound occupies a prominent position in the pleasure grounds laid out by Mr. White. How distinctly are different ages marked upon this spot! Here are the mouldering remains of a primitive race—a race whose highest achievments in the arts, was the fashioning from flint the rude weapons of war and the chase, the pipe and hatchet of stone; and here upon the other hand, is a mansion presenting good specimens

---

NOTE.— The title of this chapter would confine these notices to Holland Purchase. The author has gone a short distance beyond his bounds, to include a well defined specimen of these ancient works.

of modern architecture. Commerce has brought the materials for its chimney pieces from the quarries of Italy, and skill and genius have chiseled and given to them a mirror-like polish. Here in the midst of relics of another age, and of occupants of whom we know nothing beyond these evidences of their existence, are choice fruits, ornamental shrubbery, and graveled walks.

Directly opposite this mound upon the point formed by the junction of Tonawanda creek with the Niagara River there would seem to have been an ancient armory, and upon no small scale. There is intermingled with at least an acre of earth, chips of flint, refuse pieces, and imperfect arrows that were broken in process of manufacture. In the early cultivation of the ground, the plough would occasionally strike spots where these chips and pieces of arrows predominated over the natural soil.

On the north side of the Little Buffalo Creek, in the town of Lancaster, Erie County, there is an ancient work upon a bluff, about thirty feet above the level of the stream. A circular embankment encloses an acre. Thirty years ago this embankment was nearly breast high to a man of ordinary height. There were five gate-ways distinctly marked. A pine tree of the largest class in our forest, grew directly in one of the gate-ways. It was adjudged, (at the period named,) by practical lumbermen, to be FIVE HUNDRED YEARS OLD. Nearly opposite, a small stream puts into the Little Buffalo. Upon the point formed by the junction of the two streams, a mound extends across from one to the other, as if to enclose or fortify the point. In modern military practice, strong fortifications are invested sometimes by setting an army down before them and throwing up breast-works. May not this smaller work bear a similar relation to the larger one?

About one and a half miles west of Shelby Centre, Orleans county, is an ancient work. A broad ditch encloses in a form nearly circular, about three acres of land. The ditch is at this day, well defined several feet deep. Adjoining the spot on the south, is a swamp about one mile in width by two in length. This swamp was once, doubtless, if not a lake, an impassable morass. From the interior of the enclosure made by the ditch, there is what appears to have been, a passage way on the side next to the swamp. No other breach occurs in the entire circuit of the embankment. There are accumulated within and near this fort large piles of small stones of a size convenient to be thrown by the hand, or with a sling.* Arrow heads of flint are found in and near the enclosure, in great abundance, stone axes, &c. Trees of four hundred years growth stand upon the embankment, and underneath them have been found, earthen ware, pieces of plates or dishes, wrought with skill, presenting ornaments in relief, of various patterns. Some skeletons almost entire have been exhumed; many of giant size, not less than seven to eight feet in length. The skulls are large and well developed in the anterior lobe, broad between the ears, and flattened in the coronal region. Half a mile west of the fort is a sand hill. Here a large number of human skeletons have been exhumed, in a perfect state. Great numbers appeared to have been buried in the same grave. Many of the skulls appear to have been broken in with clubs or stones. " This," says S. M. BURROUGHS, ESQ, of Medina, (to whom the author is indebted for the description,) "was doubtless the spot where a great battle had been fought. Were not these people a branch of the Aztecs? The earthen ware found here seems to indicate a knowledge of the arts known to that once powerful nation."

The REV. SAMUEL KIRKLAND† visited and described several of these remains west of the Genesee River, in the year 1788. At that early period, before they had been disturbed by the antiquarian, the plough or the harrow, they must have been much more perfect, and better defined than now. Mr. KIRKLAND says in his journal, that after leaving "Kanawageas," ‡ he travelled twenty-six miles and encamped for the night at a place called "Joaki," ‖ on the

---

* These piles of small stone are frequently spoken of in connection with these works, by those who saw them at an early period of white settlement.

† Mr. K. was the pioneer Protestant Missionary among the Iroquois. The Rev. Dr. Wheelock, of Lebanon, Conn., who was his early tutor, in one of his letters to the Countess of Huntingdon, in 1765, says: —" A young Englishman, whom I sent last fall to winter with the numerous and savage tribes of the Senecas, in order to learn their language, and fit him for a mission among them; where no missionary has hitherto dared to venture. This bold adventure of his, which under all the circumstances of it is the most extraordinary of the kind I have ever known, has been attended with abundant evidence of a divine blessing." Connected as was the subject of this eulogy with other branches of our local history, he will be frequently referred to in the course of this work.

‡ Avon.

‖ Batavia, or the " Great Bend of the Tonnewanta," as it was uniformly called by the early travellers on the trail from Tioga Point to Fort Niagara and Canada. ☞ See account of Indian Trails. Batavia was favored with several Indian names. In Seneca, the one used by Mr K. would be *Racoon*.

river "Tonawanda." Six miles from the place of encampment, he rode to the "open fields."* Here he "walked out about half a mile with one of the Seneca chiefs to view" the remains which he thus describes : —

"This place is called by the Senecas Tegatainasghque, which imports a double fortified town, or a town with a fort at each end. Here are the vestiges of two forts; the one contains about four acres of ground; the other, distant from this about two miles, and situated at the other extremity of the ancient town, encloses twice that quantity. The ditch around the former (which I particularly examined) is about five or six feet deep. A small stream of living water, with a high bank, circumscribed nearly one third of the enclosed ground. There were traces of six gates, or avenues, around the ditch, and a dug-way near the works to the water. The ground on the opposite side of the water, was in some places nearly as high as that on which they built the fort, which might make it nessessary for this covered way to the water. A considerable number of large, thrifty oaks have grown up within the enclosed grounds, both in and upon the ditch; some of them at least, appeared to be two hundred years old or more. The ground is of a hard gravelly kind, intermixed with loam, and more plentifully at the brow of the hill. In some places, at the bottom of the ditch, I could run my cane a foot or more into the ground; so that probably the ditch was much deeper in its original state than it appears to be now. Near the northern fortification, which is situated on high ground, are the remains of a funeral pile. The earth is raised about six feet above the common surface, and betwixt twenty and thirty feet in diameter. From the best information I can get of the Indian Historians, these Forts were made previous to the Senecas being admitted into the confederacy of the Mohawks, Onondagas, Oneidas and Cayugas, and when the former were at war with the Mississaugas and other Indians around the great lakes. This must have been' near three hundred years ago, if not more, by many concurring accounts which I have obtained from different Indians of several different tribes. Indian tradition says also that these works were raised, and a famous battle fought here, in the pure Indian style and with Indian weapons, long before their knowledge and use of fire arms or any knowledge of the Europeans. These nations at that time used, in fighting, bows and arrows, the spear or javelin, pointed with bone, and the

---

* The openings, as they are termed, in the towns of Elba and Alabama; lying on either side of the Batavia and Lockport road, but chiefly, between that road and the Tonawanda Creek. The antiquarian who goes in search of the ancient *Tegatainasghque*, will be likely to divide his attention between old and new things. It was a part of Tonawanda Indian Reservation. About twenty-five years since, it was sold to the Ogden Company ; and the ancient " open fields " now present a broad expanse of wheat fields, interspersed with farm buildings that give evidence of the elements of wealth that have been found in the soil.

war club or death mall. When the former were expended, they came into close engagement in using the latter. Their warrior's dress or coat of mail for this method of fighting, was a short jacket made of willow sticks, or moon wood, and laced tight around the body; the head covered with a cap of the same kind, but commonly worn double for the better security of that part against a stroke from the war club. In the great battle fought at this place, between the Senecas and Western Indians, some affirm their ancestors have told them there were eight hundred of their enemies slain; others include the killed on both sides to make that number. All their historians agree in this, that the battle was fought here, where the heaps of slain are buried, before the arrival of the Europeans; some say three, some say four, others five ages ago; they reckon an age one hundred winters or colds. I would further remark upon this subject that there are vestiges of ancient fortified towns in various parts, throughout the extensive territory of the Six Nations. I find also by constant enquiry, that a tradition prevails among the Indians in general, that all Indians came from the west. I have wished for an opportunity to pursue this inquiry with the more remote tribes of Indians, to satisfy myself, at least, if it be their universal opinion.

"On the south side of Lake Erie, are a series of old fortifications, from Cattaraugus Creek to the Pennsylvania line, a distance of fifty miles. Some are from two to four miles apart, others half a mile only. Some contain five acres. The walls or breast-works are of earth, and are generally on grounds where there are appearances of creeks having flowed into the lake, or where there was a bay. Further south there is said to be another chain parallel with the first, about equi-distant from the lake.

"These remains of art, may be viewed as connecting links of a great chain, which extends beyond the confines of our state, and becomes more magnificent and curious as we recede from the northern lakes, pass through Ohio into the great valley of the Mississippi, thence to the gulf of Mexico through Texas into New Mexico and South America. In this vast range of more than three thousand miles, these monuments of ancient skill gradually become more remarkable for their number, magnitude and interesting variety, until we are lost in admiration and astonishment, to find, as Baron Humboldt informs us, *in a world which we call new*, ancient institutions, religious ideas, and forms of edifices, similar to those of Asia, which there seem to go back to the dawn of civilization."

"Over the great secondary region of the Ohio, are the ruins of what once were forts, cemeteries, temples, altars, camps, towns,

---

NOTE.—The traditions given to Mr. Kirkland at so early a period, are added to his account of the old Forts, to be taken in connection with adverse theories and conclusions upon the same point. As has before been observed, many of the Senecas who have since been consulted, do not pretend to any satisfactory knowledge upon the subjects.

villages, race-grounds and other places of amusement, habitations of chieftains, videttes, watch-towers and monuments."

"It is," says Mr. Atwater,* "nothing but one vast cemetery of the beings of past ages. Man and his works, the mammoth, tropical animals, the cassia tree and other tropical plants, are here reposing together in the same formation. By what catastrophe they were overwhelmed and buried in the same strata it would be impossible to say, unless it was that of the general deluge."

"In the valley of the Mississippi, the monuments of buried nations are unsurpassed in magnitude and melancholy grandeur by any in North America. Here cities have been traced similar to those of Ancient Mexico, once containing hundreds of thousands of souls. Here are to be seen thousands of tumuli, some an hundred feet high, others many hundred feet in circumference, the places of their worship, their sepulchre, and perhaps of their defence. Similar mounds are scattered throughout the continent, from the shores of the Pacific into the interior of our State as far as Black River and from the Lakes to South America."†

So much for all we can see or know of our ancient predecessors. The whole subject is but incidental to the main purposes of local history. The reader who wishes to pursue it farther will be assisted in his enquiries by a perusal of Mr. Schoolcraft's Notes on the Iroquois. But the mystery of this pre-occupancy is far from being satisfactorily explained. It is an interesting, fruitful source of theories, enquiry and speculation.

---

*Atwater's Antiquities of the West.
†Yates and Moulton's History of New York.

CHAPTER II.

THE IROQUOIS, OR FIVE NATIONS.*

Emerging from a region of doubt and conjecture, we arrive at another branch of local history, replete with interest — less obscure, — though upon its threshold we feel the want of reliable data, the lights that guide us in tracing the history of those who have written records.

The Seneca Indians were our immediate predecessors — the pre-occupants from whom the title of the Holland Purchase was derived. They were the Fifth Nation of a CONFEDERACY, termed by themselves Mingoes, as inferred by Mr. Clinton, Ho-de-no-sau-nee,† as inferred by other writers; the Confederates, by the English; the Maquaws, by the Dutch; the Massowamacs, by the Southern Indians; the IROQUOIS, by the French; by which last name they are now usually designated, in speaking or writing of the distinct branches of the Aborigines of the United States.

The original Confederates were the Mohawks, having their principal abode upon that river; the Oneidas, upon the southern shore of Oneida Lake; the Cayugas near Cayuga Lake; the Senecas, upon Seneca Lake and the Genesee River. Those localities were their principal seats, or the places of their Council fires. They may be said generally, to have occupied in detached towns and villages the whole of this State, from the Hudson to the Niagara River, now embraced in the counties of Schenectady, Schoharie, Montgomery, Fulton, Herkimer, Oneida, Madison, Onondaga, Cayuga, Seneca, Wayne, Ontario, Livingston, Genesee, Wyoming, Monroe, Orleans, Niagara, Erie, Chautauque, Cattaragus, Alle-

---

* The "Five" Nations, at the period of our earliest knowledge of them — the "Six" Nations after they had adopted the Tuscaroras, in 1712.

† "The People of the Long House," from the circumstance that they likened their political structure to a long tenement or dwelling.

ghany, Steuben and Yates. A narrower limit of their dwelling places, the author is aware, has been usually designated; but in reference to the period of the first European advent among them — 1678 — it is to be inferred that their habitations were thus extended, not only from the traces of their dwellings, and the relics of their rude cultivation of the soil, but from the records of the early Jesuit Missionaries. Their missions were at different periods, extended from the Hudson to the Niagara River, and each one of them would seem to have had several villages in its vicinity. Each of the Five Nations undoubtedly had a principal seat. They were as indicated by their names. And each had its tributary villages, extended as has been assumed. It was plainly a coming together from separate localities — a gathering of clansmen — to resist the invasion of De Nonville; and it is to be inferred from the journal of Father Hennepin that there were villages of the "Iroquois Senecas" in the neighborhood of La Salle's ship yard on the Niagara River, and the primitive garrison or "palisade," at its mouth. The Missionaries who went out from the "place of ship building," and from the "Fort at Niagara" from time to time, upon apparently short excursions, visited different villages. The Jesuit Missions upon the Mohawk, and at Onondaga would seem to have been visited, each by the inhabitants of several villages. The author rejects the conclusion, that the Tonawanda, and the Buffalo Indian villages, were not founded until after the expedition of General SULLIVAN; and concludes that these and other settlements of the Iroquois existed prior to the European advent, west of the Genesee River. While some of the Seneca Indians assume the first position, others, equally intelligent, and as well instructed in their traditions, do not pretend to thus limit the period of settlement at these points.

Their actual dominion had a far wider range. The Five Nations claimed "all the land not sold to the English, from the mouth of Sorrel River, on the south side of Lakes Erie and Ontario, on both sides of the Ohio till it falls into the Mississippi; and on the north side of these Lakes that whole territory between the Ottawa River and Lake Huron, and even beyond the straits between that and Lake Erie."* And in another place the same author says:—
"When the Dutch began the settlement of this country, all the Indians on Long Island, and the northern shores of the Sound, on

---

*Smith's History of New York.

the banks of the Connecticut, Hudson, Delaware, and Susquehannah Rivers, were in subjection to the Five Nations, and acknowledged it by paying tribute. The French historians of Canada, both ancient and modern, agree that the more Northern Indians, were driven before the superior martial prowess of the Confederates." "The Ho-de-no-sau-nee, occupied our precise territory, and their council fires burned continually from the Hudson to the Niagara. Our old forests have rung with their war shouts, and been enlivened with their festivals of peace. Their feathered bands, their eloquence, their deeds of valor have had their time and place. In their progressive course, they had stretched around the half of our republic, and rendered their name a terror nearly from ocean to ocean; when the advent of the Saxon race arrested their career, and prepared the way for the destruction of the Long House, and the final extinguishment of the Council Fires of the Confederacy.* "At one period we hear the sound of their war cry along the Straits of the St. Mary's, and at the foot of Lake Superior. At another, under the walls of Quebec, where they finally defeated the Hurons, under the eyes of the French. They put out the fires of the Gah-kwas and Eries. They eradicated the Susquehannocks. They placed the Lenapes, the Nanticokes, and the Munsees under the yoke of subjection. They put the Metoacks and Manhattans under tribute. They spread the terror of their arms over all New England. They traversed the whole length of the Appalachian Chain and descended like the enraged yagisho and megalonyx, on the Cherokees and Catawbas. SMITH encountered their warriors in the settlement of Virginia, and LA SALLE on the discovery of the Illinois." † "The immediate dominion of the Iroquois — when the Mohawks, Oneidas, Onondagas, Cayugas, and Senecas, were first visited by the trader, the Missionary, or the war parties of the French — stretched, as we have seen, from the borders of Vermont to Western New York, from the Lakes to the head waters of the Ohio, the Susquehannah and the Delaware. The number of their warriors was declared by the French in 1660, to have been two thousand two hundred; and in 1677, an English agent sent on purpose to ascertain their strength, confirmed the precision of the statement. Their geographical position made them umpires in the

---

* Letters on the Iroquois, by Shenandoah in American Review.
† Schoolcraft.

contest of the French for dominion in the west. Besides their political importance was increased by their conquests. Not only did they claim some supremacy in Northern New England as far as the Kennebeck, and to the south as far as New Haven, and were acknowledged as absolute lords over the conquered Lenappe, — the peninsula of Upper Canada was their hunting field by right of war; they had exterminated the Eries and Andastes, both tribes of their own family, the one dwelling on the south-eastern banks of lake Erie, the other on the head waters of the Ohio; they had triumphantly invaded the tribes of the west as far as Illinois ; their warriors had reached the soil of Kentucky and Western Virginia ; and England, to whose alliance they steadily inclined, availed itself of their treaties for the cession of territories, to encroach even on the Empire of France in America."*

While the citations that we have made from reliable authorities, sufficiently establish the extended dominions of the Iroquois, they also sanction the highest estimate that has been made of their bravery and martial prowess. Their strength and uniform success, are mainly to be attributed to their social and political organization. They were *Confederates.* Their enemies, or the nations they chose to make war with, for the purposes of conquest, extended rule, political supremacy — were detached, — had feuds perhaps between themselves — could not act in concert. The Iroquois were a five fold cord. Their antagonists, but single strands, and if acting occasionally in concert, it was in the absence of a league or union, of that peculiar character that made their assailants invincible. Added to this, is the concurrent testimony of historians, that the Iroquois, in physical and mental organization far excelled all other of the aboriginal nations, or tribes of our country. A position justified by our own observation and comparisons. Even in our own day, now that they are dwindled down to a mere remnant of what they were; confined to a few thousand acres of a broad domain they once posessed, (and even these stinted allotments grudgingly made, and their possession envied by rapacious pre-emptionists,) now that they have survived the terrible ordeal — a contest with our race, and all its blighting and contaminating influences, — their superiority is evinced in various ways; their supremacy apparent. Upon the banks of the Tonawanda, the Alleghany, the Cattaragus,

---

*Bancroft's History of the United States.

there are now unbroken, proud spirits of this noble race of men, who would justify the highest encomiums that history has bestowed.

If we are told that they have degenerated, the position can be controverted by the citation of individual instances. If their ambition has been crushed; if they feel, as well they may, that their condition has been changed; that they are in a measure dependants upon a soil, and in a region, where they were but a little time since, lords and masters; if they are conscious, as well they may be, that superior diplomacy, artful and over-reaching negotiation, has as effectually conquered and despoiled them of their possessions as a conquest of arms would have done; if they feel that they are aliens, as they are made by our laws, upon the native soil of themselves and a long line of ancestors.— There are yet worthy descendants of the primitive stock — the same "Seneca Iroquois," in mind, in feature, in some of the best attributes of our common nature, — that La Salle, Hennepin, Tonti, Joncair, found here in these western forests; that the seemingly partial, yet truthful historian has described. While the vices of civilization — or those that civilization has introduced — have effectually degenerated a large portion of them; debased them to a level with the worst of the whites; there are those, and a large class of them, that have, with a moral firmness that is admirable — a native, uneducated sense of right and wrong, of virtue and vice; resisted all the temptations with which they have been beset and surrounded, and command our highest esteem, not for what they, or their progenitors have been; but for their intrinsic merits. Their ancient council fires, are not extinguished; though they burn not as brightly in the allotted retreat where they are now kindled, as of yore, when they blazed in the "Long House," from Hudson to Lake Erie. Their confederacy is dwindled to a mere shadow of what it was, but it yet exists. "They have been stripped so entirely of their possessions as to have retained scarcely sufficient for a sepulchre. They have been shorn so entirely of their power as to be scarcely heard when appealing to justice from the rapacity of the pre-emptive claimants."* And yet they are a distinctive people — their Ancient League in force; their ancient rites and ceremonies are still performed. From their ancient seat at Onondaga, the council fire is transferred to Tonawanda. Here it is yet kindled. Here the representatives of

---

Shenandoah.

the Senecas, the Tuscaroras, the Onondagas, the scattered remnants of the Mohawks, Cayugas and Oneidas, yet assemble, go through with their ancient rites and ceremonies;—their speeches, dances, exhortations, sacrifices, &c.; supply vacancies that have occurred in the ranks of their sachems and chiefs, furnish a feeble but true representation of the doings of their ancient confederacy, when it was the sole conservator and legislature of two thirds of our Empire State, and held in subjection nearly that proportion of our own modern and similarly constructed Union.

The historians of the Iroquois, have found ample authority for the extended dominion, and military supremacy they have conceded to them, in the writings of the French Missionaries, and in their own well authenticated traditions; and there is still more reliable testimony. As in after times—in their wars with the French, and in the Border Wars of the Revolution, a large proportion of their prisoners were saved from torture and execution and adopted into families and tribes, for the double purpose of supplying the loss of their own people slain in battle or taken prisoners—of keeping their numbers good—and for solacing the bereaved relatives, by substituting a favorite captive in the family circle. This was not only the ancient, but the modern custom of the Iroquois. The commentators upon their institutions, have inferred that this was a part of their system and policy. This will be quite apparent in some accounts that will follow of white prisoners who were found among the Senecas in Western New York, at the earliest period of white settlement, and whose descendants are still among them. There are now upon the Tonawanda Reservation, at Cattaragus and Alleghany, descendants of Cherokee, Seminole and Catawba captives; in fact of nearly all the nations, which we are told in their traditions, they were at war with in early times. It is singular, with what apparent precision, they will trace the mixed blood, when none but themselves can discover any difference of complexion or features. Tradition must be their helper, in determining after the lapse of centuries, and a long succession of generations, where the blood of the captive is mingled with their own. They are good genealogists; far better than we are, who can avail ourselves of written records.

And there is a fact connected with this repriveing and adopting captives, that commands our especial wonder, if not our admiration. In all the numerous cases that we have accounts of, with few exceptions, captivity soon ceased to be irksome; an escape from it hardly a desirable consummation! Was the captive of their own race and color, he soon forgot that he was in the wigwam of strangers, away from his country and kindred; he was no alien; social, political, and family immunities were extended to him. He was as one of them in all respects. Had he left behind father, mother, brother, sister or wife, they were supplied him; and it baffles all our preconceived opinions of an arbitrary, instinctive sense of kindred blood affinity, when told how easily the captive adapted himself to his new relations; how soon the adopter and the adopted conformed to an alliance that was merely conventional. And so it was in a great degree with our own race. They too, were captives among the Iroquois, but wore no captive's chains. After a little there was no restraint, no coercion, no desire to escape. Upon this point, we have the recorded testimony of MARY JEMISON, of HORATIO JONES, and several others. MRS. JEMISON, who had more than ordinary natural endowments; who possessed a mind and affections adapted to the enjoyments of civilization and refinement; affirms that in a short time after she was made a captive, she was content with her condition; and she affirmed at the close of a long life, spent principally among the Senecas, that she had uniformly been treated with kindness. The author in his boyhood has listened to the recitals of captive whites among the Senecas, and well remembers how incredible it seemed that they should have preferred a continuance among them to a return to their own race. This to us seemingly singular choice, with those who were young when captured, is partly to be accounted for in the novelty of the change —the sports and pastimes—the "freedom of the woods"—the absence of restraints and checks, upon youthful inclinations. But chiefly it was the influence of kindness, extended to them as soon as they were adopted. The Indian mother knew no difference between her natural and adopted children; there were no social discriminations, or if any, in favor of the adopted captive; they had all the rights and privileges in their tribes, nations, confederacy, enjoyed by the native Iroquois.*

The Senecas have traditions of the execution of several

---

* This kind treatment of prisoners, it is not contended, was uniform. A portion of them were subjected to torture and death. It was however, one thing or the other: — death attended by all the horrors of savage custom, or adoption into a family, and the treatment that has been indicated.

prisoners, that were made captives in their wars with the Southern Indians. A stream that puts into the Alleghany, below Olean, bears the Seneca name of a Cherokee prisoner, who, their traditions say, was executed there. MRS. JEMISON* says, her husband, HIOKATOO, was engaged in 1731, to assist in collecting an army to go against the Catawbas, Cherokees, and other Southern Indians. That they met the enemy on the Tennessee River, "rushed upon them in ambuscade, and massacred 1200 on the spot;" that after that, the battle continued for two days. She names several other wars with the Southern Indians, in which her warrior husband was engaged. It is but a few years since there were surviving aged Seneca Indians, who recounted their exploits in wars waged by the Iroquois against neighboring and far distant nations.

The reader who has not made himself familiar with the history of the aboriginal pre-occupants of our region, has, perhaps, in this brief introduction of them, their wars and extended dominion — their pre-eminence among the nations of their race — the high position assigned them by historians, — been sufficiently interested to desire to know more of them; especially to know something of the organization and frame work of a political system — a confederacy so wisely conceived by the untaught Statesmen of the forest, who had no precedents to consult, no written lore of ages to refer to, no failures or triumphs of systems of human government to serve for models or comparisons; nothing to guide them but the lights of nature; nothing to prompt them but necessity and emergency.

The French historian, VOLNEY, was the first to pronounce the Iroquois the ROMANS OF THE WEST; a proud, and not undeserved title, which succeeding historians and commentators have not withheld. " Had they enjoyed the advantages possessed by the Greeks and Romans, there is no reason to believe they would have been at all inferior to these celebrated nations. Their minds appear to have been equal to any effort within the reach of man. Their conquests, if we consider their numbers and circumstances, were little inferior to those of Rome itself. In their harmony, the unity of their operations, the energy of their character, the vastness, vigor, and success of their enterprises, and the strength

---

* Life of Mary Jemison by James E. Seaver, revised and enlarged by Ebenezer Mix.

and sublimity of their eloquence, they may be fairly compared with the Greeks. Both the Greeks and Romans, before they began to rise into distinction, had already reached the state of society in which men are able to improve. The Iroquois had not. The Greeks and Romans had ample means for improvement; the Iroquois had none."* "If we except the celebrated league, which united the Five Nations into a Federal Republic, we can discern few traces of political wisdom among the rude American tribes as discover any great degree of foresight or extent of intellectual abilities."† "The Iroquois bore this proud appellation, not only by conquests over other tribes, but by encouraging the people of other nations to incorporate with them; 'a Roman principle,' says THATCHER, 'recognized in the practice as well as theory of these lords of the forest.'"‡ "From whatever point we scrutinize the general features of their confederacy, we are induced to regard it, in many respects, as a beautiful, as well as remarkable structure, and to hold it up as the triumph of Indian legislation."§ "It cannot, I presume, be doubted, that the confederates were a peculiar and extraordinary people, contra-distinguished from the wars of the Indian Nations by great attainments in polity, in government, in negotiation, in eloquence, and in war."‖

The peculiar structure of the confederacy of the Iroquois, is one of the most interesting features of our aboriginal history. A brief analysis of it is all that will be attempted. Its general features were known to their earliest historians, but it was left to a recent contributor¶ to the archives of the New York Historical Society, to investigate the subject with a zeal, industry and ability, which do him great credit; to give us a better knowledge of the legislation and laws of these sons of the forest, than we before possessed. To that source principally, with occasional reference to other authorities; the author is indebted for the materials for the sketch that follows:—

The existence of the Iroquois upon the soil now constituting Western and Middle New York, is distinctly traced back to the period of the discovery of America. Their traditions go beyond

---

* President Dwight. † Robertson's America.

‡ Yonnondio, or the Warriors of Genesee, by W. H. C. Hosmer.

§ Shenandoah. ‖ Mr. Clinton.

¶Letters on the Iroquois, Shenandoah; addressed to Albert Gallatin, President. N. Y. Historical Society.

that period—or in fact have no limits; some of their relators contending that this was *always their home;* others, that they came here by conquest; and others, that they were peaceful emigrants from a former home in the south. This involves a mooted question, which it is not necessary here to discuss, if indeed it admits of any satisfactory conclusion. They fix upon no definite period in reference to the origin of their confederacy. It existed, and was recognized by the Dutch, who were the first adventurers in the eastern portion of our state; by the earliest French Jesuits in the valley of the Mohawk, at Onondaga, and along the south shores of Lake Ontario, and upon the Niagara River; and there were evidences of a long precedent existence, that corresponded with their traditions.

Like most systems of human governments, and especially the better ones—it was undoubtedly the offspring of emergency. Protracted wars, such as their race have been subject to since our first acquaintance with it — and which has often called into requisition the mediatory offices of our government, had created the necessity of a union of strength—an alliance, for offence and defence. It was upon a smaller scale to be sure, than an alliance that followed centuries after, between the crowned heads of Europe; but was dictated by better motives, and far more wisdom; though with a history of Iroquois conquests before us, it is not to be denied, that they not only contemplated peace and union at home, but like their imitators meditated assaults upon their neighbors. The one was suggested by the autocrat of Russia, from a palace—tradition attributes the other to a "wise man[*] of the Onondaga nation," whose dwelling was but a hunter's lodge.

The confederacy in one leading feature at least, was not unlike our Federal Union. The Five Nations were as so many states, reserving to themselves some well defined powers, but yielding others for the general good.

The supreme power of the confederacy, was vested in a congress of sachems, fifty in number. The Mohawks were entitled to nine representatives; the Oneidas to nine; the Onondagas to fourteen; the Cayugas to ten; the Senecas to eight. "The office of sachem was hereditary. They were "raised up," not by their respective nations, but by a council of all the sachems. They formed the

---

[*] Dagánowedá.

"council of the League," and in them resided the Executive legislative and judicial authority. In their own localities, at home among their own people, these sachems were the government, forming five independent local sovereignties, modelled after the general congress of sachems. There were in fact five distinct local republics within one general republic. It was as it would be with our delegation in Congress, if after discharging their duties at the seat of the general government, they came home and formed a council for all purposes of local government. Although not a monarchy, it "was the rule of the few," and these few possessing what would look to us like a power very liable to abuse — the power of self creation; filling up their own ranks, as vacancies occured from time to time; and yet we are told that this formed no exception to the general well working of the system. The members of the council of the League were equals in power and authority; and yet from some provision in their organization, or from a necessity which must have existed with the Iroquois Council as with all conventional or legislative bodies, it is to be inferred that they had a head or leader — something answering the purposes of a speaker in our system of legislation, or a president, in our conventional arrangement. How all this was managed it is difficult to understand. There was always residing in the central Onondaga nation, a sachem who had at least a nominal superiority; he was regarded as the head of the confederacy, and had dignities and honors, above his fellow sachems; and yet his prerogatives were only such as were tacitly allowed or conceded; not derived as we would say, from any "constitutional" provisions. His position was an hereditary one, derived, as is affirmed by tradition, from an Onondaga chief— TA-DO-DA-HOH, a famous chief and warrior, who was co-temporary with the formation of the confederacy. He had rendered himself

---

NOTE.—Those into whose hands may chance to have fallen the pamphlet of the native Tuscarora historian, David Cusick, will remember his picture of "At-to-tar-ho." This was the real or imaginary "Ta-do-da-hoh" of Onondaga; the name varying with the different dialects. With rather more than the ordinary love of fancy and fiction, inherent in his race, the Tuscarora narrator has invested his hero with something more than human attributes; and has awarded to his memory, a wood cut — rude but graphic. He is represented as a monarch, quietly smoking his pipe, sitting in one of the marshes of Onondaga, giving audience to an embassy from the Mohawks, who have come to solicit his co-operation in the formation of a League. Living serpents are entwined around him, extending their hissing heads in every direction. Every thing around him, and the place of his residence, were such as to inspire fear and respect. His dishes and spoons were made of the skulls of enemies he had slain in battle. Him, when they had duly approached with presents, and burned tobacco in friendship, in their pipes, by way of frankincense, they placed at the head of the League as its presiding officer.

illustrious by military achievements. "Down to this day, among the Iroquois, his name is the personification of heroism, of forecast, and of dignity of character. He was reluctant to consent to the new order of things, as he would be shorn of his power, and placed among a number of equals. To remove this objection, his sachemship was dignified above the others, by certain special privileges, not inconsistent, however, with an equal distribution of powers; and from his day to the present, this title has been regarded as more noble and illustrious than any other, in the catalogue of Iroquois nobility."

"With a mere league of Indian nations, the constant tendency would be to a rupture, from remoteness of position and interest, and from the inherent weakness of such a compact. In the case under inspection, something more lasting was aimed at than a simple union of the five nations, in the nature of an alliance. A blending of the national sovereignties into one government, with direct and manifold relations between the people and the Confederacy, as such, was sought for and achieved by these forest statesmen. On first observation, the powers of the government appear to be so entirely centralized, that the national independencies nearly disappear; but this is very far from the fact. The crowning feature of the Confederacy, as a political structure, is the perfect independence and individuality of the nations, in the midst of a central and embracing government, which presents such a united and cemented exterior, that its subdivisions would scarcely be discovered in transacting business with the Confederacy. This remarkable result was in part effected by the provision that the same rulers who governed the Confederacy in their joint capacity, should, in their separate state, still be the rulers of the several nations.

"For all the purposes of a local and domestic, and many of a political character, the nations were entirely independent of each other. The nine Mohawk sachems administered the affairs of that nation with joint authority, precisely in the same manner as they did, in connection with others, the affairs of the League at large. With similar powers, the ten Cayuga sachems, by their joint councils, regulated the internal and domestic affairs of their nation. As the sachems of each nation stood upon a perfect equality, in authority and privileges, the measure of influence was determined entirely by the talents and address of the individual. In the councils of the nation, which were of frequent occurrence, all business of national concernment was transacted; and, although the questions moved on such occasions would be finally settled by the opinions of the sachems, yet such was the spirit of the Iroquois system of government, that the influence of the inferior chiefs, the warriors, and even of the women, would make itself felt, whenever the subject itself aroused a general public interest.

"The powers and duties of the sachems were entirely of a civil character, but yet were arbitrary within their sphere of action. If we sought their warrant for the exercise of power, in the etymology of the word, in their language, which corresponds with sachem, it would intimate a check upon, rather than an enlargement of, the civil authority; for it signifies, simply, 'a counsellor of the people,'—a beautiful and appropriate designation of a ruler."

There were in each of the Five Nations, and in the aggregate, the same number of War Chiefs as sachems. The subordination of the military to the civil power, was indicated upon all occasions of the assembling of the councils, by each sachem having a War Chief standing behind him to aid with his counsel, and execute the commands of his superior. If the two, however, went out upon a war party, the precedence was reversed, or in fact the sachem, who was supreme in council, was but a subordinate in the ranks. The supreme command of the war forces, and the general conduct of the wars of the confederacy was entrusted to two military chiefs raised up as the sachems were, their offices hereditary. These were, in all cases to be of the Seneca nation.*

The third class of officers was created long after the organization of the Confederacy, since the advent of Europeans among them,—the chiefs. They were elected from time to time as necessity or convenience required, their number unlimited. Their powers were originally confined to the local affairs of their respective nations; they were home advisers and counsellors of the sachems; but in process of time, they became in some respects, equal in rank and authority to the sachems.

"It is, perhaps, in itself singular that no religious functionaries were recognized in the Confederacy (none ever being raised up); although there were certain officers in the several nations who officiated at the religious festivals, which were held at stated seasons throughout the year. There never existed, among the Iroquois, a regular and distinct religious profession, or office, as

---

* They likened, as will have been seen, their political edifice, to a Long House; its door opening to the West. The Senecas occupying the door way, at the West, where hostile onsets were looked for, the location of the chief military commanders was assigned to them. It was the province of the Senecas, from their location, to first take the war path. If invaded, they were to drive back the invaders. If too formidable for them, they called upon the next allies, the Onondagas, and so on when necessary, to the Eastern end of the Long House, occupied by the Mohawks.

among most nations; and it was, doubtless, owing to the simplicity, as well as narrowness, of their religious creed.

"With the officers above enumerated, the administration of the Confederacy was entrusted. The government sat lightly upon the people, who, in effect, were governed but little. It seemed to each that individual independence, which the Hodénosaunee knew how to prize as well as the Saxon; and which, amid all political changes, they have contrived to preserve. The institutions which would be expected to exist under the government whose frame-work has just been sketched, would necessarily be simple. Their mode of life, and limited wants, the absence of all property, and the infrequency of crime, dispensed with a vast amount of the legislation and machinery, incident to the protection of civilized society. While, therefore, it would be unreasonable to seek those high qualities of mind, which result from ages of cultivation, in such a rude state of existence, it would be equally irrational to regard the Indian character as devoid of all those higher characteristics which ennoble the human race. If he has never contributed a page to science, nor a discovery to art; if he loses, in the progress of generations, as much as he gains; still, there are certain qualities of his mind which shine forth in all the lustre of natural perfection, and which must ever elicit admiration. His simple integrity, his generosity, his unbounded hospitality, his love of truth, and, above all, his unbroken fidelity,—a sentiment inborn, and standing out so conspicuously in his character, that it has, not untruthfully, become its living characteristic; all these are adornments of humanity, which no art of education can instill, nor refinement of civilization can bestow. If they exist at all, it is because the gifts of the Deity have never been debased. The high state of public morals, celebrated by the poet as reached and secured under Augustus, it was the higher and prouder boast of the Iroquois never to have lost. In such an atmosphere of moral purity, he grew up to manhood.

> 'Culpari metuit fides:
> Nullis polluitur casta domus stupris:
> Mos et lex maculosum edomuit nefas.'

If our Indian predecessor, with the virtues and blemishes, the power and weakness, which alternate in his character, is ever rightly comprehended, it will be the result of an insight into his social relations, and an understanding of the institutions which reflect the higher elements of his intellect."

In each nation there were eight tribes, which were arranged in two divisions and named as follows:—

| Wolf, | Bear, | Beaver, | Turtle, |
| Deer, | Snipe, | Heron, | Hawk. |

"The division of the people of each nation into eight tribes, whether pre-existing, or perfected at the establishment of the Confederacy did not terminate in its objects with the nation itself. It became the means of effecting the most perfect union of separate nations 'ever devised by the wit of man.' In effect, the Wolf Tribe was divided into five parts, and one-fifth of it placed in each of the five nations. The remaining tribes were subjected to the same division and distribution: thus giving to each nation the eight tribes, and making in their separated state, forty tribes in the Confederacy. Between those of the same name — or in other words, between the separated parts of each tribe — there existed a tie of brotherhood which linked the nations together with indissoluble bonds. The Mohawk of the Beaver Tribe, recognized the Seneca of the Beaver Tribe as his brother, and they were bound to each other by the ties of consanguinity. In like manner the Oneida of the Turtle or other Tribe, received the Cayuga, or the Onondaga of the same tribe, as a brother; and with a fraternal welcome. This cross-relationship between the tribes of the same name, and which was stronger, if possible, than the chain of brotherhood between the several tribes of the same nation, is still preserved in all its original strength. It doubtless furnishes the chief reason of the tenacity with which the fragments of the old Confederacy still cling together. If either of the five nations had wished to cast off the alliance, it must also have broken the bond of brotherhood. Had the nations fallen into collision, it would have turned Hawk Tribe against Hawk Tribe, Heron against Heron, in a word, brother against brother. The history of the Hodénosaunee exhibits the wisdom of these organic provisions; for they never fell into anarchy during the long period which the league subsisted; nor even approximated to a dissolution of the Confederacy from internal disorders.

"With the progress of the inquiry, it becomes more apparent that the Confederacy was in effect a League of Tribes. With the ties of kindred as its principle of union, the whole race was interwoven into one great family, composed of tribes in its first subdivision (for the nations were counterparts of each other); and the tribes themselves, in their subdivisions, composed of parts of many households. Without these close inter-relations, resting, as many of them do, upon the strong impulses of nature, a mere alliance between the Iroquois nations would have been feeble and transitory.

"In this manner was constructed the *Tribal League* of the *Hodenosaunee;* in itself, an extraordinary specimen of Indian legislation. Simple in its foundation upon the *Family Relationship;* effective, in the lasting vigor inherent in the ties of kindred; and perfect in its success, in achieving a lasting and harmonious union of the nations; it forms an enduring monument to that proud and progressive race, who reared under its protection, a wide-spread Indian sovereignty.

"All the institutions of the Iroquois, have regard to the division of the people into tribes. Originally with reference to marriage, the Wolf, Bear, Beaver and Turtle Tribes, were brothers to each other, and cousins to the remaining four. They were not allowed to intermarry. The opposite four tribes were also brothers to each other, and cousins to the first four ; and were also prohibited from intermarrying. Either of the first four tribes, however, could intermarry with either of the last four ; thus Hawk could intermarry with Bear or Beaver, Heron with Turtle ; but not Beaver and Turtle, nor Deer and Deer. Whoever violated these laws of marriage incurred the deepest detestation and disgrace. In process of time, however, the rigor of the system was relaxed, until finally, the prohibition was confined to the tribe of the individual, which among the residue of the Iroquois, is still religiously observed. They can now marry into any tribe but their own. Under the original as well as modern regulation, the husband and wife were of different tribes. The children always followed the tribe of the mother.

"As the whole Iroquois system rested upon the tribes as an organic division of the people, it was very natural that the separate rights of each should be jealously guarded. Not the least remarkable among their institutions, of which most appear to have been original with the race, was that which confined the transmission of all titles, rights and property in the female line to the exclusion of the male. It is strangely unlike the canons of descent adopted by civilized nations, but it secured several important objects. If the Deer Tribe of the Cayugas, for example, received a sachemship or warchiefship at the original distribution of these offices, the descent of such title being limited to the female line, it could never pass out of the tribe. It thus became instrumental in giving the tribe individuality. A still more marked result, and perhaps leading object, of this enactment was, the perpetual disinheritance of the son. Being of the tribe of his mother, it formed an impassable barrier against him ; and he could neither succeed his father as a sachem, nor inherit from him even his medal, or his tomahawk. The inheritance, for the protection of tribal rights, was thus directed from the descendants of the sachem, to his brothers, his sisters, children, or some individual of the tribe at large under certain circumstances ; each and all of whom were in his tribe, while his children being in another's tribe, as before remarked, were placed out of the line of succession.

"By the operation of this principle, also, the certainty of descent in the tribe, of their principal chiefs, was secured by a rule infallible ; for the child must be the son of its mother, although not necessarily of its mother's husband. If the purity of blood be of any moment, the lawgivers of the Iroquois established the only certain rule the case admits of, whereby the assurance might be enjoyed that the ruling sachem was of the same family or tribe with the first taker of the title.

"The Iroquois mode of computing degrees of consanguinity

was unlike that of the civil or canon law; but was yet a clear and definite system. No distinction was made between the lineal and collateral line, either in the ascending or descending series. The maternal grandmother and her sisters were equally grandmothers; the mother and her sisters were equally mothers; the children of a mother's sisters were brothers and sisters; the children of a sister would be nephews and nieces; and the grandchildren of a sister would be his grandchildren—that is to say, the grandchildren of the propositus, or individual from whom the degree of relationship is reckoned. These were the chief relatives within the tribe, though not fully extended to number. Out of the tribe, the paternal grandfather and his brothers were equally grandfathers; the father and his brothers equally fathers; the father's sisters were aunts, while, in the tribe, the mother's brothers were uncles; the father's sister's children would be cousins as in the civil law; the children of these cousins would be nephews and nieces, and the children of these nephews and nieces would be his grandchildren, or the grandchilden of the propositus. Again: the children of a brother would be his children, and the grandchildren of a brother would be his grandchildren; also, the children of a father's brothers, are his brothers and sisters, instead of cousins, as under the civil law; and lastly, their children are his grandchildren, or the grandchildren of the propositus.

"It was the leading object of the Iroquois law of descent, to merge the collateral in the lineal line, as sufficiently appears in the above outline. By the civil law, every departure from the common ancestor in the descending series, removed the collateral from the lineal; while, by the law under consideration, the two lines were finally brought into one.* Under the civil law mode of computation, the degrees of relationship become too remote to be traced among collaterals; while, by the mode of the Iroquois, none of the collaterals were lost by remoteness of degree. The number of those linked together by the nearer family ties, was largely multiplied by preventing, in this manner, the subdivision of a family into collateral branches.

"The succession of the rulers of the Confederacy is one of the most intricate subjects to be met with in the political system of the Hodénosaunee. It has been so difficult to procure a satisfactory exposition of the enactments by which the mode of succession was

---

* The following are the names of the several degrees of relationship, recognized among the Hodénosaunee, in the language of the Seneca:

Hoc-sote,	Grandfather.	Hoc-no-seh,	Uncle.
Uc-sote,	Grandmother.	Ah-geh-huc,	Aunt,
Ha-nih,	Father.	Ha-yan-wan-deh,	Nephew.
Noh-yeh,	Mother.	Ka-yan-wan-deh,	Niece.
Ho-ah-wuk,	Son.	Da-ya-gwa-dan-no-da,	Brothers and Sisters.
Go-ah wuk,	Daughter.	Ah-gare-seh,	Cousin.
Ka-va-da,	Grandchildren.		

regulated, that the sachemships have sometimes been considered elective; at others, as hereditary. Many of the obstacles which beset the inquiry are removed by the single fact, that the titles of sachem and war-chief are absolutely hereditary in the tribe to which they were originally assigned; and can never pass out of it, but with its extinction. How far these titles were hereditary in that part of the family of the sachem or war-chief, who were of the same tribe with himself, becomes the true question to consider. The sachem's brothers, and the sons of his sisters, are of his tribe, and consequently in the line of succession. Between a brother and a nephew of the deceased, there was no law which established a preference; neither between several brothers, on the one hand, and several sons of a sister, on the other, was there any law of primogeniture; nor, finally, was there any positive law, that the choice should be confined to the brothers of the deceased ruler, or the descendants of his sister in the female line, until all these should fail, before a selection could be made from the tribe at large. Hence, it appears, so far as positive enactments were concerned, that the offices of sachem and war-chief, as between the eight tribes, were hereditary in the particular tribe in which they ran; while they were elective, as between the male members of the tribe itself.

"In the absence of laws, designating with certainty the individual upon whom the inheritance should fall, custom would come in and assume the force of law, in directing the manner of choice, from among a number equally eligible. Upon the decease of a sachem, a tribal council assembled to determine upon his successor. The choice usually fell upon a son of one of the deceased ruler's sisters, or upon one of his brothers—in the absence of physical and moral objections; and this preference of one of his near relatives would be suggested by feelings of respect for his memory. Infancy was no obstacle: it uniting only the necessity of setting over him a guardian, to discharge the duties of a sachem until he reached a suitable age. It sometimes occurred that all the relatives of the deceased were set aside, and a selection was made from the tribe generally; but it seldom thus happened, unless from the great unfitness of the near relatives of the deceased.

"When the individual was finally determined, the nation summoned a council, in the name of the deceased, of all the sachems of the league; and the new sachem was raised up by such council, and invested with his office.

"In connection with the power of the tribes to designate the sachems and war-chiefs, should be noticed the equal power of deposition. If, by misconduct, a sachem lost the confidence and respect of tribe, and became unworthy of authority, a tribal council at once deposed him; and, having selected a successor, summoned a council of the Confederacy, to perform the ceremony of his investiture.

"Still further to illustrate the characteristics of the tribes of the Iroquois, some reference to their mode of bestowing names would not be inapt.* Soon after the birth of an infant, the near relatives of the same tribe selected a name. At the first subsequent council of the nation, the birth and name were publicly announced, together with the name and tribe of the father, and the name and tribe of the mother. In each nation the proper names were so strongly marked by a tribal peculiarity, that the tribe of the individual could usually be determined from the name alone. Making, as they did, a part of their language, they were, consequently, all significant. When an individual was raised up as a sachem, his original name was laid aside, and that of the sachemship itself assumed. The war-chief followed the same rule. In like manner, at the raising up of a chief, the council of the nation which performs the ceremony, took away the former name of the incipient chief and assigned him a new one, perhaps, like Napoleon's titles, commemorative of the event which led to its bestowment. Thus, when the celebrated RED-JACKET was elevated by election to the dignity of chief, his original name, O-TE-TI-AN-I (Always Ready) was taken from him, and in its place was bestowed SA-GO-YE-WAT-HA, (Keeper Awake,) in allusion to the powers of his eloquence.

"It now remains to define a tribe of the Hodénosaunee. From the preceding considerations it sufficiently appears, that it was not, like the Grecian and Roman, a circle or group of families; for two tribes were, necessarily, represented in every family: neither, like the Jewish, was it constituted of the lineal descendants of a common father; on the contrary, it distinctly involves the idea of descent from a common mother: nor has it any resemblance to the Scottish clan, or the Canton of the Switzer. In the formation of an Iroquois tribe, a portion was taken from many households, and bound together by a tribal bond. The bond consisted in the ties of consanguinity; for all the members of the tribe, thus composed, were connected by relationships, which, under their law of descents, were easily traceable. To the tribe attached the incident of descent in the female line, the prohibition of intermarriage, the capacity of holding and exercising political rights, and the ability to contract and sustain relationships with the other tribes.

"The wife, her children, and her descendants in the female line, would, in perpetuity, be linked with the destinies of her own tribe and kindred; while the husband, his brothers and sisters, and the descendants of the latter, in the female line, would, in like manner, be united to another tribe, and held by its affinities. Herein was a bond of union between the several tribes of the same nation, corresponding, in some degree, with the cross-rela-

---

* Like the ancient Saxons, the Iroquois had neither a prenomen, nor a cognomen; but contented themselves with a single name.

tionship founded upon consanguinity, which bound together the tribes of the same emblem in the different nations.

"Of the comparative value of these institutions, when contrasted with those of civilized countries, and of their capability of elevating the race, it is not necessary here to inquire. It was the boast of the Iroquois that the great object of their confederacy was peace: — to break up the spirit of perpetual warfare, which wasted the red race from age to age. Such an insight into the true end and object of all legitimate government, by those who constructed this tribal league, excites as great surprise as admiration. It is the highest and the noblest aspect in which human institutions can be viewed; and the thought itself — universal peace among Indian races possible of attainment — was a ray of intellect from no ordinary mind. To consummate such a purpose, the Iroquois nations were to be concentrated into one political fraternity; and in a manner effectively to prevent off-shoots and secessions. By its natural growth, this fraternity would accumulate sufficient power to absorb adjacent nations, moulding them, successively, by affiliation, into one common family. Thus, in its nature, it was designed to be a progressive confederacy. What means could have been employed with greater promise of success than the stupendous system of relationships, which was fabricated through the division of the Hodénosaunee into tribes? It was a system sufficiently ample to infold the whole Indian race. Unlimited in their capacity for extension; inflexible in their relationships; the tribes thus interleagued would have suffered no loss of unity by their enlargement, nor loss of strength by the increasing distance between their council-fires. The destiny of this league, if it had been left to work out its results among the red race exclusively, it is impossible to conjecture. With vast capacities for enlargement, with remarkable durability of structure, and a vigorous, animating spirit, it must have attained a great elevation and a general supremacy."

The Confederacy was based upon terms of perfect equality; equal rights and immunities were secured to each integral part. If in some respects there would seem to be especial privileges, and precedence, it is explained as arising from locality or convenience; as in the case of the Senecas being allowed to have the head war chiefs, the Mohawks being the receivers of tribute from subjugated nations; or the Onondagas, the central nation, supplying their Ta-do-da-hoh and his successors. "The nations were divided into classes or divisions, and when assembled in general council were arranged on opposite sides of the Council fire; on the one side stood the Mohawks, Onondagas and Senecas, who as nations, were regarded as brothers to each other, but as *fathers* to the remainder.

Upon the other side were the Oneidas and Cayugas, and at a subsequent day, the Tuscaroras; who in like manner were brother nations by interchange, but *sons* to the three first. These divisions were in harmony with their system of relationships, or more properly formed a part of it. They may have secured for the senior nations increased respect, but they involve no idea of dependence in the junior, or inequality in civil rights."

There was no annual or other fixed periods for the assembling of the general Council. It was convened only when there was occasion for it. When not in session, there was no visible general government; nor in fact, a need of any, as the local governments were so constituted as to subserve all the ordinay purposes. When events occured that concerned the general welfare, the council was convened, the business despatched, and then followed a mutual prorogation; an example worthy of imitation by modern legislators. With the Iroquois law makers, however, there was no self-sacrifice involved, no inducement to protracted sessions. Their services were gratuitous. Having no other government, the councils were the sole arbiters in all their concerns : — they made war, planned systems of offence and defence; regulated successions, their athletic games, dances and feasts. "The life of the Iroquois was either spent in the chase, or the war path, or at the council fire." Simplicity marked every feature of their system, and yet all was effective, and accomplished its purpose. Councils were convened by runners who were sent out with their belts of wampum, indicating the nature of the emergency, or the business in hand. In proportion as it was urgent, or interesting, would be the attendance of lay members, or those who constitute "the third house," in modern legislation. Upon important occasions, when matters of great moment were to be discussed and determined, the villages of the several nations would be nearly depopulated; the mass of the subjects of the League would flock to the council fire, and make a formidable lobby in its precincts. Their interests and curiosity, it is affirmed were excited by a regard for the general welfare. There were no special favors to be asked or granted. This was a long while anterior to the invention of the system of "log-rolling." The primitive children of the forest, were less sinister in all their motives and incentives, than the race that has succeeded them. Among the general powers vested in the council of the confederacy, may be enumerated those of declaring war and making peace, of admitting new nations into the league, or of incorporating fragments of nations into those existing, of extending jurisdiction over subjugated territory, of levying tribute, of sending and renewing embassies, of forming alliances, and of enacting and executing laws. Unanimity was a fundamental law.* The idea of majorities and minorities was entirely unknown to our Indian predecessors. To hasten their deliberations to a conclusion and ascertain the result, they adopted an expedient which dispensed entirely with the necessity of casting votes. The founders of the Confederacy, seeking to obviate as far as possible, altercations in council, and to facilitate their progress to unanimity, divided the sachems of each nation into classes, usually of two and three each. Each sachem was forbidden to express an opinion in council, until he had agreed with the other sachems of his class, upon the opinion to be expressed, and had received an appointment to act as speaker of his class. Thus the eight Seneca sachems, being in four classes, could have but four opinions; the ten Cayuga sachems but four. In this manner, each class was brought to unanimity within itself. A cross consultation was then held between the four sachems who represented the four classes, and when they had agreed, they appointed one of their number to express their opinion, which was the answer of the nation. The several nations having by this ingenious method become of "one mind," separately, it remained to compare their several opinions, to arrive at the final sentiment of all the sachems of the league. This was effected by a cross conference between the individual representatives of the several nations; and when they had arrived at unanimity, the answer of the Confederacy was determined.†

When the white man first entered this, the country of the Seneca Iroquois, he found deeply indented, well trodden paths, threading the forests in different directions. They led from village to village, thence to their favorite hunting and fishing grounds, or here

---

* Their war against the French was declared by a unanimous vote. After this, when the question came up of taking the British side in the war of the Revolution. the council was divided, a number of the Oneida sachems strongly opposing it, and although most of the confederates were allies of the English in that contest, it was an act of the League, but each nation chose its own position.

† The senate of the United States, in 1838, committed a great error in abrogating this unanimity principle, and substituting the rule of the majority, in reference to the sale of Seneca lands to the pre-emptionists. It was over-riding an ancient law of the confederacy, and in fact, as was the ultimate result, aiding a system of coercion and bribery, to dispossess them of their reservations.

and there marked their intercourse with neighboring aboriginal nations. They are termed Trails. They were the routes pursued by the French Missionaries and traders, by the Dutch and English in their intercourse with the Indians; by the British troops and Indians of Canada in their incursions into Western New-York, during the Revolution; by BUTLER's rangers, in all their bloody enterprises to the valleys of the Mohawk and Susquehannah; and afterwards guided our early Pioneers through the forest, enabling them to appreciate the beauty and value of this goodly land. With reference to the Holland Purchase, these trails were mainly as follows:—

The trail from the east, the valleys of the Hudson, the Mohawk, &c., passing through Canandaigua, West Bloomfield and Lima, came upon the Genesee River at Avon; crossing the River a few rods above the Bridge it went up the west bank to the Indian village a mile above the ford, and then bore off north-west to Caledonia. Turning westward, it crossed Allen's creek at Le Roy, and Black creek at Stafford, coming upon the banks of the Tonawanda a little above Batavia. Passing down the east bank of that stream, around what was early known as the Great Bend, at the Arsenal it turned north-west, came upon the openings at Caryville, and bearing westwardly across the openings it crossed the Tonawanda at the Indian village. Here the trail branched:—one branch taking a north-westwardly direction, re-crossed the creek below the village, and passing through the Tonawanda swamp, emerged from it nearly south-east of Royalton Centre, coming out upon the Lockport and Batavia road in the valley of Millard's Brook, and from thence it continued upon the Chestnut Ridge to the Cold Springs. Pursuing the route of the Lewiston road, with occasional deviations it struck the Ridge Road at Warren's. It followed the Ridge until it passed Hopkins' Marsh, when it gradually ascended the Mountain Ridge, passed through the Tuscarora village, and then down again to the Ridge Road, which it continued on to the River. This was the principal route into Canada, crossing from Lewiston to Queenston; a branch trail however, going down the River to Fort Niagara.

The other branch of the trail leaving the village of Tonawanda, took a south-west direction, and crossing Murder creek at Akron, it came upon the Buffalo road at Clarence Hollow; from thence west, nearly on the line of the Buffalo road to Williamsville, crossing Ellicott's creek it continued its westerly course to the Cold

Springs near Buffalo, and entering the city at what has since become the head of Main Street, it came out at the mouth of Buffalo creek. A branch Trail diverging at Clarence came upon the Cayuga branch of the Buffalo creek at Lancaster, thence down that stream to the Seneca village, and down the Buffalo creek to its entrance into the lake.

The Ontario trail, starting from Oswego, came upon the Ridge Road at Irondequoit Bay; then turning up the Bay to its head, where a branch trail went to Canandaigua, it turned west, crossing the Genesee River at the acqueduct, and passing down the river, came again upon the Ridge Road, which it pursued west to near the west line of Hartland, Niagara county, where it diverged to the south-west, crossing the east branch of the Eighteen-mile Creek, and forming a junction with the Canada or Niagara trail at the Cold Springs.

From Mount Morris, on the Genesee River, a trail passed up the river to Gardow, and Canadea, and from thence to Allegany River at Olean.

A trail left Little Beard's Town on the Genesee river, and crossing the east line of the Holland Purchase, entered it in the north side of T. 10 R. 1, and crossing the north-east corner of T. 10 R. 2, and south-west corner of T. 11 same range, passed through the south sides of T. 11 R. 3. T. 11 R. 4, T. 11 R. 5, entered the Seneca Reservation at the south-west corner of the latter township; and pursuing a westerly course, came upon the banks of Buffalo creek, near the Seneca Indian village.

These were the principal highways of the Seneca Iroquois. How nearly the simple primitive paths of the aborigines, correspond with our now principal thorough-fares; but how changed! The trails are obliterated in the progress of improvement, the forests that enshrouded them are principally cleared away, and in their place are turnpikes, M'Adam roads, canals, rail roads, and telegraphic posts and wires. The waters upon which they paddled their bark canoes, supply our canals; the swamps they avoided, and the ridges they traversed, are passed along and across by our steam propelled locomotives. The "forked lightning," they saw in the clouds, which occasionally scathed the tall trees of their forest home, reminding them of the power and omnipotence of the Great Spirit they adored, the Manitou of their simple creed,— is tamed, and in an instant accomplishes the purposes, that employed their swiftest runners for days!

"The wild man hates restraint, and loves to do what is right in his own eyes."* Hence there was little in all the frame work of the government of the Iroquois, of restraint or coercive laws. They seemed to have acted upon the maxim that "nations are governed too much." And this principle extended in a great degree to family government. Their children were reproved, not injured or beaten, and none but the milder forms of punishment ever resorted to. Theirs was a simple form of government—so simple as to excite a wonder that it could have been effectual;—an oligarchy, and yet cherishing the democratic principle, of the common good; an hereditary council in whom was vested all power, and yet there was no castes, no privileged orders; no conventional or social exclusiveness. Their system of government, like themselves, is a mystery. Both have been but imperfectly understood; both are well worthy of enquiry and investigation. The student, or historical reader of our country, may well turn occasionally from the beaten track of our colleges and schools—from the histories of far off ages, races and people—and taking the humble "trails" of the Iroquois, see if there is not in the history of our own country—our predecessors—that which will interest and instruct him.

As has been assumed in the preceding pages, the Seneca branch of the Iroquois were our immediate predecessors; but we gather from their traditions, and from the writings of the earliest Jesuit

---

NOTE.—At the time of the delivery of the admirable 'Letters on the Iroquois,' before the N. Y. Historical Society; or rather when that portion of them which related to the Trails was read, Dr. Peter Wilson, an educated Cayuga chief, happened to be present. He accepted an invitation to address the Society. 'He spoke with such pathos and eloquence of his people and his race, their ancient prowess and generosity—their present weakness and dependence—and especially upon the hard fate of a small band of Senacas and Cayugas which had recently been hurried into the western wilderness to perish, that all present were deeply moved by his eloquence.' 'The land of Ga-nun-no, or the 'Empire State' as you love to call it, was once laced by our Trails from Albany to Buffalo—Trails that we had trod for centuries—trails worn so deep by the feet of the Iroquois, that they became your roads of travel as your possessions gradually eat into those of my people! Your roads still traverse those same lines of communication which bound one part of the Long House to the other. Have we, the first holders of this prosperous region, no longer a share in your history? Glad were your fathers to set down upon the threshold of the Long House. Rich did they hold themselves in getting the mere sweepings from its door. Had our forefathers spurned you from it when the French were thundering at the opposite side to get a passage through, and drive you into the sea, whatever has been the fate of other Indians, we might still have had a nation, and I—I, instead of pleading here for the privilege of lingering within your borders, I—I might have had a country.'

* Bancroft.

Missionaries, that they had only possessed the country west of the Genesee river, since about the middle of the seventeenth century. In the "Relations of the Jesuits" there is a letter from Father L' ALLEMANT to the Provincial of the Jesuits in France, dated at St. Mary's Mission, May 19, 1641, in which he gives an account of a journey made to the country of the Neuter Nation the year previous, by JEAN DE BREBEUF and JOSEPH MARIE CHAUMONOT, two Jesuit Fathers. As this letter is one of the earliest reminiscence of this region, other than Indian tradition, the author copies it entire:

"JEAN DE BREBEUF and JOSEPH MARIE CHAUMONOT, two Fathers of our company which have charge of the Mission to the Neuter Nation set out from *St. Marie* on the 2d day of November, 1640, to visit this people. Father BREBEUF is peculiarly fitted for such an expedition, God having in an eminent degree endowed him with a capacity for learning languages. His companion was also considered a proper person for the enterprise.

"Although many of our French in that quarter have visited this people to profit by their furs and other commodities, we have no knowledge of any who have been there to preach the gospel except Father DE LA ROCH DAILLON, a Recollect, who passed the winter there in the year 1626.

" The nation is very populous, there being estimated about forty villages. After leaving the Hurons it is four or five days journey or about forty leagues to the nearest of their villages, the course being nearly due south. If, as indicated by the latest and most exact observations we can make, our new station, St. Marie,* in the interior of the Huron country, is in north latitude about 44 degrees, 25 minutes, then the entrance of the Neuter Nation from the Huron side, is about 44 degrees. † More exact surveys and observations, cannot now be made, for the sight of a single instrument would bring to extremes those who cannot resist the temptation of an inkhorn.

"From the first village of the Neuter Nation that we met with in travelling from this place, as we proceed south or southwest, it is about four days travel to the place where the celebrated river of the nation empties into lake Ontario, or St. Louis. On the west side of that river, and not on the east, are the most numerous of the villages of the Neuter Nation. There are three or four on the east side, extending from east to west towards the Eries, or Cat nation."

NOTE.—This would of course be along our side of the Niagara, and probably extended along the shores of lake Erie.

* A Jesuit Mission on the river Severn, near the eastern extremity of lake Huron.

† The good father is about a degree out of the way.

"This river is that by which our great lake of the Hurons, or fresh sea, is discharged, which first empties into the lake of Erie, or of the nation of the Cat, from thence it enters the territory of the Neuter Nation, and takes the name of *Onguiaahra*, (Niagara,) until it empties into Ontario or St. Louis lake, from which latter flows the river which passes before Quebec, called the St. Lawrence, so that if we once had control of the side of the lake nearest the residence of the Iroquois, we could ascend by the river St. Lawrence, without danger, even to the Neuter Nation, and much beyond, with great saving of time and trouble.

"According to the estimate of these illustrious fathers who have been there, the Neuter Nation comprises about 12,000 souls, which enables them to furnish 4,000 warriors, notwithstanding war, pestilence and famine have prevailed among them for three years in an extraordinary manner.

"After all, I think that those who have heretofore ascribed such an extent and population to this nation, have understood by the Neuter Nation, all who live south and southwest of our Hurons, and who are truly in great number, and, being at first only partially known, have all been comprised under the same name. The more perfect knowledge of their language and country, which has since been obtained, has resulted in a clearer distinction between the tribes. Our French who first discovered this people, named them the 'Neuter Nation'; and not without reason, for their country being the ordinary passage, by land, between some of the Iroquois nations and the Hurons, who are sworn enemies, they remained at peace with both; so that in times past, the Hurons and Iroquois, meeting in the same wigwam or village of that nation, were both in safety while they remained. Recently, their enmity against each other is so great, that there is no safety for either party in any place, particularly for the Hurons, for whom the Neuter Nation entertain the least good will.

"There is every reason for believing, that not long since, the Hurons, Iroquois, and Neuter Nations, formed one people, and originally came from the same family, but have in the lapse of time, became separated from each other, more or less, in distance, interests and affection, so that some are now enemies, others neutral, and others still live in intimate friendship and intercourse.

"The food and clothing of the Neuter Nation seem little different from that of our Hurons. They have Indian corn, beans and gourds in equal abundance. Also plenty of fish, some kinds of which abound in particular places only.

"They are much employed in hunting deer, buffalo, wildcats, wolves, wild boars, beaver, and other animals. Meat is very abundant this year, an account of the heavy snow, which has aided the hunters. It is rare to see snow in this country more than half a foot deep. But this year it is more than three feet.

There is also abundance of wild turkeys, which go in flocks in the fields and woods.

"Their fruits are the same as with the Hurons, except chestnuts, which are more abundant, and crab apples, which are somewhat larger.

"The men, like all savages, cover their naked flesh with skins, but are less particular than the Hurons in concealing what should not appear. The squaws are ordinarily clothed, at least from the waist to the knees, but are more free and shameless in their immodesty than the Hurons.

"As for their remaining customs and manners, they are almost entirely similar to the other savage tribes of the country.

"There are some things in which they differ from our Hurons. They are larger, stronger, and better formed. They also entertain a great affection for the dead, and have a greater number of fools or jugglers.

"The Sonontonheronons, (Senecas) one of the Iroquois nations, the nearest to and most dreaded by the Hurons, are not more than a day's journey distant from the easternmost village of the Neuter Nation, named 'Onguiaahra' (Niagara) of the same name as the river.

"Our fathers returned from the mission in safety, not having found in all the eighteen villages which they visited, but one, named '*Khe-o-e-to-a*,' or St. Michael, which gave them the reception which their embassy deserved. In this village, a certain foreign nation, which lived beyond the lake of Erie, or of the nation of the Cat, named '*A-ouen-re-ro-non*,' has taken refuge for many years for fear of their enemies, and they seem to have been brought here by a good Providence, to hear the word of God."

CHARLEVOIX says that in the year 1642, "a people, larger, stronger, and better formed than any other savages, and who lived south of the Huron country, were visited by the Jesuits, who preached to them the Kingdom of God. They were called the Neuter Nation, because they took no part in the wars which desolated the country. But in the end, they could not themselves, escape entire destruction. To avoid the fury of the Iroquois, they finally joined them against the Hurons, but gained nothing by the union. The Iroquois, that like lions that have tasted blood, cannot be satiated, destroyed indiscriminately all that came in their way, and at this day, there remains no trace of the Neuter Nation." In another place, the same author says that the Neuter Nation was destroyed about the year 1643. LA FITEU, in his "*Mœurs des Sauvages*," published at Paris in 1724, relates, on the authority of FATHER GARNIER, a Jesuit Missionary, the origin of the quarrel between the Senecas and the Neuter Nation, which is hinted at in the letter of FATHER L'ALLEMANT. He says, "the war did not terminate but by the total destruction of the Neuter Nation."

Mr. SCHOOLCRAFT assumes that the Senecas had warred upon, conquered the Neuter Nation, and come in possession of their territory, twenty-four years before the advent of LA SALLE upon the Niagara river. A writer in the Buffalo Commercial Advertiser of March, 1846, who is named in the preface of this work, says:—
"From all that can be derived from history, it is very probable, that the Kah-Kwas and the Neutral Nation were identical, that the singular tribe whose institution of neutrality has been likened by an eloquent writer, to a 'calm and peaceful island looking out upon a world of waves and tempests,' in whose wigwams the fierce Hurons and relentless Iroquois met on *neutral* ground, fell victims near this city, (Buffalo) to the insatiable ferocity of the latter. They were the first proprietors, as far as we can learn, of the soil we now occupy. Their savage spoilers gave them a grave on the spot which they died in defending, and have recently, in their turn, yielded to the encroachments of a more powerful adversary. The white man is now lord of the soil where the fires of the nation are put out forever. Around that scene, the proudest recollections and devout associations of the Senecas have long loved to linger. Let it be forever dedicated to the repose of the dead. Let the sanctity of the grave be inviolate. A simple enclosure should protect a spot which will increase in interest with the lapse of time." *

The Senecas have within few years, yielded to the importunities and appliances of the pre-emptionists, and abandoned their Reservation. It is now in the hands of another race. The plough, the pickaxe and spade, will soon obliterate all that remains of the evidences of the conquests of their ancestors. "It is a site around which the Senecas have clung, as if it marked an era in their national history; although the work was clearly erected by their enemies. It has been the seat of their government or council fire, from an early period of our acquaintance with them. It was here that RED JACKET uttered some of his most eloquent harrangues against the steady encroachments of the white race, and in favor

---

* The spot here alluded to, is upon the Reservation near Buffalo, on the creek, near the old council and mission houses. The author has included it in some preceding notices of *ancient* remains; but yielding to the better knowledge in this branch of history, of the author of the above extract, he is disposed to regard it as he has assumed, the field of final conquest of this region, by the Senecas.

of retaining this cherished portion of their lands, and transmitting them with full title to their descendants. It was here that the noted captive, DEHEWAMIS, better known as MARY JEMISON, came to live after a long life of most extraordinary vicissitudes. And it is here that the bones of the distinguished orator, and the no less distinguished captive, rest, side by side, with a multitude of warriors, chiefs and sages. But there will soon be no one left whose heart vibrates with the blood of a Seneca, to watch the venerated resting places of their dead." *

And in this connection it may be well to observe generally, that at the period when the French Missionaries and traders first reached the southern shores of lake Ontario and the Niagara river, the Neuter Nation was in possession of the region west of the Genesee river, including both sides of the Niagara river. The immediate domain of the Senecas, was east of the Genesee, until it reached that of the Cayugas. The Hurons occupied the interior of Canada West, west to lake Huron. The domain of the Eries, or Cat nation, according to HENNEPIN, commenced upon the southern shore of lake Erie, the dividing line between them and the Neuter Nation being about midway, up the lake. After the conquest of the Neuter Nation, the Senecas conquered the Eries, as is supposed, about the year 1653.

There are few into whose hand this local history will fall, who are not familiar with the general character, domestic habits, &c., of the aborigines. The first settlers of the Holland Purchase, had them for their primitive neighbors, and they even now, diminished as they are, linger among us in four localities:—at Tuscarora, Tonawanda, Cattaraugus and Alleghany. Their eloquence, their deeds of valor, their peculiarly interesting traits of character; the wrongs they have done our race, as traced in the often too highly colored, but generally truthful legends of the Mohawk and the Susquehannah; and the terrible retributions that have, in turn, been visited upon their race, in the extinguishing of most of the fires that "blazed in their Long House from the Hudson to lake Erie"—in subjecting them to the urgent and pressing overtures of pre-emptionists, who were better schooled in the diplomacy of bargain and gain, than were these men of simple habits and of honest impulses; and last and worst of all,

---

* Schoolcraft.

in visiting upon them the curse of the darker features of civilization. With all this, the reader, in most instances, will be familiar; a part of it is interwoven in the nursery tales of our region. The author has only aimed thus far to give a general idea of the Indians as found here by the first European adventurers, and afford an insight, an induction, into their political institutions, their system of government, laws, &c., which have been subjects of too recent investigation, to admit of any very general familiarity with them. He is admonished that this branch of his main subject, is occupying too much space here, inasmuch as the Seneca Iroquois especially, must be frequently mingled with the local annals of our own race, as they will occur in chronological narrative.

PART SECOND.

CHAPTER I.

EARLY EUROPEAN VOYAGES AND DISCOVERIES.

The prevailing spirit of the Monarchs of Europe, and their subjects, during the fifteenth and a greater portion of the sixteenth centuries, tended to the enlargement of their dominions, and the extension of their powers. In the latter end of the fifteenth century, COLUMBUS had discovered a New World. Spain then at the height of its prosperity and grandeur, profiting by the discoveries of an expedition that had sailed under her flag, under the auspices of her Queen had followed up the event, by farther discoveries and colonization in the Southern portion of our continent. The reigning monarch of England, HENRY VII, stimulated by regret that he had allowed a rival power to be the first in the discovery of a continent, the advantages and resources of which, as the tidings of the discovery were promulgated, dazzled the eyes and awakened the emulation of all Europe; ambitious to make his subjects co-discoverers with the subjects of the Spanish monarch; listened with favor to the theory of JOHN CABOT, a Venetian, but a resident of England — who inferred that as lands had been discovered in the southwest, they might also be in the northwest, and offered to the king to conduct an expedition in this direction.

With a commission of discovery, granted by the king, and a ship provided by him, and four small vessels equipped by the merchants of Bristol, CABOT with his son SEBASTIAN, set sail from England, in less than three years after COLUMBUS had discovered the Island of San Salvador. As the discovery of COLUMBUS was incidental to the main object of his daring enterprise — the discovery of a shorter route to the Indies, — the CABOTS, adopting his opinion that he had discovered one of the outskirts or dependencies of those countries, conceived that they had only to bear to the northwest, to find a still shorter route. Taking that course they reached the continent of North America, discovering the Islands of New Foundland and St. John, and sailed along it from the confines of Labrador to the coast of Virginia. Thus, England was the second nation that visited the western world, and the first that discovered the vast continent that stretches from the Gulf of Mexico towards the north pole. Instead of discovering a shorter route to the Indies, the one discovered a New World, and the other, by far the most important portions of it.

From dissentions and troubles that existed at home, and some schemes of family ambition that diverted his attention, CABOT found his patron king, on his return, indisposed to profit by his important discoveries. All the benefit that accrued to England from this enterprise, was a priority of discovery that she afterwards had frequent occasion to assert.

In 1498, the CABOTS, father and son, made a second expedition, with the double object of traffic with the natives, and in the quaint language of their commission, to explore and ascertain "what manner of landes those Indies were to inhabit." They sailed for Labrador by the way of Iceland, but on reaching the coast, impelled by the severity of the cold, and a declared purpose of exploring farther to the south, they sailed along the shores of the United States to the southern boundary of Maryland; after which, they returned to England.

Portugal, desirous of participating in the career of discovery, in 1501, fitted out an expedition under the command of GASPAR CORTEREAL. The most northern point he gained was probably about the fiftieth degree. The expedition resulted in a partial survey of the coast, and the taking captive of fifty Indians that were taken to Portugal and sold as slaves.

It was twenty-seven years after the last voyage of CABOT, under English auspices that FRANCIS I, King of France, awakened by the spirit of adventure, and protesting against the partition that had made of the newly discovered continent, by the Pope, between Spain and Portugal, soon after its discovery; and determined not to overlook the commercial interests of his people; extended his patronage to JOHN DE VERRAZANA, ordering him to set sail for that country "of which so much was spoken at the time in France."

The account of his first voyage is not preserved. He sailed with four ships, encountered storms in the north, landed in Britain; and going from thence to the island of Madeira, started from there with a single vessel, the Dolphin, with fifty men and provisions for eight months. After a stormy passage he arrived in latitude 34 deg. near Wilmington, North Carolina. In his own report to his king and patron, he says:—

"Great store of people came to the sea side, and seeing us approach they fled away, and sometimes would stand still and look backe, beholding us with great admiration; but afterwards, being animated and assured with signs that we made them, some of them came hard to the sea side, seeming to rejoice very much at the sight of us, and marvelling greatly at our apparel, shape, and whitenesse; shewed us by sundry signes where we might most commodiously come to land with our boate, offering us also victuals to eat. Remaining there for a few days, and taking note of the country, he sailed northwardly, and viewed, if he did not enter, the harbor of New York. In the haven of Newport he remained for fifteen days, where he found the natives the 'goodliest people' he had seen in his whole voyage. At one period during his coasting along the shores of New England, he was compelled for the sake of fresh water, to send off his boat. The shore was lined with savages 'whose countenances betrayed at the same time, surprise, joy and fear.' They made signs of friendship, and 'showed they were content we should come to land.' A boat with twenty-five men, attempted to land with some presents, but on nearing the shore were intimidated by the frightful appearance of the natives, and halted to turn back. One more resolute than the rest, seizing a few of the articles designed as presents, plunged into the water and advanced within three or four yards of the shore. Throwing them the presents, he attempted to regain the boat, but was caught by a wave and dashed upon the beach. The savages caught him, and sitting him down by a large fire, took off his clothes. His comrades supposed he was to be 'roasted and eat.' Their fears subsided however, when they saw them testify their kindness by caresses. It turned out that they were only gratifying their curiosity in an examination of his person, the 'whitenesse of his skin,' &c. They released him and after 'with great love clasping him faste about,' they allowed him to swim to his comrades. VERRAZANA found the natives of the more northern regions more hostile and jealous, from having, as has been inferred, been visited for the purpose of carrying them off as slaves. At another anchorage, after following the shore fifty leagues, 'an old woman with a young maid of 18 or 20 yeeres old, seeing our company, hid themselves in the grasse for feare; the old woman carried two infants on her shoulders, and behind her neck a child of 8 yeeres old. The young woman was laden likewise with as many; but when our men came unto them the woman cried out; the old woman made signs that the men were fled into the woods. As soon as they saw us, to quiet them, and to win their favor, our men gave them such victuals as they had with them to eate, which the old woman received thankfully, but the young woman threw them disdainfully on the ground. They took a child from the old woman to bring into France; and going about to take the young woman, which was very beautiful and of tall stature, they could not possibly, for the great outcries she made, bring her to the sea; and especially having great woodes to pass through, and being far from the ship, we purposed to leave her behind, bearing away the child onely.' At another anchorage,* 'there ran down into the sea an exceeding great streme of water, which at the mouth was very deepe, and from the sea to the mouthe of the same, with the tide which they found to raise eight foote, any great ship laden might pass up.' Sending up their boat the natives expressed their admiration and showed them where they might safely come to land. They went up the river half a league, where it made a 'most pleasant lake, about three leagues in compass, on which the natives rode from one side to the other to the number of thirty of their small boats, wherein were many people which passed from one shore to the other.' At another anchorage they 'met the goodliest people and of the fairest conditions that they had found in their voyage: — exceeding us in bigness — of the color of brasse, some inclining to whiteness, black and quick eyed, of sweete and pleasant countenance, imitating much the old fashion.' Among them, they discovered pieces of wrought copper, which they 'esteemed more than gold.' 'They did not desire cloth of silk or of gold, or of other sort, neither did they care for things made of steel or iron, which we often shewed them in our armour, which they made no wonder at; and in beholding them they only asked the art of making them; the like they did at our glasses, which when they suddenly beheld, they laughed and gave them to us again.' The ship neared the land and finally cast anchor 'in the haven,' when, continues VERRAZANA, 'we bestowed fifteen days in providing ourselves with many necessary things, whither every day the people repaired to see our ship, bringing their wives with them whereof they were very jelous; and they themselves entering aboard the ship and staying there a good space, caused their wives to stay in their boats; and for all the entreaty we could make, offering to give them divers things, we could never obtain that they should suffer to to come aboard our ship. Oftentimes one of the two kings (of this people) comming with his queene, and many gentlemen for their pleasure to see us, they all staid on shore two hundred paces from us till they sent a message they were coming. The queene and

---

* Off Sandy Hook, as has been inferred.

her maides staid in a very light boat at an island a quarter of a league off, while the king abode along space in the ship, uttering divers conceits with gestures, viewing with great admiration the ship, demanding the property of everything particularly. 'There were plaines twenty-five or thirty leagues in width, which were open, and without any impediment.' They entered the woods and found them 'so greate and thick, that any army were it never so greate might have hid itself therein; the trees whereof are oakes, cipresse, and other sorts unknown in Europe.' The natives fed upon pulse that grew in the country, with better order of husbandry than in the others. They observed in their sowing the course of the moone and the rising of certain starres, and diverse other customes spoken of by antiquity. They dwell together in great numbers, some twenty-five or thirty persons in one house. They are very pitifull and charitable towards their neighbors, they make great lamentations in their adversitie, and in their miserie, the kindred reckone up all their felicite. At their departure out of life they use mourning mixed with singing which continueth for a long space."

VERRAZANA having coasted 700 leagues of new country, and being refitted with water and wood, returned to France, arriving at Dieppe in July, whence he addressed his letter to the king. His, in all probability, were the first interviews with the natives upon all our northern, and a part of our southern coast, and for that reason his narrative which gives us a glimpse of them in the primitive condition that civilization found them, possesses a great degree of interest. "We have detailed these instances in their favor," say YATES and MOULTON, "because they occurred at a period when the warm native fountain of good feeling and disinterested charity, had not been frozen by the chilly approach and death-like contact of civilized man. We have dwelt upon these incidents as the most interesting portion of VERRAZANA's adventures. They present human nature in an amiable point of view, when unsophisticated by metaphysical subtlety, undisguised by art, or even when adorned by the refinements, the pride and circumstance of civilization. They illustrate the position which we believe is true, that the natives of this continent, before they had been exasperated by the encroachments and provocations of Europeans, when the former were confiding and unsuspicious, without any foresight of the terrible disasters which their interviews with the latter were destined to become the tragical prelude, entertained uniform feelings of kindness, of hospitality and benevolence."

"When COLUMBUS visited the new world, the natives viewed him as a super-natural being, and treated him with the veneration inseparable from a delusion, which COLON was willing to countenance. When VESPUCIUS AMERICUS landed, he also was treated as a superior being. When the CABOTS coasted this continent, when CARTIER first visited the St. Lawrence, when the French first settled in Florida as friends, when Sir HUMPHREY GILBERT, and after him the captains employed by Sir WALTER RALEIGH, first landed in Virginia, when HUDSON discovered and explored our bay and river, when the Pilgrims colonized New England, the generous reception which they all met from the natives, should stand a monumental rebuke to the shameful prejudices too prevalent among ourselves, since we supplanted their descendants on a soil which their fathers left them as a patrimony. We will cite proofs of two instances which took place thirty-seven years apart, but which are given as a general illustration of our position. In the first report of SIR WALTER RALEIGH's expedition, it is said by his captain, and those in the employ, in 1584, that they were entertained with as much bounty as they could possibly devise. They found the people most gentle, loving and faithful, void of all guile and treason, and such as live after the manner of the golden age."

The following is an extract from the first sermon ever preached in New England. It was by one of the Pilgrims, and bears date Dec. 1621:—"To us they (the Indians,) have been like lambs, so kind, so submissive and trusty, as a man may truly say many christians are not so kind and sincere. When we first came into this country we were few, and many of us were sick, and many died by reason of the cold and wet, it being the depth of winter, and we having no houses or shelter; yet when there were not six able persons among us, and that they came daily to us by hundreds with their sachems or kings, and might in one hour have made a dispatch of us, &c. yet they never offered us the least injury. The greatest commander of the country, called MASSASOIT, cometh often to visit us, though he lives fifty miles from us, often sends us presents, &c."

And yet aggressions and wrongs commenced on the part of our race in its earliest intercourse with theirs. VERRAZANA after the reception he has himself acknowledged, attempted to carry away two of their people; CABOT had carried two as a present to his sovereign HENRY VII, that were never returned. The Spaniards and Portugese immediately followed up their first intercourse with them by carrying them into captivity and slavery. Can it be wondered that in numerous instances that occurred in after attempts at settlement, in New England — upon the Hudson — in Virginia, North Carolina &c. — this primitive good feeling — the simple hospitality with which they met the first adventurers upon their shores, gave place to self-defence — perhaps revenge? Of the Spaniards, and their early intercourse with them, KOTZEBUE says: — "Wherever they moved in anger, desolation tracked their progress, — wherever they paused in amity, affliction mourned their friendship."

Well has it been observed that the Indian has had no historian of his own. Were some one of his own race, the chronicler of events; — commencing with the discovery of COLUMBUS, and coming down to our present day of pre-emption bribes, and treaties attained with wrong and outrage; — he would gather up a fearful account which would meet with no adequate offsets. It would be that which would admit of but one manner of recompense: — the careful guardianship and protection hereafter of our states and general governments, and a co-operation in all measures that tend to promote their rights, their peace and happiness, on the part of our people.

On the 20th of April, 1534, JAMES CARTIER, a mariner of St. Malo, was commissioned by Francis First, to fit out an expedition for the purpose of exploring and colonizing the new world. He sailed with two ships of sixty tons burthen, and each a crew of sixty men. He visited New Foundland, surveyed the coast, and returned. The favorable report he was enabled to make, increased the confidence of his patron, and in May, 1535, he was enabled to set sail again with a squadron of three ships, well furnished. "A solemn and gorgeous pageant," a confessional and sacrament, and the benediction of a bishop attended his departure. In this voyage he passed to the west of New Foundland and entering the Gulf of St. Lawrence, gave it its name. In September, he ascended the river as far as the Island of Orleans. Here he met with the

---

NOTE.—In ascribing the discovery of the Hudson river to the navigator whose name it bears, it is assumed that the coasting and entering of rivers, of Verrazana did not embrace it. It is generally admitted, however, that he came to anchor at Sandy Hook and that the bay within it, is the "pleasant lake," he alludes to natives of the country. Although they considered the French intruders, and wished to prevent their further advances, they nevertheless treated them with kindness and hospitality. To direct them from their purpose of advancing, they first gave them bountiful presents of corn and fish, and to discourage them they resorted to jugglery, in which they declared they had drawn maledictions from the Great Spirit, against them. They represented that there was so much ice and snow in the country above, that certain death awaited them if they advanced. Undismayed by the arts and devices of the natives, the intrepid mariner continued to ascend the river, and arrived at a principal Indian village called Hochelaga, the present site of Montreal. That region he found occupied by a branch of the Wyandot, or Huron tribe of Indians, who were there by recent conquest. "Having climbed the hill at the base of which lay the village, he beheld spread around him a gorgeous scene of woods and waters, promising glorious visions of future opulence and national strength. The hill he called Mount Royal, and this name was afterwards extended to the Island of Montreal. At that period, more than three centuries ago, the village of Hochelaga was surrounded by large fields of corn and stately forests. The hill called Montreal, was fertile and highly cultivated." The form of the village was round and encompassed with timber, with three courses of ramparts, framed like a sharp spire, but laid across above. The middlemost of them was made and built as a direct line, but perpendicular. These ramparts were framed and fashioned with pieces of timber laid along the ground, very well and cunningly joined together after this fashion:—The enclosure was in height about two rods. It had but one gate which was shut with piles, stakes and bars. Over it, and also in many places in the wall there were places to run along and ladders to get up, full of stones for its defence. In the town there were about fifty houses, about fifty paces long and twelve or fifteen broad, built of wood, covered only with the bark of the wood as broad as any board, very finely and cunningly joined together. Within their houses there were many rooms, lodgings and chambers. In the midst of these, there was a great court, in the middle whereof they made their fire. They lived in common together. Then did the husbands, wives and children, each one retire themselves to their chambers. They also had on the tops of their houses, garrets, where they kept their corn to make their bread, which they called *caraconny*."*

These Indians gave CARTIER a glimpse of the vast region that lay at the west of him and for the first time perhaps directed French enterprise to a region where it was destined to occupy so wide a space. They told him there were three great lakes and a sea of fresh water † of which no man had found the end; that a river ‡ ran south-west, upon which there was a "month's sailing to go down to a certain land where there was no ice nor snow, where the inhabitants continually warred against each other," and where "there was a great abundance of oranges, lemons, nuts and apples"; that the people ‖ there were clad as the French, lived in towns, were very honest, and had great stores of gold and copper.

By the authority of his king, and in the name of his country, CARTIER erected a cross and shield, emblazoned with the arms of France, and called the country New France.

CARTIER's report on his return from this voyage, was made with candor. "This country which he had visited abounded with no gold or precious stones and its shores were alledged to be bleak and stormy." The project of colonization was not renewed until six years after.

In 1540, FRANCIS DE LA ROQUE, SEIGNEUR DE ROBERVAL, was granted a charter by FRANCIS I, which invested him with all the powers of his sovereign, over the newly discovered and claimed colony of New France. Under his immediate auspices a squadron of five ships was fitted out, with CARTIER commissioned by the king as chief Pilot of the expedition. He was directed to take with him persons of every trade and art, and to dwell in the newly discovered territory. The expedition had an untoward commencement and ultimately resulted in but a feeble advance toward permanent settlement. As good colonists could not be obtained to go to the inhospitable and bleak northern regions, the prisons and work houses of France were resorted to to supply the demand. In addition to this, a feeling of rivalry and jealousy sprang up between

---

* The author finds this ancient account of Hochelaga, in Lanman's History of Michigan.

†Erie, Huron, Michigan. The "sea," lake Superior.

‡ The Mississippi.

‖ Florida and the Spanish colonies.

ROBERVAL and CARTIER. They neither embarked in company, nor acted in concert. CARTIER ascended the St. Lawrence and built a fort at Quebec; but no considerable advances in geographical knowledge would seem to have been made. In June, 1542 he returned to France. On the way back he met ROBERVAL on the banks of New Foundland, with more provisions and arms, and returning with him to the fort, he assumed the command, while ROBERVAL ascended the St. Lawrence. CARTIER not entering with cordiality into the views or measures of ROBERVAL, the expedition after remaining about a year returned to France.

In the career of French discovery in New France there occurs here an hiatus or suspension of over fifty years. The causes of this suspension may be found in that portion of the history of France which embraces that period; they were domestic troubles, civil war, &c., which divested the nation from all projects of discovery and colonization.

It was under the reign of ELIZABETH, that England made the first attempt at colonization in America. In 1584 Sir WALTER RALEIGH, under the patronage of the Queen, fitted out two vessels, to "visit the districts which he intended to occupy, and to examine the accommodations of the coasts, the productions of the soil, and the condition of the inhabitants." These ships approached the North American Continent by the Gulf of Florida, and anchored in Roanoke Bay, off the coast of North Carolina. This was followed the year after by seven more ships, which left 108 men at the Roanoke Colony, The immediate prospect of forming a colony was finally unsuccessful. A fleet under Sir Admiral DRAKE, that was returning home after a successful expedition against the Spaniards in the West Indies, touched at Roanoke on its homeward passage, and took the colonists home to England.

There were several other attempts to colonize by RALEIGH, and under his auspices, but were failures; amounting only to the landing of several ship loads of emigrants, illy provided for subsistance or defence; to become a prey to the natives, or perish for food. At the period of Queen ELIZABETH's death, not an Englishman was settled in America.

In 1603, BARTHOLOMEW GOSNOLD, planned an expedition in a small vessel with only thirty men—discovered a much nearer route than had hitherto been pursued—visited the coast of Massachusetts and returned with a rich freight of peltry. His favorable accoun led a few merchants of Bristol to send out two vessels, to examine the country GOSNOLD had visited. They returned, confirming his statements. Another expedition followed, which, returning, reported so many "additional particulars commendatory of the region, that all doubt and hesitation vanished from the minds of the projectors of American Colonization; and an association sufficiently numerous wealthy and powerful to undertake this enterprise, being speedily formed, a petition was presented to the King for his sanction of the plan, and the interposition of his authority towards its execution."

In April 1606, King James issued letters patent to Sir THOMAS GATES, GEORGE SOMERS, RICHARD HAKLUYT, and their associates granting to them those territories in America, lying on the sea coast between the thirty-fourth and forty-fifth degrees of north latitude, together with all the Islands situated within one hundred miles of their shores.

The patentees were divided into two companies. The territory appropriated to the first, or Southern Colony, was called Virginia. That appropriated to the Northern Colony, was called New England. They were termed the London and Plymouth companies.

Three vessels soon sailed under the auspices of the London Company, having on board one hundred and five men destined to remain in America; among the adventurers, were GEORGE PERCY, a brother of the Duke of Northumberland, GOSNOLD, the enterprising navigator, and Capt. JOHN SMITH. The squadron arrived in the Chesapeake Bay, April 1607. These colonists founded the settlement at Jamestown, and theirs was the first successful scheme of English colonization in America. In 1608, this colony first tilled the soil of what now constitutes the United States, unless the Spaniards had previously planted in Florida.

In 1607 the Plymouth company made an abortive attempt to form a colony in northern Virginia. The expedition returned to England and damped the spirit of emigration by the representations it made of the soil and climate they had visited. Six years after they fitted out two vessels, and placed one of them under the command of Capt. SMITH, who had become identified with the colony at Jamestown previously. This expedition explored with care and diligence, the whole coast from Cape Cod to Penobscot. Capt. SMITH went into the interior of the country, made a map of the coast, which on his return he presented to the King, accompanied with a highly favorable account of the country. Capt. HUNT, who commanded one of the vessels, instead of returning with SMITH, enticed a number of Indians on board his vessel, and touching at Malaga on his homeward voyage, sold them as slaves; thus upon the threshold of New England colonization, provoking the natives to abandon their pacific policy, and look upon the new comers as enemies. The very next vessel that visited the coast of New England, brought news of their vindictive hostility.

It was reserved for the pilgrim fathers, who, to escape persecution in England, had fled to Leyden, to commence the colonization of New England. Obtaining from King James a tacit acquiescence and from the Plymouth Company a grant of a portion of their territory, one hundred and twenty of their number embarked at Delft Haven, reaching the coast of America, after a long and dangerous voyage, on the 9th of November, 1620, and the coast of Massachusetts, the spot they afterwards called New Plymouth, on the 11th of December.

On the 30th day of September, 1609, two hundred and thirty-nine years ago, HENRY HUDSON an Englishman, but then in the employ of the Dutch East India Company, entered the southern waters of New York, and the next day moored his ship within Sandy Hook. He ascended the river that now bears his name, as far up as Albany, some exploring parties of his expedition having gone as far as Troy. He was from the day he passed Sandy Hook, until the fourth of October, engaged in an examination of the bay of New York, the banks of the river, &c., trafficking with the natives, gratifying his own and their curiosity, by receiving them on board his vessel, and otherwise cultivating their acquaintance and friendship.

There have been preserved minute details of this first European visit to our State. It forms a chapter in our history of great interest, not only from the fact that it informs us of the discovery of our now Empire State — of the first European advent upon the waters of the Hudson, to the site of our great northern commercial emporium, but from its giving us by far the best and most satisfactory accounts of the natives, as they were found in their primitive condition. Hudson testifies, as precedent navigators had done to their general friendly reception of the stranger European. In his four weeks' interview with the natives, nothing occured to mar its pacific character, until one of their number had been wantonly killed by one of his men. The Indian, attracted by curiosity, and having perhaps but imperfect ideas of the rights of property, stole into the cabin window, and pilfered a pillow, and some wearing apparel. The men discovering his retreat with the articles shot at and killed him. In an attempt to recover the articles, another native was killed. Previous to this, there had been what the natives construed into an attempt to carry off two of their number. Following after these events, was a concerted attempt on the part of the natives to get possession of the vessel. At the head of Manhattan Island in the inlet of Harlem river, they had collected a large force. The vessel going down the river approached the shore near the place of ambush. HUDSON discovering them, and their hostile intentions, lay off, the Indians discharging at the vessel a volley of arrows, which was returned by the discharge of muskets. This skirmishing continued as the vessel moved farther down, the Indians assaulting with their arrows, the Europeans retaliating with their muskets, and occasionally by the discharge of a cannon. Nine of the Indians were killed, none of the Europeans. How astounding to these simple warriors, armed only with their bows and arrows, must have been this their first knowledge of the use of gun-powder, and its terrible agency as an auxiliary in war! And that they were not dismayed, did not flee at the first explosion of a volley of muskets, is a matter of especial wonder.

Thus a relation, an acquaintance, that was commenced, and for some time was continued in amity, had a hostile termination. HUDSON sailed down the river and put to sea.

This first European advent to our state, was marked by another event, more important in the annals of the aborigines, than any that has occured during their acquaintance with our race. It was the inflicting upon them a curse, more terrible in its consequenses than all else combined, of the evils that have attended their relations with us; a curse equal in magnitude, in proportion to the aggregate numbers to be effected by it, to that which England has visited upon the Chinese by force of arms; (and there is some coincidence in the two events, for in both cases there was the predisposition, the physical tendency, to destructive excess):—While HUDSON's vessel lay in the river, (near Albany, as inferred from his account,) "great multitudes flocked on board to survey the wonder." In order to discover whether "any of the chiefe men of the country had any treacherie in them, our master and mate took them into the cabin and gave them so much wine and *aqua vitæ* that they were all merrie; and one of them had his wife with him, which sate sc modestly as any of our counterey womene, would doe in a strange plaice." One of them became intoxicated, staggered and fell, at which the natives were astonished. It "was strange to them, for they could not tell how to take it." They all hurried ashore in their canoes. The intoxicated Indian remaining and sleeping on board all night, the next day, others ventured on board and finding him recovered, and well, they were highly gratified. He was a chief. In the afternoon they repeated their visits, brought tobacco "and beads, and gave them to our master, and made an *oration* showing him all the country round about." They took on board a platter of venison, dressed in their own style, and "caused him to eate with them: — then they made him reverence, and departed all," except the old chief, who having got a taste of the fatal beverage chose to remain longer on board. Thus were the aborigines first made acquainted with what they afterwards termed *"fire water;"* and aptly enough for it has helped to consume them. The Indians who met HUDSON at Albany were of the Mohawk nation.

The discovery of HUDSON was followed up by several voyages from Holland, with the principal object of traffic on the river, and among the natives he had discovered. The Dutch built two small fortified trading posts, the one on Castle, and the other on Manhattan Island. The English attempted a colony upon the river, but were unsuccessful. It was not until 1623 that effectual colonization commenced. In that year, and soon after, vessels were fitted out by the Dutch company, emigrants embarked in them, forts were built, settlements founded. The colony was called New Netherland. The first governor came out in 1623.

In 1603, a company of merchants was formed at Rouen for the purpose of colonization. They were invested with authority to explore the country, and establish colonies along the St. Lawrence. SAMUEL CHAMPLAIN, an able mariner, a partner in the company,

---

NOTE.—The strong appetite of Indians for intoxicating drinks, has been observed from our earliest intercourse with them. The first navigators, who reached them, bringing "strong water," the traders who have found them ignorant of the existence of it, and fatally enticed them to its taste, have uniformly borne testimony that with few exceptions, when they have been once under the influence of it, their appetites are craving for further indulgence. The author has been informed by one who has spent most of his life among the fur traders on the head waters of the Mississippi, that he has known an Indian runner to make a journey of two hundred miles and back through deep snow, to obtain a gallon of whiskey, to finish a carousal, after having exhausted the supply of a trader.

directed the expedition. In this expedition he selected Quebec as the site of a fort. The protection of the fur trade was its principal object, though it led to a permanent establishment. A few settlers were left to build huts and clear land. It was during this expedition, as inferred by Mr. LANMAN, the intelligent historian of Michigan, that the foundation was laid for the long series of troubles that grew up between the French and the Iroquois. CARTIER, in a previous ascension of the St. Lawrence, against the wishes of the Hurons and Algonquins, had, with motives of curiosity, or to gratify it at home, taken to England three of their chiefs against their will. To win their favor, CHAMPLAIN became their ally against the Iroquois. The secret of his policy, as inferred by CHARLEVOIX, was to humble the Iroquois, in order to "unite all the nations of Canada in an alliance with the French." He did not foresee that the former, who for a long time had, single handed, kept in awe the Indians, three hundred miles around them, would be aided by Europeans in another quarter, jealous of the power of the French. It was not his fault, therefore, that circumstances he could not have anticipated, subsequently concurred to frustrate his plan.

As this expedition constitutes a distinct and important era in the history of the Aborigines of America, and their mode of warfare —the introduction of fire-arms,—the author extracts a concise account of it from the work of Messrs. YATES and MOULTON:—

"Having yielded his consent to join the expedition, he, (CHAMPLAIN) embarked with his new allies at Quebec, and sailed into the Iroquois river (now Sorrel,) until the rapids near Chambly prevented his vessel from proceeding. His allies had not apprised him of this impediment: on the contrary, they had studiously concealed it as well as other obstacles. His vessel returned; but he, and two Frenchmen who would not desert him, determined to proceed, notwithstanding the difficulties of the navigation, and the duplicity of their allies in concealing those difficulties. They transported their canoes beyond the rapids, and encamped for the night. As was customary, they sent a spy to range in the vicinity, who in a short time returned, and informed them that he saw no enemy. Without placing any guard, they prepared for repose. CHAMPLAIN, surprised to find them so stupidly incautious and confident of their safety, endeavored to prevail with them to keep watch. All the reply they made was, that people who were fatigued all day, had need of sleep at night. Afterwards, when they thought that they were approaching nearer towards the enemy, they were induced to be more guarded, to travel at night only, and keep no fires in the day time. CHAMPLAIN was charmed with the variegated and beautiful aspect of the country. The islands were filled with deer and other animals, which supplied the army with abundance of game, and the river and lake afforded abundance of fish. In the progress of their route he derived much knowledge of the Indian character as it was displayed in this warlike excursion. He was particularly amused to perceive the blind confidence which the Indians paid to their sooth-sayer or sorcerer, who in the time of one of their encampments, went through with his terrific ceremony. For several days they inquired of CHAMPLAIN if he had not seen the Iroquois in a dream. His answer being that he had not, caused great disquietude among them. At last, to relieve them from their embarrassments, or get rid of their importunity, he told them he had, in a dream, seen the Iroquois drowning in a lake, but he did not rely altogether upon the dream. The allies judged differently, for they now no longer doubted a victory. Having entered upon the great lake, which now bears the name of CHAMPLAIN, in honor of its discoverer, he and his allies traversed it until they approached towards the junction of the outlet of Lake St. Sacrament,* with Lake Champlain, at or near Ticonteroga. The design of the allies was to pass the rapids between those two lakes, to make an eruption into the mountainous regions and vallies of the Iroquois beyond the small lake, and by surprise to strike them at one of their small villages. The latter saved them the necessity of journeying so far, for they suddenly made their appearance at 10 o'clock at night, and by mere accident, met the former on the great lake. The surprise of both parties was equaled only by their joy, which was expressed in shouts, and as it was not their practice to fight upon the water unless when they were too far from land to retreat, they mutually hurried to the shore.

" Here, then, in the vicinity of Ticonderoga (a spot afterwards celebrated in the achievements of the French and Revolutionary Wars,) the two parties pitched for battle. The allies immediately labored to entrench themselves behind fallen trees, and soon sent a messenger to the Iroquois to learn whether they would fight immediately. The latter replied that the night was too dark: they could not see themselves, and the former must await the approach of day. The allies consented, and after taking the necessary precautions, slept. At break of day, Champlain placed his two Frenchmen, and some savages in the wood, to attack the enemy in flank. These consisted of two hundred choice and resolute men, who considered victory as easy and certain over the Algonquins and Hurons, whom the former did not expect, would have

---

* Lake George.

dared to take the field. The allies were equal to them in number, but displayed a part only of their warriors. They, as well as the enemy were armed with bows and arrows only, but they founded their hopes of conquest upon the fire-arms of the French; and they pointed out to CHAMPLAIN, and advised him to fire upon the three chiefs, who were distinguished by feathers or tails of birds larger than those of their followers. The allies first made a sortie from their entrenchment, and ran two hundred feet in front of the enemy, then stopped, divided into two bands to the right and left, leaving the center position for CHAMPLAIN, who advanced and placed himself at their head. His sudden appearance and arms, were new to the Iroquois, whose astonishment became extreme. But what was their dismay when, after the first report of his arquebuse from the spot where he had posted four men, the Iroquois saw two of their chiefs fall dead, and the third dangerously wounded! The allies now shouted for joy and discharged a few ineffective arrows. CHAMPLAIN recharged, and the other Frenchmen successfully fought the Iroquois, who were soon seen in disorder and flight. They were pursued warmly, many were killed, and some taken prisoners. The fugitives, in their precipitance, abandoned their maize. This was a seasonable relief for the victors, for they had been reduced to great need. They fed, and passed two hours on the field of battle in dancing and singing. Not one had been killed, although several were wounded. They prepared to return homeward, for among these people the vanquishers always retreat as well as the vanquished, and often inasmuch disorder and precipitation as if they were pursued by a victorious enemy. In their way back, they tortured one of their prisoners, whose miseries CHAMPLAIN humanely ended."

This was the first pitched battle fought upon our continent, and thus did the Iroquois learn the use of an auxiliary in war, which enabled them to extend in less than a century afterwards, their territorial dominion two thousand miles, waste the lives of their own race, and afterwards, as allies of England, to become a scourge of the border settlements of New York, in the war of the Revolution. Nor did the instructors of these amateurs in a new warfare, escape the consequences. They found them apt scholars; and in their after contests with them learned to dread the stealthy and deadly aim, in their hands, of the arms furnished them by the Dutch and English.

At nearly the same period, HUDSON had given them the taste of intoxicating liquors, at Albany. Thus were they put in possession of two agents that were finally to work their own ruin and decline. Better for them, we are apt to say, if civilization had never reached them in these their forest homes. But then comes upon us the reflection that theirs, if a sylvan abode, was not one of peace and innocence. Long before—how long their own traditions cannot inform us,—they were warring upon their own race. They too had invented weapons of war, and oppressed and trampled upon the weak; were even wanton in their wanderings upon the war path for victims. Who shall question the dispensations of Providence, or say that theirs was not the destiny he had decreed? Who shall say, that if European feet had never trod their soil, that an even worse calamity was not in store for them? That they but awaited the ebb tide of destiny? That retribution was not already coming upon them;—its ministering spirits, the leagued and exasperated of their own race, they had scourged in long years of triumph and supremacy?

With a far better knowledge of the country of New France, than had been before obtained, CHAMPLAIN returned home, and after delays and embarrassments, incident to some changes in the administration of the government of France, in 1615 embarked once more for the New World. There came out with him, monks of the order of St. Francis. "Again he invades the territory of the Iroquois in New York. Wounded and repulsed, and destitute of guides, he spends the first winter after his return to America in the country of the Hurons; and a night errant among the forests, carries his language, religion and influence, even to the hamlets of the Algonquins on Lake Nipissing."*

CARTIER is regarded as the pioneer upon the St. Lawrence, and CHAMPLAIN as the founder of a colony upon its banks. "For twenty years succeeding the commencement of the 17th century, he was zealously employed in planting and rearing that infant colony, which was destined to extend its branches to these shores and finally, to contest with its great rival, the sovereignty of North America. CHAMPLAIN discovered in his eventful life, traits of heroism, self-devotion and perseverance, which, under more favorable circumstances, would have placed him in the ranks of those, whose deeds are the land marks of history."†

Events that followed the discovery of this continent, have been thus briefly alluded to, with no intention to enlarge upon them, or

---

* Bancroft.

† Gen. Cass' Lectures before Historical Society of Michigan.

to travel over ground with which most readers will be familiar; but principally for the purpose of such a chronological introduction as will aid in connecting our own local history with the history of our entire country.

The progress of colonization was slow. In this day of PROGRESS, we may well wonder why such a country as this, did not at once invite a flood of adventurers from Europe. But a careful review of the condition of the old world at that period; the jealousies and counteracting rivalries that existed between the nations that had directed their attention to this quarter: England, France Germany and Spain; their internal dissensions, and the fluctuations in their administrations and their commercial policy; afford us chiefly the explanation. And to all these hindrances may be added, the absence of that spirit of determined and persevering national adventure, which at a later period stimulated to a more earnest and effectual searching out and occupying new fields of enterprise. In following up the slow course of events as they occurred; in noting the tardiness especially, with which England and France made their advances to this continent, even after they had through the reports of their explorers, reliable accounts of the land of promise, leads us to reflect, how it would be now, with our own people, if they could even catch a glimpse of an unoccupied field such as this was. There would be no waiting for kingly or government charters; no asking of colonial monopolies. Individual efforts, indomitable private enterprise, would take the place of all this: there would go out from our sea-ports in rapid succession, colonies of hardy adventurers, who arriving at their destinations. and finding but a moiety of the inducements, surrounded by greater obstacles, than was presented to European adventurers here — would persevere; and in the time that in the precedent case it took to deliberate at home, and determine upon a scheme of colonization, —colonies would be founded, territorial governments would be formed; and we should hear of annexation, and possibly of admission.

"Westward the star of Empire" took "its way," but dimly and slowly; giving but a feeble and flickering light to attract the nations of the earth, while its orbit was circumscribed under European auspices and dominion. It was not 'till it had the genial influences of freedom and free institutions; until it had shaken off the incubus of foreign control; that it began to shine with lustre, make its rapid transit towards the zenith, and realize the prophetic inspiration of Bishop BERKLEY.

Dating from the discovery of this continent in 1492, it was five years before CABOT discovered New Foundland, St. Johns, and the coast of Virginia; forty-two years before CARTIER discovered and sailed up the St. Lawrence; one hundred and thirty-five years before CHAMPLAIN had effectually established French settlements and dominion. Twenty years before PONCE DE LEON discovered Florida and claimed it for Spain; seventy-three years before St. Augustine was founded.* Seventy-three years before the first expedition of Sir WALTER RALEIGH entered the bay of the Chesapeake; one hundred and fifteen years before any permanent colony was established in Virginia. One hundred and twenty-nine years before the Pilgrims landed at Plymouth. One hundred and fifteen before HUDSON sailed up the river that bears his name; and one hundred thirty-one years before colonization was effectually progressing upon its banks.

The whole series of primitive discoveries upon this continent were accidental. The discoverers were in pursuit of a shorter route to the Indies, and blundered upon this fair region that lay in their way. After the discoveries, gold, other minerals, precious stones, fountains of health, predominated with the explorers, until failing in their expectations, traffic with the natives for furs and peltries, engrossed the attention of the few and far between voyagers to the New World. The great elements of wealth here, as time has demonstrated, lay dormant and undisturbed in the soil. The Acadia of France, the Eldorado of Spain, the region where the Englishman was to shovel wealth into his coffers, and the slow Dutchman was to quicken his pace in the pursuit of fortune; came far short of their expectations; and their squadrons but came and wandered lazily around the coasts, or ventured but short expeditions up our noble rivers. The wealth was here — the elements of human enjoyment, content and happiness, but they widely mistook in what it consisted. It remained for patient, persevering industry and enterprise, unshackled by tyranny; for those who fled to these shores from persecution and wrong; for young and vigorous scions of a decayed and decaying parent stock; to more than realize the hopes and expectations of the early European dreamers.

---

* St, Augustine is by forty years, the oldest town in the United States.

In 1609 the English colony at Jamestown had just begun to turn its attention to agriculture:—"yet so little land had been cultivated —not more than thirty or forty acres in all—that it was still necessary for Englishmen to solicit food from the indolent Indians; and Europeans, to preserve themselves from starving, were billeted among the sons of the forest."* In 1624, DE LAET, a director of the Dutch West India Company, under whose auspices settlement was slowly progressing upon the Hudson, attracted the attention of his countrymen by a published description of the New World. In describing New Netherland, he said:—"It is a fine and delightful land, full of fine trees and vines—wine might be made there, and the grape cultivated. Nothing is wanted but cattle, and they might be easily transported. The industry of our people might make this a pleasant and fruitful land. The forests contain excellent ship timber, and several yachts and small vessels have been built there." But it was not until several years after this first attempt to turn the attention of the Dutch from traffic to agriculture, that there was any considerable degree of success.

The Dutch trade was with the natives, upon Long Island, the banks of the Hudson, and the eastern nations of the Iroquois. By a report made to the West India Company at Amsterdam, the following exhibit was made of exports and imports for the first nine years after the regular established commerce of the colony:—

EXPORTS.

YEAR.					GUILDERS.
1624.	4,000 beavers,	700	otters,		27,125
1625.	5,295	"	463	"	35,825
1626.	7,258	"	857	"	45,050
1627	7,520	"	320	"	12,730
1628.	6,951	"	734	"	61,075
1629.	5,913	"	681	"	62,185
1630.	6,041	"	1085	"	68,012
1631.		no exports.			—
1632.	13,513	"	1661	"	143,125
					454,127
				or,	$189,219,58

IMPORTS.

YEAR.			GUILDERS.
1624.	In two ships, goods, wares,		25,569
1625.	Several ships,	"	8,772
1626.	Two ships,	"	20,384
1627.	Four ships,	"	56,170
1628.	No imports,		—
1629.	Three ships,	"	55,778
1630.	Two ships,	"	54,499
1631.	One ship,	"	17,355
1632.	One ship,	"	31,320
			272,847
		or,	$113,686,25

"The advancement of colonization in New England, [1628] was far more rapid than it had been in New Netherland; but the causes that respectively operated to produce the diversity, were altogether different in their character and tendency. In the one case, religion became the powerful motive, and it introduced as auxiliaries, talent, enterprise and skill. In the other, monopoly and aristocracy, with

---

* Bancroft.

their cold and calculating selfishness, were in collision with the freedom of trade and the genius of liberty, and the consequences were withering to the blossoms of promise which nature had so bountifully displayed in New Netherlands."*

Conflicting claims to territory upon this continent, began to arise in the earliest periods of colonization. The basis, or general principles upon which claims were to be founded, was pretty well defined by the common consent of the nations of Europe, that were interested; but disputes and collisions arose from different constructions of these general principles; and upon questions of fact, involving priority of discovery, occupation, &c.

"Discovery gave title to the government, by whose subjects, or by whose authority it was made, against all other European governments, which title might be consummated by possession. Hence, although a vacant country belonged to those who first discovered it, and who acknowledge no connexion, and owe no allegiance to any government, yet if the country be discovered and possessed by the emigrants of an existing acknowledged government, the possession is deemed taken for the nation, and title must be derived from the sovereign organ, in whom the power to dispute of vacant territories is vested by law.

"Resulting from the above principle as qualified, was that of the sole right of the discoverer to acquire the soil from the natives, and establish settlements either by purchase or conquest. Hence, also the exclusive right cannot exist in governments, and at the same time in private individuals; and hence also, the natives were recognized as rightful occupants, but their power to dispose of the soil at their own will, to whom they pleased, was denied by the original fundamental principle, that discovery gave exclusive title to those who made it.

"The ultimate dominion was asserted, and as a consequence, a power to grant the soil while yet in possession of the natives. — Hence, such dominion was incompatible with an absolute and complete title in the Indians. Consequently, from the foregoing principle, and its corollaries, the Indians had no right to sell to any other than the government of the first discoverer, nor to private

---

NOTE. — The author having found the above concise and comprehensive abstract of the basis of title to all the lands in the United States, in the work of Yates and Moulton already quoted, he transfers it to his pages. It not only contains the principles that governed the nations of Europe, in their original colonization of our country, but sets forth the main principle, and origin of pre-emption, as afterwards recognized by our general government and the states. A careful historical deduction of the title to our own region takes us back for a starting point, to the basis of title, as fixed at the primitive period of discovery and colonization.

* Yates and Moulton.

citizens without the sanction of their government. Hence the Indians were to be considered as mere occupants, to be protected indeed while in peace, in the possession of their lands, but with an incapacity of transfering the absolute title to others."

At a point we have now gained,— the commencement of permanent colonization upon this continent,— the author is admonished, in view of the local character of the work he has in hand, that he must come nearer home. Civilization is already approaching the region of Western New York. Under CHAMPLAIN, the founder of settlement upon the St. Lawrence, there have come out of France scores of adventurers; the most prominent, and far most numerous of whom, are the fur traders, the devotees of traffic and gain; and the missionaries, with the higher purposes of carrying the emblems and the tidings of salvation to the forest homes of our predecessors. The two classes, jointly, travelling together side by side, are destined to extend French dominion to the rivers and lakes of Canada west; to the head waters of lake Ontario; along the banks of the Niagara river, to the shores of lakes Erie, St. Clair, Huron, Michigan, and Superior; over the fertile plains, prairies and wood-lands of Michigan, Wisconsin, Indiania, Illinois, Missouri, Iowa, down the Mississippi to the Gulf of Mexico, and over its waters to Texas.

The missionary was seldom behind, often preceded the trader. Those of the order of St. Francis—called Franciscans,—preceded the Jesuits in the New World. They came out with CHAMPLAIN in 1615. The more formidable order, that was destined wholly to supplant them and occupy exclusively the new field of missionary enterprise, first arrived upon the banks of the St. Lawrence in 1625. Previous to this, the Franciscans, LE CARON, VIEL and SAGARD, had been instructing the tribes along the western banks of the Niagara. They were unquestionably, the first Europeans who set foot in Western New York. Their advent here was nearly co-temporary with the landing of the Pilgrims in New England. Plymouth Rock had but just re-echoed the thanksgiving of the founders of English colonization in our northern states,— the simpler and less ostentatious forms of the religious faith of the Puritans, had but just found an asylum upon our northern Atlantic coast; when the ceremonies of the Catholic church were exciting the wonder of the dwellers in the forests of our own region.

For nearly one hundred and fifty years, from the period of

effectual colonization upon the St. Lawrence, until the English conquests in 1759; the Jesuits — the disciples of LOYOLA — were almost exclusively in possession of the whole missionary ground of New France. With the exception of but brief precedent advents of the Franciscans, the Jesuits with the traders that accompanied them, were the Pioneers of civilization in Western New York. The imposing ceremonies of the ritual of the Catholic Church, awed the simple minded sons of the forest as they came to gaze upon the works of the primitive ship builders upon the Niagara; — JONCAIRE, the adopted Seneca, the successful courtier at the councils of the Iroquois, had hardly "planted himself amid a group of cabins at Lewiston," when the cross was planted in their midst. When a trading station was secured at Niagara, the Jesuit missionary erected his cabin by the side of the trader. And going out from these primitive stopping places, they threaded the narrow trails that conducted them to the scattered settlements of the Senecas west of the Genesee river, and upon its eastern banks. The advent and long career of the Jesuits upon this continent, and especially in this quarter, forms an interesting feature in our general history; a brief sketch of their founder, and his Institute, may well occupy a short chapter of our local *pioneer* annals.

CHAPTER II.

THE ORDER OF THE JESUITS.

The order of the Jesuits as it is usually termed — of the Society of JESUS, as they termed themselves — was founded in the early part of the sixteenth century. Its founder was IGNATIUS LOYOLA, a native of Navarre. Born of a noble family, bred to the profession of arms, chivalric and daring, when an army of FRANCIS I. invaded his country, he was among the gallant defenders of the besieged city of Pampeluna. While rallying and exhorting the Spanish soldiers to a desperate resistance, he was severely wounded. While an invalid, the lives of the Saints fell into his hands, and were his constant companions during the progress of a lingering cure. Their perusal excited his ardent temperament, and inspired him with ambition to signalize himself as a champion of the religious faith in which he had been educated. Retiring to a convent, he meditated and made vows to become the "Knight of the Virgin MARY," and to be "renowned for mortifications and works after the manner of saints." In his seclusion he subjected himself to the most rigid disipline of a monk of the strictest order, and after several years of solitary penance and journeyings as a mendicant, he matured a gigantic scheme of missionary enterprise, embracing the world in its designs; and which, for good and evil, is signalized as one of the most extraordinary advents that mark the pages of history.

When LUTHER publicly sustained the thesis of his apostacy in the Diet of Worms, and composed his book against monastic vows, in the solitude of Alstadt, LOYOLA was consecrating himself to his work, in the chapel of Monte Serrato, and composing his Spiritual Exercises in his retreat at Mauresa. At the time too, that HENRY the Eighth proclaimed himself spiritual head of the Anglician

Church, and ordered, under penalty of death, that the very name of Pope should be effaced from every document and from every book, LOYOLA was laying the foundations of an order that professed in a most special manner, obedience to the sovereign Pontiff, and zeal and activity in enlarging the bounds of his dominion.

The Reformation under the lead of MARTIN LUTHER, had well nigh broken the sway, prostrated the power of the Roman Church. The advent of LOYOLA was the first recoil from its effects. It was as if in battle, a powerful army had been nearly routed, its ranks thinned and broken, its leaders dismayed, appalled by the desperate onsets of the assailants — a daring spirit should spring from the ranks fitted to the emergency, and by the boldness and novelty of his designs, inspire courage to renew the contest. While the Pope and his adherents were deliberating — resolving but feebly, and often impotently essaying to execute their resolutions; an intrepid soldier—wounded in a field of carnal warfare—clothed himself in spiritual armor, and came forward the devotee and champion of a faith that had been successfully assailed by innovators, as daring and fearless in their assaults, as he was in his well arranged plan of defence. In the warfare of faiths, in which he was enlisted, — a contest to sustain the supremacy of his creed, to enable it to regain its lost ground, — LOYOLA was what NAPOLEON became after him in the political affairs of France. They were equally master spirits of the movements in which they were engaged. The one astonished the religious world with the newness and magnificence of his schemes. The other confounded and amazed the political world, by a long career of the triumphs of the one man-power that he wielded. Did NAPOLEON call to his aid the genius, the talent, the courage of France, and mould them to his will; LOYOLA equally by the attractions of his splendid conceptions, guaranteed and realized as great moral triumphs, in enlisting the co-operation of those who were fitted to his purposes. The wealth that he required to lay the foundations of his new system of propagandism, flowed into his treasury; for the possessors of it were mourning over the reverses of a religious faith that more than all others, prompts to the offerings of worldly possessions; imagined that light was again shining through the domes of St. Peters; that error,— grievous error, as they deemed it, was to be confounded by the new champion that had taken the field. Around his standard flocked the devotees of the "Church Catholic;" who, surrendering all things else, dedicated themselves to his will and his designs; set themselves apart to execute his commands, even to the farthest ends of the earth. The Church of Rome had been assailed by the bold Reformer in the seats and centres of its dominions. Its old strong fortresses were besieged. LOYOLA looked to the strengthning and extending of the out-posts; to the more than regaining all that had been lost, by sending out to the four quarters of the globe and gathering to the fold, new auxiliaries, propagating his creed in new and far off fields.

The tasks to be executed were those of difficulty and danger, but there came to his aid those who caught from him their impulses, and armed themselves with his stern resolves. Never in any missionary enterprise; (and the history of missions from the advent of christianity to the present hour, is replete with signal instances of self-sacrifice and martyrdoms; instances of the exercises of a moral and physical courage, sterner and higher than the incentives to armed encounters;) — has there been devised a scheme of missionary enterprise of equal magnitude; or one that has commanded more devoted service and extraordinary sacrifice, than the Institute which somewhat arrogantly assumed to itself the name of the "Society of Jesus."

"LOYOLA was aware, that on the day of battle, the most experienced officers stand apart, in order to watch with more composure, the conflict which they direct. A general of an army ought, by means of the orders that he issues, to be every where present to his troops. Their movements, their courage, their very life, depend on him; he disposes of them in the most absolute manner; and the very physical inaction to which, in consequence, he subjects himself, augments his intellectual energies. It is he that stimulates, that restrains, that combines the springs of action, that assumes the responsibility of events. Such was the policy of IGNATIUS LOYOLA. He dispersed his companions over the globe; he sent them forth to humiliation or to glory, to preach or to be martyred, while he from Rome, as a central point, communicated force to all, and, what was still better, regulated their movements.

"At Rome IGNATIUS followed his disciples at every step. In an age when communication was neither easy nor expeditious, and when each political revolution added to the difficulty, he found means to correspond with them frequently. He had a perfect knowledge of the state of the missions, and was acquainted with the joys and sufferings of the missionaries; he sympathised with them, and thus shared their dangers and their struggles; his orders were anxiously expected, his councils were scrupulously followed. More calm than they, for he was uninfluenced by local passions, he decided with greater discernment, he regulated with greater unity of design." *

The plan of LOYOLA not only embraced an extended missionary enterprise, but the founding of institutions of learning. Colleges of the Jesuits were founded at Rome, throughout the Papal dominions, and their branches extended to the foreign missionary grounds. They were as so many hives, from which swarmed hosts of those who were educated and fitted for the work before them. But the education of missionaries was not exclusively their province. Engrafted into the system, was the design of its founder to raise up a new class of well educated men, in all the departments of literature, the arts and sciences. The colleges were munificently endowed; learning had a new impetus given to it. There went out from the institutions of the Jesuits, not only the priest, deeply schooled in the theology of his order, but poets, philosophers and statesmen; those who were well fitted to have influence in the political and social affairs of the world, as well as those who would promote the predominating object,— the laying of a broader platform for their church, and extending its sway.

The scheme of LOYOLA, formidable as it was, excited the fears, and perhaps jealousies of the then reigning Pontiff. He regarded it an innovation, and withheld his approval; but his successor, PAUL III. clothed the institute with all the attributes necessary to make its authority ample.

"The genius of CHAMPLAIN, whose comprehensive mind planned enduring establishments for French commerce, and a career of discovery that should carry the lilies of the Bourbons to the extremity of North America, could devise no method of building up the dominion of France in Canada, but by an alliance with the Hurons, or of confirming that alliance but by the establishment of missions."† He had at first encouraged the unambitious Franciscans; but they, being excluded from New France, by the policy of the home government, in 1632, the conversion of the New World was committed to the ardent Jesuits. They had entered the land

---

* History of the Jesuits by M. Crétineu-Joly. Paris, 1844.
† Bancroft.

before, but not under the exclusive privilege of martyrdom. As early as 1611 Father BIART had opened the gospel between the Penobscot and Kennebec, and within two years a congregation of faithful red men was chanting over the territory lately disputed and along the river banks in Maine, their morning and their evening hymns. The renewal of French emigration to Canada, and the committal of this western mission to the Jesuits, were simultaneous. The fifteen who first arrived at Montreal, went principally among the Five Nations in the interior of this state.

In the immediate dominions of the Pope, throughout the cities and villages of the greater portion of Europe, the disciples of LOYOLA spread themselves, and earnestly exhorted backsliders to return to their ecclesiastical allegiance; stirred up the luke-warm, and checked the hitherto onward march of the Reformers. In 1543, the Jesuits had missionary stations in Japan and Ethiopa; in the Indies and in Peru; in Brazil and Mogul; in the remotest Archipelagos, and the bleakest Islands; in the heart of Africa and on the banks of the Bosphorus; in China; at Madras and Thibet; in Genoa.

The antagonist movements of the Reformers, the disciples of LUTHER and CALVIN, and the new school of propagandists founded by LOYOLA, came in collision upon this continent, in the very earliest periods of effectual colonization. Deeply imbued with the spirit of the Reformation, were the founders of New England, and as deeply, were the founders of New France imbued with the spirit, the impelling zeal of LOYOLA. Avarice, a desire for dominion and gain, led the way in both quarters, and the better impulses of religion and its different faiths, followed. Treading in each others footsteps were the traders and missionaries of the early New England colonists; the "gospel was opened" wherever the trafficer in furs and peltries had made a stand. On the St. Lawrence, along the great chain of Lakes and Rivers, west to the valley of the Mississippi, the chaffering of the votaries of Mammon was often merged with the devotional exercises of the disciples of LOYOLA; dividing the attention of the natives between the "tables of the money changers," and the emblems, and imposing ceremonies of the Romish church.

When the primitive, Protestant missionaries of New England, were wandering in its vallies, faithfully expounding the revealed word to their dusky auditors, gathered in their wigwams, or reclining in their forest shades, the missionaries of the church of Rome, were displaying the emblems of salvation upon the shores of lake Ontario, in the settlements of the Iroquois in the interior of our State, upon the banks of the Niagara river, and around the shores of the Western Lakes.

They were the subjects of rival nations, and the professors and propagators of rival creeds. No wonder perhaps,—and yet it was strangely at variance with the mild precepts of Him whose mediations they were offering to the inhabitants of the new world — they both brought to these shores the rankling, the spirit of contention, even to the sword, that was drenching some of the fairest portions of Europe with blood. They were contending for ecclesiastical, and it was the impulses of country and allegiance, that made them strenuous for temporal, political, dominion. Their influences were felt in the wars that succeeded between the Iroquois and the French, and the English and French. They were, more or less, participators in the competition for extended empire between those two nations.

The writers of history, and the readers of it who are in pursuit of facts it is its province to gather up, have little to do with the merits of rival creeds. The sources of instruction are ample, furnished by their respective advocates. In the history of the advents of Catholicism and Protestantism in our early colonization there is much to admire, and much to condemn.

Who will not dwell with admiration upon the details of the sufferings, martyrdoms, the self abasement of the ardent Catholic missionaries that extended civilization, planted the cross here in this western wilderness? Sincerity, ardent zeal, signalized their advent and progress. Danger was in their wilderness paths, hovered around their rude forest chapels. In winter's snows and summer's heats, they traversed the wilderness, paddled their frail canoes upon our rivers and lakes; deeming health, life, of little concern—all of temporal enjoyments, subservient to the paramount object: the gathering into the folds of the church of new converts; numbering another and another of the aboriginal nations to swell the conquests of their faith. Their system was fraught with superstition and error; yet who that reverences goodness wherever seen and by whatever name it may be called, will refuse to them a meed of praise; fail to recognize them as those who won the first triumphs for the cross, in this region; when "the wild tribes of the west bowed to the emblem of our common faith." *

> "The Priest
> Believed the fables that he taught:
> Corrupt their forms, and yet those forms at least
> Preserved a salutary faith that wrought,
> Maugre the alloy, the saving end it sought.
> Benevolence had gained such empire there,
> That even superstition had been brought
> An aspect of humanity to wear,
> And make the weal of man the first and only care."
> *Southey's Tales of Paraguay.*

This is the fair side of the picture. There are blemishes, deep and indelible ones, in the long and eventful career of the Institute of LOYOLA. In the system itself there was error, and error and wrong were mingled with its triumphs, and contributed to its decline. Elated with its successes, it sought to rule in that to which it professed itself but an auxiliary, until it encountered the jealousy, and finally the ban of the great central power at Rome it had done so much to strengthen. If not the founder of the Inquisition, in some portions of the world it availed itself of that terrible engine of ecclesiastical tyranny, crime and oppression. Its favorable aspect, is the vast amount of good it has done to the cause of learning in the various branches of science; the schools and hospitals it has founded; its early missions here and in many other benighted portions of the world. Beyond these, there is that which its advocates—those who are of the faith it upheld—cannot in our more enlightened and liberal period, look upon but with regret and disapprobation.

And Protestantism too, as connected with our early colonial history, has its pleasant and unpleasant aspects. The humble colony that for the sake of faith and conscience, embarked in a vessel illy provided, braved the winter's storms upon the ocean, and landed upon the bleak and inhospitable shores of New England; encountering disease, the tomahawk of the savage, deprivation and death, to the fearful thinning of its at best but too feeble ranks; may well claim a divided admiration with the highest exercise of religious faith and perseverance that marked the wilderness advent of the

---
* The Rev. W. J. Kipp.

disciples of Loyola. And they were unfriended; had no shield of Rome, no coffers of wealth to sustain them. Their king and country was against them. Across the ocean, in the land they had fled from, to them all was darkness; and around them on the other hand, was a wilderness in which the lurking and stealthy foe of their race was to be conciliated and appeased. No light shone in upon them but that which came from above. In process of time, (and that not long extended,) there was an Eliot and a Mayhew that contested the palm of missionary zeal and daring, with a Marquette and a Brebeuf. They furnished examples of benignity, simplicity, and heroic patience, such as the world has seldom, if ever, witnessed. The one gave the Indians a Bible in their own dialect; the other perished in an ocean voyage undertaken to bring more laborers into the field of missionary enterprise. Protestant missions early spread throughout New England, along the shores of the Hudson, up the valley of the Mohawk. They numbered in their train a band of faithful and devoted men. In the infant colonies upon the Chesapeake Bay, Harriot first displayed the Bible to the natives and inculcated its truths; and Robert Hunt, who had left behind him his happy English home, came as a peace-maker to a turbulent colony, and to act as a mediator between the natives and their molestors. Had the Jesuits among their neophytes their sainted Seneca maiden,—Catharine Tegahkouita, the "Genevieve of New France"—the Protestants upon the Bay of the Chesapeake, numbered among their converts a Pochahontas:— "the first sheaf of her nation offered to God—the consecration of her charms in early life that mercy might spare her the sight of her nation's ruin by an early death." *

But in after times Protestantism had its tyrannies and persecutions; its intemperate zeal, bigotry and coercive auxiliaries; its banishments, proscriptions, and tribunals of faith. Did the disciples of Loyola in other countries avail themselves of the inquisition; enforce cruel, world-forsaking monastic vows; the disciples of Calvin in New England, erected the gibbet and hunted to the scaffold, the non-conformist, the heretic, and the unhappy men and women whom their dark superstition accused of witchcraft.

The wrongs that were perpetrated in the old world by the institute of the Jesuits, cannot fairly be made to dim the lustre of

---

* From a friend's manuscript.

the forest advent of the faithful men of the order that pioneered the way to civilization in this region. The wrong doing—the intolerance and bigoted persecutions of the early Puritans identified with colonization in another quarter, should be hardly remembered in view of the part their descendants have finally borne, in rearing our proud fabric of religious and political freedom.

The Institute of LOYOLA has had a chequered existence; unexampled success at one period, decline and proscription at another. For a long period enjoying the high favor of a succession of Popes, then suppressed by one, to be soon restored to favor by another. It was founded near the middle of the sixteenth century, and had an almost uninterrupted career of success, upon a scale of magnificence but feebly indicated in the preceding pages. In 1759, JOSEPH I, of Portugal, declared the Jesuits traitors and rebels, confiscated their goods and banished them. In 1762 the institution was declared "incompatible with the institutions of France," and the Jesuits received orders to abandon their houses and colleges, and adopt a secular dress. Soon after, they were accused of fomenting a popular insurrection in Madrid, and expelled from Spanish territory. The example was speedily followed by the King of Naples, and the Duke of Parma. In 1773 the order was suppressed by a bull from Pope CLEMENT XIV. For forty-one years the order had no existence save in its scattered and proscribed adherents. In 1814, PIUS VII published the bull for its restoration. From that period to the present, the order has been constantly progressive. It has revived many of its missionary stations, re-opened its colleges, convents and hospitals; and again been dispersing its missionaries over the globe.

The whole number of Jesuits that came to this country from their first advent in 1611, up to 1833, was twelve hundred. When France ceded their possessions east of the Mississippi, to England in 1763, they were forbidden to recruit their numbers; thus as the old members died, the communities became extinct. The whole, or the greater part of the property of the Jesuits has been held by the British government. The Catholic institutions in the United States and Canada, have now, with few exceptions, no connection with them.

It only remains to speak of the remote results of these early missionary efforts. So far as they bear upon our country now, they may seem slight and unworthy of notice; yet they form a prominent feature in our colonial history.

The immediate results of the Jesuit missions, were hopeful and stimulating. So long as the natives had no patterns of christianity to follow but the apostle, bringing his own and his Redeemer's cross among them, they could only revere the new religion, and wrestle against it, as passion warring with conscience. Under such influences, christian virtues were blooming along the path of the messengers from Norridgewok to the bay of Che-goi-me-gon. It is a pleasing relief to turn aside from the almost unremitted din of battle which raged around the progress of settlement in this land, and the wrangling encounters of opinion within the borders of New England, to the quiet heroism of the Jesuits, as they went forth carrying the "Prayer" (as the Indians termed their religion,) building chapels where the rude wigwams had been man's only resting place, and bringing whole villages from the wild wonder of an indefinite fear, to the subdued awe of worshipping believers;— the moral prodigy, the emblem of earth's redemption, the sway of the man of peace, over the men of war. It is a singular fact that these missionaries succeeded in fixing religious principle without the tedious and patient process of literary education and subtle reasoning. In an early part of the eighteenth century an effort was made on the part of the Protestants to draw off the Abenakis from their attachments to the faith of the Jesuits. The Rev. JOSEPH BAXTER, of Medfield, Mass., was despatched on this work, but was obliged to return after being patiently heard, confessing himself foiled by the unwillingness of the natives to learn any better way. The immediate results of the Jesuit missions were blessed. Of the remote results, little is to be said in praise. It was something that, by their carrying the cross of life before the artillery of death, souls of the red men might be enrolled among the redeemed from every kindred, ere the white man had spoiled their religion and blotted out their name. But the danger which the Jesuits foresaw, came upon their converts. The remote result was as they feared. Said Father MAREST, writing from Kaskasias in Illinois:—" should any of the whites who came among us make a profession of licentiousness, or perhaps irreligion, their pernicious example would make a deeper impression upon the minds of the Indians than all that we could say to preserve them from the same disorders. They would not fail to reproach us as they have already done in some places, that we take advantage of the facility with which they believe us; that the laws of christianity are not as severe as we represent them to be; since it is not to be credited that persons as enlightened as the French, and brought up in the bosom of religion, would be willing to rush to their own destruction, and precipitate themselves into hell, if it were true that such and such an action merited a punishment so terrible." The danger was more than the missionary feared; it was first the insinuating pestilence of corruption, and then the sword of extermination. Mark the transformation in the beautiful lines of WHITTIER:

"On the brow of a hill which slopes to meet
The flowing river and bathe at its feet,
A rude and mishapely chapel stands,
Built up in that wild by unskilled hands;
Yet the traveller knows it a place of prayer,
For the holy sign of the cross is there;
And should he chance at that place to be,
 Of a Sabbath morn on some hallowed day,
Well might the traveller start to see
 The tall dark forms that take their way
From the birch canoe on the river shore,
And the forest paths to that chapel door;
And marvel to mark the naked knees,
 And the dusky foreheads bending there,—
And, stretching his long thin arms over these,
 In blessing and in prayer,
Like a shrouded spectre, pale and tall,
In his coarse white vesture, Father RALLE."

But now,

"No wigwam smoke is curling there;
The very earth is scorched and bare;
And they pause and listen to catch a sound
Of breathing life, but there comes not one,
Save the fox's bark, and the rabbit's bound;
And here and there on the blackening ground,

NOTE.—Father Ralle was a missionary among the Abenakis, in 1724. His mission station was upon the Kennebec in Maine, near the village of Norridgewok. In the war which the English and their Indian allies waged against the Abenakis, he was a victim. When a hostile band approached his village of converts, he presented himself, in hopes to save his flock; but fell under a discharge of musketry. So says the Jesuit Relations. Hutchinson says he shut himself up in a wigwam, from which he fired upon the English. A cross and a rude monument marked the spot until 1833, when an acre of land was purchased including the site of Ralle's church and his grave, and over his grave a shaft erected twenty feet high, surmounted by a cross, in the presence of a large concourse of people. Bishop Fenwick directed the ceremonies, and delivered an address. Delegates from the Penobscot, Passamaquoddy, and Canada Indians were present.

> White bones are glistening in the sun,
> And where the house of prayer arose,
> And the holy hymn at daylight's close,
> And the aged priest stood up to bless
> The children of the wilderness,
> >   There is nought save ashes sodden and dank,
> And the birchen boats of the Norridgewok,
> Tethered to tree and stump and rock,
> >   Rotting along the river bank."

The Jesuits faded away with the decline, or end of French dominion east of the Mississippi, in 1763. There is little beyond such relics as are found of Father RALLE, (*see preceding note,*) to mark their advent here. At the west, their presence can be but dimly traced; the religion they inculcated exists among some of the Indian tribes, but hardly sufficient to identify it; the rude cross occasionally found at the head of an Indian grave, is perhaps as distinct evidence as any that exists, (other than faithful records,) of the early visit and long stay of the Catholic missionaries, upon the borders of our western lakes, and in the upper vallies of the Mississippi. Among the Indians of Western New York, all that remains to mark the Jesuit missionary advent, is the form of the cross in their silver ornaments.

How different has been the destiny of the Protestant advent upon the shores of New England! The Pilgrim Fathers — cotemporary with the Jesuits,— spread their faith among the natives, with nearly as little success perhaps; but they maintained their ground, became a part of the great fabric of religious and political freedom that was rearing; their impress is indelibly stamped upon our country and its institutions.

CHAPTER III.

PROGRESS OF COLONIZATION, PROMINENT EVENTS CONNECTED WITH IT, FROM 1627 TO 1763.

This embraces a period of one hundred and thirty-six years; or, the entire French occupancy from the period of effectual colonization under CHAMPLAIN upon the St. Lawrence, to that of English conquest, and the end of French dominion east of the Mississippi.

The long succession of interesting events; the details of the French and Indian, and French and English wars; belong to our general history. For the purposes of local history it will only be necessary to embrace, with any considerable degree of minuteness, such portions of them as had a direct local relation.

But little success attended the first efforts of colonization upon the St. Lawrence. Fourteen years after the founding of Quebec, (in 1662) the population was reduced to fifty souls. The ill-success was principally owing to the hostilities of the Iroquois; that had been first excited by the unfortunate alliance of CHAMPLAIN with the Hurons; the rivalry between different interests in the fur trade; and jarring and discord arising out of a mixed population of Catholics and Protestants, who brought to the New World much of the intolerance that characterized that period. Most of the colonists were mere adventurers; more intent upon present gain, if indeed most of them had any definite purposes beyond the freedom from restraint, the perfect liberty that an ill-governed far off colony offered to them; than upon any well regulated efforts at colonization.

In order to adjust dissensions that existed in the colony, produce harmony of effort, and generally, to strengthen the colonial enterprize, in 1627 Cardinal RICHELIEU organized what was called the company of New France—or, company of an Hundred Partners. The primary object of the association, was the conversion of the Indians to the Catholic faith, by the co-operation of the zealous Jesuits; the secondary, an extension of the fur trade, of commerce generally, and to discover a route to the Pacific ocean and China through the great rivers and lakes of New France. This company was invested not only with a monopoly of trade, but with a religious monopoly; protestants and "other heretics" were entirely excluded. An inauspicious commencement:—monopoly and bigotry went hand in hand. It was in the order of Providence that neither, in whatever form they might assume, should have any permanent success upon this side of the Atlantic.

The company stipulated to send to New France, three hundred tradesmen, and to supply them with all necessary utensils for three years; after which time they were to grant to each workman sufficient land for his support, and grain for seed. The company also stipulated to colonize the lands embraced in their charter, with six thousand inhabitants, before the year 1643, and to provide each settlement with three Catholic priests, whom they were to support for fifteen years. The cleared land was then to be granted to the Catholic clergy for the maintenance of the church. Certain prerogatives were at the same time secured to the king; such as religious supremacy, homage as sovereign of the country, the right of nominating commandants of the forts and the officers of justice, and on each succession to the throne the acknowledgement of a crown of gold weighing thirteen marks. The company had also the right of conferring titles of distinction, some of which were required to be confirmed by the king. The right to traffic in peltries, and engage in other commerce, other than the cod and whale fisheries, was at the same time granted in the charter. The king presented the company two ships of war, upon condition that the value should be refunded, if fifteen hundred French inhabitants were not transported into the country in the first ten years. The descendants of Frenchmen inhabiting New France, and all savages who should be converted to the Catholic faith, were permitted to enjoy the same privileges as natural born subjects; and all artificers sent out by the company, who had spent six years in the French colony, were permitted to return and settle in any town in France.

The design of the government, was to strengthen the claims of France to territory in North America. The company, as was afterwards demonstrated, designed to benefit themselves, through the extension of the fur trade.

CHAMPLAIN was appointed Governor. For the first few years, the colony, from various causes connected with its remote position from the parent country; the hardships of the forest, and the hostility of the Iroquois, suffered extremely, and was almost upon the point of breaking down. Ships that had been sent out with supplies had been captured by Sir DAVID KERTH, then in the employment of the British Crown. The depredations of the Iroquois kept the colony in check, diminished their numbers, and crippled their exertions, until the year 1629, when the French adventurers were involved in the deepest distress. KERTH who had succeeded in cutting off several expeditions of supply vessels from France, and finally reducing them almost to starvation, sailed up the St. Lawrence and made an easy conquest of Quebec, on the 20th, July, 1629. In October following, CHAMPLAIN returned to France; most of his company, however, having remained in Canada.

About this period, a peace was concluded between England and France, by the treaty of St. Germaine. This restored to France, Quebec, with its other possessions upon this continent. CHAMPLAIN resumed the government of Canada. The Jesuits with their accustomed zeal commenced anew their efforts; and from this period to the final English conquests in 1759, a rivalship and growing hostility, partly religious and partly commercial, took place between the English and French colonists, which was evinced by mutual aggressions, at some periods, while profound peace existed between their respective sovereigns in Europe.

CHAMPLAIN in his return from France to resume his office of governor, came with a squadron provided with necessary supplies and armaments. A better organization of the colonial enterprise was had; measures were adopted to reconcile existing difficulties, growing out of the immoral principles of the emigrants, and to prevent the introduction into the colony of any but those of fair character.

NOTE.—The colonization of New France, commenced but with little regard to the character of the colonists. It was rather such as could be induced to come out, than such as the Company would have preferred. The prisons and work houses of France, a discharged soldiery, and those generally with whom no change could be for the worse, formed a large portion of the early colonists. The Baron la Hontan, who came out to Quebec in the year 1683, speaks of this as well as all things that came under his observation, with much freedom:—"Most of the inhabitants are a free sort of people that removed hither from France and brought with them but little money to set up

In 1635 a college of the order of Jesuits was established at Quebec, which was of great advantage in improving the morals of the people, that had grown to a state of open licentiousness.

At this period the colony suffered a great misfortune in the death of CHAMPLAIN. "With a mind warmed into enthusiasm by the vast domain of wilderness that was stretched out before him, and the glorious visions of future grandeur which its resources opened; a man of extraordinary hardihood and the clearest judgment; a brave officer and a scientific seaman; his keen forecast discerned, in the magnificent prospect of the country which he occupied, the elements of a mighty empire of which he had hoped to be founder. With a stout heart and ardent zeal, he had entered upon the project of colonization; he had disseminated valuable knowledge of its resources by his explorations; and had cut the way through hordes of savages, for the subsequent successful progress of the French towards the lakes."*

During the administration of MONTNEAGNY, who succeeded CHAMPLAIN, the colony made but little progress, except in the extension of its trade in furs.

The religious institutions of the Jesuits about this period, were considerably augmented; a seminary was established at Sillery, near Quebec; the convent of St. Ursula at Quebec, established by Madame de la PELTRIE, a young widow of rank, who had engaged several Sisters of the Ursulines at Tours, with whom she sailed from Dieppe in a vessel which she chartered at her own expense.

---

withal. The rest are those who were soldiers about thirty or forty years ago, at which time the regiment of Carigan was broken up." * * * "After this, several ships were sent hither from France, with a cargo of women of an ordinary reputation. The vestal virgins were heaped up, (if I may so speak), one above another, in three different apartments, where the bridegrooms singled out their brides just as a butcher does a ewe from amongst a flock of sheep. In these three seraglios there was such a variety and change of diet as could satisfy the most whimsical appetites; for here was some big, some little, some fair, some brown, some fat and some meagre. In fine, every one might be fitted to his mind:—and indeed the market had such a run, that in fifteen days time they were all disposed of. I am told that the fattest went off best, under the apprehension that these being less active, would keep truer to their engagements, and hold out better against the nipping cold of winter." * * * "In some parts of the world to which vicious European women are transported, the mob of those countries do seriously believe that their sins are so defaced by the ridiculous christening I took notice of before, that they are looked upon ever after as ladies of virtue, of honor, and untarnished conduct of life." * * * "After the choice was determined the marriage was concluded upon the spot, in the presence of a priest and a public notary; and the next day the Governor General, bestowed upon the married couple, a bull, a cow, a hog, a sow, a cock, a hen, two barrels of salt meat and eleven crowns."

* History of Illinois.

A seminary of the order of St. Sulpicious was also founded at Montreal.

The Company of New France came short of fulfilling their charter. Little was done by them either to encourage the settlement of the country, or for the advancement of agriculture, the fur trade almost engrossing their attention. In the remote points of the wilderness, forts of rude construction had been erected; but these were merely posts of defence, or depots of the trade, the dominions of which, at that early period, stretched through tracks of wilderness large enough for kingdoms. The energies of the colonists were cramped by the Iroquois, who hung like hungry wolves around the track of the colonists, seeking to glut their vengeance against the French by butchering the people, and plundering the settlements whenever opportunities occurred.

In 1640 Montreal was selected to be the nearest rendezvous for converted Indians. The event was celebrated by a solemn mass. In August of the same year, in the presence of the French gathered from all parts of Canada, and of the native warriors summoned from the wilderness, the festival of the assumption was solemnized on the Island itself. In 1647, the traders and missionaries had broken out from the St. Lawrence and advanced as far as the shores of Lake Huron. Previous to 1666, trading posts were established at Michillimackinac, Sault St. Marie, Green Bay, Chicago, and St. Joseph.

The progress of the missionaries and traders was slow around the shores of the western lakes. After one post was established, it was in most instances the work of years to advance and occupy another position. In 1665, Father CLAUDE ALLOUEZ entered the great village of the Chippeways at the bay of Che-goi-me-gon. A council was convened at the time, to prepare for threatened hostilities with the Sioux of the Mississippi. "The soldiers of France," said ALLOUEZ, "will smooth the path between the Chippeways and Quebec, brush the pirate canoes from the intervening rivers, and leave to the Five Nations, no alternative, but peace or destruction." The admiring savages, who then for the first time looked upon the face of a white man, were amazed at the picture he displayed of "hell and the last judgement." He soon lighted the Catholic torch at the council fires of more than twenty different nations. The Chippeways pitched their tents near his cabin to receive instruction. The Pottowotamies came hither from lake

Michigan, and invited him to their homes. The Sacs and Foxes imitated their example, and the Illinois, diminished in numbers and glory by repeated wars with the Sioux of the Mississippi on the one hand, and the Iroquois, or Five Nations, armed with muskets, on the other, came hither to rehearse their sorrows.

MARQUETTE was the pioneer beyond the lakes. He was early at St. Mary's, with ALLOUEZ, assisting in the conversion of the Indians, and in extending the influence of France. "He belonged to that extraordinary class of men (the Jesuit missionaries,) who, mingling happiness with suffering, purshased for themselves undying glory. Exposed to the inclemencies of nature and to savage hostilities, he took his life in his hand and bade them defiance; waded through water and through snows without the comfort of a fire, subsisted on pounded maize, and was frequently without food, except the unwholesome moss he gathered from the rocks. He labored incessantly in the cause of his Redeemer — slept without a resting place, and travelled far and wide, but never without peril. Still, said he, life in the wilderness has charms — his heart swelled with rapture as he moved over waters transparent as the most limpid fountain. Living like a patriarch beneath his tent, each day selecting a new site for his dwelling, which he erected in a few minutes, with a never failing floor of green, inlaid with flowers provided by nature; his encampment on the prairie resembled the pillar of stones where JACOB felt the presence of God, the venerable oaks around his tent — the tree of Mamre, beneath which ABRAHAM broke bread with the angels."*

The ministers of LOUIS the XIV. and COLBERT, with TALON, the intendant of the colony, had formed a plan to extend the power of France from sea to sea. A vague idea had been obtained from the natives, that a great river flowed through the country beyond the Lakes, in a southerly direction. MARQUETTE, selecting for his companion, JOLIET, a citizen of Quebec, and for his guide, a young Indian of the Illinois tribe, undertook the mission of its discovery.

Previous to his departure, a great council was held at St. Mary's. Invitations were sent to all the tribes around and beyond the head waters of lake Superior, even to the wandering hordes of the remotest north; to the Pottawatomies at Green Bay, and to the Miamis of Chicago. St. LUSAN appeared as the delegate of

---

* Brown's History of Illinois.

France. "It was then announced to the assembled envoys of the wild Republicans thus congregated together from the springs of the St. Lawrence, the Mississippi, and the Red river, that they were placed under the protection of Louis XIV., the king of France. Allouez acted as interpreter, and brilliantly clad officers from the veteran armies of Europe, mingled in the throng. 'A cross of red cedar was then raised, and the whole company bowing before the emblem of man's redemption, chanted to its glory a hymn of the seventh century;' and planting by its side a cedar column on which were engraved the arms of the Bourbons, it was supposed that the authority and faith of France was permanently united upon this continent."*

On the 10th of June, 1673, Marquette and Joliet, with five Frenchmen as companions, transported upon their shoulders, across the narrow passage which divides the Fox river of Green Bay from the Wisconsin of the Mississippi, two bark canoes, and launched them upon its waters. The Indians to whom Marquette had imparted his design, endeavored to dissuade him from it. "Those distant nations," they said, "never spare the stranger — the great river abounds with monsters which devour both men and canoes." "I shall gladly," replied Marquette, "lay down my life for the salvation of souls." "The tawny savage, and the humble missionary of Jesus, thereupon united in prayer."† "My companion," said Marquette," is an envoy of France to discover new countries; and I am an embassador from God to enlighten them with the gospel."

The party floated down the Wisconsin between alternate hills and prairies, without seeing man, or the wonted beasts of the forests, during which no sound broke the appalling silence, save the ripple of their own canoes, and the lowing of the buffalo. They entered the great "Father of waters," with a joy that could not be expressed. After descending the Mississippi about sixty leagues, they were attracted by a well beaten trail that came down to the water's edge. Halting, and tracing it for six miles they came to three Indian villages, on the banks of the Des Moines. Entering one of them, four old men advanced bearing a peace-pipe. "We are Illinois"‡ said they, and offered the calu-

---

* History of Illinois   † Bancroft.   ‡ "We are men."

met. "An aged chief received them at his cabin with upraised hands, exclaiming, 'how beautiful is the sun, Frenchmen, when thou comest to visit us. Our whole village awaits thee; thou shall enter in peace into all our dwellings.' And the pilgrims were followed by the devouring gaze of an astonished crowd."

The party descended the Mississippi to the mouth of the Arkansas, and returning, entered the mouth of the Illinois. Coming up that river, they visited the villages upon its banks, the humility and kind words of MARQUETTE conciliating and winning the favor of their inhabitants. In all the different nations and tribes the party had encountered in their long voyage, there was no demonstrations of hostility, except at one village, low down in their route on the western bank of the Mississippi. There, the natives assembled, armed for war, and threatened an attack. "Now," thought MARQUETTE, "we must indeed ask the aid of the virgin;" but trusting rather to the potency of a peace-pipe, embellished with the head and neck of brilliant birds, that had been hung round his neck by the chieftain upon the Des Moines, he raised it aloft. At the sight of the mysterious emblem, "God touched the hearts of the old men, who checked the impetuosity of the young; and throwing their bows and quivers into the canoes, as a token of peace, they prepared a hospitable welcome."* The tribe of Illinois, that inhabited its bank, entreated MARQUETTE to come and reside among them. One of their chiefs, with their young men, conducted the party by the way of Chicago to lake Michigan; and before the end of September, all were safe in Green Bay.

Thus, MARQUETTE and JOLIET, with their few companions, were the pioneer navigators of the Mississippi; above the mouth of the Arkansas;† the first Europeans to tread the soil of Wisconsin, Iowa, Illinois and Missouri. But it remained for another bold

---

NOTE.—It is worthy of remark here, that most of these Indian nations of the West hated and feared the Iroquois. The early French adventurers knew well how to profit by this. With more of good policy than truth, they were careful to represent themselves as the enemies of the Iroquois, and to add that the great captain of the French had chastised the Five Nations and commanded peace. In these first villages of the Illinois that Marquette and Joliet visited, a festival of fish, hominy, and the choicest viands from the prairies was prepared for the messengers who brought the glad tidings that the Iroquois had been subjugated.

* Jesuit Relations.

† Ferdinand De Soto, a Spanish adventurer, had in 1541, entered the mouth of the Mississippi, and ascended it probably as far up as the mouth of the Arkansas.

adventurer with more enlarged views; one who is identified prominently with our immediate local history, to complete the discovery.

And what an advent was that of the indefatigable Jesuit! He was highly educated, as were most of those of his order, that came out to the unexplored regions of the New World. He was a lover of nature in its rudeness, simplicity, beauty and grandeur. No wonder, that floating down the majestic river; viewing its banks upon either hand, their rich and variegated scenery; or up the Illinois, catching glimpses of wide prairies, skirted with wood-lands and carpeted with wild flowers, the buffalo and deer grazing and sporting upon them; flocks of swan and ducks rising upon the wing, or seeking shelter from the strangers in coves and inlets;— that he became an enthusiast; worshipped with increased devotion the Author of all things, to whose service he had dedicated himself; mingled with his prayers and thanksgivings, his admiration of the beautiful waters and landscapes that he was assisting to bring within the pale of his church, and under the temporal dominion of his king.

JOLIET returned to Quebec to announce the discoveries: MARQUETTE remained to preach the gospel among the Miamis who dwelt near Chicago. "Two years afterwards, sailing from Chicago to Mackinac, he entered a little river in Michigan. Erecting an altar, he said mass after the rites of the Catholic Church; then begging the men who conducted his canoe to leave him alone for half an hour;

> ———"in the darkling wood,
> Amidst the cool and silence, he knelt down,
> And offered to the Mightiest solemn thanks
> And supplication."

At the end of the half hour, they went to seek him, and he was no more! The good missionary, discoverer of a world, had fallen asleep on the margin of the stream that bears his name. Near its mouth the canoe-men dug his grave in the sand. Ever after the forest rangers, if in danger on lake Michigan, would invoke his name. The people of the west will build his monument." *

The success of MARQUETTE and JOLIET was destined to confirm

---

* Bancroft.

another adventurer, in his previously half formed resolutions to enter upon a broader and farther extended field of discovery; to lead another to find an uninterrupted navigation through a chain of lakes and rivers to the "country of the Illinois," and finally to trace the "great river" they had discovered, to its source.

THE FIRST VESSEL UPON THE UPPER LAKES.

An event transpiring within our borders, upon the banks of the Niagara, of so much local and general interest as the building and launching of the first sail vessel that floated upon the waters of lake Erie, demands especial notice, and more of minute detail than can be bestowed generally upon events preceding the main objects of this work. It was the pioneer advent of our vast inland commerce, the sails of which are now spread out upon our long chain of lakes and rivers, upon the borders and in the valleys of which an Empire has sprung into existence! A commerce equal to the export trade of the whole union, with foreign countries; its principal mart, the "City of the Lakes," the young, the rapidly advancing emporium of the great West, and Western New York. Here, it will only be necessary to speak of the humble beginning of all this; its first slow, and after rapid progress, will occupy succeeding pages.

ROBERT CAVALIER DE LA SALLE, was a native of France, of good family, of extensive learning, and possessed an ample fortune. He renounced his inheritance by entering the seminary of the Jesuits. After profiting by the discipline of their schools, and obtaining their praise for purity and vigilance, he had taken his discharge from their fraternity. With no companion but poverty, but with a boundless spirit of enterprise, about the year 1667, when the attention of all France was directed towards this continent, the young adventurer embarked for fame and fortune in the new world. Established at first as a fur trader at La Chine, he explored lake Ontario and ascended to lake Erie. Returning to France in 1775, by the aid of Count FRONTENAC he obtained the rank of nobility, and the grant of Fort Frontenac, now Kingston, on condition of maintaining a post there. The grant was in fact the concession of a large domain, and a monopoly of the traffic with the Five Nations.

"In the portion of the wilderness of which the young man was proprietary, cultivated fields proved the fertility of the soil; his herd of cattle multiplied; groups of Iroquois built their cabins in the environs; a few French settled under his shelter; a few Franciscans now tolerated in Canada, renewed their missions under his auspices; the noble forest invited the construction of log cabins and vessels with decks; and no canoe-men in Canada could shoot a rapid with such address as the pupils of LA SALLE."*

This was destined to be with him but a short stopping place; "flocks and herds," a small spot in the wilderness converted to rural civilized life, was not the climax of his ambition. He aspired to higher achievments than to be the patron of a village, or a trading post. The voyages of COLUMBUS, and a history of the rambles of DE SOTO, were among the books he had brought with him from home. When JOLIET returned from the west, after his tour with MARQUETTE, he took Fort Frontenac in his way, and spread the news of the brilliant discoveries they had made. LA SALLE had caught from the Iroquois a glimpse of the Ohio and its course, and some accounts of a new and hitherto undiscovered country bordering upon it. He conceived the design of making it the country of his prince. It was he who first proposed the union of New France with the valley of the Mississippi, and suggested their close connection by a line of military posts. He proposed also to open the commerce of Europe to them both, and for that purpose repaired to France.

By his earnest, bold enthusiasm,—his tone of confidence in ultimate success—he made patrons of his enterprise, COLBERT, the minister of LOUIS XIV., and at the instance of the Marquis de SEIGNEILLY, COLBERT's eldest son, he procured the exclusive right of a traffic in buffalo skins and a commission for the discovery of the Great River. The commission was as follows:—

"LETTERS PATENT
"GRANTED BY THE KING OF FRANCE TO THE SIEUR DE LA SALLE, ON THE 12TH OF MAY, 1678.

"*Louis, by the grace of God, king of France and Navarre, to our dear and well beloved Robert Cavalier, Sieur de la Salle, greeting:*—

"We have received with favor the very humble petition which has been presented to us in your name, to permit you to endeavor to discover the western part of our country of New France; and we have consented to this proposal the more willingly because there is nothing we have more at heart than the discovery of this country, through which it is probable that a passage may be found to Mexico; and because your

---
* Bancroft.

diligence in clearing the land which we granted to you by the decree of our council of the 13th of May, 1675, and by letters patent of the same date, to form habitations upon the same lands, and to put Fort Frontenac in a good state of defence, the Seigniory and government whereof we likewise granted to you; affords us every reason to hope that you will succeed to our satisfaction, and to the advantage of our subjects of the said country.

"For these reasons, and others thereunto moving us, we have permitted, and do hereby permit you, by these presents, signed by our hand, to endeavor to discover the western part of our country of New France; and for the execution of this enterprise, to construct forts wherever you shall deem it necessary; which it is our will you shall hold on the same terms and conditions as Fort Frontenac, agreeably and conformably to our said letters patent of the 13th of May, 1675, which we have confirmed as far as is needful, and hereby confirm by these presents,—and it is our pleasure that they be executed according to their form and tenure.

"To accomplish this, and every thing above mentioned, we give you full powers; on condition however, that you shall finish this enterprise in five years, in default of which their pursuits shall be void and of none effect; that you carry on no trade whatever, with the savages called Outaouacs, and others, who bring their beaver skins and other peltries to Montreal; and that the whole shall be done at your expense, and that of your company to which we have granted the privilege of trade in buffalo skins. And we call on Sieur de FRONTENAC our governor and lieutenant general, and on Sieur de CHESNEAU, intendant of justice, policy and finance, and on the officers who compose the supreme council in said country, to affix their signatures to these presents; for such is our pleasure. Given at St. Germaine en Laye, this 12th day of May, 1678, and of our reign the thirty-fifth.

[Signed]   LOUIS.
COLBERT.

Accompanied by TONTI, an Italian, and Father HENNEPIN, a number of mechanics and mariners, with military and naval stores, and goods for the Indian trade, he arrived at Fort Frontenac in 1678. In the fall of that year, a wooden canoe of ten tons, the first that ever entered the Niagara river, bore a part of his company to the foot of the rapids, at Lewiston. He established a trading post upon the present site of Fort Niagara. The work of ship-building was immediately commenced. The keel of a small vessel of sixty tons burthen, was laid at the mouth of Cayuga creek. *

---

* This locality has been questioned. Governor Cass, locates La Salle's ship yard at Erie; Mr Bancroft at the mouth of the Tonawanda, or rather did so in his history of the United States, In a letter to the author, dated London May 17th, 1848, he says:— "As to the ship building of La Salle above Niagara Falls, Mr. Catlin is quite confident it took place upon the opposite or Canada side of the river. His local knowledge is greater than mine, and his opinion merits the most respectful consideration." In coming to this conclusion, Mr Catlin must have set aside the authority of Hennepin, who was present and taking note of all that was passing at the time. He says the ship-building was commenced "two leagues above the Falls." This to be sure does not determine which side of the river it was; but it is determined in a portion of his journal that follows, that the portage of these first adventurers was upon this side. After the vessel was built Hennepin went to Fort Frontenac, and returning to join his comrades

Tonti and Hennepin, venturing among the Senecas, established relations of amity; while La Salle urged on the completion of his vessel; gathering, at the same time, furs from the natives, and sending on messengers with merchandize to trade for furs and skins, and to apprise the Illinois of his intended visit, and prepare the way for his reception.

"Under the auspices of La Salle, Europeans first pitched a tent at Niagara; it was he who in 1679, amid the salvo from his little artillery, the chanting of the Te Deum, and the astonished gaze of the Senecas, first launched a wooden vessel, a bark of sixty tons, on the upper Niagara river, and in the Griffin, * freighted with a colony of fur traders for the valley of the Mississippi, on the 7th. day of August, unfurled a sail to the breezes of lake Erie."

The following is Hennepin's account of the advent of La Salle upon the Niagara river, the building and launching of the Griffin, &c.:—

"On the 14th day of January, 1679, we arrived at our cabin at Niagara, to refresh ourselves from the fatigues of our voyage. We had nothing to eat but Indian corn. Fortunately, the white fish, of which I have heretofore spoken, were just then in season. This delightful fish served to relish our corn. We used the water in which the fish were boiled in place of soup. When it grows cold in the pot, it congeals like veal soup.

"On the 20th, I heard, from the banks where we were, the voice of the Sieur de La Salle, who had arrived from Fort Frontenac † in a large vessel. He brought provisions and rigging necessary for the vessel we intended building above the great fall of Niagara, near the entrance into lake Erie. But by a strange misfortune, that vessel was lost through fault of the two pilots, who disagreed as to the course.

"The vessel was wrecked on the southern shore of lake Ontario, ten leagues from Niagara. The sailors have named the place *La*

---

who had gone up with the vessel to the "mouth of lake Erie" they cast anchor "at the foot of the *three mountains*," and he speaks of the difficulty they had in ascending the three mountains with their provisions, munitions of war, &c. The three mountains were evidently.—first, the high river bank at Lewiston; secondly, the distinct offset which may be seen near the residence of S. Scovel and thirdly, the upper ledge or terrace, upon the map inserted in Baron La Hontan's "voyages to North America" published in London, in 1703, the landing place at Lewiston is distinctly marked, and the "three mountains" of Hennepin, are called the "*Hills*." Additional evidence could be cited. The place where the Griffin was built is clearly designated, and should no longer be questioned.

* In compliment to Count Frontenac whose armorial bearings were adorned by two griffins, as supporters.

† Now Kingston.

Cap Enrage, (Mad Cap.) The anchors and cables were saved, but the goods and bark canoes were lost. Such adversities would have caused the enterprise to be abandoned by any but those who had formed the noble design of a new discovery.

"The Sieur de LA SALLE informed us that he had been among the Iroquois Senecas, before the loss of his vessel, that he had succeeded so well in conciliating them, that they mentioned with pleasure our embassy, which I shall describe in another place, and even consented to the prosecution of our undertaking. This agreement was of short duration, for certain persons opposed our designs, in every possible way, and instilled jealousies into the minds of the Iroquois. The fort, nevertheless, which we were building at Niagara, continued to advance. But finally, the secret influences against us were so great, that the fort became an object of suspicion to the savages, and we were compelled to abandon its construction for a time, and content ourselves with building a habitation surrounded with palisades.

"On the 22d we went two leagues above the great falls of Niagara, and built some stocks, on which to erect the vessel we needed for our voyage. We could not have built it in a more convenient place, being near a river which empties into the strait, which is between lake Erie and the great falls. In all my travels back and forth, I always carried my portable chapel upon my shoulders.

"On the 26th, the keel of the vessel and other pieces being ready, the Sieur de LA SALLE sent the master carpenter named MOYSE, to request me to drive the first bolt. But the modesty appropriate to my religious profession, induced me to decline the honor. He then promised ten louis d'or for that first bolt, to stimulate the master carpenter to advance the work.

"During the whole winter, which is not half as severe in this country as in Canada, we employed in building bark huts one of the two savages of the Wolf tribe, whom we had engaged for hunting deer. I had one hut especially designed for observing prayers on holidays and Sundays. Many of our people knew the Gregorian chant, and the rest had some parts of it by rote.

"The Sieur de LA SALLE left in command of our ship yard one TONTI, an Italian by birth, who had come to France after the revolution in Naples, in which his father was engaged. Pressing business compelled the former to return to Fort Frontenac, and I conducted him to the borders of lake Ontario, at the mouth of the river Niagara. While there he pretended to mark out a house for the blacksmith, which had been promised for the convenience of the Iroquois. I cannot blame the Iroquois for not believing all that had been promised them at the embassy of the Sieur de LA MOTTE.

"Finally the Sieur de LA SALLE undertook his expedition on foot over the snow, and thus accomplished more than eighty leagues.

He had no food, except a small bag of roasted corn, and even that had failed him two days' journey from the fort. Nevertheless he arrived safely with two men and a dog which drew his baggage on the ice.

"Returning to our ship yard, we learned that the most of the Iroquois had gone to war beyond lake Erie, while our vessel was being built. Although those that remained were less violent, by reason of their diminished numbers, still they did not cease from coming often to our ship yard, and testifying their dissatisfaction at our doings. Some time after, one of them, pretending to be drunk attempted to kill our blacksmith. But the resistance which he met with from the smith, who was named LA FORGE, and who wielded a red hot bar of iron, repulsed him, and together with a reprimand which I gave the villian, compelled him to desist. Some days after, a squaw advised us that the Senecas were about to set fire to our vessel on the stocks, and they would, without doubt, have effected their object, had not a very strict watch been kept.

"These frequent alarms, the fear of the failure of provisions, on account of the loss of the large vessel from Fort Frontenac, and the refusal of the Senecas to sell us Indian corn, discouraged our carpenters. They were moreover enticed by a worthless fellow, who often attempted to desert to New York, (*Nouvelle Jorck,*) a place which is inhabited by the Dutch, who have succeeded the Swedes. This dishonest fellow would have undoubtedly been successful with our workmen, had I not encouraged them by exhortations on holidays and Sundays after divine service. I told them that our enterprise had sole reference to the promotion of the glory of God, and the welfare of our Christian colonies. Thus I stimulated them to work more diligently in order to deliver us from all these apprehensions.

"In the meantime the two savages of the Wolf tribe, whom we had engaged in our service, followed the chase, and furnished us with roe-bucks, and other kinds of deer, for our subsistence. By reason of which our workmen took courage and applied themselves to their business with more assiduity. Our vessel was consequently soon in a condition to be launched, which was done, after having been blessed according to our church of Rome. We were in haste to get it afloat, although not finished, that we might guard it more securely from the threatened fire,

"This vessel was named The Griffin, (*Le Griffon*) in allusion to the arms of the Count de FRONTENAC, which have two Griffins for their supports. For the Sieur de LA SALLE had often said of this vessel, that he would make the Griffin fly above the crows. We fired three guns, then sung the *Te Deum*, which was followed by many cries of joy.

"The Iroquois who happened to be present, partook of our joy and witnessed our rejoicings. We gave them some brandy to drink, as well as to all our men, who slung their hammocks under the deck of the vessel, to sleep in greater security. We then left our bark huts, to lodge where we were protected from the insults of the savages.

"The Iroquois having returned from their beaver hunt, were extremely surprised to see our ship. They said we were the *Ot-kon*, which means in their language, *penetrating minds*. They could not understand how we had built so large a vessel in so short a time, although it was but sixty tons burthen. We might have called it a moving fort, for it caused all the savages to tremble, who lived within a space of more than five hundred leagues, along the rivers and great lakes.

"I now went in a bark canoe, with one of our savage hunters, to the mouth of lake Erie. I ascended the strong rapids twice with the assistance of a pole, and sounded the entrance of the lake. It did not find them insurmountable for sails, as had been falsely represented. I ascertained that our vessel, favored by a north or northeast wind, reasonably strong, could enter the lake, and then sail throughout its whole extent with the aid of its sails alone; and if they should happen to fail, some men could be put on shore and tow it up the stream.

"Before proceeding upon our voyage of discovery, I was obliged to return to Fort Frontenac, for two of our company to aid me in my religious labors. I left our vessel riding at two anchors, about a league and a half from lake Erie, in the strait which is between that lake and the great falls. I embarked in a canoe with the Sieur de CHARON, and a savage; we descended the strait towards the great falls, and made the portage with our canoe to the foot of the great rock of which we have spoken, where we re-embarked and descended to lake Ontario. We then found the barque which the Sieur de la FOREST had brought us from Fort Frontenac.

"After a few days, which were employed by the Sieur de la FOREST in treating with the savages, we embarked in the vessel, having with us fifteen or sixteen squaws, who embraced the opportunity, to avoid a land passage of forty leagues. As they were unaccustomed to travel in this manner, the motion of the vessel caused them great qualms at the stomach, and brought upon us a terrible stench in the vessel. We finally arrived at the river *A-o-ou-e-gwa*,* where the Sieur de la FOREST traded brandy for beaver skins. This traffic in strong drink was not agreeable to me, for if the savages drink ever so little, they are more to be dreaded than madmen. Our business being finished, we sailed from the southern to the northern shore of the lake, and, favored by fair winds, soon passed the village which is on the other side of Keute and Ganneousse. As we approached Fort Frontenac the wind

---

* Probably the Genesee River.

failed us, and I was obliged to get into a canoe with two young savages, before I could come to land.'

* * * * * *

"A few days after, a favorable wind sprung up, and fathers GABRIEL DE LA RIBOURDE, and ZENOBE MAMBRE, and myself, embarked from Fort Frontenac in the brigantine. We arrived in a short time at the mouth of the river of the Senecas, (Oswego river,) which empties into lake Ontario. While our people went to trade with the savages, we made a small bark cabin, half a league in the woods, where we might perform divine service more conveniently. In this way we avoided the intrusion of the savages, who came to see our brigantine, at which they greatly wondered, as well as to trade for powder, guns, knives, lead, but especially brandy, for which they are very greedy. This was the reason why we were unable to arrive at the river Niagara before the thirtieth day of July.

"On the 4th of August I went over land to the great falls of Niagara with the sergeant, named LA FLEUR, and from thence to our ship yard, which was six leagues from lake Ontario, but we did not find there the vessel we had built. Two young savages slyly robbed us of the little biscuit which remained for our subsistence. We found a bark canoe, half rotten, and without paddles, which we fitted up as well as we could, and having made a temporary paddle, risked a passage in the frail boat, and finally arrived on board our vessel, which we found at anchor a league from the beautiful lake Erie. Our arrival was welcomed with joy. We found the vessel perfectly equipped with sails, masts, and every thing necessary for navigation. We found on board five small cannon, two of which were brass, besides two or three arquebuses. A spread griffin adorned the prow, surmounted by an eagle. There were also all the ordinary ornaments, and other fixtures, which usually adorn ships of war.

"The Iroquois, who returned from war with the prisoners taken from their enemies, were extremely surprised to see so large a vessel, like a floating castle, beyond their five cantons. They came on board, and were surprised beyond measure, to find we had been able to carry such large anchors through the rapids of the river St. Lawrence. This obliged them to make frequent use of the word *gannoron*, which, in their language signifies, how wonderful. As there were no appearances of a vessel when they went to war, they were greatly astonished now to see one entirely furnished on their return, more than 250 leagues from the habitations of Canada, in a place where one was never seen before.

"I directed the pilot not to attempt the ascent of the strong rapids at the mouth of lake Erie until further orders. On the 16th and 17th, we returned to the banks of lake Ontario, and ascended with the barque we had brought from Fort Frontenac, as far as the great rock of the river Niagara. We there cast anchor at the foot of the *three mountains,* where we were obliged to make the portage caused by the great falls of Niagara, which interrupt the navigation.

"Father GABRIEL, who was sixty-four years old, underwent all the fatigues of this voyage, and ascended and descended three times the three mountains, which are very high and steep at the place where the portage is made. Our people made many trips, to carry the provisions, munitions of war, and other necessaries, for the vessel. The voyage was painful in the extreme, because there were two long leagues of road each way. It took four men to carry our largest anchor, but brandy being given to cheer them, the work was soon accomplished, and we all returned together to the mouth of lake Erie.

* * * * * *

"We endeavored several times to ascend the current of the strait into lake Erie, but the wind was not yet strong enough. We were therefore obliged to wait until it should be more favorable.

"During this detention, the Sieur de LA SALLE employed our men in preparing some ground on the western side of the strait of Niagara, where we planted some vegetables for the use of those who should come to live in this place, for the purpose of keeping up a communication between the vessels, and maintaining a correspondence from lake to lake. We found in this place some wild chervil and garlic, which grow spontaneously.

"We left father MELITHON at the habitation we had made above the great falls of Niagara, with some overseers and workmen. Our men encamped on the bank of the river, that the lightened vessel might more easily ascend into the lake. We celebrated divine service on board every day, and our people, who remained on land, could hear the sermon on holidays and Sundays.

"The wind becoming strong from the northeast, we embarked, to the number of thirty-two persons, with two of our order who had come to join us. The vessel was well found with arms, provisions and merchandise, and seven small cannon.

"The rapids at the entrance into the lake are very strong. Neither man, nor beast, nor ordinary bark can resist them. It is therefore almost impossible to stem the current. Nevertheless, we accomplished it, and surmounted those violent rapids of the river Niagara by a kind of miracle, against the opinion of even our pilot himself. We spread all sail, when the wind was strong enough, and, in the most difficult places, our sailors threw out tow lines, which were drawn by ten or twelve men on shore. We thus passed safely into lake Erie.

"We set sail on the 7th of August, 1679, steering west south west. After having chanted the *Te Deum,* we fired all the cannon and arquebuses in presence of many Iroquois warriors, who had brought captives from *Tintonha*, that is to say, from the *people of the prairies*, who live more than 400 leagues from their cantons. We heard these savages exclaim, *gannoron*, in testimony of their wonder.

"Some of those who saw us did not fail to report the size of our vessel to the Dutch at New York, (*Nouvelle Jorck*), with whom the Iroquois carry on a great traffic in skins and furs; which they exchange for fire arms, and blankets, to shelter them from the cold.

"The enemies of our great discovery, to defeat our enterprises, had reported that lake Erie was full of shoals and banks of sand, which rendered navigation impossible. We therefore did not omit sounding, from time to time, for more than twenty leagues, during the darkness of the night.

"On the 8th, a favorable wind enabled us to make about forty-five leagues, and we saw almost all the way, the two distant shores, fifteen or sixteen leagues apart. The finest navigation in the world, is along the northern shores of this lake. There are three capes, or long points of land, which project into the lake. We doubled the first, which we called after St. Francis.

"On the 9th, we doubled the two other capes, or points of land, giving them a wide berth. We saw no islands or shoals on the north side of the lake, and one large island, towards the southwest, about seven or eight leagues from the northern shore, opposite the strait which comes from lake Huron.

"On the 10th, early in the morning, we passed between the large island, which is toward the southwest, and seven or eight small islands, and an islet of sand, situated towards the west. We landed at the north of the strait, through which lake Huron is discharged into lake Erie.

"Aug. 11. We sailed up the strait and passed between two small islands of a very charming appearance. This strait is more beautiful than that of Niagara. It is thirty leagues long, and is about a league broad, except about half way, where it is enlarged, forming a small lake which we call Sainte Claire, the navigation of which is safe along both shores, which are low and even.

"This strait is bordered by a fine country and fertile soil. Its course is southerly. On its banks are vast meadows, terminated by vines, fruit trees, groves and lofty forests, so arranged that we could scarcely believe but there were country seats scattered through their beautiful plains. There is an abundance of stags, deer, roe-bucks and bears, quite tame and good to eat, more delicious than the fresh pork of Europe. We also found wild turkeys and swans in abundance. The high beams of our vessel were garnished with multitudes of deer, which our people killed in the chase.

"Along the remainder of this strait, the forests are composed of walnut, chestnut, plum and pear trees. Wild grapes also abound, from which we made a little wine. There are all kinds of wood for building purposes. Those who will have the good fortune some day to possess the beautiful and fertile lands along this strait, will be under many obligations to us, who have cleared the way, and traversed lake Erie for a hundred leagues of a navigation before unknown."

The Griffin cast anchor in Green Bay. After being freighted with a rich cargo of furs, it started upon its return voyage. From the period of its departure, no tidings ever came of the vessel or crew. Capricious and dangerous as the navigation of the lakes has since proved; especially in the advanced season of navigation at which the Griffin must have attempted a return; there is little wonder that the small craft, imperfectly built as she must have been, with the stinted means that the bold projector could only have had, met with the fate that in after years of more perfect architecture, and experience in lake navigation, so many others have been subjected to.

Change, progress and improvement, will meet us at every step in tracing our local history; prompting to a halt, and a comparison of the present with the past; but not often as urgently as here. This was the humble beginning of our lake commerce. Here, upon the banks of the Niagara, were a small band of adventurers, headed, cheered on and encouraged by one who was in advance of his own age — should have belonged to this. How abstracted from the then civilized world, were these primitive ship builders! A vast unexplored wilderness, a broad expanse of waters, of lakes and rivers, their surfaces as yet undisturbed but by the bark canoes of the natives, lay before them; behind, but a feeble colony of their countrymen who were hardly able to protect themselves from a stealthy foe that had rejected overtures of peace with their pale faced stranger visitors. In mid winter, with but stinted facilities,

---

NOTE. — The translation is by O. H. Marshall of Buffalo. It first appeared in the Buffalo Commercial Advertiser, in 1845, and is copied by Mr. Schoolcraft in his notes on the Iroquois. It is from the French edition of Hennepin, published at Amsterdam in 1698. The original text is regarded as the best that has reached this country; — the only reliable one in fact; — and the faithfulness of the translation is fully guaranteed by the integrity and literary qualifications of the translator. The interest derived from the perusal of the early French Jesuits and travellers, is much increased by having their own fresh and vivid impressions detailed in their own words. This consideration, in connection with the fact that Hennepin's account has not heretofore been published in any form to render it generally accessible, induces the author to give it entire, omitting only a few paragraphs that have no necessary relation to the main subject.

they erected for themselves cabins and commenced the work of ship building! When the difficult work was consummated, the frail bark launched, their sails set to catch the breeze, they knew not to what disturbed waters and inhospitable shores it would carry them. They had witnessed the hostile demonstrations of the Iroquois, and had no warrant that the nations they were to meet in their new track would be any better reconciled to their further advance. They had but dim lights to guide them. They saw and heard the rush of waters; the earth beneath their pilgrim feet, as they threaded the dark forest that lay between their "place of ship building" and the "three mountains," trembled with the weight and descent of the mighty volume. And yet they knew little of the vast sources from which such an aggregate proceeded. They had the glimpses of the "Great River" that MARQUETTE and JOLIET had given them, but knew not where it mingled with the ocean. Theirs was the mission to first traverse our great chain of lakes and rivers; to pass over the dividing lands, strike a tributary of the Mississippi, and pursue that river to the Gulf of Mexico. Theirs, the first European advent that extended across from the northern to the southern shores of the Atlantic. One hundred and thirty nine years ago, the Griffin set out upon its voyage, passed up the rapids of the Niagara, and unfurled the first sail upon the waters of the Upper Lakes.

Intrepid navigator and explorer! High as were hopes and ambition that could alone impel him to such an enterprise; farseeing as he was; could the curtain that concealed the future from his view, have been raised, his would have been the exclamation;—

"Visions of glory spare my aching sight;
Ye unborn ages rush not on my soul!"

He deemed himself but adding to the nominal dominions of his king; but opening a new avenue to the commerce of his country; founding a prior claim to increased colonial possessions. He was pioneering the way for an empire of freemen, who, in process of time, were to fill the valleys he traversed; the sails of whose commerce were to whiten the vast expanse of waters upon which he was embarking!

How often, when reflecting upon the triumphs of steam navigation, do we almost wish that it were admitted by the dispensations of Providence, that FULTON could be again invested with mortality, and witness the mighty achievments of his genius. Akin to this would be the wish that LA SALLE could rise from his wilderness grave in the far off south, and look out upon the triumphs of civilization and improvement over the vast region he was the first to explore.

Ours is a country whose whole history is replete with daring enterprises and bold adventures. Were we prone, as we should be, durably to commemorate the great events that have marked our progress, here and there, in fitting localities, more monuments would be raised as tributes due to our history and the memory of those who have acted a conspicuous part in it. Upon the banks of our noble river, within sight of the Falls, a shaft from our quarries would soon designate the spot where the Griffin was built and launched; upon its base, the name of LA SALLE, and a brief inscription that would commemorate the pioneer advent of our vast and increasing lake commerce.

On his way up, LA SALLE, while passing through the "verdant Isles of the majestic Detroit," had debated planting a colony upon its banks; and he had planted a trading house at Mackinaw. After the Griffin had left, with the portion of his company he had retained, in bark canoes, he ascended to the head of lake Michigan, or rather, to the mouth of the St. Joseph, where ALLOUEZ had preceded him and gathered a village of the Miamis. Anticipating the return of his ill-fated vessel, he remained and added to the small beginning that had been made there, a trading house with pallisades, which was called the fort of the Miamis. Despairing of the return of the Griffin, leaving ten men to guard the fort, with HENNEPIN, two other missionaries, TONTI and about thirty followers, he ascended the St. Joseph, descended the Kankakee to its mouth, reaching an Indian village near Ottawa. From thence he descended the Illinois as far as lake Peoria, where he met large parties of Indians, who, desirous of obtaining axes and fire-arms, offered him the calumet and agreed to an alliance. Of the Griffin no tidings came; his men deeming their leader ruined by its loss, grew discontented. LA SALLE, who never desponded, exerted all his means to revive their hopes. "Our strength and safety" said he, "is in our union. Remain with me till spring and none shall remain thereafter, except from choice." He commenced building a fort. Thwarted by destiny, in allusion to his misfortunes, he called it Creve Cœur.* He despatched HENNEPIN to explore the Upper Mississippi, and renewed the unlucky business of ship building.

HENNEPIN, with two companions, ascended the Mississippi, to the Falls which he named St. Anthony, as a tribute due to ST. ANTHONY of Padua, whose protection and guidance he had invoked when starting on his expedition. On a tree near the cataract he engraved the cross and the arms of France, and by the way of the Wisconsin and Fox rivers returned to the French mission at Green Bay. What wanderers! Even now, in 1848, when steam boats in fleets, are upon the Lakes and the Mississippi, and canals and rail-roads are in their vallies, a visit to the Falls of St. Anthony is more than an ordinary adventure.

LA SALLE set his men to sawing "trees into plank," and in March, with three companions, set off on foot for Fort Frontenac to procure recruits, and sails and cordage for the vessel that was going upon the stocks. Taking the ridge of high lands which divide the basin of the Ohio from that of the Lakes, the small party, with " skins to make moccasins, a musket and pouches of powder and shot, trudged through thickets and forests, waded through marshes and melting snows; without drink except water from the brooks, without food except supplies from the gun." Arriving at Fort Frontenac, which still acknowledged him for its lord, additional supplies were at once furnished, and new adventurers flocked to his standard. With these he returned to the garrison he had left on the Illinois.

There he found little to revive the spirits which must have been dead within him, if he had been a man of ordinary mould. A party of Iroquois had descended the river, attacked the Fort, massacred the aged Franciscan Father RIBOURDE, and obliged TONTI and a few others, to flee to the Pottowattomies on lake Michigan for protection; LA SALLE and his companions repaired to Green Bay, recommenced trade, and established a friendly intercourse with the natives; found TONTI and his party, embarked from thence, left Chicago on the 4th of January, 1682, and after building a spacious barge on the Illinois river, in the early part of that year, descended the Mississippi to the sea. On his way he raised a cabin on the Chickasaw Bluff, a cross at the mouth of the Arkan-

---

* Creve Cœur: — The Fort of the Broken Hearted.

9

sas, and planted the arms of France near the gulf of Mexico. He claimed the country for France, and called it Louisiana.

He returned to France in 1683, and reporting to his government his brilliant discoveries, preparations were made to supply him with ample means for colonization; and in July, 1684, he sailed with a fleet of four vessels, for the Mississippi; on board of which were one hundred soldiers, six missionaries, "mechanics of various skill," and young women.

The sequel is a chapter of disasters: — The colonists were badly selected; the mechanics "ill versed in their arts;" the soldiers, "spiritless vagabonds without discipline or experience;" the volunteers, generally rash adventurers, having "indefinite expectations;" so says JOUTEL, the military commander, and faithful historian of the expedition. BEAUJEAU, the naval commander, was deficient in judgment, unfit for his station, envious, proud, self-willed and self-conceited; incapable of any sympathy with the magnanimous heroism of LA SALLE. The fleet sailing as often wrong as right; (LA SALLE always right, but opposed by his naval commander;) after a tedious voyage of five months, reached, instead of its destination, the Bay of Matagorda in Texas. Here the store ship was wrecked by the careless pilot; the ample stores provided by the munificence that marked the plans of LOUIS XIV., lay scattered on the sea. LA SALLE obtained boats from the fleet, and by great efforts saved a part of the stores for immediate use. To heighten their distress, the natives came down from the interior to plunder the wreck, and two of the soldiers, or volunteers, were slain.

The fleet returned, taking with it many who were tired of the expedition, and deserted. "There remained upon the beach of Matagorda, a desponding company of about two hundred and thirty souls, huddled together in a fort constructed with the fragments of their ship-wrecked vessel, having no hopes but in the constancy and elastic genius of LA SALLE."* A shelter was built at the head of the bay—a rude fortification, which was called St. Louis; LA SALLE himself marking the beams and tenons. He took possession of the country in the name of his king. It was this that made Texas a province of France, or a part of Louisiana.

As soon as the encampment was completed, LA SALLE started

---

* Bancroft.

with a party in canoes, to seek the mouth of the Mississippi. After an absence of four months, and the loss of fourteen of his followers, he returned in rags, having entirely failed in his object. Spending most of the year 1686, with twenty companions in New Mexico,—enticed there by the brilliant fictions of the rich mines of St. Barbe, the El Dorado of Northern Mexico. He found there no mines, but a "country unsurpassed in beauty and fertility."

Returning to his colony in Texas, he found it diminished to about forty; among whom, "discontent had given place to plans of crime." Leaving twenty of them to maintain the fort, he started with sixteen on foot to return to Canada for the purpose of getting farther recruits and means to prosecute enterprises not yet abandoned, though so often thwarted. No Spanish settlement was nearer than Pamico—no French settlement, than Illinois. "With wild horses obtained from the natives to transport his baggage, he followed the track of the buffalo, pasturing his horses at night upon the prairie; ascended streams of which he had never yet heard—marched through groves and plains of surpassing beauty, amid herds of deer, and droves of buffaloes; now fording the rapid torrent, now building a bridge by throwing some monarch of the forest across the stream, till he had passed the basin of the Colorado, and reached a branch of the Trinity river."*

Of his company was Duhaut and L'Archiveque. The former had long shown a spirit of mutiny. "The base malignity of disappointed avarice,"(they had both embarked capital in the enterprise,) "maddened by suffering, and impatient of control, awakened the fiercest passions of ungovernable hatred. Inviting Moranget† to take charge of the fruits of a buffalo hunt, they quarrelled with him, and murdered him. Wondering at the delay of his return, La Salle, on the 20th of March, went to seek him. At the brink of a river, he saw eagles hovering, as if over a carrion; and he fired an alarm gun. Warned by the sound, Duhaut and L'Archiveque crossed the river; the former skulked in the prairie grass; of the latter, La Salle asked:—'where is my nephew?' At the moment of the answer, Duhaut fired; and without uttering a word, La Salle fell dead! 'You are down now, grand Bashaw! you are down now!' shouted one of the conspirators, as they despoiled his

---

* Bancroft. † The nephew of La Salle.

remains, which were left on the prairie, naked and without burial, to be devoured by wild beasts."*

Thus perished the pioneer navigator of our lakes, the father of colonization in the great central valley of the west, ROBERT CAVALIER DE LA SALLE! Well did he merit the eulogy bestowed upon his memory, by the accomplished historian, (Mr. BANCROFT,) who has given him and his achievements, his successes and his reverses, a conspicuous place in our national annals. "For force of will and vast conceptions; for various knowledge and quick adaptation of his genius to untried circumstances; for a sublime magnanimity, that resigned itself to the will of Heaven, and yet triumphed over affliction by energy of purpose, and unfaltering hope,—he had no superior among his countrymen."

Retribution in part was at hand. DUHAUT and another of the conspirators, attempting afterwards to convert to their use an unequal share of the spoils, were themselves murdered, and their reckless associates joined the savages. JOUTEL, who commanded the expedition, the nephew of LA SALLE, and four others, procured a guide and sought the Arkansas. They reached a beautiful country above the Red river, and afterward, with the exception of one only, who was drowned while bathing in a river, they all reached the Mississippi in safety, on the 24th of July, 1687. Upon its banks they discovered a cross, and near it a cabin occupied by four of their countrymen. TONTI, the faithful companion of LA SALLE, had descended the river in search of his friend. Failing to find him, he had erected the cross and cabin, and left the men that JOUTEL found there, to guard them. On the 14th of September

---

* Joutel.

NOTE,—The account of Hennepin differs from that of Joutel. It is as follows:— "He, (La Salle,) was accompanied by Father Anastasi, and two natives who had served him as guides. After travelling about six miles, they found the bloody cravat of Saget, (one of La Salle's men,) near the bank of the river, and at the same time, two eagles were hovering over their heads, as if attracted by food on the ground. La Salle fired his gun, which was heard by the conspirators on the other side of the river. Duhaut and L'Archiveque immediately crossed over at some distance in advance. La Salle approached, and, meeting the latter, asked for Moranget, and was answered vaguely that he was along the river. At that moment Duhaut, who was concealed in the high grass, discharged his musket and shot him through the head. Father Anastasi was standing by his side and expected to share the same fate, till the conspirators told him they had no design upon his life. La Salle survived about an hour, unable to speak, but pressing the hand of the good father, to signify that he understood what was said to him. The same kind friend dug his grave, buried him, and erected a cross over his remains."

they reached the head quarters of TONTI, in Illinois, and soon after passed through Chicago to Quebec, and from thence to France.

Little is known of the after life of TONTI beyond what is gathered from a petition signed by him, and addressed to the French minister of Marine, in 1690. In that he asks for the command of a company to embark again in the service of his country, and recounts the services he had already rendered. He says that he remained at the Fort in Illinois till 1684, where he was attacked by two hundred Iroquois, whom he repulsed, with great loss on their side: that after spending a year in Quebec, under the orders of M. de la BARRE, he returned to Illinois, and in 1686, in canoes, with forty men, he descended the Mississippi to the Gulf of Mexico, in search of LA SALLE. Returning to Quebec, he put himself under the orders of DE NONVILLE, and was with him at the head of a band of Indians and a company of Canadians, at the battle with the "Tsonnonthouans," (Senecas,) where he forced an ambuscade. ☞ See account that follows, of DE NONVILLE'S expedition to Irondequoit Bay, and battle with the Senecas. That he went again to Illinois in 1689, and again in search of LA SALLE's colony, but was deserted by his men, and unable to execute his designs. The petition is endorsed by Count FRONTENAC, who says:—"Nothing can be truer than the account given by the Sieur de TONTI in his petition."

NOTE.—La Salle, and the early Jesuits supposed the Griffin was driven ashore in a gale, the crew murdered by the Indians, and the vessel plundered. Such was undoubtedly the fact, and the author is enabled to fix with a considerable degree of certainty, upon the spot where this occurred. In the Buffalo Commercial Advertiser of January 26th, 1848, there is a communication from James W. Peters, of East Evans, Erie county, in which he says:—"Some thirty-five or forty years ago, on the Ingersoll farm, in Hamburgh, a short distance below the mouth of the Eighteen Mile Creek, and on the summit of the high banks, in the woods, was found by the Messrs. Ingersoll, a large quantity of wrought iron, supposed to be seven or eight hundred weight. It was evidently taken off a vessel. It was of superior quality, much eaten by the rust, and sunk deep in the soil. A large tree had fallen across it, which was rotted and mixed with the earth. There were trees growing over the iron from six to twelve inches in diameter, which had to be grubbed up before all the iron could be got. Some twenty-six or seven years since, a man by the name of Walker, immediately after a heavy blow on the Lake, found on the beach near where the irons were found, a *cannon*, and immediately under it a second one. I saw them not forty-eight hours after they were found. They were very much destroyed by age and rust—filled up with sand and rust. I cleared off enough from the breach of one to lay a number of letters bare. The words were French, and so declared at the time. The horns, or trunions, were knocked off." In a letter from the venerable David Eddy, of Hamburgh, to the author, received while this work was going to press, he says that in the primitive settlement of that region—in 1805, there was found upon the lake shore, where a large body of sand and gravel had been removed during a violent gale, a "beautiful *anchor*." It was taken to Buffalo and Black Rock, excited a good deal of curiosity at the time, but no one could determine to what vessel it had belonged.

The expedition of La Salle traced to its disastrous and fatal termination; the western lake region, and the whole valley of the Mississippi, added to the dominions of France; let us return to the region of western New York, the banks of the St. Lawrence, to colonization under English auspices, advancing in this direction from the northern Atlantic coast.

Previous to the building of the Griffin, La Salle had "enclosed with pallisades a little spot at Niagara." This was the first blow struck, the first step taken as an earnest of occupation by Europeans, in all the region of New York west of Schenectady, if we except the short stay of the Jesuits, and perhaps some mission stations they may have established upon the Mohawk, and in the vicinity of Onondaga lake. It is to be presumed that the post at Niagara was after this, with but little intermission, used as a partially fortified trading station, until it was finally made a French garrison and occupied by an armed force.

The French continued to extend their establishments. Following the track of Marquette and La Salle, they soon occupied prominent points in the upper vallies of the Mississippi, in what is now Illinois, Wisconsin and Iowa. The Hurons of Canada were their fast allies. They conciliated and won the favor of all the Indian nations around the western lakes, except the Foxes and Ottagamis, who dwelt principally in that part of Michigan which lies upon Detroit river. "It was the studied policy of the French to secure the good will of the natives. The French explorers, traders and missionaries, advanced to their remotest villages in the prosecution of their several objects. They lodged with them in their camps, attended their councils, hunting parties and feasts; paid respects to their ceremonies, and were joined in the closer bonds of blood. The natural pliancy of the French character led them into frequent and kind associations with the savages, while the English were cold and forbidding in their manners. Besides, the Jesuit missionaries exerted no small influence in strengthening the friendship of the Indians. They erected little chapels in their territory, carpeted with Indian mats and surmounted by the cross; took long journeys through the wilderness, performed the ceremo-

---

There is no record of any vessel being wrecked here previous to 1805. The French and the English vessels were few upon the lakes, numbering not more than two or three at any one time. A record of the loss of one at a later period than that of the advent of La Salle, would in all probability have been preserved. May we not well conclude that the iron, the cannon, and the anchor, were those of the Griffin?

nies of their church in long black robes, and showed their paintings and sculptured images, which the savages viewed with superstitious awe. Added to all this, they practiced all the offices of kindness and sympathy for the sick, and held up the crucifix to the fading vision of many a dying neophyte." *

But the French had but partial success with the proud, warlike, self-dependent Iroquois. The relation between them and the Five Nations, was never one of perfect amity, though they were at times on good terms with the Senecas, and had missions and trading establishments with the Onondagas. The acquaintance had an untoward commencement as we have seen. CHAMPLAIN, in his unfortunate alliance with a foe of their own race, had shown them the use of fire-arms. The Dutch and English supplied them with the new weapons. It not only enabled them to push their conquests over the Indian nations of the west, but helped them to stand out against the French and resist their inroads into their territories. The Iroquois, from the first European advent to this country, did not view the visitors with favor. They seemed to have had a clearer view by far, than other Indian nations of North America, of the ultimate tendency of it, and its fatal result to their race. Their first position was one of independence; a refusal to be allies of either the French, Dutch or English: —"We may guide the English to our lakes. We are born free. We neither depend on ONNONDIO or CORLEAR." This was the tone and bearing of a Seneca chief, in reply to some complaints of the French-Governor, in 1684. But the Dutch, to secure their trade, aided them to arm against the French, and maintained for the period they held dominion upon the Hudson, with but slight exceptions, a friendly relation, which the English, their successsors, inherited, and by every means in their power, assiduously cultivated, for the two-fold purpose of securing their trade, and preventing French encroachments upon what they regarded English territory. "The Dutch" said they, "are our brethren; with them we keep but one council fire. We are united by a covenant chain. We have always been as one flesh. If the French come from Canada, we will join the Dutch nation and live or die with them. With the English and French the contest was for territorial dominion and Indian trade, and the English early saw the advantages that would accrue to them from

---

* History of Illinois.

keeping the Iroquois in close alliance. As the Iroquois were at war with almost all other Indian nations, those other nations saw their advantage in having the protection of the French, who lost no opportunity of impressing upon them exalted ideas of the power of their king and country, of their ability not only to stay the march of conquest of the Iroquois,— to throw a shield around those of their own race they had persecuted and oppressed; but also to humble the pretensions of the English.

The Onondagas, Cayugas and Senecas, who for a time had been influenced by the Jesuits, to occupy something like a neutral position, in 1689 met the governors of New York and Virginia at Albany, and pledged to them peace and alliance. "Although England and France for many years after, sought their alliance with various success, when the grand division of parties throughout Europe was effected, the Bourbons found in the Iroquois implacable opponents: and in the struggle that afterwards ensued between England and France, they were allies of the former, and their hunting grounds were transformed into battle fields. Western New York, it would seem, was severed from Canada by the valor of the Mohawks," * or rather the author should have said, it was never but partially under the dominion of France, for the reason that the Seneca Iroquois, whose territory it was, were never their allies; never acknowledged any French sovereignty.

The Marquis d'ARGENSON was appointed Governor General of New France in 1658. The condition of the colony continued to be much depressed. In addition to the bad working of the colonial system under the auspices of the Company, the Iroquois grew more and more irreconcilable to French encroachment; more and more determined to uproot the French from this quarter of the continent. Hostile bands hung upon the borders of the French settlements upon the St. Lawrence.

In 1661 the Governor was recalled on account of ill-health, and the Baron d'AVANGOUR, a man of extraordinary energy, was appointed in his place. Encouraging the king by his representations of the advantages in prospect in the new country, four hundred new troops were sent out. But for this timely assistance, it is supposed that the Iroquois would have executed their threat of an extermination of the French.

---

* History of Illinois.

In 1664, the company of New France surrendered their charter. Its privileges were transferred to the Company of the West Indies, under whose auspices a better system of government was organized. Reinforcements arrived from the West Indies, and a number of officers, to whom had been granted lands with the rights of *seigneurs*, settled in the colonies. Forts were erected on the principal streams in Canada, where it was thought necessary to keep the Iroquois in check. In 1668 the affairs of New France seemed much improved. Count FRONTENAC, a nobleman of distinguished family, a man of energy and arbitrary will, was soon after invested with the office of home administrator of the affairs of the French colonies. He made extraordinary efforts to develope the resources of the country, and build up the scattered colonial establishments. In 1683, however, such had been the slow progress, the untoward events in New France, the population did not exceed nine thousand.

De la BARRE was Governor General of New France in 1684. incensed at the Iroquois for favoring the English, and introducing parties of them to the borders of the lakes to trade with the Indians, he resolved upon gathering an army at Fort Frontenac, to intimidate them; to try peaceful negotiation with a large force to back him; and if that failed, to invade their country. For this purpose, all the disposable troops at Montreal, Quebec, Niagara, and the western posts, were ordered to rendezvous at Fort Frontenac. His whole force assembled there, was from seventeen to eighteen hundred, including four hundred Indian allies. It was in the month of August, during the prevalence of fevers that prevailed upon the borders of lake Ontario, which those of our own people who were pioneer settlers upon its southern shore, have had occasion to know something about;* the French soldiers were unacclimated, and the larger portion of them were confined to the hospital. In the crippled condition of his army, De la BARRE concluded that he should be unable to effect any thing save by treaty. Despatching orders to Mons. DULBUT, who was

---

* Our old resident physicians, who have had some experience in "lake fevers," will be amused at the theory of the disease, which La Hontan says, De la Barre's physician advanced: — It was, that the excessive heat of the season put the vapors, or exhalations into an over rapid motion; that the air was so over rarified that a sufficient quantity of it was not taken in; that the small quantity inhaled was loaded with insects and impure corpusculums, which the fatal necessity of respiration obliged the victim to swallow, and that by this means, nature was put into disorder." The Baron adds, that the "system was too much upon the *Iroquois* strain."

advancing from Mackinaw with six hundred Frenchmen and Indians, to hasten his march, he embarked upon lake Ontario with his Indian allies, and such of his French soldiers as were able to join the expedition, and landed upon the southern shore of lake Ontario, at *La Famine*.* Col. Dongan, the English Governor of New York, apprised of the movement, had sent his Indian interpreter to persuade the Five Nations not to treat with the French. De la Barre despatched Le Moine, who had much influence with the Iroquois, to bring with him some of their chief men. In a few days he returned, bringing with him Garangula, a noted Seneca chief, called by his people Haaskouan, accompanied by a train of thirty young warriors. As soon as the chief arrived, De la Barre sent him a present of bread and wine, and thirty salmon trout, "which they fished in that place in such plenty, that they brought up a hundred at one cast of a net;" at the same time congratulating him on his arrival. La Hontan says, that De la Barre had taken the precaution of sending the sick back to the colony that the Iroquois might not perceive the weakness of his forces; instructing Le Moine to assure Garangula that the body of the army was left behind at Frontenac, and that the troops that he saw, were only the Governor's guards. "But unhappily one of the Iroquois, that had a smattering of the French tongue, having strolled in the night time towards our tents, overheard what was said, and so revealed the secret. The chief, after taking two days to rest and recruit himself, gave notice to De la Barre that he was ready for the interview.†

The speeches that succeeded, which the author copies from a good English translation of La Hontan, will not only materially aid the reader to understand the then existing relations of the French, Iroquois, and English, but furnish one of the earliest and best specimens of native eloquence, and the proud bearing and spirit of independence, of our wild and unschooled forest predecessors.

De la Barre, through the interpreter Le Moine, said:—

"The King, my master, being informed that the five Iroquois

---

* Or, Hungry Bay, so named at the time, from the stinted allowance of food which they had there.

† La Hontan has a drawing of the interview between De la Barre and Garangula. De la Barre is in front of his camp, with the interpreter and his officers near him. "The Garangula" is in front of his thirty warriors, who sit in a half circle upon the ground.

nations have for a long time made infractions upon the measures of peace, ordered me to come hither with a guard, and to send *Akouesson* to the canton of the *Onnotagues*, in order to an interview with their principal leaders in the neighborhood of my camp. This great monarch, means that you and I should smoke together in the great *calumet* of peace, with the proviso, that you engage in the name of the *Tsonnontouans, Goyogouans, Onnotagues, Onnoyoutes,* and *Agnies*, to make reparation to his subjects, and to be guilty of nothing for the future that may occasion a fatal rupture.

"The *Tsonnontouans, Goyogouans, Onnotagues, Onnoyoutes,* and *Agnies*, * have stripped, robbed and abused all the forest rangers that travelled in the way of trade to the country of the *Illinese*, of the *Oumamis*, and of the several other nations who are my master's children. Now this usage being in high violation of the treaty of peace concluded with my predecessor,† I am commanded to demand reparation, and at the same time to declare that in case of their refusal to comply with my demands, or of relapsing into the like robberies, war is actually proclaimed. This makes my words good. [Giving a belt.]

"The warriors of these Five Nations have introduced the English into the lakes belonging to the King my master, and into the country of those nations of whom my master is a father:— This they have done with a desire to ruin the commerce of his subjects, and to oblige those nations to depart from their due allegiance; notwithstanding the remonstrances of the late Governor of New York, who saw through the danger that both they and the English exposed themselves to. At present, I am willing to forget those actions; but if ever you be guilty of the like for the future, I have express orders to declare war. This belt warrants my words. [Giving a belt.]

"The same warriors have made several barbarous incursions upon the country of the *Illinese* and *Oumamis*. They have massacred men, women and children; they have took, bound, and carried off an indefinite number of the natives of those countries, who thought themselves secure in their villages in times of peace. These people are my master's children, and must therefore cease to be your slaves. I charge you to restore them to their liberty, and to send them home without delay; for if the Five Nations refuse to comply with this demand, I have express orders to declare war. This makes my words good. [Giving a belt.]

"This is all I had to say to the GARANGULA, whom I desire to report to the Five Nations, this declaration, that my master commanded me to make. He wishes they had not obliged him to

---

* Senecas, Cayugas, Oneidas, Onondagas, and Mohawks.

† The predecessor of De la BARRE had concluded a treaty of peace with the Iroquois, which was of short duration.

send a potent army to the Fort of *Cataracony*,* in order to carry on a war that will prove fatal to them; and he will be very much troubled if it so falls out, that this fort, which is a work of peace, must be employed for a prison to your militia. These mischiefs ought to be prevented by mutual endeavors:—The French, who are the brethren and friends of the Five Nations, will never disturb their repose, provided they make the satisfaction I now demand, and prove religious observers of their treaties. I wish my words may produce the desired effect; for if they do not, I am obliged to join the Governor of New York, who has orders from the king his master, to assist me to burn the villages and cut you off. † This confirms my words. [Giving a belt.]

La Hontan says:—"While De La Barre's interpreter pronounced this harangue, the Garangula did nothing but look upon the end of his pipe. After the speech was finished, he rose, and having took five or six turns in the ring that the French and the savages made, he returned to his place, and standing upright, spoke after the following manner to the general, (De La Barre,) who sat in his chair of state."

"Yonnondio!‡ I honor you, and all the warriors that accompany me do the same. Your interpreter has made an end of his discourse, and now I come to begin mine. My voice glides to my ear, pray listen to my words.

"Yonnondio! In setting out from Quebec you must needs have fancied that the scorching beams of the sun had burnt down the forests that render our country inaccessible to the French; or else, that the inundations of the lake had surrounded our castles, and confined us as prisoners. This certainly was your thought; and it could be nothing else than the curiosity of seeing a burnt or drowned country, that moved you to take a journey hither. But now you have an opportunity of being undeceived, for I, and my warlike retinue come to assure you that the *Tsonnontouans, Goyoguans, Onnotagues, Onnoyoutes and Agnies*, are not yet destroyed. I return you thanks in their name, for bringing into the country the calumet of peace, that your predecessors received at their hands. At the same time I congratulate your happiness, in having left underground the bloody axe that has so often been dyed with the blood of the French. Hear, Yonnondio! I am not asleep; my eyes are open; and the sun that vouchsafes the light gives me a clear view of a great captain at the head of a troop of soldiers, who speaks as if he were asleep. He pretends that he does not approach to this lake with any other view than to smoke with the

---

* The Indian name of Fort Frontenac, and lake Ontario.

† De la Barre seems to have been ignorant of the fact, that the English governor had been persuading the Iroquois to stand out against French diplomacy.

‡ The Iroquois called the Governor of New France, whoever he might be, Yonnondio, and the Dutch or English Governor, Corlear.

Onnotagues in the great calumet; but the *Garangula* knows better things; he sees plainly that the YONNONDIO mean'd to knock 'em on the head if the French arms had not been so much weakened.

"I perceive that the YONNONDIO raves *in a camp of sick people whose lives the Great Spirit has saved, by visiting them with infirmities.* Do you hear YONNONDIO? Our women had taken up their clubs, and the children and the old men had visited your camp with their bows and arrows, if our warlike men had not stopped and disarmed them, when *Akouessan,* your ambassador, appeared before my village. But I have done, I will talk no more of that.

"You must know, YONNONDIO, that we have robbed no Frenchmen but those who supplied the *Illinese* and the *Oumamis,* (our enemies,) with fusees, with powder and with ball. These indeed we took care of, because such arms might have cost us our life. Our conduct in that point, is of a piece with that of the Jesuits, who stave all the barrels of brandy that are brought to our cantons, lest the people getting drunk, should knock them on the head. Our warriors have no beavers to give in exchange for all the arms they have taken from the French; and as for the people, they do not think of bearing arms. This comprehends my words. [Giving a belt.]

"We have conducted the English to our lakes in order to traffic with the *Outaouas,* and the *Hurons*; just as the *Algonkins* conducted the French to our cantons in order to carry on a commerce that the English lay claim to as their right. We are born freemen, and have no dependence either on the YONNONDIO or the CORLEAR. We have a power to go when we please, to conduct those whom we will to the places we resort to, and to buy or sell where we see fit. If your allies are your slaves or your children, you may e'en treat 'em as such, and rob 'em of the liberty of entertaining any other nation but your own. This contains my words. [Giving a belt.]

"We fell upon the *Illinese* and the *Oumamis* because they cut down the tree of peace that served as limits, or boundaries to our positions. They came to hunt beavers upon our lands, and contrary to the custom of all the savages, have carried off whole stocks, both male and female.* They have engaged the *Chaouanous* in their interest, and entertained them in their country. They supplied 'em with fire-arms after the concerting of ill designs against us. We have done less than the English and the French, who, without any right, have usurped the grounds they are now possessed of; and of which they have dislodged several nations, in order to make way for their building of cities, villages and forts. This, CORLEAR, contains my words. [Giving a belt.]

"I give to you to know, YONNONDIO, that my voice is the voice

---

* The Indians regarded it a great offence to wholly exterminate a beaver colony.

of the Five *Iroquese* cantons. This is their answer; pray incline your ear and listen to what they represent.

"The *Tsonnontouans, Goyogouans, Onnotagues, Onnoyoutes,* and *Agnies,* declare that they interred the axe at *Cataracouy,* in the presence of your predecessor, in the very center of the fort; and planted the tree of peace in the same place that it might be preserved; that 'twas then agreed that the fort should be used as a place of retreat for merchants, and not a refuge for soldiers; and that instead of arms and ammunition, it should be made a receptacle only of beaver skins and merchandise goods. Be it known to you, YONNONDIO, that for the future you ought to take care that so great a number of martial men as I now see, being shut up in so small a place, do not stifle and choak the tree of peace. Since it took root so easily, it must needs be of pernicious consequence to stop its growth, and hinder it to shade both your country and ours with its leaves. I do assure you, in the name of the Five Nations, that our warriors shall dance the calumet dance under its branches; that they shall rest in tranquility upon their matts and will never dig up the axe to cut down the tree of peace; till such times as the YONNONDIO and the CORLEAR do either jointly or separately offer to invade the country that the Great Spirit has disposed of in the favor of our ancestors. This belt preserves my words, and this other, the authority which the Five Nations have given me." [Giving two belts.]

Then, GARANGULA, addressing himself to the interpreter LE MOINE, said:—

"*Akouessan,* take heart; you are a man of sense; speak and explain my meaning; be sure you forget nothing, but declare all that thy brethren and thy friends represent to thy chief YONNONDIO, by the voice of the GARANGULA, who pays you all honor and respect, and invites you to accept of this present of beavers, and to assist at his feast immediately. This other present of beavers is sent by the Five Nations to the YONNONDIO."

When the Iroquois chief had finished his speech, De la BARRE "returned to his tent much enraged at what he had heard." The GARANGULA prepared his feast, several of the French officers becoming his guests. Two days afterwards he returned to his people.

The army of De la BARRE broke up, that part of it belonging at Quebec and Montreal, going down the St Lawrence; those belonging to Fort Frontenac and the western posts returning some by water and some by land. "Thus a very chargeable and fatiguing expedition (which was to strike the terror of the French name, into the stubborn hearts of the Five Nations,) ended in a scold between the French General and an old Indian."*

EXPEDITION OF DE NONVILLE AGAINST THE SENECAS IN 1687

The Marquis de NONVILLE, a colonel in the French dragoons, succeeded De la BARRE in the local government of New France, in 1685. CHARLEVOIX says he was "equally esteemed for his valor, his wisdom, and his piety." At the commencement of his administration, the Iroquois had renewed their wars against Indian nations at the west, with whom the French were in alliance, and continued, as GARANGULA had assured De la BARRE they would, to introduce the English around the borders of the lakes.† De NONVILLE brought out with him a large reinforcement for the army, and at once resolved upon a series of measures having in view the humbling of the Iroquois by making them allies or neutrals and the security of the French dominion and trade upon the Lakes. Prominent in these measures, was a formidable attack upon the Senecas, who, from their location and partiality for the English, were most in the way of the French interests; and the building of a fort at Niagara. His first steps were to accumulate ample provisions for his army at Fort Frontenac, and gather the whole disposable military force of New France, at Montreal. The commandants of the French posts at the west, were ordered to rendezvous at Niagara with their troops, and the warriors of their Indian allies in that quarter.

At this period, England and France were at peace, or rather a treaty had been signed between them, to the effect that whatever differences might arise at home or elsewhere, neutral relations

---

* Colden's History of the Five Nations. Mr. Clinton, in his discourse before the New York Historical Society in 1811, says of the speech of Garangula:—"I believe it to be impossible to find, in all the effusions of ancient or modern oratory, a speech more appropriate or convincing. Under the veil of respectful profession, it conveys the most biting irony; and while it abounds with rich and splendid imagery, it contains the most solid reasoning. I place it in the same rank of the celebrated speech of Logan; and I cannot but express my astonishment at the conduct of two respectable writers who have represented this interesting interview, and this sublime display of intellectual power, as a "scold between the French General and an old Indian."

† It should be observed here, that the English claimed dominion over all the country of the Iroquois south of the lakes, including of course the site of Fort Niagara. The French claimed the Iroquois' country, from priority of discovery and occupation by the Jesuits, La Salle, &c.

should be observed by their subjects in North America. The Iroquois, apprised by the movements of DE NONVILLE, but not knowing where he intended to strike, communicated their apprehensions to Governor DONGAN, who immediately wrote to DE NONVILLE that the great collection of supplies at Fort Frontenac convinced him that an attack was meditated upon the Iroquois;—that they were the subjects of the crown of England, and any injury to them, would be an open infraction of the peace which existed between them and their two kings. He also stated that he understood the French intended to build a fort at Niagara, which astonished him exceedingly, as "no one could be ignorant, that it lay within the jurisdiction of New York." DE NONVILLE replied that the Iroquois feared chastisement because they deserved it; and dissimulating, endeavored to convey the impression that no more supplies were ordered to Frontenac than were necessary for the use of the troops stationed there. He said that the pretensions of England to the land of the Iroquois were unfounded, as the French had taken possession of them "long before there was an Englishman in New York;" at the same time admonishing the English governor that while their kings and masters were living in perfect peace and amity, it would be unwise for their lieutenant generals to embroil themselves in war. Governor DONGAN took no measures to counteract the designs of the French, but to confirm the Iroquois in their apprehensions, and supply them with arms and ammunition; but while the French preparations for war were going on, the English were sending trading parties to the Lakes, and assiduously improving a slight foot-hold they had obtained among a few Indian nations that were inclining to their interests. The English used one weapon, almost as potent —(in some instances more so,)— as Jesuit influence, and insinuating French diplomacy. They had learned the fatal appetite of the Indian for strong drink, and took advantage of it, by introducing brandy and rum wherever they made their advances among them. The Jesuit priests kept up a continual warfare with the French traders, against the introduction of intoxicating liquors, and generally prevailed. The Catholic church had, at that early period, their Father MATTHEWS in this far off wilderness. And here it is no falsifying of historical record, to add, that generally, the French policy and conduct, looked far more to the ultimate good of the natives, than those of the English. The presence of the Jesuit missionary, modified and checked the sordid desire of gain with the trader. English cupidity had no such check.

DE NONVILLE employed the winter of 1687 in making ready for the expedition. The previous summer, as he says in his journal, was passed in negotiations, which terminated in an agreement that both parties should meet at Fort Frontenac to take measures for the conclusion of a general peace. "But the pride of that nation, (the Iroquois,) accustomed to see others yield to its tyranny, and the insults which they have continued to heap upon the French and our savage allies, have induced us to believe that there is no use in negotiating with them, but with arms in our hands, and we have all winter been preparing to make them a visit."

The French army, consisting of about sixteen hundred men, accompanied by four hundred Indian allies, set out from Montreal on the 13th of June, in three hundred and fifty batteaux, and after a slow passage up the St. Lawrence, encountering many difficulties, arrived at Fort Frontenac on the 30th. On the 4th day of July, it started for its destination; taking the route by the way of La Famine Bay, and coasting along the south side of lake Ontario, encamping upon the shore each night, arrived at *Ganniagataronta-gouat*,* on the 10th. Previous to leaving Fort Frontenac, DE NONVILLE had despatched orders to the commandant at Niagara to meet him with his troops, and the French and Indian allies who had come down from the west. This reinforcement amounted to about five hundred and eighty French and Indians. The two divisions of the army met at Irondequoit within the same hour.

The next day was employed in constructing pallisades, facines and pickets for the protection of provisions, batteaux and canoes. On the 12th, after detaching four hundred men to garrison their landing place, the French and Indians took up their line of march toward the villages of the Senecas. Passing up the east side of Irondequoit Bay, they encamped at night, a few miles above its head, near the village of Pittsford. The Indian village of Ganna-garo, which was situated near the present village of Victor, Ontario county, was to be the first point of attack. Continuing their march on the 13th, they arrived about 3 o'clock, at a defile near

---

* Irondequoit. The name given above, is the one by which the French designated it, and was borrowed from the Mohawks. The Seneca name is *Ongiudaondagwat.*

the Indian village, when they were attacked by a large party of Senecas, that lay in ambush: —

"They were better received than they anticipated, and were thrown into such consternation that most of them threw away their guns and clothing to escape under favor of the woods. The action was not long, but there was heavy firing on both sides. The three companies of Ottawas who were stationed on the right, distinguished themselves, and all our christian savages farther in the rear, performed their duty admirably, and firmly maintained the position which had been assigned to them on the left. As we had in our front a dense wood, and a brook bordered with thickets, and had made no prisoners that could tell us positively the number of Indians that had attacked us; the fatigues of the march, which our troops, as well the French as the Savages, had undergone, left us in no condition to pursue the enemy. They had fled beyond where we had sufficient knowledge of the paths, to be certain which we should take to lead us from the woods into the plain. The enemy left twenty-seven dead on the field to our knowledge, besides a much larger number of wounded, judging from the traces of blood which we saw. We learned from one of the dying that they had more than eight hundred men under arms, either in the action or in the village, and were daily expecting assistance from the neighboring Iroquois. Our troops being much fatigued, we rested during the remainder of the day at the same place, where we found sufficient water for the night. We maintained a strict watch, waiting for day, in order to enter the plain, which is about a league in extent, before proceeding to the village.

"The next day, which was the 14th, a heavy rain, which lasted till noon, compelled us to remain until that time at the place where the battle occured. We set out in battle array, thinking the enemy entrenched in the new village, which is above the old. In the mean time we entered the plain without seeing any thing but the relics of the fugitives. We found the old village burnt by the enemy, and the entrenchments of the new deserted, which were distant from the old about three-quarters of a league. We encamped on the height of the plain, and did nothing this day but protect ourselves from the rain which continued until night." *

Two old men who had been left by the Senecas in their retreat, told DE NONVILLE that the ambuscade consisted of two hundred and twenty men stationed on the hill side to attack the French in the rear, and five hundred and thirty in front; and beside this,

---

* De Nonville's Journal.

there were three hundred in their fort, situated on a very advantageous height: that there were none but Senecas in the battle the Cayuga and Onondaga warriors not having arrived.

The Senecas setting fire to all their villages, retreated before the French army, and sought refuge among the Cayugas. The French army remained in the Seneca country until the 24th. The deserted villages were entered, large quantities of corn and beans destroyed; the Indian allies scouting the country and tomahawking and scalping such straggling Senecas as fell behind in the flight, or remained in consequence of infirmity. Such was the spirit of the western Indians, and determination to execute vengeance upon those who had so often warred upon them, that the French could not induce them to save such prisoners as fell into their hands.

DE NONVILLE estimates the amount of corn destroyed in all the "four villages of the *Sonnontouans*," 1,200,000 bushels! A great exaggeration, undoubtedly, as the Senecas were never sufficiently numerous nor agricultural, to warrant the conclusion that they had any thing approaching to that amount in all their territory. He was making a report to "the king his master," and it is quite likely made his exploits as formidable as possible. He differs materially in his account of the expedition from Baron LA HONTAN who was one of his officers.

LA HONTAN's account of the invasion of the Seneca country is as follows:

"On the third day of July, 1687, we embarked from Fort Frontenac, to coast along the southern shore, under favor of the calms which prevail in that month, and at the same time the Sieur de LA FORET left for Niagara by the north side of the lake, to wait there for a considerable reinforcement.

"By extraordinary good fortune we both arrived on the same day, and nearly the same hour, at the river of the Tsonnontouans, by reason of which our savage allies, who draw predictions from the merest trifles, foretold, with their usual superstition, that so punctual a meeting infallibly indicated the total destruction of the Iroquois. How they deceived themselves the sequel will show.

"The same evening on which we landed, we commenced drawing our canoes and batteaux upon land, and protected them by a strong guard. We afterwards set about constructing a fort of stakes, in which four hundred men were stationed, under the command of the Sieur DORVILLIERS, to guard the boats and baggage.

"The next day a young Canadian, named LA FONTAINE

Marion, was unjustly put to death. The following is his history: This poor unfortunate became acquainted with the country and savages of Canada by the numerous voyages he made over the continent, and after having rendered his King good service, asked permission of several of the Governors general to continue his travels in further prosecution of his petty traffic, but he could never obtain it. He then determined to go to New England, as war did not then exist between the two Crowns. He was very well received, on account of his enterprise and acquaintance with nearly all the Indian languages. It was proposed that he should pilot through the lakes, those two companies of English which have since been captured. He agreed to do so, and was unfortunately taken with the rest.

"The injustice of which they were guilty, appears to me inexcusable, for we were at peace with the English, besides which they claim that the Lakes of Canada belong to them.

"On the following day we set out for the great village of the Tsonnontouans, without any other provisions than the ten biscuit which each man was compelled to carry for himself. We had but seven leagues to march, through immense forests of lofty trees and over a very level country. The *Coureurs de bois* formed the vanguard, with a part of the savages, the remainder of which brought up the rear — the regulars and militia being in the center.

"The first day, our scouts marched in advance without making any discoveries. The distance which we accomplished was four leagues. On the second day the same scouts took the lead, and advanced even to the fields of the village, without perceiving any one, although they passed within pistol shot of five hundred Tsonnontouans lying on their bellies, who suffered them to pass and repass without interruption.

"On receiving their report, we marched in great haste and little order, believing that as the Iroquois had fled, we could at least capture their women, children and old men. But when we arrived at the foot of the hill on which they lay in ambush, distant about a quarter of a league from the village, they began to utter their ordinary cries, followed with a discharge of musketry.

"If you had seen, sir, the disorder into which our militia and regulars were thrown, among the dense woods, you would agree with me, that it would require many thousand Europeans to make head against these barbarians.

"Our battalions were immediately separated into platoons, which ran without order, pell mell, to the right and left, without knowing whither they went. Instead of firing upon the Iroquois, we fired upon each other. It was in vain to call '*help, soldiers of such a battalion,*' for we could scarcely see thirty paces. In short we were so disordered, that the enemy were about to fall upon us, club in hand, when our savages having rallied, repulsed and pursued them so closely, even to their villages, that they killed more than eighty, the heads of which they brought away, not counting the wounded who escaped.

"We lost on this one occasion ten savages and a hundred Frenchmen; we had twenty or twenty-two wounded, among whom was the good Father ANGELRAN, the Jesuit, who was shot in those parts of which ORIGEN wished to deprive himself, that he might instruct the fair sex with less scandal.

"When the savages brought the heads to M. De NONVILLE, they inquired why he halted instead of advancing. He replied that he could not leave his wounded, and to afford his surgeons time to care for them, he had thought proper to encamp. They proposed making litters to carry them to the village, which was near at hand. The general being unwilling to follow this advice, endeavored to make them listen to reason, but in place of hearing him, they reassembled, and having held a council among themselves, although they were more than ten different nations, they resolved to go alone in pursuit of the fugitives, of whom they expected to capture at least the women, children, and old men.

"When they were ready to march, M. De NONVILLE exhorted them not to leave him or depart from his camp, but rest for one day, and that the next day he would go and burn the villages of the enemy, and lay waste their fields, in consequence of which they would perish by famine. This offended them so much that the greater part returned to their country, saying that 'the French had come for an excursion rather than to carry on war, since they would not profit by the finest opportunity in the world; that their ardor was like a sudden flash, extinguished as soon as kindled; that it seemed useless to have brought so many warriors from all parts to burn bark cabins, which could be rebuilt in four days; that the Tsonnontouans would care but little if their Indian corn was destroyed, since the other Iroquois nations had sufficient to afford them a part; that finally, after having joined the Governors of Canada to no purpose, they would never trust them in future, notwithstanding any promises they might make.'

"Some say that M. De NONVILLE should have gone farther, others think it was impossible for him to do better. I will not venture to decide between them. Those at the helm are often the most embarrassed. However, we marched the next day to the great village, carrying our wounded on litters, but found nothing but ashes, the Iroquois having taken the precaution to burn it themselves. We were occupied five or six days in cutting down Indian corn in the fields with our swords. From thence we passed to the two small villages of The-ga-ron-hies and Da-non-ca-ri-ta-oui, distant two or three leagues from the former, where we performed the same exploits, and then returned to the borders of the lake. We found in all these villages, horses, cattle, poultry, and a multitude of swine. The country which we saw is the most beautiful, level and charming in the world. The woods we traversed abounded in oak, walnut and wild chestnut trees."

COLDEN, the historian of the Iroquois, says that five hundred of the Senecas lay in ambush; that they "lay on their bellies and let the French scouts pass and repass without disturbing them;" but that when the main body of the army came up "the *Senekas* suddenly raised the war shout, with a discharge of their fire arms. This put the regular troops, as well as the militia, into such a fright, as they marched through the woods, that the battalions immediately divided and ran to the right and the left, and in the confusion fired upon one another. When the Senekas perceived their disorder they fell in upon them pell mell, till the French Indians, more used to such mode of fighting, gathered together and repulsed the Senekas. There were, (according to the French accounts,) a hundred Frenchmen, ten French Indians, and about four score Senekas killed in the rencounter. Monsieur DE NONVILLE was so dispirited with the fright that his men had been put into that his Indians could not persuade him to pursue. He halted the remainder of the day. The next day he marched on with a design to burn the village, but when he came there he found that the Senekas had saved him the trouble; for they had laid all in ashes before they retired. The French stayed five or six days to destroy the corn, and then marched to two other villages, at two or three leagues distance. After they had performed the like exploits in tnese places, they returned to the banks of the lake."

There are some traditions among the Senecas, in reference to DE NONVILLE's expedition which are worthy of note:—WILLIAM JONES, a native Seneca, who married a relative of RED JACKET, states that he has heard the chief often say, that when he was a boy he used to hear the old men speak of a large party of French soldiers who penetrated the Indian country along the Genesee to a place called in the Seneca language, *Sgohsaisthah*. He did not admit that the Indians suffered any serious defeat.

JOHN BLACKSMITH, a chief of the Senecas, residing on the Tonawanda Reservation, hunted in his youth over the country embraced in the counties of Monroe, Livingston and Ontario, and thus acquired an intimate knowledge of old Indian localities. He was asked if he had ever heard that a French army penetrated the Seneca country in olden time? He related the following tradition:—

"About four generations ago, a French army landed secretly and unexpectedly at a place called by the Senecas, *Gannyeodathah*, which is a short distance from the head of *Onyiudaondagwat*, or Irondequoit Bay, as it is called by the whites. They immediately marched into the interior towards the ancient village of the Senecas, called *Gaosaehgaah*, following the main beaten path which led to that place.

"As soon as the Indians residing at the village, received intelligence of their approach, they sent news to the neighboring town of *Gahayanduk*. On being reinforced by them, they met the French as they advanced towards the former village, and a severe battle ensued. On account of their inferior numbers, the Indians were defeated, and fled to a village then located near the foot of Canandaigua lake. The French advanced, burned the village, and laid waste the adjacent corn fields. As soon as they had accomplished the above object, they retraced their steps towards the landing. Runners having been despatched by the Senecas to their principal towns, to give notice of the presence of the enemy, a large force was soon collected to defend the village and capture the French. When they reached *Gaosaehgaah*, nothing remained of that village but its smoking ruins. They immediately pursued the French, and arrived at the Bay a short time too late. The place where the battle occurred, was near a small stream with a hill on one side, and was known to the Senecas by the name of *Dyagodiyu*, or the 'place of a battle.'"

The four Indian villages which DE NONVILLE visited, are supposed to have been situated as follows:—*Gannagaro*, as the French called it, *Gaosaehgaah* in Seneca, was upon Boughton's Hill, in Victor, Ontario county;—*Gannogarae*, in the town of East Bloomfield, about three and a half miles from Boughton's Hill, near where the old Indian trail crossed Mud Creek; *Totiakto*, *Deyudihaakdoh* in Seneca, was the north-east bend of the Honeoye outlet, near West Mendon, in Monroe county;—*Gannounata*, in Seneca *Dyudonsot*, about two miles south-east of East Avon, at the source of a small stream which empties into the Conesus, near Avon Springs.

The precise place where the battle occurred is a short distance north-west of the village of Victor, on the north-eastern edge of a large swamp, and on the northerly side of a stream called Great Brook. On the first settlement of the country it was partly covered with a thick growth of timber, and dense underbrush, forming a very advantageous place for an Indian ambuscade. It is about a mile and a quarter north-west of the old Indian village on Boughton's Hill, called by DE NONVILLE, *Gannagaro*.

The height on which the Fort mentioned by DE NONVILLE was located, is about a mile and a quarter westerly from the site of *Gannagaro,* a wide valley intervening. It is now known as Fort Hill. Although nearly defaced by the plough, the works can be traced with sufficient certainty to identify the spot; and the solitary spring that supplied the French army, still oozes from the declivity of a hill, an existing witness of the locality. There are indications of extensive Indian settlements in the neighborhood of Victor, within a circuit of three miles. Thousands of graves were to be seen by the pioneer settlers, and the old French axes supplied them with iron when it was difficult to obtain it from other sources. At an early period the old Indian trail pursued by DE NONVILLE from Irondequoit Bay to Victor, was distinctly visible. The fortification that DE NONVILLE made, in which he left a detachment of his army to guard his stores and bateaux, at the bay, was described to the author during the last summer, by OLIVER CULVER of Brighton, who was in the country as early as 1796. French axes, flints, &c. were plenty there at that early period of settlement.

The author is indebted to GEORGE HOSMER, of Avon, for the following account of a relic which unquestionably belongs to the period of the French invasion of the Seneca Iroquois: —

"In the spring of 1793, I was present, when in ploughing a piece of new land on the Genesee bottom, near the river, on a farm then owned by my father, the plough passed through a bed of ashes several inches in thickness, and near that turned up an instrument which was called a French *couteau.* The blade was about twenty inches in length, and three inches wide. It was covered with rust, which upon being scoured off, exhibited the *fleur de lis* and armorial bearings of France, and a date referring to the age and reign of LOUIS XIV. The relic elicited a momentary attention. It was cleared of rust, ground to an edge, and used in my father's kitchen as a cleaver. The haft was eight or ten inches long, and made of buckhorn, or bone. I was then but a boy, but in after years have often regretted that it had not been preserved with care, as an item of evidence to illustrate the early history of the country."

The author indulges in a feeling of local pride, in noticing, in this connection, the poem,* "*Yonnondio,*" founded upon the advent of DE NONVILLE to the valley of the Genesee, once the favorite home

---

* "Yonnondio, or the Warriors of the Genesee : — a tale of the seventeenth century. By Wm. H. C. Hosmer."

of the Seneca Iroquois, as it is now, that of a prosperous and happy people of our own race. It is a "woof of fiction, woven upon a warp of fact." The author is of pioneer stock, as the reader will learn in some subsequent portions of this work; born and reared in the "realm of the Senecas," a remnant of that noble race of men associated with his earliest recollections; the tales of his nursery were of them, "their eloquence and deeds of valor;" and going out in manhood, wandering in the peaceful vale that echoed their war shouts, inspired by the reminiscences with which he was surrounded; he has seized the lyre, and in its silver tones are beautifully blended the facts and the romance of local history. It is replete with more striking and truthful delineations of the red man and his character, than any other poem upon the same subject, extant.

As a specimen of this first successful essay to mingle the charms of verse with the local history of our region; and in fact, as a help to the better understanding of the causes that induced the invasion of DE NONVILLE, and the spirit, the proud and haughty bearing of the Senecas in resisting it; the author selects some of the concluding portions of the speech that the poet attributes to CANNEHOOT, a Seneca chief, who is supposed to be closing a council of war, preparatory to the fierce onslaught that the undisciplined soldiers of the forest made upon the ranks of the French invaders:—

"Regardless of our ancient fame,
Our conquests, and our dreaded name,
Fierce YONNONDIO and his band
Are thronging in our forest land;
And ask ye why with banner spread
His force the Frank hath hither led?
We scorched with fire the skulking hounds.
Who dared to cross our hunting grounds,
A trading, base, dishonest band,
Who in exchange for pelts had given
Guns, lead, and black explosive sand,
To tribes our power had western driven:" *

* * * * * *

"Shall warriors who have tamed the pride
Of rival nations far and wide,
At their own hearths be thus defied ?
Shall it be said the beast of prey
His den abandoned far away,

---

* See speech of De la Barre, and Garangula's reply.

And, seeking out the hunter, found
His aim less true, less deep the wound ?
Shall it be told in other days,
The tomahawk we feared to raise,
While the green hillocks, where repose
The cherished dust of woodland-kings
Insulted by the march of foes,
   Gave back indignant echoings ?
Base is the bosom that will quake
With one degrading throb of fear,
When fame and country are at stake,
Though an armed troop of fiends are near!
Oh! never can such craven tread
The happy chase grounds of the dead;
Between him and that fount of bliss
Will yawn a deep and dread abyss;
And doomed will be his troubled ghost
To range that land forever more,
Upon whose lone and barren coast,
The black and bitter waters roar.
The clime of everlasting day,
Where groves, all red with fruitage, wave,
And beauty never fades away,
Is only trodden by the brave."

   *   *   *   *   *   *

" In answer to the bold harangue,
Each warrior from his bear-skin sprang,
And, ominous of coming strife,
Clashed tomahawk and scalping knife.
A signal by the chief was made,
To close the council, and obeyed:
His eloquence of look and word,
Dark depths of every heart had stirred."

Before leaving the Seneca country DE NONVILLE made the following " procès verbal," of the act of taking possession:—

"On the 19th day of July, in the year 1687, the troops commanded by the Honorable RENE DE BRISAY, Chevalier, Seigneur Marquis of De Nonville and other places, Governor and Lieutenant General for the King in the whole extent of Canada, and country of New France, in presence of HECTOR, Chevalier de Calliere, Governor of Montreal in said country, commanding the camp under his orders, and of PHILIP DE RIGAND, Chevalier de Vaudreuil, commanding the troops of the King, which being drawn up in battle array, there appeared at the head of the army, CHARLES AUBERT, Sieur de la Chenays, citizen of Quebec, deputed by the Honorable JEAN BOCHART, Chevalier, Seigneur de Champigny, Horoy, Verneuil and other places, Counsellor of the King in his councils, Intendant of Justice, Police and Finances in all Northern France, who asserted and declared, that at the requisition of the said Seigneur de Champigny, he did take possession of the village of Totiakton, as he had done of the three villages named Gannagaro, Gannondata, and Gannongarae, and of a fort distant

HOLLAND PURCHASE. 155

half a league from the said village of Gannagaro, together with all the lands which are in their vicinity, however far they extend, conquered in the name of his Majesty; and as evidence thereof has planted in all the said villages and forts, the arms of his said Majesty, and has proclaimed in a loud voice, "*vive le roi*," after the said troops have vanquished and put to flight eight hundred Iroquois Tsonnontouans, and have laid waste, burnt and destroyed their provisions and cabins. And on account of the foregoing, the Sieur de la Chenays, AUBERT, has required evidence to be granted to him by me, PAUL DUPUY, Esquire, Counsellor of the King, and his Attorney at the Court of the Provost of Quebec.

"Done at the said village of Totiakton, the largest village of the Tsonnontouans, in presence of the Reverend Father VAILLANT, Jesuit, and of the officers of the regulars and militia, witnesses with me the said attorney of the King. Subscribed the day and year above mentioned, and signed in the original by Charles Aubert de la Chenays, J. René de Brisay, Monsieur de De Nonville, Le Chevalier de Calliere, Fleutelot de Romprey, de Desmeloizes, de Ramezay, Francois Vaillant of the Company of Jesus, de Grandeville, de Longueil, Saint Paul and Dupuy.

"Compared with the original remaining in my hands, by me, the undersigned, Counsellor, Secretary of his Majesty, and chief Register of the Sovereign Council of Quebec."

Signed,   PENURET."

The fair inference, from all the evidence that has been preserved is that the French gained little honor, and less advantage, by this rencounter. COLDEN says, "the French got nothing but dry blows by this expedition."

After despatching one of the bateaux to Fort Frontenac, to carry the news of the result of the expedition, the whole army set sail for Niagara on the 26th, adverse winds delaying its arrival there until the morning of the 30th. "We immediately, (says the journal of DE NONVILLE), set about choosing a place, and collecting stakes for the construction of a fort which I had resolved to build at the extremity of a tongue of land between the river Niagara, and lake Ontario, on the Iroquois side.* In three days the army had so fortified the post as to put it in a good condition of defence, in case of an assault. DE NONVILLE says his object in constructing the fortification, was to afford protection for their Indian allies, and enable them to continue in small detachments, the war against the Iroquois. A detachment of an hundred

---

* It is remarked by Mr. Marshall, in a note accompanying his translation of De Nonville's journal, that the geographical designation given here "removes all doubt as to the original location of this fortress." The circumstance of Joncaire persuading the Senecas to permit him to fix his residence "in the midst of a group of cabins at Lewiston," has undoubtedly led some historians to conclude that it was originally the site of the Fort. La Hontan, writing from the spot, while the fort was building, says: "The Fort stands on the south side of the Straight of *Herrie* lake, upon a hill; at the foot of which that lake falls into the lake of *Frontenac*."

Troyes, with provisions and ammunition for eight months. They were closely besieged by the Senecas, and a sickness soon broke out which proved fatal to nearly all of them.

The Indian allies of the French, returning to Niagara with De Nonville, had declared their intention at Irondequoit, after what they regarded the failure of the expedition, not to join them in another one; but on seeing the fort erected, they became reconciled, concluding that it would favor their retreat in any expedition against the Iroquois. Upon parting with De Nonville, they made a speech, in which, among other things they said:—

"That they depended upon his promise to continue the war till the Five Nations were either destroyed or dispossessed of their country; that they earnestly desired, that part of the army should take the field out of hand, and continue in it both winter and summer, for they would certainly do the same on their part; and in fine, that for as much as their alliance with France was chiefly grounded upon the promises the French made of listening to no proposals of peace, 'till the Five Nations should be quite extirpated; they therefore hoped they would be as good as their word."*

De Nonville left Niagara on his return to Montreal, on the 2d day of August, reaching his destination on the 13th; resting a day or two at Fort Frontenac, and leaving at that post one hundred men under the command of M. D'Orvilliers. The Senecas soon returned and occupied the ground they had deserted. As the French Indians predicted, it is probable that the other branches of the Confederacy supplied them with corn in the place of what the French had destroyed, and game and fish were abundant. The early French journalists often speak of the abundance of salmon in lake Ontario. On the lake shore, somewhere between the Genesee and Oswego rivers, a party of Indian allies that had been sent from Niagara in advance of the main army of De Nonville, encamped until it came up with them; and more fortunate in hunting deer, than in hunting the Senecas, had piled up at their camp two hundred for the use of the army.

La Hontan, much against his inclination, as it would appear from a letter dated at Niagara, was ordered to take command of a

---

* La Hontan.

detachment and go west with the returning western Indian allies. He says he was "thunderstruck with the news," that he had "fed himself all along with the hope of the returning to France." He concluded, however, to make the best of it, as he had been supplied with "brisk, proper fellows," his "canoes are both new and large," and TONTI and DULBUT were to be his companions. His detachment came up to Lewiston, or the "place where the navigation stops," and carried their canoes up the "three mountains," launching them again at Schlosser. He says that in "climbing the mountains, one hundred Iroquese might have knocked them on the head with stones." And, incredible as it may seem, so soon after their route and dispersion, a large body of those indefatigable warriors were upon his track. Their stopping place, on their retreat a few days before, had been at the foot of Canandaigua lake. From that point they had sallied out to post themselves in the vicinity of the Falls, to fall in with the French troops on their return to the west, or their Indian allies, towards whom they entertained a more fierce and settled hostility. The French and Indians had but just embarked at Schlosser, when a "thousand Iroquese" made their appearance upon the bank of the river. With such enemies lurking in the vicinity, LA HONTAN thought he had "escaped very narrowly," as on his way up, he and "three or four savages" had left the main body to go and look at "that fearful cataract." In his fright, or apprehension of danger, he must have taken but a hurried view of the Falls, for he made an extravagant estimate of their height:—"As for the water-fall of Niagara, 'tis seven or eight hundred foot high, and half a league [a mile and a half] broad. Towards the middle of it we descry an island that leans towards the precipice, as if it were ready to fall. All the beasts that cross the water within a half a quarter of a league above this unfortunate island, are sucked in by force of the stream: and the beasts and fish that are thus killed by the prodigious fall, serve for food for fifty *Iroquese* who are settled about two leagues off, and take 'em out of the water with their canoes. Between the surface of the water that shelves off prodigiously, and the foot of the precipice, three men may cross in abreast, without any further damage than a sprinkling of some few drops of water."

The party were apprehensive of an attack from the pursuers, while getting up the rapids of the Niagara, but, having reached the lake they were secure, the heavy canoes of the Iroquois not being able to overtake the lighter ones of the French. They coasted along the northern shore of lake Erie. The navigators of that lake at the present day, will smile when they are told that these early navigators made a portage of Long Point, carrying their canoes and baggage over land. LA HONTAN speaks of an abundance of game, deer, turkeys, &c., which they found upon the lake shore, as well as upon the islands. The party stopped upon several of the small islands of lake Huron, and, driving the "Roe-bucks" (deer) into the water, would overtake them with their canoes and knock them upon the head with their oars.

The detachment of LA HONTAN took possession of the fort of St. Josephs, relieving the force that had been stationed there. The provisions which DE NONVILLE had promised, failing to arrive during the winter, the garrison was obliged to depend principally upon the chase.

During the winter, a party of Hurons set out over land for the garrison at Niagara, determined to enter the country of the Iroquois, as a marauding party to kill and capture detached parties of beaver hunters. On their way they came across a party of Iroquois hunters, sixty in number, and while they were sleeping in their camps, killed and made prisoners of the whole party. The Hurons returned in triumph to the post at Mackinaw. Some of the Iroquois prisoners told LA HONTAN that they were of the party of one thousand, that intended to capture him and his command at the Falls of Niagara; that when they left, eight hundred of their warriors had blocked up Fort Niagara; and that famine and disease were fast reducing the small French force there; news that proved too true, as the reader will have already learned. They also gave LA HONTAN to understand that, after succeeding at Niagara, the Iroquois would try the same experiment upon his post. He was not apprehensive that they would attack him, but feared they would cut off his hunters and stop his supplies. To guard against this, he employed additional hunters and laid in a large supply of meat. The Iroquois not coming to attack him, in the course of the season he joined a large party of the western Indians, and invaded the country of the Iroquois on the south side of lake Erie, and had several engagements with them.

Soon after De NONVILLE's expedition, Gov. DONGAN met a deputation of the Five Nations at Albany, and praised and scolded them in turn, as would best enable him to maintain the appearance of neutrality, and at the same time encourage them to persevere against the French. He told them they were subjects of the King of England, that he claimed dominion over their territory; that they must not enter into any treaty with the French, except with his advice and consent. Dr. COLDEN says that Gov. DONGAN was not averse to a peace between the French and Iroquois, but he wished the French to solicit his assistance to bring it about, and in doing so acknowledge the dependence of the Five Nations on the crown of England. He was, however over-ruled by King James, and ordered to assist in bringing the Iroquois to consent to a peace on terms dictated by the French. He was soon after removed from his government.

The French so often foiled by the Iroquois, and so annoyed by them and their wars upon other Indian nations, were determined upon measures of peace. De NONVILLE, in the summer of 1688, ordered a cessation of hostilities, and succeeded in getting a large delegation from the Five Nations to repair to Montreal, for the purpose of negotiation. Five hundred of the Iroquois appeared as negotiators; while twelve hundred of their warriors, were awaiting the result near Montreal, ready to fall upon the French settlements, if no treaty was effected.

The confederates insisted that twelve of their people who had been taken prisoners the year previous, and sent by De NONVILLE to the galleys of France, should be returned to their country; that Forts Frontenac and Niagara should be razed; and that the Senecas should be paid for the destruction of their property. De NONVILLE declared his willingness to put an end to the war if all his Indian allies were included in a treaty of peace; if the Mohawks and Senecas would send deputies to signify their concurrence; and Fort Frontenac might remain in their hands, and continued as a depot of trade.

The French and English accounts differ as to the terms of peace finally agreed upon. But a treaty was concluded, which was frustrated by an unforeseen occurrence.

Among the French Indian allies, was KONDIARONK, or LE RAT, a Huron chief, powerful in council and in arms. He had leagued with De NONVILLE to aid in warring upon the Iroquois, his enemies, and the enemies of his nation. From no love for the English, (for he hated them because they were the friends of the Iroquois,) but for the sake of making a good sale of his furs, he had seemed to favor some of their trading parties that had been among the Hurons. This had excited the jealousy of the French; to remove which, he repaired to Fort Frontenac with an hundred warriors. Arriving there, he was told by the commandant that De NONVILLE was in hopes of concluding a peace with the Iroquois, and that the presence of him and his warriors might obstruct the negotiations. Feigning acquiescence, he determined upon a plan not only to prevent a peace, but to punish his French allies for breaking the league they had made, to continue the war. Under the pretence of returning to his country, he took another direction, and repairing to one of the falls of the St. Lawrence, he placed his warriors in ambush, and when a large party of the Iroquois came up, on their return from Montreal, he attacked them, killing a part, and making prisoners of the remainder. He gave the prisoners to understand that he was acting in concert with the French; that De NONVILLE had told him when he could best interrupt the party on its way from Montreal. When told by his prisoners that they were peace ambassadors, he affected great surprise and indignation; and addressing them, said:—"Go, my brethren, I untie your hands, and send you home again, though our nations be at war. The French Governor has made me commit so black an action, that I shall never be easy after it, till the Five Nations shall have taken full revenge."

As the wily Huron chief had anticipated, the discharged prisoners spread the news of French perfidy, (as it seemed to them,) on their return to their country, and measures for the renewal of the war, and revenge, soon followed; those of the Five Nations who had been friendly to the French zealously co-operating. An army of twelve hundred warriors was soon ready for the field. On the 26th of July, 1688, they landed on the south side of the Island of Montreal, while the French were in perfect security; burnt their houses, sacked their plantations, and put to the sword all the men, women, and children, without the skirts of the town. "A thousand French were slain in the invasion, and twenty-six carried into captivity and burnt alive. Many more were made prisoners, in another attack, in October, and the lower part of the Island wholly destroyed. Only three of the confederates were lost in all this scene of misery and desolation."*

---

* Smith's History of the "Province of New York," the statement is upon the author-

As soon as the news reached Fort Frontenac, that post was hurriedly abandoned. On leaving, the French designed to have blown up the works, but the match which was to fire the magazine did not accomplish its purpose. The Iroquois hearing that the fort was deserted, repaired to it, and secured a large amount of plunder, a part of which, was twenty-eight kegs of powder.

The news of these disasters spreading among the French Indian allies at the west, had the effect to alienate most of them and incline them to the English interests. In fact all but two Nations, were thus affected. The whole range of country from Quebec to the western posts, was possessed by the Iroquois or scoured by their war parties; and nothing saved the western posts, but the inability of the Indians to attack successfully fortified places. Added to the other misfortunes of the French upon the St. Lawrence, was a threatened famine. The war and the fur trade, had diverted from agriculture, and supplies failed to reach them from France. Shut up in their fortifications, the Iroquois were ready to fall upon them whenever they ventured out. SMITH, the early historian of New York, says; "but for the uncommon sagacity of Sieur PEROT, the western Indians would have murdered every Frenchman among them." Dr. COLDEN says: "I say, whoever considers all these things, [disadvantages he enumerates under which the Iroquois carried on the war, growing out of the want of an entire unity among themselves, and other wars in which they were engaged,] and what the Five Nations did actually perform, will hardly doubt that they of themselves, were at that time an over match for the French of Canada."

The English taking advantage of the emergency in which the French were placed, held a conference at Albany with the Mohawks. A Mohawk chief assuming to speak for the entire confederacy, said;—"We have burned Montreal, we are allies of the English, we will keep the chain unbroken."

While all this was transpiring upon the American continent the revolution in England was consummated by the elevation of the Prince of Orange to the English throne. This changed the whole complexion of English and French affairs, at home as well as in

---

ity of Dr. Colden. Charlevois says the attack upon Montreal was late in August, and that the Iroquois were 1500 strong; that the loss of the French was only two hundred souls.

NOTE.—When the war was renewed with the French, the Senecas were at war with three Western Nations;—the Utawawas, Chicktaghicks and Twightwies.

their colonies. James II. had been accused of partiality to the French and the colonial measures he had dictated were more favorable to French interests in America than the English colonists and the Protestant party in England, had hoped to see adopted. The recall of Gov. DONGAN, and the position of neutrality the King had dictated to the English colonists, in the war between the French and the Iroquois, were among the colonial measures that were complained of. The policy of DONGAN would have excluded the Jesuits and their powerful influence from the country of the Five Nations, as well as other territory claimed by the English; while King James was too much of a Catholic to second his views.

France declared war against England, soon after the revolution of 1689. Among the offensive measures immediately adopted, were those which not only contemplated a regaining of all lost ground in America, but the conquering of the English colonies and the perfecting of exclusive French dominion.

De NONVILLE was recalled, and Count de FRONTENAC ordered to sail for New France, and assume the local government.

Previous to the arrival of FRONTENAC, the Iroquois had abandoned Montreal. He arrived at Quebec, Oct. 2d, 1689. His vigorous measures soon gave to French affairs a different aspect. Remaining but a few days at Quebec, he pushed on to Montreal. There he summoned a general council of the western Indians. "There, as a representative of the Gallic monarch, claiming to be the bulwark of christendom — Count FRONTENAC, himself a peer of France, now in his seventieth year, placed the murderous hatchet in the hands of his allies; and with the tomahawk in his own grasp, chanted the war song, danced the war dance, and listened, apparently with delight, to the threats of savage vengeance.* An alliance with all the Indians between lake Ontario and the Mississippi was perfected. Fort Frontenac was again garrisoned with a detachment of French troops. The new French governor took every means in his power to win the Five Nations to his interest, realizing how important their friendship would be, in the contest with the English, that he was about to engage in. FRONTENAC brought with him from France the Iroquois that DE NONVILLE had sent home as prisoners, one of whom was a chief of some note. With an eye to the use he could make of them in peace negotiations, he had treated them with much kindness.

---

* Bancroft.

Retaining the chief TAWARAHET, he sent the other four to Onondaga with overtures of peace. A council of eighty sachems was convened; previous to which, however, the magistrates of Albany had been apprised of what was going on, and had sent messengers to the council, to oppose any peace measures. An Onondaga chief, SADEKANAGHTIE, opened the council, stating that the French governor had brought back the prisoners from France; had sent four of them to their own country, and retained the rest at Montreal as hostages; that he had invited the Iroquois to meet him at *Cadarackui* to "treat about the old chain." A chief of the "praying Indians,"* that had accompanied the discharged peace ambassadors, rose up in the council and presented a belt, saying it was from TAWARAHET, the captive chief, in token that he had suffered much in his long captivity, and desired that they would meet the French governor as he desired. The messengers of the magistrates of Albany delivered their message which urged that no overtures that the French might make, should be listened to. CANEHOOT, the Seneca sachem, whose stirring eloquence had roused the Senecas to resist the invasion of DE NONVILLE, informed the council that during the previous summer, as many as seven of the western Nations had made peace with the Senecas and had "thrown away the axe that YONNONDIO had put into their hands;" assuring them that they should no more hearken to YONNONDIO, but, like the Iroquois, be on terms of peace with the English. The Onondaga chief who had opened the council, said:—"Brethren, we must stick to our brother *Quider*,† and look on YONNONDIO as our enemy, for he is a cheat." The Albany messengers assured the council that, as France and England were at war, a great many English soldiers had been sent over; that an expedition was fitting out in New England to conquer New France, &c. The council determined upon not entertaining the proposition of the French governor, but to assist the English to "strike at the root, that the trunk being cut down, the branches fall of course." ‡ An answer to the French governor was agreed upon, which was in substance:—"That they were glad he had brought back their

---

* Such of the Iroquois as the Jesuits had converted, were so called. There was a settlement of them near Montreal.

† Peter Schuyler, the mayor of Albany.

‡ Meaning an attack on Quebec.

people from France, but that the French had acted deceitfully so often, that they could not trust them;" that they could not meet him as he wished at *Cadarackui,* for their council fire was "extinguished with blood." Their ultimatum was, that their chief, TAWARAHET must first be sent home; and after that, they might "speak of peace." They proposed to save the lives of all their French prisoners until spring, and release them upon condition that the French released all their people.

In the winter of 1690, a party of one hundred and fifty French and Indians, left Montreal, and "wading through snows and morasses, through forests deemed before impervious to white men, and across rivers bridged with frost, arrived on the 18th of February, at Schenectady."* With the general features of this expedition, and its fatal termination, the reader will be familiar. There have been several versions of it—most of them imperfect. Among the Paris Documents, brought to this country by Mr. BROADHEAD, is a minute relation of all that appertained to the expedition, written at the time, and sent to the celebrated M. de MAINTENON. The author uses a translation of it, which has been recently published in the Albany Argus. This is, of course, French authority; our accounts heretofore have been wholly from English sources:—

"The orders received by M. le COMTE (de FRONTENAC) to commence hostilities against New England and New York, which had declared for the Prince of Orange, afforded him considerable pleasure, and were very necessary for the country. He allowed no more time to elapse before carrying them into execution, than was required to send off some despatches to France — immediately after which he determined to organize three different detachments, to attack those rebels at all points at the same moment, and to punish them, at various places, for having afforded protection to our enemies, the Mohawks. The first party was to rendezvous at Montreal, and proceed towards Orange (Albany;) the second at Three Rivers, and to make a descent on New York, at some place between Boston and Orange, and the third was to depart from Quebec, and gain the seaboard between Boston and Pentagouet, verging towards Acadia. They all succeeded perfectly well, and I shall now communicate to you the details.

* * * * * *

The detachment which formed at Montreal, may have been

---

* Bancroft.

composed of about two hundred and ten men, namely: eighty savages from the Sault, and from La Montagne; sixteen Algonquins; and the remainder Frenchmen—all under the command of the Sieur LE MOYNE DE SAINTE HELENE, and Lieutenant DAILLEBOUT DE MANTET, both of whom were Canadians. The Sieurs le MOYNE D'IBERVILLE and REPENTIGNY DE MONTESSON commanded under these. The best qualified Frenchmen were the Sieurs de BONREPOS and de LA BROSSE, Calvinist officers, Sieurs la MOYNE DE BLAINVILLE, LE BERT DU CHENE, and la MARQUE DE MONTIGNY, who all served as volunteers. They took their departure from Montreal at the commencement of February.

"After having marched for the course of five or six days, they called a council to determine the route they should follow, and the point they should attack.

"The Indians demanded of the French what was their intention. Messieurs de SAINTE HELENE and MANTET replied that they had left in the hope of attacking Orange, (Albany) if possible, as it is the Capital of New York and a place of considerable importance, though they had no orders to that effect, but generally to act according as they should judge, on the spot, of their chances of success, without running too much risk. This appeared to the savages somewhat rash. They represented the difficulties and the weakness of the party for so bold an undertaking. There was even one among them who, with his mind filled with the recollection of the disasters which he had witnessed last year, enquired of our Frenchmen, 'since when had they become so desperate?' It was our intention, now, to regain the honor of which our misfortunes had deprived us, and the sole means to accomplish that, we replied, was to carry Orange, or to perish in so glorious an enterprise.

"As the Indians, who had an intimate acquaintance with the localities, and more experience than the French, could not be brought to agree with the latter, it was determined to postpone coming to a conclusion until the party should arrive at the spot where the two routes separate—the one leading to Orange, and the other to Corlear (Schenectady). In the course of the journey, which occupied eight days, the Frenchmen judged proper to diverge towards Corlear, according to the advice of the Indians; and this road was taken without calling a new council. Nine days more elapsed before they arrived, having experienced inconceivable difficulties, and having been obliged to march up to their knees in water, and to break the ice with their feet in order to find a solid footing.

"They arrived within two leagues of Corlear, about 4 o'clock in the evening, and were there harangued by the Great AGNIEZ, the chief of the Iroquois from the Sault. He urged on all to perform their duty, and to lose all recollections of their fatigue, in the hope of taking ample revenge for the injuries which they had received from the Mohawks at the solicitation of the English, and of washing themselves in the blood of the traitors. This savage was, without contradiction the most considerable of his tribe — an honest man — as full of spirit, prudence, and generosity as it was possible, and capable at the same time of the grandest undertakings. Shortly after, four squaws were discovered in a wigwam who gave every information necessary for the attack on the town. The fire found in this hut served to warm those who were benumbed, and they continued their route, having previously detached GIGUIERES, a Canadian, with nine Indians, on the look out. They discovered no one, and returned to join the main body within one league of Corlear.

"At eleven of the clock that night, they came within sight of the town, resolved to defer the assault until two o'clock of the morning. But the excessive cold admitted of no further delay.

"The town of Corlear forms a sort of oblong square, with only two gates — one opposite the road we had taken; the other leading to Orange, which is only six leagues distant. Messieurs de SAINTE HELENE and de MANTET were to enter at the first, which the Squaws pointed out, and which in fact was found wide open. Messieurs D'IBERVILLE and de MONTESSON took the left, with another detachment, in order to make themselves masters of that leading to Orange. But they could not discover it, and returned to join the remainder of the party. A profound silence was every where observed, until the two commanders, who separated, at their entrance into the town, for the purpose of encircling it, had met at the other extremity.

"The wild Indian war-whoop was then raised, and the entire force rushed simultaneously to the attack. M. de MANTET placed himself at the head of a detachment, and reached a small fort where the garrison was under arms. The gate was burst in after a good deal of difficulty; the whole set on fire, and all who defended the place were slaughtered.

"The sack of the town began a moment before the attack of the fort. Few houses made any resistance. M. de MONTIGNY discovered some, which he attempted to carry sword in hand, having tried the musket in vain. He received two thrusts of a spear — one in the body and the other in the arm. But M. de SAINTE HELENE having come to his aid, effected an entrance, and put every one of the garrison to the sword. The massacre lasted two hours. The remainder of the night was spent in placing sentinels and taking some rest.

"The house belonging to the minister was ordered to be saved, so as to take him alive, to obtain information from him. But, as it was not known, it was not saved any more than the others. He was slain and his papers burnt before he could be recognized.

"At daybreak, some men were sent to the dwelling of Mr. COUDRE, who was Major of the place at the other side of the river. He was not willing to surrender, and began to put himself on the defensive, with his servants and some Indians; but as it was resolved not to do him any harm, in consequence of the good treatment which the French had formerly experienced at his hands, M. D'IBERVILLE and the Great AGNIEZ proceeded thither alone, promised him quarter for himself, and his people and his property, whereupon he laid down his arms, on parole; entertaining them in his fort, and returned with them to see the commandants of the town.

In order to occupy the savages, who would otherwise have taken to drink, and thus rendered themselves unable for defence, the houses had already been set on fire. None were spared in the town but one house belonging to COUDRE, and that of a widow who had six children, whither M. de MONTIGNY had been carried when wounded. All the rest were consumed. The lives of between fifty and sixty persons, old men, women and children, were spared, they having escaped the first fury of the attack. Some twenty Mohawks were also spared, in order to show that it was the English and not they, against whom the grudge was entertained. The loss on this occasion in houses, cattle and grain, amounted to more than four hundred thousand livres. There were upwards of eighty well built and well furnished houses in town.

"The return march commenced with thirty prisoners. The wounded, who were to be carried, and the plunder, with which all the Indians and some Frenchmen were loaded, caused considerable inconvenience. Fifty good horses were brought away. Sixteen only of these reached Montreal. The remainder were killed for food on the way.

"Sixty leagues from Corlear, the Indians began to hunt, and the French not being able to wait for them, being short of provisions, continued their route, having detached Messieurs D'IBERVILLE and DU CHESNE with two savages before them to Montreal. On the same day, some Frenchmen, who doubtless were very much fatigued, lost their way. Fearful that they should be obliged to keep up with the main body, and believing themselves in safety, having eighty Indians in their rear, they were found missing from the camp. They were waited for next day until eleven o'clock, but in vain, and no account has since been received of them.

"Two hours after, forty men left the main body without acquainting the commander, continued their route by themselves, and arrived within two leagues of Montreal one day ahead, so that there were not more than fifty or sixty men together. The evening on which they should arrive at Montreal, being extremely fatigued from fasting and bad roads, the rear fell away from M. de SAINTE HELENE, who was in front with an Indian guide, and who could not find a place suitable for encamping nearer than three or four leagues of the spot where he expected to halt. He was not rejoined by M. de MANTET and the others, until far advanced in the night. Seven have not been found. Next day on parade about 10 o clock in the forenoon, a soldier arrived, who announced that they had been attacked by fourteen or fifteen savages, and that six had been killed. The party proceeded somewhat afflicted by this accident, and arrived at Montreal at 3 o'clock, P. M.

"Such, Madame, is the account of what passed at the taking of Corlear (Schenectady). The French lost but twenty-one men, namely, four Indians and seventeen Frenchmen. Only one Indian and one Frenchman were killed at the capture of the town. The others were lost on the road."

Another French party, of but fifty three persons, left the Three Rivers, and fell upon an English settlement on the Piscataqua in Maine, and after a bloody engagement, burnt houses, barns and cattle in their stalls, and captured fifty-four persons, chiefly women and children.

The French and English war continued until 1697. The details of it enter largely into our general history. It was a war, so far as the colonies were concerned, growing out of disputed boundary and dominion; the chief or immediate interest at stake, being the fur trade and the fisheries upon our northern coast. In all the war, each nation had its Indian allies, who were left, in most instances, to prosecute their own mode of warfare. At times during the war, Frontenac was enabled to succeed partially with some portions of the Five Nations, through the influence of the Jesuits and the christian Indians, in occasionally securing their neutrality; but for the most part, they were the implacable enemies of the French. In the distracted condition of the English, the dissensions and political rivalries in their colonies; the feebleness with which they prosecuted war measures, as all must have observed, who are familiar with the history of those times; had it not been for the aid of the Iroquois, who occupied an advantageous position to form a barrier against French incursions in a defenceless quarter, the English colonies would have suffered much worse, if indeed French conquest had not been consummated. After the disaster of Schenectady, the

---

NOTE.— Colden says the number of inhabitants massacred was sixty-three, and that twenty-seven were carried away prisoners. In reference to the attack upon the French in their retreat, he says:—"The care the French took to soothe the Mohawks, had not entirely its effect, for as soon as they heard of this action, a hundred of their readiest young men pursued the French, fell upon their rear, and killed and took twenty-five of them." The English accounts generally, state, that the citizens of Schenectady, not apprehensive of an attack from Montreal at such a season of the year, were all asleep, with their gates unclosed.

remnant of a settlement left there, were for abandoning their possessions. They were encouraged to remain by the Mohawks, who assured them that the Five Nations had beat the French every where, single handed, and could easily control them, if the English would do their part. The Five Nations were indignant at what they deemed the temerity of some portion of the citizens of Albany, who contemplated fleeing to New York.

During the whole period of this war, the Iroquois had uninterrupted possession of all the region west of Onondaga lake, and in fact of the whole west of Schenectady, with the exception of some incursions of the French which will be noticed. It was an interim generally of quiet with them and other Indian nations. They made several incursions, down the St. Lawrence, attacking the French near Montreal, with considerable success.

The English soon after the breaking out of the war, made formidable preparations for the conquest of Quebec and Montreal, as the starting point for putting an end to French dominion in this portion of the continent. The measures of FRONTENAC, as has been before observed, looked to an end of English dominion. Little was accomplished by either in furtherance of their ultimate designs. The English expeditions to the St. Lawrence were failures ; and the French incursions were but marauding expeditions, marked with all the horrors and barbarities of savage warfare. In reference to the results of the year 1691, and the failures of the English expeditions, Mr. BANCROFT remarks — "Repulsed from Canada, the exhausted [English] colonies, attempted little more than the defence of their frontiers. Their borders were full of sorrow, of captivity and death."

After the English had abandoned their designs upon the head quarters of the French upon the St. Lawrence, FRONTENAC turned his attention to the Five Nations, whom he alternately, by missions and treaties, endeavored to win, and by invasions to terrify into an alliance. In February, 1692, three hundred French, with Indian confederates, were sent over the snows, against the hunting parties of the Senecas in Upper Canada, near the Niagara."* In 1693, a large party invaded the country of the Mohawks, destroyed several castles, at one of which a small band of warriors so well resisted the invaders as to cause them the loss of thirty men.

---

* Bancroft.

Frontenac had ordered no quarters to be given, except to women and children, but a more humane policy of his Indian allies prevailed. They attempted to carry away prisoners, but a small force collected by Peter Schuyler, of Albany, pursued and liberated the captives.

Toward the close of the war, in 1696, Frontenac, then seventy-four years of age, headed the last French expedition to Western New York. Assembling a large force at Fort Frontenac, he crossed over to Oswego, and marching thence to the chief settlement of the Onondagas, found it deserted. This central nation of the Iroquois had followed the example of the Senecas and set fire to their wigwams.

The only prisoner taken, was an aged chief, who had refused to fly, or probably from weakness and infirmity, could not. The Indian allies of the French were allowed to torture him; but he "scoffed at his tormentors as the slaves of those he despised." They gave him mortal wounds, and expiring under them, his last words were;—"You should have taken more time to learn to meet death manfully! I die contented; for I have no cause of self reproach. You Indians their allies, you dogs of dogs, think of me when you shall be in the like state."

Dr. Colden says the Onondagas were deterred from remaining and defending their houses, by the frightful accounts that a Seneca gave them, who had deserted from the French. He said the French army was as numerous as "the leaves on the trees; that they had machines which threw balls up into the air, and which falling on their castle would burst to pieces and spread fire and death every where; against which, their stockades could be no defence."

The Chevalier de Vaudreuil was detached with a large force to ravage the country of the Oneidas and destroy their crops. The Oneidas were less hostile to the French than the rest of the confederacy. Thirty or forty of them remained to make the French welcome, but they were made prisoners and taken to Montreal.

Frontenac was urged by some of his officers to extend the conquest, but he declined, saying "it was time for him to repose." He concluded he had so far intimidated the Five Nations as to incline them to peace. It is plain, however, that the French had learned to dread the Iroquois and their stratagems, and were fearful that the retreat from their towns was, but to collect in full force, and perhaps surprise their invaders by an ambuscade. Colden, who, as an

Englishman, and the historian of the Five Nations, inclines to cavil generally upon the French expeditions, says;—"all that can be said for this expedition, is, that it was a kind of *heroic dotage ;*" and it would seem to have been somewhat of that complexion.

The French army returned to Montreal, not, however, without being harassed on their way by the Onondagas. But a few weeks had elapsed before war parties of the Five Nations appeared in the vicinity of Montreal, making attacks upon the French settlements. "Thus," says COLDEN, "the war was continued until the peace of Ryswick, by small parties of Indians on both sides, harrassing, surprising, and scalping the inhabitants of Montreal and Albany."

The war settled nothing in the way of respective boundary and dominion, except perhaps a kind of mutual acknowledgment of what each had claimed before. It left Western New York to continue to be a bone of contention. The French had conceded to them the whole coast and adjacent Islands, from Maine to beyond Labrador and Hudson's Bay, besides Canada, the western Lake region, and the valley of the Mississippi.

In adjusting the boundaries, the English commissioner claimed all the country of the Five Nations, and that it extended west, so far even as to include Mackinaw, This extravagant ambition was treated with derision; the French still claiming the whole country of the Five Nations, from discovery and precedent occupancy, by a garrison at Niagara, and their missionaries and traders. "Religious sympathies" says BANCROFT "inclined the Five Nations to the French, but commercial advantages brought them always into connection with the English." About the period of the attempt to settle the question of boundary in New York, the English passed a law for hanging "every Popish priest that should come voluntarily into the province;" including, of course, the disputed ground, as that was claimed to be a part of the province. "The law ought forever to continue in force," says SMITH, the first historian of New York, who had strong prejudices against the French and their religion. Mr. BANCROFT, in a better spirit, concludes that his predecessor was "wholly unconscious of the true nature of his remark." While the French and English both laid claim to Western New York, the rightful owners and occupants never for a moment assented to either of the claims but insisted upon their independence.

In 1700 a peace was ratified between the Iroquois on the one side, and France and her Indian allies on the other. The Rat, the Huron chief who had so craftily played the part of an Iago, in preventing a previous peace, said at a council at Montreal:—"I lay down the axe at my father's feet;" the deputies of the four tribes of Ottawas echoed his words. All the western Indians agreed to terms of peace. A general exchange of prisoners took place, as well between the hostile Indian nations, as between the French and the Five Nations.*

Count FRONTENAC died soon after the close of the French and English war, and was succeeded in the government of New France, by DE CALLIERS, who had been first in rank under him in his military expeditions. Lord BELLAMONT, succeeded Colonel SLOUGHTER, as Governor of the English provinces. The new French Governor insisted upon French jurisdiction of the Iroquois, and that question remained unsettled, while all others were adjusted.

The peace between England and France was of short duration. The smoke of what was termed "King William's War," had hardly cleared away, when "Queen Anne's War" commenced. In the month of may, 1702, war was declared between Queen ANNE and her allies, the Emperor of Germany and the States

---

* "I shall finish this Part by observing that, notwithstanding the *French* Commissioners took all pains possible to carry Home the *French* that were Prisoners with the *Five Nations*, and they had full Liberty from the *Indians*, few of them could be persuaded to return. It may be thought that this was occasioned by the Hardships they endured in their own Country, under a tyrannical Government and a barren Soil. But this certainly was not the only reason; for the English had as much Difficulty to persuade the people that had been taken Prisoners by the *French Indians*, to leave the *Indian* Manner of living, though no People enjoy more Liberty, and live in greater Plenty than the common Inhabitants of *New York* do. No Arguments, no Intreaties, nor Tears of their Friends and Relations, could persuade many of them to leave their New *Indian* Friends and Acquaintance; several of them that were by the Caressings of their Relations persuaded to come Home, in a little time grew tired of our Manner of living, and run away again to the *Indians*, and ended their Days with them. On the other Hand *Indian* Children have been carefully educated among the *English*, clothed and taught, yet I think there is not one Instance, that any of these, after they had Liberty to go among their own People, and were come to Age, would remain with the *English*, but returned to their own Nations, and became as fond of the Indian manner of Life as those that knew nothing of the civilized Manner of living. What I now tell of Christian Prisoners among *Indians*, relates not only to what happened at the Conclusion of the War, but has been found true on many other occasions."

COLDEN,

NOTE.—The captive chief Tawarahet died in Montreal. Colden says the French gave him a christian burial, in a pompous manner; the Priest that had attended him at his death having declared he died a true christian; for, said the Priest, while I explained to him the passion of our Savior, whom the Jews crucified, he cried out:— "Oh! had I been there, I would have revenged his death, and brought away their scalps."

General, of Holland, and France and Spain. It was soon extended to the colonies, and another long and bloody war ensued. By this time the French, through the influence of the Jesuit Missionaries, and the diplomacy of VAUDREUIL, had fully reinstated themselves in the good will of the western Indians, and made allies of the most powerful nations of New England. This gave them by far the vantage ground throughout the war. The Province of New York took but little part in the contest, and its chief burden fell upon New England. The Indians, within their own limits, reinforced by the Indians of Canada, and not unfrequently accompanied by the French, made incursions into all parts of the eastern English Provinces, falling upon the frontier settlements with the torch, the tomahawk and knife, and furnishing a long catalogue of captivity and death, that mark that as one of the most trying periods in a colonial history upon almost every page of which we are forcibly reminded how much of blood and suffering it cost our pioneer ancestors to maintain a foothold upon this continent.* The war on the part of the English colonies, was principally directed against Port Royal, Quebec, and Montreal. Most of the expeditions they fitted out were failures; there was a suspicion of shipwreck, badly framed schemes of conquest; organization of forces but to be disbanded before they had consummated any definite purposes; "marching up hills and marching down again."

Such being the geographical features of the war; the Province of New York having assented to the treaty of neutrality between the French and Five Nations, and contenting itself with an enjoyment of Indian trade, while their neighboring Provinces were struggling against the French and Indians; there is little to notice having any immediate connection with our local relations.

Generally, during the war, the Five Nations preserved their neutrality. They managed with consummate skill to be the friends of both the English and French. Situated between two powerful nations at war with each other, they concluded the safest way was to keep themselves in a position to fall in with the one that finally triumphed. At one period when an attack upon Montreal was contemplated, they were induced by the English to furnish a large auxiliary force, that assembled with a detachment of English

---

* From the year 1675, to the close of Queen Anne's War, in 1713, about six thousand of the English colonists, had perished by the stroke of the enemy or by distempers contracted in military service.

troops at Wood Creek. The whole scheme amounting to a failure, no opportunity was afforded of testing their sincerity, but from some circumstances that transpired, it was suspected that they were as much inclined to the French as to the English. At one period during the war, five Iroquois sachems were prevailed upon to visit England for the purpose of urging renewed attempts to conquer Canada. They were introduced to the Queen, decked out in splendid wardrobe, exhibited through the streets of London, at the theatres, and other places of public resort; feasted and toasted, they professed that their people were ready to assist in exterminating the French, but threatened to go home and join the French unless more effectual war measures were adopted. This was a lesson undoubtedly taught them by the English colonists who had sent them over to aid in exciting more interest at home in the contest that was waging in the colonies. The visit of the sachems had temporarily the desired effect. It aided in inducing the English government to furnish the colonies with an increased force of men and vessels of war; in assisting in a renewed expedition against Montreal and Quebec, which ended, as others had, in a failure. They got nothing from the Five Nations but professions; no overt act of co-operation and assistance. The governor of the province of New York, all along refused to urge them to violate their engagements of neutrality; for as neutrals, they were a barrier to the frontier settlements of New York, against the encroachments of the French and their Indian allies.

The treaty of Utrecht, in April, 1713, put an end to the war. France ceded to England, " all Nova Scotia or Acadia, with its ancient boundaries, also the city of Port Royal, now called Annapolis Royal, and all other things in those parts, which depend upon the said lands." France stipulated in the treaty that she would " never molest the Five Nations subject to the dominion of Great Britain," leaving still undefined their boundaries, to form with other questions of boundary and dominion, future disagreements.

In all this contest, France lost no foothold at the West; but had kept on strengthening and extending its trading establishments in that quarter; following up the new impulse which had been given to their interests there, at the close of King William's war, through the successful diplomacy of FRONTENAC. In June, 1701, De la TOTTE CADILLAC, with a Jesuit Missionary and one hundred

Frenchmen took possession, and became the founders of Detroit. At that period there were three numerous Indian villages in the immediate vicinity of the French post.

In 1722, WILLIAM BURNET, Governor of the Province of New York and New Jersey, who had acquired an accurate and thorough knowledge of the interior geography of Western New York, considered it very important to get command of lake Ontario. To accomplish this object, strengthen English influence over the Six Nations; and defeat the French project of a continuous line of forts, stretching from Quebec to the Gulf of Mexico, he established a trading house at Oswego in the country of the Senecas. The French having repaired the fort at Niagara, and built a large store house in 1725, he in 1726, at his own expense, built a fort at Oswego. In a report of the "committee of the council" of New York, in 1724, they say "the government has built a public trading house upon *Cataraqui* lake, at *Irondequat*, on the *Sennekas*' lands, and another is to be built next spring on the *Onondagas*' (Oswego) river." In a letter written by "J. A. Esq., to Mr. P. C.," of London, dated New York, 1740, on the subject of the measures taken by Gov. BURNET, for "redeeming the Indian trade out of the hands of the French," it is said:—"Gov. BURNET, through his earnest application, and at first chiefly with his money, credit and risk, erected a trading house and fortification at the mouth of the Onondagues river, called Osneigo, where the province of New York supports a garrison of soldiers, consisting of a Lieutenant and twenty men, which are yearly relieved. At this place a very great trade is carried on with the remote Indians, who formerly used to go down to the French, at Montreal, and there buy our English goods, at second hand, at about twice the price they now pay for them at *Osneigo*."

About the period of the occupation of Oswego by the English, and the re-occupation of Niagara by the French, a warm contest arose in the Province of New York, growing out of the fact that the French had taken the advantage of the interim of peace, and were buying their Indian goods in New York. The English Indian traders, by representing that this was helping the French to almost wholly engross the Indian trade, and aiding in alienating the Indians from the English, procured the passage of an act forbidding merchants in the Province of New York, selling Indian goods to the French. The law was not to the liking of the New

York merchants, who made bitter complaints of its effects. Growing out of this controversy, was a memorial which stated the relative advantages of bringing goods into the country by the way of Montreal, and Quebec, and New York. After enumerating the great expenses and disadvantages of the northern French route, they speak of the facilities the French enjoy after getting upon the lakes and the Mississippi:—there is opened to them, says the memorial, "such a scene of inland navigation as cannot be paralleled in any other part of the world." With reference to the English route to the lakes and the Mississippi, they say:—"From Albany, the English traders commonly carry their goods over-land sixteen miles to the Mohawk river at Schenectady, the charge of which carriage is nine shillings New York money, or five shillings sterling, each wagon load. From Schenectady they carry them in canoes up the Mohawk river, to the carrying place between the Mohawk river and the river which runs into the Oneida lake; which carrying place between is only three miles long, except in very dry weather, when they are obliged to carry them two miles farther. From thence they go down with the current the Onondaga river to Cataracui lake." This, the author ventures to assume, is the earliest written document having reference to the inland navigation of our state. Its date is 1724.

The peace of Europe was again interrupted by a war in which England, Spain, France and Austria, were ultimately, involved; together with the American colonies of the three first named. The events that distinguished it, however interesting and important as matters of general colonial history, have little or no relation to this section of country. The frontiers of Florida and Georgia became involved. OGLETHORPE, the Governor of Georgia, conducted an expedition against St. Augustine, with forces raised in the newly settled province. An English fleet, commanded by VERNON, captured Porto Bello, destroyed the fort at Chargres, and demolished the fortifications at Carthagena, in the West Indies. England sent out to the Gulf of Mexico the largest naval armament that had ever before sailed upon its waters. Four battalions were demanded of the colonies north of Carolina to accompany it. The colonies complied with the requisition, and furnished the troops. England set out with the intention of conquering the richest Spanish provinces in America; but, after all her efforts and losses, she made no permanent acquisitions at the south. An English fleet having met, engaged, and gained a victory over a French fleet in the Mediterranean.

In America, the scene of contest was now transferred from the southern to the northern portion of the continent. The New England colonies planned and fitted out the successful expedition that besieged and captured Louisburgh, on the Island of Cape Breton. A plan for the entire conquest of Canada was formed, preparations were made; but it was not carried out.

At length a treaty of peace was negotiated between the warring nations, and signed at Aix la Chapelle, October 7th, **1748**. Though peace prevailed in Europe, yet so far as the French and English colonies were concerned, it was only nominal, never real. The repose and quietness they so much needed, never came. Both England and France immediately entered upon the system of mutual aggression, that finally proved so fatal to the power of the latter on this continent. By the terms of the treaty, England restored to France all the conquests she had made, and no change was made in the colonial possessions of either.

Though not strictly relative to our subject, we will note a matter of general interest, in this connection. While England and Spain were at war, a proposal was made to the British Minister, in **1739**, to tax the English colonies in America. The reply which the minister made is worthy repetition; and had the lesson of wisdom which it taught been learned and regarded by those who, a generation after, stood in his place, how different might have been the annals, not only of our own region, but the entire history which commemorates the achievements and progress of the fortunes and destiny of Britain and America:—" Taxation," said Sir ROBERT WALPOLE, " That, I will leave for some of my successors who may have more courage than I have, and be less a friend to commerce than l am. It has been a maxim with me during my administration, to encourage the trade of the American colonies in the utmost latitude."

THE TUSCARORAS.

The remnant of this once powerful nation are located upon the Mountain Ridge, in the town of Lewiston. Their introduction at this stage of our history, is due to the chronological arrangment it is intended to preserve. They were adopted by the Iroquois, and became the Sixth Nation of the confederacy, in 1712.

They came originally from North Carolina—from the upper country, on the Rivers Neuse and Tar. In 1708 they had "fifteen towns, and could count twelve hundred warriors." In 1711 a rupture occured between them and the colonists. There was a question of territory; of alledged aggression upon their lands. That they were aggrieved and wronged in the onset, is plainly to be inferred from concurrent history. Their new neighbors, the trespassers upon their territory, were not of a character to have a very nice sense of right and wrong.* With as little ceremony, and with as little show of justice, as was exhibited in a later period in the partition of Poland the "Proprietaries" of North Carolina commenced parcelling out their lands to the German fugitives. DE GRAFFENRIED, who had charge of the establishment of the exiles, accompanied by a surveyor, named LAWSON, traversed the Neuse in their territory to determine the character of the country through which it flowed. This and previous demonstrations, convinced the Tuscaroras of the intended aggressions, and they seized the agent and surveyor, and conveyed them to one of their villages. Here, before a general council of the principal men of the various tribes, in which was recounted the wrongs they had suffered from the English, and especially their having "marked some of their territory into lots for settlers," the prisoners were condemned to death. The Indian ceremonies, a feast and festive dances, the kindling of a fire, were preliminary to the execution. On the morning of the appointed day, a new council decreed a reprieve of GRAFFENRIED, but renewed the sentence of LAWSON. GRAFFENRIED was retained as a prisoner for five weeks, and discharged upon a promise that as chieftain of the German emigrants, he would occupy no land without the consent of the Indians.

While all this was transacting in one quarter, and a suspension of aggression and retribution, agreed upon; in another, hostilities had commenced. A band of Tuscaroras and Corees in concert, made a descent upon the scattered German settlers upon the Roanoke

---

* In allusion to an epitaph upon the tomb stone of one of the early Governors, which says that "North Carolina enjoyed tranquility during his administration," Mr Bancroft says;—"It was the liberty of freemen in the woods; a wild independence." Gov. Spotswood of Virginia said, "it was a country without any form of government." And a severe commentator has said;—"In Carolina every one did what was right in his own eyes, paying tribute neither to God nor Cæsar."

and Pamlico Sound, carrying there, and to the Albemarle Sound, the utmost rigors of savage warfare. A portion of the Tuscaroras did not countenance this sudden resort to the knife and tomahawk.

South Carolina came to the relief of the whites in North Carolina. A commander named BARNWELL, at the head of an allied force of South Carolinians, Cherokees, Creeks, Catawbas, Yamasses,* and a few North Carolinians, besieged a fort the Tuscaroras had constructed in Craven County. Thus situated, failing in a co-operation which the people of North Carolina refused from a feeling unfriendly to those who had brought on the war, BARNWELL, to avoid the doubtful issue of a battle, negotiated a treaty of peace. The peace was of but short duration; in violation of its terms, the returning forces of BARNWELL seized the inhabitants of Tuscarora villages, and carried them into captivity and slavery. Retaliation, such as before had been made, was renewed. In warlike measures, however, the Tuscaroras were divided, Gov. SPOTSWOOD, of Virginia, having succeeded in making neutrals of a large portion of them. In Dec., 1713, the country of the Tuscaroras was again invaded from South Carolina by a large force of Indians, and a few white men, under the command of JAMES MOORE. Assembled in a fort on the Neuse, eight hundred of the Tuscaroras became the captives of the invaders. The legislature of North Carolina, entering into the contest with more harmony in their councils, men and money were raised, and the woods were patrolled by the "red allies, who hunted for prisoners to be sold as slaves, or took scalps for a reward."

Thus defeated and persecuted, driven from their lands and homes by the adverse result of a contest provoked by wrong and aggression; with not only the colonial authorities of North and South Carolina to contend with, but their own race, to gratify an arrant spirit of revenge, basely becoming the active allies of their enemies; the Tuscaroras who had remained in arms, migrated to New York.

The author, thus far, has relied chiefly upon the authority of

---

* Why the neighboring nations were found ready to take up arms against the Tuscaroras, as allies of the English, is probably explained by a recurrence to previous events. They had been at war with them; and in the long wars waged against the southern Indians, by the Confederated Five Nations of this region, the Tuscaroras had been allies of the northern invaders. And this was probably the affinity that led them afterwards to seek a home at the north, instead of their being "kindred of the Iroquois," as Mr. Bancroft infers.

Mr. BANCROFT, with reference to the events that preceded the emigration of the Tuscaroras. He is enabled to add two other accounts. The first was written but sixteen years after the events, by WM. BOYD, of Westover, Virginia, who was one of the early commissioners to run a boundary line between Virginia and Maryland; and was first published in 1841. The second is from CARROLL's Historical Collections of South Carolina:—

"These Indians were heretofore very numerous and powerful, making, within time of memory, at least a thousand fighting men. Their habitation, before the war with Carolina, was on the north branch of Neuse river, commonly called Connecta creek, in a pleasant and fruitful country. But now the few that are left of that nation, live on the north side of Moratuck, which is all that part of Roanoke below the great Falls, towards Albemarle Sound. Formerly there were seven towns of these savages, lying not far from each other, but now their number is greatly reduced. The trade they have had the misfortune to drive with the English has furnished them constantly with rum, which they have used so immoderately, that, what with the distempers, and what with the quarrels it begat amongst them, it has proved a double destruction. But the greatest consumption of these savages happened by the war about twenty-five years ago, on account of some injustice the inhabitants of that province had done them about their lands. It was on that provocation they resented their wrongs a little too severely upon Mr. LAWSON, who, under color of being Surveyor General, had encroached too much upon their territories, at which they were so enraged, that they way-laid him, and cut his throat from ear to ear, but at the same time released the Baron de GRAFFENRIED, whom they had seized for company, because it appeared plainly he had done them no wrong. This blow was followed by some other bloody actions on the part of the Indians, which brought on a war, wherein many of them were cut off, and many were obliged to flee for refuge to the Senecas, so that now there remain so few, that they are in danger of being quite exterminated by the Catawbas, their mortal enemies. These Indians have a very odd tradition amongst them, that many years ago, their nation was grown so dishonest, that no man could keep any of his goods, or so much as his loving wife to himself. That, however, their God, being unwilling to root them out for their crimes, did them the honor to send them a messenger from heaven to instruct them, and set them a perfect example of integrity and kind behavior towards one another. But this holy person, with all his eloquence and sanctity of life, was able to make very little reformation among them. Some few old men did listen a little to his wholesome advice, but all the young fellows were quite incorrigible. They not only neglected his precepts, but derided and evil-entreated his person. At last, taking upon him to reprove some young rakes of the Connecta clan very sharply for their impiety, they were so provoked at the freedom of his rebukes, that they tied him to a tree, and shot him with arrows through the heart. But their God took instant vengence on all who had a hand in that monstrous act, by lightning from heaven, and has ever since visited their nation with a continued train of calamities, nor will he ever leave off punishing and wasting their people, till he shall have blotted every living soul of them out of the world.

"Among the many errors which HEWIT has committed in his history of Carolina, he has fallen into none more careless and inexcusable, than his account of this war. Dr. RAMSAY, whose history of South Carolina is an exact copy of HEWIT'S, as far as he goes, has been guilty of the same misstatement of facts. The true history of this insurrection of the Indians, as collected from WILLIAMSON, and the authors quoted by him, is this: JOHN LAWSON, had in discharge of his duty, as Surveyor General of Carolina, marked off some of the lands, claimed by the Tuscarora Indians, on the Neuse river. In consequence of this encroachment upon their rights, added to the frequent impositions of fraudulent traders among them, they seized LAWSON, and after a brief trial, put him to death. Becoming alarmed at this outrage, they hoped to escape punishment, by murdering, on a given day, all the colonists south of Albemarle Sound. Dividing themselves into small parties, they commenced their horrid purpose on the 22d of September, 1711; on which memorable day, 130 persons fell a sacrifice to their revenge. To put down this insurrection, aid was demanded from South Carolina; and Colonel BARNWELL, with a small party of whites, and a considerable body of friendly Indians, of the Cherokee, Creek, and Catawba tribes, was despatched for the purpose. This officer, after killing fifty of the hostile Indians, and taking 250 of them prisoners, came upon one of their forts on the Neuse river, in which were enclosed six hundred of the Tuscaroras. Instead of carrying the fort by storm, which he could easily have done, he concluded a peace with the enemy, who proving faithless, renewed hostilities in a day or two afterwards. Colonel BARNWELL, immediately after this treaty, returned to South Carolina. A second demand was made upon that state for aid, and Col. MOORE, with forty whites, and eight hundred Ashley Indians, set out in the month of December, to meet the enemy. After a

---

NOTE.—The reader will bear in mind that this remarkable tradition of the Tuscaroras was written one hundred and twenty years ago, at which time it was current among them. It is strikingly coincident with the mission and crucifixion of the Savior. Many able scholars and divines believe that our American Indians descended from the ten Lost Tribes. Is not this tradition another link in the chain tending to strengthen that opinion?

fatiguing march through deep forests and swamps, and having encountered much delay by snow storms, and freshets in the rivers, he at length came upon the hostile Indians who had thrown up fortifications on the Taw river, about 50 miles from its mouth. Though Colonel MOORE found the enemy well provided with small arms, he soon taught them the folly of standing a seige. Advancing by regular approaches, he, in a few hours, completely entered their works, and eight hundred Tuscaroras became his prisoners. These were claimed by the Ashley Indians as a reward for their services, and were taken to South Carolina, where they were sold for slaves. The Swiss baron, who, HEWIT says, was killed by the Indians, made a treaty with the Tuscaroras, and he, together with all the Palatines who had emigrated with him, escaped the massacre."

The Tuscaroras, having been merged in the Iroquois confederacy, there is but little in their history since their arrival in this state, of a distinctive character. We in fact mostly lose sight of them, until the commencement of the Revolution. In that contest, as is well known, most of the Six Nations adhered to the English, and their warriors, as allies of England, under the JOHNSONS, the BUTLERS, and BRANT, were a scourge to the border settlers upon the Mohawk, and the Susquehannah. A portion of the Oneidas and Tuscaroras were neutrals, or rather regarded as friendly to the colonists. There is but little mention made of them in all the accounts we have of the border wars. Col. GANSEVOORT, in giving an account to Gen. SULLIVAN, of his expedition, says:—"Agreeable to my orders, I proceeded by the shortest route to the Lower Mohawk Castle, passing through the Tuscarora and Oneida Castles, where every mark of hospitality and friendship was shown to the party. I had the pleasure to find that not the least damage nor insult was offered to any of the inhabitants."

In the instruction of Gen. SULLIVAN to Col. GANSEVOORT, he was ordered to capture and destroy all the Indians he should find at the Mohawk castle, but to spare and treat as friends the Oneidas, meaning, probably, to include the friendly Tuscaroras.

Such portions of the Tuscaroras and Oneidas as had been allies of the English, in their flight from the total route of Gen. SULLIVAN, embarked in canoes, upon the Oneida lake, and down the Oswego river, coasted along up lake Ontario to the British garrison at Fort Niagara. They encamped during the winter of 1780 near the garrison, drawing a portion of their subsistence, in the form of rations. In the spring a part of them returned, and a part of them took possession of a mile square upon the Mountain Ridge, given them by the Senecas. The Holland Company afterwards donated to them two square miles, adjoining their Reservation, and in 1804 they purchased of the company four thousand three hundred and twenty-nine acres; the aggregate of which several tracts, is their present possessions. The purchase of the Holland Company was made by Gen. DEARBORN, then Secretary of War, in trust for them. The purchase money, $13,722, was a portion of a trust fund held by the United States, possessed in pursuance of a final adjustment of their claims upon North Carolina.

They thus became residents in this region seventeen years previous to the advent of the Holland Company, and nineteen or twenty years before the settlements by the whites commenced.

The surviving pioneer settlers at Lewiston and its neighborhood, bear witness to the uniform good conduct of the Tuscaroras, and especially to the civility and hospitality they extended to the early drovers and other adventurers upon the trail that passed through their villages. Previous to 1803 the traveler upon this trail, saw no habitation after leaving the Tonawanda village, until he arrived at Tuscarora. Even Indian habitations helped to relieve the solitude of their wilderness path. The primitive settlers found them kind and obliging; and good neighbors at a time they most needed the benefits of a good neighborhood.

In the war of 1812 they were uniformly and decidedly in the American interests. Of this, and some other matters connected with them, it will be necessary to speak farther on in our work.

FORT NIAGARA.

It will be recollected that LA SALLE first occupied the site of Fort Niagara. It was his first stopping place, before he commenced building the Griffin at Cayuga Creek. He intended it only as a trading station, but protected it with "pallisades," as the French did all their trading posts. In 1687, DE NONVILLE built a "fort of four bastions," a place of temporary and weak defence, as we are to infer from the short time employed in its construction. For the greater portion of the time that elapsed, after its desertion by the remnant of the hundred troops that DE NONVILLE left there, (most of them having perished by disease),* until 1725, it would seem to have been a deserted post. CHARLEVOIX visited this region in 1721. In a letter dated at Niagara, he says:—"Towards 2 o'clock in the afternoon, we entered the river Niagara formed by the great fall, whereof I shall speak presently; or rather it is the river St. Lawrence, which proceeds from lake Erie, and passes through lake Ontario after fourteen leagues of narrows. After sailing three leagues, you find on the left some cabins of Iroquois, Tsonnonthouans, and of the Mississaugues as at Catarocoui. The Sieur de JONCAIRE, lieutenant of our troops, has also a cabin at this place, to which they have beforehand given the name of fort: for it is intended that in time this will be changed into a great fortress. I here found several officers who were to return in a few days to Quebec." He was evidently writing from Lewiston, as there are other evidences that JONCAIRE's residence was there. In a note to an edition of CHARLEVOIX's journal, published in London in 1761, it is remarked:—"A fort has since been built *in the mouth of the river Niagara on the same side*, and exactly at the place where M. DE NONVILLE had built one, which subsisted not long. There even begins to be formed a French town." The inference from this is, that for a considerable period after the desertion of the fort that DE NONVILLE built on the present site of Fort Niagara, there was no French occupation there; but that JONCAIRE's negotiations with the Senecas had reference only to his "cabin," at Lewiston, which, from the presence of French officers which CHARLEVOIX found there, must have grown into a military post; though if a "fort" was erected there, as CHARLEVOIX says, it could have been no more than a trading post picketed in after the then French fashion. Mr. BANCROFT says:— "JONCAIRE (in 1721) planted himself in the midst of a group of cabins at Lewiston, on the site where LA SALLE had driven a rude pallisade, and where DE NONVILLE had designed to lay the foundations of a settlement."

The two locations are here merged; an error undoubtedly, as it is clear that DE NONVILLE built his fort where the fort now stands,

---

* In a note which Mr. Marshall appends to his translation of De Nonville, it is observed:—"The cause of the sickness was ascribed to the climate, but was probably owing to the unwholesome food with which they were provided. They were so closely besieged by the Iroquois that they were unable to supply themselves with fresh provisions. The fortress was soon after abandoned and destroyed, much to the regret of De Nonville."

HOLLAND PURCHASE.   185

and JONCAIRE his cabin at Lewiston. All that CHARLEVOIX relates in the extract which follows, of the negotiations of JONCAIRE, the jealousies of the English, &c., has reference to Lewiston. It is possible, and probable, however, that his influence was put in requisition two or three years afterwards, when the French re-occupied the site of Fort Niagara, as mentioned in a preceding page, built one story of the old Mess-house, and for the first time made it a substantial fortress;—such as (with occasional additions and improvements that took place from 1725 to 1759,) it was found at the English siege and capture. The building in 1725 was strongly opposed by the Senecas, as was the occupation of Oswego by the English governor by the Onondagas; though from the close of the war in 1713 the French had been far more successful in winning the favor of the Confederates than the English. The following tradition, which is common in our histories, is adopted by SAMUEL DE VEAUX in some sketches he made of the Falls and its vicinity, in 1839. The author was a resident at the fort at an early period, after the settlement of this region commenced, and the intelligence and good sense with which he is prone to make historical investigations, is a guarantee of the truth of the relation, though the author finds no authority for it in early history, but the general fact that the Iroquois neither yielded to the French nor the English any right to occupy their territory with fortifications:—"It is a traditionary story that the Mess-house which is a very strong building, and the largest in the fort, was erected by stratagem. A considerable, though not powerful body of French troops had arrived at the point. Their force was inferior to the surrounding Indians, of whom they were under some apprehensions. They obtained consent of the Indians to build a wigwam, and induced them, with some of their officers, to engage in an extensive hunt. The materials were made ready, and while the Indians were absent, the French built. When the hunting party returned, they found the French had so far advanced with their work as to cover their faces, and to defend themselves against the savages in case of an attack. In progress of time it became a place of considerable strength. It had its ravines; its ditches and pickets; its curtains and counterscarp; its covered way, draw-bridge, and raking batteries; its stone towers, laboratory, and magazine; its mess-house, barracks, and bakery, and blacksmith's shop; and for worship, a chapel, with a large ancient dial over the door to mark the course of the sun. It was indeed a little city of itself, and for a long period the greatest place south of Montreal, or west of Albany. The fortification originally covered a space of about eight acres. At a few rods from the barrier gate is a burying ground; it was filled with the memorials of the mutability of human life; and over the portals of the entrance was painted the word 'REST.'"

The history of JONCAIRE's negotiations with the Senecas, is thus given in CHARLEVOIX's letter from Niagara, referred to in a preceding page:—

"I have already had the honor to acquaint you, that we have a scheme for a settlement in this place; but in order to know the reason of this project, it will be proper to observe, that as the English pretend, by virtue of the treaty of Utrecht, to have sovereignty of all the Iroquoise country and by consequence, to be bounded on that side by lake Ontario only; now it is evident, that, in case we allow of their pretensions, they would then have it absolutely in their power to establish themselves firmly in the heart of the French colonies, or at least entirely to ruin their commerce. In order therefore, to prevent this evil, it has been judged proper, without, however, violating the treaty, to make a settlement in some place, which might secure to us the free communication between the lakes, and where the English should not have it in their power to oppose us. A commission has therefore been made to M. DE JONCAIRE, who having, in his youth, been prisoner among the Tsonnonthouans, so insinuated himself into the good graces of those Indians, that they adopted him, so, that even in the hottest of their wars with us, and notwithstanding his remarkable services to his country, he has always enjoyed the privileges of his adoption.

"On receiving the orders I have been now mentioning to you, he repaired to them, assembled their chiefs, and after having assured them that his greatest pleasure in this world would be to live amongst his brethren; he added, that he would much oftener visit them had he a cabin amongst them, to which he might retire when he had a mind to be private. They told him that they had always looked upon him as one of their own children, that he had only to make choice of a place to his liking in any part of the country. He asked no more, but went immediately and made choice of a spot on the banks of a river, which terminates the canton of Tsonnonthouan, where he built his cabin. The news of this soon reached New York, where it excited so much more the jealousy of the English, as that nation had never been able to obtain the favor granted to Sieur DE JONCAIRE in any Iroquoise canton.

"They made loud remonstrances, which being seconded with presents, the other four cantons at once espoused their interest. They were, however, never the nearer their point, as the cantons are not only independent of each other, but also very jealous of this independence. It was therefore necessary to gain that of Tsonnonthouans, and the English omitted nothing to accomplish it; but they were soon sensible they should never be able to get JONCAIRE dismissed from Niagara. At last they contented themselves with demanding, that at least they might be permitted to have a cabin in the same place; but this was likewise refused them. 'Our country is in peace, said the Tsonnonthouans, the French, and you will never be able to live together, without raising disturbances. Moreover, added they, it is of no consequence that JONCAIRE should remain here; he is a child of the nation; he enjoys his right, which we are not at liberty to take from him.'

"Now, Madame, we must acknowledge, that nothing but zeal for the public good could possibly induce an officer to remain in such a country as this, than which a wilder and more frightful is not to be seen. On the one side you may see just under your feet, and as it were at the bottom of an abyss, and which in this place is like a torrent by its rapidity, a whirlpool formed by a thousand rocks, through which it with difficulty finds a passage, and by the foam with which it was always covered; on the other, the view is confined by three mountains placed one over the other, and whereof the last hides itself in the clouds. This would have been a very proper scene for the poets to make the Titans attempt to scale the heavens. In a word, on whatever side you turn your eyes, you discover nothing which does not inspire a secret horror.

"You have, however, but a very short way to go, to behold a very different prospect. Behind those uncultivated and uninhabitable mountains, you enjoy the sight of a rich country, magnificent forests, beautiful and fruitful hills, you breathe the purest air, under the mildest and most temperate climate imaginable, situated between two lakes, the least of which is two hundred and fifty leagues in circuit.

"It is my opinion, that had we the precaution to make sure of a place of this consequence, by a good fortress, and by a tolerable colony, all the forces of the Iroquoise and the English conjoined, would not have been able at this time to drive us out of it, and that we ourselves would have been in a condition to give law to the former, and to hinder most part of the Indians from carrying their furs to the second, as they daily do with impunity. The company I found here with M. de JONCAIRE, was composed of the baron de LONGUEIL, the marquis de CAVAGNAL, captain, son of the marquis de VAUDREUIL, the present governor of New France; M. de SENNEVILLE, captain; and the Sieur de la CHAUVIGNERIE, ensign, and interpreter of the Iroquoise language. These gentlemen are about negotiating an agreement, of differences, with the canton of

Onontague, and were ordered to visit the settlement of the Sieur de JONCAIRE, with which they were extremely well satisfied. The Tsonnonthouans renewed to them the promise they had formerly made to maintain it. This was done in a council, in which JONCAIRE, as they told me, spoke with all the good sense of a Frenchman, whereof he enjoys a large share, and with the sublimest eloquence of an Iroquoise."

[Among the residents at Fort Niagara, at an early period of its occupancy by American troops, was Dr. JOSEPH WEST. He was there from 1805 until 1814, at which time he was transferred to Philadelphia, when a declining health, that had induced his change of residence, terminated in death. At an early period of sale and settlement under the auspices of the Holland Company, he purchased a farm upon the lake shore, a short distance below the garrison grounds, where his aged widow and one surviving daughter now reside. In 1822 or 3, Mrs. W. became the wife of JOSEPH LANDON, then resident at Lockport as a canal contractor, who was an early and widely known tavern keeper at Buffalo. He died but a few years since. To the surviving daughter of Dr. WEST, the author is indebted for the following "REMINISCENCES OF FORT NIAGARA." Although the sketch introduces events that belong to a later period, the author has thought its insertion in this connection, not inappropriate. It derives additional interest from having been made generally from personal observation; an interest that the author will aim to mingle with his narrative, whenever it can be made available.]

Fort Niagara! How many associations crowd into my mind at the bare mention of thy name. There I first drew my breath, and passed the earliest years of childhood under the eye of a kind father, who was taken from his young family by consumption, caused by a severe cold caught in the damp dungeons of the old Mess-house, while attending the wounded and dying, after the battle of Queenston. Although I have a distinct recollection of the appearance it then presented, it is the recollection of early years, which, perhaps, does not enable me to describe it with strict accuracy. It was then surrounded on three sides with strong pickets of plank, firmly planted in the ground, and closely joined together; a heavy gate in front, of double plank, closely studded with iron spike. This was enclosed by a fence, with a large gate just on the brow of the hill, called the barrier gate. The fourth side was defended by embankments of earth, under which were formerly barracks, affording a safe, though somewhat gloomy

---

NOTE. — The reader will not hesitate in concluding that Charlevoix was describing Lewiston; and that in the interim between the desertion of the Fort upon the present site, in 1698, and the re-building and re-occupancy in 1725, — immediately preceding the latter event, — there was a military station at Lewiston, and a design to locate the Fort there.

retreat for the families of soldiers, but which had been abandoned, and the entrances closed, long before my remembrance; having been so infested with rattlesnakes that had made their dens within, that it was hardly safe to walk across the parade.

But the Lake has done as much as time, towards changing the aspect of the place. At that time there was a yard some thirty or forty feet wide between the Mess-house and pickets; and beyond them a spot sufficiently wide to admit of two persons walking abreast; affording a delightful promenade. But now the waves dash against the house, or rather did until recently, a stone wall having been erected, of immense strength, to prevent further encroachments. The old house, however, remains very much the same, except some slight alterations which have been made in the arrangements of the rooms. On its massive stone walls, time has yet made no ravages, although nearly two centuries* have elapsed since the first story was built by the French. After the English obtained possession, they added another story and made very comfortable quarters for the officers; and there has since, at intervals, been improvements made, but it still retains its air of gloomy grandeur; many gay scenes have I there witnessed, both in my childhood, and after an absence of long years, when I had returned to the home of my youth. I have seen it lit up for festive hours, enlivened by the smiles of beauty, the cheering voice of friendship, mingled with the strains of gay music; the old walls decorated with our country's banners; the eagle's broad wing chalked beneath our feet; the light arms tastefully arranged in our room, and manly forms ready to use them, (if needs be,) flitting past in the gay dance. Then have I looked back through the long vista of years, and thought of the multitudes who had passed through those old halls, until I could fancy I heard the Indian's wild whoop, and see their hideously painted forms, mingled with those of gay, chattering Frenchmen. Then came the proud Englishmen, in their glittering uniform; they in their turn succeeded by our own noble and brave army.

My father received the appointment of Surgeon to the garrison, and, contrary to the present practice, was allowed to remain there ten years. There was a constant interchange of civilities and kindnesses, between the officers of Fort Niagara and the British Fort

---

* But one hundred and twenty-three years since the structure was commenced by the French, that our fair correspondent is describing.

George, and the inhabitants of the little town of Niagara, until the war of 1812 severed many ties of friendship. I well remember the Sunday previous to the receipt of the declaration of war; being at church at Niagara; on our return Gen. BROCK accompanied us to the boat, and, taking myself and sisters by turns in his arms, said:—"I must bid good bye to my little rosy cheeked Yankees;" then extending his hand to my father, said:—"Farewell, Doctor; the next time we meet it will be as enemies." Then came the official declaration of war, the reception of which is as vivid in my memory as if it had occured but last week. We were aroused by the Sentinel's cry, "who goes there?"—then the call to the Corporal of the guard to conduct the intruder to the Captain, who no sooner received the document from his hands than he hastened to consult with my father. I fancy I can see him now, seated on the side of the bed half dressed, with the most rueful countenance, saying:—"What shall we do?—we are liable to attack at any moment, with our fortifications out of repair. We have but one company, and scarcely any arms and ammunition." Sleep was banished from all eyes for the remainder of that night. At dawn of day, we heard the sound of the artificer's hammer mingled with those of other implements of toil. The old well in the hall, which had been covered up as unfit for use, was uncovered and cleaned out to be used in case of necessity. A heavy cannon was drawn into the porch; every crack and crevice in the pickets closed up; new embankments made, and old ones repaired; cannon mounted; and everything done that circumstances would admit of, to strengthen the garrison. Then came company after company of militia, pouring in from all quarters, gay with all sorts of uniform, and as raw and undisciplined as ever stood their ground, or ran from a foe. The families of the officers were obliged to vacate their quarters to make room for them, and we were sent into the country. On our way up the river, we met about one hundred of the Tuscarora Indians, headed by their chief, all powerful, active young men, decorated with their war paint and armed with tomahawk and hatchet, on their way to offer their services at the fort.

We returned after an absence of four weeks to a residence near the fort. Father remained day and night at his post, attending to his professional duties, while our family were safely at the farm; unmolested, except occasionally by the enemy landing from their boats and plundering the hen-roost. At one time the voice of a

British officer was heard, and recognizing us as acquaintances, observed: "there are no American officers here, and we do not war with women, let us get some fowls and be off." At another time an English vessel remained all day, making ineffectual attempts to reach the house with their cannon balls, but when near enough to do so, they could not clear the high bank of the lake. They did not probably wish to annoy the family, but they well knew that not many hours passed without some of the officers from the fort being there. There were a large number there on the day of the cannonading.

The news of the capture of "Little York"—(now *large* Toronto)—was preceded by the report of the explosion of the magazine, which jarred our house, and was distinctly heard at the fort. It was soon followed by dispatches, bringing the gratifying intelligence of the capture of the town, and the sad intelligence of the death of the brave Gen. PIKE. Then came our gallant soldiers who had fought so bravely under the command of Gen. DEARBORN. Many were the wounded and dying that were brought over. They were conveyed to the shore by boats from the fleet, and encamped in a field directly opposite our house. Day and night we heard the groans of the sufferers, and well do I remember walking with my father between the rows of white tents, stopping in front of them while he made his professional visits. To some we were admitted. And, oh, what scenes of sorrow and suffering! Here lay a poor soldier without an arm, or the hand gone and the arm hanging loosely by his side; there one without a leg; there one with most of his face shot off. Many died, and were buried in the same field. Gen. DEARBORN and his staff, and many others whose names now stand foremost in the ranks of the army, were quartered at our house, as every apartment at the fort, and every inch of ground there was occupied. As many as could find room in the house spread their matrasses upon the floor, (none but the general officers expecting the luxury of a room and bed;) the rest occupying the yard with their marquees much to my chagrin, as the continual pacing of the sentinels defaced the green sward; and Col. SCOTT, (now the gallant Commander-in-Chief of our Army,) even went so far as to order his tent pitched upon my favorite rose bush.

[Our correspondent here gives some account of the battle of Queenston, and the cannonading between Fort Niagara and Fort

George, which is omitted, as those subjects must necessarily be embraced in some sketches of the local events of the war of 1812.]

Gen. DEARBORN and his staff, and many others, returned and took up their quarters at our house, where they remained until they again made an attack upon Canada. The capture of Fort George and Niagara followed. Soon after, owing to my father's continued ill health, we left the frontier, and I can recollect but little more that is not familiar to all readers of American history. In our absence, in connection with the news that the British were in possession of Fort Niagara, we heard that our house, with every other on the lines, was in ashes.

In after years, when visiting the fort, my blood has boiled and my cheeks have been tinged with shame, on being shown the place where the British entered, and hearing a recital of the affair. They entered at a place where twenty men could have successfully opposed hundreds, had the commander been at his post. But he had gone home that night, (his family living about two miles off in the country,) and laid down by the fire for a few moments with his clothes on, his horse being saddled at the door ready for an immediate return.—He was awakened by the firing, and springing upon his horse, lost no time in reaching the fort, where he was met by a British soldier who immediately took him prisoner. It is true that he might not by his presence have saved the fort, but he would have saved his reputation, a court-martial, and dismissal from the army.

EARLY NOTICES OF NIAGARA FALLS.

It is difficult to conclude who was the first European that saw Western New York, or the Falls of Niagara. There are some accounts from which it may be inferred that CHAMPLAIN was upon lake Ontario at different times, from 1614 to 1640, and LE ROUX in 1628, but no hint occurs in connection, that they visited its southern shore. French traders are said to have visited the Falls as early as 1610, '15, but there are no authentic accounts to confirm the statement. JOSEPH DE LA ROCHE DALLION, a Franciscan Father, a missionary of ardent religious zeal and enterprise, was in this region as early as the year 1626 or '7, and was probably the first European adventurer who saw Western New York, but there is no evidence that he visited the Falls. He made but a short stay, the severity of the winter, and the hostility of the Iroquois to his presence and mission, obliging him to retreat. There are no reliable accounts of any further attempts to explore this region until 1641. ☞ See Father ALLEMONT's account of BREBEUF and CHAUMANOT's visit, page 65. DUCREUX, the author of "Historiæ Canadensis," has noted the Falls on a map dated 1660, but does not allude to them in his narrative.* The earliest dates which have been discovered, engraved upon the rocks at the Falls, are of 1711, 1712 1726, and 1745. There is a date 1745, on a tree on Goat Island, which shows that the French must have had access to the Island while occupants of this region.

HENNEPIN, who, as will have been seen, was with LA SALLE at the primitive commercial advent upon the Lakes in 1688, has given us the earliest description of the Falls that has found its way into our histories; if indeed it is not the earliest description of them, in any form, extant.† He thus describes them:—

"Betwixt the lakes Ontario and Erie, there is a vast and prodigious cadence of water which falls down after a surprising and astonishing manner, insomuch that the universe does not afford its parallel. 'Tis true, Italy and Switzerland boast of some such things, but we may well say that they are sorry patterns, when compared with this of which we now speak. At the foot of this horrible precipice, we meet with the river Niagara, which is not above a quarter of a league broad, but is wonderfully deep in some places. It is so rapid above this descent, that it violently hurries down the wild beasts while endeavoring to pass it to feed on the other side, and not being able to withstand the force of its current, which inevitably casts them headlong above six hundred feet high.

"This wonderful downfall is compounded of two great crossstreams of water, and two falls into an isle sloping along the middle of it. The waters which fall from this horrible precipice, do foam

---

* The generally correct and indefatigable gleaner of history, antiquarian and naturalist, Dr. Barton, of Philadelphia, is in error in concluding that the Falls were "described and delineated" by Frenchmen, as early as 1638.

† The following is the title of his book: "A new discovery of a vast country in America, extending above four thousand miles between New France and New Mexico, with a description of the great Lakes, Cataracts, Rivers, Plants and Animals; also the manners, customs, and languages of the several native Indians, and the advantages of commerce with those different nations, with a continuation giving an account of the attempts of the Sieur De La Salle upon the mines of St. Barbe, &c. The taking of Quebec by the English; with the advantages of a shorter cut to China and Japan. Both parts illustrated with maps and figures, and dedicated to His Majesty K. William. By L. Hennepin, now resident in Holland. To which is added several new discoveries in North America, not published in the French edition. London, 1698."

and boil after the most hideous manner imaginable, making an outrageous noise, more terrible than that of thunder; for when the wind blows out of the south, their dismal roaring may be heard more than fifteen leagues off.

"The river Niagara having thrown itself down this incredible precipice, continues its impetuous course for two leagues together, to the great rock, above mentioned, with an inexpressible rapidity; but having past that, its impetuosity relents, gliding along more gently for two other leagues, till it arrives at lake Ontario or Frontenac.

"From the great fall into this rock, which is to the west of the river, the two banks of it are so prodigious high, that it would make one tremble to look steadily over the water, rolling along with a rapidity not to be imagined. Were it not for this vast Cataract, which interrupts navigation, they might sail with barks or greater vessels, more than 450 leagues, crossing the lake of Hurons, and reaching even to the further end of lake Illinois; which two lakes we may easily say are little seas of fresh water.

"After these waters have thus discharged themselves into this gulf, they continue their course as far as the three mountains, which are on the east of the river, and the great rock which is on the west, and lifts itself three fathoms above the waters, or thereabouts."

The exaggerated account of LA HONTAN, follows next in order of time. [☞ See page 157.] In 1721, CHARLEVOIX gave a description of the Falls, in connection with his account of the diplomacy of JONCAIRE in obtaining permission to fix his residence at Lewiston. His is the first description made with any considerable degree of accuracy.

"The officers having departed, I ascended those Mountains,* in order to visit the famous fall of Niagara, above which I was to take water; this is a journey of three leagues, though formerly five; because the way then lay by the other, that is, the west of the river, and also because the place for embarking lay full two leagues above the Fall. But there has since been found, on the left, at the distance of a half a quarter of a league from this cataract, a creek † where the current is not perceivable, and consequently a place where one may take water without danger. My first care after my arrival, was to visit the noblest cascade perhaps in the world; but I presently found the Baron LA HONTAN had committed such a mistake with reference to its height and figure, as to give

---

* The "Three Mountains" of Hennepin, the "Hills" of La Hontan; at Lewiston.
† Gill Creek.

grounds to believe he had never seen it. It is certain that if you measure its height by that of the three mountains, you are obliged to climb to get at it, it does not come much short of what the map of M. DELISLE makes it; that is, six hundred feet, having certainly gone into this paradox either on the faith of baron LA HONTAN or Father HENNEPIN; but after I arrived at the summit of the third mountain, I observed that in the space of three leagues, which I had to walk before I came to this piece of water, though you are sometimes obliged to ascend, you must still descend still more, a circumstance to which travellers seem not to have sufficiently attended. As it is impossible to approach it but upon one side only, and consequently to see it, excepting in profile or side-ways, it is no easy matter to measure its height with instruments. It has, however, been attempted by means of a pole tied to a long line, and after repeated trials it has been found only one hundred and fifteen or one hundred and twenty feet high. But it is impossible to be sure that the pole has not been stopped by some projecting rock; for although it was always drawn up wet, as well as the end of the line to which it was tied, this proves nothing at all, as the water which precipitates itself from the mountain, rises very high in foam. For my own part, after having examined it on all sides, where it could be viewed to the greatest advantage, I am inclined to think we cannot allow it less than one hundred and forty or fifty feet.

"As to its figure, it is in the shape of a horse shoe, and it is about four hundred paces in circumference; it is divided in two, exactly in the centre, by a very narrow Island, half a quarter of a league long. It is true these parts very soon unite; that on my side, and which I could only have a side view of, has several branches which project from the body of the cascade, but that which I viewed in front, appearing to me quite entire. The Baron de LA HONTAN mentions a torrent, which, if this author has not invented it, must certainly fall through some channel on the melting of the snows.

"You may easily guess, Madame, that a great way below this fall, the river still retains strong marks of so violent a shock, accordingly it becomes only navigable three leagues below, and exactly at the place where JONCAIRE has chosen for his residence. It should by right, be equally unnavigable above it, since the river falls perpendicularly the whole space of its breadth. But besides the Island, which divides it into two, several rocks which are scattered up and down above it, abate much of the rapidity of the stream; it is notwithstanding so very strong, that ten or twelve Outaways trying to cross over to the Island to shun the Iroquoise who were in pursuit of them, were drawn into the precipice, in spite of all their efforts to preserve themselves.

"I have heard say that the fish that happen to be entangled in the current, fall dead into the river, and that the Indians of those parts were considerably advantaged by them; but I saw nothing, of this sort. I was also told that the birds that fly over were sometimes caught in the whirlwind formed by the violence of the torrent. But I observed quite the contrary, for I saw small birds flying very low, and exactly over the fall, which yet cleared their passage very well.

"This sheet of water falls upon a rock, and there are two reasons which induce me to believe that it has either found, or perhaps in process of time hollowed out a cavern of considerable depth. The first is, that it is very hollow, resembling that of thunder at a distance. You can scarce hear it at M. de JONCAIRE's, and what you hear in this place, may possibly be that of the whirlpools, caused by the rocks, which fill the bed of the river as far as this. And so much the rather, as above the cataract you do not hear it near so far. The second is, that nothing has ever been seen again that has once fallen over it, not even the wrecks of the canoes of the Outaways, I mentioned just now. Be that as it will, OVID gives us the description of another cataract, situated according to him in the delightful valley of Tempe. I will not pretend that the country of Niagara is as fine as that, though I believe its cataract much the noblest of the two."

"Besides, I perceive no mist above it, but from behind, at a distance, one would take it for smoke, and there is no person who would not be deceived with it, if he came in sight of the isle, without having been told before hand that there was so surprising a cataract in the place."

In reflecting upon these early advents to this now great center of attraction, the mind is prone to wander back and associate with it the vast wilderness, its silence only broken by the ceaseless roar —in which was but occasionally mingled the sound of human voices—the war whoop, the festive shout of the Iroquois, or the stranger sounds of the Gallic dialect, uttered by the trader or missionary, in their unfrequent visits. The European adventurer, as Mr. GREENWOOD beautifully expresses it:—"stood alone with God!" Yes, alone! communing with the Great Architect, in the presence of the triumphs of His Omnipotence! where, gathering the waters of vast inland seas, it would seem that He

> * * * "Poured them from His hollow hand,"
> * * * * * *
> "And spoke in that loud voice which seemed to him
> Who dwelt in Patmos for his Savior's sake,
> 'The sound of many waters;' and had bade
> The flood to chronicle the ages back
> And notch His centuries in the eternal rocks." *

---

* Brainard.

The early adventists were men of devout minds, and upon errands of devotion. How, when the mighty scene was first presented, must they have anticipated the sublime conceptions of the poet in an after age:—

> "Deep calleth unto deep. And what are we,
> That hear the question of that voice sublime?"
> * * * * * *
> "Yea, what is all the riot man can make
> In his short life, to thy unceasing roar!
> And yet, bold babbler, what art thou to Him
> Who drowned a world and heaped the waters far
> Above its loftiest mountains?—a light wave
> That breaks and whispers of its Maker's might."

Theirs must have been the thoughts that in after years found utterance in the verse of another of the gifted in the annals of American literature;—theirs, the feelings that were embodied in her exclamation of mingled wonder, awe, and chastened admiration:

> "Flow on forever in thy glorious robe
> Of terror and of beauty! God hath set
> His rainbow on thy forehead, and the cloud
> Mantled around thy feet, and He doth give
> The voice of thunder power to speak of Him
> Eternally—bidding the lip of man
> Keep silence, and upon thy rocky altar pour
> Incense of awe-struck praise." *

How wild and magnificent this panorama of the wilderness, as it must have appeared to those solitary wanderers! It was unheralded; no traveller had spread before them maps or descriptions; the sound of its rushing waters, booming over the unbroken forest, and assailing their ears as they were leaving the "Lake of Frontenac," and entering the "Streights of Herrie Lake," first attracted their attention. Approaching the "great waterfall" by stealth—watchful of the poisonous reptile that coiled in their path—fearful of the Iroquois that lurked in the dark surrounding forests—stunned by the sounds that fell heavier and heavier upon the ear, as they approached their source;—they emerged from behind the forest curtain, and the scene in all its lonely, primeval grandeur, like a flood of light, burst upon their view! It was Nature in her retreat. Hid away in the bosom of this then vast

---

* Mrs. Sigourney,

wilderness, before unknown to any portion of the civilized world, was one of the mightiest achievements of Creative Power.

How primitive the scene! All but the roar of the mighty cataract was hushed silence. That, rioted in a monopoly of sound, as does the rolling thunder in the heavens, when, as the voice of God, it chastens all things else to stillness and humility.

At each crackling beneath their footsteps, the wild beast started from his lair in the ever-green shades that crown the lofty palisades of rock;— the timid deer, as if transfixed, gazed for a moment upon strange faces, and bounded to his forest retreat; the eagle, frightened from his eyrie, sailed away, in an atmosphere of spray and fleeting cloud, the tints of the rainbow that spans the deep abyss, reflected from his glossy wing. Onward! Onward! came the avalanche of waters! Ages have passed,— all but that has changed! Civilization, the arts, the highest achievements of genius, human progress, are placing their triumphs by its side, and claiming a divided admiration. Tens of thousands, gathered from almost every portion of the habitable globe, come annually, pilgrims and sojourners, to gaze upon the works of God, and the feebler yet interesting consummations of Art. How vividly, do thoughts, contrasts of the past and present, cluster around this spot!

The general narrative, which has been interrupted by the introduction of distinct local topics, will be resumed.

The treaty of Aix la Chapelle, as other treaties, had left matters of dispute between England and France unsettled. Either nation was at liberty, whenever its interests might be promoted by so doing, to revive any of the vexed and difficult questions of discovery, boundary and occupancy, that had frequently involved them and their distant colonies, in war, disasters and ruin. Their contending armies had enjoyed but a short armistice — hostilities on the extended frontier of their colonial settlements had but just ceased — the conquests that had been made, had hardly been surrendered and re-occupied — when the French began a system of encroachments, which they intended should result in confining the English colonies within the comparatively narrow limits between the Alleghanies and the Atlantic, and secure to themselves undisputed possession of all the territory west and south-west, around the Lakes, and in the vallies of the Mississippi and its tributaries. The warlike preparations and collisions that occurred during the two years immediately preceding the public declaration of war on the part of England, in 1756, were the immediate consequences of the far-reaching policy deliberately adopted and steadily pursued by France. Both England and France were anxious to gain the good will and aid, alliance and trade, of the Indian nations yet occupying and owning the contested dominions. Their respective agents made use of every means to win their favor, make treaties of friendship with them, and fill their minds with hatred and enmity;—induce them to believe that either one nation or the other was their exclusive friend and protector. The Indians regarded these two European nations as perpetual enemies, for they were almost always wrangling at the council fires, interrupting each other's trade, or making the battle field the arbitrer of their disputes. They were never united against the Indians as a common enemy; and the Indians, in turn, generally sided with the one that offered the best terms. Especially was this the case with the Iroquois; the French missionaries, and the French faculty generally, of adapting themselves to wild forest life, and the habits and customs of the Indians, gave them decidedly the vantage ground among the less independent and politic nations of the West. If the Indians attacked the frontier settlements, or committed any acts of hostility, one nation was sure to charge it to the instigation of the other, and hold the implicated party responsible. Out of this state of things, and out of the desire which both had to maintain their rival and irreconcilable claims— to strengthen their influence and ascendency—arose mutual suspicions, distrusts, jealousies, and open acts of aggression. Both became watchful and vigilant that one should not obtain the advantage of the other. Each nation had formed a firm determination to defend what it regarded its just rights, and was secretly, though efficiently, preparing itself for the great struggle which was to decide the fate of their colonial dependencies in North America. Both were ambitious to extend and widen their western boundaries, and consolidate the power by which they held and governed them. When both were so sensitive and watchful, it needed only a slight occasion to terminate a peace which gave any thing but repose and quietness to the parties that professed to observe it; and to cause a war which involved the destiny of the contestants in its issues, and the possession of empires in its fortunes.

The seizure of English fur traders by the French; the establishment, by the latter, of military posts on the Ohio, and refusal to surrender them on the demand of the colonial authorities, in 1753; the expedition conducted by WASHINGTON* to the western frontiers of Virginia,—and the skirmishes he had with the French and Indians in the Great Meadows, in 1754; the extensive preparations made by both parties for active campaigns; the expeditions planned by the English against forts Du Quesne, Crown Point and Niagara; the forcible expulsion of the French from Nova Scotia; the repulse and death of Col. EPHRAIM WILLIAMS, by Baron DIESKAU, and the final overthrow of the latter by Sir WILLIAM JOHNSON, at the battle of lake George; the occupation and fortification of Ticonderoga by the French, in 1755, were the principal events that took place in the wide and extended field of operations, before the two contending nations, with their savage allies, began to struggle in earnest for the undivided possessions they had respectively claimed, within the more immediate region of our researches.

---

* The venerated name of the Father of his Country, is here first incident to our narrative. The reader who has not had the opportunity of admiring Mr. Bancroft's beautiful introduction of it into his pages, will thank us for embracing it in a note. He has seized upon an earlier occasion, and other than a military advent, but his admirable episode is so framed as to admit of being appropriately blended with the events we are tracing:—" At the very time of the congress of Aix la Chapelle, the woods of Virginia sheltered the youthful GEORGE WASHINGTON, the son of a widow. Born by the side of the Potomac, beneath the roof of a Westmoreland farmer, almost from infancy his lot had been the lot of an orphan. No Academy had welcomed him to its shades, no College crowned him with its honors:—to read, to write, to cypher—these had been his degrees in knowledge. And now at sixteen years of age, in quest of an honest maintenance, encountering intolerable toil; cheered by being able to write to a school-boy friend, 'Dear Richard, a doubloon is my constant gain every day, and sometimes six pistoles;' 'himself, his own cook, having no spit but a forked stick, no plate but a large chip;' roaming over the spurs of the Alleghanies, and along the banks of the Shenandoah; alive to nature, and sometimes 'spending the best of the day in admiring the trees and the richness of the land;' among skin clad savages, their scalps and rattles, or uncouth emigrants 'that would never speak English,' rarely sleeping in a bed; holding a bear skin a splendid couch; glad of a resting place at night upon a little hay, straw or fodder, and often camping in the forests, where the place nearest the fire was a happy luxury;—this stripling surveyor in the woods, with no companion but his unlettered associates, and no implements of service but his compass and chain, contrasted strongly with the imperial magnificence of the congress of Aix la Chapelle. And yet God had selected, not Kaunitz nor Newcastle, not a monarch of the house of Hapsburgh, nor of Hanover, but the Virginia stripling, TO GIVE AN IMPULSE TO HUMAN AFFAIRS, AND AS FAR AS EVENTS CAN DEPEND UPON AN INDIVIDUAL, HAD PLACED THE RIGHTS AND DESTINIES OF COUNTLESS MILLIONS IN THE KEEPING OF THE WIDOW'S SON."

Governor SHIRLEY of Massachusetts, who commanded the English forces destined to attack forts Niagara and Frontenac, after much delay, embarrassment and a tedious march through the wilderness, arrived at Oswego, the 21st of August, 1755. Having ascertained that the garrison in the fort was reduced to about sixty French soldiers, and one hundred Indians, but was in daily expectation of reinforcements, the British General made every exertion in his power to attack it immediately. But his scanty means of transportation, the desertion of batteau men, the scarcity of wagons on the Mohawk river, and the desertion of sledge men at the great carrying place, the slow and lingering conveyance of provisions and military stores, occupied about four weeks. The council of war that Gov. SHIRLEY assembled on the 18th of September, recommended that an attempt be made on Fort Niagara. Six hundred regulars were drafted for that object. The artillery and military stores were first put on board the Sloop *Ontario*, part of the provision on another vessel, and the remainder were to be transported in small row boats. The long and drenching rains that now set in, rendered it dangerous to attempt a venture upon the lake before the 26th of the month. Orders to embark were promptly given, but it was found impossible to execute them. Winds from the west blew violently, followed by a rain which lasted thirteen days. Sickness and disease then rapidly began to diminish the strength and numbers of the army, and the Indians to desert. The season for active operations was now far gone. Another council of war was held on the 27th, which resulted in a determination to put off the expedition until next year. Col. MERCER was left at Oswego with a garrison of seven hundred men, with orders to erect two new forts for the better protection of the place. Gov. SHIRLEY returned with the rest of his army.

Thus this expedition, like the others that had been planned, and were to be carried on by the skill and bravery, experience and prudence of the combined colonial and English forces, ended in disaster and failure; to be followed by a brilliant triumph of the arms of France, when she should again make this place the scene of bloody conflict, level to the ground the battlements which England had raised, under the brave but finally unfortunate Marquis de MONTCALM.

Though open hostilities had existed for two years, war was not formally declared by Great Britian until the 17th of May, 1756. France not only persevered in her encroachments, but sent out a large armament with troops and munitions of war. Every hope that the questions of dispute could be amicably settled was now gone. The court of France endeavored to conceal and cover their real designs by the most solemn assurances of pacific sentiments and intentions. To do this more effectually, their ambassador at the court of St. James was deceived, and while he was instructed to give the most positive pledges of the friendship of France, orders were at the same time transmitted to the French authorities in Canada still to strengthen and hold their posts at all hazards. France, true to her policy of erecting a barrier beyond which English territorial authority should not go in North America, was pursuing a similar policy at the same time in India. It soon became inevitable that the fortunes of war must decide the destinies of both nations, so far, at least, as concerned their colonial possessions on the eastern portions of this continent.

MONTCALM, the successor of DIESKAU, as commander in chief of the French forces of Canada, led an army of five thousand men, composed of regulars, militia and Indians, against Oswego, and invested the English fort there. On the 12th. of August, at midnight, after the completion of every necessary arrangement, with thirty-two pieces of artillery besides howitzers and mortars, he opened a terrible cannonade from his trenches. The small amount of ammunition the garrison had, having been exhausted, Col. MERCER, the commanding officer, spiked his guns, abandoned the fort, retreated across the river without the loss of a single man, and took position in Little Fort Oswego. MONTCALM immediately entered the deserted fort, and from it he poured a destructive fire upon the English, during which Col. MERCER was killed. Dismayed at the loss of their commanding officer, defeated in an effort to open a communication with Fort George, (situated about four miles up the river, under the command of Gen. SCHUYLER,) the English offered to capitulate on the 14th, on condition that they should not be plundered by the Indians, but treated with humanity. The two regiments that surrendered amounted to about one thousand four hundred men. A large quantity of military stores and provisions, one hundred and twenty-one pieces of artillery, and fourteen mortars, fell into the hands of the French. As soon as MONTCALM was in possession of both forts, he ordered them to be demolished and destroyed, in the presence of his enemies and allies. Then was enacted a tragedy, as contrary to every sentiment of humanity, as it was in violation of the faith that had been pledged to prevent it. MONTCALM, against his promise and treaty, gave twenty of his prisoners to the custody and tortures of his savage allies, as victims for an equal number of Indians that had been killed during the siege. The rest of the prisoners were also exposed to the insults of the French Indian allies.

When these calamitous events became known, the British authorities abandoned all plans of further offensive operations that season, which was then nearly passed. The high and splendid anticipations, that the campaign would end in a series of brilliant achievments, were all disappointed, and a feeling of gloom and despondency followed, in the English colonies.

Thus was struck down the red cross of St. GEORGE, to float no more over these chequered scenes of desolation and conflict, where many a brave and gallant youth found an untimely grave, until it waved triumphantly over the then entire northern portion of the continent that rallied around a hostile standard—each of which, ere long, in its turn—even before that generation passed away—when friends turned oppressors, and enemies became allies—was to give place to another banner, that was not then in existence,—its emblematic stars had not yet risen above the horizon of empires;—but which is now the banner of a nation great and glorious, alike in the arts of war, and the far nobler arts of peace.

The victories of the French gave them command of lake Champlain and lake George. Their success at Oswego confirmed their control over the western Lakes, and the valley of the Mississippi. Their occupation of Fort Du Quesne, enabled them to cultivate the friendship, and continue their influence over the Indians west of the Alleghanies. Their line of communication reached from Canada to Louisiana, and they were masters of the vast territories that spread out beyond it. Their supremacy upon this continent was now at its zenith; henceforward all change tended to decline and final dispossession. The time speedily came, when the victors were to be vanquished, and their dominions ruled by their enemies.

In 1758, WILLIAM PITT, afterwards Earl of Chatham, was at the head of the British ministry. Soon every department of the public service felt the animating influence of his commanding and lofty spirit. His energetic and vigorous measures inspired hope and confidence at home and abroad. The brave soldiers who had been so often humbled in defeat, kindled with ardor for an opportunity to assert their title to honor and fame, and have a share in the glorious deeds which the future promised. Incompetent commanders were re-called, and officers of military genius and experience succeeded them. Three expeditions were planned. Louisburg was again captured. The French deserted Fort Du Quesne on the approach of an English army. That against Crown Point and Ticonderoga alone was defeated, and relinquished; but out of its failure arose the successful expedition against Fort Frontenac, at the suggestion of Colonel BRADSTREET, who commanded it.

At the head of about three thousand men, with eight cannon and three mortars, Col. BRADSTREET left the camp of the defeated army, which had retreated to its former position on the south side of lake George. Arriving at Oswego, he lost no time in embarking his men. Crossing the lake, he landed about one mile from the fort, on the evening of August 25th.* He urged forward his preparations for an attack with such rapidity, that within two days, he opened his batteries so near the French works as to make every discharge produce an effect. The French commander; deserted by his Indian allies, and satisfied that his capture was inevitable, surrendered at discretion, on the 27th. One hundred and ten prisoners, nine vessels, sixty cannon, sixteen mortars, a large number of light arms, great quantities of military stores, provisions, and merchandise, were taken. The fort was dismantled and demolished. The vessels and such other things as could not be carried away, were destroyed. Col. BRADSTREET then marched his detachment back and joined the main army.

The success of this expedition aided that which was marching

---

* Fort Frontenac is thus described in the "Journals of Major Robert Rogers," an officer justly distinguished as a daring and skillful commander of a company of "Rangers," who visited it soon after it was taken by the English:

"This fort was square faced, had four bastions with stone, and was near three-quarters of a mile in circumference. Its situation was very beautiful, the banks of the river presenting, on every side, an agreeable landscape, with a fine prospect of lake Ontario, which was distant about a league, interspersed with many Islands that were well wooded, and seemingly beautiful. The French had formerly a great trade at this fort with the Indians, it being erected on purpose to prevent their trading with the English, but it is now totally destroyed."

against Du Quesne. French re-inforcements from Niagara and Frontenac, could not now come. Conscious of their inability to dispute successfully the possession of the fort, with a force so formidable as that of the English, the French voluntarily abandoned it, silently passing down the Ohio river. With them also departed the powerful influence they had long exercised over the surrounding Indian nations, never again to be revived. No sooner was the British flag floating over the embattlements France had raised, than they called councils, and entered into treaties of peace and alliance with the British. The Indians said that the Great Spirit, having deserted the French, would no more protect them, and would be angry with all who helped them. The French line of communication between the northern and southern extremities of their possessions was now effectually broken. The reverse which took place in the fortunes of the contending nations, was not more striking, than was the change of feeling manifested by the different parties, at the close of the campaign.

In 1759, Major General AMHERST succeeded as commander of the British forces in North America. The success which had attended the British arms, encouraged the adoption of measures which contemplated the entire conquest of Canada. The three strong positions still held by the French were all to be attacked at the same time. General JAMES WOLF, who had distinguished himself at Louisburg, was to besiege Quebec. General AMHERST was to march against Ticonderoga, and Crown Point, and after taking those places, cross lake Champlain, and join WOLF. General PRIDEAUX, accompanied by Sir WILLIAM JOHNSON, was to command the expedition against Fort Niagara. General STANWIX commanded a detachment, which was to watch and guard lake Ontario, and reduce the remaining French posts on the Ohio.

Early in the spring, Gen. AMHERST established his head-quarters at Albany, where he concentrated his forces about the end of May. The summer was well advanced before he was able to cross lake George. He reached Ticonderoga, July 22d. When he was ready to open his batteries on the French, who appeared determined to defend this position, he suddenly discovered that after blowing up their magazines and doing all the injury they could, the enemy had retreated during the night, to Crown Point. The British took possession of the fort without firing a gun, the next day. After reparing its damaged fortifications, Gen. AMHERST proceeded to Crown Point. On his approach the French retired before him, and took up a position on the Isle Aux Noix, at the northern end of lake Champlain. At that point the French force was about three thousand five hundred strong. They had a large train of artillery and four armed vessels. Gen. AMHERST was anxious to dislodge them, but this could not be done without a naval force able to meet the enemy's. He hastily built two boats, and succeeded in destroying two belonging to the French. The season was now far gone. In October he fixed his winter quarters at Crown Point, and employed the time in repairing the works there and at Ticonderoga.

The arrangements for the expedition against Fort Niagara having been completed, General PRIDEAUX, with an army composed of European and Provincial troops and Indians, marched to Oswego, coasted along the southern shore of lake Ontario, and without opposition landed at the mouth of the Four Mile creek on the 6th of July.

The author derives the following minute accounts of the investment and final capture of Fort Niagara, from files of the Maryland Gazette, published at Baltimore at that early period of newspaper enterprise in the American colonies, that have been perserved in the archives of the Maryland Historical Society. The preceding accounts, it will be observed, are from English sources, in the form of letters from correspondents, and items of news by the editor, derived either from New York and Philadelphia papers, or from correspondents in those cities. The heading to the account that follows, is sufficiently explanatory of the source from which it is derived. Taken altogether, the reader will probably conclude that it is a much better account of this locally important military enterprise, than has before been incorporated in history. The author adopts the accounts as he finds them in the ancient newspaper files, believing that a cotemporary relation of the events will be far more interesting to the reader, than any he could derive from other sources:

"NIAGARA, July 25th, 1759.

"Yesterday morning a party of French and Indians, consisting of 1500, of which 400 were Indians, about 8 o'clock, came upon our right, where a breast-work was thrown up, as we had intelligence of their coming; and as ten of our people were crossing the lake above, they began to fire on them, which gave our people time to get all their piquets, the 46th regiment, part of the 44th, 100 New Yorkers, 600 Indians, ready to oppose them: we waited and received their fire five or six times, before our people returned it, which they did at about 30 yards distance, then jumped over their breast-work, and closed in with them, upon which they immediately gave way and broke; their Indians left them, and for a while we made a vast slaughter. The whole being defeated, the prisoners were brought in, among which were above 16 or 17 officers, several of distinction, and about 60 or 70 men; the whole field was covered with their dead. After the General took the names of all the officers taken, he sent Major HARVEY, by the desire of Monsieur D'AUBREY, the commanding officer of the whole party, to the commanding officer of the fort, who disputed his having them, and kept Major HARVEY in the fort, and sent an officer to the General; when they found it was true, and all their succors cut off, they began to treat on conditions of surrender, which continued till near 8 o'clock in the evening before they were concluded; however, our grenadiers, with the train, marched in this morning, and the whole garrison was surrendered to Sir WILLIAM JOHNSON, who succeeded to the command after the death of General PRIDEAUX.

"The ordnance stores found in the Fort at Niagara when Gen. JOHNSON took possession of it, were two 14 pounders; 19 twelve pounders; one eleven pounder; 7 eight pounders; 7 six pounders; 2 four pounders; 5 two pounders — all iron: 1500 round 12 pound shot; 40,000 pound musket ball; 200 weight of match; 500 hand grenades; 2 cohorns and 2 mortars, mounted; 300 bill-axes [?]; 500 hand hatchets; 100 axes; 300 shovels; 400 pick-axes; 250 mattocks; [hoes]; 54 spades: 12 whip-saws, and a considerable number of small arms, swords, tomahawks, scalping-knives, cartouch-boxes, &c.

A letter from Niagara, dated July 25th, has the following particulars:—

"Your old friend Sir WILLIAM JOHNSON, has gained immortal honor in this affair. The army have the highest opinion of him, and the Indians adore him, as his conduct has been steady and judicious; he has carried on the siege with spirit. The Mohawks have done wonders, serving in the trenches and every place where Sir WILLIAM was."

We are informed, that upon Gen. AMHERST's receiving the news of the death of Brigadier Gen. PRIDEAUX, he immediately appointed Brigadier General GAGE, of the Light Infantry, commander-in-chief of the forces before Niagara; and that Gen. GAGE was at Albany, when the orders from Gen. AMHERST came to him; but it was impossible for him to reach Niagara before it surrendered to Sir WILLIAM JOHNSON. Col. HALDIMAN, we are told, embarked from Oswego for Niagara, the very day it surrendered, the 24th ult.

All the prisoners taken at Niagara, amounting in the whole to about 800, are coming down to this city [*i. e.* New York], and are on their way; so that we may expect them every day. The women and children taken in the fort, Gen. JOHNSON has sent to Montreal, we are told.

From Oswego we have the following interesting intelligence, dated July 28th, 1759:

"This day Lieutenant MONCRIEF, aid-de-camp to the late Gen. PRIDEAUX, arrived here from Niagara, which he left the 26th instant, on his way to Gen. AMHERST. From the said gentleman we have the following particulars, viz:—That after the melancholy accident of the 20th, which carried off the General, the command of the army devolving on Sir WILLIAM JOHNSON, he continued to pursue the late General's vigorous measures, and erected his third battery within 100 yards of the flag bastion; having intelligence from his Indians, of a large party being on their march from the Falls to relieve the fort, Sir WILLIAM made a disposition to prevent them. The 23d, in the evening, he ordered the Light Infantry, and picquets of the lines, to lie near the road on our left, leading from the Falls to the fort; these he reinforced in the morning of the 24th, with the Grenadiers, and part of the 46th regiment, all under the command of Lieut. Col. MASSEY: Lieut. Col. FARQUAR, with the 44th battalion, was ordered to the tail of the trenches, to support the guard of the trenches, commanded by Major BECKWITH. About eight in the morning our Indians advanced to speak to the French Indians, which the enemy declined. The action began soon after, with screams, as usual, from the enemy; but our troops were so well disposed to receive them in front, and our Indians on their flanks, that in less than an hour's time their whole army was ruined. The number of the slain was not ascertained, as the pursuit was continued for three miles. Seventeen officers were made prisoners, among whom are Monsieur D'AUBREY, chief in command, wounded; Monsieur de LIGNERY, second in command, wounded also; Monsieur MARINI, leader of the Indians; Monsieur de VILLIE, REPENTINI, MARTINI, and BASONC, all captains, and several others.* After this defeat, which was in sight of the garrison, Sir WILLIAM sent Major HARVEY into the fort, with a list of the officers taken, recommending it to the commanding officer to surrender before more blood was shed, and while he had it in his power to restrain the Indians. The commanding officer, to be certain of such a defeat, sent an officer of his to see the prisoners; they were shown to him; and, in short, the capitulation was finished about ten at night of the 24th, by which the garrison surrendered, with the honors of war, which Lieutenant MONCRIEF saw embarked the morning he came away, to the number of 607 private men, exclusive of the officers and their ladies, and those taken in the action. We expect them here to-morrow on their way to New York.

Saturday afternoon an express arrived in town [New York City] from Albany, which place he left about 6 o'clock on Thursday morning, with the following agreeable news, which was brought to Albany a few hours before, from Sir WILLIAM JOHNSON at Niagara, viz:—That on the 24th of July, as Sir WILLIAM lay before the fort of Niagara, with the forces under his command, besieging it, he received intelligence by a party of his Indians that were sent out on a scout, that there was a large body of French and Indians, coming from Venango, as a reinforcement to the garrison of Niagara. Gen. JOHNSON thereupon ordered 600 chosen men from the 44th and 46th regiments, 100 New York provincials, and 600 Mohawks, Senecas, &c. to march immediately, and way lay them, which they accordingly did, and threw up a breast-work at a place where they knew the French must pass by on their way to the fort; and sent a batteau with 10 or 12 men down the river a little way, to fire when the enemy were near at hand, which would give them warning to prepare themselves for their reception; and in a short time after their breast-work was finished, they heard the alarm given by the batteau, that was sent forward, on which they all prepared themselves to receive the enemy, each man having two balls and three buck-shot in his gun, and were squatted. However, the enemy perceived them in their entrenchment, and fired six times on them before our people returned the fire; but as soon as the enemy came close, all the English rose up and discharged their pieces, which made the utmost slaughter imaginable among them, and repeated their fire three times, when the enemy's Indians that were left alive, left them; immediately upon which our people jumped over their breast-work, and flew on the enemy, sword in hand, still continuing to make great slaughter among them, and took 120 prisoners, among which were 17 officers, some of which are of distinction, with their chief commander. The havoc we made at the end was great, 500 of the enemy at least being left on the field of

---

* The battle ground is a mile and a half below the Five Mile Meadows, at a place called Bloody Run. Skulls and other human bones, bill-axes, pieces of muskets, &c., were strewn over the ground there, long after the settlement of the country commenced.

battle. Those that could, made their escape, and went down the river. Upon the return of our troops to Gen. JOHNSON with the prisoners, he immediately sent a flag of truce in to the commander of the fort, and demanded a surrender, telling him of the defeat of the reinforcement he expected; but the French commandant would not give credit to what Gen. JOHNSON said, till he had sent a flag of truce with a drum, into our camp, and found it but too true; and immediately on the officer's return to the fort, the French commandant offered to capitulate, provided Gen. JOHNSON would permit the garrison to march out with all the honors of war, which was agreed to; but that they must immediately, upon their coming out, lay down their arms, and surrender themselves, which they accordingly did; and Gen. JOHNSON took possession of the fort directly after. The garrison consisted of 607 men, among which were 16 officers, 7 of which were captains, besides the chief commander, and we hear they are shortly after their surrender, embarked on board of batteaux, and sent up to Oswego, and from thence were to be sent down to New York, and may be expected here every day. The number of our killed and wounded in the defeat of the reinforcement from Venango, we cannot as yet justly ascertain, but there were five of the New Yorkers among the slain in that affair. It is said we had not lost 40 men in the whole, since the landing of the troops at Niagara. The Indians were allowed all the plunder in the fort, and found a vast quantity of it, some say to the value of £300 a man. The fort, it is said, is large enough to contain 1000 fighting men, without inconvenience; all the buildings in and about it are standing, and in good order; and it is thought, had our forces stormed the place (which was intended) they would have met with a warm reception; and beating the Venango party, will undoubtedly crown with laurels the ever deserving JOHNSON '"*

From the Maryland Gazette, Aug. 23d, 1759: Under Philadelphia head, Aug. 16th:

By a letter from Niagara, of the 21st. ult. [?], we learn that by the assiduity and influence of Sir William JOHNSON, there were upwards of eleven hundred Indians convened there, who, by their good behaviour, have justly gained the esteem of the whole army: That Sir William being informed the enemy had buried a quantity of goods on an Island, about twenty miles from the fort, sent a number of Indians to search for them, who found to the value of eight thousand pounds, and were in hopes of finding more, and that a French vessel, entirely laden with beaver, had foundered on the Lake, where her crew, consisting of forty-one men, were all lost.†

From the Maryland Gazette, Thursday, Aug. 30, 1759.

"NEW YORK, August 20, 1759.

JOURNAL OF THE SIEGE OF NIAGARA, TRANSLATED FROM THE FRENCH:

Friday, July 6, 1759. About seven at night a soldier, who was hunting, came with all diligence to acquaint Monsieur POUCHOT, that he had discovered at the entrance

---

* The following eloquent description of the battle scene upon the river bank, occurs in Graham's Colonial History: — "The French Indians having raised the fierce, wild yell, called the war-whoop, which by this time had lost its appalling effects on the British soldiers, the action began by an impetuous attack from the enemy; and while the neighboring Cataract of Niagara, pealed forth to inattentive ears, its everlasting *voice of many waters*, the roar of artilley, the shrieks of the Indians, and all the martial clang and dreadful revelry of a field of battle, mingled in wild chorus with the majestic music of nature."

† Some may be disposed to infer that the anchor, cannon, &c. which the author has assumed, were those of the Griffin, are as likely to have belonged to the shipwrecked vessel here spoken of. But forty-six years intervened between the loss of this vessel, and the finding of the relics near the mouth of the Eighteen Mile creek; not a sufficient period to allow of the appearance those relics presented: the anchor deeply embedded in sand and gravel, the timber growth, &c.

of the wood, a party of savages, and that they had even fired on some other hunters. Mons. POUCHOT immediately sent M. SELVIERT, Captain in the regiment of Rousillon, at the head of one picquet, a dozen Canadian volunteers preceded them, and on their coming to the edge of the woods, a number of Indians fired upon them which they returned, and were obliged to retire. They took Messrs. FURNACE and ALOQUE, Interpreters of the Iroquois, two Canadians, and two other gentlemen. They made another discharge and retired. Monsieur POUCHOT fired some cannon upon them. Mons. SELVIERT lay all night, with 100 men, in the Demilune,* and the rest of the garrison was under arms on the ramparts till midnight.

Saturday, July 7th. We perceived 7 barges on the Lake, a league and a half distance from the fort; we judged by that it was the English come to besiege us: Mons. POUCHOT ordered the general to be beat, and employed all hands to work on the batteries, to erect embrasures,† all being *en barbet* ‡ before. He immediately despatched a courier to Mons. CHEVERT, to give him notice of what happened; he also sent out Monsieur LA FORCE,|| Captain of the Schooner Iroquois, to destroy the English barges where he could find them. All that day several savages showed themselves on the edge of the desert. Monsieur LA FORCE fired several cannon shot at them; and perceived they were working at an entrenchment at the Little Swamp,¶ which is a league and a half from the fort. The guards this night as the night before.

Sunday, 8th July. The schooner continued to cruise and fire on the English camp. About nine in the morning, an English officer brought a letter from Brigadier PRIDEAUX, to Mons. POUCHOT, to summons him, proposing him all advantages and good treatment, all which he very politely refused, and even seemed to be unwilling to receive the English General's letter. The remainder of this day the English made no motions.

[There is no entry for Monday.]

Tuesday, 10th. At 2 o'clock all our men were on the ramparts, and at day-break we perceived they had opened their trenches, at the entrance of the wilderness, at about three hundred toises from the fort; we made a very hot fire upon them all day. M. CHABOURT arrived with the garrison of the Little Fort,§ and seven or eight savage

---

* The work in front of the curtain or main breast-work.

† A narrow orifice through which the cannon is fired.

‡ In a condition to allow of cannon being fired over them.

|| We first hear of this early navigator upon lake Ontario, in Washington's diary of his mission to the Ohio, in 1753. He accompanied him in a part of his tour, and in the ensuing spring was captured and sent a prisoner to Williamsburg. He was the French leader and Indian negotiator in the early contest between the French and English in the neighborhood of Fort Du Quesne, (Pittsburgh). He was the JONCAIRE of that region, though not as successful, as was the adopted son of the Senecas. He broke jail at Williamsburg, and going at large, excited terror among the border settlers of Virginia, by whom he was regarded as a dangerous ally of the Indians. In his attempted escape, he was arrested by a back woods-man, who resisted his offers of wealth and preferment, and conveyed him back to prison, where he was loaded with a double weight of irons and chained to the floor of his dungeon. Washington, hearing of the hard fate of his old acquaintance, remonstrated with Gov. DINWIDDIE, but failed to excite his sympathies. LA FORCE remained in prison two years. The next we hear of him, he is captain of the "Schooner Iroquois" on lake Ontario. Cruising on the lake, he escaped the fate of his countrymen at Niagara.

¶ The Little Swamp is forty rods west of the mouth of the Four Mile Creek. Some of the remains of the battery are still there.

§ At Schlosser

Iroquois and Missagoes. Monsieur POUCHOT went to palisade the ditches: The service as usual, only the addition of two officers to lie in the covered way. About 11 o'clock at night, orders were given to make all the picquets fire from the covered way, to hinder the workmen of the enemy. M. LA FORCE sent his boat on shore for Monsieur POUCHOT's orders.

Wednesday, 11*th July*. The works continue on both sides. At noon a party of about fifteen men, soldiers and militia, went very nigh the trenches of the enemy, and perceived them sally out between four and five hundred, who came towards them at a quick pace, but they were stopped by our cannon. They began on the other side of the swamp, which is the left of their trench, another about twenty yards; and at 5 o'clock they began to play two Grenadoe Royal Mortars. At 6 o'clock two savages of the Five Nations, who were invited by one CAYENDESSE, of their nation, came to speak to Monsieur POUCHOT; the firing ceased on both sides during this parley. At 10 o'clock we began to fire again, and then we found the English had eight mortars.

Night between the 11*th and* 12*th*. The enemy ran their parallel from their first trench to the lake side, where it seemed they intended to establish a battery. At two in the afternoon, [of the 12th, doubtless,] four chiefs of the Five Nations came to us on parole, and said they were going to retire to Belle Famille. The enemy wrought the rest of that day, and perfected their night's work. Monsieur LA FORCE had orders to proceed to Frontenac, and to return immediately. In the night between the 12th and 13th they fired many bombs. I went with thirty men to observe where the enemy wrought.

Friday, 13*th July*. A canoe arrived from Monsieur DE VILLE, to hear how we stood at this post (or rather for the Canada post.) The enemy threw a great many bombs all this day, and continued to work to perfect their trenches: we fired a great many cannon shot. Many of their savages crossed the river, and desired to speak with us; there were but two of those nations with us. I went out with five volunteers, to act as the night before. The enemy fired no bombs till about midnight.

Saturday, 14*th July*. At day-break we found they had prolonged their trenches to the lake shore, in spite of the great fire from our cannon and musketry, during the night, and perfected it during the day time; they have placed four mortars and thrown many bombs. All our garrison lay in the covered way, and on the ramparts.

Sunday, 15*th July*. In the morning we perceived they had finished their works begun the night before. During the night they threw three hundred bombs; the rest of the day and night they threw a great many, but did not incommode us in any shape.

Monday, 16*th July*. At dawn of day we spied, about half a league off, two barges, at which we discharged some cannon, on which they retired. In the course of the day they contined to throw some bombs. They have already disabled us about twenty men. All our men lie on beaver, or in their clothes, and armed. We do what we can to incommode them with our cannon.

Tuesday, 17*th July*. Until six this morning we had a thick fog, so that we could not discern the works of the enemy; but it clearing a little up, we saw they had raised a battery of three pieces of cannon, and four mortars on the other side of the river; they began to fire about 7 A. M., and Monsieur POUCHOT placed all the guns he could against them: The fire was brisk on both sides all day, they seemed most inclined to batter the house where the Commandant lodges. The service as usual for the night.

Wednesday, 18*th July*. There was a great firing as on the preceding day; we had one soldier dismembered, and four wounded by their bombs.

Thursday, 19*th July*. At dawn of day we found the enemy had begun a parallel eighty yards long in front of the fort. The fire was very great on both sides. At 2 P.

M. arrived the Schooner Iroquois, from Frontenac, and laid abreast of the fort, waiting for a calm, not being able to get in, the enemy having a battery on the other side of the river. Monsieur POUCHOT will have the boat on shore as soon as the wind falls.

Friday, 20th July. The English have made a third parallel, towards the lake; they are to-day about one hundred and sixty yards from the fort. They cannot have worked quietly at the Sappe, having had a great fire of musketry all night long, which they were obliged to bear. During the day they made a great firing with their mortars, and they perfected their works begun the night of the 19th to the 20th. We had one man killed, and four wounded. The fire of the musketry was very hot on both sides till eleven at night, when the enemy left off, and we continued ours all night. Two canoes were sent on board the schooner, which are to go to Montreal and Tironto.

Saturday, 21st. During the night the enemy made a fourth parallel, which is about one hundred yards from the fort, in which it appears they will erect a battery for a breach in the flag bastion. They have hardly fired any cannon or bombs in the day, which gives room to think they are transporting their cannon and artillery from their old battery to their new one. The service as usual. Their battery on the other side fired but little in the day. The schooner went off to see two canoes over to Tironto, one of which is to post to Montreal, and from thence she is to cruise off Oswego, to try to stop the enemy's convoys when on their way. The company of volunteers are always to pass the night in the covered way.

Sunday, 22d. All the night was a strong conflict on both sides. We had one man killed by them and by our own cannon. We fired almost all our cannon with cartridges. They worked in the night to perfect all their works begun the night before. The enemy began to fire red-hot balls in the night; they also fired fire-poles.* All day they continued at work to establish their batteries. They fired, as usual, bombs and cannon. The service as usual for the night of the 22d and 23d. They worked hard to perfect their batteries, being ardently sustained by their musketry.

Monday, 23d. We added two pieces of cannon to the bastion of the lake, to oppose those of the enemy's side. At 8 A. M. four savages brought a letter from Monsieur AUBREY to Monsieur POUCHOT, by which we learn, that he has arrived at the Great Island,† before the Little Fort, at the head of twenty-five hundred, half French and half savages. Monsieur POUCHOT immediately sent back four savages with the answer to Monsieur AUBREY's letter, informing him of the enemy's situation. These savages, before they came in, spoke to the Five Nations, and gave them five belts to engage them to retire from the enemy. They saw part of the enemy's camp, and told us the first or second in command was killed by one of our bullets, and two of their guns broken and one mortar. We have room to hope, that with such success we may oblige the enemy to raise the siege, with the loss of men, and as they take up much ground, they must be beat, not being able to rally quick enough. At 2 P. M. they unmasked another battery of —— pieces of cannon, three of which were eighteen-pounders, the others twelve and six. They began with a brisk fire, which continued two hours, then slackened. About 5 P. M. we saw a barge go over to Belle Famille, on the other side of the river, and some motions made there. One of the four savages which went off this morning, returned his Porcelain (*i. e.* wampum), he had nothing new. The service of the night as usual. We worked hard to place two pieces, twelve-pounders, on the middle of the curtains, to bear upon their battery.

---

* Fire-balls.

† Navy Island, which the French may have regarded as but a continuation of "Great" or Grand Island

Tuesday, 24th July. The enemy began their fire abount 4 o'clock this morning, and continued to fire with the same vivacity the rest of the day. At 8 A. M. we perceived our army was approaching, having made several discharges of musketry at Belle Famille. At 9 the fire began on both sides, and lasted half an hour. We wait to know who has the advantage of those two. At 2 P. M. we heard by a savage, that our army was routed, and almost all made prisoners, by the treachery of our savages: when immediately the English army had the pleasure to inform us of it, by summoning us to surrender."

The above with some letters, were found in an embrasure, after we were in possesssion of the fort, since which, translated, and the original given to Sir WILLIAM JOHNSON.

Since our last seven sloops arrived here [N. Y.] from Albany, with about six hundred and forty French prisoners, officers included, being the whole of the garrison of Niagara. Among the officers are Monsieur POUCHOT, who was commander-in-chief of the fort, and Monsieur VILLARS, both captains, and knights of the order of St. Louis. There are ten other officers, one of which is the famous Monsieur JOINCŒUR, a very noted man among the Seneca Indians, and whose father was the first that hoisted French colours in that country. His brother, also a prisoner, is now here, and has been very humane to many Englishmen, having purchased several of them from the savages."

While British arms were achieving victories at Ticonderoga, Crown Point, Frontenac, Du Quesne, and Niagara, Gen. WOLFE was at the same time, vigorously carrying forward his operations before Quebec. In the midst of his exertions, he received intelligence of the capture of Niagara and the retreat of the French before Gen. AMHERST. The advanced period of the season, the strong French force at the isle Aux Noix, satisfied WOLFE that the union of the force under Gen. AMHERST with that under himself, could not take place. Neither was it probable that Sir WILLIAM JOHNSON would be able to march against Montreal, to divide the forces and divert the attention of the French. Notwithstanding all this, WOLFE resolved to continue the siege, make superior caution and daring, activity and bravery supply the place of numbers and strength. Though in body so weak and feeble from the effects of a painful and wasting malady, that he was often confined to his room, Gen. WOLFE, by his cheerful and confident bearing, inspired the minds of all around him with the highest expectation, that under him their brightest hopes would be fully realized—their toils and sufferings be rewarded with the noblest triumph British valor had ever before achieved on the American continent.

With an army of eight thousand men, under a convoy of British vessels, Gen. WOLFE landed on the Isle of Orleans, lying in the St. Lawrence, a few leagues below the city of Quebec, near the close of June, 1759. Here he had a full view of the dangers and embarrassments that he must encounter, and of the bold yet cautious course he would have to adopt and pursue, in order to succeed. Nobly exclaiming that "a victorious army finds no difficulties," WOLFE resolved to hazard every thing to gain every thing. With the hope that MONTCALM, the French commander, might be induced to change his strong and well chosen position and enter into a general engagement, WOLFE brought about the battle of Montmorency, and was repulsed with the loss of five hundred of his best men. At this critical juncture, the daring resolution was made to carry on all future operations above the town. At the greatest risk and the most imminent danger, by a bold and master movement, the English finally gained the Heights of Abraham, which overlooked and commanded the city. So great were the astonishment and surprise of MONTCALM, when first informed of this sudden change of the enemy's position, that he refused to believe it possible. He saw that a fatal battle could not much longer be avoided—a battle that inevitably would decide the fate of the empire of France in America—and he made his preparations accordingly. An engagement soon after took place between the two armies, in which the steady, unflinching bravery of the British, and the reckless, impetuous courage of the French were both tried and proved. The English were victorious and to them the French surrendered Quebec—their last remaining strong hold that had not yet fallen into the possession of their enemies.

WOLFE and MONTCALM, the commanding generals, were foemen worthy of each other. The wonderful coincidence and contrast presented in the closing scene of their fortunes and life, have forever blended their memory in glorious union on the Historian's page, the Painter's canvass, and in the Poet's numbers. Both had distinguished themselves during the war—both were in the thickest and fiercest of the battle storm—both led their emulous columns on to the deadly charge—both were mortally wounded and reluctantly carried from the field—both died—one as the shouts of victory were ringing louder and louder in his failing ears, and words of peaceful resignation were falling from his closing lips,—the other, with the fervent aspiration that he might not "live to see the surrender of Quebec," and his country's dominions pass into the hands of his conqueror.

The loss of these two brave and accomplished commanders was deeply lamented and regretted by their respective nations — their names united and honored by their enemies. With what truth and beauty does their kindred fate illustrate, though under widely different circumstances, how often it is,

> "That the paths of glory lead but to the grave."*

Thus triumphantly with the English, ended the campaign of 1759; but not the mutual exertions of the French and English for supremacy over the Indian nations. After the conquest of Quebec, two Indians of the Six Nations, at the suggestion of the English, it is presumed, visited a settlement of their people that had removed to Canada and were in the French interest. They endeavored to persuade their people to make a timely secession from the French, and come home to their own country; telling them that "the English, formerly women, were now all turned into men, and were growing as thick in the country as trees in the woods, that they had taken the French forts at Ohio, Ticonderoga, Louisburg and Quebec, and would soon eat all the French in Canada, and the Indians that adhered to them." The French Indians were incredulous; they said to their visitors: — "Brothers you are decieved; the English cannot eat up the French; their mouths are too little, their jaws too weak, and their teeth not sharp enough. Our father, Yonnondio, has told us, and we believe him, that the English, like a thief have stolen Louisburg and Quebec from the great king, while his back was turned, and he was looking another way; but that he has turned his face, and sees what the English have done, he is going into their country with a thousand great canoes, and all his warriors; and he will take the little English king and pinch him till he makes him cry out and give back what he has stolen, as he did about ten summers ago, and this your eyes will see." The French Indians came near making converts of the English agents. The result of the visit was at least to make the Six Nations more

---

*An affecting incident is related of Gen. Wolfe, which presents his character in the most amiable light. It is said that when Wolfe and his army were noiselessly floating down the St. Lawrence, at midnight, to the place where they were to land and begin their difficult ascent to the Heights above, he, in a low, tender tone, repeated the whole of Gray's plaintive and touching "Elegy in a Country Church Yard," in which occurs the *prophetic* line above quoted; and at the conclusion of it, he remarked:—"Now, gentlemen, I would rather be the author of that poem, than take Quebec." What a noble tribute for a Warrior to render a Poet.

wavering in their adherence to the English, and distrustful as to their final supremacy.

While this war had been waging, as in those that had preceded it, there were frequent incursions of French and Indians to the frontiers of Massachusetts and New Hampshire; but their visits were less sanguinary and barbarous in their character, than those of former years. Bounties were paid, to encourage the Indians to deliver all English prisoners alive.

French determination to maintain their ground, was revived after a short recoil from the capture of their strong hold; and new and large levies of troops were made from the English colonies. No sooner had the English fleet retired from the St. Lawrence than LEVI, who had succeeded MONTCALM, resolved to attempt the recovery of Quebec. In April, 1660 he embarked with a strong army from Montreal, and having by means of armed frigates, the control of the St. Lawrence, he took position at Point au Tremble, within a few miles of Quebec. In a few days, Gen. MURRAY, who had succeeded WOLFE, sallied out and attacked the French in their then position, near Sillery. He retreated, after a severe engagement, and the loss of one thousand men; the French loss still larger. The French soon after, opened trenches against the town, and commenced an effectual fire upon the garrison. It was vigorously resisted, but so well conducted was the siege, that the fate of the English was only decided by a squadron of theirs passing a French armament that had been sent out, and entering before it the mouth of the St. Lawrence. The English ships attacked the French frigates that had come down from Montreal, destroyed a part of them, and obliged the others to retreat up the river. The siege was raised; the whole French army making a hasty and rapid retreat to Montreal.

The Marquis de VAUDREUIL, Governor General of Canada, had fixed his head quarters at Montreal, and resolved to make his last stand for French colonial empire. For this purpose he collected around him the whole force of the French colony. He infused his own spirit, confidence and courage, in the hemmed up colony, cheering the desponding by promises of help and succor from France.

The English in the mean time, were not idle. Arrangements were made for a combined attack on Montreal. A detachment of English troops advanced from Crown Point, and took possession of

Isle Aux Noix. Gen. AMHERST, with an army of about ten thousand regulars and provincials, left the frontiers of New York and advanced to Oswego, when he was joined by a thousand warriors of the Six Nations, under the command of Sir WILLIAM JOHNSON. Embarking on lake Ontario, they arrived at Isle Royal, reducing that post, and proceeding down the St. Lawrence, arrived at Montreal, simultaneously with the command under Gen. MURRAY. Arrangements were made to invest the city with this formidable consolidated army. VAUDREUIL, rightly estimating the strength of his assailants, and his own inability successfully to resist them, resolved upon capitulation. On the day after the arrival of the British army,—the 7th of September, 1760, Montreal, Detroit, and all other places of strength within the government of Canada, were surrendered to the British crown. Gen. MURRAY was appointed Governor of Montreal, and a force left with him of two thousand men; and returning to Quebec, his force was augmented to four thousand.

The French armament, that has before been noticed, on learning that the English had entered the St. Lawrence, took refuge in the Bay of Chaleurs, on the coast of Nova Scotia, where it was soon pursued by a British fleet from Louisburg, and destroyed.

Thus ended the colonial empire of France in North America; or rather its efforts to resist by regular military organizations, fortified forts, &c., English dominion. With the fall of Montreal, they had surrendered all their possessions upon this continent, east of the Mississippi, and beyond that, possession was merely nominal, consisting of but little more than the feeble colony of Louisiana.

Soon after these events, most of the eastern Indian nations inclined to the English, but the anticipated entire alliance and pacific disposition of the Indians around the borders of the western lakes, was not realized. Indian fealty did not follow but partially, the triumph of the English arms. The French had gained a strong hold upon the western Indians, which was not unloosed by the reverses they had encountered. The Indian nations became alarmed at the rapid strides of the English, jealous of its consequences to them, and the French lost no opportunity to increase this feeling, and induce them to believe that the next effort of English ambition and conquest, would be directed to their entire subjugation, if not extermination.

"There was then upon the stage of action, one of those high and heroic men, who stamp their own characters upon the age in which they live, and who appear destined to survive the lapse of time, like some proud and lofty column, which sees crumbling around it, the temples of God and the dwellings of man, and yet rests upon its pedestal, time worn and time honored. This man was at the head of the Indian confederacy, and had acquired an influence over his countrymen, such as had never before been seen, and such as we may not expect to see again. To form a just estimate of his character, we must judge of him by the circumstances under which he was placed; by the profound ignorance and barbarism of his people; by his own destitution of all education and information, and by the jealous, fierce, and intractable spirit of his compeers. When measured by this standard, we shall find few of the men whose names are familiar to us, more remarkable for all they professed and achieved, than PONTIAC. Were his race destined to endure until the mists of antiquity could gather around his days and deeds, tradition would dwell upon his feats, as it has done in the old world, upon all who, in the infancy of nations have been prominent actors, for evil or for good."* PONTIAC was an Ottawa.

Major ROGERS, commanded the British troops that took possession of Detroit under the treaty of capitulation at Montreal. When he was approaching his destination, the ambassadors of this forest king met him and informed him that their sovereign was near by, and that he desired him to halt until he could see him; that the request was in the name of "PONTIAC, the king and lord of the country." Approaching Major ROGERS, PONTIAC demanded his business. An explanation followed, and permission was granted for him and his troops to take the place of the French; acts of courtesy even attending the permission.

This friendly relation was not destined to be permanent. In 1763, PONTIAC had united nearly all the Indian nations of the west, in a confederacy, the design of which, was to expel the English from the country, and restore French ascendancy. "His first object was to gain his own tribe, and the warriors who generally attended him. Topics to engage their attention and inflame their passions were not wanting. A belt was exhibited which he pretended to have received from the king of France, urging him to drive the British from the country, and to open the paths for the return of the French. The British troops had not endeavored

---

* Governor Cass.

to conciliate the Indians, and mutual causes of complaint existed. Some of the Ottawas had been disgraced by blows, but above all, the British were intruders in the country, and would ere long conquer the Indians as they had conquered the French, and wrest from them their lands."* His first step was to convene a large council of the confederates at the river Aux Ecorces. The speech he delivered upon that occasion, was ingeniously framed to further his object. By turns he appealed to the pride of country, the jealousy, the warlike spirit, the superstition, of the assembled councillors. He assumed that the Great Spirit had recently made a revelation to a Delaware Indian, as to the conduct he wished his red children to pursue. He had directed them to "abstain from ardent spirits, and to cast from them the manufactures of the white man. To resume their bows and arrows, and skins of animals for clothing." "Why," said the Great Spirit indignantly, to the Delaware, " do you suffer these dogs in red clothing to enter your country, and take the land I gave you? Drive them from it, and when you are in distress I will help you." The speech had its desired effect. In the month of May following, all things were arranged for a simultaneous atttack upon each of twelve British posts, extending from Niagara to Green Bay, in the north-west, and Pittsburg in the south-west. Nine of these posts were captured. The posts at Niagara and Pittsburg were invested but successfully resisted. Detroit was closely besieged by the forces of PONTIAC, and the siege, and his war generally, was protracted beyond the reception of the news of the treaty of peace between France and England; in fact, until the expedition of Gen. BRADSTREET, of which some account will be given in another place. The incidents of PONTIAC'S war are among the most horrid in Indian war history. The officers and soldiers of most of the captured garrisons were tomahawked and scalped. The details do not come within our range.

A treaty of peace was definitely concluded at Paris, between England and France, on the 10th of February, 1763. To prevent any future disputes as to boundary, it was stipulated, that "the confines between Great Britain and France on the continent of North America should be fixed irrevocably by a line drawn along the centre of the Mississippi, from its source as far as the river

---

* Gov. Cass.

Iberville; and from thence, by a line drawn along the middle of the river, and by the lakes Maurepas and Ponchartrain, to the sea." It was stipulated that the inhabitants of the countries ceded by France, should be allowed the enjoyment of the Roman Catholic faith, and the exercise of its rights as far as might be consistent with the laws of England; that they should retain their civil rights, while they were disposed to remain under the British government, and yet be entitled to dispose of their estates to British subjects, and retire with their produce, without hindrance or molestation to any part of the world.

Never, perhaps, was a treaty of peace more acceptable, or hailed with livelier feelings of joy and congratulation, than was this by the English colonists in America. Harassed through long years, upon all their borders, their young men diverted from the peaceful pursuits of agriculture, to fill the ranks of the army in a long succession of wars, they had been longing for repose. But it was the will of Providence, in directing and controlling the destinies of men — in shaping a higher and more glorious inheritance for the wearied colonists than colonial vassalage — that the repose should be of but short duration. "Amidst the tumultuous flow of pleasure and triumph in America, an intelligent eye might have discerned symptoms, of which a sound regard to British ascendancy required the most cautious, forbearing, and indulgent treatment; for it was manifest that the exultations of the Americans was founded, in no small degree, upon the conviction, that *their own proper strength* was augmented, and that they had attained a state of security which lessened at once their danger from neighboring hostility, and their dependence on the protection, so often delusive and precarious, of the parent state." And few will fail to observe how well calculated were the events we have just been considering, to prepare the sympathies, and shape the policy of France, in the struggle to which this peace was but a prelude.

We have now come to the end of French dominion upon this portion of the continent of North America. The treaty of Paris consummated what the fall of Quebec and Montreal had rendered inevitable. In one chapter, the events of a long period — from 1627 to 1763, one hundred and thirty-six years — have been embraced. How chequered and fluctuating the scene! How full of vicissitudes, of daring adventures, of harassing rivalry, suffering, privation and death! It was the contest of two powerful nations of Europe, for supremacy upon this continent. The stakes for which they were contending, were colonial power, extended dominion and GAIN—the last, the powerful stimulus that urged to the battle field, or prompted the bloody, stealthy assault. How little, the thoughtful reader will say, the rights, the interests, the dignity, the elevation, the freedom of MAN—was involved in this long, almost uninterrupted, sanguinary conflict. Nothing of all this was blended with the motives of the promoters of these wars. The fields of contest, the banks of the St. Lawrence, of the lakes, our own fair, but then wilderness region,—were drenched with some of the best blood of England and France; the colonies of New England sent out those to an untimely grave that would have adorned and strengthened her in a not far off, and more auspicious period. They "bravely fought and bravely fell;" but there was little in the cause in which they were engaged to shed a halo of glory around the memory of its martyrs. And yet remotely, those most unprofitable struggles, (viewed in reference to any immediate result,) were to have an important bearing upon the destiny of our now free, happy, and prosperous Republic.

How slight the causes that often, seemingly, govern great and momentous events! And yet, what finite reason would often construe as accidental, may be the means which Infinite Wisdom puts in requisition to accomplish its high purposes. Had the French fleet gained the mouth of the St. Lawrence before that of the English, Quebec, in all probability, would have been restored to France, and French dominion would have held its own upon this continent, if indeed, with the Indian alliances that the French had secured, and were securing, they had not subjugated the English. Then comes the enquiry whether any of the same causes would have existed under French colonial dominion, that arose under English rule? Some, prominent ones, we know, would not. And yet, in the main, English colonial rule, was more liberal than that of the French. Had the contest for separation and independence been against France, England, as in the reversed case, would not have been the ally of the weaker party, struggling against its deep-seated notions of legitimacy and kingly rule. But it was best as it was; and speculation like this is unprofitable, especially when it can work out in its imaginings no more glorious result, than the one that was realized.

It was during the war with France, that some of the most distinguished officers and soldiers of the Revolution, that commanded and filled the ranks of our armies so skillfully and successfully, rendered their first military services. WASHINGTON fought his first battle at the Great Meadows; he was at BRADDOCK's defeat, where buds of promise appeared, that in a better conflict bloomed and shed abroad their fragrance — their cheering influences, in years of doubt and despondency — their matured and ripened fruit, a cluster of sovereign states, constituting a glorious Union. PUTNAM, the self-taught, rough man of sterling virtues, — New England's bravest, if not most prudent leader, was at Ticonderoga, in 1756; GATES was at BRADDOCK's defeat, as was MORGAN. STARK, afterwards the hero of Bennington, was a captain of Rangers in that war. And who, of middle age, has not listened to the mingled recitals of events of the French war, and the war of the Revolution, coming from the veterans who helped to fill the ranks of the armies of both?

The reader will have observed that the trade in furs and peltry, constituted the main object of French enterprise. The cultivation of small patches of ground around the military and trading posts, and a narrow strip of some twenty miles in length on the Detroit river, constituted mainly the agricultural efforts of the French, in all their long occupancy of this region. They early introduced at Detroit, apple trees, (or seeds,) from the province of Normandy.* The first apples that the pioneer settlers of the Holland Purchase had, come from that source, and from a few trees that had a like origin, at Schlosser, on the Niagara river. The trees at Schlosser are existing, and bearing a very pleasant flavored natural fruit. They are the oldest apple trees in Western New York. Those found in the vicinity of Geneva, Canandaigua, Honeyoye flats, and upon the Genesee river, were either propagated from them, or from seeds given the Seneca Indians by the Jesuit Missionaries.

The Hudson's Bay Company was organized in 1696, by the English. Its operations were confined to the northern regions, but in process of time, its branches came in collision with the French

---

* History of Michigan.

traders upon the lakes. It was a monopoly, opposed not only to French, but to English private enterprise. "The consequences were injurious to the trade, as the time and energies which might have been employed in securing advantages to themselves, were devoted to petty quarrels, and the forest became a scene of brawls, and a battle ground of the contending parties. The war was organized into a system. The traders of the Hudson's Bay Company followed the Canadians to their different posts, and used every method to undermine their power."

During the winter of 1783, the north-west company was established. It was composed principally of merchants who had carried on the trade upon their own individual accounts. For a long period, both companies made vast profits. Some idea of the extent of the trade, may be formed by the following exhibit of the business for one year:—

106,000	Beaver skins,	600	Wolverine skins,
2,100	Bear "	1,650	Fisher "
1,500	Fox "	100	Racoon "
4,000	Kitt Fox "	3,800	Wolf "
4,600	Otter "	700	Elk "
16,000	Muskquash "	750	Deer "
32,000	Martin "	1,200	Deer skins dressed,
1,800	Mink "	500	Buffalo robes, and a
6,000	Lynx "		quantity of Castorum,

"There was necessarily, extensive establishments connected with the trade, such as store-houses, trading-houses, and places of accommodation for the agents and partners of the larger companies. The mode of living on the Grand Portage, on lake Superior, in 1794 was as follows:— The proprietors of the establishment, the guides, clerks, and interpreters, messed together; sometimes to the number of one hundred, in a large hall. Bread, salt pork, beef, butter, venison and fish, Indian corn, potatoes, tea and wine, were their provisions. Several cows were kept around the establishments, which supplied them with milk. The corn was prepared at Detroit by being boiled in a strong alkali, and was called "hominee." The mechanics had rations of this sort of provisions, while the canoe-men had no allowance but melted fat and Indian corn. The dress of the traders, most of whom had been employed under the French government, consisted of a blanket coat, a shirt of striped cotton, trowsers of cloth, or leather leggins, similar to

---

NOTE.—☞ See Hennepin's account of the difficulties of getting the Griffin up the rapids of the Niagara river, page 124. The planting he speaks of must have been near the village of Waterloo, on the Canada side. These were the first seeds planted by Europeans, in all the region west and south of Schenectady and Kingston, and east of the Mississippi.

those of the Indians, moccasins wrought from deer-skins, a red or parti-colored belt of worsted, which contained suspended, a knife and tobacco pouch, and a blue woolen cap or hat, in the midst of which stuck a red feather. Light hearted, cheerful and courteous, they were ever ready to encamp at night among the savages, or in their own wigwams, to join in the dance, or awaken the solitudes of the wilderness with their boat-songs, as they swept with vigorous arm across the bosom of the waters.*

"Even as late as 1810, the island of Mackinaw, the most romantic point on the Lakes, which rises from the altar of a river-god, was the central mart of the traffic, as old Michilimackinac had been a century before. At certain seasons of the year it was made a rendezvous for the numerous classes connected with the traffic. At these seasons the transparent waters around this beautiful island were studded with the canoes of Indians and traders. Here might then be found the merry Canadian voyageur, with his muscular figure strengthened by the hardships of the wilderness, bartering for trinkets along the various booths scattered along its banks. The Indian warrior, bedecked with the most fantastic ornaments, embroidered moccasins and silver armlets; the North-Westers, armed with dirks—the iron men who had grappled with the grizzly bear, and endured the hard fare of the north; and the South-Wester, also put in his claims to deference.†

"Fort William, near the Grand Portage, was also one of the principal ports of the Northwest Company. It was the place of junction, where the leading partners from Montreal met the more active agents of the wilderness to discuss the interests of the traffic. The grand conference was attended with a demi-savage and baronial pomp. The partners from Montreal, clad in the richest furs, ascended annually to that point in huge canoes,

---

* The author is indebted to a friend for the following literal translation, of one of the gay and frivolous, yet characteristic songs of these "forest mariners." It is said even now to be heard occasionally upon our north-western lakes:—

Every spring
So much novelty,
Every lover
Changes his mistress,
Good wine doth not stupefy,
Love awakes me.

Every lover
Changes his mistress,
Let them change who will,
As for me, I'll keep mine,

Good wine doth not stupefy,
Love awakes me.

On my way, I have met,
Three cavaliers, each mounted,
Tol, lol, laridol da,
Tol lol, laridon da.

Three cavaliers, each mounted,
One on horseback, the other on foot,
Tol lol, laridon da,
Tol lol, laridol da.

† The American Fur Company, now in existence, and extending its operations from the shores of the Lakes to those of the Pacific, modelled in its operations somewhat after the old French and English companies, had its trading establishments scattered through the forest.

manned by Canadian voyageurs, and provided with all the means of the most luxurious revelry. The Council-House was a large wooden building, adorned with the trophies of the chase, barbaric ornaments, and decorated implements used by the savages in war and peace. At such periods the post would be crowded with traders from the depths of the wilderness and from Montreal; partners of the Company, clerks, interpreters, guides, and a numerous host of dependents. Discussions of grave import, regarding the interests of the traffic, made up the arguments of such occasions; and the banquet was occasionally interspersed with loyal songs from the Scotch Highlander, or the aristocratic Britain, proud of his country and his king. Such were the general features of a traffic which constituted for a century, under French and English governments, the commerce of the North-western lakes. It was a trade abounding in the severest hardships, and the most hazardous enterprises. This was the most glorious epoch of mercantile enterprise in the forests of the North-west, when its half savage dominion stretched upon the lakes over regions large enough for empires; making barbarism contribute to civilization."*

While the Jesuit missionary, as we have before had occasion to remark, left but feeble traces of his religion to mark his advent—the French traders, other adventurers, and those who, becoming prisoners in the long wars with the Indians, were adopted by them, left more enduring impressions. The French blood was mixed with that of the Indian, throughout all the wide domain that was primitively termed New France. In all the remnants of Indian nations that a few years since existed around the borders of the western lakes and rivers, the close observer of merged races, could discover the evidences of the gallantries, (and not unfrequently, perhaps, the permanent alliances,) of these early adventurers. Among the remnants of the Iroquois, now residing in our western counties, the mixed blood of the French and Indian, is frequently observed.†

---

*History of Michigan.

† John Green, an intelligent pioneer settler upon the Alleghany river, said to the author, during the last summer, when speaking of the Indians on the Alleghany Reservation, that there were but a small proportion there of pure Indian blood. That the prisoners taken by their ancestors in the French wars, and war of the Revolution, intermarried, and the white blood now predominates. "Take an instance now," said our informant, "where either father or mother is mixed blood, they have large families —when both are full blood Indians, they have but small families."

PART THIRD.

CHAPTER I.

BRIEF NOTICES OF EVENTS UNDER ENGLISH DOMINION.

There is but little of local importance to embrace in our narrative, occurring between the close of the French and English war, by the treaty of Paris, in 1763, to the commencement of the American Revolution, in 1775.

The English strengthened and continued the captured French garrison at Niagara, and other important posts along the western frontiers, for the purpose of protecting their scattered settlements, and trading with, and conciliating the Indians. The questions of difference between England and her colonies—the disputes that were hastening to a crisis—did not reach and disturb these remote and then but partially explored solitudes;—where none but the fearless hunter, the adventurous traveller, the soldier, and the native inhabitants were seen. The only connection then between the eastern and western portion of our state, was kept up by commerce with the Indians, and such relations as existed between the military posts. This region was then far removed from civilization and improvement. Nearly a quarter of a century was to pass away before the tide of emigration reached its borders.

The Senecas, it would seem, from the earliest period of English succession at Fort Niagara, were not even as well reconciled to them as to the French. There is very little doubt of their having been generally in the interests of PONTIAC, and co-operators with him in his well arranged scheme for driving the English from the grounds the French had occupied. Some other portions of the Six Nations were also diverted from the English, as we find that a body of Iroquois were engaged in the attack on Fort Du Quesne.*

---

* Graham, in his colonial history, says the Senecas were co-operators in the designs of Pontiac, but that, by the "indefatigable exertions of Sir William Johnson, the other

MARY JEMISON, in relating a history of her captivity, &c., to her biographer, says that when she first arrived upon the Genesee river, the Senecas were making active preparations to join the French in the re-taking of Fort Niagara. That the expedition resulted, (not in any attack upon the garrison, as we are to infer,) but in a successful resistance to an English force that had sallied from the garrison to get possession of the small French post at Schlosser.* The English were driven back with considerable loss. This, she says, was in the month of November, 1759. Two English prisoners, that were taken, were carried to the Genesee river and executed.

TRAGEDY OF THE DEVIL'S HOLE.

There are few of our readers who will not be familiar with the main features of this event. It was fresh in the recollection of the few of the white race, that were found here, when settlement commenced, and Seneca Indians were then living, who participated in it. The theatre of this tragedy — the locality that is figuratively designated as one of the fastnesses of the great embodiment of sin and evil — was in the high banks of the Niagara river, three miles below the Falls, and half a mile below the Whirlpool. It is a deep, dark cove, or chasm. "An air of sullen sublimity prevades its gloom; and where in its shadowy depths you seem cut off from the world and confined in the prison-house of terror. To appearance it is a

---

of the Six Nations were restrained though with great difficulty, from plunging into the hostile enterprise, which seemed the last effort of the Indian race to hold at least divided empire with the colonists of North America."

*Fort Schlosser—called by the French Little Fort—took its name, under English possession, from a Captain Schlosser, who was the first to occupy the place as an English post. In Dec. 1763, he was in New York. The Moravian Indians at Bethlehem, apprehending an attack from the whites, and the horrid fate that afterwards befel them, appealed to Gen. Gage and Sir William Johnson, for protection, sending a deputation to New York for that purpose. Capt. Schlosser, with one hundred and seventy men, were detached to accompany the deputation back, and defend the Moravian settlement. In Loskriel's History of the Moravian Missions, it is said:—"These soldiers had just come from Niagara, and had suffered much from the savages near Lake Erie, which rendered them in the beginning, so averse to the Indians, that nothing favorable could be expected from them;—God in mercy, changed their dispositions; their friendly behavior soon softened into cordiality; and they conversed familiarly with the Indian brethren, relating their sufferings with the savages." In Heckwelder's Indian Narrative, p. 83, that good Moravian Missionary, speaking of the same event, says of Captain Schlosser, the commander of the guard:—"An officer deservedly esteemed by all good men, for his humanity and manly conduct, in protecting these persecuted Indians."

fit place for a demon-dwelling; and hence, probably, derives its name."* The road along the river bank passes so near, that the traveller can look down from it into the frightful gulf—to the bottom of the abyss, one hundred and fifty feet. It would seem that a huge section of rock had been detached, parting off and leaving the high banks almost perpendicular—over-hanging in fact, at some points. A small stream—the Bloody Run—taking its name from the event of which we are about to give some account, pours over the high pallisade of rock. Trees of the ordinary height of those common in our forests, rise from the bottom of the "Hole," their tops failing to reach the level of the terrace above.

Hitherto our accounts of the tragedy enacted there, have been derived from traditionary sources; no cotemporary written statement of it has as yet appeared in any historical work, or in any printed form. Among the London documents brought to this country by Mr. BROADHEAD, and deposited in the office of the Secretary of State at Albany, is a letter from Sir WILLIAM JOHNSON, to the Board of Trade in New York, dated at Johnson's Hall, (on the Mohawk) September 25th, 1763, to which is appended the following Postscript:—

"P. S.—This moment I have received an express informing me that an officer and twenty-four men who were escorting several wagons and ox-teams over the carrying place at Niagara, had been attacked and entirely defeated, together with two companies of Col. Wilmot's regiment who marched to sustain them. Our loss on this occasion, consists of Lieuts. Campbell, Frazier and Roscoe, of the Regulars. Capt. Johnson and Lieut. Drayton of the Provincials; and sixty privates killed with about eight or nine wounded. The enemy, who are supposed to be Senecas of the Chenussio, [Genessee,] scalped all the dead, took all their clothes, arms and amunition, and threw several of their bodies down a precipice."

In a "Review of the Indian trade," by the writer of the above, dated four years after, speaking of this furious outbreak of the Indians, it is said:—"They totally destroyed a body of Provincials and regulars of about one hundred men in the Carrying Place of Niagara, but two escaping." There is some discrepancy in the two statements. The first account was probably sent to Sir WILLIAM by a messenger despatched from Niagara as soon as the affair was known there, and before the full extent of the loss was ascertained. In 1764 the writer was at Niagara, holding a treaty with the Senecas, where he probably learned the facts as he last

---

* Orr's Guide to Niagara Falls.

stated them. The statement that but two escaped the massacre, agrees, as will be seen from what follows, with the traditionary accounts, though the fate of the "eight or nine wounded," is left to conjecture.

JESSE WARE was the successor of the STEDMANS at Schlosser, and before his death related to the compiler of the first edition of the Life of MARY JEMISON, the story as he assumed to have heard it from WILLIAM STEDMAN, the brother and successor of JOHN STEDMAN, who was one of the two that escaped. The relation was in substance as follows:—

After the possession of Fort Niagara and Schlosser, by the English, Sir WILLIAM JOHNSON made a contract with JOHN STEDMAN to construct a portage road between Lewiston and Schlosser, to facilitate the transportation of provisions and military stores from one place to the other. The road was finished on the 20th of June, 1763, and twenty-five loaded wagons started to go over it, under the charge of STEDMAN, as the contractor for army transportation; accompanied by "fifty soldiers and their officers," as a guard. A large force of Seneca Indians, in anticipation of this movement, had collected and laid in ambush near what is now called the Devil's Hole. As the English party were passing the place, the Indians sallied out, surrounded teams, drivers, and guard, and "either killed on the spot, or drove off the banks," the whole party, "except Mr. STEDMAN, who was on horseback." An Indian seized his bridle reins, and was leading him east to the woods, through the scene of bloody strife, probably for the purpose of devoting him to the more excruciating torments of a sacrifice; but while the captor's attention was drawn in another direction for a moment, STEDMAN with his knife, cut the reins near the bits, at the same time thrusting his spurs into the flanks of his horse, and dashing into the forest, the target of an hundred Indian rifles. He escaped unhurt. Bearing east about two miles, he struck Gill creek, which he followed to Schlosser. ☞ See some subsequent remarks upon the claim instituted by the STEDMANS, or their successor, to lands, based upon this flight, and a consequent Indian gift.

"From all accounts," says the biographer we have relied upon for the above statement, "of this barbarous transaction, Mr. STEDMAN was the only person belonging to this party who was not either driven, or thrown off into the Devil's Hole." Tradition has transmitted to us various accounts of the fate of some few others of the party; that is, that one, two, or three others escaped with life, after being driven off the bank, although badly wounded, and maimed by the fall. Most of the accounts agree in the escape of a little drummer * who was caught while falling, in the limb of a tree, by his drum-strap.

Mrs. JEMISON says that no attempt was made to procure plunder, or take prisoners. The object, sanguinary as was the means used to accomplish it, was not mercenary, but formed a part of a general concerted plan to rid the country of the English.

The account of Sir WILLIAM JOHNSON, which the author, considering that it is both cotemporary and official, is disposed to rely upon, rather than the traditional accounts, gives a different complexion to the whole affair, than the hitherto generally accredited version. The inference would be from his statement, that the cavalcade of wagons, teamsters, and guard of twenty-four men, was first attacked, and was reinforced after the attack by the two companies, who, he says, "marched to sustain them." This would protract the action beyond a sudden attack, and such a summary result as has before been given; and favor the conclusion that the advance party was first attacked as stated, and that those who came to their relief, shared a similar fate. Though the discrepancy is perhaps not material.

HONAYEWUS, or Farmer's Brother, an active Seneca war chief in the Border Wars of the Revolution, was in this battle, or rather surprise and massacre. It was one of his earliest advents upon the war-path.

The pioneer settlers upon the frontier, especially in the neighborhood of Lewiston and the Falls, say that at an early period relics of this horrid tragedy were abundant, in this deep gorge. They consisted of skulls, of human bones, and bones of oxen, pieces of wagons, gun barrels, bayonets, &c., &c.

---

* The story of the drummer is mainly true. Seeing the fate that awaited him, he leaped from the high bank; the strap of his drum catching upon the limb of a tree, his descent, or fall, was broken, and he struck in the river, near the shore, but little injured by the terrible leap of one hundred and fifty feet! His name was Matthews. He lived until within a few years, in the neighborhood of Queenston, to relate the story of his wonderful preservation.

NOTE.—Mrs. Jemison says the first neat cattle that were brought upon the Genesee river were the oxen that the Senecas obtained of the English in the previous affair at Schlosser. As that was an attack upon a military expedition, where no oxen would be likely to have been used, it is probable that those she speaks of were such as were preserved at the affair of the Devil's Hole.

BATTLE NEAR BUFFALO.

In a few weeks after this too successful onslaught of the Senecas upon the English, they followed it up by an attack upon a detachment of English troops, on their way from Niagara to Detroit:—

From the Maryland Gazette, December 22, 1763.

"*New York*, December 5.—Last Monday, Capt. GARDINER of the 55th, and Lieut. STOUGHTON, came to town from Albany. They belonged to a detachment of 600 men under the command of Major WILKINS, destined for Detroit, from Niagara; but on the 19th of October, at the east end of Lake Erie, one hundred and sixty of our people being in their boats, were fired upon from the beach by about eighty Indians, which killed and wounded thirteen men, (and among them Lieut. JOHNSON, late of Gorham's, killed,) in the two stern-most boats, the remainder of the detachment being ahead about half a mile. Capt. GARDINER, who was in the boats adjoining, immediately ordered the men, (fifty) under his command, ashore, and took possession of the ground from which the enemy had fired; and as soon as he observed our people landing, he with Lieut. STOUGHTON, and twenty-eight men pursued the Indians. In a few minutes a smart skirmish ensued, which lasted near an hour, in which three men were killed on the spot, and Capt. GARDINER, with Lieut. STOUGHTON and ten others, badly wounded. During the skirmish, the troops that did not follow the Indians formed on the bank, and covered the boats."

The attacks upon the English at Schlosser, the Devil's Hole, and at the foot of lake Erie, were all the out-breaks of the Senecas, during the disaffection that followed the English advent, of which there is any record, or well authenticated tradition. From some correspondence which occurred between General AMHERST and Sir WILLIAM JOHNSON, which have been preserved in the Broadhead documents, it would seem that the English attributed the hostilities of the Senecas to the evil influences of the French who remained among them as traders, or as adopted Senecas. This is likely to have been the case, though it is apparent that all along the Seneca branch of the Iroquois especially, had resolved to maintain their independence, and resist the encroachments of both the French and the English. After the French were conquered, it was natural for the Senecas to adopt them as allies in any contest they had with the conquerors.

But after the failure of the scheme of PONTIAC at the west, the promulgation of the peace of Paris here, and the consequent submission of the French to the rule of their conquerors, the Senecas, as did the Indian nations generally, concluded that acquiescence and non-resistance was the best policy. By a letter from Lieut. Gov. COLDEN to the Board of Trade, dated Dec. 19th, 1763, it seems that they had then sued for peace. In MANTE's History of the French War, the preliminary articles of this peace are given. It was entered into at JOHNSON's Hall, April 3d, 1764, between Sir WILLIAM JOHNSON and eight deputies of the Seneca nation, viz:— Tagaanedie, Kaanijes, Chonedaga, Aughnawawis, Sagenqueraghta, Wanughsisiae, Tagnoondie, Taanjaqua.

They were to cease all hostilities immediately; never more to make war on the English, or suffer their people to commit acts of violence on the persons or property of any of his Majesty's subjects; forthwith to collect and deliver up all English prisoners, deserters, Frenchmen and negroes; and neither more to harbor or conceal either. They ceded as follows:—"To His Majesty, and his successors forever, in full right, the lands from Fort Niagara extending easterly along lake Ontario about four miles, comprehending the Petit-Marais, or landing place, and running from thence southerly about fourteen miles to the creek above Fort Schlosser or Little Niagara, and down the same to the river, or strait, and across the same, at the great cataract; thence northerly to the banks of lake Ontario, at a creek, or small lake about two miles west of the fort; thence easterly along the banks of lake Ontario, and across the river, or strait, to Fort Niagara; comprehending the whole carrying place, with the lands on both sides of the strait, [or river,] and containing a tract of about fourteen miles in length, and four in breadth. And the Senecas do engage never to obstruct the passage of the carrying place, or the free use of any part of the said tract; and will likewise give free liberty of cutting timber for the use of His Majesty, or that of the garrisons, in any other part of their country, not comprehended therein."*

---

* This is the first tract of land to which the Indian title was extinguished, in Western New York. The reader will have no difficulty in determining the boundaries. It included both banks of the Niagara river, the Falls, Schlosser, Lewiston, Fort Niagara, Niagara, C. W. and the mouth of the Four-mile-creek. It will be observed of course, that the Senecas here assumed that their dominion extended over the Niagara river. This is based undoubtedly upon their conquest over the Neuter Nation ☞ See pages 66, 67, 68.

They farther agreed to grant a free passage through their country, from that of the Cayugas to Niagara, or elsewhere, for the use of His Majesty's troops forever; and the free use to His Majesty forever, of the harbors within the country on lake Ontario, or any of the rivers; immediately to stop all intercourse of their people with the hostile Shawnees, and to assist His Majesty's arms in bringing them to proper punishment. Sir WILLIAM grants a free pardon for past transgressions.

This treaty was to be fully ratified by Sir WILLIAM JOHNSON and the Senecas, the ensuing summer at Fort Niagara. But the Senecas, even after this, proved somewhat refractory. In the ensuing summer, Sir WILLIAM accompanied the expedition of Gen. BRADSTREET as far as Niagara, to attend there a congress of friendly Indian nations, convened to exchange with the English sentiments of peace and alliance, make purchases, receive presents, and some of them to offer themselves as volunteers under Gen. BRADSTREET. About seventeen hundred had assembled; but the Senecas were not among them. Sir WILLIAM sent them repeated messages to come in and ratify their treaty, which they answered by repeated promises of attendance. It was found that they were in council deliberating whether they should renew the war or confirm the peace. Gen. BRADSTREET sent them a peremptory message, in substance, that if they did not repair to Niagara and fulfill their engagements in five days, he would send a force and destroy their settlements. This brought them in. They ratified their treaty, and received some presents.

BURNT SHIP BAY—NIAGARA RIVER.

It will have been seen that the small French garrison at Schlosser, held out and successfully resisted the first attack. The fall of Quebec, however, convinced them that all was lost, and anticipating another attack, they resolved on the destruction of two armed vessels, lying in the river, having on board their military stores. The vessels were taken into the arm of the river that separates a small Island from the foot of Grand Island, and burned down to the water's edge; after which the hulls sunk. In low water, the wrecks are now plain to be seen. In an early period of settlement of the frontier, the hulls were partly exposed;

anchors, chains, cannon balls, grape and cannister shot, irons belonging to the upper rigging, used to be taken from them by the early settlers. The hulls are now mostly covered with mud, sand and gravel. The Bay derives its name from the circumstances here related.*

GENERAL BRADSTREET'S EXPEDITION.

By far the best account of this expedition that has come under the author's observation, is contained in Mante's History, already cited; a rare work, which but a small portion of our readers can have seen. From that source, mainly, our brief notice of it is derived. The expedition was the result of the war that Pontiac and his confederates had waged at the west, and was intended to over-awe the hostile Indians, recover the captured garrisons, and secure a general peace. Gen. Bradstreet, who had headed the successful expedition against Fort Frontenac, was the leader in this. His orders were to "give peace to all such nations of Indians as would sue for it, and chastise those who would continue in arms." The expedition, consisting of about twelve hundred troops, came from Albany to Oswego, where it was joined by a band of warriors of the Six Nations.† From Oswego it came by water, to Fort Niagara, where it halted and remained until Sir William Johnson, had perfected his treaty with the Senecas. Still distrustful of the Senecas, Lieut. Montressor had been ordered to throw up a chain of redoubts, from the landing place at the Four-mile-creek, to Schlosser, "in order to prevent any insults from the enemy, in transporting the provisions, stores and boats, from one lake to another, and likewise to erect a fort on the banks of Lake Erie, for the security of vessels employed upon it; and these services were effectually performed before the arrival of the army."‡

---

* Pieces of the wreck are now often procured, as relics of olden time. The author procured from one of them, during the last summer, an oak plank. The timber — after remaining 89 years under water, is sound, and when the water is dried out, is very hard, and susceptible of a fine polish.

† It may not be generally known, even to those familiar with colonial history, that Israel Putnam, once trod the soil of Western New York. He was in the expedition of Bradstreet, a Lieut. Colonel of the Connecticut battalion, as the newspapers of that day clearly show.

‡ This was the origin of Fort Erie. The author finds no authority for assuming (as some tourists and authors of Sketch Books have,) that the French ever had a post at that point.

The army moved to Fort Schlosser on the 6th of August, when it halted until the 8th, for the arrival of an additional Indian force which was to accompany it. It consisted of three hundred Senecas, who, Mr. MANTE says, Gen. BRADSTREET "thought himself compelled to regard as spies, rather than employ them as auxiliaries." The aggregate force of the expedition now amounted to about three thousand. The army moved up the Niagara, to Fort Erie, and from thence, on the 10th, continued its route along the south side of the lake, agreeable to the instructions of Gen. GAGE. In the morning of the 12th, while detained at *l'Anse-Aux-Feuilles* [Bay of Leaves]* by contrary winds, he received a deputation from the Shawnees, the Delawares, the Hurons of Sandusky and the Five Nations of the Sciota Plains, sueing for a peace; and in the evening he gave them an audience in the presence of the sachems, and other chiefs of the Indians who accompanied him. These Indians made excuses for hostile conduct, and begged forgiveness, which Gen. BRADSTREET granted, and proceeded to Detroit, where he held other conferences. On his way up he had burned the Indian corn-fields and villages at Sandusky, and along the Maumee, and dispersed the Indians wherever he had found them. The confederates of PONTIAC, with the exception of the Delawares and Shawnees, finding they could not successfully compete with such a force, laid down their arms, and concluded a treaty of peace.

PONTIAC, sullenly, stood aloof from the negotiations. He went to Illinois, yielding none but a tacit aquiescence to measures of necessity, in which he clearly foresaw the dispersion and gradual extinction of his race, which has followed the events we have been narrating. He was assassinated by a Peoria Indian. The Ottawas, the Pottawottamies, and the Chippewas, made common cause in avenging his death, by waging war, and nearly exterminating the tribes of the murderer. "The living marble and the glowing canvass may not embody his works; but they are identified with the soil of the western forest, and will live as long as the remembrance of its aboriginal inhabitants, the Algonquin race." †

---

*Maumee Bay.
† Lanman's History of Michigan.

CHAPTER II.

EARLY GLIMPSES OF WESTERN NEW YORK.

A primitive glimpse of the western portion of this state, has been reserved for insertion here,—though not in its order of time. It is by far the earliest notice, of any considerable detail, which we derive from English sources; if in fact it is not the earliest record of any English advent to our region. The author is disposed to conclude that the writer was the first Englishman that saw the country west of the lower valley of the Mohawk. His advent was but three years after the English took final possession of the Province of New York, and ten years previous to the expedition of DE NONVILLE. It is taken from "*Chalmer's Political Annals of the United Colonies,*" a work published in London, in 1780:—

"OBSERVATIONS OF WENTWORTH GREENHALPH.
"*In a journey from Albany to the Indians westward,* [*the Five Nations,*]—*begun the 28th of May,* 1677, *and ended the 14th of July following.* *

[NOTE.—What is said of the "Maquas, (Mohawks,) Oneydoes, Onondagoes, and Cayugas," is omitted, and the journal commences with the Senecas.]

"The Senecas have four towns, viz:—Canagorah, Tistehatan, Canoenada, Keint-he. Canagorah and Tistehatan lie within thirty miles of the Lake Frontenac; the other two about four or five miles to the southward of these; they have abundance of corn. None of their towns are stockadoed.

"Canagorah lies on the top of a great hill, and, in that as well as in the bigness, much like Onondagoe, [which is described as 'situated on a hill that is very large, the bank on each side extending itself at least two miles, all cleared lands, whereon the corn is planted,'] containing 150 houses, north-westward of Cayuga 72 miles.

---

* Mr. Chalmers purports to derive the journal "from New York papers" meaning as is presumed, the manuscripts of the New York "Board of Trade."

"Here the Indians were very desirous to see us ride our horses, which we did. They made feasts and dancing, and invited us, that, when all the maids were together, both we and our Indians might choose such as liked us to lie with.

"Tistehatan lies on the edge of a hill: not much cleared ground; is near the river Tistehatan, which signifies *bending*.* It lies to the northward of Canagorah about 30 miles; contains about 120 houses, being the largest of all the houses we saw; the ordinary being 50 or 60 feet, and some 130 or 140 feet long, with 13 or 14 fires in one house. They have good store of corn growing about a mile to the northward of the town.

"Being at this place, on the 17th of June, there came 50 prisoners from the south-westward, and they were of two nations; some whereof have a few guns, the other none. One nation is about ten days' journey from any Christians, and trade only with one great house,† not far from the sea; and the other, as they say, trade only with a black people. This day, of them were burnt two women and a man, and a child killed with a stone. At night we heard a great noise, as if the houses had all fallen; but it was only the inhabitants driving away the ghosts of the murdered.

"The 18th, going to Canagorah, we overtook the prisoners. When the soldiers saw us, they stopped each his prisoner, and made him sing and cut off their fingers and slashed their bodies with a knife; and, when they had sung, each man confessed how many men he had killed. That day, at Canagorah, there were most cruelly burned four men, four women and one boy; the cruelty lasted about seven hours: when they were almost dead, letting them loose to the mercy of the boys, and taking the hearts of such as were dead to feast on.

"Canoenada lies about 4 miles to the southward of Canagorah; contains about 30 houses, well furnished with corn.

"Keint-he lies about 4 or 5 miles to the southward of Tistehatan; contains about 24 houses, well furnished with corn.

"The Senekas are counted to be in all about 1000 fighting men.

```
"Whole force—Magas,..............................300
             Oneydoes,..............................200
             Onondagoes,...........................350
             Cayugas, ..............................300
             Senekas, ..............................1000
                                     2150 fighting men."‡
```

---

* The Tistehatan, or bending River, must refer to the Genesee.

† Probably among the Swedes on the Delaware — Penn had not yet commenced his settlement.

‡ "Among the manuscripts of Sir William Johnson, there is a census of the northern and western Indians, from the Hudson River to the great Lakes and the Mississippi, taken in 1763. The Mohawk warriors were then only 160; the Oneidas 250; Tuscaroras, 140; Onondagas 150; Cayugas, 200; Senecas, 1050; total, 1950. According to the calculation of a British agent, several of the tribes must have increased between the close of the French war and beginning of the American Revolution, as it

"*Remark.*—During the year 1685 an accurate account was taken by order of the Governor, of the people of Canada, [New France]; which amounted to 17,000, of whom three thousand were supposed to be able to carry arms. We may thence form a judgment with regard to the comparative strength of the two beligerent powers, whose wars were so long and destructive."—*Chalmer's Annals.*

The Rev. SAMUEL KIRKLAND, whose name we have had occasion to introduce in connection with the antiquities of this region, left the mission station at Johnson's Hall, on the Mohawk, Jan. 16th, 1765, in company with two Seneca Indians, upon a mission which embraced all the settlements of the Iroquois, travelling upon snow shoes, carrying "a pack containing his provisions, a few articles of clothing, and a few books, weighing in all about forty pounds."—Leaving the last vestige of civilization, (Johnson's Hall,) his only companions, two Indians with whom he had had but a short acquaintance, the young missionary shaped his course to the westward, encamping nights (with his two guides with whom he could hold no conversation except by signs,) beneath hemlock bows, and sleeping upon ground cleared from snow, for his temporary use. Arriving at Onondaga, the central council fire of the Iroquois, a message, from Sir WILLIAM JOHNSON secured him a friendly reception. After remaining there one day, the party left, and came on to Kanadasagea, the principal town of the Senecas. Halting at the skirts of the town, (a courtesy that his Mr. K.'s Indian guides told him by signs, was customary,) a messenger came out to enquire, "whence they came, whither they were going, and what was their desire." His guides replied:—"We are only bound to this place, and wish to be conducted to the house of the chief sachem." The embassy was conducted into the presence of the sachem, to whom, as at Onondaga, a message was delivered from Sir WILLIAM JOHNSON. The reception was friendly, except with a few, "whose sullen countenances" Mr. K. says "he did not

---

was computed that, during the latter contest, the English had in service, 300 Mohawks, 150 Oneidas, 200 Tuscaroras, 300 Onondagas, 230 Cayugas, and 400 Senecas.

NOTE.—There can be but little doubt that the four villages mentioned by Mr. Greenhalph, are those that were ten years afterwards destroyed by De Nonville. The over-estimate of distances, made by this early adventurer, may well be attributed to the absence of any means to ascertain them correctly. In the names, as given by De Nonville, and by Mr. Greenhalph, there is sufficient analogy to warrant the identity.

quite like." The head sachem treated him with every kindness and attention, and it was after much deliberation and consultation among the Indians, determined that he should fix his residence with them. Through a Dutch trader, who had preceded him, and located at Kanadasagea, he communicated freely with the Indians. A few weeks after his arrival, he was formally adopted as a member of the family of the head sachem. This adoption was attended with formalities—a council, speeches, &c. The council having assembled, "the head sachem's family being present and sitting apart by themselves," Mr. KIRKLAND was waited upon and invited to attend. On his entrance, after a short silence, one of the chiefs spoke:—

"Brothers,—open your ears and your eyes. You see here our white brother who has come from a great distance, recommended to us by our great chief, Sir WILLIAM JOHNSON, who has enjoined it upon us to be kind to him, and to make him comfortable and protect him to the utmost of our power. He comes to do us good. Brothers,—this young white brother of ours, has left his father's house, and his mother, and all his relations, we must now provide for him a house, I am appointed to you and to our young white brother, that our head sachem adopts him into his family. He will be a father to him, and his wife will be a mother, and his sons and daughters, his brothers and sisters."

The head sachem then rose, called him his son, and led him to his family. Mr. K. thanked him, and told him he hoped the Great Spirit would make him a blessing to his new relations. The zealous and enterprising young missionary, says in his journal:—"A smile of cheerfulness sat on every countenance, and I could not refrain from tears; tears of joy and gratitude for the kind Providence that had protected me through a long journey, brought me to the place of my desire, and given me so kind a reception among the poor savage Indians."

Mr. K. applied himself diligently to learn the Seneca language, and by the help of two words, "*atkayason,*" (what do you call this,) and "*sointaschnagati,*" (speak it again,) he made rapid progress. He was made very comfortable and treated very kindly.

All things were going on well, but friendly relations were destined to an interruption. The missionary had been assigned a residence with an Indian family, whose head was a man of much influence with his people;—"sober, industrious, honest, and telling no lies." Unfortunately, in a few days after Mr. K. had become an inmate of his wigwam, he sickened and died. Such of the Senecas as were jealous of the new comer, seized upon the circumstance to create prejudice against him, even alledging that the death was occasioned by his magic, or if not, that it was an "intimation of the displeasure of the Great Spirit at his visit and residence among them, and that he must be put to death." Councils were convened, there were days of deliberation, touching what disposition should be made of the missionary — the chief sachem proving his fast friend, and opposing all propositions to harm him. During the time, a Dutch trader, a Mr. WOMP, on his way from Niagara east, stopped at Kanadaseaga, and he was the only medium through which Mr. K. could learn from day to day, the deliberations of the council. At length his friend, the sachem, informed him joyfully, that "all was peace."

Some proceedings of the Council afterwards transpired, that Mr. KIRKLAND was enabled to preserve in his journal. It was opened by an address from the chief sachem:—

"Brothers,— this is a dark day to us; a heavy cloud has gathered over us. The cheering rays of the sun are obscured; the dim, faint light of the moon *sympathises with us.* A great and awakening event has called us together, the sudden death of one of our best men; a great breach is made in our Councils, a living example of peace, *sobriety* and industry, is taken from us. Our whole town mourns, for a good man is gone. He is dead. Our white brother had lived with him a few days. Our white brother is a good young man. He loves Indians. He comes recommended to us by Sir WILLIAM JOHNSON, who is commissioned by the great king beyond the waters to be our superintendent. Brothers, attend! The Great Spirit has supreme power over life. He, the upholder of the skies, has most certainly brought about this solemn event by his will, and without any other help, or second cause. Brothers, let us deliberate wisely; let us determine with great caution. Let us take counsel under our great loss, with a *tender mind.* This is the best medicine and was the way of our fathers."

A long silence ensued, which was broken by a chief of great influence, who was ambitious of supreme control. He made a long and inflammatory harrangue against the missionary. Among other things, he said:—

"This white skin, whom we call our brother, has come upon a

dark design, or he would not have travelled so many hundred miles. He brings with him the *white people's Book.* They call it *God's Holy Book.* Brothers attend! You know this book was never made for Indians. The Great Spirit gave us a book for ourselves. He wrote it in our heads. He put it into the minds of our fathers, and gave them rules about worshipping him; and our fathers strictly observed these rules, and the Upholder of the skies was pleased, and gave them success in hunting, and made them victorious over their enemies in war. Brothers attend! Be assured that if we Senecas receive this white man, and attend to the Book made solely for white people, we shall become miserable. We shall soon loose the spirit of true men. The spirit of the brave warrior and the good hunter will be no more with us. We shall be sunk so low as to hoe corn and squashes in the field, chop wood, stoop down and milk cows, like the negroes among the Dutch people.* Brothers, hear me! I am in earnest, because I love my nation, and the customs and practices of our fathers; and they enjoyed pleasant and prosperous days. If we permit this white skin to remain among us, and finally embrace what is written in his book, it will be the complete subversion of our national character, as true men. Our ancient customs, our religious feasts and offerings, all that our fathers so strictly observed, will be gone. Of this are we not warned by the sudden death of our good brother and wise sachem? Does not the Upholder of the skies, plainly say to us in this:— 'Hear, attend, ye Senecas! Behold, I have taken one, or permitted one to be taken from among you in an extraordinary manner, which you cannot account for, and thereby to save the nation?' Brothers, listen to what I say. Ought not this white man's life to make satisfaction for our deceased brother's death?"

A long discussion and investigation followed. Mr. KIRKLAND'S papers were carried to the council house and examined; the widow

---

* The Indian orator, had probably been to Schenectady and Albany, and observed the slaves among the Dutch.

NOTE.—The author derives this account of the primitive advent of a protestant missionary among the Senecas, from Spark's American Biography. The name of the chief sachem of Kanadasegea—Mr. Kirkland's adopted father, and friend—does not transpire. The chief who so eloquently spoke for his nation, and ingeniously wrought upon the jealousy and superstition of the council, was Onoongwandeka. The speeches are given, (as is what else transpired at the time,) as communicated to Mr. Kirkland by Mr. Womp. The reader will bear in mind that in this case, as well as in all reports of the speeches of uneducated Indians, the reporters, have but caught the ideas of the native orators, and substituted their own manner of expression. An eloquent idea— a beautiful figure of speech—can of course, only be faithfully reported, in corresponding words and sentences. For instance, we are not to suppose that the Seneca sachem said:—"the dim faint light of the moon sympathises with us," but he did probably make use of a beautiful figure of speech that justified Mr. Kirkland, in such an interpretation.

of the deceased was questioned: — she gave a good account of the "young white brother," said "he was always cheerful and pleasant, and they had began to love him much." Said one of the opponents of Mr. K., "did he never come to your husband's bed-side and whisper in his ears, or puff in his face?" "No, never, he always sat, or lay down, on his own bunk, and in the evening after we were in bed, we would see him get down upon his knees and talk with a low voice." This testimony, and the closing speech of the head sachem, brought matters to a favorable issue. The speech was an able reply to ONOONGWANDEKA — not in opposition to his views, as to the effect generally of admitting the white man and his Book, but generally, in reference to the witchcraft and sorcery charged upon Mr. KIRKLAND, in connection with the sudden death of his host. The speech bore down all opposition, and was followed by shouts, and applause, in which only fifteen refused to participate. The chief sachem said, "our business is done. 1 rake up the council fire."

After this, Mr. KIRKLAND "lived in great harmony, friendship and sociability." Another trouble ensued in the shape of a famine. The corn crop for the year previous, had been short, and game was scarce at that season of the year, (March.) He wrote to a friend that he had "sold a shirt for four Indian cakes, baked in the ashes, which he could have devoured at one meal, but on the score of prudence had ate only one." He lived for days, on "white oak acorns, fried in bear's-grease." He gives a long detail of suffering and privation, as severe as any of his Jesuit predecessors had endured; which terminated in making a return journey through the wilderness to Johnson Hall, where he procured a supply of provisions.

Mr. KIRKLAND was a missionary among the Six Nations, for eight years previous to the Revolution; during that struggle he was useful in diverting some portions of them from adhering to the British interests; and his name and services are often blended in the Indian treaties that followed after the war, and resulted in the extinguishment of their title to lands in Western New York. In these latter connections, frequent reference to him will occur in subsequent pages.

ACCOUNT OF A FRENCH COLONY,
Established at Onondaga in 1655.

DABLON, a Jesuit, established himself in 1655 on or near the spot where Salina now stands.* The same year he was joined by Sieur DUPUYS, an officer from the garrison at Quebec, with fifty Frenchmen. The enterprise was encouraged by the Superior General of the Catholic Missions, who was desirous of establishing at this central Iroquois canton a permanent missionary establishment. It was favored by the Onondagas, but encountered the hostility of the Mohawks from its first inception. They attacked the party of DUPUYS on its way up the St. Lawrence, but were repulsed.

The reception of the party, on their arrival at their destination, was cordial and hospitable. Father MERCEIR, (the Superior General,) had accompanied the expedition, and he spared no pains to give the arrival an imposing appearance, impress the natives with awe and veneration for the religion he wished to introduce, and win their friendly regards. Dwellings were erected, and for nearly two years, the establishment prospered.

At length a conspiracy which extended itself through the Iroquois cantons, was formed against them. DUPUYS, was kept advised of all that was transpiring, by friendly Indians. Deliberating whether he would fortify himself and sustain a siege, or retreat to Quebec, he resolved on the latter.

"To effect his escape M. DUPUYS required first to construct some canoes, for they had not taken the precaution to reserve any. But to work at them publicly would be to announce his retreat, and thereby render it impossible. Something must be resolved on immediately, and the commandant adopted the following plan. He immediately sent an express to M. D' AILLEBOUT to inform him of the conspiracy. He then gave orders for the construction of some small light batteaux; and to prevent the Iroquois from getting the wind of it, he made his people work in the garret of the Jesuit's house, which was larger and more retired than the others.

"This done, he warned all his people to hold themselves in readiness to depart on the day which he named to them, and he supplied each one with provisions sufficient for the voyage, and charged them to do nothing in the mean time to excite the suspicions of the Iroquois. It only remained now to concert measures for embarking so secretely that the savages should have no knowl-

---
* Barber and Howe's Historical Collections.

edge of their retreat until they should have advanced so far as not to fear pursuit, and this they accomplished by a stratagem singular enough.

"A certain young Frenchman who had acquired great influence with the Indians, had been adopted into one of their most respectable families. According to the custom of the Indians, whoever was adopted by them became entitled to all the privileges that belonged to native members of the families. This young man went one day to his adopted father, and told him that he had on the night before dreamed of one of those feasts where the guests eat every thing that is served, and that he desired to have one of the kind made for the village; and he added, that it was deeply impressed upon his mind he should die if a single thing were wanting to render the feast just such a one as he described. The Indian gravely replied that he should be exceedingly sorry to have him die, and would therefore order the repast himself and take care to make the invitations, and he assured him that nothing should be wanting to render the entertainment every way such an one as he wished. The young man having obtained these assurances, appointed for his feast the 19th of March, which was the day fixed upon for the departure of the French. All the provisions which the families through the village could spare were contributed for the feast, and all the Indians were invited to attend.

"The entertainment began in the evening, and to give the French an opportunity to put their boats into the water and to load them for the voyage without being observed, the drums and trumpets ceased not to sound around the scene of festivity.

"The boats having now been launched and every thing put in readiness for a departure, the young man, at the signal agreed upon, went to his adopted father and said to him, that he pitied the guests, who had for the most part asked quarter, that they might cease eating, and give themselves to repose, and adding, that he meant to procure for every one a good night's sleep. He began playing on the guitar, and in less than a quarter of an hour every Indian was laid soundly to sleep. The young Frenchman immediately sallied forth to join his companions, who were ready at the instant to push from the shore.

"The next morning a number of Indians went, according to their custom on awaking, to see the French, and found all the doors of their houses shut and locked. This strange circumstance, joined to the profound silence which everywhere reigned through the French settlement, surprised them. They imagined at first that the French were saying mass, or that they were in secret council; but after having in vain waited for many hours to have the mystery solved, they went and knocked at some of the doors. The dogs who had been left in the houses replied to them by barking. They perceived some fowls also through the palings, but no person could be seen or heard. At length, having waited until evening, they forced open the doors, and to their utter astonishment found every house empty.*

Previous to the Revolution, white settlement did not advance beyond the lower Mohawk valley. The period of the early settlement of Schenectady will have been noticed.

The pioneer emigrants, that began the march of civilization and improvement, west of Schenectady, were as the Plymouth colonists of New England, refugees for the sake of religion and conscience. "Early in the eighteenth century, near three thousand German Palatines emigrated to this country under the patronage of Queen ANNE; most of them settled in Pennsylvania; a few made their way from Albany, in 1713, over the Helleberg, to Schoharie creek, and under the most discouraging circumstances, succeeded in effecting a settlement upon the rich alluvial lands bordering upon that stream. Small colonies from here and from Albany, and Schenectady, established themselves in various places along the Mohawk, and in 1722, had extended as far up as the German Flats, near where stands the village of Herkimer; but all the inhabitants were found in the neighborhood of those streams; none had ventured out in that unbroken wilderness, which lay to the south and west of these settlements." †

This branch of the emigrating Palatines, (there were three thousand, in all, that arrived in New York,) consisted of about seven hundred persons. Their location, "began on the little Schoharie kill, in the town of Middleburg, at the high water mark of the Schoharie river, at an oak stump burned hollow, which is said to have served the Mohegan and Stockbridge Indians, the purposes of a corn-mill; and ran down the river to the north, taking in the flats on both sides of the same, a distance of eight or ten miles, containing twenty thousand acres." ‡ They settled in Indian villages, or dorfs, under the direction of seven individuals, as captains, or commissaries. As these were primitive adventurers, in this direction—and as their names are associated intimately, with early times; and even now are blended with almost every reference to the valley of the Mohawk, and especially "Old

---

* Manuscript history, of the Rev. J. W. Adams, Syracuse.
† Campbell's Annals of Tryon County.
‡ Simm's History of Schoharie and the Border Wars.

Schoharie," — the author inserts such of them as he finds in Mr. SIMM's history: — There were the Keysers, Boucks, Rickards, Rightmyers, Warners, Weavers, Zimmers, Mathers, Zeks, Bellingers, Borsts, Schoolcrafts, Kryslers, Casselmans, Newkirks, Earharts, Browns, Merkleys, Foxes, Berkers, Balls, Weidhams, Deitzs, Manns, Garlocks, Sternbergs, Kneiskerns, Stubrachs, Enderses, Sidneys, Bergs, Houcks, Hartmans, Smidtz, Lawyers.

Their lands were granted them by the Queen, as were provisions, while emigrating; but after leaving Albany they had to depend upon their own resources, and they were as few perhaps as were ever possessed by any forest pioneers, in the settlement of a new country. Upon game, ground-nuts, fish, and a little grain they could procure by going on foot to Schenectady, pursuing an Indian path, they contrived to subsist for the first year, when getting a little ground cleared, they managed to raise some wheat and corn, without any ploughs or teams to use them with. They raised the first wheat in 1711. It was cultivated with the hoe, like corn. For several years, when going to Schenectady to mill, or upon other errands, they went in large parties, as a precaution against the attacks of wild beasts.

In 1735, small settlements of Germans had been made at Canajoharie and Stone Arabia.

In 1739, a Scotchman by the name of LINDSAY, who had obtained by assignment from three other partners, a tract of 8000 acres of land, which is embraced in the town and village of Cherry Valley, became a resident there. His family consisted of his wife and father-in-law, a Mr. CONGREVE, and a few domestics. His location was named "Lindsay's Bush." The proprietor cultivated the friendship of the Indians. His nearest white neighbors, were fifteen miles off, upon the Mohawk, and he had no way of approaching it except by a difficult Indian trail. He was a Scotch gentleman; — a taste for the romantic — a fondness for the chase, which was fully gratified by abundance of wild game in that region, had prompted him to adopt a back-woods life; but he soon began to experience some of its hardships. The snow fell to a great depth in the winter of 1740, — he was short of provisions, and could not get to the settlements for a supply. He was relieved by a friendly Indian, who making his journeys on snow shoes, obtained food for him and his house-hold, for the winter. In 1741 he was joined by the Rev. Samuel Dunlop, David Ramsay,

Willam Galt, James Campbell, William Dickinson, and one or two others, with their families; in all about thirty persons. In 1744, they had a grist and saw-mill, and an increasing, flourishing settlement. It was however harrassed, during the French and English war, by some portions of the Six Nations, in the French interests. Its inhabitants were frequently, during the war, called out to defend the northern frontiers. This was the germ of the settlement of a large district of country, which in our early histories, was included under the name of Cherry Valley.

SIR WILLIAM JOHNSON.

The year 1740, is signalized by the advent upon the Mohawk, of one who was destined to exercise an important influence, and occupy a conspicuous place in our colonial history. Sir WILLIAM JOHNSON was a native of Ireland. He left his native country in consequence of the unfavorable issue of a love affair. His uncle, Sir PETER WARREN, an Admiral in the English navy, owned by government grant, a large tract of land—15,000 acres—within the present town of Florida, Montgomery county. Young JOHNSON became his agent, and located himself in the year above named, at Warren's Bush, a few miles from the present village of Port Jackson. He now began that intercourse with the Indians which was to prove so beneficial to the English, in the last French war that soon followed, the influences of which were to be so prejudicial to the colonial interests, in the war of the Revolution. He made himself familiar with their language, spoke it with ease and fluency; watched their habits and peculiarities; studied their manners, and by his mildness and prudence, gained their favor and confidence, and an unrivalled ascendancy over them. In all important matters he was generally consulted by them, and his advice followed. In 1755, he was entrusted with a command in the provincial service of New York. He marched against Crown Point, and after the repulse of Col. WILLIAMS, he defeated and took DIESKU prisoner. For this service the Parliament voted him five thousand pounds, and the King made him a Baronet. The reader will have noticed his effective agency in keeping the SIX Nations in the English interests, and his military achievement at Niagara.

From the following notice, which appeared in a contemporary

publication—the London Gentleman's Magazine, for September, 1755—it will be seen how well adapted he was to the peculiar offices and agencies that devolved upon him. It is an extract of a journal written in this country:—

"Major General JOHNSON (an Irish gentleman,) is universally esteemed in our parts, for the part he sustains. Besides his skill and experience as an officer, he is particularly happy in making himself beloved by all sorts of people, and can' conform to all companies and conversations. He is very much of the fine gentleman in genteel company. But as the inhabitants next him are mostly Dutch, he sits down with them and smokes his tobacco, drinks flip, and talks of improvements, bear and beaver skins. Being surrounded with Indians, he speaks several of their languages well, and has always some of them with him. His house is a safe and hospitable retreat for them from the enemy. He takes care of their wives and children when they go out on parties, and even wears their dress. In short, by his honest dealings with them in trade, and his courage, which has often been successfully tried with them and his courteous behaviour, he has so endeared himself to them, that they chose him one of their chief sachems or princes, and esteem him as their common father."

Miss ELEANOR WALLASLOUS, a fair and comely Dutch girl, who had been sold to limited service in New York, to pay her passage across the ocean, to one of his neighbors, soon supplied the place of the fair one in Ireland, whose fickleness had been the means of impelling him to new scenes and associations in the back-woods of America. Although taking her to his bed and board, and for a long period acknowledging her as his wife, he was never married to her until she was upon her death-bed, a measure necessary to legitimatize his three children, who afterwards became, Sir JOHN JOHNSON, Mrs. GUY JOHNSON, and Mrs. Col. CLAUS. His next wife, was MOLLY BRANT, sister of the conspicuous chieftain of that name. He was married to her a few years before his death, for the same purpose that was consummated in the previous instance.

COLDEN says of Sir WILLIAM, that "he dressed himself after the Indian manner, made frequent dances after their customs when they excite to war, and used all the means he could think of, at a considerable expense, to engage them in a war against Canada."

The liberal patronage of the English government, and the facility with which he could procure grants of the Indians, made him an extensive land-holder. He obtained one grant, in a manner

which has made it the subject of a familiar anecdote, from HEN-
DRICK, a Mohawk chief, of one hundred thousand acres, situated in
the now county of Herkimer. He had before his death laid the
foundation of perhaps as large an individual landed estate, as was
ever possessed in this country. His heirs, taking sides against the
colonies, in the Revolution, at its close, the whole estate was
confiscated.

The JOHNSON family are so mingled with our early colonial
history, and the border wars of the Revolution, that most readers
will be familiar with a subject that has been introduced here, only
to assist in giving a brief sketch of the progress of settlement
west of the Hudson previous to the Revolution; and to aid a clear
understanding of some local events in that contest.

Sir WILLIAM JOHNSON died on the 24th of June, 1774—having
for nearly thirty-five years, exercised an almost one man power,
not only in his own immediate domain, but far beyond it. In his
character were blended many sterling virtues, with vices that are
perhaps to be attributed in a greater degree to the freedom of a
back-woods life,—the absence of the restraints which the ordinances of civilization imposes,—than to radical defects. His
talents, it must be inferred, were of a high order; his achievements
at Niagara alone, would entitle him to the character of a brave
and skillful military commander; and in the absence of amiable
social qualities, he could hardly have gained so strong a hold upon
the confidence and respect of the Six Nations, as we see he
maintained up to the period of his death.

He died just as the great struggle of the colonies commenced.
Had he lived to have participated in it he would probably have
been found on the side of the mother country. In his case, to the
ordinary obligations of loyalty, were added those of gratitude for
high favors and patronage. Though it has been inferred that in
anticipation of the crisis that was approaching, he was somewhat
wavering in his purposes. Mr. SIMMS, the local historian of the
Mohawk Valley, upon information derived from those who lived at
that period, and in the vicinity, favors the conclusion that he died
by his own hand, to escape a participation in the struggle, which
his position must have forced upon him:—"As the cloud of colonial difficulty was spreading from the capital of New England to
the frontier English settlements, Sir WILLIAM JOHNSON was urged
by the British crown, to take sides with the parent country. He

had been taken from comparative obscurity, and promoted by the government of England, to honors and wealth. Many wealthy and influential friends around him were already numbered among the advocates of civil liberty. Should he raise his arm against that power that had thus signally honored him? Should he take sides with the oppressor against many of his tried friends in many perilous adventures? These were serious questions, as we may reasonably suppose, which often occupied his mind. The Baronet declared to several of his friends, as the storm of civil discord was gathering, that 'England and her colonies were approaching a terrible war, but that he *should never live to witness it.*'* At the time of his death, a court was sitting at Johnstown, and while in the court-room on the afternoon of the day of his death, a package from England of a political nature was handed him. He left the court-house, went directly home, and in a few hours was a corpse."

While it must remain perhaps, a subject of speculation how Sir WILLIAM JOHNSON would have used his powerful influence, had he lived, it is quite certain that it would not have been as hurtful to the colonies, as that portion of it was, which was inherited, with his title, by his son and son-in-law. While they were not his equals in talent — had not many of the good qualities he possessed — they used the influence that he transmitted to them in a manner that we are justified in inferring, it would not have been used, had he lived to exercise it.

Sir WILLIAM was succeeded in his titles and estate, by his son Sir JOHN JOHNSON; his authority as General Superintendent of Indian Affairs, fell into the hands of Col. GUY JOHNSON, his son-in-law, who had long been his assistant, as deputy; in which office he was assisted by Col. DANIEL CLAUS, who had married another daughter of the Baronet.

Before the close of the French and English war, small settlements were begun in the neighborhood of the colony commenced by Mr. LINDSAY. Previous to the American Revolution, a family of HARPERS, distinguished in that contest, had left Cherry Valley and commenced a settlement at Harpersfield, Delaware county.

---

* Col. Stone, in his life of Brant, rejects the inference that Sir William committed suicide; or that he was embarrassed in reference to the course he should pursue. He says, he " visited England for the last time in the autumn of 1773, returning the next spring. He probably came back with his loyal feelings somewhat strengthened."

The Rev. WILLIAM JOHNSON had succeeded in planting a flourishing little colony, on the east side of the Susquehannah, a short distance below the forks of the Unadilla, and several families were scattered through Springfield, Middlefield, (then called New-Town Martin,) and Laurens and Otego, called Old England District. In the year 1716, PHILIP GROAT, made a purchase of land in the present town of Amsterdam. He was drowned in removing his family to his new home. His widow and her three sons made the intended settlement. They erected a grist mill at what is now called Crane's Village, in 1730. One of the brothers, LEWIS GROAT, was captured by the Indians in the French and English war, and kept in captivity four years. In this war, these primitive settlers upon the Mohawk were often visited by the French Indian allies, and had a foretaste of the horrid scenes that were to follow, in a few years. The valley of the Mohawk was the theatre of martyrdom and suffering, in two wars.

In the year 1740 a small colony of Irish emigrants, located in the present town of Glen. The Indian disturbances alarmed them, and after a few years they returned to Ireland.

GILES FONDA was the first merchant west of Schenectady. His customers were the few settlers upon the Mohawk, and the Indians of the Six Nations. He had branches, or depots, at Forts Schuyler, Stanwix, Oswego, Niagara and Schlosser. His principal business was to exchange blankets, trinkets, ammunition and rum for furs, peltries, and ginseng.

A church was erected at Caughnawaga, partly under the patronage of Sir WILLIAM JOHNSON, in 1765. Churches were erected at Stone Arabia, Palatine and German Flats, before the Revolution. At an early period a small church was constructed of wood, near the Upper Mohawk Castle. A bell that was in use then, was brought away by the Mohawks, in their flight westward, and was used in the temporary Mohawk settlement at Lewiston. ☞ See JOHN MOUNTPLEASANT's account of the church, bell, &c.

Toward the close of the French war, the public debt of the Province of New York, obliged a resort to a direct tax. The amount levied upon the inhabitants of the "Mohawk Valley," which designation then embraced the whole State west of Albany, was £242,176.

In 1772, three years previous to the Revolution, Tryon county was taken from Albany.* It embraced all the present state of New York, west of a line drawn north and south nearly through the center of Schoharie county. It was divided into five districts. The first court of *"general quarter sessions of the peace,"* was held in Johnstown, Sept. 8th, 1772. The Bench consisted of

Guy Johnson, *Judge.*
John Butler, Peter Conyne, *Judges.*
Sir John Johnson, Knight, Daniel Claus, John Wells, Jelles Fonda, *Asst. Judges.*
John Collins, Joseph Chew, Adam Loucks, John Fry, Francis Young, Peter Ten Broek, *Justices.*

A glimpse has thus been furnished the reader, of the condition of things, in the county of Tryon, preceding a crisis which was to make it the theatre of sanguinary scenes; its few and scattered inhabitants, sufferers, and not unfrequently martyrs, in the harassing border war that came upon them to multiply three fold the ordinary endurances of the pioneers of the wilderness.†

---

* Named in honor of William Tryon, then Governor of the Province.

† "The population of Cherry Valley was short of three hundred, and that of the whole county of Tryon but a few thousand, when the Revolution commenced."—*Campbell's Annals.*

CHAPTER III.

THE BORDER WARS OF THE REVOLUTION.

In the condition of settlement that has been briefly stated, the reader will perceive that all Western New York could have had but a remote connexion with the long and eventful struggle that ended in a separation of the colonies, and the blessings of a free and independent government. While the author has presumed in his preceding pages, that there was much of early colonial history, having a distinct local relation, with which most of those into whose hands his work will fall were not familiar, he will not regard it necessary to embrace any portion of a general history—the causes and prominent events of the Revolution—which is as "familiar as house-hold words," with his readers—formed a portion of their nursery tales, and are incorporated with the rudiments of our primary schools.

Foremost in its loyalty, effective and vigilant in its services, in the French war that had closed by the triumph of the English arms,—the province of New York was not backward in preparations for asserting its rights, when the period arrived in which England, proud of her colonial possessions, but oppressive in its government of them, provoked resistance to its unjust requirements. "During the long and harrassing French wars, her levies both of men and money, considering her population and resources, were immense. Her territory was the principal scene of action, and she seconded with all her powers the measures adopted by the English to destroy the French influence in America."* But loyalty, faithful and enduring as it had been, began to be forfeited, and the Province of New York was early in so regarding it.

Its resistance to the stamp act in 1765, paved the way for the convening of a congress in New York, the same year.

---

* Annals of Tryon County.

A public meeting of citizens of Palatine district, in Tryon county, was assembled as early as August, 1774. The Boston Port Bill had gone into operation in the preceding June. The resolutions of that meeting declared unaltered and determined allegiance to the British crown, but strenuously remonstrated against an act which it regarded as "oppressive and arbitrary," and "subversive of the rights of English subjects." The meeting approved of a previous act of their brethren in New York, in sending five delegates to the approaching congress in Philadelphia; and appointed a committee of correspondence, consisting of five persons, to correspond with committees of Albany and New York.

The ball thus put in motion, its progress was retarded by all the influence of the JOHNSON family and their adherents. In the spring of 1775, after the proceedings of the Philadelphia congress had been promulgated, during the session of a court at Johnstown, a declaration was drawn up and circulated by the loyalists of Tryon county, opposing the proceedings of that congress. It occasioned much altercation, but was finally signed by most of the grand jury, and nearly all the magistrates. Public meetings soon followed in most of the districts of the county, in opposition to the sentiments expressed in the Johnstown declaration. On a day appointed, the little church at Cherry Valley, was crowded with all ages and sexes. THOMAS SPENCER, an Indian interpreter, addressed the meeting in a strain of "rude, though impassioned eloquence." * Articles of association were adopted at this and at similar district meetings, approving the proceedings of the Philadelphia congress, and declaring that the Johnstown proceeding was a measure which would assist to "entail slavery upon America." On the 8th of May, the Palatine committee, wrote a letter to the Albany committee, in which they say that they are busy in circulating petitions, and enlisting the citizens of Tryon county, on the side of the colonies, but they say:—

"This county has for a series of years been ruled by one family, the different branches of which are still strenuous in persuading people not to come into congressional measures; and even have, last week, at a numerous meeting of the Mohawk District, appeared with all their dependents armed, to oppose the

---

* Mr. Campbell says:—"The noblest efforts of an Henry and an Otis, never wrought more sensibly upon the feelings of the congresses they addressed, than did the harangue of this unlettered patriot, upon that little assembly."

people considering of their grievances:—their number being so large, and the people unarmed, struck terror into the most of them, and they dispersed. We are informed that Johnson Hall is fortifying by placing swivel guns around the same, and that Col. JOHNSON has had part of his regiment of militia under arms, yesterday, no doubt with the design to prevent the friends of liberty from publishing their attachment to the cause, to the world. Besides which, we are told, that about an hundred Highlanders, (Roman Catholics,) are armed, and ready to march upon the like occasion. We are informed that Col. JOHNSON, has stopped two New Englanders, and searched them, being as we suppose, suspicious that they came to solicit aid from us or the Indians, whom we dread most, there being a current report through the county, that they are to be made use of in keeping us in awe. We recommend it strongly and seriously to you to take it in your consideration, whether any powder and ammunition, ought to be permitted to be sent up this way, unless it is done under the inspection of the committee, and consigned to the committee here, and for such particular shop-keepers, as we in our next shall acquaint you. We are determined to suffer none in our district, to sell any, but such as we approve of, and sign the association. When any thing particular comes to our knowledge relating to the Indians, (whom we shall watch), or anything interesting, we shall take the earliest opportunity in communicating the same to you. And as we are a young county, remote from the metropolis, we beg you will give as all the intelligence in your power. We shall not be able to send down any deputies to the Provincial Congress. as we cannot possibly obtain the sense of the county soon enough to make it worth our while to send any, but be assured we are not the less attached to American liberty. For we are determined, although few in number, to let the world see who are, and who are not such; and to wipe off the indelible disgrace brought upon us by the declaration signed by our grand jury, and some of our magistrates; who in general, are considered by a majority of our county, as enemies to their country. In a word, gentlemen, it is our fixed resolution to support, and carry into execution every thing recommended by the Continental Congress, and to BE FREE OR DIE."

At the next meeting of the Palatine Committee, in the same month, two intercepted letters were read. The first, was a letter from the Mohawk, to the Oneida Indians. Translated into English, it was as follows:—

"Written at GUY JOHNSON's, May 1775. This is your letter, you great ones, or Sachems. GUY JOHNSON says he will be glad if you get this intelligence, you Oneidas, how it goes with him now, and he is now more certain concerning the intention of the Boston people. GUY JOHNSON is in great fear of being taken prisoner by the Boston people. We Mohawks are obliged to watch him constantly. Therefore we send you this intelligence, that you shall know it, and Guy Johnson assures himself and depends upon your coming to his assistance, and that you will without fail be of that opinion. He believes not that you will assent to let him suffer. We therefore expect you in a couple of day's time. So much at present. We send but so far as to you Oneidas, but afterwards perhaps, to all the other nations. We conclude, and expect that you will have concern about our ruler, Guy Johnson, because we are all united."

The letter was signed by Joseph Brant as Secretary to Guy Johnson, and by four other chiefs. The other letter was from Guy Johnson to the magistrates and others, of the upper districts of Tryon county:—

"Guy Park, May 20, 1775.

Gentlemen,—I have lately, repeated accounts, that a body of New Englanders, or others, were to come and seize, and carry away my person, and attack our family, under color of malicious insinuations that I intended to set the Indians upon the people. Men of sense and character know that my office is of the highest importance to promote peace among the Six Nations, and prevent their entering into any such disputes. This I effected last year, when they were much vexed about the attack on the Shawnees, and I last winter appointed them to meet me this month, to receive the answer of the Virginians. All men must allow that if the Indians find their council fire disturbed, and their superintendent insulted, they will *take a dreadful revenge*. It is therefore the duty of all the people to prevent this, and to satisfy any who may have been imposed upon, that their suspicions, and allegations, they have collected against me, are false, and inconsistent with my character and office. I recommend this to you as highly necessary at this time, as my regard for the interests of the country and self preservation, has obliged me to fortify my house, and keep men armed for my defence, till these idle and malicious reports are removed."

Upon the reading of these letters, the Committee adopted a set of strong resolutions confirming their former positions, and severely condemning the conduct of Sir Guy, in keeping about him a body of armed Indians, fortifying his house, and "stopping and searching travellers upon the King's highway." It was resolved,—"That as we abhor a state of slavery, we do join and unite together, under all the ties of religion, honor, justice, and a love for our country, never to become slaves, and to defend our freedom with our lives and fortunes."

Before the Committee adjourned, it addressed another letter to the Albany Committee,—in which they say, that they have ordered the inhabitants of the district to provide themselves with arms and ammunition, and be ready at a moment's warning; that Johnson has five hundred men to guard his house; that he has stopped all communication between the counties of Tryon and Albany; that there was not fifty pounds of powder in their district; that they propose, jointly, with the Committees of other districts, to force a communication with Albany; that JOHNSON had invited the upper Indian nations to go down to his neighborhood, but as many of the Indians were dissatisfied with him, they should endeavor to make a diversion in their favor; and that they wish the Albany Committee to send them some one or two who would be able to make the Indians understand the true nature of the dispute with the mother country. They say:—"We are gentlemen, in a worse situation than any part of America is at present. We have an open enemy before our faces, and treacherous friends at our backs;" but they assure the Albany Committee that they are very unanimous in the Palatine and Canajoharie districts, and are "determined neither to submit to the acts of Parliament, or Col. JOHNSON's arbitrary conduct." In answer to a communication from GUY JOHNSON, the Albany Committee used conciliatory language; said they were disposed to believe in the sincerity of his professions; that they are sorry that reports prejudicial to his character had gone abroad; and trusted that he would "pursue the dictates of an honest heart, and study the interests, peace and welfare of his country." They also, addressed a communication to the committees in Tryon county, advising as the prudent course, not to attempt to open a communication with Albany, as they had intended. Before adjourning, in reference to a threat they had understood JOHNSON had made, of procuring the imprisonment of those who took a conspicuous part in the proceedings that were going on, they resolved to "stand by each other, and rescue from imprisonment any who were confined in an illegal manner." Secresy, was enjoined upon all the members. It was resolved to have no social intercourse, or dealings, with those who had not joined the association. The owners of slaves were enjoined not to suffer them to go from home, except with a certificate that they were on their master's business.

On the 25th of May, an Indian council was convened at Guy Park. Delegates were present from Albany and Tryon counties. The Indians, through LITTLE ABRAHAM, a Mohawk chief, assured them that they did not wish to have a quarrel with the inhabitants. That during Sir WILLIAM JOHNSON's life time, and since, they had been peaceably disposed. The delegations, and Indians, parted with mutual assurances of continued friendship; though the Mohawks declared that they were under great obligations to

Sir WILLIAM JOHNSON, had a great respect for his memory, and they must guard and protect every member of his family.

On the 22d of June, 1775, a meeting of the Committees of Tryon county was held; being joined for the first time, by a Committee from the Mohawk district, which district had hitherto kept aloof, through the influence of the JOHNSONS. This meeting addressed a letter to GUY JOHNSON, in which they assured him that the people of Tryon county, made common cause with their brethren of Massachusetts Bay; they recapitulated generally, the grievances complained of on the part of the colonies; that possessing as he did, very large estates in the county, they could not think that he differed with them upon the subject of American freedom; and they complained that peaceable meetings of the Mohawk district, had been disturbed, and a man in their interests, had been inhumanly treated, &c.

JOHNSON in his answer, persevered in pacific assurances; said he had fortified his house, because he was apprehensive of an attack, and in doing so, he had only exercised the prerogative of all English subjects. While he professed loyalty to his king, he assured the Committee that he should continue to so discharge the duties of his office, as to best do his duty to his country, and preserve its peace; that his family had been the benefactors of the country, &c. He said the movements of the people were premature, that they should wait and see what would be the final action of the home government upon the matters complained of; that they should have "nothing to apprehend from his endeavors," but that he should "be glad to promote their true interests."

Notwithstanding such professions, it would seem that he had early been ambitious to seize upon the influence he had inherited from his father-in-law, mould the Six Nations to his will, and subserve the two-fold purpose of gratifying a personal ambition, and making an exhibition of his loyalty, to his family's patron, GEORGE the Third. Under the pretence that he could better control the Indians, and keep them peaceable, by withdrawing them from the irritating influences that surrounded them in the Mohawk Valley, he removed with his retinue to Fort Stanwix, and from thence farther west, where he was met by thirteen hundred warriors in council. From his then location, under date of July 8th, he wrote to Mr. LIVINGSTON, the President of Congress, a letter which concludes thus:—"I should be much obliged by your promises of discountenancing any attempts against myself, did they not appear to be made on conditions of compliance with *continental* or *provincial* Congresses, or even Committees, formed or to be formed, many of whose resolves may not consist with my conscience, duty or loyalty;"—still he assures Mr. LIVINGSTON that he shall always "manifest more humanity than to promote the destruction of innocent inhabitants of a colony, to which I have been always warmly attached."

He retired to Montreal, where he took up his residence, and "continued to act during the war as an agent of the British government, distributing to the Indians liberal rewards for their deeds of cruelty, and stimulating them to further exertions." *

The Mohawks, almost the entire body of them, had accompanied JOHNSON and his family to the west. † In June, the Rev. SAMUEL KIRKLAND, then missionary to the Oneidas, held a conference with the Oneidas and Tuscaroras, to induce them to remain neutrals during the war. Knowing his influence with the Oneidas, the JOHNSONS had not been idle in attempts to prejudice them against him. They told him that Mr. K. "was a descendant of those New England, or Boston people, who had formerly murdered their king, and fled to this country for their lives;" that the New England ministers "were not true ministers of the gospel." All this did not succeed however, in depriving him of his influence, or the attachment of the Oneidas to him. Most of them remained neutrals during the war—a large portion of them offered to take up the hatchet in behalf of the colonies, but it was preferred to dispense with their services, except in a few instances. Some of them rendered important services, as runners, in apprising the border settlers of approaching danger.

JOSEPH BRANT—THAYENDANEGA.

An elaborate history ‡ having been written of this noted Indian chief, no farther biographical sketch of him will be attempted, than is incidental to local narrative.

The place of his birth, parentage, &c., have been differently

---

* Spark's American Biography.
† Guy Johnson was accompanied by Joseph Brant, and John and Walter Butler.
‡ Life of Brant, by William L. Stone.

stated by historians. It was assumed by Dr. STRACHAN, of Toronto, in some sketches he wrote many years since, and published in the Christian Register, that BRANT was born on the Ohio river, whither his parents had emigrated from the valley of the Mohawk, and where they are said to have sojourned for several years. This information was derived from the Rev. Dr. STEWART, formerly a missionary in the Mohawk Valley. Col. STONE concedes that he was born on the Ohio river, but assumes that it was during a hunting excursion from the Mohawk, in which his parents participated; and that his father was a full blooded Mohawk of the Wolf tribe. The friend of the author, (Mr. L. C. DRAPER,) to whom reference is made in the preface to this work, assumes that he was a native Cherokee, upon some evidence he has discovered in his indefatigable researches. If this is so, we are to infer that his parents were adopted Cherokee captives.

The home of his family was at the Canajoharie Castle. In July, 1761, he was sent by Sir WILLIAM JOHNSON, to the "Moor's Charity School," at Lebanon, Conn., established by the Rev. Dr. WHEELOCK, with several other Mohawk boys. He made good progress in education, and on his return from school, was employed by his patron in public business. His first military exploits, had preceded his education; when quite young, he had been upon several expeditions with Sir WILLIAM JOHNSON.

Under the circumstances—the friendship and patronage, and the family alliance that has been already spoken of—it is easy to perceive how his position was determined in the border wars; and why he followed the fortunes of the JOHNSON family. Mr. CAMPBELL, himself a descendant of severe sufferers in that terrible crisis, and enjoying good opportunities to estimate the character of BRANT, says in his Annals.—"Combining the natural sagacity of the Indian, with the skill and science of the civilized man, he was a formidable foe. He was a dreadful terror to the frontiers. His passions were strong. In his intercourse, he was affable and polite, and communicated freely, relative to his conduct. He often said that during the war he had killed but one man in cold blood, and that act he often regretted. He said he had taken a man prisoner, and was examining him; the prisoner hesitated, and he thought equivocated. Enraged at what he considered obstinacy, he struck him down. It turned out that the man's obstinacy arose from a natural hesitancy of speech."

The statement that he had been guilty of but one assassination, does not correspond with well authenticated tradition; though he may, to have satisfied his own conscience, made a nice distinction in some instances, as to what constituted a taking of life in "cold blood." That the bad features of his character, and his atrocities, have been much magnified, there is no doubt, as have nearly all of the events in the border wars. It is difficult to reconcile the character of JOSEPH BRANT, as given in many of our histories, with the accounts we have of him from living cotemporaries, who knew him well.

He was the companion of Judge PORTER, in a journey he made from Albany to Canandaigua, in 1794. The chief was returning from a visit to the then seat of government, (Philadelphia,) to his residence at Brantford, C. W. The Judge speaks of him as an intelligent, gentlemanly, travelling companion. The journey was on horseback. It was the first time BRANT had travelled the valley of the Mohawk, since the Revolution, and on leaving Albany, he was somewhat apprehensive of the treatment he would receive. Peace, however, and the obligations it imposed, saved him from any harm or insult, from those in whose memory the scenes with which he was associated, were painfully fresh and vivid. While he avoided being drawn into any conversation connected with the border wars, he pointed out such things upon the Mohawk as were associated in the reccollections of his boyhood.

JOHN GOULD, of Cambria, Niagara county, was a resident at Brantford, as early as 1791, or '2; says he has often heard BRANT relate the story of his visit to England; how he was feasted and toasted in London, &c. After his return, his house at Brantford was the resort of many of the British officers, and prominent citizens of Canada. He was hospitable, had good social qualities, and was much esteemed by the early residents of Brantford, and its vicinity. The patronage of the government had enabled him to live much in the style of an English gentleman. He retained the slaves he had brought from the Mohawk. Mr. GOULD remembers well the death of his son ISAAC, from a stab inflicted by his father. "When sober," says Mr. G. "Isaac was a good Indian—when in liquor, he was a devil. He committed many depredations. I once invited him to a raising. He excused himself on the ground, that if he went he should get a taste of liquor and commit some outrage. One day he became intoxicated, went to his father's house and attacked him with a knife—they had a desperate fight, which ended in Isaac's death. No one at the time blamed the old man, but all considered it was an act of necessary self-defence. Isaac had before killed a saddler upon Grand River, upon some slight provocation."

Judge Hopkins, of Lewiston, Niagara county, was a resident, near the Brants, in 1800 and 1801, and confirms generally, the statement of Mr. Gould.

Others, who were early residents of Canada, and neighbors of the subject of this sketch, in the latter years of his life, have given the author many interesting reminiscences of him, derived from personal observation and conversation; but a few of which can be made available without transcending prescribed limits.

In speaking of the attack and massacre at Minisink, he excused himself upon the ground that the Americans came out under pretence of holding a parley, and fired several shots, some of which were aimed at him.* Provoked at this, he gave orders for an attack in which no quarters were to be given. He assumed that he saved the life of Capt. Wood, had him taken to Niagara, as a prisoner, where he remained until peace. He acknowledged to an informant of the author, that he took the life of Lieut. Wisner, at Minisink, very much as the inhuman act is already detailed in history; but excused the act upon the ground, that he had either to leave him to become a prey to wild beasts in his wounded and helpless condition, be encumbered with him in a retreat through an enemy's country, or adopt the terrible alternative he did. He claimed to have saved many prisoners, upon other occasions,—and generally to have been governed by the incentives of humanity; though it is difficult to reconcile these professions, even with his own versions. At Oriskany he said:—"I captured a man who had hid behind a stump; his name was Waldo or Walbridge; he begged, and I ordered the Indians to save him. He conducted myself and party to his home, a mile distant; arriving there, we found that Indians had preceded us, and had bound for sacrifice, a 'beautiful girl,' the sister of our prisoner. I ordered her release."

Says another informant:—"I first knew Joseph Brant in 1797. He resided at the Mohawk village. He was the patroon of the place—his authority nearly absolute, with both Indians and whites.

---

* Not consistent with authentic history.

He was in high favor with Gov. SIMCOE, and the Canadian authorities generally. The governor was often a partaker, with others, of his hospitalities. I have heard Capt. BRANT say, he could not regret the death of his son ISAAC; but, much regretted that he had been obliged to take the life of a son."

Few mooted points of history have been more often discussed, than the question whether BRANT was present at the Wyoming massacre. The poet CAMPBELL, in his widely read and admired poem, "Gertrude of Wyoming," in a passage purporting to be a part of the speech of an Oneida chief, pending the battle, or massacre, says:—

> "'But this is not a time' ;— (he started up,
> And smote his breast with wo-denouncing hand) —
> 'This is no time to fill the joyous cup,
> The mammoth comes — the foe — the monster, BRANT!
> With all his howling, desolating band;
> These eyes have seen their blade, and burning pine;
> Awake at once, and silence half your land.
> Red is the cup they drink; but not with wine;
> Awake and watch to-night, or see no morning shine.
> Scorning to wield the hatchet for his bribe,
> 'Gainst BRANT himself I went to battle forth:
> Accursed BRANT! he left of all my tribe,
> Nor man, nor child, nor thing of living birth;
> No, not the dog that watched my household hearth,
> Escaped that night of blood upon our plains:
> All perished! I alone am left on earth!
> To whom nor relative, nor blood remains —
> No — not a kindred drop that runs in human veins."

This was admired verse, but destined to be questioned fact. JOHN BRANT, a son of the old chief, visited London in 1822. While there, he caused to be exhibited to Mr. CAMPBELL, documentary evidence, showing that he had done great injustice to the memory of his father; and that he was not present at the massacre at Wyoming. Mr. CAMPBELL immediately addressed the young chief a respectful letter, in which after justifying himself by citing numerous authorities in favor of the conclusion he had favored in his poem, frankly acknowledged that the evidence presented to him had induced him to change his opinion; to which he added an expression of regret that he had been led to favor the imputation.

W. L. STONE, in his life of the Mohawk chief, assumes that he was not at Wyoming. The publication of his history was followed by a paper published in the Democratic Review, attributed to CALEB CUSHING; in which it is assumed that BRANT was at Wyoming; and the biographer is called upon to show where he was at the time, if he was not there?* Col. STONE replied to this, and pretty effectually justified his position.

In a conversation that took place between Col. BUTLER and JOSEPH BRANT, at Brantford, many years after the Revolution, (well remembered by one who related it to the author,) BRANT was complaining that much was laid to his charge of which he was innocent. "They say," said he, "that I was the Indian leader at Wyoming; *you*, Colonel, *know* I was not there." To which, BUTLER replied:—"To be sure, I do,—and if you had been there, you could have done no better than I did; the Indians were uncontrollable."

The author inclines to the opinion of Col. STONE, (though deeming him in the main, too partial to his semi-civilized hero;) the terrible instrument in the hands of his British prompters, in scenes of stealthy assault, captivity and death; the foremost and most formidable scourge of the border settlers of our state, in a crisis that found them exposed to all the evils of savage warfare — enhanced by the aid and assistance of a portion of their own race, who had not savage custom and usage to plead in extenuation of their atrocities and villanies.

JOSEPH BRANT died at his residence at Burlington Bay, on the 24th of November, 1807, aged 64 years. Previous to his death, he had become a communicant of the Episcopal church, and in his life time had aided that church materially in its missionary labors among the Indians, by translating some portions of the scriptures, and the Book of Common Prayer, into the Mohawk language.

Where the first stopping place of the Mohawks was, after leaving their home upon the Mohawk, with GUY JOHNSON and BRANT, (if they had any intermediate abiding place,) before reaching Lewiston, the author has nowhere seen named. In an early period of the border wars, BRANT's residence was at Lewiston,— his dwelling a block house, standing near what is called "Brant's Spring," on the farm of ISAAC COOK. His followers, forming a considerable Indian village, were located along the

---

* A difficult task, the reader will conclude: — to go back beyond a half century, and show where the leader of a band of Indians was, whose range was a then wilderness comprising half of our entire state, a part of Pennsylvania, and a part of Canada West; his location changing with the vicissitudes of a predatory warfare.

Ridge Road between the Academy and the road that leads up to the Tuscarora village. There were remains of the huts standing when white settlement commenced. It would seem by reference to the books of the land office, that for several farms there, the purchasers were charged an extra price, in consequence of the improvements the Mohawks had made during their residence there. There was a log church in which the Episcopal service was usually read upon Sundays, by some one attached to the British garrison at Niagara, and occasionally a British army chaplain, or a missionary would be present. That church, in any history of its origin and progress, in Western New York may well assume that beyond the garrison at Niagara, Lewiston, BRANT's rude log church, was the spot where its services were first had. Upon a humble log church there could, of course, then, be no belfry or steeple. The bell that was brought from the Mohawk, was hung upon a crossbar, resting in the crotch of a tree, and rang by a rope attached. The crotch was taken down by the COOK family, after they had purchased the land. In 1778, JOHN MOUNTPLEASANT, then but eight years old, says his Tuscarora mother used to take him down to the church, where he remembers seeing his father, Capt. MOUNTPLEASANT, then in command of the garrison at Niagara. He speaks of the crotch and the bell, as objects that attracted his especial attention.

Our brief narrative of events in the border war, having been interrupted—to admit of some reminiscences of one who was so conspicuous in its memorable scenes—it will be resumed, but only with reference generally, to events connected with the western portion of our state.

The Tryon county General Committee, after the departure of GUY JOHNSON, and his retinue, were active in perfecting its organization, and enlisting the co-operation of the citizens of the county. Sir JOHN JOHNSON had remained behind, converted his house into a rendezvous and focus of loyalty, and was actively engaged in counteracting the movements of the Committee. The public authorities of the county—the Judges of the court, the Magistrates, were mostly with him and against the Committee. The sheriff of the county, ALEXANDER WHITE, had early demonstrated his position and sentiments, by using his official authority to disperse the primitive meeting in the Mohawk district, made himself especially obnoxious with the people. In a letter from the Committee to the Provincial Congress, they say:—"We must further hear that Gov. TRYON shall have again granted a commission to the great villain, ALEXANDER WHITE, for High Sheriff in our county, but we shall never suffer any exercise in our county, of such office by said WHITE." In such an emergency, the Committee formally declared, that there was an end to the previously constituted authorities of the county, and constituted themselves the local government, exercising as a demand of necessity, in most matters, arbitrary authority. It was in fact, thus early, revolution, so far as *our* county of Tryon was concerned.

In September, 1775, the Committee say in a letter to Congress, "there is a great many proved enemies to our association and regulations thereof, being Highlanders, amounting to 200 men, according to intelligence. We are daily scandalized by them, provoked and threatened, and we must surely expect a havoc of them upon our families if we should be required and called elsewhere upon our country's cause." It was ascertained that JOHNSON kept up a continual correspondence with GUY JOHNSON at Montreal, after his retreat. In October, the Committee wrote to Sir JOHN, wishing to know if he would "allow the inhabitants of Johnstown and Kingsborough, to form themselves into companies according to the regulations of our Continental Congress;" whether he would lend his personal assistance to such a measure; and whether he pretended a "prerogative to our county court house and goal, and would hinder or interrupt the Committee making use of the same?" He replied that he should not hinder his tenants from doing as they pleased, but that they were not disposed to engage in the cause of Congress, &c.; as to himself, he said, "sooner than lift his hand against his King, or sign any association, he would suffer his head to be cut off;" as to the court house and jail, they should be used only for the purposes for which they were built, until he was paid seven hundred pounds, advanced for their erection; and closed by charging that "two of the Canajoharie and German Flatts people had been forced to sign the association."

The Provincial Congress, addressed a letter to the committee, advising forbearance and moderation, and suggesting that they had in some particulars asked too much of Sir JOHN, yet the Congress denied that he had any right to control the court-house, as that was conveyed by Sir WILLIAM, for the use of the county. But the Congress advised the Committee, that as it might lead to serious consequences, they had better not confine persons in the jail "inimical to our country," but procure some other convenient place, and also advised against in any way, molesting Sir JOHN, as long as he was inactive.

In the following winter, Sir JOHN made preparations to fortify Johnson's Hall, and the rumor gained ground, that when completed, he would garrison it with three hundred Indians, besides his own men. In January, Gen. SCHUYLER, Gen. TEN BROEK, and Col. VARICK, came into Tryon county with a small party of soldiers, where they were joined by the Tryon county militia, ordered out by Gen. HERKIMER. The rendezvous was but a few miles from Johnson's Hall. From the camp, a correspondence was carried on for several days with Sir JOHN JOHNSON. It resulted in his surrendering himself a prisoner, and disarming his tenants. This produced quiet for the winter, but in May, Sir JOHN broke a parole he had entered into, and accompanied by a large number of his tenants, went to Montreal. There, or at some point in Canada, he organized a military corps of refugees, known throughout the war, as "Johnson's Greens."

The first delegates to the Provincial Congress, from Tryon county, were JOHN MARLATT and JOHN MOORE. In May, 1776, the Tryon county committee, instructed their delegates in the Provincial Congress, to vote for the entire independence of the Colonies; and the Declaration of Independence, of the 4th of July following, was hailed by the people of Tryon county with joy.

For nearly a year after this, there were but little of war movements, in the Mohawk valley. In June, 1777, BRANT appeared at Unadilla with seventy or eighty Indians, where he sought an interview with some militia officers, and the Rev. Mr. JOHNSTONE. He told them his party were in want of provisions, and that if they could not get them peaceably, they must by force. He admitted he had joined his fortunes and that of his tribe, to the King, who "was very strong," that he and his people were "natural warriors, and could not bear to be threatened by Gen. SCHUYLER." He demanded that the Mohawk people he had left behind, should be made free, to pass out of the country when they pleased. This advent was attended only by levying some supplies from the inhabitants.

In July following, Gen. HERKIMER went to Unadilla with a corps of three hundred and eighty militia; where BRANT again appeared with one hundred and eighty warriors. He was as insolent as before. He repeated a declaration of his intention to espouse the cause of the King; said the King would "humble the Boston people that Gen. HERKIMER had joined;" and intimated that those he served, were much better able to make Indians presents, than were Gen. H. and his associates. Col. Cox, who was present, said to BRANT if he had determined to espouse the cause of the King, the matter was ended. At some intimation from BRANT, his warriors raised a shout, and repaired to their camp about a mile distant, when seizing their arms, they fired several guns and raised the Indian war whoop. Returning to the conference ground, Gen. HERKIMER assured BRANT that he had not come to fight; at which BRANT motioned to his warriors to keep their places; and addressing Gen. HERKIMER, in a threatening attitude, told him if his purpose was war, he was ready for him. He then proposed that Mr. STEWART the missionary among the Mohawks, (who was supposed to lean to the English side,) and the wife of Col. BUTLER, should be permitted to pass from the upper to the lower Mohawk castle. Gen. HERKIMER offered to comply upon the condition that some tories and deserters were given up to him; to which condition BRANT would not yield, but closed the conference with a threat that he would go to Oswego and hold a treaty with Col. BUTLER; or rather the conference was ended by a violent storm which obliged both parties to retreat for shelter.

This was the last conference that was held with any of the Six Nations except the Oneidas, to prevent them from engaging in the war. It is supposed that Gen. HERKIMER's forbearance, his neglect to urge matters to extremes when provoked by BRANT, was dictated by the hope that amicable arrangements would eventually be made.

On the 5th of July, 1777, Gen. BURGOYNE had obtained possession of Ticonderoga. The presence of so large a British armed force there, with the feeble means as it seemed of resisting their further conquests, spread alarm throughout the country, and especially in Tryon county. On the 15th of July, an Oneida sachem, returned from Canada and brought news that Col. JOHN JOHNSON with his family, and Col. CLAUS and his family, were at Oswego, with "700 Indians, 400 regulars, and 600 tories," and that preparations were making for an attack on Fort Schuyler;* that Col. BUTLER had arrived at Oswego from Niagara, with an additional force, &c.

In April preceding this, Col. GANSEVOORT had garrisoned this frontier post with the 3d regiment N. Y. line of state troops, and had been busily engaged in strengthening it. Alarm increased in consequence of the news from the west. Secret information of movements had been industriously circulated among the disaffected inhabitants of Tryon county. Insinuations of an alarming nature were thrown out, and not without effect. The Indians, it was said, would ravage the whole intervening country. "Many," says Mr. CAMPBELL, "who had not acted before decidedly, now espoused the cause of the mother country, and in small parties, stole away and went to the enemy." On the 17th of July, Gen. HERKIMER issued a proclamation, that two thousand troops "christians and savages," had collected at Oswego, with intention to invade the frontiers. He announced his intention, in case the enemy approached, to order into service, every male person, being in health, between the ages of sixteen and sixty;—"and those above sixty, or unwell and incapable to march, shall assemble also, armed, at the respective places, where women and children will be gathered together, in order for defence against the enemy, if attacked, as much as lies in their power." He also ordered that the disaffected should be arrested, and kept under guard; appealed in urgent language upon all to discharge their duty, in the approaching crisis; and closed his stirring proclamation as follows:—"Not doubting that the Almighty Power, upon our humble prayers, and sincere trust in him, will then graciously succor our arms in battle, for our just cause, and victory cannot fail on our side."

On the 2d of August, Gen. St. LEGER, having advanced from Oswego, with an army of seventeen hundred men, (including BRANT and his Indian forces,) arrived before Fort Schuyler, where

---

*"This fort occupied a part of the site of Rome, in the present county of Oneida, situated at the head of navigation of the Mohawk, and at the carrying place between that river and Wood Creek, from whence the boats passed to Oswego; it was a post of great importance to the western part of New York. The French, with their usual sagacity, in endeavoring to monopolize the Indian trade, had erected a fortification at this place. At the commencement of the war, it seems to have gone to decay; a few families had settled there, forming the extreme outposts of civilization, save the forts of Oswego and Niagara. It was called Fort Schuyler, in honor of Gen. Schuyler. It has been confounded by some with Fort Schuyler, which was built in the French wars, near where Utica now stands, and named in honor of Col. Schuyler, the uncle of Gen. Schuyler." — *Campbell's Annals.*

he soon found there was no disposition to surrender. He soon after published a proclamation, high toned and insolent; he recapitulated the offences of the citizens of the Mohawk Valley against his sovereign, the King, and announced that he had come at the head of a competent force to punish the aggressors, and afford relief to those who were not engaged in "rebellion." He declared his intention first to adopt conciliatory measures, and if those failed, he deemed himself justified in "executing the vengeance of the state against the willful outcasts." "The messengers of justice and wrath," said the confident leader of the royalist force, "await them in the field, and devastation and famine and every concomitant horror that a reluctant but indispensable prosecution of military duty, must occasion, will bar the way to their return."

Gen. HERKIMER was advancing to join his force—about seven hundred—with that of Col. GANSEVOORT, in the fort. Apprised of this, St. LEGER detached BRANT and BUTLER with a body of Indians and Tories to intercept him. They resolved upon a surprise, and for this purpose chose a spot well suited to the purpose. Gen. HERKIMER advancing with his force without any suspicion of danger; the joint forces of BUTLER and BRANT, favored in their ambuscade by the thick foliage of the forest, arose and poured a destructive fire upon them. The advance guard was entirely destroyed; those who survived the first onslaught, became victims of the tomahawk. The rear regiment fled in confusion, and were pursued by the Indians. The forward division, facing out in every direction, sought shelter behind the trees, and returned an effectual fire. "The fighting had continued for some time, when Major WATSON, a brother-in-law of Sir JOHN JOHNSON, brought up a detachment of Johnson's Greens. The blood of the Germans boiled with indignation at the sight of these men. Many of the 'Greens' were personally known to them. They had fled their country, and were now returned in arms to subdue it. Their presence under any circumstances, would have kindled up the resentment of those militia; but coming as they now did, in aid of a retreating foe, called into exercise the most bitter feelings of hostility. They fired upon them as they advanced, and then rushing from behind their covers, attacked them with their bayonets, and those who had none, with the but ends of their muskets. This contest was maintained, hand to hand, for nearly half an hour. The Greens made a good resistance, but were obliged to give way under the fury of their assailants."* Major WATSON was taken prisoner, but left upon the field.

Col. WILLETT, with two hundred and seven men, made a sally from the fort, and attacked the enemy in camp, to make a diversion in favor of Gen. HERKIMER, and after an engagement of two hours compelled a retreat. After he had secured a part of the spoils the enemy had left, and destroyed the remainder, he was upon his return back to the fort, attacked by two hundred regulars from St. LEGER's army, which, aided by a fire of cannon from the fort he soon compelled to retreat. He returned into the fort without the loss of a single man. This successful sally, the hearing that their camp was taken, and a shower of rain, induced the detachment that was in conflict with Gen. HERKIMER, to withdraw, and thus ended the events of the day. The loss of the Provincials was about 200 killed, and as many wounded.

Gen. HERKIMER was wounded; one of his legs fractured by a musket ball. Refusing to leave the field, he had himself placed in a position a little distance from the theatre of action, when facing the enemy, he deliberately lit and smoked his pipe. Surrounded by a few men he continued to issue his orders with firmness. A few days after the battle, his leg was amputated; mortification ensued and caused his death. Thus were the patriotic men of the valley of the Mohawk, deprived of the services of their brave leader, in a crisis when the services of such as him would seem to have been indispensable.

Of the other officers of the Tryon county militia, Col. Cox, Majors Ersinlord, Klepsattle, and Van Slyck were killed, as was also Thomas Spencer, whose eloquence had stirred up the people of Cherry Valley, in a primitive period of the war. Major Frey, and Col. Bellinger were taken prisoners. The British Indian allies had one hundred killed; the Senecas alone, over thirty. The loss in killed, of the regulars and tories was computed at one hundred.

St. LEGER, though effectually defeated, resolved not to regard the events of the day in that light; but to use them even to aid

---

*Campbell's Annals.

NOTE.— In an address before the New York Historical Society, Governeur Morris said:—"Let me recall gentlemen to your reccollection, the bloody spot on which Herkimer fell. There was found the Indian and the white man born on the banks of the Mohawk, their left hand clenched in each other's hair, the right grasping in a grasp of death, the knife plunged in each other's bosom; thus they lay frowning."

him in obtaining a surrender of the fort. He compelled Col. Bellinger and Major Frey, who were in his camp as prisoners, to address a letter to Col. Gansevoort, exaggerating the disasters of the day, and strongly urging a surrender; telling him how strong were his beseigers; that no succor could reach him; and assuming that Burgoyne was already before Albany. After repeated demands of a surrender, a correspondence, and some verbal messages, the finale of which was a short answer from Col. Gansevoort, in which he declared his fixed determination of holding out and resisting the seige, St. Leger threw up some redoubts, and brought his artillery to bear upon the fort, but with little effect. The siege continued until the 22d of August, when the besiegers had advanced within one hundred and fifty yards of the fort. Gen. Schuyler on hearing of the attack upon Gen. Herkimer and its results, despatched Gens. Learned and Arnold, (Benedict,) with a brigade of men to its relief; at the same time writing a letter to Col. Gansevoort exhorting him to hold out, and encouraging him with flattering accounts of the prospects of staying the march of Burgoyne. On the 22d of August, Gen. Arnold, in advance of Learned, arrived with his force at the German Flatts. From there, he also addressed Col. Gansevoort, telling him he should soon be with him, to be under no apprehensions, that he "knew the strength of the enemy and how to deal with them." He included in his letter the announcement that Stark had gained a signal victory at Bennington; that Howe with the shattered remnant of his army were on ship-board; that "Burgoyne was retreating to Ty."

In the camp of Gen. Arnold, was a refugee—Han Yost Schuyler—he gave him his liberty on condition that he would proceed to the camp of St. Leger, announce his approach, and give an exaggerated account of the advancing force under his command; retaining the brother of the refugee as an hostage to secure a faithful discharge of the duties he had engaged to perform. The Indians in St. Leger's camp were already dissatisfied; they had suffered severely, and despaired of being remunerated with plunder. This was greatly enhanced by the arrival of Han Yost, who told them that Gen. Arnold's force was "as numerous as the leaves on the forest trees." The Indians refused to remain any longer. Thus crippled, on the 22d, of August, St. Leger, retired in disorder and confusion, leaving the greater portion of his baggage behind. He went by the way of Oswego to Montreal, and from thence, through lake Champlain to join Gen. BURGOYNE.

Thus ended the siege of Fort Schuyler.

Having thus opened the campaign upon the Mohawk — sketched briefly the leading events up to the first principal conflict of arms, and given its main features and results — the author is admonished of the necessity of disposing of the Border War, with but brief chronological sketches of what followed, to its termination, except in reference to two prominent events. The whole subject forms an interesting and instructive branch of the local history of a large portion of our State; and he indulges the hope that he has been enabled to introduce enough of it in his work — and in a manner — to invite the younger portion of his readers especially, to sources of greater detail, and farther extended enquiry and research. — In the entire history of our revolutionary struggle, there are few pages we can read, which in a greater degree serves to remind us of the sufferings and sacrifices that purchased the blessings we so eminently enjoy — than those upon which are inscribed a faithful narrative of the Border War of New York and Pennsylvania.

After the siege of Fort Schuyler, the Indians still hung like a "scythe of death," on the frontiers of New York. In the remote and less thickly inhabited parts, single individuals and whole families disappeared — no one could tell by what means, or how. Relative, friend, or traveler, came to the place which he knew was once the residence of those he sought, but the charred fragments of their dwellings, were all he found.

BRANT opened the Indian campaign of 1788 by an attack upon the town of Springfield, near the head of Otsego lake. He imprisoned all who did not fly, burnt every building but one, into which he gathered all the women and children, and left them unhurt.

On the first of July, a skirmish occurred between a party of militia, and a large body of Indians, at Cobbleskill. The militia were compelled to retreat. Several dwellings were burned, after being plundered; houses and cattle were all killed or taken off. The whole of the Schoharie region was constantly visited by predatory bands of Indians and Tories, during the whole war.

MASSACRE OF WYOMING.

There are few events connected with Indian border warfare that have called forth more sympathy and condemnation than the massacre of Wyoming. The settlers in this peaceful retreat were removed from the theatre of war. Its secluded situation seemed to hide it from the observation of both parties. Most of the settlers were in favor of the Colonies, and a considerable number belonged to the revolutionary army. Though there was a kind of understanding that the troops enlisted there, should not be removed from the valley, but kept there for its security and defence; still such was the emergency of the country that they had been called away, and about three hundred more enlisted. Most of those who remained were either too young or too old to be very serviceable as soldiers. Such was the defenceless state of Wyoming, when its inhabitants discovered some indications that war was to be brought to their doors. Their distance from other settlements destroyed all hope of obtaining help from abroad, and the suddenness with which the attack probably would be made, rendered assistance from the regular army very doubtful.

In 1778, a band of Tories and Indians, under the command of Col. JOHN BUTLER, marched into this quiet valley, and made it the scene of desolation and suffering. The expedition "moved from Niagara, across the Genesee country, down the Chemung, to Tioga Point, whence they embarked upon the Susquehannah, and landed about twenty miles above Wyoming." Col. ZEBULON BUTLER, who had been in the French war, and was now an officer in the Revolutionary army, happened to be home on a visit at the time of the invasion. At the urgent solicitation of the people, he assumed command of the militia. An attempt was made to attack the enemy by surprise, but the scout was accidentally discovered by an Indian, who fired at him, and immediately gave the alarm. When the Americans came up they found the enemy ready to receive them. A bloody battle ensued, in which one party fought with the desperation of men knowing their fate if conquered, and the other with the savage ferocity of revenge. The Tories and Indians gave no quarter, but pursued the flying party, killing all they could and afterwards murdering all they took. The fugitive army first sought shelter in what was called "Fort Forty." From this, those who still survived, fled to Fort Wyoming, which was shortly surrounded by Indians and Tories. This fort was filled with women and children; it was in no condition to be defended, or to withstand a siege. A capitulation took place, in which it was stipulated that the inhabitants might return to their farms but were not to take up arms during the war. The Tories were allowed to return to their lands. The English commanding officer pledged his influence to have the Indians respect private property. This promise was totally disregarded. The Indians prowled through the valley, plundering and burning every house that was not occupied by a Tory — carrying misery and wretchedness into the bosom of many a happy home, and spreading ruin and suffering through the whole valley.

Early in the month of September, BRANT desolated the German Flatts. Fortunately, the inhabitants had warning in time to enable them to make their escape. It was evening when BRANT arrived. It being rainy and dark, and supposing his presence in the neighborhood not known, he waited until morning, when his party almost simultaneously fired all the dwellings. Disappointed at not finding the inhabitants, he destroyed every thing they had left behind, without attacking the fort in which the people were collected.

The flourishing settlements in Cherry Valley were next doomed to suffer the horrors of an Indian invasion. LAFAYETTE, observing its exposed condition, early in the spring of 1778, ordered a fortification to be built, in which the inhabitants deposited their property, and went for protection in seasons of danger. In the autumn of that year, supposing all danger passed, and relying on the vigilance of the commanding officer of the fort, to warn them of the approach of the enemy, they returned to their dwellings. Col. ALDEN received timely notice that the enemy were on their way, and where was their destination. Refusing to believe the reports of the intended attack, promising to take every necessary measure to prevent surprise — he made others feel the same security, and thus all was left completely exposed. Even after the attack had been begun, when told by a wounded settler, who had barely escaped with life, he still doubted. The enemy had ample time to make complete their plans for striking a terrible blow. Particular houses where officers of the garrison were staying, were ascertained by the Indians. With hardly a moment's notice, when least expected, the quiet villagers were aroused to a sense of their fearful situation by the sound of death-shots, the slashes of the tomahawk, and the shrieks of devoted victims. Fire and hatchet were busily engaged in accomplishing their work of terror — slaughter and pillage marked the course of civilized and savage foe. The fort was surrounded and assaulted, but being met with spirit and firmness, the Indians soon shrunk from the steady fire that was poured upon them, run to the houses, to plunder, destroy, and kill without mercy or check. The same evening thirty or forty prisoners were marched into the wilderness. When they arrived at the place of encampment, large fires, in a circular form were kindled, and the captives, without shelter from the inclement weather, or any regard to age, health or sex, were all put indiscriminately in the centre. Their dreadful situation was rendered still more awful, by the startling yells and savage revelry kept up all night by the Indians while dividing the spoils. In the morning, the prisoners with their captors, set out on their journey; but before they had gone far, the women and children were voluntarily released, with the exception of Mrs. CAMPBELL and her four children, and Mrs. MOORE and her children. The invaders then went back to Niagara from whence originated most of these expeditions of pillage and bloodshed.

NOTE. — Mrs. Campbell and her children were carried to Kanadasaega, (Geneva,) then the chief town of the Senecas. She and her children were adopted into an Indian family, to supply the place of lost relations. Nobly resolving to adapt herself to her new condition, she exerted herself in getting in favor with her captors, and making herself useful to them. She made garments for the squaws, and in various ways, acquired an influence which greatly meliorated her condition. One day an Indian came to her, and observing that she wore caps, said he would give her one; upon presenting it he told her he had obtained it "at Cherry Valley." She recognized it as the cap of Miss Jane Wells, who had been most barbarously massacred at Cherry Valley. It had a cut in the crown made by a tomahawk, and was spotted with blood! "She could not but drop a tear to her memory, for she had known her from her infancy, a pattern of virtue and loveliness." The Indian acknowledged himself the murderer. Mrs. Campbell preserved the relic, and afterwards presented it to the friends of the deceased. When Col. Butler went to Canada, he had left his wife and children, who were retained as hostages. A proposition was made to exchange them for Mrs. Campbell and her children. Col. Campbell, the husband and father, receiving the proposition in writing, laid it before Gov. Clinton and Gen. Schuyler, and it was acceded to. Early in the spring Col. Butler went to Kanadasaega and proposed the release of Mrs. Campbell; after a council of several days, with much reluctance, on the part of the Indians, he succeeded in his mission. She was taken to Niagara in June, 1779, but her children were retained at Kanadasaega. About this time news was received at Niagara, of the march of Gen. Sullivan; anticipating his arrival there, the garrison was recruited and strengthened. Col. Butler did not succeed in getting Mrs. Campbell's children, until the Senecas, fleeing before Gen. Sullivan, sought refuge at Niagara, bringing them along in their flight. Mrs. Campbell remained at Niagara a year from the period of her first arrival there; in June, 1780, she and her children were taken down to Montreal, where she found Mrs. Butler and her children, and her own son, a small boy, with them. After a delay of several months, the family were

GEN. SULLIVAN'S EXPEDITION.

The desolating and terrible Indian incursions with which the frontiers of New York and Pennsylvania had been visited in 1777 and 1778, induced Congress to authorize General WASHINGTON to send an expedition into the country of the Six Nations, lay waste their villages, destroy their haunts, and make them suffer some of the evils they had inflicted on others. The ultimate design of the expedition was the capture of Fort Niagara, the head quarters of the British and their Indian allies.

The distance of the Senecas, upon the banks of the Seneca lake, and in the valley of the Genesee, from the immediate vicinity of hostile operations, had screened them from assault and retributive justice; while they could sally out whenever a runner from Butler, Brant, or the Johnsons, told them there was work of blood in hand; or when an ambitious chief among them took the war path upon his own account, to scourge with the double motive of revenge and plunder;—finding a safe retreat when their sanguinary missions were executed.

The Six Nations had at this period, made considerable advances in some of the arts of civilized life. They had begun to depend less upon the chase for subsistence, than upon the cultivation of the soil. They had more permanent places of residence, and were less wandering in their habits, than most of their race upon this continent. They had numerous villages, cultivated fields, orchards, and rude gardens. They were enjoying many of the comforts and conveniences of civilization.

Gen. SULLIVAN was appointed commander of the expedition. After some delay and embarrassment he assembled his division at Wyoming, marched to Tioga, and formed a junction with the eastern division, under the command of Gen. JAMES CLINTON. On the 22d of August, 1779, the two divisions united and made an effective force of five thousand men. Gen. SULLIVAN marched up

---

sent to Albany, and ultimately, reached their home at Cherry Valley. When Gen. WASHINGTON traversed the valley of the Mohawk, in the summer of 1784, accompanied by Gov. CLINTON and others, they were the guests of Col. Campbell in the rude log cabin he had erected after the war. Gov. Clinton observed to Mrs. Campbell, in reference to her boys:— "They will make fine soldiers in time." "I hope my country will never need their services," was the response of one who had seen enough of war and its consequences. "I hope so too madam," said Gen. WASHINGTON, for "I have seen enough of war."

the Tioga and Chemung, taking every precaution to guard against surprise and ambuscades.

The estimate made by Gen. SULLIVAN in his report of the strength of the Indians and Tories, at fifteen hundred, materially differs from the official report of Col. JOHN BUTLER, who assumes that he had but six hundred British and Indians. The Indians were under the command of JOSEPH BRANT, and the Rangers under Col. JOHN BUTLER, who held the chief command.* The British and Indians had taken position and thrown up some rude fortifications about a mile below Newtown, now Elmira. Col. BUTLER states in his official account of the battle, that the Senecas, and the few Delawares he had with him, had selected this spot and obstinately resolved to make a stand there, in spite of the opposition of himself and BRANT.

After destroying on his way all the Indian towns and planted fields that could be reached, on the 29th of August, Gen. SULLIVAN prepared to attack the British and Indians in their own position. In the battle that followed, a portion of the Indians maintained their ground firmly and bravely, fought as long as there was any hope of victory. BRANT and another chief named KIANGARACHTA, particularly distinguished themselves, flying from point to point, animating and sustaining their warriors, by encouraging words, and daring deeds. Col. BUTLER bitterly complains of the conduct of some of his Indian allies in the early part of the engagement, who became frightened and panic struck by the explosion of some shells thrown beyond them, which they supposed came from an opposite direction, and led them to think that they were about to be surrounded, and all means of escape cut off. The battle having continued near two hours, the enemy became fearful of being completely hemmed in, precipitately abandoned his works and fled. Gen. SULLIVAN pursued him for nearly two miles, destroying every thing that could possibly be of any service to the Indians. Col. BUTLER acknowledged the loss of only five rangers, killed or taken; five Indians killed, and nine wounded. It is evident that he underestimated his loss, for Gen. SULLIVAN found eleven dead on the field, and it is a well known Indian custom, to carry off as many of their dead as possible. Beside the eleven, fourteen were found

---

* The statement made by Col. Stone, in his life of Brant, that the Johnson's were present, participating in the movements against Gen. Sullivan, is contradicted by the official report of Col. John Butler.

partially buried under the leaves. So effectual was the dispersion of the Indians as to render it impossible that Col. BUTLER should be able to ascertain his precise loss. The loss of the Americans was only five or six killed, and forty or fifty wounded — a very small loss considering the force they had to contend with, and the fierceness with which the battle was fought.

Gen. SULLIVAN promptly followed up his advantage. The Indians seemed to be disheartened from a conviction that they could not make a successful stand against Gen. SULLIVAN, arrest his onward march, and the consequent ruin and devastation which they knew would inevitably attend it.

They made no more serious and united opposition to the invaders. When they heard that Gen. SULLIVAN was approaching to their villages on the Genesee, they did indeed think of making another attempt. They selected a position between the head of Connesus lake and Honeoye outlet. They intended to await the approach of SULLIVAN in ambuscade. They, however, retreated when SULLIVAN came up, and fled before him. He continued his march, leaving burning villages and devastated fields, the witnesses of his presence. While Gen. SULLIVAN was constructing a bridge over a creek which led to Little Beard's town, Lieut. BOYD was sent out to observe the situation of the village. After a long, fatiguing march, continued far into the night, the party came to a village that appeared to have been lately deserted, as fires were yet burning in the huts. They passed the remainder of the night there, sending two of their number back to the main army to report.* BOYD having been discovered in the morning, resolved to reach the main army as soon as possible. He met with no difficulty until he came within a mile and a half of Gen. SULLIVAN's camp, when they encountered a party of observation belonging to the enemy. Lieut. BOYD's brave but devoted little band were soon surrounded, and their only chance of escape was to cut their way through the ranks of their foe. Twelve of BOYD's men were soon shot down, and himself and PARKER taken prisoners, the other seven making their escape. BOYD immediately asked for an interview with BRANT, which was granted. While in the presence of BRANT, he, by signs, gave him to understand, that enemies though they might be on the battle field, yet there was one

---

* Mary Jemison's Narrative.

relation in which they were sacredly bound to regard each other as "brothers." BRANT recognized the appeal, and promised to protect him from injury. BOYD, placing the utmost confidence in the assurance of BRANT, refused to answer any questions that Col. BUTLER asked, relative to the condition, strength, and designs of Gen. SULLIVAN's army, although threatened with being delivered over to the Indians, if he refused to give the desired information. Confident of BRANT's protection, he still declined. BUTLER, meaning all that he threatened, gave BOYD and PARKER up to the Indians. After inflicting on BOYD the most cruel tortures—throwing hatchets at his head, tearing off his nails, cutting off his tongue, ears and nose, putting out one of his eyes, taking out an end of his intestines, tying it to a small tree and then driving him around as long as they could, they finally ended his sufferings by cutting off his head. PARKER was also killed, but they cut off his head, without any torture.

Gen. SULLIVAN now employed some time in completing the work of desolation and destruction up and down the river, whereever were found villages, wigwams, fields, orchards, gardens, corn, cattle, or anything that is necessary to support life—all were swept away. The capture of Niagara, the general place of rendezvous of the Indians, whence they sallied on those bloody excursions which made them a terror to all the frontier settlements, was not effected. Gen. SULLIVAN returned with his army, and went into winter quarters, in New Jersey, having prepared the way for the famine and want which the Indians soon felt. The destruction of so many of their villages, and the total loss of their planted fields, just as they were ripening for the harvest, and as the previous year's supply was exhausted, caused hundreds of Indians, with their wives and children, to flock to Fort Niagara for the means of subsistence the ensuing winter—the memorable winter of 1779 and 1780. The British Canadian Governor, Sir JOHN JOHNSON, was obliged to make great exertions to furnish sufficient

---

NOTE.—In 1841, a public tribute of respect was paid to the memory of Boyd, by citizens of the Genesee Valley. A large concourse assembled at the village of Cuyler. The venerable revolutionary patriot, Maj. MOSES VAN CAMPEN, with other revolutionary soldiers were present. The burial place of Boyd having been identified, his remains were deposited in an urn, and suitable exercises were had in a grove near by; including a pertinent and timely historical and biographical discourse, by ―――― TREAT, Esq. The next day the remains, attended by a large military and civil escort, were taken to Mount Hope cemetery, where their interment was attended by an address from Gov. SEWARD, and suitable military and religious exercises.

supplies for them. The following paragraph from a manuscript letter of the Delaware chief, KILLBUCK, to Col. DANIEL BROADHEAD, at Pittsburgh, dated at Salem, on the Muskingum, June 7th, 1780, will give some idea of the sufferings that were experienced: "Some days ago, one man and an old woman, came from Niagara, who acquaint me that last winter, three hundred Indians died at that place of the flux."

The destruction of the Onondagas formed a part of the general plan of SULLIVAN's campaign against the Six Nations and preceded it. The command of the eastern division of that expedition having been assigned Gen. JAMES CLINTON, he detailed Col. VAN SCHAICK, assisted by Col. WILLETT and Major COCHRAN for the one against the Onondagas. Gen. CLINTON instructed Col. VAN SCHAICK to sweep away their villages and fields — to take as many prisoners as he could, with as little bloodshed as possible. On the 19th of April, 1779, with about five hundred and fifty effective men, Col. VAN SCHAICK left Fort Schuyler. Notwithstanding bad and rainy weather, swollen streams and morasses, he arrived at the Onondaga settlements on the third day. For the purpose of falling upon as many towns at the same time as possible, the men were divided in detachments with orders to make their attacks simultaneously. The detachments suddenly came upon the Indian hamlets that were scattered through the valley of the Onondaga Creek, and began their devastating work. Indian villages were soon wrapt in flames, cultivated fields destroyed, gardens spoiled, provisions wasted, and cattle of all kinds killed. When they discovered that an enemy had so unexpectedly rushed into their very midst, and was spreading ruin on every side, they fled so precipitately that they left every thing behind them, even their guns and other weapons of war. From a state of security and plenty, in a day, the Onondagas were reduced to misery and want — became houseless and destitute. Though they professed to be friendly to the Americans, their war parties had long hovered on the borders of the frontiers and around Fort Schuyler, scalping and murdering, imprisoning and torturing all the white inhabitants they could. The influence of this expedition was salutary on the Oneidas, who were really friendly in their feelings to the Americans. The Oneidas and Tuscaroras sent a deputation to Fort Schuyler, and renewed their promises of friendship. Having successfully accomplished the objects of the expedition Col. VAN SCHAICK marched back to Fort Schuyler, without loosing a single man.

In the spring and summer of 1780, the Mohawk valley was again invaded, Sir JOHN JOHNSON heading the expedition—Johnstown the point of attack. BRANT was again upon the war path. He attacked Canajoharie, burning houses, wasting property, and putting to death, and making captive, the inhabitants. Jointly the two leaders, one of the loyalists, and the other of the Indians, extended the incursions into Schoharie. They re-enacted the terrible scenes that have been described, occurring upon previous visits. The next year, 1781, the Indians in alliance with the corps of JOHNSON and BUTLER, harrassed the frontiers, and kept the settlers in a state of dread and alarm.

In August, Major Ross and WALTER BUTLER, came from Canada by the way of Sacondaga to Johnstown, with a force of five hundred regulars, Tories and Indians, and encamped near Johnson Hall. They were attacked by Col. MARINUS WILLETT with a force of three hundred men, in the end obliged to give way. They retreated up the Mohawk, hotly pursued by their conqueror, Col. WILLETT.

In the month of January, 1783, Gen. WASHINGTON, not having yet been apprised of the treaty of peace, conceived the plan of surprising and obtaining possession of the important fortress of Oswego. The possession of this post and Niagara had given the enemy great advantage throughout the war. Oswego was then one of the most formidable military defences on the continent. The hazardous enterprise was confided to Col. WILLETT. There is now residing in Bloomfield, Ontario county, a venerable pioneer of western New York,—BENJAMIN GOSS—who was with Col. WILLETT in this expedition. From him, the author received some account of it during the last summer:—With great secresy, as the original intention was a surprise, Col. WILLETT assembled his force at Fort Herkimer on the 8th of February, and there provided a large portion of them with snow shoes, as they had no beaten track to follow, and the snow was from two feet and a half to three feet deep. The men thus provided, went ahead and made a track for a cavalcade of two hundred sleighs that followed, carrying the remainder of the troops, and the baggage. The expedition crossed

Oneida lake on the ice, and arriving at Fort Brewington, at the foot of the lake, the sleighs were left. Here a large number of the pressed militia, having seen enough of a winter campaign in the wilderness, deserted. An Oneida Indian was selected as the pilot through the woods to Oswego. He, by mistake, or purposely, misled the expedition, which occasioned great delay in arriving at the garrison, and much suffering from cold and hunger. When they supposed themselves near the garrison, and began to prepare for the attack, they discovered that they had gone in another direction, were lost in the forest, the deep snow adding much to their perplexity and embarrassment. Changing their course, they arrived within four miles of the place of destination, but in a condition that did not justify an attack upon a strong fortification. The men had been three days without provision, were wearied by marching in the deep snow, and their ammunition had become much injured.—Col. WILLETT upon consultation with his officers, resolved reluctantly to forego the attack, and retrace his steps. The retreat was attended with even more suffering than the advance. From the time the expedition left Fort Plain until its return there, it was twelve days of almost constant suffering from cold or hunger, or both combined. Many of the men had their feet frozen, our informant among the number. On the return of the expedition to Albany, it was met by the welcome news of peace, proclaimed by the town clerk at the city Hall.

"The incursion of Ross and BUTLER was the last made into the county of Tryon. Indeed, there was no longer any thing to destroy. The inhabitants lost all but the soil they cultivated; their beautiful county, except in the vicinity of the forts, was turned into a wilderness. During the war, famine sometimes appeared inevitable, and it was with difficulty that they preserved from the ravages of the enemy sufficient grain to support their families during the winter. The resistance of the inhabitants on the frontier settlements, however unimportant it may seem, because no great battles were fought, or important victories won, was of very considerable moment in the cause for which they struggled; they kept back the enemy from the towns of the Hudson, and thus frustrated the plan of the British for establishing a line of posts along that river. And while we admire the heroism and patriotism of those worthies of the Revolution, whose names have come down to us surrounded with a halo of glory, we should not withhold our praise from those obscure individuals in the frontier settlements, who, amid the most appalling dangers, surrounded on all sides by enemies and traitors, still refused to submit to oppression and arbitrary exactions, though allured by assurances of safety and promises of reward. Many left their homes; many fell in battle in the regular army, and in skirmishes and battles with the enemy at home, and many fell silently by the rifle, the tomahawk, and the scalping knife of the Indian."*

Having now travelled over a period of one hundred and seventy-five years—from the advent of CHAMPLAIN upon the St. Lawrence to the close of the American Revolution—we have done, for a while, with wars,† and mostly, with the "rumors of wars"—and enter upon the more pleasing task of recording the peaceful triumphs of civilization and improvement—of enterprise and industry.

The settlement of Western New York followed soon after the peace of 1783. Our national independence achieved—the glorious prospect of future peace and prosperity, opening upon our country—men's minds soon began to turn to the extension of the bounds of civilization and improvement—the enlargement of the theatre upon which the experiment of free government and free institutions was to be enacted. The war closed—the armies discharged—there were many, poor in purse, but rich in all the elements that fitted them to become the pioneers of the wilderness, the founders of new settlements. There had come along with SULLIVAN to the regions of Western New York, a great number of those who, looking forward to the end of the war, converted the expedition to the two-fold purpose of quelling the disturbers of the border settlers, and viewing the country they inhabited, with an eye to future enterprises. They passed through the vallies of the Mohawk, of our interior lakes, of the Susquehannah, delighted at every step with the beautiful prospects that surrounded them, until arriving at the valley of the Genesee, it realized their highest hopes and most extravagant anticipations. They returned to their homes to mingle with the narratives of an Indian war, descriptions of the country they had seen; resolved themselves to retrace their steps upon the

---

* Campbell's Annals.

† With the exception of some brief references to the campaigns of St. Clair and Wayne.

more peaceful mission of emigration and settlement; and their representations turned the attention of others in this direction. Thus War—as it is often its province to do—as if it was the will of Providence to make evils productive of blessings—aided in hastening and achieving one of the noblest triumphs of Peace.

[Before commencing to trace the progress of settlement westward, brief biographical sketches of individuals who were in Western New York, previous to white settlement, captives, one of them a voluntary exile;—will be inserted in a separate chapter.]

CHAPTER IV.

BRIEF BIOGRAPHICAL SKETCHES.

HORATIO JONES.

Horatio Jones, an Indian captive, was born in December, 1763, in Bedford county, Pennsylvania. His father was a blacksmith, and intended that his son should follow the same business. But at a very early age, Horatio's love of adventure and military life, showed itself by his voluntarily going off with companies of soldiers as a fifer, and cheerfully enduring all the privations of the camp. He was active, enterprising, fearless—possessed of a powerful frame, capable of enduring any amount of fatigue, a sure and accomplished marksman. Though but a boy, hardly capable of fully understanding the merits of the contest, yet with the ardent enthusiasm of youth, he joined the patriot ranks, ready and willing to face any danger and perform any duty. In 1781, he enlisted as a soldier in the army of the United States, and belonged to a company called "Bedford Rangers." This company repaired to a neighboring fort, to be reinforced, and then to march into the Indian country. When the company arrived at the fort, the garrison there was found so weak that no soldiers could be spared. Notwithstanding this, Capt. Dunlap, the commander of the company, resolved to proceed with the small force he had with him. He had not gone far, before he was surrounded by Indians, who simultaneously fired upon him, killed nine of his men, took eight prisoners, among the latter of whom, was himself and young Jones. Jones tried to make his escape by flight, but he fell down, was overtaken and captured.

The captives were carried into the wilderness. For two days they were entirely without food, and on the third day only the entrails of a bear was allowed them. Capt. DUNLAP was wounded. Showing some slight evidence of exhaustion, an Indian, fearing that he might be troublesome, silently stepped up behind him, and without a warning word, struck a hatchet deep into the back of his neck, stripped off his scalp, and left him to die. For the first two or three days after their capture, the Indians were very cautious and watchful; they would hardly allow a gun to be fired, lest the sound might guide their pursuers. After the fourth day, they began to relax their vigilance. A hunting party had been out and prepared some food. The Indians pointed it out to JONES, who supposed that they intended it as an invitation to dine; so he commenced running toward the spot, and they after him; when he reached it, he stopped. The Indians, supposing that he was trying to make his escape, laid him on his back, tied each limb to a tree, drove pronged sticks over his arms and legs, and in that condition kept him all night, his face upwards and the rain falling in it. During their forest journey, they regarded JONES with so much favor that they relieved him of his burden. Observing that one of his fellow-captives, older and feebler than himself, was overloaded, he generously took part of his load and carried it for him. When they arrived at the Indian settlement, at Nunda, Alleghany county, he was informed that a council had been held, and the Great Spirit had interposed in his behalf. He was taken to a height near the village, by an Indian, who showed him a wigwam at a considerable distance, and said if he could reach that unhurt, all would be well — if he passed through the fearful trial safely, he would be adopted and regarded as one of themselves. He immediately began the perilous race, swiftly pressing his way forward through a shower of clubs, stones, knives, hatchets and arrows — skillfully dodging and evading them all — he reached his destination and was received as one of their nation.

JONES possessed those qualities both of mind and body which the Indians most admire and respect. He was strong and finely proportioned, and able to rival any of them in those feats which they regard as tests of manliness. He was bold and fearless. By his care and prudence he soon gained their confidence and esteem. He became familiar with their language, and was often employed as an interpreter.

The life which he led among his new associates seems to have been marked by all the vicissitudes which distinguish the Indian state. He accommodated himself to his new situation, and made himself as happy as circumstances would allow. Though surrounded by savages, he had the courage to resent any insults they ventured to offer. When they threw hatchets at him he threw them back, and often with better success than they had. On one occasion, an Indian named SHARPSHINS, commenced the play of throwing tomahawks at JONES, in earnest. JONES threw them back with such effect as to endanger the life of SHARPSHINS, and render his recovery from the wound doubtful. He however, got well, and was careful how he provoked the "pale face warrior." He made himself very useful to them in repairing their hunting implements and weapons of war.

In the chase successful, swift on the race course, often outstripping their fleetest runners—temperate in his habits—cheerful in his dispositions—with a firm and fearless spirit, he soon became a great favorite with the Indians, he acquired a power and influence over them which he always exercised on the side of humanity, and saved captives from the lingering tortures of an Indian execution. He was often chosen arbiter to decide their disputes, and so uniformly just were his decisions, that he used to draw acknowledgements of the correctness of his judgements from those against whom he decided.

The history of his residence among the Indians is full of thrilling incidents and daring adventures. Without any very strict adherence to order, we shall speak of some of them: —

He had not been with them long before a "young brave" began to amuse himself at the expense of JONES, who warned him in vain to desist. At dinner one day, the young Indian renewed his sport; JONES jumped up, ran to the fire, seized a boiling squash by the neck, gave chase, overtook the Indian, and thrust the hot squash between his loose garments and bare skin. After this he was permitted to eat his dinner in peace.

JONES often saved the lives of prisoners. Major VAN CAMPEN, with two others, having fallen into their hands, they were placed under a guard of seven Indians. The prisoners managed to get loose during the night, kill all the Indians, except one, who ran away with VAN CAMPEN's hatchet sticking in his back. The White prisoners made their escape. VAN CAMPEN became an object of their deadly hatred. He soon after fell into their hands again. A council was assembled to determine his fate. JONES knew that he was the man who "lent JOHN MOHAWK the hatchet," but wished to conceal it from the rest of the Indians. In the midst of the council sat VAN CAMPEN, calm, unmoved, self possessed, closely watching every new comer, expecting soon to see JOHN MOHAWK enter with the fatal loan. JONES leaped over the heads of the Indians, and acted as interpreter, asking questions and answering them. The Indians were induced to refer the case to their prophet, who decided that the life of the prisoner should be spared.

JONES, with his Indian father and family, were in the habit of making annual visits to their relatives, living on Grand river, in Canada. They went through Tonawanda village, down the south side of the creek, to its mouth and were anxious to get across that night to camp at Schlosser. A canoe lay opposite them, on the north side of the creek. JONES wanted to swim across and get it, but his Indian father told him no one ever attempted to swim the Tonawanda, but was drowned by the witches—sunk under the water, and never seen afterwards. JONES told him that he belonged to a nation that could control the witches in the water, and said he could bring the canoe over. His Indian mother told him to mind his father, as he was a man of sense and years. JONES and his brothers being set to work to make a camp fire, he watched his opportunity, plunged into the water, and, much to the surprise of the Indians, succeeding in swimming across, and in bringing the canoe over. When he came back he was caressed by the party for his miraculous escape. They encamped that night at Fort Schlosser. The next morning they went down to Niagara. A British officer wanted to purchase JONES — having bought two prisoners of the same family before. The Indian father refused the offer, because JONES was his adopted son. The officer offered gold and told how rich his father, the King, was. "Go and tell your father the king, that he is not rich enough to buy Ta-e-da-o-qua," replied the Indian. The triumph of JONES over the witches at Tonawanda made him valued more than before among the Indians.

At one period of his life he became dissatisfied with his manner of living, and resolved to visit the home and scenes of his childhood. He accordingly started and traveled a day; night came, and he began to reflect how few of his youthful associates would remember him; how fewer still might be the number remaining there, and how coldly he might be received. The morning found him retracing his steps, with no more thoughts of changing his condition.

When this whole region of country was a wilderness, and the roads, that are now lined on either side by well cultivated fields, were not even marked out, Capt. HORATIO JONES was often employed to convey money and dispatches from one distant place to another. He was always faithful and trust worthy, never failing to transact the business on which he was sent. These journeys, which he often performed alone, were then attended with difficulties and dangers few can now appreciate. The thickest leaved tree was his only shelter from the storm when night came on; the pure spring his only hotel, where he partook of his frugal meal, which he carried with him. Yet with a brave heart and cheerful spirit, would he start off on these journeys, heedless of the perils that he might have to encounter.

The change made in his course of life by his captivity, he seems never to have regretted, but to have voluntarily acquiesced in, when it was in his power to return to his former home. He loved forest-life — its unrestrained liberty — its comparative freedom from want and care — the opportunities which it afforded him for indulging in his favorite pursuits of hunting and fishing, and beholding and admiring nature in its primitive beauty and grandeur.

Settlement, civilization, came to him; he did not seek it; though adapting himself again to the associations from which he had long been an exile, he made himself useful in the early period of emigration to the Genesee valley. — When his brother, JOHN H. JONES, came to the Seneca lake in Oct. 1788, he found him there, surrounded "with quite a little settlement — every house was covered with barks, no boards or shingles to be had." His son, WM. W. JONES, now residing at Leicester, Livingston Co., was born at Geneva, in Dec. 1786, and was the first white male child born west of Utica. In the spring of 1790, Capt. JONES and family, went upon the Genesee river, occupying at first, an Indian house, in Little Beard's town.

Soon after the treaty of peace, between the United States and the Six Nations, President WASHINGTON appointed Capt. JONES Indian Interpreter, which office he held until within a year or two of his death. For near forty years he discharged the duties of the office with ability and fidelity.

At a council held by the Six Nations, at Genesee river, Nov. 1798, it was decreed that a present should be made to Capt. JONES and Capt. PARRISH. To this end a speech was made by FARMER's

BROTHER, which was intended as a communication to the Legislature of this state, asking its co-operation in the matter. The title was finally confirmed. An extract from the speech is inserted:—

"BROTHERS:—This whirlwind," (the Revolution,) "was so directed by the Great Spirit above, as to throw into our arms two of your infant children, HORATIO JONES and JASPER PARRISH. We adopted them into our families, and made them our children. We nourished them and loved them. They lived with us many years. At length the Great Spirit spoke to the whirlwind, and it was still. A clear and uninterrupted sky appeared. The path of peace was opened, and the chain of friendship was once more made bright. Then these adopted children left us to seek their relations. We wished them to return among us, and promised, if they would return and live in our country, to give each of them a seat of land for them and their children to sit down upon.

"BROTHERS:—They have returned, and have for several years past been serviceable to us as Interpreters, we still feel our hearts beat with affection for them, and now wish to fulfill the promise we made them, for their services.—We have therefore made up our minds to give them a seat of two square miles of land lying on the outlet of lake Erie, beginning at the mouth of a creek, known as Suyguquoydes creek, running one mile from the Niagara river, up said creek, thence northerly, as the river runs, two miles, thence westerly, one mile to the river, thence up the river as the river runs, two miles to the place of beginning, so as to contain two square miles."

Capt. JONES died at his residence upon the Genesee river, in 1836, at the age of seventy-five years;—in the full possession and excercise of all his mental faculties—his eye undimmed—his nerves unstrung—full of years, and without reproach.

NOTE.—Those from whom the author derived the information contained in this biographical sketch, did not name the fact of his having left the Indians for a short period after the Revolution; which fact is to be inferred from the language of Farmer's Brother. Whatever may have been the fact with regard to a temporary residence among the whites, it would seem that he had returned, and had a family upon the Seneca lake as early as 1786.

JASPER PARRISH.

Capt. JASPER PARRISH was born in March, 1766, in Windham Connecticut. He was quite young when his parents moved to Luzerne county, Pennsylvania. Soon after the Massacre of Wyoming, when only eleven years old, he was taken captive by a party of Delawares, and carried away by them from his home. During the seven years of his captivity, he was often transferred from one tribe to another among the Six Nations, and exposed to all the hardships and privations of Indian life. While he was among them, by his prudent and conciliatory conduct, he managed to gain their confidence and good will. He learned and became familiar with the language of five different nations, and he could speak them all with fluency and correctness. In the treaty negotiated at Fort Stanwix between the United States and the Six Nations, in 1784, the Indians agreed to surrender all their prisoners and captives. PARRISH, with others was accordingly released. He was shortly appointed Indian Interpreter, and afterwards a sub-agent of Indian affairs, by the government of the United States. He discharged the duties of these offices in a manner entirely satisfactory to his own government and the Indians, for more than thirty years. He was an early pioneer in Ontario county, having settled at Canandaigua as early as 1792.

At a very tender age, when he could hardly begin even to appreciate its consequences, he was destined to experience how sudden and awful are some of the misfortunes of life. We can scarcely conceive of a more startling and fearful change, than to be suddenly taken from the midst of civilization, and carried into barbarism;— to be compelled to relinquish the comforts, usages and associations of the one, and be forced to submit to the hardships, privations and customs of the other. It was the lot of PARRISH, as it had been the lot of others, to suffer such a reverse of fortune. But he seems to have met it with manly fortitude, and even to have profited by it. In 1836, at the age of sixty-nine, he died, respected and happy in the varied relations of life.

What in all human probability, appeared to have been the greatest evil that could have befallen these captives individually, perhaps was the source of the greatest good to the country generally. During their captivity, they gained a more thorough and extensive knowledge of the character, language, habits, manners, &c. of the Indians, than they could otherwise have acquired. They were adopted by the Indians into their families, regarded as members of their nations. These captives saw them in war, and in peace — around the council fire and on the battle field — at home and abroad. Our government redeemed them whenever it could — and availed itself of their knowledge and experience, employed them as interpreters and agents, consulted and advised with them; and with their assistance, the proprietorship and possession of a whole continent has been essentially changed; civilization has taken the place of barbarism;— the works of man, his art and his science, are transforming the whole face of nature, and giving a new and different direction, to its course and destiny.

MARY JEMISON.

The interesting and instructive narrative of the captivity and life of MARY JEMISON, written as she herself related the story to her biographer before the faculties of her mind were impaired, though more than three quarters of a century afterwards, has made most readers familiar with her strange fortunes.

In the summer of 1755, during the French and Indian wars, her father's house, situated on the western frontier of Pennsylvania, was surrounded by a band, consisting of six Indians and four Frenchmen. They plundered and carried away whatever they could that was valuable, and took the whole family captive, with two or three others, who were staying with it, at the time. They were all immediately hastened away into the wilderness, murdered and scalped, with the exception of MARY and a small boy, who were carried to Fort Du Quesne. Little MARY was there given to two Indian sisters, who came to that place to get a captive to supply the place of a brother that had been slain in battle. They took her down the Ohio to their home, adopted her as their sister, under the name of DEHHEWAMIS — a word signifying "a beautiful girl." The sorrow and regret which so sudden and fearful a change in her condition produced, gradually yielded under the

---

NOTE — The prominent position of Capt. Parrish at an early period of the settlement of Western New York, would suggest a more extended biography than the author could obtain materials to make. He found himself in possession of no data beyond a brief obituary notice in the Ontario Repository.

influence of time; and she began to feel quite reconciled to her fate, when an incident occurred, which once more revived her hopes of being redeemed from captivity and restored to her friends. When Fort Pitt fell into the possession of the British, MARY was taken with a party who went there to conclude a treaty of peace with the English. She immediately attracted the notice of the white people, who showed great anxiety to know how one so young and so delicate came among the savages. Her Indian sisters became alarmed, and fearing that they might lose her, suddenly fled away with her, and carried her back to their forest home. Her disappointment was painful and she brooded over it for many days, but at length regained her usual cheerfulness, and contentment. As soon as she was of sufficient age, she was married to a young Delaware Indian, named SHENINJEE. Notwithstanding her reluctance at first to become the wife of an Indian, her husband's uniform kind treatment and gentleness, soon won her esteem and affection, and she says:—" Strange as it may seem, I loved him!"—and she often spoke of him as her "kind husband." About 1759, she concluded to change her residence. With a little child, on foot, she traveled to the Genesee river, through the pathless wilderness, a distance of near six hundred miles, and fixed her home at Little Beard's Town. When she came there, she found the Senecas in alliance with the French; they were making preparations for an attack on Fort Schlosser; and not a great while after, enacted the tragedy at the Devil's Hole. Sometime after her arrival, she received intelligence of the death of her husband, SHENINJEE, who was to have come to her in the succeeding spring. They had lived happily together, and she sincerely lamented his death.

When the war between England and France ended, she might have returned to the English, but she did not. She married another Indian, named HIAKATOO, two or three years after the death of SHENINJEE. When Gen. SULLIVAN invaded the Genesee country, her house and fields shared a common fate with the rest. When she saw them in ruins—with great energy and perseverance, she immediately went to making preparation for the coming winter. Taking her two youngest children on her back, and bidding the other three follow, she sought employment. She found an opportunity to husk corn, and secured in that way twenty-five bushels of shelled corn, which kept them through the winter.

After the close of the Revolution, she obtained the grant of a large tract of land, called the "Gardeau Reservation," which was about six miles in length and five in breadth. With the exception of some deeply afflicting domestic calamities, and the uneasiness and discontent which she felt as the white people gathered around, and her old Indian associates departed, but little occurred in her after life which need be noticed here. In 1831, preferring to pass the remainder of her days in the midst of those with whom her youth and middle age had been spent, she sold the rest of her land at Gardeau Flatts, purchased a farm on the Buffalo Reservation, where the Senecas, among whom she had long lived, had settled some five years previous. She passed the remainder of her days in peace and quietness, embraced the Christian religion, and on the 19th of September, 1833, ended a life that had been marked by vicissitudes, such as it is the lot of but few to experience.

The story of her family, of her son JOHN, especially,—his murder of his brothers, &c., has been well narrated in the small work originally written by JAMES E. SEAVER, and afterwards enlarged and improved by EBENEZER MIX. The author in his boyhood, has often seen the "White Woman," as she was uniformly called by the early settlers; and remembers well the general esteem in which she was held. Notwithstanding she had one son who was a terror to Indians, as well as the early white settlers, she has left many descendants who are not unworthy of her good name. JACOB JEMISON, a grand son of hers, received a liberal education, passed through a course of medical studies, and was appointed an assistant surgeon in the U. S. Navy. He died on board of his ship, in the Mediterranean.

Soon after the war of 1812, an altercation occurred between DAVID REESE, of Buffalo—(who was at the time the government blacksmith for the Senecas upon the Reservation near Buffalo)—and a Seneca Indian called YOUNG KING, which resulted in a severe blow with a scythe, inflicted by REESE, which nearly severed one of the Indian's arms; so near in fact, that amputation was immediately resorted to. The circumstance created considerable excitement among the Indians, which extended to Gardeau, the then home of the JEMISON family. JOHN JEMISON, headed a party from there, and went to Buffalo, giving out as he traveled along the road, that he was going to "kill REESE." The author saw him on his way, and recollects how well he personated the ideal "angel of death." His weapons were the war club and tomahawk; red paint was daubed upon his swarthy face, and long bunches of horse hair, colored red, were dangling from each arm; his warlike appearance was well calculated to give an earnest to his threats. REESE was kept secreted, and thus in all probability, avoided the fate that even kindred had met at the hands of JOHN JEMISON.

Mrs. BLACKMAN, a surviving daughter of PETER PITTS, the early pioneer upon the Honeoye Flatts, says:—"Mrs. JEMISON used to be at our house frequently, on her journeys from Gardeau to Canandaigua and back. BILL ANTIS at Canandaigua used to do her blacksmithing. She was a smart intelligent woman. She used often to sit down and tell my father stories of her captivity; but always avoided doing it in the hearing of her Indian husband, HIAKATOO."

☞ See notice of burial place of MARY JEMISON, p. 69.

EBENEZER, ALIAS, "INDIAN ALLAN."

It has been, in all periods of history, a marked, prominent result of War, to draw out, develope the character of men. The flint, inert of itself, is not more sure, when brought in quick contact with hardened steel, to produce fire, than are the exigencies of War, to produce daring, adventurous spirits;—both good and bad. No people, or age, dwelling in peace and quiet, undisturbed, know how much of the elements of good and evil, in men's characters, are slumbering, awaiting a stimulus, or call to action. How well was this illustrated by the whole history of our Revolution! The great colonial exigencies occurred—separation—war;—a great necessity was created; and men were found equal to it. There came out from the quiet walks of life, here and there, often from whence least expected, the bold, the daring—the men to lead in field and council—fitted to the terrible emergency; gifted with the skill, bravery and prudence, to carry it to a successful termination.

The history of the border wars, cotemporary with the Revolution, and prolonged beyond it; those that have succeeded them upon our western and northwestern frontiers; are replete with illustrations. They partook largely of the character of civil or internal commotions—of feuds between joint occupants of a soil or country; they were predatory—governed little by any settled rules or regulations; dependent upon skill, cunning, stratagem; the stealthy onset, and when necessary, the quick and irregular retreat. The assailants knew no rules of regular warfare; the assailed must adapt themselves to the exigency; and well did they do so. There is hardly to be found in the whole range of history, an account of war, or wars, so full of personal adventure, of individual daring, of all that would interest and instruct, if gathered up and recorded, as is all that relates to the border wars of New York. The truthful historian, finds a marked extraordinary character, or characters, in every prominent feature of the bloody contest; in after times the novelist may find a basis of truth, for a wide range of fancy.

These are thoughts that have occurred, after a brief review of some memorandums, made in conversation of those who knew EBENEZER ALLAN; and the perusal of some notices of him in the life of MARY JEMISON; and yet they are mainly not applicable to him; for he was no hero,—but rather a desperado. He warred against his own race, country and color; vied with his savage allies in deeds of cruelty and blood-shed. As a portion of his life was spent in Western New York; and especially, as he was prominent in an early period of settlement, some notice of him may be regarded as coming within the scope of local history.

He was a native of New Jersey; joined himself to the backwoodsmen of the valley of the Susquehannah, who under BRANT and BUTLER, were allies of England—leagued, and co-operating with the Indians.* Mrs. JEMISON says she has "often heard him relate ♦his inglorious feats, and confess crimes, the rehearsal of which made my blood curdle, as much accustomed as I was to hear of bloody and barbarous deeds." A detail of the enormities he confessed—though it is said, with some professions of regret—would be but a recapitulation of tales of horror, with which narratives of the border wars abound.

---

* Little is known of his early history, birth, parentage &c. Mrs. GEORGE HOSMER, of Avon speaks of a sister of his, as her early tutor, at a period when there were no schools. She had married a British soldier, named Dugan, and resided upon a farm of Allan's at "Dugan's creek," a small stream emptying into the Genesee river a few miles below Avon Springs; and at another period, at Allan's mill. Mrs. Hosmer speaks of her as a well educated, and otherwise accomplished woman, who had connected herself in marriage to one in every way unworthy of her. She had been in the capacity of governess in the family of Lord Stirling, in New Jersey; others, who knew her in her singularly chosen retreat, in the wilderness—dependant principally, for support upon a brother who seems to have fled from civilized life because he was unworthy of a participation in its blessings—speak of her in high terms of praise and commendation.

Near the close of the Revolutionary war, ALLAN, then a young man, made his first appearance on the Genesee river. He had acquired the habits of Indian life, made Mrs. JEMISON's house his residence;—seemed an adventurer, alienated by his own acts from kindred and home; and partly from choice, and partly from necessity, seeking a permanent abode with his war associates.

As it was a preliminary step to after feats of gallantry, in which he seems to have had a sovereign contempt for the usages of savage as well as civilized life, it may be mentioned here, that he had not been long at Gardeau, when he disturbed the domestic relations of a white tenant of Mrs. JEMISON, who had married a squaw. Unfortunately the two had a similarity of tastes. This, after an open rupture and separation, resulted in a reconciliation, a condition of which, was to remove away from the captivating influences of the new comer.

He turned his attention to agriculture; worked the fine flats of Mrs. JEMISON, until after the peace, in 1783, when he ventured to Philadelphia, and returned with a horse and some dry-goods; built a house, and settled at Mount Morris. He seemed disposed to peace. Learning that the British and Indians, upon this frontier, and in Canada, were determined to prolong the war, and continue their attacks upon the settlements in the Mohawk valley, he forestalled their action by an ingenious fraud. Just before an expedition was to start, he procured a belt of wampum and carried it as a token of peace to the nearest American post. The Indians were very unexpectedly informed that the overtures of peace were accepted. The wampum, although presented without their consent, was a sacred thing with them, and they determined to bury the hatchet—go no more out upon the war path with their British allies. The British at Fort Niagara, however, and the Indians, mutually resolved to punish ALLAN. For months he was pursued; but skulking in the woods, hiding in the cleft rocks, approaching the hospitable wigwam of his friend the White Woman, stealthily, at night, and getting food; he managed to keep out of their clutches. The matter apparently dying away, the chase abandoned, ALLAN, "all in tatters, came in;" HI-A-KA-TOO, the husband of Mrs. JEMISON, giving him a blanket and a piece of broadcloth, with which he made himself some trousers. Dressed up, and recruited a little, he turned his attention to matrimony;—married a squaw, whose name was SALLY. The news of all this transpiring at Niagara, a party was sent down, who succeeded in arresting him. Just as they were arriving at the garrison, a house near by took fire, the guard went to extinguish the flames; ALLAN took to his heels. Arriving at Tonawanda, he armed himself, got some refreshments, and went on to Little Beard's Town, where he found his wife SALLY. Attempting to go to Gardeau, he discovered a party of British and Indians in pursuit of him. Then followed weeks of skulking, lying in wait by his pursuers, a search of all the fastnesses of the forest; frequent approaches of the fugitive by night, to get food from the benevolent hand of the White Woman; until the pursuit was again abandoned,—the pursuers returning to Niagara. ALLAN again ventured out with assurances of protection by the Indians, who by this time, were generally his friends, and in favor of an armistice being extended to him;—believed "that the Niagara people were persecuting him without just cause." The chief, LITTLE BEARD, had given orders for his protection. His persecutors had appropriated his horse and goods, but all this time, Mrs. JEMISON had been the faithful depository of a "box of money and trinkets." Thus situated, in fancied security, the party again came on from Niagara, took him by surprise, and carried him bound to the garrison, where he was confined for the winter. In the spring, he was taken to Montreal for trial, and acquitted. There was probably no law, or precedent, for punishing the offence of carrying wampum to the enemy. It was a novel offence; and the proof must have been difficult to obtain. It probably aided in putting an end to the cruel warfare upon the border settlers upon the Mohawk and Susquehannah, stimulated and encouraged from the British, in this quarter—the authorities of Canada, the officers of Fort Niagara, at Kingston and Oswego, after peace had been concluded; and even after their allies of the Six Nations, wished to bury the tomahawk and scalping knife.* For so much, let "Indian Allan," be credited.

He went immediately to Philadelphia, and purchased on credit, "a boat load of goods," bringing them to Mount Morris, by the way of Conhocton. He bartered them for ginseng and furs, which he sold at Niagara. He then planted corn, raised a large crop, and after harvesting it, moved down to the mouth of "Allan's creek"

---

* It is evident from the whole narration, that it was the British, and not the Indians, who wished to punish Allan: that the Senecas, were even glad of the excuse to refuse farther participation in the war.

where he lived with his squaw SALLY, who by this time had made him the father of two daughters, named MARY and CHLOE. He next season, entered into an arrangement with PHELPS and GORHAM, in pursuance of which they gave him 100 acres of land, at the Genesee Falls, in consideration of his building a grist and saw-mill, to accommodate the few settlers in the surrounding country.*

His friend, Mrs. JEMISON, signalizes this advent of ALLAN as an early miller of this region, by two murders, and the obtaining of two additional wives. While conveying down the river some materials, an old German named ANDREWS, in his employ, gave him some offence, and as is supposed, he pushed him out of the canoe. ANDREWS was never afterwards heard of; ALLAN still resided at Allan's creek.

While at the Falls, superintending the erection of his mills, a white man came along, emigrating to Canada. He had a young daughter, that took ALLAN's fancy; there was a summary courtship; the young woman, "nothing loth," consented; the ambitious emigrant parents, thought the suitor rich, unmarried of course, consented. They were married. "Miss LUCY,"—that was her name—had her dream of happiness soon interrupted. She was introduced to the domicile of her suddenly acquired husband, where she found a dark complexioned "SALLY," a joint tenant, and co-partner in bed and board. She had none of her own race to appeal to for redress, the parents had gone on their way, and she, perhaps prudently, resolved to stay and make the best of it.

The backwood's "BLUE BEARD" was about this time in a marrying way, and did not know where to stop. On a visit to Mrs. JEMISON, at Gardeau, a short time after this, he saw a "young woman with an old husband," and deemed that circumstance, a justification for his gallantry. (Fatal to the happiness of many an old dotard, would such a deduction in moral ethics be in these latter days of January and May matches!) He poured into her ears the

---

* The author has in his possession a quit claim deed, or rather an assignment of his right to this 100 acre tract, to Benjamin Barton, the father of Benjamin Barton, Jr. It would seem he had at the date of it, no written title to the land, but he authorises Messrs. Phelps and Gorham to deed to Mr. Barton. The consideration was "Two hundred pounds, N. York currency." It is in the hand writing of Samuel Ogden, and witnessed by "Gertrude Ogden," by which it would seem that it was executed in the city of New York. The signature is well executed. It is written "E. Allan"—not Allen. The land is described as being on the "west side of Genesee river in Ontario county:—bounded east by the river, so as to take in the mills recently erected by the said Allan." The instrument is dated March, 1792.

story of his wealth—his possessions at Allan's creek—his "Mills" —his influence;—and succeeded so far as to induce his victim to persuade her "old man" to accompany him home with his wife. ALLAN under pretence of showing him his flats on Allan's creek, took him out, and pushed him into the river. He saved himself from drowning, but died in a few days, in consequence of the fall and struggle. The young widow, remained in the harem for a year, and left.

He removed from the creek, back to Mt. Morris, in the summer of 1792, it is presumed, as he sold the mill tract, early in that season. He built a house there; moved his remaining two wives into it; and soon resolved to fill the vacancy occasioned by the departure of the widow. He married MILLE M'GREGOR, the daughter of a white settler upon the Genesee flats. Taking her home, there was soon trouble in his domicil:—SALLY and LUCY united, and whipped the new comer, MILLE. She was provided with a separate residence. This is a sad picture, it is confessed, of morals and matrimony, in our region, at a primitive period; and yet it is a truthful record. It is a specimen of "freedom in the backwoods."

In 1791, the Seneca Indians deeded to ALLAN in trust, for his two daughters, four square miles on the Genesee river, the tract which now embraces the beautiful village of Mount Morris. The deed commences by setting forth the reasons why the gift is made: —"It has been the custom of the nation from the earliest times of our forefathers, to the present day, to consider every person born of a Seneca woman as one of the nation, and as having equal rights with every one in the nation to lands belonging to it. And whereas, KYENDANENT, named in English, SALLY, has had two daughters born of her body, by our brother JENUHSHIO, named in English, EBENEZER ALLAN; the names of said daughters being in English, MARY ALLAN, and CHLOE ALLAN,"&c. It was provided in the deed that ALLAN should have the care of the land, until his daughters were married, or became of age; that out of its proceeds he should cause the girls to be instructed "in reading and writing, sewing and other useful arts, according to the custom of the white people." SALLY, the mother, was to have comfortable maintenance during her natural life, or as long as she "remained unjoined to another man." The deed is signed by the sachems and chiefs of the Seneca nation, and by TIMOTHY PICKERING as U. S. Commissioner;

witnessed by Horatio Jones, Jasper Parrish, Oliver Phelps, Ebenezer Bowman.

In pursuance of the provisions of the deed, ALLAN took the two daughters to Philadelphia and placed them in a school. Mrs. BLACKMAN, to whom allusion has been made in a preceding page, remembers well when ALLAN returned with his daughters from Philadelphia, and staid at her fathers house over night. She says: — "The party were on horseback, attended by a white man and a white woman, as waiters. ALLAN would not allow them to sit at table with him and his daughters. The daughters were fine looking well behaved girls. The early settlers here did not like ALLAN. I remember when he came near being burned up when dry grass caught fire on Genesee Flatts, and that people generally were sorry that he escaped. He has sit in my father's house often, and boasted of the murders he had committed on the Susquehannah, and his other exploits there." Mrs. B. says that ALLAN got the irons for his mill at Rochester, at Conhocton, and hired Indians to take them to Rochester on pack horses.

JOHN M' KAY, of Caledonia, says: — "I knew ALLAN well. He was about fifty years of age when I first came upon the Genesee river. He was tall and strait — light complexion — genteel in appearance — of good address. Capt. JONES told me the story of ALLAN'S carrying the wampum to the American commissioner, (not to the commandant of a post.) The Indians were very angry, but said JONES, such was the influence he had over them, they dared not to punish him." Mr. M' KAY thinks it was not a disinterested act; but that the goods he carried to Mount Morris were the proceeds of the pacific enterprize.

In 1797, finding the white settlers getting too thick around him — the restraints of civilized life, that he had fled from in his youth, likely to interfere with his "perfect freedom" — he sold his property at Mount Morris, and moved to Delawaretown, on the Thames, (C. W.) taking with him his white wife, and leaving SALLY and MILLE behind. Gov. SIMCOE granted him 3000 acres of land, upon condition, that he should build a saw-mill, grist-mill, and a church; all but the church, to be his property. He performed his part of the contract, and the title to his land was confirmed. In a few years, he had his mills, a comfortable dwelling, large improvements, was a good liver; and those who knew him at that period, represent him as hospitable and obliging. In two or three years after he left for Canada, MILLE followed him, and when he was flourishing there, he had the two wives under one roof. SALLY soon followed, remained in the neighborhood about a year, when she was driven away by the persecutions of the two white wives. An acquaintance of the author, who was for a long period his neighbor, says he once asked him how he could manage two women. He replied that he "ruled them with a rod of iron." The reader must have, ere this, discovered that he was the man thus to rule his household.

About the year 1806 or '7, reverses began to overtake him. At one period, he was arrested and tried for forgery; at another, for passing counterfeit money; at another, for larceny. He was acquitted of each offence, upon trial. He was obnoxious to many of his white neighbors, and it is likely, that at least two of the charges against him, arose out of a combination that was prompted by personal enmity. All this brought on embarrassments, which terminated in an almost entire loss of his large property. He left Delawaretown, and went upon some land that had been leased to his daughters by the Indians.

Soon after the breaking out of the war of 1812, he was suspected by the Canadian authorities, of being friendly to the Americans, of holding a correspondence with Gen. HULL at Detroit; arrested and confined in jail at Niagara. He was bailed out upon condition that he should in no way interfere against the government. He took no part in the war; though he was evidently in favor of the Americans; alledging that the British government had illy requited his services. He died in 1814.

His wife MILLE, was the mother of six children; LUCY of one; and there were beside, the two half-breed daughters of SALLY. An elderly lady of the author's acquaintance, knew these daughters well after they went to reside upon the Thames. They were tolerably educated, amiable and reputable. They died after having become the wives of white men, and the mothers of several children, who are supposed to be still living in Canada West. His son SENECA ALLAN, is a resident of one of the western states.

NOTE.—Allan conveyed the land at Mount Morris, that was given to his daughters, to Robert Morris; by what right, it does not appear upon the records. Allan's creek, heading in Wyoming, passing through Warsaw, Le Roy, and emptying into the Genesee river at Scottsville, derives its name from the subject of our biographical sketch. He had a farm where Scottsville now is.

PART FOURTH.

CHAPTER I.

PROGRESS OF SETTLEMENT WESTWARD, AFTER THE REVOLUTION.

In the treaty of peace which ended the Revolution, Great Britian made no provisions for her Indian allies. Notwithstanding their strong and well founded claims to British regard and protection they were left to take care of themselves, and get out of the difficulties in which an unsuccessful war had involved them, as best they could. They were much offended and disappointed; they complained of this conduct as unjust and ungrateful, in view of the sacrifices they had made, and losses they had sustained, all along through the war. They were sagacious enough to conclude, that if the arms of the "Thirteen Fires," had conquered them and their British allies united, there was little use in their contending single handed. A portion of them however, were not disposed to yield. Prompted by British agents, they were for leaguing with the North Western Indians, and reviving the war. Among these, was the youthful, subtle, and eloquent Red Jacket. But Corn Planter, and some others of the more influential Indians, counciled peace, and peaceable councils prevailed.

Accordingly the sachems, chiefs and warriors, of the Six Nations, and the commissioners in behalf of the United States, assembled at Fort Stanwix in October, 1784, and concluded a treaty of peace and friendship. Oliver Wolcott, Richard Butler and Arthur Lee, acted as commissioners for the United States. The Six Nations agreed to surrender all their captives, and relinquish " all claims to the country lying west of a line beginning at the mouth of Oyowagea creek, flowing into lake Ontario, four miles east of Niagara; thence southerly, but preserving a line four miles east of the carrying path, to the mouth of the Tehoseroron, or Buffalo creek; thence to the north boundary of Pennsylvania; thence east to the end of that boundary; and thence south along the Pennsylvania line to the river Ohio."*

"The cession of their hunting grounds north-west of the Ohio, was vigorously, though unavailingly opposed by the red men. Sagoyewatha, or Red Jacket, then young and nameless among the head men, rose rapidly in favor with the Senecas for his hostility to the measure—while the popularity of their great chief Cornplanter, suffered severely among his race for his partiality to the whites, in the arrangement." * * * "The patriotism of Red Jacket was then thoroughly aroused, and his wisdom and eloquence were generally zealously employed to vindicate the rights of the red man against the encroaching influence of the pale faces. He was elected a chief among the Senecas, soon after this treaty, and his influence was great in the Indian confederacy for upwards of forty years."†

After the conclusion of this treaty, the United States commissioners, in consequence of the then condition of the Six Nations, and in pursuance of the humane and liberal intentions of the government whose agents they were, distributed a large quantity of goods in the form of presents.

It will be observed that at the treaty above referred to, the Indians made no cession of territory, but simply defined their

---

* A bad definition of boundaries, but the reader will have no difficulty in seeing what was intended.

† History of Rochester and Western New York.

NOTE.—Lafayette was present at the treaty of Fort Stanwix. After the lapse of forty years, the generous Frenchman, the companion of Washington, and the Seneca orator again met. The author was present at the inteview. A concourse of citizens had been assembled for nearly two days, awaiting the arrival of the steam boat from Dunkirk, which had been chartered by the committee of Erie county, to convey Lafayette to Buffalo, and among them was Red Jacket. He made, as usual, a somewhat ostentatious display of his medal—a gift from Washington—and it required the especial attention of a select committee to keep the aged chief from an indulgence—a " sin that so easily beset him,"—which would have marred the dignity, if not the romance of the intended interview. The reception, the ceremonies generally, were upon a staging erected in front of "Rathbun's Eagle." After they were through with, Red Jacket was escorted upon the staging, by a committee. "The Douglass in his hall,"— himself, in his native forest—never walked with a firmer step or a prouder bearing! There was the stoicism of the Indian—seemingly, the condescension, if it existed, was his, and not the "Nation's Guest." He addressed the General in his native tongue, through an interpreter who was present. During the interview, Lafayette not recognizing him, alluded to the treaty of Fort Stanwix: "And what" said he, "has become of the young Seneca, who on that occasion so eloquently opposed the burying of the tomahawk?" "He is now before you!" replied Red Jacket. The circumstance, as the reader will infer, revived in the mind of Lafayette, the scenes of the Revolution, and in his journey the next two days, his conversation was enriched by the reminiscences which it called up.

boundaries, rocognizing and somewhat enlarging the bounds of the " carrying place " at Niagara, which they had granted under English dominion.

This treaty was the first ever made by the United States with the Indians.

At Fort Herkimer, on the Mohawk, in June, 1785, a treaty was held with the Oneidas and Tuscaroras, by George Clinton and other commissioners. For a consideration of eleven thousand five hundred dollars, those nations ceded to the State of New York, the land lying between the Unadilla and Chenango rivers, south of a line drawn east and west between those streams, and north of the Pennsylvania line, &c.

On the 12th of September, 1788, the Onondagas, by a treaty at Fort Stanwix, ceded to the State of New York, all their territory, saving a reservation around their chief village. It was stipulated that the Onondagas should enjoy forever, the right of fishing and hunting in the territory thus relinquished. The " Salt Lake," and the land around the same for one mile, was to remain forever for the common use of the State of New York, and the Onondagas, for the purpose of making salt, and not to be disposed of for other objects. The consideration was a thousand French crowns in hand, two hundred pounds value in clothing; and a perpetual annuity of five hundred dollars. Upon a full confirmation of the treaty, in 1790, the state gave as a gratuity, an additional five hundred dollars.

On the 22d of September 1788, the Oneidas, who had before ceded a part of their lands, made an additional cession, including all their lands except a small reservation for themselves, and another for the Brothertown Indians, which they had previously given them. The consideration was two thousand dollars in hand, two thousand dollars in clothing, one thousand dollars in provisions, five hundred dollars to build a grist mill on their reservation; and a perpetual annuity of five hundred dollars.

By a treaty at Albany, in 1789, the Cayugas ceded to the State of New York all their lands, saving a reservation of one hundred square miles exclusive of the waters of Cayuga lake, about which the reservation was located. The consideration was five hundred dollars in hand; an agreement to pay one thousand five hundred and twenty-five dollars, in June following; and a perpetual annuity of five hundred dollars. Upon the final confirmation of the treaty, the State paid the Cayugas as a gratuity, one thousand dollars.

In 1793, the Onondagas ceded to the state some portions of their reservation. The consideration was four hundred dollars in hand, and a perpetual annuity of four hundred dollars.

On the 29th of March, 1797, the Mohawks, who had mostly fled to Canada during the Revolution, by their agents, Capt. Joseph Brant and Capt. John Deserontyon, relinquished to the State of New York all claims to lands within the state, for the sum of one thousand dollars, and six hundred dollars in the form of a fee for traveling expenses, &c. advanced to the above named agents.

Numerous treaties and cessions of reservations followed, with the five easterly nations of the confederacy, but the cessions that have been noticed embraced the great body of their lands. In all these cessions the Indians reserved the right of fishing and hunting, and stipulated to lend their assistance in keeping off intruders upon the lands.

A treaty was held at Canandaigua on the 11th of September, 1794, between the United States and the Six Nations — Timothy Pickering acting in behalf of the United States. The object of President Washington in ordering this treaty, was to remove some existing causes of complaint, and establish a firm and permanent friendship with the Indians. These two objects were consummated. It was stipulated on the part of the United States that the Indians should be protected in the free enjoyment of their reservations, until such times as they chose to dispose of them to the United States. This had reference to the reservations east of the Massachusetts pre-emption line. At this treaty, the boundaries of the lands of the Senecas were defined, as including all lands west of Phelps and Gorham's Purchase, in this state, excepting the carrying place upon the Niagara river. "In consideration of the peace and friendship hereby established, and of the engagements entered into by the Six Nations; and because the United States desire with humanity and kindness to contribute to their comfortable support, and to render the peace and friendship hereby established strong and perpetual," the United States delivered to the Six Nations ten thousand dollars worth of goods, and for the same consideration, and with a view to promote the future welfare of the Six Nations and of their Indian friends aforesaid, the United States added $3000 to the $1,500 previously allowed them by an article dated

23d, April, 1792, (which $1,500 was to be expended annually in purchasing clothing, domestic animals, and implements of husbandry, and for encouraging useful artificers, to reside in their villages,) making in the whole $4,500, the whole to be expended yearly in purchasing clothing, &c. as just mentioned, under the direction of the Superintendant appointed by the President.

"Lest the firm peace and friendship now established should be interrupted by the misconduct of individuals, the United States and Six Nations agree that, for injuries done by individuals on either side, no private revenge or retaliation shall take place; but, instead thereof, complaint shall be made by the party injured to the other, and such prudent measures shall then be pursued as shall be necessary to preserve our peace and friendship, until the Legislature (or the great Council of the United States) shall make other equitable provisions for the purpose.

"A note in the treaty says:—'It is clearly understood by the parties to this treaty, that the annuity stipulated in the sixth article is to be applied to the benefit of such of the Six Nations, and of their Indian friends united with them aforesaid, as do or shall reside within the boundaries of the United States; for the United States do not interfere with nations, tribes, or families of Indians elsewhere resident.'"

The state of New York, by its legislature, in 1781, resolved to raise forces to recruit the army of the United States. The period of enlistment was fixed at three years, or until the close of the war, and the faith of the State was pledged that each soldier who enlisted and served his time according to his enlistment, should receive six hundred acres of land as soon after the close of the war as the land could be surveyed.

On the 25th of July, 1782, the legislature of the state passed another act, setting apart a certain district of country, described therein, to meet its engagements contained in the first mentioned act. The district so set apart, contained the territory now included in the counties of Onondaga, Cayuga, Seneca, Cortland, the southwest part of Oswego, the north part of Tompkins, the east part of Wayne, and small parts of Steuben and Yates; containing, besides, the reservations afterwards made therein by the Indians, one million, six hundred and eighty thousand acres.

On the 28th day of February, 1789, a third act was passed by the legislature, *appropriating* the lands devoted to the payment of the Revolutionary soldiers; the Indian title to which, had at length been extinguished by treaties with the Onondagas and Cayugas; which was soon after surveyed into townships, and those townships subdivided into lots of six hundred acres each: the state of New York thus redeemed its pledge given to the Revolutionary soldiers by the act of July 25th, 1782.

Although the military tract may truly be considered a proud and splendid monument of the gratitude of the state of New York to her Revolutionary heroes; the soldiers, whose patriotic valor earned the full reward, in many cases, realized but little from the bounty of their country; as many of the patents for six hundred acres of excellent land, were sold as late as ten years after the close of the war at from eight to thirty dollars each.

It has been already indicated that at the close of the Revolution, in 1783, settlement had not advanced beyond the lower valley of the Mohawk. In May, 1784, Hugh White, with his family, advanced beyond the then bounds of civilization, located at what is now Whitestown, near Utica. In 1786, a considerable settlement had been made there. In the same year that Whitestown was settled, James Dean, who had acted as an Indian agent during the war, settled upon a tract of land given him by the Indians, near Rome. In 1784, the county of Tryon had its name changed to Montgomery, its citizens preferring the name of a Revolutionary patriot, to that of an English colonial governor. In 1786, a Mr. Webster became the first white settler of the territory now comprised in the county of Onondaga. In 1788, Asa Danforth and Comfort Tyler located at Onondaga Hollow. In 1793, John L. Hardenbergh settled at what was for many years called "Hardenbergh's Corners,"—now the village of Auburn. In 1789, James Bennet and John Harris settled upon opposite sides of the Cayuga lake, and established a ferry. These primitive beginnings will however, best be indicated in sketches that will follow of some relations of early adventurers.

GLIMPSES OF WESTERN NEW YORK AFTER THE REVOLUTION.

NOTE. — [The author at this point, to connect the chain of events as nearly as possible in chronological order, will avail himself of the preceding portion of narratives he has had from some of the earliest adventurers to the regions of Western New York; reserving for their order of time, the remainder. Since he commenced the preparation of this work, he has had interviews with a large number, who yet survive to tell the story of their wilderness advents. As far as consistent with a brevity which it is necessary to observe, he will endeavor to preserve that interest in the narratives, which the relators in their own language and manner, could alone impart to them.]

SILAS HOPKINS, of Lewiston, Niagara county, started from New Jersey, in the summer of 1787, to assist his father in driving a drove of cattle to Niagara. Twelve or thirteen other young men came along, to assist in driving the cattle, and to see the country. Party came to Newton Point, thence to Horse Heads, Catherine's Town at the head of Seneca lake, Kanadesaega, Canandaigua, and from thence upon the Indian trail via Canawagus, the "Great Bend of the Tonewanta," Tonawanda Indian village, to Niagara. Route up the Susquehannah, to Tioga, was principally in the track of Sullivan's army; after that almost wholly upon Indian trails. Saw the last white inhabitant at Newtown Point. There were a few Indians at Catherine's Town, and among them the old squaw that is named in accounts of Sullivan's expedition. At this period, nine tenths of the settlers upon the frontiers in Canada, were Butler's Rangers. They had all got lands from the British government, two years supply of provisions, and were otherwise favored. The New Jersey drovers sold their cattle principally to them, and to the garrisons at Queenston and Niagara.

"I came out twice the next summer with my father upon the same business. Upon one of these occasions, I went with my father to the residence of Col. Butler near Newark, (Niagara.) He was then about fifty five or sixty years old; had a large, pretty well cultivated farm; was living a quiet farmer's life. He was hospitable and agreeable, and I could hardly realize that he had been the leader of the Rangers.

"In all our journeyings in those early days, we were well treated by the Indians. They had a custom of levying a tribute upon all drovers, by selecting a beeve from each drove as they passed through their principal towns. This they regarded as an equivalent for a passage through their territories; and the drovers found it the best way to submit without murmuring. At Geneva, there was an Indian trader named Poudrey, and another by the name of La Berge. There were several other whites there; they were *talking of putting up a building*. We happened to be at Canandaigua at a treaty. Phelps and Gorham bought several head of cattle of my father, to butcher for the Indians. When I went to Canada the first time, Gov. Simcoe was residing at 'Navy Hall,' near old Fort George. He was esteemed as a good Governor, and good man.

"In 1789, on one of our droving excursions there was an unusual number of drovers collected at Lewiston. We clubbed together and paid the expenses of a treat to the Indians,—gave a benefit. They were collected there from Tonawanda, Buffalo, Tuscarora, and some from Canada. There were two or three hundred of them; they gave a war-dance for our amusement. We had as guests, officers from Fort Niagara. The Indians were very civil. After the dance, rum was served out to them, upon which they became very merry, but committed no outrage. We had a jolly time of it, and I remember that among our number was a minister, who enjoyed the thing as well as any of us.

"In 1790, after I had sold a drove of cattle at Lewiston, (to go over the river, and at Fort Niagara,) I met with John Street, the father of the late Samuel Street, of Chippewa, C. W. He then kept a trading establishment at Fort Niagara. He was going to Massachusetts, and said he should like my company through the wilderness, as far as Geneva. Waiting a few days, and he not getting ready, I started without him. He followed in a few days, and was murdered at a spring, near the Ridge Road, a mile west of Warren's. The murderers were supposed to be Gale and Hammond. Gale lived near Goshen, in this State. I knew his father, a Col. Gale. Hammond had been living on the Delaware river. They were arrested in Canada, by authority of the commanding officer at Fort Niagara; sent to Quebec for trial; Hammond turned King's evidence, divulged the whole affair, charging the offence principally upon Gale, but made his escape. Gale was afterwards discharged. When I came up the next season, I camped at the spring. Some fragments of Mr. Street's clothes were hanging upon the bushes. His body had been discovered by some travelers, stopping at the spring; their dog brought to them a leg with a boot upon it. His friends in Canada, gathered up fragments of the body, and carried them home for burial. He was robbed of a considerable sum of money."

Judge Hopkins remarked at this point in his narrative, that the fact having become generally known that drovers with considerable sums of money, and emigrants to Canada, were every few days passing on the "Great Trail from the Susquehannah to Niagara," robbers had been attracted to it. It was soon enough after the close of the border wars, to have remaining upon the outskirts of civilization, men fitted to prowl around the wilderness path, and solitary camp of the traveler.

"My father being at Niagara, on one occasion, a letter was sent to him by Col. Hollenbeck who was on the Susquehannah, warning him against starting on his return journey alone, as he was satisfied that a couple of desperadoes, in his neighborhood were intending to waylay him somewhere on the trail. He handed the letter to the commandant at Fort Niagara; a couple of men soon made their appearance in the neighborhood answering the description of Col. Hollenbeck. They were arrested and detained at the garrison until my father had time to reach the settlements on the Susquehannah.

"When but sixteen years of age, my father had some business in Canada that made it necessary to send me there from N. Jersey. I came through on horseback, the then usual route. I encamped the last night of my journey, on Millard's branch of the Eighteen-milecreek, about a mile above where it crosses the Chestnut Ridge, five miles east of Lockport. In the morning, my hoppled horse having gone a short distance off, I went for him, and on my way stumbled upon a silver mounted saddle and bridle, and a little farther on lay a dead horse that had been killed by a blow on the head with a tomahawk. I carried the saddle and bridle to Queenston, where they were recognized as those of a traveler who had a few days before come down from Detroit, on his way to New York. Nothing more was ever known of the matter."

In narrating this, the Judge remarks that the howling of the wolves in the Tonawanda swamp, all night, deprived him of sleep. A boy, sixteen years old, alone far away from civilization; the howling of the wolves, his forest lullaby; the relics of a murdered traveler, presented to him in the morning! He acknowledges that he left his camping ground with less delay than usual.

"I spent most of the summer of 1788, at Lewiston, purchasing furs. I bought principally, beaver, otter, muskrat, mink. The Indian hunting grounds for these animals, were the marshes along the Ridge Road, the bays of the Eighteen, Twelve, and Fourmile-creeks. The marsh where I now live, (six miles east of Lewiston,) was then, most of the year a pond, or small lake. The only white inhabitant at Lewiston, then was Middaugh. He kept a tavern—his customers, the Indians, and travelers on their way to Canada. I carried back to New Jersey, about four hundred dollars worth of furs, on pack horses. At that period, furs were plenty. I paid for beaver, from four to six shillings; for otter, about the same; for mink and muskrat, four cents. There were a good many bears, wolves, and wild-cats; but a few deer.

"Immediately after the defeat of St. Clair, the Indians were very insolent and manifested much hostility to the whites.

"In 1778, or '9, I was returning from Niagara, to New Jersey, in company with a dozen or fifteen men. When we arrived upon the Genesee river, we found a white settler there—Gilbert Berry;*— he had arrived but a few days before with his wife and wife's sister; had made a temporary shelter, and had the body of a log house partly raised. He had tried to raise it with the help of Indians, and failed. We stopped and put it up for him. The next day, we found at the outlet of the Honeoye, a settler just arrived by the name of Thayer. He had logs ready for a house, but had no neighbors to help him. We stopped and raised his house."

The narrator of these early events is now seventy-five years old; his once vigorous and hardy constitution, is somewhat broken by age, but his mental faculties are unimpaired. In the war of 1812, he was early upon the frontier, as a Colonel of militia, and has well filled many public stations. He was the first Judge of Niagara, after Erie was set off.

JOHN GOULD, Esq. of Cambria, Niagara county, came from New Jersey in 1788, as a drover; came by Newton, Painted Post, Little Beard's village, Great Bend of Tonawanda, &c.—stopped with drove at Little Beard's village over night. In the morning, Little Beard pointed out a fine ox, and an Indian boy shot him down with a bow and arrow. This was the usual tribute, mentioned by Judge Hopkins. "The Great Bend of the Tonnewanta," was a well known camping ground for Butler's Rangers, in their border war excursions, and after emigration to Canada; for early drovers, and other travellers.

"Col. Hunter, was then in command at Fort Niagara. Our cattle and pack horses were ferried across to Newark in batteaux and Schenectady boats. Nothing then at Newark, (Niagara village,) but an old ferry house and the barracks that had been occupied by Butler's Rangers. The Massaguea Indians were numerous then in Canada. They had no fixed habitations; migrated from camping ground to camping ground, in large parties; their principal camping grounds Niagara and Queenston. There were their fishing grounds. Sometimes there would be five or six hundred encamped at

---

* Gilbert Berry was an Indian trader. After his death, his widow kept a public house, early, and long known, as "Mrs. Berry's," at Avon. His two daughters are Mrs. George Hosmer of Avon, and Mrs. E. C. Hickox, of Buffalo.

Niagara. They were small in stature, gay, lively, filthy; and much addicted to drunkenness.

"We sold our cattle principally to Butler's Rangers. They were located mostly at the Falls, along the Four and Twelve Mile Creeks. Oxen brought as high as £50, cows £20.

"In June, after I arrived, I was at Fort Niagara, and witnessed the celebration of King George's birth day:—there was firing of cannon, horse racing, &c. The Tuscarora Indians were there, in high glee. It was upon this occasion that I first saw Benjamin Barton, sen.

"Butler's Rangers had taken a sister of my mother's captive, upon the Susquehannah. She afterwards became the wife of Capt. Fry, of the Mohawk, who had gone to Canada during the Revolution. She had induced my mother and step father, to emigrate to Canada in 1787. I found them located upon the Six Mile creek. At the time my aunt was taken prisoner, there were taken with her several children of another sister: their names were Vanderlip.

"When I came through in '88, I saw no white inhabitant after leaving Newton, till I arrived at Fort Niagara. At Newton there was one unfinished log house. 'Painted Post' was at the junction of Indian trails. It was a post, striped red and white.

"Along in '88, '90, eagles were plenty on Niagara river and shores of lake Ontario. Ravens were plenty; when they left, the crows came in. Black birds were a pest to the early settlers; they seemed to give way to the crows. The crows are great pirates. I think they robbed the nests of the black birds. There used to be myriads of the caween duck upon the river. In the breaking up of the ice in the spring, they would gather upon large cakes of ice, at Queenston, and sailing down to the lake, return upon the wing, to repeat the sport; their noise at times would be almost deafening."

"In '99, on my return to New Jersey, I went by Avon, Canandaigua, &c. Widow Berry was keeping tavern at Avon; settlers were getting in between there and Canandaigua; there were a few buildings in Canandaigua; a few log buildings at Geneva. On my return the next year, emigration was brisk; the military tract, near Seneca lake was settling rapidly."

Mr. Gould is now 78 years old; vigorous; but little broken by age; relaxing but slightly in an enterprise and industry, that has been crowned with a competency, which he is enjoying in the midst of his children, grand children, and great grand children.

JOHN MOUNTPLEASANT, a native of Tuscarora, is now sixty-eight years old. His father was Captain Mountpleasant, of the

British army; at one period commandant of Fort Niagara; his mother was an Oneida; emigrated to Canada during the Revolution, and afterwards came to Tuscarora. His father and mother, residing for two years at Mackinaw; that was his birth place, although almost his entire life has been spent at Tuscarora. He had a sister, who became the wife of Capt. Chew, of the British army. Capt. Mountpleasant was ordered to Montreal when his children were quite young; he was not entirely unmindful of them; occasionally sent them presents.

"The earliest white people I can recollect, were the English at Fort Niagara, and a small guard they used to keep at Lewiston, to guard the portage. When I was a boy, the portage used to employ five or six teams. I remember well when the early emigrants used to come through on the trail, going to Canada. Their children were frequently carried in baskets, strung across the backs of horses." ☞ See his account of Brant's Mohawk village on Ridge Road. "The Middaughs, came from North River; when they first came they occupied one of the old houses left by the Mohawks. Hank Huff, and Hank Mills, were early at Lewiston. Huff had a Mohawk wife, and used to live in the house that Brant left. When I was a small boy, I used to go through to Genesee river, with my mother. There was Poudery at Tonnawanda, 'a white man' (Berry,) keeping a ferry over the Genesee river.

"Deer were not plenty in this region, the wolves hunted them; driving them into the lake, they would wait until they were wearied with swimming, and catch them as they came on shore. In periods of deep snows and crusts, they used to make great havoc among them. As the wolves grew scarce, the deer became plenty. A strip of land between Ridge and lake, used to be a great resort for bears. Our best hunting grounds used to be off toward Genesee river. Secord was an early and successful white trapper in this region. Some Tuscarora hunters once killed a panther, in the marsh near Pekin. There were no crows until after the war of 1812. The bittern, was often seen about the marshes. The white owl used occasionally to make his appearance here. Flocks of swans were often seen about the Islands above the Falls.

"When I was a boy, most of the marshes in Niagara county, were open ponds. I have been with my mother, picking cranberries, in open marshes, where there was then but small bushes; now there are tamaracks, soft maples, black ash, &c. as large as my body. The beaver dams were in a good state of preservation as long as I can remember,— though then but few beaver left. I have taken salmon in Eighteen mile creek, where Lewiston road crosses near Lockport, and below the Falls of the Oak Orchard, with my hands, three feet in length.

"My mother's second husband was a white man named James Pemberton, who was taken prisoner at the same time that Jasper Parrish was. He was brought to Lewiston with the Mohawks. He remained with the Tuscaroras after the Mohawks went to Canada, and until his death.

"I remember when the Indian family—Scaghtjecitors—lived at the creek at Black Rock that derives its name from them. They moved back to Seneca village, after the land was sold. One of the family was murdered at 'Sandy Town,' and robbed of twelve dollars. The murderers were never detected.

"When I was a boy, two schooners used to come to Lewiston—armed, King's vessels—the 'Seneca,' and 'Onondaga.' There was another afterwards, called the 'Massasagua.' I used to see batteaux come up, taken out of the river, and conveyed over the Portage; manned by jolly Frenchmen, who used to sing, keeping time with their oars, as they came up the river.

"For many years I followed the business of stocking rifles. I learned to do it from seeing Bill Antis do it at Canandaigua. For many years he stocked rifles for us without pay, being employed for that purpose by the government; afterwards we paid him half price.

"I remember when Gov. Simcoe first came to Niagara. He had a thousand troops with him called 'Queen's Rangers.' They wore green uniform. Their barracks were at Queenston,—thence the the name."

The narrator resides at Tuscarora with his sons, who are good farmers, educated and intelligent. His fine form would serve as a model for a sculpture. Tall, unbent by age; with a countenance, mild, benevolent, and expressive.

NOTE.—The author is indebted to Judge Cook of Lewiston, for some additional particulars which he adds to the brief narrative of John Mountpleasant. When James Pemberton, was brought a prisoner to Lewiston, it was decreed that he should be burned at the stake, to revenge the death of some Mohawk warrior. Brant interested himself in saving him; proposed that he should be saved and adopted. He told the Indians that he was a man of fine proportions, (as he really was,) that he would become useful to them. He interested the squaws in behalf of the captive, by promising that some one of them should have him for a husband. Managing to divert the attention of the Indians from their victim, Brant pointed out to Pemberton a way of escape, which he pursued with sufficient fleetness of foot, to enable him to reach Fort Niagara, where he was protected. The Indians had compelled Pemberton to collect the brush and dry wood for his own destruction. He was stripped naked—all was ready for the terrible sacrifice, when Brant's scheme in his behalf saved him. The place of the intended burning at the stake, is a small spot of level ground, between the dwelling of Seymour Scovell, Esq., and the Ferry. Pemberton pointed it out to Judge Cook, and told him the story of his fortunate escape. He remained at Niagara until the peace of '83, then went to Tuscarora and married the mother of John Mountpleasant. He died in 1806 or '7. His children and grand children reside at Tuscarora. [*See next page.*

THOMAS BUTLER, Esq. is a grandson of Col. John Butler, and resides upon the farm where his grandfather located after the Revolution, near Niagara, C. W. He is an associate Judge of the court of Queen's Bench. He was educated at Union College, Schenectady, residing there, in the family of the late Gov. Yates, who was his cousin. The author avails himself of a brief narrative he derived from him during a visit to his residence last summer, in search of some old manuscripts which had fallen into his hands as an attorney for one of the early Pioneers of Western New York:

"In 1797, during a vacation in college, I came home to Niagara. Joseph Ellicott, a surveyor named Thompson, and six or eight others, were just starting from Schenectady with batteaux, on their way to the Holland Purchase. I came in company with them. I found Mr. Ellicott a very agreeable traveling companion. Our route was via Oswego, and lake Ontario. Mr. Ellicott's party landed at fort Niagara, their goods went to Lewiston, and from thence over the Portage, to Schlosser; thence to Buffalo.

"Col John Butler died in 1794. Was, up to the period of his death, superintendent of Indian affairs for Upper Canada; was a half pay Lieut. Colonel. His remains are buried upon his estate. He organized at Niagara the corps he commanded during the Revolution. Butler's Barracks were originally built for their use.

"Col Claus died at Niagara seven or eight years ago. His two sons, John and Warren reside here now. Warren is an Attorney at law; at present, the Surrogate of the Niagara District.

"When Gov. Simcoe came to Niagara he issued a proclamation to all those who, in the Revolution, had adhered to the 'United Empire, (thence the name, U. E. Loyalists,'*) to come and take possession of lands. The different corps that drew lands, were, Butler's Rangers, who drew their lands in this part of Canada; Jessup's Corps, who drew their lands in the lower portion of the upper province; Johnson's Greens, who drew their lands about the Bay Quinte. Jemima Wilkinson claimed to be a U. E. Loyalist,

---

The first husband of the sister Mountpleasant speaks of, was a Capt. Elmer, of the U. S. army, stationed at Niagara. She lived with him at the garrison—he acknowledged her as his wife—and when ordered to New-Orleans, and prohibited by his superior officer from taking her with him, the parting was one which gave evidence of strong affection. To use the language of one who knew her at that period: "she was a beautiful woman." After the separation, she became the wife of Capt. Chew, a British Indian Agent at Niagara. She died a few years since, at an advanced age. Her eldest son is now head chief of the Tuscaroras.

* Judge Butler showed the author one of these deeds. It was one that had been given to Johnson Butler, for services as a Lieutenant in Butler's Rangers. The seal of white wax, would weigh three ounces. Each side is impressed with a die; the British coat of arms, &c.

and at one time came near deceiving Gov. Simcoe, and drawing a large tract of land.*

"The travel over-land from Tioga to Niagara, on the great trail was very large, at one period. I have heard it observed that in winters, one party, on leaving their camp, would build up large fires for the accommodation of those who followed them; and in this reciprocal way, fires were kept burning at the camping grounds.

In June, 1795, a French nobleman, LA ROCHEFOUCAULD LIAINCOURT, in company with others, who wished to see a large Indian settlement, passed through Buffalo, on his way to the Seneca village, on Buffalo creek, which he describes as situated about four miles from Lake Erie. He mentions Farmers Brother as a distinguished Indian chief and warrior. He complains of unbridged streams, bad and difficult roads to the town, and was disappointed in not finding it as large as he expected; but says that for many miles wigwams were scattered either way along the creek. He observes that though the whole country was filled with "miry and pestilential swamps," the Indians were healthy.

The following truthful sketch of Buffalo, as it actually appeared, but little more than half a century ago, to one who, perhaps, had visited the ancient and renowned capitals of the Old World, and had taken an adventurous journey in search of that novelty and freshness he no longer found there, will be interesting to all who can only know from such sources, the original condition in which the Pioneer settlers found the seats of now large and flourishing cities:

"We at length arrived at the post on Lake Erie, which is a small collection of four or five houses, built about a quarter of a mile from the Lake.

"We met some Indians on the road and two or three companies of whites. These encounters gave us great pleasure. In this vast wilderness, a fire still burning; the vestiges of a camp, the remains of some utensil which has served a traveller, excite sensations truly agreeable, and which arise only in these immense solitudes.

"We arrived late at the inn, and after a very indifferent supper, were obliged to lay on the floor in our clothes. There was liter-

---

* This was about the period of her difficulties with the early settlers on Seneca lake. She started for Canada, with a portion of her followers, got as far as Oswego, to embark on lake Ontario, and was met by the news that Gov. Simcoe had changed his mind, and refused to recognize her as a U. E. L.

ally nothing in the house, neither furniture, rum, candles, nor milk. After much trouble the milk was procured from the neighbors, who were not as accommodating in the way of the rum and candles. At length some arriving from the other side of the river, we seasoned our supper, as usual, with an appetite that seldom fails, and after passing a very comfortable evening, slept as soundly as we had done in the woods.

"Every thing at *Lake Erie*—by which name this collection of houses is called—is dearer than at any other place we visited, for the simple reason that there is no direct communication with any other point. Some were sick with fever in almost every house."

JOSHUA FAIRBANKS resides at Lewiston. His first visit to western New York, was in the winter of 1791. He had been recently married to Miss Sophia Reed, the daughter of Col. Seth Reed, of the Revolutionary army, at Uxbridge, Massachusetts. Col. Reed had the winter previous moved his family to Geneva— or rather to where Geneva now is. In the winter of '91, Mr. F. set out with his wife, to join him. They were in a sleigh. The narrative of the journey is taken up after they had passed Whitesborough:—

"Half way from Whitesborough to Onondaga Hollow, night overtook us, and fortunately, we found a settler who had just got in, and had a log house partly finished. There were some Indians at the house; the first that Mrs. F. had seen. I do not recollect the name of our obliging pioneer host; but he was the first settler between Whitesborough and Onondaga Hollow. We staid the next night at Onondaga Hollow. The only settler there was Gen. Danforth. Here Mrs. F. remarked that she thought there must have been others in the neighborhood, as there was a small dancing party at the General's that night. The next night we camped out; found the remains of an Indian tent; struck a fire; Mrs. F. cooked a supper, and we passed the night pretty comfortably. It was in February; snow from eighteen inches to two feet deep. Staid next night at Cayuga lake with —— Harris, who kept a ferry when the lake was not closed; we crossed on the ice. We arrived at Col. Reed's the next day."

Mr. Fairbanks had brought along with him a few goods to trade with the Indians. He remained at Geneva with Col. Reed, until the fall of 1793. He has an old deed of two village lots in Geneva. It is dated in August, 1790. The grantor is Peter Bortle. —— Ryckman would seem to have been one of the proprietors of the original village plot. The lot conveyed, was "91, on west side of Front street." The instrument is witnessed by Albert Ryckman and John Taylor. During the time of Mr. Fairbanks' residence at Geneva, a court was held—he thinks by Judge Cooper of Cooperstown.* It was then, says Mr. F. considered a good day's walk, or ride, to Canandaigua. The inhabitants that he recollects at Geneva, at that period, were:—Ezra Patterson, Thomas Sisson, the Reed family, Peter Bortle, —— Talmadge, —— Van Duzen, Benjamin Barton, —— Butler, —— Jackson, Dr. Adams; and Dr. Coventry, lived over the lake. Mr. Fairbanks has preserved an old bill of a part of the goods he brought to Geneva. They were bought of "Reed & Rice, Brookfield, Massachusetts." A few of the articles and prices are noted:—

```
11  yds. Ratteen, 4s. pr. yd.
30   "   Cotton Cord, ribbed, 3s. 4d.
 7½  "   Corduroy, 5s.
63   "   Shalloon, 2s. 4d.
25  lbs. Bohea Tea, 2s. 8d.
```

"About the 1st of September, 1793, I started with my wife, Giles Sisson, and William Butler, in a batteau; went down the Seneca river, Oswego river to Falls, where we had our batteau, goods, &c. to carry over a portage of one and a half miles; thence down to the British garrison at Oswego. The commanding officer, as ex-officio, revenue inspector, searched our goods. There was one settler at the portage—Oswego Falls. There was one company of troops, and a small gun boat at Oswego—no settler.

"We coasted up lake Ontario; going on shore and camping nights. We were seventeen days making the journey from Geneva to Queenston. The only person we saw on the route, from Oswego to Niagara, was William Hencher, at the mouth of Genesee river. We made a short call at Fort Niagara, reporting ourselves to the commanding officer. He gave us a specimen of British civility, during the *hold over* period, after the Revolution. It was after a protracted dinner sitting, I should think. He asked me where I was going? I replied, to Chippewa. "Go along and be d——d to you," was his laconic, verbal passport. There was then outside of the garrison, under its walls, upon the flatts, two houses. No tenement at Youngstown.

"I landed at Queenston—went into a house, partly of logs, and partly framed, and commenced keeping tavern. There was then a road from Fort Niagara to Fort Erie. At Queenston, Hamilton had a good house built, the rest were small log huts."

---

*Judge HOWELL thinks this Court was in June 1793; and says that the presiding Judge was John Sloss Hobart, one of the Judges of the Supreme court of this State; one of the first three who were appointed Judges of that Court. It was the first Court of Oyer and Terminer, &c. held in Ontario county. There was a grand jury sworn and charged, but no other business done.

Mr. Fairbanks, remained at Queenston and Chippewa, until 1805. Mrs. Fairbanks names the circumstance, that while keeping the tavern at Queenston, they had as guests, Aaron Burr, and his daughter Theodosia, and her husband, Mr. Allison. The party traveled on horse back, attended by servants. It was upon their trip to Niagara Falls.

"In 1794, I took passage on board of a British armed schooner, at Fort Erie, commanded by Capt. Cowen. I wished to see the country; the vessel was going up to bring down a British engineer, who had been employed on some of the western posts. Went to Detroit; Col. England was there in command of a British regiment. On our return we entered the Maumee Bay and anchored off the mouth of the Au Glaize. It was soon after the battle of Wayne with the Indians. We saw many of the Indians who were in the fight. Taking advantage of the little knowledge I had of their language, I asked one of them, who I learned had retreated at a pretty early hour in the engagement, why he came away? Suiting the action to the word, he replied: — "Pop, pop, pop,—boo, woo, woo-o-o, oo,— whish, whish,—boo, woo!—kill twenty Indians one time; no good by d—n."*

"The armed vessel upon which I took passage, and some few gun boats, constituted all the British armament then on the Lakes. I think there was then no merchant vessel."

Deacon HINDS CHAMBERLIN, a venerable early Pioneer, aged eighty-three years, resides at Le Roy, Genesee county. He came to Avon in 1790. In 1789, previous to any settlement west of Avon, his brother-in-law, Isaac Scott, and family, and two other families, had settled at Scottsville. These, with William Hencher, were the first settlers west of Genesee river.

"In 1792, I started from Scottsville with Jesse Beach and Reuben Heath; went up Allen's creek, striking the Indian trail from Canawagus, where Le Roy now is. There was a beautiful Indian camping ground—tame grass had got in; we staid all night. Pursuing the trail the next morning, we passed the Great Bend of the Tonawanda, and encamped at night at Dunham's Grove; and the next night near Buffalo. We saw one whiteman — Poudery — at Tonawanda village. We arrived at the mouth of Buffalo creek the next morning. There was but one white man there, I think; his name was Winne, an Indian trader. His building stood first as you descend from the high ground. He had rum, whiskey, Indian

---

* This, the reader will observe, was an imitation, as near as the Indian could make it, of the firing of small arms, of cannon, and the whizzing and bursting of bombs;— a specimen of the entertainment served up to the Indians by "Mad Anthony."

knives, trinkets, &c. His house was full of Indians; they looked at us with a good deal of curiosity. We had but a poor night's rest; the Indians were in and out all night, getting liquor.

"Next day we went up the beach of the lake to mouth of Cattaraugus creek where we encamped; a wolf came down near our camp. We had seen many deer on our rout, during the day. The next morning we went up to Indian village; found "Black Joe's" house, but he was absent; he had however seen our tracks upon the beach of the lake, and hurried home to see what white people were traversing the wilderness. The Indians stared at us; Joe gave us a room where we should not be annoyed by Indian curiosity, and we stayed with him over night. All he had to spare us in the way of food was some dried venison. He had liquor, Indian goods, and bought furs. Joe treated us with so much civility, that we stayed with him till near noon. There was at least an hundred Indians and Squaws, gathered to see us. Among the rest, there was sitting in Joe's house, an old Squaw, and a young delicate looking white girl, with her, dressed like a Squaw. I endeavored to find out something about her history, but could not. I think she had lost the use of our language. She seemed not inclined to be noticed.

"With an Indian guide that Joe selected for us, we started upon the Indian trail for Presque Isle. Wayne was then fighting Indians. Our Indian guide often pointed to the west, saying, 'bad Indians there.'

"Between Cattaraugus and Erie, I shot a black snake, a racer, with a white ring around his neck. He was in a tree, twelve feet from the ground, his body wound around the tree. He measured seven feet and three inches.

"At Presque Isle, (Erie,) we found neither whites nor Indians; all was solitary. There were some old French brick buildings, wells, block houses, &c. going to decay; eight or ten acres cleared land. On the peninsular, there was an old brick house, forty or fifty feet square; the peninsular was covered with cranberries.

"After staying there one night, we went over to La Boeuf, about sixteen miles distant, pursuing an old French road. Trees had grown up in it, but the track was distinct. Near La Boeuf, we came upon a company of men, who were cutting out the road to Presque Isle; a part of them were soldiers, and a part Pennsylvanians. At La Boeuf, there was a garrison of soldiers—about one hundred. There were several white families there, and a store of goods.

Myself and companions were in pursuit of land. By a law of Pennsylvania, such as built a log house, and cleared a few acres of land, acquired a pre-emptive right; the right of purchase, at £5 per one hundred acres. We each of us made a location near Presque Isle.

On our return to Presque Isle, from Le Boeuf, we found there

Col. Seth Reed and his family. They had just arrived. We stopped and helped him build some huts; set up crotches; laid poles across, and covered with the bark of the cucumber tree. At first the Colonel had no floors; afterwards he indulged in the luxury of floors made by laying down strips of bark. James Baggs, and Giles Sisson came on with Col. Reed. I remained for a considerable time in his employ. It was not long before eight or ten other families came in.

"On our return we again staid at Buffalo over night, with Winne. There was at the time a great gathering of hunting parties of Indians there. Winne took from them all their knives and tomahawks, and then selling them liquor, they had a great carousal.

The author finds the following incorporated in the pamphlet of Mr. WILLIAMSON to which reference will be made in a subsequent page. It is there said to be "an account of a journey of a gentleman into the Genesee country, in February, 1792."

"On the 15th February 1792, I left Albany, on my route to the Genesee river, but the country was thought so remote, and so very little known, that I could not prevail on the owner of the stage to engage farther than Whitestown, a new settlement on the head of the Mohawk, 100 miles from Albany. The road as far as Whitestown had been made passable for wagons, but from that to the Genesee river, was little better than an Indian path, sufficiently opened to allow a sled to pass, and some impassable streams bridged. At Whitestown, I was obliged to change my carriage, the Albany driver getting alarmed for himself and horses, when he found that for the next 100 miles we were not only obliged to take provisions for ourselves, but for our horses, and blankets for our beds. On leaving Whitestown we found only a few straggling huts, scattered along the path, from 10 to 20 miles from each other; and they affording nothing but the conveniency of fire, and a kind of shelter from the snow. On the evening of the third day's journey from Whitestown, we were very agreeably surprised to find ourselves on the east side of Seneca Lake, which we found perfectly open, free of ice as in the month of June; the evening was pleasant and agreeable, and what added to our surprise and admiration was to see a boat and canoe plying on the lake. After having passed from New York, over 360 miles of country completely frozen, the village of Geneva, though then only consisting of a few log-houses, after the dreary wilderness we had passed through, added, not a little to the beauty of the prospect; we forded the outlet of the lake, and arrived safe at Geneva.

" The situation of this infant settlement on the banks of a sheet of water 44 miles long, by 4 to 6 wide, daily navigated by small craft and canoes, in the month of February, was a sight as gratifying as unexpected. It appeared that the inhabitants of this delightful country, would by the slight covering of the snow on the ground, have all the convenience of a northern winter; and by the waters of the lake being free from ice, have all the advantages of this inland navigation, a combination of advantages perhaps not to be experienced in any other country in the world.

"From Geneva to Canandarqua the road is only the Indian path a little improved, the first five miles over gentle swellings of land, interspersed with bottoms seemingly very rich, the remainder of the road to Canandarqua, the county town, 16 miles, was the greatest part of the distance through a rich heavy timbered land; on this road there were only two families settled. Canandarqua, the county town, consisted of two small frame houses and a few huts, surrounded with thick woods; the few inhabitants received me with much hospitality, and I found abundance of excellent venison. From Canandarqua to the Genesee river, 26 miles, it is almost totally uninhabited, only four families residing on the road; the country is beautiful and very open, in many places the openings are free of all timber, appearing to contain at least 2 or 300 acres beautifully variegated with hill and dale; it seemed that by only enclosing any of them with a proportionable quantity of timbered land, an inclosure might be made not inferior to the parks in England. At the Genesee river I found a small Indian store and tavern; the river was not then frozen over, and so low as to be fordable. Upon the whole, at this time, there were not any settlements of any consequence in the whole of the Genesee country; that established by the Friends on the west side of the Seneca lake, was the most considerable, consisting of about forty families. At this period the number of Indians in the adjoining country was so great, when compared with the few white inhabitants who ventured to winter in the country, that I found them under serious apprehensions for their safety. Even in this state of nature, the county of Ontario shews every sign of future respectability; no man has put the plough in the ground, without being amply repaid, and through the mildness of the winter the cattle brought into the country the year before on very slender provision for their subsistence, were thriving well; the clearing of land for spring crops is going on with spirit; I also found the settlers abundantly supplied with venison."

CHAPTER II.

LAND TITLES—PHELPS AND GORHAM'S PURCHASE—EARLY EVENTS.

James I, King of Great Britain, in the year 1620, granted to the Plymouth Company, a tract of country denominated New England; this tract extended several degrees of latitude north and south, and from the Atlantic to the Pacific ocean east and west. A charter for the government of a portion of this territory, granted by Charles I, in 1628, was vacated in 1684, but a second charter was granted by William and Mary in 1691. The territory comprised in this second charter extended on the Atlantic ocean from north latitude 42° 2′ to 44° 15′, and from the Atlantic to the Pacific ocean.

Charles I, in 1663, granted to the Duke of York and Albany, the province of New York, including the present state of New-Jersey. The tract thus granted extended from a line twenty miles east of the Hudson river, westward rather indefinitely, and from the Atlantic ocean north to the south line of Canada, then a French province.

By this collision of description, each of those colonies, (afterwards states,) laid claim to the jurisdiction as well as to pre-emption right of the same land, being a tract sufficiently large to form several states. The State of New York, however, in 1781, and Massachusetts, in 1785, ceded to the United States all their rights, either of jurisdiction or proprietorship, to all the territory lying west of a meridian line run south from the westerly bend of lake Ontario. Although the nominal amount in controversy, by these acts, was much diminished, it still left some nineteen thousand square miles of territory in dispute, but this controversy was finally settled by a convention of Commissioners appointed by the parties, held at Hartford, Conn., on the 16th day of December, 1786.

According to the stipulations entered into by the convention, Massachusetts ceded to the state of New York all her claim to the government, sovereignty and jurisdiction of all the territory lying west of the present east line of the state of New York; and New York ceded to Massachusetts the pre-emption right, or fee of the land subject to the title of the natives, of all that part of the state of New York lying west of a line, beginning at a point in the north line of Pennsylvania, 82 miles west of the north-east corner of said state, and running from thence due north through Seneca lake, to lake Ontario; excepting and reserving to the state of New York, a strip of land east of and adjoining the eastern bank of Niagara river, one mile wide, and extending its whole length. The land, the pre-emption right of which was thus ceded, amounted to about six millions of acres.

In April, 1788, Massachusetts contracted to sell to Nathaniel Gorham of Charlestown, Middlesex county, and Oliver Phelps of Granville, Hampshire county of said state, their pre-emption right to all the lands in Western New York amounting to about six million acres, for the sum of one million dollars, to be paid in three annual instalments, for which a kind of scrip, Massachusetts had issued, called consolidated securities, was to be received, which was then in market much below par.*

In July 1788, Messrs. Gorham and Phelps purchased of the Indians, by treaty, at a convention held at Buffalo, the Indian title to about 2,600,000 acres of the eastern part of their purchase from Massachusetts. This purchase of the Indians being bounded west by a line beginning at a point in the north line of the state of Pennsylvania due south of the corner or point of land, made by the confluence of the Kanahasgwaicon (Cannaseraga) creek with the waters of Genesee river; thence north on said meridian line to the corner or point at the confluence aforesaid; thence northwardly along the waters of said Genesee river to a point two miles north of Kanawageras (Cannewagus) village; thence running due west twelve miles; thence running northwardly, so as to be twelve miles distant from the westward bounds of said river, to the shore of lake Ontario.

---

* It must be understood that Messrs. Gorham and Phelps although acting in their own names only, in this transaction, were merely the representatives of a company, consisting of themselves and a number of others, who had formed an association for the purchase of these lands.

On the 21st day of November, 1788, the state of Massachusetts conveyed and forever quitclaimed to N. Gorham and O. Phelps, their heirs and assigns forever, all the right and title of said state to all that tract of country of which Messrs. Phelps and Gorham had extinguished the Indian title. This tract, and this only, has since been designated as the "Phelps and Gorham Purchase."

According to the original plan of the proprietors the tract was, as soon as practicable, surveyed into townships about six miles square, and those townships subdivided into lots of different sizes; and so promptly was the execution of the design commenced, that through the industry and perseverance of Mr. Phelps, the acting and efficient conductor of the whole enterprise, Capt. William Walker, a surveyor and his assistants, arrived on the territory about the time the sale was perfected, to wit., in the fall of 1788, and surveyed several township lines before the inclemency of the winter weather put a stop to their labors.

The proprietors offered this tract for sale by townships or parts of townships; and during the summer of 1789, several families settled on, and near, the site of the old Indian village at Canandaigua; at Bloomfield, and on Boughton Hill now in the town of Victor. During this season the first productions of the earth were brought forth by the cultivation of white people, and the first wheat was sown on the tract. So rapid were the sales of the proprietors that before the 18th day of November, 1790, they had disposed of about fifty townships, which were mostly sold by whole townships or large portions of townships, to sundry individuals and companies of farmers and others, formed for that purpose. On the 18th day of November, 1790, they sold the residue of their tract, (reserving two townships only,) amounting to upwards of a million and a quarter acres of land, to Robert Morris of Philadelphia, who soon sold the same to Sir William Pultney, an English gentleman, who appointed Capt. Charles Williamson his general and resident agent, to superintend his interest in, and dispose of the lands by sale in small or large quantities. These lands lay somewhat scattered over Phelps and Gorham's purchase, although mostly on the south and north parts. This property, or such parts of it as was unsold at the time of the decease of Sir William, together with other property which he purchased in his lifetime in its vicinity, is now called the "Pultney Estate."

OLIVER PHELPS.

OLIVER PHELPS, was a native of Windsor, Conn. and soon after his majority became a citizen of Suffield, Massachusetts. At the commencement of the revolutionary war, he took an active part and in various capacities, remained with the American army to its close. It was at this period that he became acquainted with Robert Morris; Mr. Phelps being superintendant of army purchases, for Massachusetts, it led to an acquaintance with Mr. Morris, who as will be seen was the chief financier of the Revolution. He removed with his family, to Canandaigua Ontario county, in March, 1802, and resided there until the period of his death, in 1809. He was appointed first Judge of the county of Ontario, and elected a member of Congress from his district. An inscription upon his tomb stone, closes as follows:—

"Enterprise, Industry, and Temperance, cannot always secure success, but the fruits of those virtues, will be felt by society."

Like his revolutionary acquaintance, and afterwards co-operator in the purchase and settlement of Western New York, Robert Morris, he was destined to close his life in the midst of reverses. His business became much extended; his purchase of large tracts of wild land, had extended even to Georgia and Mississippi. In 1795, he estimated his property at nearly one million of dollars,— his debts at less than eighty-five thousand; and yet at his death, in 1809, he was much embarrassed; what was saved from his estate, being the result of good management with those upon whom its administration devolved. A memorandum in his own hand writing would show that he lost over three hundred and thirty thousand dollars, by bad debts and bad titles. Among the early Pioneers of Western New York, who knew him well, it is common to hear him alluded to in terms of respect and esteem; to hear the expression of sincere regret for the misfortunes attending his last years, mingled with their recollections of early events.

He left one son and one daughter. His son Leicester Phelps, after graduating at Yale College, assumed the name of Oliver Leicester Phelps. He died in 1813, leaving seven children, of whom the present Judge Oliver Phelps of Canandaigua—a worthy descendant of his Pioneer ancestor,—is one.

By the side of that of her husband, in the village cemetery, at Canandaigua, is the tomb stone of "Mary, wife of Oliver Phelps, and daughter of Zachariah and Sarah Seymour;—died 13th September, 1826, aged seventy four years." It is said of her:

"She was alike unaffected in prosperity and adversity."

The late Jesse Hawley, has left upon record the following tribute to the memory of the subject of our necessarily limited memoir:—

"Oliver Phelps may be considered the *Cecrops* of the Genesee Country. Its inhabitants owe a Mausoleum to his memory, in gratitude for his having pioneered for them the wilderness of this CANAAN of the West."

NATHANIEL GORHAM, Esq., the partner of Mr. Phelps, in the land purchase, was a citizen of Boston, Massachusetts, was never a resident upon the purchase, and had but little to do with the details of its management. His son, NATHANIEL GORHAM, became an early resident of Canandaigua, and died there in 1826, leaving a widow, son and daughter.

CHARLES WILLIAMSON.

Soon after the purchase of Sir William Pultney, [in 1792,] Captain CHARLES WILLIAMSON was appointed his agent, and came upon the purchase. He came by the way of Williamsport, Pennsylvania, and located at Bath, Steuben county. He was an Englishman, (or a Scotchman,) well educated, with liberal views; though as it proved perhaps, not as well calculated to lead the way as the patroon of new settlements, as if he had seen more of backwoods life.

In his first advent, he was accompanied by his wife, his friend and relative, Mr. Johnstone, a servant, and one laborer. Mr. Maude, an English traveller in this region, in '99, and 1800, says:—

"On Capt. Williamson's first arrival, he built a small hut where now is Bath. If a stranger came to visit him, he built up a little nook for him to put his bed in. In a little time, a boarded or framed house was built to the left of the hut; this was also intended as but a temporary residence, though it then appeared a palace. His present residence, a very commodious, roomy, and well planned house, is situated on the right of where stood the log hut, long since consigned to the kitchen fire.　*　*　* On the first settlement of the country, these mountainous districts were thought so unfavorably of when compared with the rich flats of Ontario county, (or the Genesee country,) that none of the settlers could be prevailed upon to establish themselves here till Capt. Williamson himself set the example, saying:—'As nature has done so much for the northern plains, I will do something for these southern mountains;' though the truth of it was, that Capt. Williamson saw very clearly, on his first visit to this country, that the Susquehannah, and not the Mohawk, would be its best friend. Even now, it has proved so, for at this day (1800) a bushel of wheat is better worth one dollar at Bath, than sixty cents at Geneva. This difference will grow wider every year; for little, if any improvement can be made with the water communication from New York, while that to Baltimore, will admit of extensive and advantageous one."*

Few agents in the sale and settlement of a new country, have manifested more enterprise and liberality than Capt. Williamson. In addition to his early expenditures at Bath, he built a large hotel at Geneva, contributed to the opening of roads, and other primitive beginnings in the wilderness. He was a useful helper in time of need. The author knows little of his personal biography, yet a separate notice of one so early and prominently identified with pioneer history, has been deemed requisite. He left Western New York; was appointed by the British government, governor of one of the West India Islands, and died on his passage.

There are many reminiscences that associate his memory with early times in Western New York; not the least of which are a series of letters which he wrote in 1799, published at the time in a pamphlet form:—"Description of the settlement of the Genesee country, in the State of New York, in a series of letters from a gentleman to his friend." The intention of the pamphlet was evidently, to circulate in the older portions of this country, and in England,—to attract public attention to the region where his prin-

---

* The reader will smile at the prophecies of this early tourist; and yet his conclusions were quite natural ones at the time. For all the region he speaks of, the Susquehannah then seemed the prospective avenue to the Atlantic; Baltimore, the commercial mart. But how changed the whole course of trade, by the achievments of our state, in the works of internal improvement! Millions have been, and are now expending, to enable the district of country of which Mr. Maude was speaking, to reach the great artery of internal commerce—the Erie Canal. A prosperous and wealthy valley,—its beautiful young city, planted among the hills, almost in the immediate neighborhood of Bath, extends an arm to reach it, and fall in with the great current of trade through the valley of the "Mohawk."

cipal had become so largely interested; yet it was ably and truthfully written, with the ken of prophecy it would almost seem; "visions of glory" were indulged in, but not a tithe hardly, of the splendid consummations that have been realized.

Such was the rapidity of the settlement of this wilderness, isolated as it was, from contiguous territory occupied by civilized communities, that by a census taken in December, 1790, recorded in "Imlay's Topographical description of the western territory of North America, London edition," it appears that thirty-four of the townships were then more or less settled; that it contained one hundred and ninety families, consisting of five hundred and five (white) males over sixteen years old; one hundred and eighty of that age and under; two hundred and ninety seven females; two free negroes; eleven slaves, and one Indian, making in the whole nine hundred and ninety six inhabitants; of these inhabitants, township No. 10, range 2, (Hopewell) contained six families, thirteen males and *no* females; T. 10, R. 3, (Canandaigua) contained eighteen families, seventy-eight males and twenty females; T. 8, R. 4, (Bristol) contained four families, twenty males and *no* females; T. 10, R. 4, (Bloomfield) contained ten families, forty-four males and twenty females; and T. 11, R. 4, (Boughton Hill or Victor) contained four families, fifteen males and four females.

The foregoing enumeration does not include the settlement of "Friends" the adherents of Jemima Wilkeson, consisting of about two hundred and sixty persons, who had established themselves near the outlet of Crooked lake, nor does it include the settlement at Geneva, supposed to consist of one hundred inhabitants, nor the inhabitants from thence, north to lake Ontario, as they were on what has been since called the "Gore," and was not then supposed to be included in Phelps and Gorham's purchase. The same census notes, that there were west of the Genesee river on the Indian lands, eleven families, (one of which was that of Hon. John H. Jones at old Leicester) composed of fifty-one individuals.

Thus rapidly progressed the settlement of this tract, notwithstanding it had more than the ordinary difficulties in settling a new country to overcome; such as reports of the unusual unhealthiness of the climate, want of provisions to support life, and deficiency of title, set afloat by persons interested in the settlement of rival districts of country; the absolute attack of the Indian chiefs, on the validity of the title, supported or rather assisted by an attack of the British authorities in Canada. One of the usual and almost universal difficulties in settling all new countries, is the prevalence of diseases engendered by change of climate, extra fatigue and unusual exposures, of which this settlement had at least a moderate share—as well as the fear of Indian incursions.

In a letter written by Mr. Phelps to his co-proprietor, Mr. Gorham, dated, Canandaigua, August 7, 1790, from which the following are extracts, the situation of the settlement is more truly described, and better depicted, than the most vivid description written at the present time could portray. Mr. Phelps writes:—

"I arrived at this place the 29th ult. and found the people in this settlement very sickly, but the most of them are getting better, a bilious fever has been the prevailing distemper. Capt. Walker, my nearest neighbor, is now supposed to be dying with the bilious cholic. He will be much lamented as he was one of the most thorough farmers on the ground. We have suffered much for the want of a physician. Dr. Atwater has not been in the country. We have now a gentleman from Pennsylvania attending on the sick, who appears to understand his business. The two Wadsworths [Messrs. William and James Wadsworth who settled at Geneseo,] who brought a large property into the country, have been very sick, and are now on the recovery, but are low-spirited. They like the country, but their sickness has discouraged them. The settlement goes on as well as could be expected, there is a great number of people settled in the country. English grain is good, and we are now in the midst of our harvest."

"The Indians are now in great confusion on account of some Indians being inhumanly killed by the white people; I am this moment setting out with an agent from Pennsylvania, to make them satisfaction for the two Indians murdered. I hope to be able to settle the matter, if I should not succeed, they will retaliate; I never saw them more enraged than they are at this time."

It appears, however, that the mission of Mr. Phelps and the Pennsylvania agent, had no other effect than to induce the Indians to issue a kind of summons, dated August 12, 1790, directed to the Governor and Council of Pennsylvania, signed by Little Beard, (Beaver Tribe) Sangoyeawatau, Gisseharke, (Wolf Tribe) and Caunhisongo, of which the following is an extract:—

"Now we take you by the hand and lead you to the Painted Post, or as far as your canoes can come up the creek, where you will meet the whole of the tribe of the deceased, and all the chiefs, and a number of the warriors of our nation, when we expect you will wash away the blood of your brothers and bury the hatchet, and put it out of memory, as it is yet sticking in our head.

"Brothers, it is our great brother, your Governor, who must come to see us, as we will never bury the hatchet until our great brother himself comes and brightens the chain of friendship, as it is very rusty.—Brothers, you must bring the property of your brothers, you have murdered, and all the property of the murderers, as it will be great satisfaction to the families of the deceased. Brothers, the sooner you meet us the better, for our young warriors are very uneasy, and it may prevent great trouble."

What the sequel of this transaction proved to be, we have not data to determine, although it undoubtedly was brought to an amicable termination; but that such a state of things must strike consternation over a new settlement, where the healthy inhabitants, have a sufficient task to provide for and take care of the sick, may well be conceived. As an instance of the assassin-like attacks made on this settlement, especially when it is considered that of all the privations incident to a new settlement, the want of provisions was less felt in this district than in any other as remote from old settlements; attacks made, it must be presumed, by men having rival interests to subserve, the following will suffice:—

From the Maryland Journal, July 31st, 1789.

"Extract of a letter from Northumberland County, dated July 2d:"—'The people of the Genesee and Niagara country are crowding in upon us every day, owing to the great scarcity of provisions; the most of them who have gone there lately are starving to death, and it is shocking to humanity to hear of the number of the families that are dying daily for the want of sustenance. Since I wrote the above, I have heard from the Genesee and Niagara country, that the scarcity of provisions has increased since the last accounts, so much, that flour was sold for £4 per hundred, and it is a fact that a cow, valued at £7 10s., was given by a man for a bushel of rye, to keep a wife and children from the jaws of death. The wild roots and herbs that the country affords, boiled and without salt, constitute the whole food of most of the unhappy people, who have been decoyed there, through the flattering accounts of the quality of the lands. You have my permission to publish this, in order to deter others from going, and it is thought that unless they get supplies from this and the neighboring counties, they will be compelled to quit the place, as their crops have universally failed. Several boat loads of flour that were carried from here, have been seized by force by the people."

A more infamous libel on the character of the Genesee country and its inhabitants could not have been penned. At the time the printer issued this paper there was not to exceed fifteen families on the whole tract, who had come on within three months previous to that time, and those were mostly wealthy farmers who had emigrated from Massachusetts and Connecticut into the country, bringing with them, what was estimated to be a year's provision. They had not been in the country long enough to try the success or failure of crops; but had it been otherwise, who that has ever entered into a log cabin in the Genesee country does not know that in times of scarcity of provisions, every man of the New England pioneers who would not divide with his necessitous neighbors without money and without price, would be considered as an outlaw in society.

The attack of Cornplanter and other Indian chiefs, on the title of Phelps and Gorham to this tract was well calculated to arrest the sale of lands and the progress of the settlement. In 1790 and 1791, Cornplanter, Half Town, and Great Tree, or Big Tree, sent serious complaints against Mr. Phelps contained in several memorials to the President of the United States, which if true might operate to invalidate the title of Phelps and Gorham to their purchase. The first memorial usually called "Cornplanter's speech," the following extract from which, contains most of the charges against Mr. Phelps and his transactions during the treaty for the lands set forth in the whole. To these charges Mr. Phelps was cited to answer, by the President. Mr. Phelps, as soon as they could be obtained, which however took him some time to effect, produced depositions, certificates, letters and other documentary testimony, signed by such persons as Timothy Pickering, Judge Hollenbeck, Rev. Samuel Kirkland, Joseph Brant, and others which clearly proved that the charges contained in the memorials against him where untrue, as appears from the report of a committee of the United States Senate made January 27, 1792, in the following words:—

"Mr. Butler from the Committee on Indian affairs, to whom was referred the speeches of Cornplanter, of the 9th, of December, 1790; 10th, of January, 7th, of February, and 17th, of March, 1791; made the following report:—

"That Oliver Phelps of whom Cornplanter makes mention, produced some affidavits and other papers, relating to the purchase of lands made by him of the Indians, which your Committee have examined, and are of opinion, that the said affidavits and other papers should be filed in the Secretary's office; and that your Committee be discharged from the further consideration of this subject."

Extracts from Cornplanter's Speech.

"The voice of the Seneca Nation speaks to you, the great counsellor, in whose heart the wise men of all the Thirteen Fires have placed their wisdom. It may be very small in your ears, and we therefore entreat you to hearken with attention; for we are about to speak of things which are to us very great. When your army entered the country of the Six Nations, we called you the Town Destroyer, and to this day, when that name is heard, our women look behind them and turn pale, and our children cling close to the necks of their mother's. Our counsellors and warriors are men, and cannot be afraid; but their hearts are grieved with the fears of our women and children, and desire that it may be buried so deep as to be heard no more. When you gave us peace, we called you father, because you promised to secure us in the possession of our lands. Do this, and, so long as lands shall remain, that beloved name will live in the heart of every Seneca.

"FATHER: our nation empowered John Livingston to let out part of our lands on rent, to be paid to us. He told us, that he was sent by Congress to do this for us, and we fear he has deceived us in the writing he obtained from us; for since the time of our giving that power, a man of the name of Phelps has come among us, and claimed our whole country northward of the line of Pennsylvania, under purchase of that Livingston, to whom he said he had paid twenty thousand dollars for it. He said, also, that he had bought, likewise, from the council of the Thirteen Fires, and paid them twenty thousand dollars more for the same. And he said, also, that it did not belong to us, for that the great King had ceded the whole of it, when you made peace with him. Thus he claimed the whole country north of Pennsylvania, and west of the lands belonging to the Cayugas. He demanded it; he insisted on his demand, and declared that he would have it *all*. It was impossible for us to grant him this, and we immediately refused it. After some days he proposed to run a line, at a small distance eastward of our western boundary, which we also refused to agree to. He then threatened us with immediate war, if we did not comply.

"Upon this threat our chiefs held a council, and they agreed that no event of war could be worse than to be driven, with their wives and children, from the only country which we had a right to, and, therefore, weak as our nation was, they determined to take the chance of war, rather than submit to such unjust demands, which seemed to have no bounds. Street, the great trader at Niagara, was then with us, having come at the request of Phelps, and as he always professed to be our great friend, we consulted him on this subject. He also told us, that our lands had been ceded by the King, and that we must give them up.

"Astonished at what we heard from every quarter, with hearts aching with compassion for our wives and children, we were thus compelled to give up all our country north of the line of Pennsylvania, and east of the Genesee river, up to the fork, and east of a south line drawn from that fork to the Pennsylvania line. For this land Phelps agreed to pay us ten thousand dollars in hand, and one thousand dollars a year for ever. He paid us two thousand and five hundred dollars in hand, part of the ten thousand, and he sent for us to come last spring, to receive our money; but instead of paying us the remainder of the ten thousand dollars, and the one thousand dollars due for the first year, he offered us no more than five hundred dollars, and insisted that he had agreed with us for that sum to be paid yearly. We debated with him for six days, during all which time he persisted in refusing to pay us our just demand, and he insisted that we should receive the five hundred dollars; and Street, from Niagara, also insisted on our recieving the money as it was offered to us. The last reason he assigned for continuing to refuse paying us, was, *that the King had ceded the lands to the Thirteen Fires*, and that he had bought them from you and *paid you for them*.

"We could bear this confusion no longer, and determined to force through every difficulty and lift up our voice that you might hear us, and to claim that security in the possession of our lands, which your commissioners so solemnly promised us. And we now entreat you to enquire into our complaints and redress our wrongs.

"FATHER: Our writings were lodged in the hands of Street, of Niagara, as we supposed him to be our friend; but when we saw Phelps consulting with Street, on every occasion, we doubted of his honesty towards us, and we have since heard, that he was to receive for his endeavors to deceive us, a piece of land two miles in width, west of the Genesee river, and near forty miles in length, extending to lake Ontario; and the lines of this tract have been run accordingly, although no part of it is within the bounds which limit his purchase. No doubt he meant to deceive us.

"FATHER: You have said that we are in your hand, and that, by closing it, you could crush us to nothing. Are you determined to crush us? If you are, tell us so, that those of our nation who have become your children, and have determined to die so, may know what to do. In this case, one chief has said he would ask you to put him out of pain. Another, who will not think of dying by the hand of his father, or of his brother, has said he will retire to Chatauque, eat off the fatal root, and sleep with his fathers in peace."*

---

* The translator of this speech has taken the liberty to give the English orthography to the name of the lake. In Seneca, it was Jadaqueh; i. e. the place where a body

And there was rivalry and misrepresentation to contend with in another quarter. The Upper Province of Canada had commenced settling—there were land dealers there too, who wished to divert settlers from Western New York, and promote the interests of themselves and their localities. John Gould, Esq., who has already been cited, says, that at the period of his earliest residence in Canada, reports were spread prejudicial to the settlements then just commencing in Western New York. It was said that the country was sickly, the Livingston claim and others, were named as adverse titles. He observes, that on leaving Canada in 1804 to settle in the States, Esq. ——— told him he would not give his farm in Canada for "all the land between Niagara and the Cayuga lake." And now, said the old gentleman to the author, as he looked out upon the broad well cultivated acres he and his children possess:— "I would not give my farm for Esq. ———'s, and half a dozen more like it."

The new settlers were threatened with even more formidable difficulties than those that have so far been enumerated. Although the treaty of peace in 1783, between the United States and Great Britain, caused an immediate suspension of hostilities, and a withdrawal from all the posts held by the British in the Eastern States, there were still many delicate and difficult questions that remained to be settled, and which were a source of continual irritation and embarrassment. The posts at Oswego and Niagara, and all the western posts were not surrendered until 1796. The singular spectacle was presented here in Western New York, of surveys and settlement going on under the auspices of one government, while the battlements of fortified places, occupied by the troops of

---

ascended, or was taken up. Cornplanter had allusion to a Seneca tradition:—A hunting party of Indians was once encamped upon the shores of this lake; a young squaw of the party, dug and eat a root that created thirst; to slake it, she went to the lake, and disappeared forever. Thence it was inferred, that a root grew there, which produced an easy death—a vanishing away from the afflictions of life. The author is aware that the name of the lake has been ascribed to another tradition, and that other derivations have been given. His authority is information derived from a native Seneca.

Note.—The Livingston claim, otherwise called the Lessee claim was founded on the circumstance, that John Livingston and others had leased from the Indians, for 999 years on a rent of two thousand dollars per annum, a large tract of land which was alledged to include the whole of the Massachusetts pre-emption tract: but as the whole transaction has been declared to be illegal by the legislation and judicial authorities of the State, and is now abandoned, although it has afforded a pretext for the Lessees, to receive donations from the state and from Phelps and Gorham; but with the Holland Company, their application, although commenced by a suit in ejectment, was less successful.

another, were frowning upon the peaceable operations of enterprise and industry.

The pretext for withholding these posts, was, that the United States had not fulfilled some of its treaty stipulations; the one that guarantied the payment of debts due from American to British subjects, being a special subject of complaint. But while such were the avowed reasons for not surrendering them, it is quite apparent, that they were not the real ones. A peace—a surrender of an empire such as this was, had been as we well know, a sacrifice to necessity, humbling to the pride of England. A suspension of hostilities had been reluctantly consented to, with the lingering hope and expectation, that something might occur, to prevent the final consummation of separation and independence. The holding of this line of posts afforded a feeble prospect of a successful renewal of the struggle, through a continued alliance with the Indians, and the placing of obstacles in the way of the peaceable overtures made to them by our government. And perhaps England entertained hopes that free government was a thing to talk about, and pretty successfully fight for—but would not admit of final consummation. There were differences of opinion they well knew, —radical ones—among those who were to frame the new system; the whole matter looked to them, as it really was, surrounded with difficulties and embarrassments. There might be a failure. Should it be so, here, in the possession of these posts—an alliance with the Indians—was a prospective nucleus for renewing the war and recovering the lost colonies; restoring the precious jewel that had dropped from England's crown. And here it may be remarked, upon the authority of circumstances, too strong to admit of much doubt, that the last vestige of such hopes with England, was not obliterated until the treaty of Ghent, that closed the war of 1812.

Under the instructions of Congress, President Washington, immediately after the peace of '83, despatched Baron Steuben to Quebec to make the necessary arrangements with Sir Frederick Haldimand, for delivering up the posts that have been named. His mission not only contemplated the delivery of the posts to him, but preparations for their occupancy and repairs. The Baron met Gen. Haldimand at the Sorel, on a tour to the Lakes. He was informed by him that he had received no instructions from his government to evacuate the posts, nor for any overt act of peace, save a suspension of hostilities. He regarded himself as not at liberty to enter into any negotiations — complained of a non-fulfilment of treaty stipulations — and even refused the Baron a passport to Detroit. Thus ended the mission; and a long succession of negotiations and embarrassments followed, which belong to the province of general history. Our object here has only been to furnish an induction to local events.

The withholding of the posts, was coupled with the assumption of jurisdiction and guardianship over the Indians, the Six Nations included. Extracts from the Maryland Journal:—

"WHITESTOWN, July 9, 1794."

"We learn by a gentleman immediately from the county of Onondaga, that the greatest part of the Onondaga tribe of Indians, who have heretofore resided in that part of the country, and annually received an annuity of 500 dollars from the State, have removed into the British territory of the Province of Upper Canada. That on the 25th ult., those Indians who were on their way, and had collected at the Onondaga Salt Springs, to take leave of the few who remained behind, and could not be prevailed on (notwithstanding the most insinuating and indefatigable exertions of the British lions of the North) to quit their country; the Indians were collected in council, and the inhabitants, alarmed at the movement of those tawny sons of cruelty, were also collected."

"PHILADELPHIA, Sept. 1, 1794."

"An Express arrived at the War Office on Saturday last from the Genesee country (within the State of New York) with despatches for the Executive of the United States, which were immediately laid before the President. Several private letters, received by the same conveyance, advise that a peremptory order had been issued by Col. Simcoe, the Governor of Upper Canada, requiring an immediate removal of the inhabitants who have been for some time settled on a tract of land in that country, within the bounds of the United States, agreeably to the treaty of peace. They likewise inform, that Capt. Williamson, and the other citizens of the United States, who are principally concerned in the settlement of those lands, were determined to resist the said order, and were preparing to oppose any force that may be sent to deprive them of their lawful rights and property."

"PHILADELPHIA, Sept, 1, 1794."

"SIR:—If after the information, upon which my letter of the 20th of May, was founded, any considerable doubt had remained, of Gov. Simcoe's invasion, your long silence, without a refutation of it, and our more recent intelligence, forbid us to question its truth. It is supported by the respectable opinions, which have been since transmitted to the Executive, that in the late attack on *Fort Recovery*, British officers and British soldiers were, on the very ground, aiding our Indian enemies.

"But, Sir, as if the Governor of Upper Canda was resolved to destroy every possibility of disbelieving his hostile views, he has sent to the Great Sodus—a settlement begun on a bay of the same name on Lake Ontario—a command to Captain Williamson, who derives a title from the State of New York, to desist from his enterprise. This mandate was borne by a Lieutenant Sheaffe, under a military escort; and in its tone corresponds with the form of its delivery, being unequivocally of a military and hostile nature: —

"I am commanded to declare that during the inexecution of the treaty of peace

between Great Britain and the United States, and until the existing differences respecting it shall be mutually and finally adjusted, the taking possession of any part of the Indian territory, either for the purposes of war or sovereignty, is held to be a direct violation of his Britannic Majesty's rights, as they unquestionably existed before the treaty; and has an immediate tendency to interrupt, and, in its progress, to destroy that good understanding which has hitherto subsisted between his Britannic Majesty and the United States of America. I therefore require you to desist from any such aggression. R. H. SHEAFFE,
Lieutenant and Qr. Mr. Gen'l Dept. of his Britannic Majesty's service."

Captain Williamson being from home, a letter was written to him by Lieutenant Sheaffe, in the following words:

"SODUS, 16th August, 1794."

"SIR:— Having a special commission and instructions for that purpose from the Lieutenant Governor of his Britannic Majesty's Province of U. Canada, I have come here to demand by what authority an establishment has been ordered at this place, and, to require that such a design be immediately relinquished, for the reasons stated in the written declaration accompanying this letter; for the receipt of which protest I have taken the acknowledgment of your agent, Mr. Little. I regret exceedingly in my private as well as public character, that I have not the satisfaction of seeing you here, but I hope on my return, which will be about a week hence, to be more fortunate. I am, Sir, your most obedient servant. R. H. SHEAFFE,
Lt. 5th Regt. Q. M. G. D."

"The position of Sodus is represented to be seventy miles within the territorial line of the United States — about twenty from Oswego, and about one hundred from Niagara.

"For the present, all causes of discontent, not connected with our western territory, shall be laid aside; and even among these shall not be revived the root of our complaints, the detention of the posts. But while peace is sought by us through every channel, which honor permits, the Governor of Upper Canada is accumulating irritation upon irritation. He commenced his operations of enmity at the rapids of the Miami. He next associated British with Indian force to assault our fort. He now threatens us, if we fell our own trees and build houses on our own lands. To what length may not Governor Simcoe go? Where is the limit to the sentiment which gave birth to these instructions? Where is the limit of the principle which Governor Simcoe avows?

"The treaty and all its appendages we have submitted to fair discussion, more than two years ago. To the letter of my predecessor of the 29th of May, 1792, you have not been pleased to make a reply, except that on the 20th of June 1793, the 22d of November, 1793, and the 21st of February, 1794, no instructions had arrived from your court. To say the best of this suspension, it certainly cannot warrant any new encroachments, howsoever, it may recommend to us forbearance under the old.

"It is not for the Governors of his Britannic Majesty to interfere with the measures of the United States towards the Indians within their territory. You cannot, Sir, be insensible that it has grown into a maxim, that the affairs of the Indians within the boundaries of any nation, exclusively belong to that nation. But Governor Simcoe, disregarding this right of the United States, extends the line of usurpation in which he marches, by referring to the ancient and extinguished rights of his Britannic Majesty. For, if the existing condition of the treaty keeps them alive on the southern side of Lake Ontario, the Ohio itself will not stop their career.

"You will pardon me, Sir, if under these excuses of Governor Simcoe, I am not discouraged by your having formerly disclaimed a control over, and a responsibility for, the Governors of his Britannic Majesty, from resorting to you on this occasion. You are addressed from a hope, that if he will not be restrained by your remonstrances, he may at least be apprized, through you, of the consequences of self-defence.

I have the honor to be, Sir, &c.

Hon. GEORGE HAMMOND,   EDM. RANDOLPH.
Minister Plenipotentiary of his Britannic Majesty."

To this letter of Secretary Randolph, Mr. Hammond replied, under date, New York, Sept. 3, 1794, that he should transmit copies of Mr. Randolph's letter by the earliest opportunity, to Gov. Simcoe and His Majesty's ministers in England. The invasion of Gov. Simcoe referred to at the commencement of Mr. Randolph's letter, was the marching of British troops by Gov. Simcoe's orders, and taking post and erecting a fort on the Maumee river, early in 1794.

Between these movements of Gov. Simcoe, and a passage in the "Travels of the Duke de la Rochefoucauld Liancourt," which has already been quoted in another connection, there is a remarkable coincidence. The Duke visited the Governor at Niagara, about the period of these acts of aggression. The passage is as follows: "He," (Gov. Simcoe,) "discourses with much good sense, on all subjects, but his favorite topics are, his projects and war, which seem to be the objects of his leading passions. He is acquainted with the military history of all countries; no hillock catches his eye without exciting in his mind the idea of a fort which might be constructed on the spot, and with the construction of this fort, he associates the plan of operations for a campaign, *especially of that which is to lead him to Philadelphia.*" It is not presuming too much, to conclude that his aim was to embroil the frontiers of Western New York, and the North West Territory in difficulties, which he designed should eventuate in war; and he, at the head of a British Army, take the high road to Philadelphia, and to fame.

From the Maryland Journal, of Nov, 21, 1794.

"WHITESTOWN, Nov. 5."

"A gentleman directly from Canandarquie, informs that 1600 Indians had come in to the treaty on Monday Se'nnight—and also that Wm. Johnson, a British Indian agent, and a Mr. Steel, the Indian interpreter from Niagara, were also there, and had found means to collect 26 chiefs in a bye-place, and were haranguing of them in the most eloquent and flattering manner, when discovered by the inhabitants, they were using the most persuasive acts, together with offers of large presents, to induce the Indians to turn their arms against the United States. The meeting broke up in a disorderly manner. The inhabitants were greatly exasperated at this insolent conduct of British agents; and it is said that they gave out that if Col. Pickering did not cause their arrest, they would inflict upon them the Yankee punishment of tar and feathers."

From same paper, of Dec. 9, 1794.

"ALBANY Nov. 27."

" The Genesee treaty, we are informed, has terminated much to the satisfaction of the commissioner of the United States, and of the Six Nations of Indians, who have relinquished all right and title to the Presque Isle territory, and a tract of land four miles wide, from Johnston's Landing to *Fort Slauser*, including Fort Niagara; and also granted to the United States, the right of passing and repassing through their country."

The disposition to renew the war, the work of mischief that was commenced and carried on among the Indians—perhaps the beligerent spirit of Gov. Simcoe, had been greatly promoted by a measure of Lord Dorchester, after the defeat of St. Clair. Viewing it now, after the lapse of over half a century, it is impossible to construe it in any other way than as a premeditated attempt to renew the Indian border wars; and as his Lordship had but recently returned from a visit to England, it would seem that he acted under home influences which contemplated a recommencement of hostilties upon a much larger scale. Having been waited upon by a deputation of Indians, of the west, for advice in reference to their existing boundary difficulties with the United States, he answered them in the following speech:—

"CHILDREN:—I was in expectation of hearing from the people of the United States what was required by them. I hoped that I should have been able to bring you together and make you friends.

"CHILDREN:—I have waited long and listened with great attention, but I have not heard one word from them.

"CHILDREN:—I flatter myself with the hope that the line proposed in the year eighty-three, to separate us from the United States, which was immediately broken by themselves as soon as the peace was signed, would have been mended, or a new one drawn, in an amicable manner. Here, also, I have been disappointed.

"CHILDREN:—Since my return, I find no appearance of a line remains; and from the manner in which the people of the United States rush on, and act, and talk, on this side; and from what I learned of their conduct towards the sea, I shall not be surprised if we are at war with them in the course of the present year, and if so, a line must be drawn by the warriors.

"CHILDREN:—You talk of selling your lands to the state of New York. I have told you that there was no line between them and us. I shall acknowledge no lands to be theirs which have been encroached on by them since the year 1783. They then broke the peace, and as they keep it not on their part, it doth not bind on ours.

"CHILDREN:—They then destroyed their right of pre-emption.

Therefore all their approaches towards us since that time, and all the purchases made by them, I consider as an infringement on the King's rights. And when a line is drawn between us, be it in peace or war, they must lose all their improvements and houses on our side of it. Those people must all begone who do not obtain leave to become the King's subjects. What belongs to the Indians, will of course, be secured and confirmed to them.

"CHILDREN:—What farther can I say to you? You are witnesses that on our parts, we have acted in the most peaceable manner, and borne the language and conduct of the people of the United States with patience. But I believe our patience is almost exhausted."

As we have no information beyond the correspondence introduced, in reference to the affair between Lieut. Sheaffe* and Capt. Williamson, we are left to infer that the spirited communication of Secretary Randolph induced His Brittanic Majesty's plenipotentiary, to curb the further raging of loyal wrath in the bosom of Gov. Simcoe.

It can well be imagined how all that we have been alluding to, helped to throw obstacles in the way of settlement, and perplex the backwoods adventurers. There was a long succession of harassing events, of fearful apprehensions and danger. The Six Nations of Indians not wholly reconciled, in their midst; far outnumbering them; conquered but not subdued; their jealousies and prejudices excited by such powerful influences as have been alluded to; their tomahawks and scalping knives still stained with the blood of their victims in the border wars; in whose bosoms rankled dire revenge for the retributive justice so lately inflicted upon them by Gen. Sullivan. Although there were no Indians on the Phelps and Gorham tract, yet numerous villages, teeming with their warriors, were in its immediate neighborhood,—the barrier of distance not intervening as a shield against their stealthy incursions. In the year 1793, after the defeat of Generals Harmer and St. Clair, in the Northwestern Territory, in which British officers and soldiers, as well as some of our own Indians participated with

---

* The then Lieut. Sheaffe, was afterwards the Maj. Gen. Sheaffe, of the war of 1812. At the commencement of the Revolution, he was a lad, residing with his widowed mother, in Boston. Earl Percy's quarters were in his mother's house. He became his protege, received from him a military education and a commission in the army, from which he rose to the rank of Major General. The commencement of the war of 1812 found him stationed in Canada. He professed a reluctance to engage in it, and wished rather a transfer to some other country, than a participation in a war against his countrymen. For his exploit at Queenston Heights, he was created a Baronet. These facts are derived from a note in Stone's life of Brant.

our enemy, and before the victory obtained by Gen. Wayne, over those Indians in 1794, the "Genesee Indians behaved very rudely, they would impudently enter the houses of the whites (in the Genesee country,) and take the prepared food from the tables without leave, but immediately after the event of the battle (Wayne's victory,) was known, they became humble and tame as spaniels." It was a fact known only at the time to Judge Hosmer and Gen. Israel Chapin, Superintendent of Indian affairs, residing at Avon and Canandaigua, "that the Genesee Indians were ready to rise upon the frontier dwellers of this state, as soon as it should be known that the Indians had been victorious over Wayne, which they did not doubt." Judge Hosmer and Gen. Chapin received this information from an American gentleman, living at Newark, (Niagara) Upper Canada. This gentleman's name, whose character stood high in the confidence of government, was ever kept a secret by those two gentlemen, nor was the rumor suffered to spread among the inhabitants, as it would probably have depopulated the country; but it put these two gentlemen on the guard until the contingency was settled.

For the foregoing information, we are indebted to George Hosmer, Esq.

Though there was no concerted or formidable participation of the Six Nations, in the war going on at the west, it is plain that they meant to keep themselves in a position to take advantage of any ill success of Wayne's expedition. It is inferred by Col. Stone that there were Seneca Indians in the final battle with Wayne, or if not, runners of that nation stationed near the scene of action, from the fact that the Indians of Western New York, were apprized of the result before the whites were.

The inference of the following letter from Gen. Wayne, to Cornplanter, and two other Seneca chiefs, is, that the position of the Senecas was an undefined one; that although it was professedly one of inaction, or neutrality, the government through the agency of Gen. Wayne, found it necessary, while quelling the western Indians, to lay anchors to the windward, to guard against the participation of the Senecas in the disturbances it was endeavoring to quell. The letter is copied from the original manuscript; attached to which, is the autograph signature of the brave, impetuous, but successful "Mad Anthony." There is no date to the letter, but the contents indicate about the period it was written:—

BROTHERS!—

"It was the sincere wish and desire of the President (General Washington) to see you in Philadelphia at the Grand Council Fire of the Fifteen United States of America, whilst the chosen Counsellors were assembled together from every part of this great Island:

"He, therefore, commanded me to send to invite you to come to Philadelphia to meet him in that Council & to inform you that he had sent to invite Red *Jacket* and other Chiefs to meet him also.—

"Pursuant to this command of the President, I sent Mr. Rosecrantz with a message to you from Pittsburgh on the 14th day of November last (more than four moons since) inviting you to that Council Fire:

"You returned for answer "that you could not come at present, as you had so much business to do among yourselves, which you must first attend to."

"At the same time you were so good & friendly as to communicate the proceedings & result of the Grand Council of the Hostile and other Chiefs assembled at Au-Glaize which I received by Mr. Rosecrantz and Cayendoe, now present.

"They were partly the same as had been communicated to General Washington by you & the other Chiefs of the Six Nations from Buffalo Creek some time before.

"But the President still wishing to see & talk with you at the Grand Council Fire then kindled in Philadelphia, ordered me to send you a second message to meet him there that he might hear & understand from your own lips the terms upon which the Hostile Indians would agree to make peace — and which would be more fully & better explained viva voce or, by word of mouth,—than in writing, as many questions might occur that were not thought of at the time of writing.

"In obedience to those orders, I sent you another invitation by Mr. Rosecrantz and Cayendoe to meet the President in Philadelphia at the Council Fire, hoping that by that time you had settled the business you had to transact among yourselves:

"You have now come forward — but, it is too late; the fire is extinguished — and will not be rekindled until November next, i. e. between eight & nine moons from this time.

"I am however, happy to inform you that the Farmers brother, the young King the Infant, the Shining breast-plate & two others of inferior rank went forward and met the President & Grand Council of the Fifteen Fires in Philadelphia agreeably to the invitation which I mentioned had been sent to them by the President and from whom it is probable that the President and Council have received the required information; those Chiefs must have returned to their towns about the time that you set off to come to this place: and will be able to inform you of the Council held with them.

"I will now fully inform you of the intelligence I have just received from Gen'l Knox the Secretary: viz. agreeably to the request of the Six Nations assembled at Buffalo Creek last November.—The President & Grand Council of the Fifteen Fires of the United States have appointed three Commissioners to hold a conference with the Hostile Indians about the first day of June next at the Lower Sandusky: they will probably be at Niagara about the middle of May; from whence it's also probable that you with the other Chiefs of the Six Nations will accompany them to the treaty and use your influence & good offices to procure a permanent peace; so much the true interest of all parties concerned.

"But if after all your good & friendly offices, aided by the sincere wish & desire of the President & Grand Council of the United States for *Peace*, it cannot be obtained but by the sacrifice of National Character & Honor, I hope and trust that there will be but one voice and mind to prosecute the war with that vigor and effect — that the

Hostile Indians will have cause to lament that they did not listen to the voice of peace.

"Having thus communicated to you all the information that I have received respecting the proposed treaty and having spoken my mind openly & freely as a Warrior ever ought to do when speaking to friends & brothers,—

"I have now to request that you will also speak your minds freely & without reserve: so that we may perfectly understand each other: this is what you requested me to do—and what I have done.

"You will therefore make your minds easy—and consider yourselves in the midst of your friends and brothers.—

ANT'Y WAYNE,
Major General & Commander in Chief of the troops
of the United States of America.

THE CORNPLANTER,
NEW ARROW,
GEYESUTHA and
STIFF KNEE (alias) BIG TREE.
} *Chiefs of the Alleghany."*

The effect of the decisive victory of Gen. Wayne, his thorough scourging of the hostile Indians of the west and northwest, put an end to all existing Indian disturbances. Its happy influences extended to all the interests of our country. The Indian wars had come when the government and people were tired of war, and were looking forward to peace and repose. But no where was the consummation hailed with greater joy, than among those who struggling with all the usual hardships and privations of new settlements, had been encountering the additional obstacle, the fear that the scenes of the border war, were to be re-enacted in their midst.

With the Six Nations, it was followed by the burying of the tomahawk, "never to be dug up." Settling down upon their Reservations, they became gentle and inoffensive; friendly to the new settlers as they began to drop in around them; the faithful allies of the United States, in the contest of 1812; emphatically, it may be said, that in all the time that has intervened, from the period we have been speaking of, to the present, they have been far more " sinned against, than sinning."

The Society of Friends, of Philadelphia—or rather, what is termed the "Philadelphia yearly meeting,"—were the early, and have been the constant guardians of the welfare and interests of the Senecas, as the reader will observe in some of the early annals that will follow. Their good offices were interposed in counselling peace and the pursuit of peaceful avocations. Among some old manuscripts the author has in his possession, which belonged to Cornplanter and Red Jacket, is the following letter, which it will be observed bears date a few months after Wayne's victory. It breathes a kind spirit, and was well calculated to promote the interests not only of the Indians, but of those who were becoming their neighbors:—

PHILADELPHIA 1st. month, 24th, 1795.

My good friend the Farmers Brother.

By Capt. Chapin I thought proper to inform thee, & thy Nation, that me and all my friends who attended the Treaty at Canandarqua, arrived safe home and found our friends well — we Reflect frequently on your friendly Disposition towards us, & the Issue of the Treaty which we hope will be the means of a Lasting peace Between you & the United States — we hope you will keep the Remainder of your Land in your hands, and learn to Cultivate it & that you will by all means keep in Peace with the White People as well as with your Indian Brethren & all men — this will be your greatest happiness, if we your friends the Quakers of Philadelphia Can be of any Service to you we are Ready & willing at any time, & we Desire you may be free in applying to us — with a great Deal of Regard & Desire for your Welfare, I am your friend,

WILLIAM SAVERY.

Among the same manuscripts, is the following, by which it would seem that soon after taking possession of Fort Niagara by the troops of the United States, there was an assembling there of the sachems and warriors of the Six Nations, to interchange sentiments of peace, friendship, and mutual aid. Nothing accompanies the manuscript to explain it; the author has no cotemporary history of the council it would indicate; but it is an interesting relic; and its contents have a direct bearing upon early local events:—

Sachams and Brother warriors of the six nations residing within the territory of the United States; I welcome you to Niagara.

We have meet,—BROTHERS — to brighten that chain of friendship which is strectched out to you;— to your brethern on the western waters;— and to the whole world. A proof of this — these Western posts that have so long been witheld, are at length given up without the spilling of blood; and a good understanding now subsists between the United States and the British Government: Lines are fixed and so strongly marked between us that they cannot be mistaken, and every precaution taken to prevent a misunderstanding. Within these lines you hold large tracts of land:— in the sure and peaceable possession of which the United States have taken care to guard you as their own children and citizens: and if any rememberance of former animosities yet remain — let us burry them in the grave of forgetfulness.

BROTHERS:— As we have become near neighbors — it will be our interest that we shall also be good friends: be assured, you will experience in us a disposition to cultivate harmony and a good understanding; and that we hope to find the same disposition in you: As a pledge of the sincerity of these professions, and as a token of regard the president of the United States has charged me with — and I now have the honour to present you a flag of our nation: may the luster of its stars illuminate the western world; and while the increase of its stripes give to our friends a confidence of our ability, to protect them; may they, also, admonish such as would disturb our peace;— of our power to chastise them.

BROTHERS:—Thus far (I conceive) I have spoken by authority derived from the father of our country — the president of the United States: indulge me a moment while I speak in behalf of this garrisson, the command of which he has honoured me with, you know (better than I do) that there is no road by which cured provisions and other necessaries can be sent us from our settlements; that in winter all communication by water is cut off; that the land between this and Genesee river is yours, and without your permission, we will not attempt to widen, mend or straighten your road, which at present is scarcely passable, but which if done, will not only be an accomodation to this garrisson; — to our settlers on the genesee, and our British neighbors on the opposite shore; — but to yourselves also: nor will our making use of it in common with you, injure your property — or invade your rights: the road as well as the country, being yours. I wish you therefore, to consult together, and if you agree with me in sentiment; give us permission to widen, mend and straighten, the road to Connowagoras.

BROTHERS: — As guardian of the honour, rights and interest of my country in this quarter — my duty makes it necessary for me to take notice of a practice — I have already represented to the British commandant on the opposite shore as wrong. While the British held this post, they also claimed the souvreignty of the country quite to our settlements: It was then a practice (and the precedent is yet contended for) to imploy indians to pursue deserters on the American side of the line to the Genesee river: such pursuits are now improper. The British will not permit them on their side the water: because they (justly) consider it an infraction of the rights of nations: — what is a violation of rights on one side, must be so on the other. This practice therefor, if persisted in — may involve the two governments in very disagreeable disputes (now perhaps in your power to prevent) but which if you encourage; may terminate very unpleasent to both countries and yourselves. I therefore request, that you will admonish your brethren not to meddle with disputes between white people, of so delicate a nature — our differences (experience may have taught you) will not benefit you, but your interference may involve us very disagreeably. For if I know the interest & wish of my country, it is for peace: — but however thus disposed, she ought not, she cannot, and I am persuaded, will not tamely suffer her territory to be violated — her sovereignty on this the water to be disputed, and her rights contemptuously to be trampled on. I beg you, therefore, to restrain your people from a practice the pernicious consequences of which I have taken some pains to put in a proper light.

BROTHERS: — Yesterday you reccived some refreshment — to day there is a further supply provided and ready for you; when we have finished our business, (which I hope will be soon,) I have a barrel of rum to present you; that you may with your brethren you left to keep up your fires in your absence, drink prosperity to the United States — health and long life to our President. I wish my supplies would afford you those necessaries you solicit, have been in the habit of receiving here; and appear to want. But when you reflect that I command but the advance of the American troops intended for this post — and that my stores must consequently be small — you cannot expect much — such as they are; you have partaken of. May your stay here be pleasant — may we part satisfied, and on your return, may the Great Spirit take you under his care — so that you may arrive safely at your respective homes, and find all you left behind in security — your friends and connexions will.

NIAGARA, September 23d, 1796.   J. BRUFF, *Captain Commanding.*"

The following, derived from the same source, though not of a local character, is inserted chiefly to preserve a relic of one, the bare mention of whose name excites the liveliest recollections of our war of independence, and those foremost in achieving it. It was an invitation of the Senecas to join in St. Clair's expedition; an expedition in which the brave and chivalric writer of the autograph we transcribe, was a victim to the tomahawk and scalping knife, after he was carried from the field to have wounds dressed previously received: —

"BROTHERS OF THE FIVE NATIONS:—

The bearer hereof Mons'r De Bartzch having express'd a Desire to assist and go with such of your people as may be inclin'd (and you think proper to send) to join Governor St. Clair & accompany the Army of the U. S. against the Western Hostile tribes of Indians — As you & Mons'r De Bartzch are acquainted, should any of your People join the Governor & Troops, and that he is still inclin'd to go on the Expedition, and that it is agreeable to you and your People that he should be with you, it will be very agreeable to me as I believe him to be a Gentleman, and of very honorable Character—I am Brothers your Real Friend

RICH'D BUTLER,
Maj'r Gen'l in the U. S. Army.

PITTSBURGH, June 5th, 1791.
To the CORNPLANTER, and other Chiefs and Warriors of the Five Nations."

ROBERT MORRIS.

A short biography of one eminently useful in our Revolutionary struggle, is suggested by his after identity with our local region. He was as will have been seen, at one period, the proprietor of the whole of Western New York west of Phelps and Gorham's Purchase, by purchase from Massachusetts, and the Seneca Indians.

In the attempt of feeble colonies, to throw off the yoke of oppression, there was work to be done in council as well as in the field — at the financier's desk, as well as in the more conspicuous conflicts of arms. If raw troops, called from the field and workshop, were to be enrolled and disciplined, upon a sudden emergency, provisions were to be made for their equipment and sustenance. Both were tasks surrounded with difficulty and embarrassment; both required men and minds of no ordinary cast. Fortunately they were found. WASHINGTON was the chief, the leader of our armies, the master spirit that conducted the struggle to a glorious termination; MORRIS was the financier. They were heads of co-ordinate branches, in a great crisis, and equally well performed their parts.

Robert Morris was born in Liverpool, in 1733. His father emigrated to the United States in 1745, and settled at Port Tobacco, in Maryland, engaging extensively in the tobacco trade.

He met his death in a singular manner, when the subject of this sketch was but a youth. He was the consignee of a ship that had arrived from a foreign port; the custom then was to fire a gun when the consignee came on board. As if he had a presentiment that the ceremony would prove fatal to him, he had requested its omission. The captain had so ordered, but a sailor, not having understood the order, and supposing the omission accidental, seized a match, and fired the gun as Mr. Morris was leaving the ship. A portion of the wadding fractured his arm, mortification and death ensued.

Previous to the death of his father, Robert Morris had been placed in the counting house of Mr. Charles Willing, an eminent merchant of Philadelphia, where he soon acquired a proficiency in mercantile affairs that recommended him as a partner of the son of his employer.

When the first difficulties occurred between the colonies and the mother country, though extensively engaged in a mercantile business that was to be seriously affected by it, he was one of other patriotic Philadelphia merchants who promoted and signed the non-importation agreement, which restricted commercial intercourse with Great Britain to the mere necessaries of life.

When the news of the battle of Lexington reached Philadelphia, Mr. Morris was presiding at a dinner usually given on the anniversary of St. George. He participated in putting a sudden stop to the celebration in honor of an English saint, and helped to upset the tables that had been spread. His resolution was fixed. It was one of devotion to the cause of the colonies; and well was it adhered to.

In 1775 and '76 he was a member of Congress, and became a signer of the Declaration of Independence. A few days after the battle of Trenton, it became a matter of great importance to the commander-in-chief, to obtain a sum of money in specie, in order to keep himself well advised of the movements of the enemy. He applied to Mr. Morris for that purpose, and received the following answer: —

"Philadelphia, Dec. 30, 1776.

"Sir — I have just received your favor of this day, and sent to Gen. Putnam to detain the express until I collected the hard money you want, which you may depend shall be sent in one specie or other with this letter, and a list thereof, shall be enclosed herein. I had long since parted with very considerable sums of hard money to Congress, and therefore must collect from others — and as matters now stand, it is no easy thing. I mean to borrow silver and promise payment in gold, and then collect the gold the best way I can. Whilst on this subject, let me inform you, that there is upwards of twenty thousand dollars of silver at Ticonderoga. They have no particular use for it, and I think you might as well send a party to bring it away, and lodge it in a safe place convenient for any purposes for which it may hereafter be wanted. Whatever I can do shall be done for the good of the cause.

I am dear Sir, yours, &c.
ROBERT MORRIS."

When Washington had re-crossed the Delaware for the second time, in Dec. 1777, the time of service of nearly all the eastern troops had expired. To induce them to engage for another six weeks, he promised a bounty of ten dollars each; and for the necessary funds applied to Mr. Morris. In the answer of Mr. Morris, accompanying the sum of fifty thousand dollars, he congratulates the commander-in-chief upon his success in retaining the men, and assures him that "if farther occasional supplies of money are wanted, you may depend on my exertions either in a public or private capacity."

In March, 1777, he was chosen with Benjamin Franklin and others, to represent the assembly of Pennsylvania in Congress; and in November following, was associated with Mr. Gerry, and Mr. Jones, to repair to the army and confidentially consult with the commander-in-chief upon the best plan of conducting the winter campaign. In August, 1778, he was appointed a member of the standing committee of finance.

The years 1778, and '79, were the most distressing periods of the war. The finances were in a wretched condition, and Mr. Morris, not only advanced his money freely, but put in requisition an almost unlimited individual credit.*

---

* Judge Peters relates the following anecdote:—"We (the Board of War,) had exhausted all the lead accessible to us; having caused even the spouts of houses to be melted; and had unsuccessfully offered the equivalent of two shillings specie, (25 cents,) per lb. for lead. I went on the evening of a day in which I received a letter from the army, to a splendid entertainment given by Don Mirailles, the Spanish minister. My heart was sad, but I had the faculty of brightening my countenance even under gloomy disasters; yet it seems not then with sufficient adroitness, for Mr. Morris, who was one of the guests, and knew me well, discovered some casual trait of depression. He accosted me in his usual frank and ingenuous manner, saying:—'I see some clouds passing across the sunny countenance you assume; what is the matter?' After some hesitation I showed him the general's letter which I had brought from the office, with the intention of placing it at home, in a private cabinet. He played with my anxiety, which he did not relieve for some time. At length however, with great and sincere delight, he called me aside and told me that the Holker privateer had just arrived at his wharf with ninety tons of lead which she had brought as ballast. 'You shall have' said Mr. Morris 'my half of this fortunate supply: there are the owners of the other half,' (indicating gentlemen in the department.) The other half was obtained. Before morning, a supply of cartridges was made ready and sent off to the army."

In 1781, (a period of despair,) in addition to other contributions of money and credit, Mr. Morris supplied the almost famishing troops with several thousand barrels of flour. This timely aid came when it was seriously contemplated to authorize the seizure of provisions wherever they could be found; a measure which would have been unpopular with the whole country, and probably turned back the tide of public feeling flowing in favor of the Revolution.

There is upon record a long catalogue of transactions similar to those which have been related. Not only the commander-in-chief but Generals of divisions, found Mr. Morris the dernier resort when money and provisions were wanted. To private means that must have been large, and a large credit, he added astonishing faculties as a financier. When he had no other resource, he would compel others to use their money and credit. In financial negotiations, with him, to will a thing was to do it.

He was appointed to the office of "Financier," or what was equivalent to the now office of Secretary of the Treasury. Never perhaps, in any country, was a minister of finance placed over a treasury the condition of which was worse. To use a phrase of the play-house, it was a

"Beggarly account of empty boxes."

It had not a dollar in it, and was two millions and a half in debt. Those who have seen Gen. Washington's military journal, of the 1st of May, 1781, can form some idea of the condition of the army, and the finances.

It was the province of Mr. Morris to financier for Congress, and a country and cause, in such a crisis. He began by restoring credit and establishing confidence; promulgated the assurance that all his official engagements would be punctually met; and put in requisition his private means, the means of his friends, to fulfill the promises he had held out. When apprized of his appointment to the management of financial affairs, he replied:—"In accepting the office bestowed upon me, I sacrifice much of my interest, my ease, my domestic enjoyment, and internal tranquility. If I know my own heart, I make these sacrifices with a disinterested view to the service of my country. I am willing to go further, and the United States may command every thing I have except my integrity, and the loss of that would effectually disable me from serving them more."

Among his financial expedients, to resuscitate public credit, was the establishment of the Bank of North America. Collateral security was given for the performance of the engagements of the institution in the form of bonds, signed by wealthy individuals. Mr. Morris heading the list with a subscription of £10,000.

In a private interview with Washington the subject of an attack on New York was broached. Mr. Morris dissented; assuming that it would be at too great a sacrifice of men and money; that the success of the measure was doubtful; that even if successful the triumph as to results, would be a barren one; the enemy having command of the sea could at any time land fresh troops and retake it, &c. Assenting to these objections, the commander-in-chief said:—"What am I to do? The country calls on me for action; and moreover my army cannot be kept together unless some bold enterprise is undertaken." To this Mr. Morris replied: "Why not lead your forces to Yorktown? there Cornwallis may be hemmed in by the French fleet by sea, and the American and French armies by land, and will ultimately be compelled to surrender." "Lead my troops to Yorktown!" said Washington, appearing surprised at the suggestion. "How am I to get them there? One of my difficulties about attacking New York arises from the want of funds to transport my troops thither. How then can I muster the means that will be requisite to enable them to march to Yorktown?" "You must look to me for funds," rejoined Mr. Morris. "And how are you to provide them?" said Washington. "That," said Mr. Morris, "I am unable at this time to tell you, but I will answer with my head, that if you will put your army in motion, I will supply the means of their reaching Yorktown." After a few minutes reflection, Washington said:—"On this assurance of yours, Mr. Morris, such is my confidence in your ability to perform any engagement you make, I will adopt your suggestion."

When the army arrived at Philadelphia, Mr. Morris had the utmost difficulty in furnishing the supplies he had promised, but at last hit upon the expedient of borrowing twenty thousand crowns from the Chevalier de Luzerne, the French Minister. The Chevalier objected that he had only funds enough to pay the French troops, and could not comply unless two vessels with specie on board for him arrived from France. Fortunately, about the time the troops were at Elk, preparing to march for Yorktown, the ships arrived, the money was procured, and especial pains taken to parade the specie in open kegs, before the army. The troops were paid, and cheerfully embarked to achieve the crowning triumph of the Revolution.*

John Hancock, President of Congress, writing to Mr. Morris in a severe crisis of the Revolution, says:—"I know however, you will put things in a proper way, all things depend upon you, and you have my hearty thanks for your unremitting labor." Gen. Charles Lee said to him in a letter, when he assumed the duties of Secretary of an empty treasury:—"It is an office I cannot wish you joy of; the labor is more than Herculean; the filth of that Augean stable is in my opinion too great to be cleared away even by your skill and industry."

Paul Jones made Mr. Morris his executor, and bequeathed him as a token of his high regard, the sword he had received from the King of France. Mr. Morris gave it to Commodore Barry, with a request that it should fall successively into the hands of the oldest commander of the American Navy.

The Marquis de Chastellux, was in the United States, in 1780, 1781, and 1782, a Major General in the French Army, serving under the Count de Rochambeau. In a book of Travels of which he is the author, (a work well worthy of being more generally known than it is,) he gives the following account of Mr. Morris. He visited him at his house in Philadelphia:—

"He was a very rich merchant, and consequently a man of every country, for commerce bears every where the same character. Under monarchies, it is free; it is an egotist in republics; a stranger, or if you will, a citizen of the universe, it excludes alike the virtues and the prejudices that stand in the way of its interests. It is scarcely to be credited, that amidst the disasters of America, Mr. MORRIS, the inhabitant of a town just emancipated from the hands of the English, should possess a fortune of eight millions, (between three and four hundred thousand pounds, sterling.) It is, however, in the most critical times, that the greatest fortunes are acquired. The fortunate return of several ships, the still more successful cruises of his privateers, have increased his riches beyond his expectations, if not beyond his wishes. He is, in fact, so accustomed

---

* Mr. Morris anxious to enlist the feelings of the Chevalier and secure his co-operation, took him into his carriage and was proceeding to Elk, when they met on the road, an express rider. Mr. Morris called out to him and enquired for whom he had despatches? "For Robert Morris," he replied. On opening the paper, it proved to be the announcement that the French frigates had arrived in the Delaware with the specie on board!

to the success of his privateers, that when he is observed on Sunday to be more serious than usual, the conclusion is, that no prize has arrived the preceding week. This flourishing state of commerce at Philadelphia, as well as in Massachusetts Bay, is entirely owing to the arrival of the French squadron. The English have abandoned all their cruises, to block it up at Newport, and in that they have succeeded ill, for they have not a single sloop coming to Rhode Island, or Providence. Mr. Morris is a large man very simple in his manners; his mind is subtle and acute, his head perfectly well organized, and he is as well versed in public affairs as in his own. He was a member of Congress in 1776, and ought to be reckoned among those personages who have had the greatest influence in the revolution of America. He is the decided friend of Dr. Franklin, and the decided enemy of Mr. Read. His house is handsome, resembling perfectly the houses in London; he lives there without ostentation, but not without expense, for he spares nothing which can contribute to his happiness and that of Mrs. MORRIS to whom he is much attached."

The account of Mr. Morris' wealth, at the period named, is not perhaps exaggerated. During the Revolution the commercial house in which he continued a partner, was prosecuting a successful business. The translator of a London edition of the Travels of the Marquis de Chastellux, speaks of vast money making facilities Mr. Morris enjoyed through the French consul, resident in Philadelphia, by means of special permits to ship cargoes of flour, &c. in a time of general embargoes. At one period, says the translator, he circulated his private notes throughout the country, as cash.

The close of the Revolution, must have found him in possession of immense wealth, exceeding that by far of any individual citizen of the United States. But he was destined to a sudden reverse of fortune. There followed the Revolution a mania for land speculation, as great perhaps in porportion to the then number of persons to participate in it, as one that has been witnessed in our own times. Mr. Morris participated largely in it; investing in large tracts of wild land, as they came into market in different parts of the United States; realizing for a time vast profits upon sales. A reaction ensued, which found him in possession of an immense landed estate, and largely in debt for purchase money. From the opulence that we have been speaking of, he was reduced to poverty; and ultimately, some merciless creditors, made him for a long time the tenant of a prison.

It has been stated that his misfortunes were partly owing to sacrifices he made during his financial agencies in the Revolution. This error is corrected in a letter with which the author has been favored from a surviving son of his, the venerable THOMAS MORRIS,

Esq. a resident of the city of New York:—"My father's pecuniary losses were not owing to his public engagements in the war of Independence. Heavy as those engagements were, (the last two years of the war having been supported almost entirely by his advances and by his credits,) he was eventually reimbursed by the public."

The author has in his posession two autograph letters, from Mr. Morris, addressed to "Mr. Benjamin Barton," the father of the late Benjamin Barton, Jr. The first, was written but a few weeks after the Treaty with the Indians on the Genesee river, at which the Indian title was extinguished to all the lands in this state west of Phelp's and Gorham's Purchase. It is inserted entire:—

"Hills, near Philadelphia, Oct. 18, 1797.

Sir.—I received your letter dated at Newark, the 12th inst. only yesterday, and am sorry to see thereby the several unfortunate accidents you have met with, and particularly as your affairs have become deranged thereby. In consequence of the purchase lately made by the Indians, our surveyors, will immediately set to work and survey and lay out that country; and as my son Thomas, who lives at Canandaigua, Ontario county, will have a principal share in selling lands, and establishing settlements there, I think you had better apply to him; but your application will be time enough by or before next spring, when he comes to Albany in the winter, to meet the Legislature.

You did not furnish me with an account of the lumber you sent down, which I wish you would do, with the cost thereof.

I am, Sir, Your obt. serv't. ROBERT MORRIS."

At the date of this letter, he was a "Merchant Prince," living in affluence, writing of the purchase and intended sale and settlement of vast tracts of land. Upon him had devolved the financiering for our country in a period of peril and embarrassment. When the army of Washington, unpaid, were lacking food and raiment; murmuring as they well might be; it was his purse and credit that more than once prevented its dispersion, and the failure of the glorious achievement of Independence. His ships were upon the ocean, his notes of hand forming a currency, his drafts honored every where among capitalists in his own country, and in many of the marts of commerce in Europe.

A reverse of fortune, saddening to those who are now enjoying the blessings to which he so eminently contributed—who wish that no cloud had gathered around the close of his useful life—intervened between the dates of the two letters. The second one is dated "Philadelphia, Dec. 11, 1800," and after disposing of some business enquiries that had been made, closes as follows:—

"You have now the clearest information I can give you. I have been frequently applied to about this affair, but hope there is an end of it. If however, you should find it necessary to write again, be good enough to pay the postage of your letters, for *I have not a cent to spare from the means of subsistence.*

I am, Sir, Your very obt. serv't.
ROBERT MORRIS.

Mr. BENJAMIN BARTON, Sussex Co. N. J."

Mr. Morris died at Morrisania, N. J., Nov. 6th, 1806, aged 73 years.

NOTE.— During the life of Mrs. Morris, she had an annuity of fifteen hundred dollars, paid her by the Holland Company, as an equivalent for the release of dower, in the lands they purchased of her husband. "This was all that was left of that splendid fortune which we have seen to have been lavished in loans for the public service, when its return was most doubtful." Robert Morris was not only connected with this region as a primitive proprietor, but the project of the Erie Canal was promoted by his efforts.

AUGUSTUS PORTER.

Few names were earlier, have been more intimately, and none more honorably, associated with the entire history of settlement and progress in Western New York, than that of AUGUSTUS PORTER. Entering it in his youth—sitting down in the primitive log cabins erected by the first settlers west of the Mussachusetts pre-emption line;—going out with compass and chain and traversing the wilderness, over hill and dale, the trails of the Indian that he occasionally crossed, the only evidences that human advent and agency had preceded him;—his rude camp in the fastnesses of the forest, pitched upon streams and by the side of springs that had flowed and gurgled until then, unknown to his race;—changing his wilderness itineracy for a position and agency that equally blended him and his name with the primitive settlement of that now empire of wealth and substantial prosperity,—"Phelps and Gorham's Purchase." Remaining there but to see settlement fairly commenced, then coming farther on, first as surveyor and then as a settler to prominently participate in pushing settlement and improvement to a new field of enterprize—to the western boundaries of the Holland Purchase;—he lives to witness the mighty change that has been wrought! With a memory and a judgment unimpaired by age and more than its usual physical infirmities, he yet lives to contribute valuable and essential reminiscences to the Pioneer history of a region he has seen converted —and helped to convert—from the hunting grounds of the migratory Indian, to the fairest and most prosperous region of our Empire State.

There are few whose days are lengthened out as his have been; fewer by far who have had cognizance of, and participation in, so extended a period of interesting events in the history of our country. Change, progress, the conversion of a wilderness to what Western New York now is, in the short space of a little over half a century, is a wonder of itself—and how far enhanced is the wonder, when in view of the average amount of years that are allotted to an active participation in the affairs of this life, we listen to, or read the recital of events from a living witness, commencing with the earliest advents of our race, in the work of settlement and improvement!

His studies at school in the years immediately preceding his

AUGUSTUS PORTER.

majority, were interrupted by a transfer to farm labor, to help supply the places of those who had gone out to fill the ranks of an army raised by a few feeble colonies struggling for separation and Independence. He has lived not only to see a glorious consummation of that struggle, but lives to see those colonies a mighty empire of states, fulfilling the highest destinies fondly anticipated by its founders.

The hand that helped to make some of the primitive township and farm surveys of the region between the Seneca lake, and the east line of the Holland Purchase,—a region now embracing a city with over thirty thousand inhabitants; large and prosperous villages; dotted throughout its entire length and breadth with comfortable farm houses and highly cultivated farms; traversed by canals, rail roads and telegraphic wires;—is spared to make a record of events of his own times, that in the old world would be witnessed but by successive generations, and mark the lapse of centuries!

Penetrating the wilderness region still farther on—locating at the Falls of Niagara, and prominently pioneering in clearing away the forest that enshrouded them—in commencing there the work of settlement and improvement—in surveying and opening the primitive roads; he lives to see there, a prosperous and growing village; to see it the termination of rail roads and telegraphs; the deep gorge, or basin, into which he has seen the mighty volume of water pour but to affright the wild beasts in their favorite haunts, spanned by one of the highest perfections of modern art; to see where stood the rude, semi-log cabin resting place of an occasional visitor, palace-like hotels erected, annually crowded by those who throng to the great centre of attraction.

Where now is a city of over forty thousand inhabitants, the great mart of the commerce of prosperous states, he has set down and partaken of backwoods fare, in a log-cabin, the only place of entertainment. There he has waited for a change of wind, to enable him and his companions to coast along the shores of lake Erie, in a batteau, over waters then but seldom disturbed but by the elements, and the Indian's bark canoe. He lives to see those waters whitened by the sails of commerce; "floating palaces," steam-propelled, in fleets, competing for the travel and transportation of a young but already extended and prosperous empire of the west!

How blended with change, progress, the mighty achievements of our age and race, is the name, the reminiscences, of this early Pioneer! The reader will not be surprised that the author has, for a few moments, arrested the course of narrative, for comments, such as he has indulged in; nor deem it inappropriate, to have availed himself of the skill of the artist, to give a faithful portrait of his venerable features.

Judge PORTER was born on the 18th of January, 1769; is a native of Salisbury, Connecticut; the son of Joshua Porter, who was, for fifty years, a practicing physician and surgeon, in that town. He died in 1825, at the advanced age of ninety-five years. The subject of our brief memoir acquired the rudiments of education in the common school of his native town; his regular attendance at school being confined, as was the case with most boys of New England at that period, to the winter months. In 1786, in the sixteenth year of his age, he had the advantage of a few month's study of mathematics, and particularly surveying, under the tuition of Mr. Nathan Tisdale, of Lebanon. His tutor dying, he returned to labor upon his father's farm, remaining under the paternal roof until the spring of 1789, when he first started for the new field of enterprise, then just opening in Western New York. A continuation of the Judge's personal biography, in this form, is rendered unnecessary, as it is embraced in a narrative of early events, which he has furnished, at the request of the Buffalo Young Men's Association; much of which, as it will be observed, the author has transferred to his pages.

In June 1806, he became a resident of the Holland Purchase — locating himself at the Falls of Niagara, where he still resides, at the advanced age of eighty years. He may be said to constitute a connecting link between two generations — or rather between two distinct classes; so far as habits of life are concerned. He is one of the survivors of a race of Pioneers, hardy, industrious and frugal; men of iron constitutions they must have been, to encounter the hardships and privations of the wilderness. Living now in an age of luxury, of increasing effeminacy; surrounded by all the comforts of life; with ample means to enjoy its luxuries; he emphatically belongs to the old school; preserving the simple, frugal habits of his youth and middle age, his habits of industry and economy; his love of the substantial and sensible things of this life; leaving to those who have acquired wealth through a less rugged path, their choice of show and ostentation. In this respect, as well as others, his life and example furnish a useful lesson; a protest against the moral and physical degeneracy he lives to witness.

He came to the western country as will have been seen, young; with a good New England constitution; healthy and muscular. In all of his early life he enjoyed good health; interrupted occasionally by diseases incident to the climate, and extraordinary exposures. In 1843, then seventy-four years of age, he was engaged with his laborers, in prying up a stick of timber. Standing himself upon the pry, the whole weight of the stick came upon it, throwing him off with such violence as to partially break a hip bone; to which casualty is to be attributed, a present lameness; added to which is the troublesome and at times painful infirmity — hernia — and a hereditary deafness, that increases with age, and renders the use of an ear trumpet essential in ordinary conversation. And yet, under all these disabilities, the greater portion of each day, is spent in the out-of-door general management of a largely extended and varied business.*

[During the last winter, as a preliminary step in the preparation of this work, the author called upon Judge Porter for such assistance as his long residence, retentive memory, and intelligent observation enabled him to give. He cheerfully and obligingly complied, and devoted several days to a patient answering of such enquiries as were made of him; the author taking notes during the interview. These are principally applicable of the early settlement of the Holland Purchase, and will be used in a detached form, as the necessity of their use occurs. About this period the Judge had been applied to by a committee of the Young Men's Association of Buffalo, for historical reminiscences, with a view to preservation in the archives of their Association; which request he was complying with. With his consent, and that of the Association, that portion of his written narrative of events, having reference to settlement as it was approaching the Holland Purchase, is used by the author. It saved the narrator from travelling twice over the same ground, and insured a greater degree of correctness, than could have been relied upon from notes of conversation. The narrative is taken up as it came from his hands; with such portions omitted as have been embraced in other forms; that in reference to land titles being the principal omission in all that relates to the progress of settlement in Western New York.]

In the year 1789, Capt. Wm. Bacon, Gen. John Fellows, Gen. John Ashley, and Elisha Lee, Esq., of Sheffield, Mass., Deacon John Adams of Alford, Mass., and my father, having become the purchasers of Township No. 12, 1st Range (now Arcadia, Wayne Co.,) and No. 10, in the 4th Range, (now East Bloomfield, Onta-

---

* This is from a note made in the author's memorandum book, a year previous to the publication of his work.

rio Co.,) then in the county of Montgomery, New York, I entered into an agreement with them to go out and survey the tracts. I, accordingly, in pursuance of previous arrangements, made with Capt. Bacon, met him at Schenectady, early in May, 1789. Here I found Capt. B. had collected some cattle, provisions, and farming utensils, for the use of the settlers who were going forward in company with Deacon Adams and his family, whom I also met at the same place, and who took charge of the cattle. The provisions were taken into two boats. I assisted in navigating one of the boats, each carrying about twelve barrels, and known as Schenectady batteaux, and each navigated by four men. Leaving Schenectady, we proceeded up the Mohawk to Fort Stanwix (now Rome.) In passing Little Falls of the Mohawk, the boats and their contents were transported around on wagons. At Fort Stanwix, we carried our boats, &c., over a portage about one mile, to the waters of Wood creek. This creek affords but little water from the portage to its juncture with the Canada creek, (which falls into Wood creek seven miles west of Fort Stanwix.) At the portage there was a dam for a saw mill, which created a considerable pond. This pond, when filled, could be rapidly discharged, and on the flood thus suddenly made, boats were enabled to pass down. We passed down this stream, which empties into Oneida Lake, and through that lake and its outlets to the Three River Point, and thence up the Seneca River and the outlet of Kanadasaga Lake, (now Seneca Lake,) to Kanadasaga settlement, (now Geneva.) The only interruption to the navigation to this river and the outlet, occurred at Seneca Falls and Waterloo, (then known as Scoys.) At Seneca Falls we passed our boats up the stream empty, by the strength of a double crew, our loading being taken around by a man named Job Smith, who had a pair of oxen and a rudely constructed cart, the wheels of which were made by sawing off a section of a log, some two and a half or three feet in diameter. At Scoys, we took out about half our load to pass, consisting mostly of barrels, which were rolled around the rapids.

From the time we left Fort Stanwix, until we arrived at Kanadasaga, we found no white persons, except at the juncture of Canada and Wood creeks, where a man lived by the name of Armstrong;— at Three River Point, where lived a Mr. Bingham, and at Seneca Falls, where was Job Smith. Geneva was at that time the most important Western settlement, and consisted of some six or seven families, among whom was Col. Reed, (father of the late Rufus Reed, of Erie, Pa.,) Roger Noble and family, of Sheffield, Mass., and Asa Ransom, late of Erie county, who had a small shop, and was engaged in making Indian trinkets. At Geneva we left our boats and cargoes in charge of Capt. Bacon, who had come from Schenectady to Fort Stanwix, on horseback, and there took passage on our boats. Joel Steel, Thaddeus Keyes,

Orange Woodruff, and myself, took our packs on our backs, and followed the Indian trail, over to Canandaigua.

At Canandaigua, (then called Kanandarque) we found Gen. Chapin, Daniel Gates, Joseph Smith, (Indian interpreter) Benjamin Gardner and family, Frederick Saxton, (Surveyor) and probably some half a dozen others, all of whom except Smith and Gardner had come on with Gen. Chapin, some ten or fifteen days before, in boats from Schenectady, by Fort Stanwix, Wood creek, Oneida Lake, &c., and up the Canandaigua outlet, into the lake itself. This is the only instance to my knowledge of the ascent of boats for transportation so high up; the ordinary point of landing, afterwards, being at Manchester, seven miles down. The only houses in Canandaigua were of logs. One occupied by Gen. Chapin near the outlet; one a little further north, on the rising ground occupied by Smith, and one by Gardner near the old Antis house, as at present known; and the other on the lot where Oliver Phelps' house stands, which had been built the fall before by Mr. Walker, an agent of Mr. Phelps. In this house, Caleb Walker, his brother, died in 1790, and was the first person buried in the graveyard at Canandaigua.

From Canandaigua, I went to township, No. 10, in the 4th Range (now East Bloomfield,) where I found Jonathan Adams, one of the proprietors of the town, who had come on from Schenectady with cattle and horses, accompanied by his large family, consisting of the following persons; himself and wife, his sons, John, William, Abner, and Joseph; his sons-in-law, Ephraim Rew, and Lorin Hull, and their wives, (his daughters) Wilcox, another son-in-law, and a younger daughter, afterwards the wife of John Keyes; Elijah Rose a brother-in-law, wife and son, and the following named persons: Moses Gunn, Lot Rew, John Barns, Roger Sprague, Asa Heacock, Benjamin Goss, John Keyes, Nathaniel Norton, and Eber Norton. Here Mr. Adams had erected two small log houses, and one large one, in which for the time being, all these people found a shelter. Mr. Adams in compliance with an arrangement with the proprietors, furnished me with the necessary hands and provisions to fit out my surveying party, and I' then commenced to survey the town.

After finishing the survey of this township, Fredrick Saxton and myself, surveyed and allotted township 9, in 6th Range, (now Livonia, Livingston Co.,) which proved to be one of the best townships of land in the Genesee country. To show however, the inconsiderable value put upon it at that time, I mention the fact that Gen. Fellows offered to sell the whole township to Mr. Saxton and myself at twenty cents per acre.

After completing the survey of this township, Mr. Saxton assisted me in the survey of township No. 12, 1st Range, (Arcadia, Wayne Co.) Col. Hugh Maxwell, a surveyor, had contracted with Phelps and Gorham, the previous year, to run out into townships the whole of that part of their purchase to which the Indian title had been extinguished. Not having completed the work, he entered into an agreement with Mr. Saxton and myself, to survey a portion, consisting of about forty townships, which now constitute part of Steuben county. We entered immediately on this survey, and completed it in the course of the season. While engaged in it we made our head quarters at Painted Post on the Conhocton river, at the house of old Mr. Harris and his son William. These two men, Mr. Goodhue who lived near by, and a Mr. Meade, two miles up the river, at the mouth of a stream since known as "Meade's creek," were the only persons then on the territory we were surveying. Before we left, however, Solomon Bennet, Mr. Stevens, Capt. Jameson, and Mr. Crosby, arrived from Pennsylvania in search of a township for purchase and for future settlement, and fixed on township No. 3 in the 5th, and No. 4 in the 6th, Ranges, both lying on the Canisteo river, and soon after settled by these men. They are now known in whole or in part as the town of Canisteo.

In the fall I returned to my father's, in Salisbury, by the water route, in company with several persons from New England, who, having spent the summer at the west, were returning home to spend the winter.

In addition to the persons mentioned by me as found at Canandaigua, in the spring of this year, (1789) the following came during the summer, viz: Abner Barlow, Israel Chapin, Jr., Othniel Taylor, Nathaniel Gorham, Dr. Moses Atwater, Judah Colt, John Call, Amos Hall, Gen. Wells, John Clark, Daniel Brainard, John Fanning, Stephen Bates, Aaron Heacock, James Fisk, Jairus Rose, Hugh Jameson, Mr. Truman, Orange Brace, Martin Dudley, and Luther Cole. The following came to Victor: Hezekiah Boughton, Jr., Enos Boughton, Jared Boughton, Seymour Boughton, 2d, Lyman Boughton, Zebulon Norton, Joel Scudder, Mr. Smith, and Mr. Brace. Into Bristol: Gamaliel Wilder, Jonathan Wilder, Wm. Gooding, Elnathan Gooding. Into Geneva: Roger Noble, Phineas Stevens, Elias Jackson, Mr. Jennings, Wm. Patterson, Peter Bortle. To Palmyra: Gen. John Swift. To Pittsford: Israel Stone, Simon Stone, Paul Richardson, Mr. Allen, and Mr. Acker. To Irondequoit Landing: Mr. Lusk. To Brighton: Orange Stone and Chauncey Hyde, Capt. John Gilbert from Lenox, Mass. (father of John Gilbert, now of Ypsilanti, Mich.) who surveyed the town into lots. To Perrinton; Glover Perrin and Caleb Walker. To Livonia: Solomon Woodruff. To Avon: Timothy Hosmer, Gilbert Berry, Capt. Thompson, and Mr. Rice (whose wife gave birth to the first child born on the Phelps and Gorham Purchase, whose name was "OLIVER PHELPS RICE.") To Vienna: Decker Robinson. To Middleton: (at the head of Canandaigua lake,) Col. Clarke, Capt Watkins, Lieut. Cleveland, and Ensign Parrish. To Lima: Abner Miles and Doctor Minor.

Among the incidents of this year (1789) in this western region, then just beginning to be inhabited, was the following: A Mr. Jenkins, who went out for the proprietors, John Swift and others, to survey township 12, 2d range, (Palmyra) commenced his labors early in the season, and erected for the accommodation of his party a small hut of poles. One night, when the party were asleep, two Indians attacked them, first firing their rifles through the open cracks of the hut, and then rushing in. One of Jenkins' men was killed by the first fire, but Jenkins and his party after a brief struggle, succeeded in driving the savages off without further loss. He went the next morning to Geneva, where he learned that the party to which they probably belonged had gone south. He accordingly, in company with others, followed in pursuit, as far as Newtown, (Elmira) on the Chemung river, near which place the murderers were captured. Newtown was then the principal, indeed almost only settlement, in that region of country. The Indians were examined before an informal assembly, and the proof being in their opinion, sufficient to establish their guilt, the question arose as to how they should be disposed of. The jail of the county, (then Montgomery) was at Johnstown, and it was not deemed practicable to transport them so great a distance, through an Indian wilderness. It was therefore determined summarily to execute them, and this determination was carried immediately into effect, — an account of which I received from Jasper Parrish and Horatio Jones (afterwards Indian interpreters) who were eye witnesses of the execution.* Another incident occured at Canandaigua this year, worthy, perhaps, of notice.

The year was one of unusual scarcity among the Indians. Indeed, they were almost reduced to starvation. Oliver Phelps having made a treaty with them the year previous, they were to

---

* The narrator will be gratified to learn that his recollections of an event that transpired almost sixty years since, are mainly corroborated by printed, cotemporary record, as will be seen by an extract of a letter published in the Maryland Journal of April 14th, 1789, dated at Wyoming, March 27th, 1789:—" Major John Jenkins, Solomon Earl, —— Baker, and William Ransom, about the 10th instant, were surveying lands near the Lakes. One morning about 2 o'clock, four Tuscarora Indians, and a squaw, made an attack upon them in their cabin. The Indians put the muzzles of their guns into the cabin and each fired. Baker was killed and Earl badly wounded. This awoke Jenkins and Ransom; the Indians rushed on with the knife and tomahawk, but Jenkins by an instantaneous effort of bravery, caught hold of an axe and knocked down two Indians; afterwards Ransom assisted and beat the Indians off, and took each of their guns, tomahawks, &c. Jenkins and his surviving companion lodged that night in said cabin with the dead and wounded; next day they returned with Earl to Geneva. A scout was immediately sent after the said Indians. When the party arrived at the cabin they found the Indians had been back and taken off all their provisions; the object of this bloody attack. Four Indians are sent in quest of the villians, and have pledged their honor they will not return without their bodies, or their scalps. God preserve their honor!" So it seems that Baltimore was the place to look for news of local events in Western New York, at one period. Mr. Boughton, who is introduced in a subsequent page, says, that when he arrived at the foot of Seneca lake in February 1790, he "saw there the man that was shot at Palmyra; the ball had gone through his jaw."

meet him this year to receive their stipulated annuities. As is usual on such occasions, presents were provided for distribution among them, as well as articles of subsistence, of which it was known they stood in great need. The number of Indians assembled, however, greatly exceeded his expectations, (increased, doubtless, by their starving condition,) amounting, propably, to two thousand. The stock of provisions proving inadequate to their wants, they were driven to the necessity of devouring every thing that could satisfy their hunger, consuming with voracity even the entrails of the animals that had been slaughtered. They parted with almost every thing they had to purchase food, and did not disperse until they had nearly produced a famine among the white inhabitants. Another occurrence of this season was the opening of a road, from Geneva to Canandaigua, which was the first piece of road opened west of Westmoreland (now Oneida,) county. The winter of 1789-90, I spent at my father's in copying my field notes, and finishing up my surveys.

During the winter of 1789-90, I entered into an agreement with Gen. John Fellows, one of the proprietors of East Bloomfield, to join him in the erection of a saw-mill, on Mud creek, in that town, about five miles west of Canandaigua. In pursuance of this plan, we collected at Schenectady a stock of provisions, tools, &c., necessary for the purpose. In May, I embarked again at Schenectady, for the west, taking with me these articles, and proceeded by nearly the same route as in the previous year, except that I passed up the Canandaigua outlet to Manchester, now called, and thence transported my loading by teams to East Bloomfield. One of my companions in this expedition was Dr. Daniel Chapin, who resided many years in Bloomfield, and afterwards removed to Buffalo, where he died,— also Oliver Chapin and Aaron Taylor and family.

I have heretofore remarked that the mode adopted to render Wood creek navigable, was to collect the water by means of a mill dam, thus creating a sudden flood to carry boats down. Sometimes boats did not succeed in getting through to deep water in one flood, and were consequently obliged to await a second one. As we were coming down the creek during the voyage on our first flood, we overtook a boat which had been grounded after the previous one, the navigators of which were in the water, ready to push her off as soon as the coming tide should reach them. Among these persons, was James Wadsworth, of Geneseo, with whom I then first became acquainted. He was then on his way west, to occupy his property at Geneseo, which has since become so beautiful and valuable an estate. Gen. Fellows set out for Bloomfield on horseback, having sent on a team, (two yoke of oxen and a wagon,) with a moderate load, and four or five cows. These were driven on by some person coming on to assist in building the mill, and among them, Mr. Dibble, the millwright. Gen. F. parted with the wagon near Utica.

During the previous winter, the legislature of New York had appropriated a township of land (called "the Road township") situated in what is now called Madison county, the proceeds of which were to be applied to opening a road west from Westmoreland. The job had been taken by contract, and Gen. Fellows found the party cutting out the road not far from the present settlement at Onondaga. After Gen, F. reached Bloomfield, fearing that the team might not be able to get through with the materials for the mills, dispatched me back to meet the party, and help them along. At Cayuga lake I met Mr. Dibble, the millwright, from whom I learned that the team had left its load at Onondaga, and that the men with the cattle and wagons were coming on with a large number of settlers, as fast as the persons employed in opening the road, with their assistance, progressed with the work. I, therefore, concluded to return to Manchester and take the boat I had left there and go to Onondaga for the loading. Taking Mr. Dibble and three other men with me, I went to Onondaga and returned with the loading. The men and the teams of the party reached Bloomfield at about the same time we did. I spent the summer chiefly in attending to the erection of the saw-mill, occasionally doing some surveying, particularly town 13, 4th range, (now Penfield, Monroe Co.) which had been purchased of Phelps and Gorham by Jonathan Fasset. The mill was finished in the fall, and was, I believe, the third one erected on Phelps and Gorham's Purchase.

In Dec. of this year, (1790) I went, in company with Orange Brace and two other persons, on foot, to Connecticut. The journey was a tedious and painful one, being made through a deep snow the whole distance, a part of which was accomplished on snow shoes. The following are some of the persons who came into the country during this year, viz: To Canandaigua: Nathaniel Sanburn, Lemuel Castle, Seth Holcomb. To Victor: Hezekiah Boughton, Senr., Seymour Boughton, Senr. To Bristol: Deacon Codding, Francis Codding and Ephraim Wilder. To Pittstown, (now Richmond:) Peter, Gideon, William and Samuel Pitts. To Geneseo: James Wadsworth and William Wadsworth. To West Bloomfield. Benjamin Gardner, (from Canandaigua,) Robert Taft, Mr. Miller, Clark Peck, Esq. Curtis, Jasper P. Sears, Nathan Marvin, Lorin Wait, Amos Hall. To Avon: Gad Wadsworth, Mr. Ganson. To Farmington: oldMr. Comstock, and his sons Jared, Darius, John, Otis, and Isaac Hathaway. During the session of the Legislature in 1789–90, a law was passed erecting the county of Ontario, to consist of all that portion of the state lying west of the Eastern line of Phelps and Gorham's Purchase. This was the first county set off from Montgomery. The following were the officers appointed: Oliver Phelps, first Judge; Timothy Hosmer, (afterwards himself first Judge) Arnold Potter, and Israel Chapin, side Judges; Judah Colt, Sheriff; Nathaniel Gorham, Clerk.

I spent a part of the winter of 1790–91 at my Father's, and in February I left again for the west. I made the journey in company with John Fellows, son of Gen. Fellows, and two others, in a two horse sleigh. At that time, the only white settlements between Westmoreland and the Seneca Lake, were at Onondaga Hollow, where Gen. Danforth and Comfort Tyler had settled, and at what is now Eldridge, Cayuga Co., where Mr. Buck had located himself. On this journey we encamped for the night in a fine hemlock grove, on the east side of Owasco outlet, where Auburn now stands.

During the early part of this season (1791) in carrying on the saw mill, and making improvements on land, with occasional surveying, I became acquainted, for the first time, with OLIVER PHELPS. This was an important event in my life at the west, for it led not only to my permanent and steady employment for more than ten years, (first for Phelps and Gorham, but always under the direction of Mr. P. himself,) during which I became familiar with most of the transactions relating to land sales, surveys, &c., but was followed by a personal intimacy with him, from which I derived many important advantages. His friendship for, and confidence in me, never faltered, and I have consequently always retained the highest personal respect for his name and memory.

* * * * * * *

On the 12th of May, 1788, Mr. Phelps, accompanied by Col. Hugh Maxwell, a Revolutionary officer, of Heath, Mass., as surveyor, then fifty-seven years old — and William Walker, of Lenox, as assistant, proceeded to Kanadasaga, (now Geneva) for the purpose of making arrangements for holding a treaty with the Indians for the purchase of the possessory right to the whole or a part of the territory. On arriving at Kanadasaga, he found the Indians assembled in council with John Livingston, of Columbia Co., and Caleb Benton, of Greene Co., who represented a company known at that time as "the Lessee Company," for the lease of the tract lying immediately east of the Massachusetts claim. Mr. Phelps at once commenced negotiations, but as the Indians were not very numerously represented, further proceedings were adjourned to a treaty agreed to be held at Buffalo about the last of June. This treaty was held at Buffalo in pursuance of this adjournment. Mr. Phelps was anxious to purchase all their lands within the Massachusetts pre-emption claim. But the Indians were unwilling to sell any part of the country west of the Genesee river, alledging that "the Great Spirit" had fixed that stream as the boundary between the white and the red man.

Mr. Phelps, finding them quite immoveable on this point, then represented to them that he was very desirous of getting some land west of the river, at the great Falls, for the purpose of building thereon mills, for the use and convenience of the white settlers coming into the country, and that these mills, when built, would be very convenient for the Indians themselves. The Indians then asked him how much land he wanted for his Mill Seat. He replied that he thought a piece about twelve miles wide, extending from Canawagas village, on the west side of the river to its mouth (about twenty-eight miles) would answer his purpose. To this the Indians replied that it seemed to be a good deal of land for a Mill Seat, but as they supposed the Yankees knew best what was required, they would let him have it. After the treaty was concluded, the Indians told Mr. Phelps, that it being customary for them to give to the man with whom they dealt, a name, they would give him one. They also said they should expect from him "a treat" and a walking staff (meaning some spirits,) to help them home. The name they gave Mr. Phelps, on this occasion, was that by which he was ever afterwards known among them, viz: Scaw-gun-se-ga, which translated, is "the Great Fall." This purchase, which comprised what is now the city of Rochester, was thereafter called "the Mill Seat Tract."*

The result of this treaty was the purchase of this Mill Seat Tract, and the whole of the eastern portion of the Massachusetts claim, bounded as follows: North by lake Ontario: East by the east line of the Massachusetts claim (which passes through a part of the Seneca lake at Geneva); south by the Pennsylvania north line; and west by the Genesee river, as far as the mouth of the Canascraga creek, and by a line running due south to the Pennsylvania line. The lands thus purchased at this treaty, I shall hereafter have occasion to refer to as "Phelps and Gorham's Indian Purchase."

At the same time the Lessee Company concluded their arrangements with the Indians, renting from them, for 999 years the tract lying east of Phelps and Gorham's purchase. The object of this company in taking their conveyance from the Indians in the form of a lease, was to evade the pre-emptive right. It was, however, so palpable a fraud on that right, that the State of New York at once refused to recognize it, and it was declared void by the Legislature at its next session. The lands were subsequently appropriated by the State of New York to the payment of military bounties, and hence have since been known as the Military Tract. The agents of the Lessee Company, Messrs. Livingston and Benton, at this treaty, rendered important services in aiding Mr. Phelps in his negociations, and received from him two townships of lands in what is now Yates county, which were afterwards known as "the Lessee Townships," one of which is now named "Benton," after the grantee above mentioned.

Messrs. Phelps and Gorham and the Lessees, as soon as their treaties were concluded, determined at once to send surveyors to run out the line which was to divide their property on the east line

---

*" Its contents are about 200,000 acres."

of the Massachusetts claim. Geneva was then a small settlement beautifully situated on the bank of Seneca lake, rendered quite attractive from its lying adjoining an old Indian settlement, in which was an orchard. This orchard had been destroyed by Gen. Sullivan, in his celebrated campaign, in 1779, but sprouts had grown up from it into bearing trees. As it was known the line must pass near this place, some anxiety was felt as to which party it might belong. Col. Maxwell, on the part of Phelps and Gorham, and Mr. Jenkins on the part of the Lessees, as surveyors, proceeded to the point of beginning at the 82d mile stone, on the north line of Pennsylvania, and ran through to lake Ontario a line known as the Preemption line, which passed about a mile and a quarter west of Geneva, and which was the basis of the surveys, made by Phelps and Gorham. This line afterwards was proved to have been incorrectly run, and it was charged that the incorrectness was in part a fraud of Jenkins, whose object was to secure to his employers, the Lessee Company, the location of Geneva. The suspicion of fraud led to a re-survey of this line, under the direction of Robert Morris.* The line being run, Col. Maxwell commenced immediately the survey of the tract west of it, and in the course of the season run out about thirty townships and began the survey and allotment of Canandaigua.

The supposition was quite common, that on ascertaining the western boundary of the Massachusetts claim (being the east line of the New York and Massachusetts cession to the United States) it would be found to include the harbor and town of Presque Isle (now Erie, Pa.) The state of Pennsylvania was anxious to secure to itself that point, and in the winter of 1788-89 had made propositions to Phelps and Gorham for the purchase of it. At the request of Phelps and Gorham, the U. S. Government sent out the Surveyor General, Andrew Ellicott, in 1789, for the purpose of running and establishing this line. Frederick Saxton went with him on behalf of Phelps and Gorham. As the line was to commence at the west end of Lake Ontario, there was some hesitation in the outset in determining whether it should commence at the western extremity of Burlington Bay, or at the Peninsula separating the Bay from the lake. But it was at length fixed at the Peninsula, and on the completion of the survey, by first running some distance south, and then offsetting around the east end of lake Erie, it was found to pass some twenty miles east of Presque Isle. This line now forms the western boundary of the State of New York, between lake Erie and the old north line of Pennsylvania, and is the Eastern line of a tract known as the

---

* This re-survey was made by Andrew Ellicott, United States surveyor General, assisted by Judge Porter. It corrected the previous survey, by establishing the line about as far east of Geneva as that had west of it. The care taken in this last survey was well calculated to ensure correctness, and in fact its correctness was never questioned.

"Presque Isle triangle," which was afterwards purchased by Pennsylvania of the United States, and is now a part of that State.

After the conclusion of the Indian treaty at Buffalo, in 1788, and as soon as the progress of surveys would permit, Phelps and Gorham commenced making sales, and up to the middle of the year 1789, had sold some thirty or forty townships, receiving small payments, chiefly in Massachusetts final settlement notes, with an understanding that future payments, might be made in the same securities at par. It was in consequence of this system of sales, that they were so large.

In consequence of the adoption of the Constitution of the United States, not long after the purchase by Phelps and Gorham, it was anticipated that the General Government would assume the indebtedness of the several states growing out of the Revolution. The effect of this was to make the holders of the State securities less willing to sell at low rates, so that Messrs. Phelps and Gorham, instead of being able to continue to sell rapidly, for this species of payment, sold comparatively little after about the middle of 1789; and during the year 1790, Congress did, in fact, assume the payment of certain State debts, among which were included these Massachusetts final settlement notes. The consequence of this assumption was to raise them at once to par, and even above.

Having failed to make the payment of the installment due to Massachusetts in 1789—90, the state commenced a suit against Phelps and Gorham and their sureties. Phelps and Gorham were, however, enabled to effect a compromise with the State, by which it was agreed that P. and G. should re-convey to Massachusetts all that portion of their purchase to which they had not extinguished the Indian title, viz: All west of the Genesee river up to the mouth of the Canascraga, and thence due south to the Pennsylvania line, except the mill seat tract above mentioned, and retain to themselves the remainder, supposed to be about one-third of the whole, paying therefor a sum proportioned to the amount retained. It being understood that the final settlement notes were worth only four shillings on the pound when the purchase was made, the amount to be paid was to be estimated on that basis. This agreement was carried into effect in 1790, or thereabouts.

Meantime, the rise of these public state securities, which had prevented Phelps and Gorham from fulfilling their contract with Massachusetts, in like manner, prevented the early purchasers under them from making their payments. Consequently, a considerable part of these lands sold, reverted to Phelps and Gorham in after years, or were bought by Oliver Phelps, and sold by him to other persons.

[The portion of Judge Porter's manuscript omitted here—several pages—has reference principally to surveys in which he participated, connected with the boundaries of Phelps and Gorham's purchase, its sub-divisions,— and to matters necessarily connected with our chain of land titles.]

In the spring of 1794, I again returned to Canandaigua, and was employed during the whole season in making surveys of various tracts for Mr. Phelps. In the fall I again returned with him to Suffield, where I spent part of the winter, and the remainder with him in New York, where he effected his large land sale to De Witt Clinton, and other large sales to other persons.

During the summer of 1794, the court house of Ontario county was erected at Canandaigua. Thaddeus Chapin came this year to Canandaigua.

* * * * * * *

In the spring of 1795, I again left Suffield for Canandaigua. At Salisbury I was joined by my brother, Peter B. Porter, who had decided to settle at Canandaigua, in the practice of the law. During this season I acted as agent for Mr. Phelps in the management and sale of his lands, and in surveying for him. In the latter part of August, this year, I went to Presque Isle (now Erie Pa.) in company with Judah Colt. At this time all that part of the state of New York, lying west of "Phelps and Gorham's Indian Purchase," was still occupied by the Indians, their title to it not being yet extinguished. There was of course no road leading from Buffalo eastward, except an Indian trail, and no settlement whatever on that trail. We traveled on horseback from Canawagus (now Avon,) to Buffalo, and were two days in performing the journey. At Buffalo there lived a man of the name of Johnstone, the British Indian interpreter,—also a Dutchman and his family, by the name of Middaugh, and an Indian trader by the name of Winne. From Buffalo we proceeded to Chippewa, U. C. where we found Capt. Wm. Lee, with a small row-boat, about to start for Presque Isle, and waiting only for assistance to row the boat. Mr. Colt, Mr. Joshua Fairbanks, now of Lewiston, and myself, joined him. Two days of hard rowing brought us to that place where we found surveyors engaged in laying out the village, now called Erie. Also a military company under the command of Gen. Irwin, ordered there by the Governor of the state, to protect the surveyors against the Indians. Col. Seth Reed, (father of Rufus S. Reed, and grandfather of Charles M. Reed,) was there with his family, living in a marquee, having just arrived.* A Mr. Reese, was also there, acting as agent for the "Population Company," for selling and managing their lands, of whom Mr. Colt and I purchased two thousand acres. We returned in the same boat to Chippewa, and from thence on horseback by way of Queenston, on the Indian trail through Tonawanda Indian village to Canandaigua.

During this expedition from Buffalo to Erie, a very remarkable

---

* It would appear by the date of Judge Porter's visit to Erie, that Deacon Chamberlin was in error as to the year he was there. Mr. Fairbanks, who married the daughter of Col. Reed, agrees with Judge Porter as to the period of his settlement at Erie.

circumstance presented itself, the like of which I had never before seen, nor have I since witnessed. Before starting from Buffalo, we had been detained there for two days by a heavy fall of rain, accompanied by a strong northeast gale. When off Cattaragus creek, on our upward passage, about one to two miles from land, we discovered, some distance ahead, a white strip on the surface of the lake, extending out from the shore as far as we could see. On approaching this white strip, we found it to be some five or six rods wide, and its whole surface covered with fish of all the varieties common to the lake, lying on their sides as if dead. On touching them, however, they would dart below the surface, but immediately rise again to their former position. We commenced taking them by hand, making our selection of the best; and finding them perfectly sound, we took in a good number (indeed, if we had desired, we might have loaded our boat with them.) On reaching Erie, we had some of them cooked and found them perfectly good. The position of these fish on their sides in the water placed their mouths partly above and partly below the surface, so that they seemed to be inhaling both water and air, for at each effort in inhaling, bubbles would rise and float on the water. It was these bubbles that caused the white appearance on the lake's surface. I have supposed that these fish had, from some cause, growing out of the extraordinary agitation of the lake by the gale from the eastward, and the sudden reflux of water from west to east, after it subsided, been thrown together in this way, and from some unknown natural cause, had lost the power of regulating their specific gravity, which it is said they do, by means of an air bladder, furnished them by nature. I leave to others, however, to explain this phenomenon.

During this season, (1795) Nathaniel W. Howell, of Canandaigua, and Gen. Vincent Mathews, late of Rochester, first came to Canandaigua to attend court, their residence being, at that time, at Newtown, now Elmira.

* * * * * * *

In the fall of 1796, I returned to Suffield, and spent most of the winter in making up my surveys and maps of the Reserve, and in closing up my business with the Connecticut Land Co., having concluded not to remain longer in their service, although they were desirous I should. But as I had now a family, and had spent most of my time for seven years in the fatigues and hardships of a woods life, I determined to settle at Canandaigua and accept the agency offered me by Mr. Phelps, of his land business. In accordance with this determination, in the latter part of February, 1797, I left Suffield with my family, in a sleigh for Canandaigua, where I arrived early in March. I immediately entered into the service of Mr. Phelps, in selling and surveying his lands, and in collecting his debts. One of the first acts of my agency was to sell three or four farms on the road leading north towards Farmington. In running them out as it was necessary I should, I caught a severe cold in the swamps through which I was obliged to make my way by wading. From this circumstance I date the commencement of my deafness, which has since so much afflicted me.

During the winter past, (of 1797,) Gideon King and Zadock Granger, two of the proprietors of the tract of 20,000 acres in the north part of township one, short range, (which included the land on which Rochester now stands,) and two or three other families from Suffield, had gone to the tract and commenced thereon a settlement. Mr. Phelps, my brother Peter B., and myself, were also proprietors. This 20,000 acre tract was sold originally by Phelps and Gorham, in 1790, to a company of gentlemen of Springfield and Northampton, Massachusetts, among whom was Ebenezer Hunt, Quartus Pomeroy and Justin Ely. The tract was bounded north and west by the north and west lines of the township, east by the Genesee river, and south by a line parallel with the north line, so far distant therefrom as to contain 20,000 acres, excepting and reserving therefrom 100 acres, which had been previously sold to Ebenezer Allan, for the purpose of erecting a mill thereon, which one hundred acres was to be located in as near a square form as the windings of the river would permit, commencing at the centre of the mill, and extending an equal distance up and down the river, then back so far as to contain the 100 acres in the above form. The lines of this 20,000 acres had been run by Frederick Saxton in the summer of 1790. It may not be uninteresting to state here that this 100 acres embraces the most densely and valuably built part of the city of Rochester;—and that all the titles within it are derived from Allan, who never himself had any other known paper title than that which is derived by implication from the exception above mentioned in Phelps and Gorham's deed to the Springfield and Northampton Company.

* * * * * * *

I omitted to mention in the proper place, that in returning to Canandaigua, after completing the survey for Robert Morris, in company with Joseph Ellicott, we traveled down the lake to Buffalo, chiefly on the beach, there being no road, and as yet, none other than an Indian trail from Buffalo to Canawagus (now Avon.) There was then (1797) but one dwelling house between the two places, which was owned by a Mr. Wilbur. It was situated at the point where Mr. John Ganson afterwards built a large house, and kept a tavern many years, and is about one mile and a half east of Le Roy.

In 1800, I built a dwelling house in Canandaigua, opposite the Academy, in which I resided until the year 1806, when, on removing with my family to this place, I sold it to John Greig, Esq., by whom it was occupied many years. Here, except during the war of 1812, I have continuously resided. In 1813, an invasion by the

British troops took place, which resulted in laying all the settlements on the frontier, Buffalo included, in ashes. My dwelling, mills, &c., at this place, shared in the common desolation. The alledged justification of this system of warfare, was the burning of Newark, (now Niagara) by troops of the United States, under the command of Gen. George McClure, on his evacuating Fort George, a few weeks previous.

During the last years of my residence in Canandaigua, I was interested with Mr. Phelps and Nathaniel and Birdseye Norton, in a contract with the United States for the supply of provisions to the garrisons of Niagara, Detroit, Mackinaw, Chicago, and Fort Wayne. This connection with Mr. Phelps, continued until his death, which occurred in the winter of 1809. In 1810, I took this contract in my own name, and supplied the above posts until 1813, except during the period of their occupation by the enemy, after the surrender of Detroit, by Gen. Hull. These transactions led to my early connection with the commerce of the lakes, some account of which is contained in a communication I furnished to the editors of the Buffalo Commercial Advertiser, and which was published in that paper under date of 27th March, 1846.

So much interest appears to have been recently manifested for collecting and preserving the early incidents of western settlement, and so many contributions are about to be offered in aid of this object, by others, that I think it advisable to leave to them (who will no doubt perform the duty far more acceptably than I can,) the task of presenting matters of subsequent occurrence, to the close of the last century. My early cotemporaries in western life, (with so far as I can learn, two or three solitary exceptions,) are in their graves. On account of my advanced age, and the busy though humble part I have borne as one of the very earliest of the Pioneers of Western New York, I can well imagine that a record of my experience and adventures might be supposed to possess some interest with those who are seeking such materials for preservation from an actor himself. What I have written, I am sensible, will fall very far short of expectation, but I must, in justice to myself, say, that it is but the hitherto unwritten reminiscences of a very aged man, prepared without memoranda, and without the opportunity, by reference to, and consultation with, a solitary cotemporary, of quickening my recollection of many events, doubtless of some interest, but which have long since faded from my memory. Truth is, of course, my aim; and it may be supposed I incur some hazard in drawing on my memory alone at this late period in life. To this I will only say, that having been personally an actor and participator in most by far, of the events spoken of, I feel a strong degree of confidence in claiming, for this simple narrative the concession of at least ordinary authenticity.

I cannot close what I have to say without expressing the gratitude I have ever felt, for the kind and friendly treatment, patronage, and confidence, extended to me on my first arrival in the Genesee country in 1789, by many of the most distinguished of the early Pioneers. Among these I refer with pleasure to the names of Gen. ISRAEL CHAPIN, Judge OLIVER PHELPS, Judge NATHANIEL GORHAM, Major ADAM HOOPS, THOMAS MORRIS, Esq. JAMES WADSWORTH, Esq. and CHARLES WILLIAMSON, Esq.

TIMOTHY HOSMER.

The early advent and prominent position held by this gentleman as a pioneer in Western New York, as well as his numerous descendants, the elder generation of whom may well be classed among the junior pioneers, entitles him to some biogaphical notice.

The subject of this memoir was born in Hartford, Conn., in Sept. 1745. He passed through a course of medical studies with Dr. Dickinson in Middletown, and settled in Farmington, in the same State, and married his wife, soon after his admission to practice.

About this period the troubles precursory to the American Revolution commenced, and he was one of the earliest to resist the encroachments of British power. He, together with John Treadwell (afterwards Governor of Connecticut,) and one or two others, openly proclaimed resistance to oppression in that then loyal town, so that they were for some time in great personal peril, from the violence of their loyal neighbors; but they persevered in retaining their patriotic position, until that town became distinguished for its zeal in the cause of the Revolution.

Dr. Hosmer early entered the public service as a surgeon of the sixth continental regiment. On the appearance of the small pox in the army, he was assigned to the charge of the Hospital in Danbury, and the subjects sent there for inocculation, he being one of the few phycians who at that time, were acquainted with the practice of inocculation, wherein he was singularly successful. He was with the army throughout the struggle on Long Island, and on its retreat.

At the close of the war he retired from the service happy in the recollection of the glorious result, but poor and pennyless, with a growing family dependant on his professional exertions for support.

His extensive acquaintance formed in the army, rendered him personally and professionally known, to most of the families in the state, the consequence of which was, that he at once entered into an extensive practice, which continued to the time of his removing to Western New York.

He first came into this country in 1789, or '90 and with four others, purchased Township No. 10, in the 7th Range, now the town of Avon, Livingston county, at one shilling and six pence per acre; and in the early part of 1792, he moved with his family to the banks of the Genesee river where he remained until his death, which happened Nov. 29th, 1815, being a few weeks over seventy years of age.

Upon the organization of the county of Ontario he was appointed one of the Judges of the Court of Common Pleas for said county, and upon Oliver Phelps declining to accept the office of first Judge of that court, he received that appointment, and continued to hold that office until he arrived at the age of sixty years, when he was incapacitated from longer holding the same by the constitution of the state. In taking leave of the bench and bar, he received the most gratifying testimonials of their respect and kindness.

The Indians early experienced the benefits of his services in the treatment of diseases; for which they were ever grateful: nor is their memory of him yet dimmed, for in numerous instances, they have manifested their gratitude to his surviving descendants. In the wilds of Wisconsin they have cordially greeted the children of At-a-gus, (healer of diseases,) by which name he was known.

He was distinguished for a lively and cheerful disposition, for his active benevolence, ready wit and indifference to the acquisition of wealth; his professional services were as readily extended to the poor and helpless, as to the wealthy; his philanthrophy made all who knew him his friends, and it is not known that he ever had a personal enemy. He died as he had lived, in peace with all men, and in reconciliation with his Creator.

NOTE. — A venerable pioneer, an early neighbor of Judge Hosmer, in a few words, furnished the author an eulogy to his memory, worthy of record: —"He was" said he, "an excellent hearted man; he practised medicine all through the valley; and was kind and obliging to all the new settlers." And not forgetting the wife of the Judge, he said she was a practical sister of charity and benevolence, in the new settlement.

JARED BOUGHTON.

This gentleman who was an inhabitant of Stockbridge, Mass. in the month of July, 1788, started on an exploring expedition to find himself a new home in the western country. He attended the Indian council at Geneva, in which Phelps and Gorham extinguished the Indian title to their Genesee Purchase. Being satisfied with the appearance of the country, but being unable to purchase until the country was surveyed, he returned to Stockbridge. His brother Enos Boughton who was the clerk and an assistant to William Walker, Phelps and Gorham's surveyor, purchased that fall, Township No 11, Range 4, of that tract, now the town of Victor, Ontario county, at the price of twenty cents per acre.

In the spring of 1789, Mr. Boughton, his brother Enos Boughton, a brother-in law, Horatio Jones, surveyor, and several hired hands, went on to the township purchased by Enos. They surveyed it into lots and prepared it for retailing. Jared Boughton commenced the first improvement made by white labor in this town. He cleared the land, raised two acres of buckwheat, sowed three acres of wheat, and built a log cabin, on what has since been called "Boughton Hill." At the approach of winter the whole party returned to Stockbridge, except Jacob Lobdell, who stayed to feed and take care of thirteen or fourteen head of cattle belonging to the Boughton family. These cattle were wintered on grass cut the season before on an old clearing on Boughton Hill, supposed to be the site of an ancient Indian village.*

In February, 1790, Mr. Boughton started from Stockbridge for his new home, with his wife, two children and his younger brother Seymour Boughton, as an assistant on the journey and to return with the horses and sleigh. After a long and fatiguing journey through an uninhabited wilderness, in which formidable obstacles were to be surmounted, they arrived at Boughton Hill on the 7th day of March. This was the first white family, and Mrs. Boughton and her infant daughter Malania, were the first white females who settled in the town of Victor, and Mrs. Boughton's second son Frederick was the first white child born in that town; his birth was on the first of June next after their arrival:—

---

* See "Gaosaehgaah," in account of De Nonville's expedition, p. 151.

"I will give you my own experience of settling a new country, which has probably been similar to that of hundreds of others. I came from Stockbridge with my family in the winter of 1790, in a sleigh, by the way of Schenectady. At Utica there was a small frame store, old John Post, an Indian trader—and a large log house kept as a tavern. There were one or two families, the Blackmores, at Westmoreland. Two or three families between Westmoreland and Utica—Esquire Blackman's was the last house until we arrived at Oneida Castle. It was but a wood's road. At Oneida Castle, there was a Dutchman, who had hired an Indian house to accommodate travellers. We arrived there about 12 o'clock at night and found no lodgings except the floor, all the beds being occupied by emigrating families. The road was very bad. We got our sleigh 'stuck,' which hendered us a day. We came to Onondaga Hollow—no settlement between Oneida Castle and there—arrived at Col. Danforth's, who kept a tavern. Comfort Tyler and Ephraim Webster, an Indian interpreter, with his squaw wife lived there; they were the only inhabitants.

"We travelled thirteen miles the day we left Col. Danforth's. Col. Reed's family and mine, fourteen in number, camped that night under a hemlock tree, built a camp of hemlock boughs, had a warm brisk fire—made chocolate—and although my wife had a young child, we had a comfortable time of it.

"Next night we arrived at the east shore of Cayuga lake—there were two families there—Judge Richardson's was one—we stayed with him all night, and crossed the lake on the ice in the morning. The next night we got to the foot of Seneca lake—found there a man by the name of Earl; he had a log cabin, but no floor in it; we stayed there all night; Earl had a scow to ferry us across the outlet of the lake. Next morning we went home with Mrs. Reed and family—found Col. Reed at home, waiting for the arrival of his family. His house stood on the bank of the lake, in Geneva; the place then contained ten or twelve families.

"From Geneva to Canandaigua there was no house; Flint creek, half way between those places was very high, and frozen at the edges; there was no bridge; had to fall trees to get my family, sleigh, and goods over; had to draw the horses over with ropes. About five miles from Canandaigua, we stayed all night at 'Wells' cabin;' Wells had been there and sowed wheat, but had left; the weather was very cold. Next morning we arrived at Canandaigua; the outlet of the lake was not bridged, and we had a hard time in getting over. From Canandaigua, we pursued our journey to Boughton Hill, where we arrived in good health, March 7, 1790.

"Although we were somewhat prepared for living, we still had to bring on our supplies—very little flour, however, as we had buckwheat, and wheat harvest was not far off. A small log mill had been set in motion for grinding corn, in the present town of Avon, by a Mr. Ganson. The stones were of the native rock, no doubt; to this mill I carried my buckwheat, on horse-back, twenty miles.

"As wheat harvest approached, some preparations for the event were necessary. A floor was to be laid, of split basswood or linden, with such joints as the axe and drawing-knife could produce, the surface smoothed by the axe and carpenter's adz; cradles and rakes to be made by very unskillful hands — nay, further, we found on examination, that there was chaff growing with our wheat, and, as none of the thousand and one pedlars of fanning-mills happened along at that juncture, we were compelled to devise some plan to separate the two articles.

"A large oak tree was felled, a piece split from it, dressed to the thickness of a half bushel rim, six or eight feet long and twelve or thirteen inches wide in the widest part. This forms the curve or back-side of the machine. The bottom or horizontal part was made of part of a pine sleigh-box, and two semi-circular handles completed the article. This we presumed to denominate a Corn Fan. The sieve or riddle was of black ash splinters."

The subject of the previous biographical remarks, and writer of the foregoing graphic sketches of a woodsman's life; together with his wife, the long tried partner of his sorrows and his joys, of his toils and their fruits, now reside in East Bloomfield, Ontario county, to which place they lately moved from Victor — himself 82 years of age, and his wife 79, having raised twelve children, and being now the ancestors of fifty five living descendants, are spending the remainder of their days in the midst of peace and competency.

A Scotch colony in the vicinity of Caledonia Springs, were among the earliest adventurers west of Genesee river. Their advent was in 1798. They came from Broadalbin, in the Highlands of Perthshire; arriving first at a settlement of their countrymen at Johnstown, Montgomery county; they were induced by the solicitations of Col. Williamson to settle at Caledonia. They were Presbyterians of the "Old Kirk," poor, with little to help them make their

---

NOTE.— Few family names are more blended in the history of Western New York, than that of BOUGHTON. The four brothers that helped to commence settlement on Phelps and Gorham's purchase, were: — Enos, Jared, Seymour and Hezekiah. The last named died as early as 1793; he was the father of the late Col. Claudius V. Boughton, of Victor, and of George H. Boughton, Esq. of Lockport. Col. Seymour Boughton was killed at the battle of Black Rock, in the war of 1812. Enos Boughton, died at Lockport, in 1826. At the great celebration, the year previous, he was introduced to Gov. Clinton as the man who built the first framed barn, the first stick chimney, and planted the first orchard west of Seneca lake. The author has been shown a letter, from Hezekiah Boughton, dated in the Genesee country, in the winter of 1793, to his wife in Stockbridge. He mentions that there had not been sleighing enough for a "single team to venture to Onondaga for salt;" and says he is about to start for Niagara, and has been "fortunate enough to secure company through the woods." The father of the four brothers, came to Victor in 1790, aged 65 years, and died in '98.

way in a new country, but stout hearts, industry and frugality. Col. Williamson sold them their land at three dollars per acre, on a credit of ten years, supplied them with a year's provisions, some teams, cows, &c. The five of their number who came out to make the selection of lands, were:—John M'Vean, Hugh M'Dermott, Donald M'Pherson, James M'Laren, and John Anderson.

In their new location the early Scotch adventurers had been preceded by one who had given the place a very bad reputation. His name was Peterson, a Dane, had been a sea captain—and tradition says, a pirate. He built a house, near the spring and entertained travellers, cooking himself and affording very good fare; afterwards marrying a girl that lived with Dugan, at Dugan's creek. He was strongly suspected of taking advantage of his secluded position, for the purpose of robbery and murder; and a surviving witness states that Dugan, once during a quarrel with him charged him with a specific offence, naming the victim. There was much uneasiness among the new settlers in reference to him, and their suspicions at one time led to an arrest and commitment to the jail at Canandaigua. He was finally obliged to run away, and afterwards died at sea. He was the first tavern keeper west of the Genesee river; certainly, a very untoward commencement of that branch of business.

Mrs. Chamberlin, the wife of Deacon Chamberlin, whose narrative has already been introduced, is one of the few survivors of the original colonists. Her first husband, was Malcolm M'Laren. The other survivors, are; John M'Naughton, Mrs. M'Vean, widow of Donald M'Vean, and Hugh M'Dermott.

The introduction here of portions of a narrative furnished by JOHN M'KAY, Esq. of Caledonia, will not only afford some glimpses of early settlement there, but of previous events upon the Genesee river.

"I came to what is now Groveland, on the Genesee river, in 1793, in my 16th year. Col. Williamson had laid out a village at Williamsburgh, (near Geneseo;) fifteen or twenty buildings were erected there. I remained at Groveland, for several years working at the carpenter's trade. Among the early events that now occur to me, was the firing of lands by the Indians for the purpose of taking game. It was in 1795. The Indians to the number of at least five hundred assembled. At 12 o'clock in the day, they set a train of fire which enclosed an area of about seven miles square, of the oak openings between the Canascraga and Conesus lake. Placing themselves inside of the area as the fire advanced and lessened its size, the game was driven in and shot. It was a brisk time during the afternoon; seventeen deer, several bear, and a large amount of other game, was the result of the fire hunt. Shanks, a celebrated Indian hunter, came in contact with a bear during the afternoon, that he had wounded. It was fight Indian, fight bear; the bear getting decidedly the advantage. He sprang upon Shanks, tore and lacerated his flesh — actually eating off the calves of his legs! The Indians found Shanks almost lifeless; the bear having left him for dead. He was cured of his wounds by Indian remedies, and lived for many years.

"I was at Morris' treaty; should think there were three thousand Indians assembled for several days. Those who were there to effect the treaty, bought up beef cattle and distributed the beef freely to the Indians.

"I came to Caledonia in 1803; there was then but two houses at the Springs. I purchased two hundred acres of land, including the Big Spring and the mill site at Slab City, (or Mumfordville;) Capt. Williamson had built a small grist mill, with one run of stones, to accommodate the Scotch settlers, about eighteen months before I came. I paid for the whole property, a little over two thousand dollars. My customers for some time, were from most of the then settled portions of the Holland Purchase; they came from as far as Buffalo, when they could not cross the river to Canada, on account of the ice; in fact, at times, from all the region west of me. The next mills built were those of the Holland Company, at Batavia, and Stoddard and Platt's, at Leroy. The first merchant at Caledonia was John Cameron; he came with a few goods in 1804 or '5.

"When I first came to the springs, trout were abundant in it; and it will surprise trout fishers of the present day — and would perhaps old Isaac Walton himself, if he were living — to learn that they were comparatively tame. When we wanted them, we used frequently to catch them with our hands, as they lay under the roots of the cedar trees that grew along the banks. There would be occasionally one weighing as high as three pounds. It is the habit of the speckled trout to breed in none but running water, consequently they would never breed in the spring, but resorted to its outlet. There was never any other fish in the spring; they have been gradually diminishing, not only in numbers, but in size.*

"My brother Robert came here in 1808, had been a clerk for some of the early merchants in Geneseo.

---

* This last resort, almost, of the speckled trout in all the northern portion of Western New York, has within a few years, been threatened with entire desertion, or extinction. There is now a law in operation, limited to three years duration, which makes fishing in the spring or its outlet, a penal offence. The trout, as if ready to co-operate in this attempt to protect them in this their seeming "Reservation," are now rapidly increasing in numbers and size. It is almost a wonder that some greedy Pre-emptionists — say a shoal of horned "Bull Pouts"— are not contesting their rights.

"I have often heard of buying wives, but have known, I think, of but one actual sale, and afterwards peaceable and quiet possession. Phelps, the early settler at Queenston, was a Ranger. In 1794, or '5, getting tired of a bachelor's life, he went down to Geneva, bought the wife of one Jennings, for six hundred dollars, cash down, taking her directly to Queenston. I have heard that the transfer was a fortunate one for all concerned; she making him a good wife.

"When I first came upon the Genesee river, Little Beardstown, now Cuylerville, contained about fifteen hundred Indians, at Big Tree, (Geneseo,) there was a small Indian settlement, forty houses, perhaps. There was a large Indian settlement at Squawky Hill, and a small one at Mt. Morris. The white woman, had a number of families upon her reservation at Gardeau.

"When I came west of the river, in 1803, Isaac Smith* lived at the Hosmer place, mid way between the river, and Caledonia; he had located there as early as 1801. There was a family of Bakers, squatters, upon the flatts. These were all except the Scotch, on and near the Buffalo road, between Caledonia and the river. The Indian settlement of Canawagus, (now the Newbold farm,) contained at least forty wigwams."

The two brothers, John and Robert M'Kay, are both surviving residents at Caledonia. The one, still owning and carrying on the mills that did the grinding at one time for "all west" of their location, to the western extremity of the State; the other, resides upon his farm, a short distance from the springs.

JEHIEL KELSEY, an aged Pioneer resides in a pleasant retreat, surrounded by all the comforts of life, a short distance north of Avon Springs. He cheerfully suspended his field labor, in which he was industriously engaged, and gave the author a short account of his early advent:—

"I came to Avon, in 1794, purchased the farm where I now reside, for one dollar fifty cents per acre, about ten years afterwards. I had to labor several years to get the means of purchase. I think I brought the first salt, in any considerable quantity, to the Genesee Valley. I took pork to Onondaga, exchanged pounds for

---

* It is worthy of note here, that Major Smith was not only a Pioneer landlord, but he was the father of six daughters, five of whom were Pioneer wives and mothers. There are few primitive log cabins in Western New York, from beneath the roof of which there have gone out more and better helpers, in the settlement of a new country. One of the daughters became the wife of Isaac Sutherland of Batavia; another, of James D. Faulkner of Dansville; two others, of Sylvester and Sidney Hosmer; and another, of John M'Kay, of Caledonia. The sixth, and youngest, is Mrs. Kimberly, formerly of Batavia. Major Smith died in 1814.

bushels; brought my salt via Oswego, and mouth of Genesee river; sold it here, for ten dollars fifty cents per barrel.

"The first grist mill built in this region, was by Capt. Ganson, before I came on. Judge Hosmer built a saw mill on the Conesus, as early as 1796, the first one in this region. The Wadsworths built one the same year, on the same stream. ——— Starr, who was the father of Horatio Jones' first wife, built the first framed house in the Genesee Valley. In '94, all the inhabitants on the river, from Williamsburgh to its mouth, were:—Judge Hosmer, Gad Wadsworth, Gilbert R. Berry, Wm. Markham, Ransom Smith, Peter Shaeffer, William Hencher, Ebenezer Merry.

"I helped to put up the first bridge, over 'Deep Hollow' below Rochester. We had previously, to go up three-fourths of a mile to get over this gulf. To raise the bridge, all able bodied men had to go from Avon, and some from above. In '98 or '9, Peter Shaeffer put up a framed barn; it took all the men in this region—twenty, all told.

"When the Holland Company surveyors first came on, they came here to buy much of their provisions, and grain and hay for their pack horses.

"Our first meetings were held in a log school house on the present public square, of Avon, Judge Hosmer usually reading the Episcopal service. Mr. Crane, an Episcopal clergyman, was here, as early, I think, as 1800, or '1. At an early period, the Rev. Mr. Mills, father of Gen. Mills, a Presbyterian minister, used to come down to Avon and hold meetings.

"I must tell you" said the old gentleman to the author, "how one of our young men got his wife, in an early day. Ebenezer Merry, Jr. the son of an early settler I have already named, pushed on still farther ahead, and settled on the Reserve, in Ohio, at Painsville. He built him a log hut, kept bachelor's hall, and commenced making an opening in the woods. He came back here on a visit, and told me it was pretty lonesome up there, in the woods. I told him he must take back a wife with him. 'Well' said he, disposed to make a prompt business matter of it, 'who shall I get?' I replied, there is the daughter of Aaron Adams, she would make just such a wife as you want. The young man went to see Miss Adams, they struck up a bargain, were married, and in a few days, were off through the woods to the Reserve; the young wife on horseback, and he on foot. He was one of the founders of the village of Milan, became prominent, among the early settlers of Ohio, was a member of the State Legislature. He died a few years since, leaving a large circle of descendants.

"It was very sickly through the whole Genesee valley in all the early years. If the settler escaped the bilious fever the first year, he was sure to have it the next."

Pittstown, originally, afterwards Honeoye, now Richmond, dates its first settlement at the early period of 1789. The township and a part of Bristol were purchased of Phelps and Gorham, by a company of individuals of Dighton Massachusetts; thence they were called the "Dighton Company." The land was divided among the proprietors by lottery; Capt. Peter Pitts drew his share, three thousand acres, and was so fortunate as to get the Honeoye flatts, embracing the site of an old Indian town that Sullivan had destroyed, large patches of cultivated ground, and some apple trees. Gideon Pitts, the eldest son of Capt. Pitts, came out to view lands about the period of Phelps and Gorham's purchase of the Indians, saw the lands about the Honeoye lake, and informed the Dighton company, of their desirable character.

"In 1789, Gideon and William Pitts went upon their father's land, carrying their goods in on an ox sled. Their first shelter was made of their sled box; afterwards they erected a cabin and for two years lived alone, putting in crops upon the old Indian grounds."

Capt. Pitts and the remainder of the family came in 1791, living, for nearly four years, alone, Capt. Tafft, of Bloomfield, being nearest neighbor, north, the Wadsworths, nearest west, James Goodwin, in Bristol, nearest east, and a few settlers at the head of Canandaigua lake, nearest south. There came into Pittstown, in 1794, Dr. Lemuel Chipman, Dr. Cyrus Chipman, Philip Reed, Roswell Turner, (himself, bringing in his family next year,) Edward Hazen. In '95, Jonas Belknap and Elijah Parker. In '96 and '7, settlers came in rapidly.

Aaron Hunt, Col. Green, James Garlinghouse, Jacob Holden, Nicholas Burby, settled at Hunt's Hollow, (head of Honeoye lake,) in '94. Solomon Woodruff was in Livonia as early as '93; Philip Short, at the foot of Hemlock lake, in '95.

Peter Allen went into Pittstown in '96; in '7, his brother, Nathaniel, who had worked as a journeyman blacksmith, in Canandaigua, followed him, and erected the first blacksmith's shop in the town, getting together a few tools, and supplying himself with iron, by bringing it from Canandaigua, on horseback.*

---

* This early blacksmith was well known upon the Niagara frontier, in the war of 1812, as army contractor and paymaster; afterwards, as sheriff of Ontario county, and representative in Congress, from that district. In the latter years of his life, he was a contractor upon a work of the general government, upon the Erie and Oswego canals,

The brief glimpse of early settlement thus given, is from information derived from Peter Pitts, the only surviving son of Capt. Peter Pitts, aged 67. The other survivor of the family, is the Mrs. Blackman, whose name has already been introduced in another connection. To her the author is indebted for the following reminiscences:—

"Zadoc Hunn, a Presbyterian minister, who lived at the old Sheldon place, near Canandaigna, held meetings at my father's house, as early as 1793. He first preached in Canandaigua, afterwards, a log meeting house was built for him, in Bristol. We used to have good meetings in those days; better ones than we do now.

"My father's house was, for several years, a home for the new settlers, land explorers, land agents, and surveyors. When Louis Philippe visited Western New York, he wished to see our neighborhood. He came with his companions, to our house, bringing a letter of introduction, from Thomas Morris, Esq., of Canandaigua. He was very sociable, and much pleased with the country. He remained over night. There were some Indians encamped on the lake shore; the party went down to see them, taking my brother Peter, then a small lad, along with them. He could talk Indian; Louis Philippe was highly pleased at being enabled to communicate with them through the agency of so young an interpreter. The first few years after our family came in, there were many Indians passing our house daily, and hunting parties were encamped nearly all the time, in the neighborhood.

"The old Indian castle that Sullivan burned down, stood about one hundred rods from the foot of the lake. After we came here, there were many remains of wigwams that Sullivan had destroyed, and the bones of his pack horses"

Capt. Peter Pitts, died in 1812, aged 74 years. His descendants are numerous, many of them occupying the lands he left them;— the flats of the Honeoye—conspicuously beautiful even now, when surrounded with rural landscapes, that would oftener tempt the traveler from the great thoroughfares, could he realize what a panorama of lakes, broad highly cultivated fields, flocks and herds,

---

and lastly, for the construction of the canal around the falls of the Ohio, at Louisville, where he died in 1833 or '4. The village of Allen's Hill grew up on a part of his fine farm, and took its name from him. His successor, at the old homestead, is the Hon. Robert L. Rose, who married his daughter; the present Representative in Congress, from Ontario; the original farm in his hands, having had accessions of hundreds of acres, and now forming one of the finest agricultural estates in Western New York. The elder brother, Peter Allen, whom Mrs. Blackman also names, was in Queenston battle, in command of a regiment, when he was made prisoner. He will be remembered by our older class of readers, as the one who gave the name to the "Peter Allen Legislature," of this state. He emigrated to Terra Haute, on the Wabash, in 1816, where he ended an enterprising and useful life, in 1836.

villages, more than comfortable farm houses, is spread out in the southern portions of Ontario and Livingston.

Mrs. Blackman, is enjoying with her descendants, a competence of worldly blessings, cheerful and happy; even disposed to be humorous. She gave as a reason why she did not go to the "Holland Purchase," when many of her neighbors were pushing on there, in 1804, '5 and '6, that her husband had then "got land enough cleared, so they could see out by looking straight up," and she did not wish to make a new beginning. The old gentleman, who had been almost as early a pioneer as herself, was at work on the highway, (June, 1848.)

BURGOYNE KEMP, is an aged pioneer, living in Newfane, Niagara county. A small portion of a narrative he has furnished the author, belongs to this period: —

"My father's family consisting then of eleven persons, came from New Jersey, to Niagara, C. W. in 1786, on pack horses, pursuing the then usual route, via Tioga Point, and the Indian trail. We saw no white inhabitant after leaving Tioga Point, until we arrived at Lewiston. At Newton, logs had been cut to build two houses. At Painted Post, we were passed by a young man who was deaf and dumb; from signs we learned that his destination was Queenston. He never arrived; and from the fact that an Indian was afterwards in possession of his clothes, there is no doubt but he was murdered; though it may have been by a white brigand, the Indian afterwards taking the clothes from the body.

"We had a small drove of cattle and sheep; arriving at the Genesee river, they swam across, the family crossing in a canoe. We were much troubled several times on our route by the Indians stealing our horses, when they wandered a short distance from our camp."

Mr. Kemp, as will be seen farther on, became an early settler upon the Holland Purchase.

OLIVER CULVER, Esq. of Brighton, Monroe county, still survives to tell the story of his early wilderness advent. His life has been one of more than ordinary enterprize and industry. Coming to Western New York, in 1796, but nineteen years old, he has been a hired laborer, a trapper, a navigator of the lakes, a contractor on one of our largest public works, a legislator, and the patroon of his neighborhood. An ample fortune is the reward of a long life of enterprize and toil. His intellect is yet vigorous, and the iron frame that in youth and middle age, enabled him to encounter the diseases and privations of a new country, has yielded far less than usual to the advance of years.

"I came from Vermont in 1796, on foot, my companion a young man by the name of Samuel Spafford. Reaching Farmington, Ontario county, I got a job of making sap troughs for Jonathan Smith. Hearing that something was going on at Irondequoit, I came on to see the place. Judge Tryon, of Lebanon, Conn. had purchased three hundred acres of land and laid out a village. There was one settler upon the village plat—a mulatto by the name of Samuel Dunbar. Remaining at Irondequoit a few weeks, five batteaux came up, with surveyors and provisions, bound for the New Connecticut tract. Myself and companion hired out to the company, and embarked for the west.

"At Erie, we found Col. Seth Reed keeping a tavern in a double log house. On our way up the lake, we left a settler by name of Gunn, at Conneaut, and his family; he was the Pioneer there. We landed at the mouth of the Cuyahoga, (Cleveland,) built a store-house and a dwelling for the surveyors, and hands. One of our hands, ——— Stiles, had his wife with him, built a house. He was the first settler at Cleveland. During the first winter, Mrs. Stiles was confined; her only female attendants being squaws; the child was the first born on the Reserve, and had a present of land from the proprietors.

"After remaining there for one season, myself and Spafford went back to Vermont, returning to Irondequoit the next spring. Having brought traps with us, we followed for a while the business of trapping and hunting. Game was very plenty about the Bay. Wild geese, with their broods of young goslins, were especially abundant. We trapped and bought furs of Indians."

[Another surveying party for Ohio arriving, Mr. Culver and his companion again accompanied them. His narrative embraces many interesting events connected with the primitive survey and settlement of the Reserve, witnessed during this and a third advent there. In 1798 he helped cut out the road from Pennsylvania line across the Reserve. On his way up he was taken sick at Buffalo —no physician to be had—Middaugh's wife took care of him.]

"In the year 1800 I purchased the farm where I now reside; went to work upon it, going through the woods by marked trees to Major Orange Stone's, for my meals and lodging; cleared seven acres and got it into wheat. Suspecting that I had an imperfect title to my land, I did no more upon it until 1805, when the title was made perfect. During this time, I worked at the Bay for Tryon and Adams, who by this time had a store there and an ashery. In 1804, there was a grist and saw mill, built by ——— Smith, on a stream that crosses the road from Rochester to Pittsford. The mill stones were taken from the old Allan mill at Rochester, that had run down. The trade of Tryon and Adams, extended to Pittsford, Penfield, Mendon; divided the trade with Canandaigua, of the whole region. The ashery was of great use to the new settlers; enabling them to sell their ashes for a shilling a bushel when they stood in need of the proceeds. I remember that in 1803, Tryon and Adams shipped one hundred and three barrels of pearl ashes to Montreal. In 1804, when I left the Bay, four or five families had come in. The father of Oliver Grace, Esq., of Lewiston, was a general agent, or clerk, for Tryon and Adams; was well educated, social and pleasant; an agreeable accession to our back woods' settlement.*

"In the early years, the whole region about the Bay, was a favorite hunting ground; deer and bear were very plenty. There were a few beaver in this region when I first came in. I trapped a couple of young ones at Braddock's Bay, in 1797; found one of their houses, or lodges. It was built in a conical form, of brush and rushes, plastered with clay. Their bed was elevated above the water, and dry. The sticks they had carried into their lodge for their winter's food, were piled up outside with the bark all gnawed off. I have seen the stumps of trees they had gnawed off one foot in diameter. They select their sites for dams with all the nice judgment that man would use in locating mill dams. The beaver dams were numerous in all the lake Ontario region.

"I married and settled upon my farm in 1805. In that year and the following, myself and four neighbors:—George Daly, Orange Stone, Samuel Spafford, and Miles Northup, with the help of fifty dollars appropriated by the then town of Northfield, cut out the road two rods wide, for the distance of four miles from the river, east. I am the only person now living in the town of Brighton, who was here, an adult, in 1796."

The author is indebted to Mr. J. B. Taylor, of West Webster,

---

* The author has one of the old account books of this primitive mercantile establishment. Each page is dated "Gerundegut Landing." Some names as they occur through its pages, will remind the reader of early times:—Seymour Boughton, Miles Bristol, Jonathan Brown, Capt. Abraham Burchard, William Bacon, James Brooks, James Cronk, John Dailey, Levi Van Fossen, Wm. and Daniel Gould, Nathaniel Rowley, Paul Roberts, John Stoughton, Noah Smith, Asa Taft, Nathan Tolls, Gideon Thayer, Stephen Tinker, Matthew Warner, Ashael Warner, Aaron Watkins, Ezra Norton, Zebulon Norton, James Annibal, Amherst Humphrey, Samuel Stephens, Samuel Miles, James Maxwell, John Porter, Elijah Morgan, Samuel Bullin, Samuel Carr, Martin Lewis, Asa Porter, Solomon Hovey, Abner Sheldon, Wm. Keyes, Solomon Sylvester, Wm. Tanner, James Henry, Richard Smith, Reuben Thayer, Benjamin Barton, Paul Davison Elisha Brockway, Aaron Watkins, Noah Smith, Jasper Sears, Wait Lewis, Joel Brace, John Daily, Wheelock Wood, Thaddeus Keyes, Smith Wilcox, Levi Boughton, Abel Baker, Joel Henderson, Abel Rowe, John Chapman, Stephen Hopkins, Oliver Tracy, Augustus Porter, Peter B. Porter, Oliver Culver, James Walsworth, Glover Perrin, Samuel Stone, Oliver Grace, Oliver Phelps, John Ray, John F. Taylor, Thomas King, Wm. Hencher.

Monroe county, for the information contained in the following extracts of a letter:—

"My mother, now quite advanced in years, resides with her sister, Mrs. M'Laren, near Benedict's Corners, on Ridge Road, east of Rochester. I gather from her the statement, that she came with my father, to Braddock's Bay, in 1797. There had been living there, then, for three or four years, three brothers:—Bezeal, Stephen, and John Atchison. The names of the others there, were:—John Madden, —— Goodhue, —— Labon, —— Bennet. Wm. Hencher lived at the mouth of Genesee river; a rather singular sort of personage; a second Daniel Boone. Some emigrants settled four or five miles from him, at which he became very indignant; said he did not wish to have neighbors so near him."*

The following is a copy of the first tax roll ever made out for the region west of the Genesee river; it being then all embraced in one town—Northampton. It is entire, with the exception of fifteen or sixteen names, torn from the first page of the roll. It was furnished to the editor of the Rochester Democrat, by Donald M'Kenzie, Esq., of Caledonia. It is dated October 6th, 1800; and signed by Augustus Porter and Amos Hall, as commissioners of taxes for Ontario county. The assessors for the town of Northampton, were:—Cyrus Douglas, Michael Beach, Eli Griffith, and Philip Beach; Peter Shaeffer, (still living,) was the collector. There were not then, as it appears, over twelve taxable inhabitants upon the Purchase; in Buffalo, only Johnston, Middaugh and Lane.

	Value real and pers'l estate.	Am't of Tax.		Value real and pers'l estate.	Am't of Tax.
Curtis, William	$30	$0 06	Conatt, Samuel	38	06
Carter, William	94	18	Chamberlin, Joshua	60	12
Chamberlin, Hinds	284	40	Cary, Joseph	948	1 61
Curtis, Augustus	500	61	Coots, Timothy	396	54
Curtis, Jonathan	387	54	Dugan, Christopher	1306	1 63
Campbell, Peter	52	09	Douglas, Cyrus	78	14
Chapin, Henry	3000	6 50	Davis, Daniel	572	72
Chapman, Asa	112	23	Davis, Garret	350	45
Cumins, Joseph	20	04	Davis, Bela	105	22

* This first settler at the mouth of Genesee river—and first, in fact, in all that region—has been several times alluded to, by others. He had held a commission under Shay, in the Massachusetts rebellion. When the force was disbanded, he had taken so conspicuous a part in the rebellion, that he feared to remain, and came first to Chemung, where he remained two or three years. The following extract of a letter, dated in 1791, from one of his daughters, who was with him, to another, in Massachusetts, would show that he came to Western New York, about that period:—"We are waiting at Chemung, to get rid of the fever and ague; as soon as we do, we are going to the Genesee country. Father has been out there and returned." Mr. Hencher died in 1821, leaving a large number of descendants. Mrs. Donald M'Kenzie, of Caledonia, is one of his daughters. Mrs. Richardson, of Cambria, Niagara county, widow of Jonathan Richardson, is a sister of the early pioneer.

HOLLAND PURCHASE

Name	Value real and pers'l estate.	Am't of Tax.	Name	Value real and pers'l estate.	Am't of Tax.
Davis, Samuel	312	37	Rhau, Alexander	85	12
Ellicott, Benjamin	600	71	Stimson, Leonard	52	11
Fish, Josiah	1516	1 86	Stimson & Jones	200	29
Farewell, Elisha	288	37	Stoughton, Amaziah	164	21
Fuller, David	80	12	Sheffer, Peter	4260	5 36
Forsyth, John	330	43	Scott, Isaac	1108	1 45
Granger, Eli	100	14	Shelly, Phiros	150	18
Goodhue, George	176	20	Scott, Salmon	796	95
Ganson, John, Jr.	1640	2 10	Scoonover, Jacob	731	1 00
Ganson, James	12	02	Thompson Abriandner	30	07
Griffith, Eli	658	98	Utley, Asa	901	1 17
Hencher, Wm.	1036	1 64	Olmstead, Jeremiah	120	29
Hicks, Samuel	44	09	Wilber, Charles	60	31
Heth, Reuben	40	09	Walther, Frederick	488	68
Hunt, Elijah	68	14	Wemple, Henry	27	17
Harris, Alpheus	72	15		42	10
Hall, Friend	200	30	King, Thomas	30	07
Hunt, Joseph	64	13	King, Simeon	40	10
Hopkins, Timothy	42	09	Hender, Stephen	12	02
Hayne, John	50	11	Ransom, Asa	410	61
Hawley, Chapman	112	18	Erwin, John	428	96
Hall, Gilbert	370	52	Woolman, John	162	36
Hoit, Stephen	153	34	Philips, William	30	07
Jones, H. John	140	23	Carver, John	316	40
Jones, Elizabeth	153	24	Eli, Justin	5000	9 91
Johnson, Moses	800	1 07	Barnard, Ebenezer } Perkins, Enoch }	1950	3 87
Johnson, Wm.	2034	3 50			
Kith, M. Michael	42	09	Phelps, Oliver	4437	8 80
Kimball, John	700	1 03	Hartford, Charles	2333	4 62
Kent, Elijah	96	14	King, Gideon, heirs	4500	5 36
Lane, Ezekiel	114	24	Granger, Zadoc	4500	8 92
Laybourn, Christopher	470	62	Hinkley, Samuel } Stone, John } Graves, Silas }	5000	9 91
Lyon, John	40	08			
Leonard, Jonathan	40	06			
Lewis, Seth	60	14	Wadsworth, James	34,500	68 38
Mills, Wm.	714	94	Williamson, C. & others	34,500	68 28
Mills, Lewis	72	16	Gilbert, Warren	2,190	2 60
Mills, Alexander	80	19	Colt, Judah	1,320	2 61
Mills, Samuel	250	30	Morris, Thomas	4,200	8 32
Morton, Simeon	50	11	Hall, Amos	700	1 38
Mading, Timothy	128	16	Holland Company	3,300,000	5231 62
McCloning, John	40	09	Williamson, Charles	155,150	307 41
McCloning, John, Jr.	12	02	Williamson & Phelps	100,000	219 14
Middaugh, Martin	45	09	Craigie, Andrew	50,000	73 96
Mayle, Lewis	30	09	Ogden, Samuel	50,000	109 57
	84	19	Cottinger, Garrit	50,000	109 57
Mulkins, Henry	54	11	Church, Phillip	100,000	219 14
Nettleton, Philemon	592	80	Unknown	27,210	59 41
Morgan, Joseph	870	1 11	Leroy & Bayard	82,000	179 68
M'Naughton, John	48	11	Leroy & Bayard	40,000	87 66
McPherson, Dan	100	22	Phelps & Jones	—	—
Patterson, Lawrence	500	90	Supposed to be owned by Thomas Morris }	40,960	89 36
Pebody, Stephen	86	18			
Palmer, John	482	72	Joseph Fitts Simmons } Joseph Higby }	600,000	1314 84
Pangman, William	300	66			
Quivey, Norton	70	15			
Redford, John	130	19	Total	$4,785,368	8,387 11

NOTE—The names were, many of them, wrong, in the transcript copied from. After such corrections as the author is enabled to make by reference to other records, there are yet, it is presumed, some errors.

BENJAMIN BARTON.

He was a native of Sussex county, New Jersey; born in 1771. When but seventeen years of age — in the year 1787 — he accompanied his father to assist in driving a drove of cattle and sheep purchased for the use of the British Commissariat at Niagara. The route was the one that has already been described; the Indian trail, that was then the only route to Fort Niagara and Canada. On reaching the Genesee river, the party rested for a few days to allow the cattle and sheep to recruit, and while there, erected a small log cabin, for their own convenience, and the convenience of other drovers; which is supposed to be the first tenement erected by white men, between Whitestown on the Mohawk and the western frontiers of the state.

Major Barton came to Geneva in 1788; and in the year 1790, purchased from Poudery, a Frenchman, who had married a squaw, (and to whom the Indians had given the land,) a valuable farm on the Cashong creek, seven miles from Geneva.

This farm was formerly the site of an Indian town which had been destroyed by the army of Gen. Sullivan in 1779. More than one hundred acres of it had been improved from time immemorial; so long, that the stumps had rotted away, and there were a great many old apple trees growing upon it, many of which were more than a foot and a half in diameter. These were the only things on it that escaped the destruction inflicted upon all Indian towns he reached, by Gen. Sullivan. In payment for this farm, he gave all the money and property he had, even to parting with a portion of his raiment. He had great difficulty in getting the purchase ratified by the State, but succeeded finally, through the great kindness and assistance rendered to him by Gov. George Clinton.

In 1792, Major Barton, was married at Canandaigua to the kind and affectionate companion who yet survives him, and with whom he lived nearly half a century. After his marriage he settled in Geneva, where his first child, a daughter, was born; and in 1794 removed on to his farm, where he continued to reside until the spring of 1807, when he removed to Lewiston in Niagara county. He was employed a long time by the Surveyor General in surveying the State military tract lying east of Ontario, to, and including Onondaga county; as well as rendering much service in that way in Ontario county.

Between 1801 and 1805, he was three or four years the Sheriff of Ontario county, which then embraced all the territory of New York (except the county of Steuben,) west of Seneca lake, and from the Pennsylvania line to lake Ontario, which has since been subdivided into thirteen counties.

During the time he held the office, he had to serve a criminal process upon an Indian residing on the Buffalo reservation for the crime of murder, he having killed a man in a drunken brawl at a little log tavern, near where the Mansion House in this city now stands. At that period of time the Indians were much the stronger party in the country, and a process like this could not be executed without their consent. The chiefs objected to the arrest being made; said they regretted the circumstance, but they understood the white people in a case of murder, in trying and punishing a man who committed it, they made no difference whether he was drunk or sober at the time, that they did, their young warrior was drunk when he committed the act, and they would punish him; at all events they would not consent that he should be taken and tied on a horse like a thief, and carried through the country to the jail at Canandaigua. Major B. represented to them, that as the offence was a crime against our laws and within the jurisdiction of the state, the arrest must be made, even if it took a large force to do it, and they had better consent, but they positively forbid his making it. It was then mutually agreed between him and the chiefs, that they should go to Fort Niagara, then commanded by Major Moses Porter, and consult with him what was best to be done. Even here a positive refusal was adhered to, not to permit the arrest to be made. They were willing to pledge their words as chiefs, that the man should be in Canandaigua when the court met, and that the Sheriff might go home. This agreement was faithfully performed. The Indian had his trial, was convicted and sentenced to be hung, but subsequently pardoned by Gov. George Clinton and banished the state. He went by the English name of Stiff-arm George, and is yet, or was a few years ago, residing in the state of Pennsylvania.

Previous to the surrender of Fort Niagara, in 1796, under Jay's treaty, and while held by the British Government, no white man could travel on the frontier, without being liable to be arrested by the Indians and taken to the fort under suspicion of being a deserter, unless he could exhibit to the Indians a pass, from the commander of the fort; which pass, as the Indians could not read, was a card or thick piece of paper having on it a large wax seal, bearing a particular impression. Major B. has been once or twice thus arrested, and at other times had to dodge and run away from drunken and troublesome Indians.

During his early rambles on this frontier, he foresaw the brilliant prospects and immense trade which would in time flow through these great inland seas. As soon as the Mile Strip on the Niagara river was surveyed into farm and village lots, by the State who was the owner, he attended the sale at the Surveyor General's office in Albany, in 1805. Here he met with Judge and General Porter on the same business. They formed a connection of friendship and business, which continued unbroken to the day of his death. They purchased several farm lots, including the property around the Falls, and bid off, at public auction, the landing places at Lewiston and Schlosser, for which they received a lease for twelve or thirteen years. In 1806, under the firm of Porter, Barton & Co., they commenced the carrying trade around the Niagara Falls, on the American side; they were connected with Matthew M'Nair of Oswego, and Jonathan Walton & Co. of Schenectady; and this was the first regular and connected line of forwarders that ever did business from tide-water to lake Erie on the American side of the Niagara river.

After Major Barton removed to Lewiston, in 1807, then in the county of Genesee, he was for one or two years the Sheriff; after which he never asked for nor held any civil office, except such as supervisor or other town office, which are rather burthensome than otherwise, but he always held that it was every one's duty to bear his share of such tasks. He was an American in heart and principle, and loved his country and her republican institutions before all others. He was a strong advocate for the war of 1812, and during the early part of it, gave his whole efforts and influence to its support. In 1813 when the Niagara frontier was invaded and laid waste with fire and sword by the enemy, Major Barton was a large sufferer; his houses, stores, mills, and other property being burned up or otherwise destroyed; for all of which he received but a partial remuneration from the Government. This severe pecuniary loss, flowing from the progress of the war which he had aided in bringing about, and to which he had given his untiring zeal in supporting, did not in the least change his views or feelings in what he considered a just and proper act of the Government; but on the contrary called him more fully into action.

In the spring of 1814, when his friend and partner, General Porter, raised his Brigade of Volunteers, which during the campaign so much distinguished themselves, Major B. joined them as special quarter master for the corps, under a commission from Gov. Tompkins. In this department, his services were soon found so useful, that in July, while the American army lay on Queenstown Heights, he received from the President, a commission as Deputy Quarter Master General in the regular army, in which he continued to the close of the war.

After the restoration of peace, Major B. returned with his family (who left at the commencement of the war,) to Lewiston, his favorite place, and commenced rebuilding and repairing the injury his property had received during the war. For the last fifteen or twenty years of his life, he gave up all cares of business, except agriculture, to which he was much attached. He originally had a most uncommonly robust constitution; but from early exposure in surveying the country, by exposure in winter and summer to rains and snows, and hard fare in living, he became, as age creeped on, subject to rheumatism and other chronic complaints, which entirely broke him up; and, for the last five years, he enjoyed but little good health.

During a long life, Major Barton has been eminently a useful man. Thrown, in his minority, upon the world, to work his own way, without a shilling to aid him, but possessing talents, industry, perseverance and economy, he overcame all obstacles, and rose to the enjoyment of wealth and honors. He was naturally modest and unobtrusive; decisive and firm in purpose; honest and upright in all his dealings; never oppressive to those indebted to him, but rather extending to them additional assistance; generous and obliging in his disposition, and always ready to bear his portion in any public improvement; without any desire for, or attempt at show or ostentation, for which he had a perfect contempt; but treating with great respect and civility, worth and merit, whether covered with the humble garb of poverty or more rich attire; a kind husband, an affectionate father, a good neighbor, and an unflinching friend.

He died at Lewiston, in 1842, aged 72 years.

NOTE.—The portrait accompanying the biography, is from a painting made when the subject of it was but a little over fifty years of age; there being no later one. With

CHAPTER III.

MORRIS' PURCHASE—GENERAL DISPOSITION OF "MORRIS' RESERVE."

Messrs. Phelps and Gorham, who had paid about one third of the purchase money of the whole tract purchased of Massachusetts, in consequence of the rise of the value of "Massachusetts consolidated stock," (in which the payments for the land were to be received) from twenty per cent. to par, were unable further to comply with their engagements and consummate the conditions of the sale on their part, and Massachusetts commenced suits on their bonds. After a long negotiation between the parties in which many propositions were made, accepted and abrogated by mutual consent, the whole transaction relative to the purchase of those lands was settled and finally closed on the tenth day of March, 1791, by Messrs. Phelps and Gorham relinquishing to Massachusetts that portion of the land, and Massachusetts relinquishing to the said Phelps and Gorham, their bonds for the payment of the purchase money therefor.

On the 12th day of March, 1791, the state of Massachusetts agreed to sell to Samuel Ogden, who was acting for and in behalf of Robert Morris, all the lands ceded to the said state, by the state of New York, except that part thereof which had been conveyed by Massachusetts to Phelps and Gorham. *See Sec. Office, Massachusetts Exemp. Records, fol. 1.*

In conformity with this agreement the state of Massachusetts conveyed to Robert Morris, on the 11th day of May, 1791, the whole of said land in five different deeds—the first including all

---

those who have only known him in later years, broken in health, as has been observed, it will not be recognized as a faithful likeness; while those who knew him when he had but just passed the prime of life, consider it generally, correct.

the land on said tract lying east of a meridian line beginning at a point in the north line of Pennsylvania, twelve miles west of the southwest corner of Phelps and Gorham's tract, and running due north to lake Ontario, supposed to contain about five hundred thousand acres. *See Sec. Office, Albany, Book of Deeds*, 23, *fol.* 231. The second deed included all the land between the last described tract and a meridian line beginning at a point in the north line of Pennsylvania, sixteen miles west of the southwest corner of the last described tract, thence running due north to lake Ontario. *See Sec. Office, Albany, Lib.* 23, fol. 234. The third deed included all the land lying between the last mentioned tract, and a meridian line, beginning at a point in the north line of Pennsylvania, sixteen miles west of the southwest corner of the last described tract, and thence running due north to the shore of lake Ontario. *See Sec. Office, Albany, Lib.* 23, fol. 235. The fourth deed contained all land lying beetween the last mentioned tract, and a meridian line, beginning at a point in the north line of Pennsylvania, sixteen miles west of the southwest corner of the last described tract, and thence running due north to the shore of lake Ontario. *See Sec. Office, Albany, Lib.* 23, fol. 232. The fifth and last deed included all the land owned by the state of Massachusetts in this state, lying west of the last described tract. *See Sec. Office, Albany, Lib.* 23, fol. 237. The four last mentioned tracts included about three million, three hundred thousand acres.

One undivided sixtieth part of the whole of the land included in these five deeds, had been reserved by Massachusetts, in their original agreement with Samuel Ogden, Morris' agent, to meet the demands of John Butler, who had contracted with Phelps and Gorham for the purchase of the same, prior to the surrender of their claim to Massachusetts. Butler, however, subsequent to the surrender, and before the execution of the conveyances above recited, assigned his right to said sixtieth part to Robert Morris, which enabled him to acquire a title to the whole at the same time.

The tract of land described in and conveyed by the first mentioned deed, took the name of Morris' Reserve, from the fact that he retained that tract in the sale which he afterwards made to the Holland Company. Mr. Morris sold out in parcels from forty, to one hundred and fifty thousand acres each, to wit: he sold to Leroy, Bayard and M'Evers the triangular tract, bounded south-easterly by the Phelps and Gorham purchase west of Genesee river, west by a line beginning at the southwest corner of said Phelps and Gorham's tract, and running due north to lake Ontario and north by said lake Ontario, containing about eighty seven thousand acres. The next sale which Mr. Morris made (which was before he sold the land described in the other deeds to the Holland Company,) was one hundred thousand acres to Watson Cragie and Greenleaf, bounded east by said triangular tract, north by lake Ontario, west by a line running parallel with the west line of the triangle and six miles distant therefrom, and south by an east and west line so far south of lake Ontario as that the tract shall contain one hundred thousand acres. This sale was made under the fullest confidence (on what authority it is not known) that the full width of the tract fell on the land described in the first mentioned deed, executed to Mr. Morris by Massachusetts, which appears to have been an erroneous assumption.

This tract after several transfers, was conveyed in 1801, to the State of Connecticut (being purchased with a portion of their school fund) and Sir William Pultney, one undivided half each, which was divided between them in 1811, portions of the share of each being interspersed through the whole tract. The lands falling to the one share being called Connecticut lands and to the other Pultney estate lands, although the whole tract is usually designated the Connecticut Tract.

Mr. Morris then sold fifty thousand acres, south of and adjoining the Connecticut Tract to Andrew Cragie. This sale, however, was made after Mr. Morris had sold the land included in the other four deeds from Massachusetts, to the Holland Company, or to persons in trust for them. This tract was bounded east, partly by the Triangular Tract, and partly by a line run due south from the southern angle thereof, in the whole one hundred four chains and sixty seven links; north by the Connecticut tract six miles; west by a line parallel to, and six miles west from the east boundary of the tract, one hundred four chains and sixty-seven links, and south by an east and west line, parallel to the north bounds of the tract, one hundred four chains and sixty-seven links south therefrom: this is generally called the Cragie Tract. Mr. Morris sold to Samuel Ogden fifty thousand acres described as lying south of, and adjoining the Cragie Tract, and of the same length and breadth:

this is called the Ogden Tract. He likewise sold one other tract containing fifty thousand acres to Gerrit Cotringer, lying south of, and adjoining the Ogden Tract, of the same length and breadth.

Mr. Morris sold forty thousand acres to Wilhem and Jan Willink, bounded east by the Genesee river, north by Phelps and Gorham's Purchase west of Genesee river, twelve miles; west by a line running due south from the southwest corner of said Phelps and Gorham's Purchase, and south by a line parallel with the north bounds of the tract and so far south as to include forty thousand acres: this is called "The Forty Thousand Acre Tract." Of this tract Mr. Morris sold to John B. Church, one hundred thousand acres, being six miles wide, lying east of, and adjoining the lands sold by him to the Holland Company and extending nearly from the Pennsylvania line to the Cotringer Tract. One undivided half of this tract fell into the hands of the creditors of J. B. Church and the other half became the property of his son Judge Philip Church, which parts have since been separated.

The tract six miles wide, east of the Cotringer tract and Church's tract, containing one hundred and fifty thousand acres, was sold by Mr. Morris to Samuel Sterrett, and the lands between the Sterrett tract and the forty thousand acre tract, except the Mount Morris tract, part of Gardeau Reservation, &c. is generally known as Morris' honorary creditor's tract. It will be understood that the foregoing mentioned sales as well as that to the Holland Company or their trustees, was made before the Indian title to the lands was extinguished, with an agreement on his part, to effect that object. In regard to the settlement of these several tracts, the Connecticut Tract could not be offered for sale until after its division between Connecticut and the Pultney Estate, in 1811. The owners of the Cragie Tract, Ogden Tract, Cotringer Tract and Sterrett Tract, neglected to put their lands in market, until great progress had been made in settling the adjacent lands west on the Holland Purchase. There were some early settlers on the Triangular Tract, Forty thousand acre Tract, and Church's Tract, but these settlements progressed slowly at first, especially on Church's Tract, the only one of these which joined the Holland Purchase. We know of no reason for the tardy progress of the settlement on Mr. Church's Tract, as the proprietor located himself on the premises in 1804, and expended large sums of money to give it its primary impetus, unless it was that Mr.

Church, who was educated in Europe and had associated with its aristocracy, was better qualified to support the high character of his hospitable mansion, overflowing with the substantials, and well stored with all the delicacies and luxuries produced in or imported to this region; than to mete out the hills and dales of the earth by the acre, to the huge-framed axe-man, and long-limbed Bill Purdys of the exploring pioneers. Judge Church resides two and a half miles southwest of the village of Angelica, the county town of Alleghany county, at his beautiful country seat, Belvidere, on the banks of the Genesee river.

PART FIFTH.

CHAPTER I.

HISTORICAL DEDUCTION OF HOLLAND COMPANY TITLE — SURVEYS.

The last four tracts described in the conveyances of the land purchased of Massachusetts by Robert Morris, were conveyed by him by four separate deeds, as follows: 1st, deed from Robert Morris and wife, to Herman Le Roy and John Linklaen, for one and a half million acres, dated December 24th, 1792. 2d, deed from Robert Morris and wife, to Herman Le Roy, John Linklaen and Gerrit Boon for one million acres, dated February, 27th 1793. 3rd, deed from Robert Morris and wife to Herman Le Roy, John Linklaen and Gerrit Boon, for eight hundred thousand acres, dated July 20th, 1793. Deed from Robert Morris and wife, to Herman Le Roy, William Bayard and Matthew Clarkson, for three hundred thousand acres, dated July 20th, 1793.

These tracts were purchased with the funds of certain gentlemen in Holland, and held in trust by the several grantees for their benefit, as they, being aliens, could not purchase and hold real estate, in their own names, according to the then existing laws of the State. After several changes in the trustees, and transfers of portions of the land, sanctioned by the Legislature, the whole tract was conveyed by the trustees by three separate deeds, to the Holland Company, or rather, to the individuals, in their own names, composing three separate branches of that Company.*

Although these deeds of conveyance were given to three distinct companies of proprietors, their interests were so closely blended, several of the same persons, having large interests in each of the three different estates; they appointed one general agent for the whole, who managed the concerns of the tract generally, as though it all belonged to the same proprietors, making

---

* For a deduction of the title of the Holland Land Company, including a synopsis of those three deeds, see Appendix.

no distinction which operated in the least on the settlers and purchasers, but simply keeping the accounts of each separate, when practicable, and apportioning, *pro rata*, all expenses when blended in the same transaction for the benefit of the whole. The general agent likewise appointed the same local or resident agent for the three companies owning this tract in Western New York.* The only difference between its consisting of one or more tracts discernable by the purchaser of lands, was, that in executing contracts or conveyances, the agents used the names of the respective proprietors of each tract. Under this state of things, we shall denominate the whole of the proprietors holding under these three deeds, " The Holland Company," and the lands conveyed by those deeds, the " Holland Purchase."

It is a curious fact, that when the Dutch proprietors were parcelling out the tract among the three different branches of the company, it was mutually agreed among the whole, that Messrs. Wilhem Willink, Jan Willink, Wilhem Willink the younger, and Jan Willink the younger, should have three hundred thousand acres, located in such part of the whole tract as they should select. In making their selection, they located their three hundred thousand acres, in nearly a square form, in the southeast corner of the tract, for the reason *that it was nearest Philadelphia,* the residence of their agent general. This selection contained the territory now composing the towns of Bolivar, Wirt, Friendship, the east part of Belfast, Genesee, Clarksville and Cuba, in Allegany county, Portville, and the east parts of Hinsdale and Rice in Cattaragus county. This location will give the reader who is acquainted with the localities of the country, some idea of the knowledge, or rather want of knowledge, of the Dutch proprietors, of the situation and relative advantages of the different portions of their vast domains.

This sale by Robert Morris to the Holland Company was made before the Indian title to the land was extinguished, accompanied by an agreement on his part to extinguish that title, with the assistance of the Company, as soon as practicable; therefore at a council of the Seneca Indians, held at Geneseo, on Genesee river, in the month of September, 1797, at which Jeremiah Wadsworth attended as Commissioner for the United States, and William Shepherd as

---

* The same proprietors or a portion of them, owned tracts of land in the middle section of this state and in Pennsylvania which was under the supervision and control of other local or resident agents.

agent for Massachusetts, Robert Morris in fulfilment of his several contracts with the Holland Company, and the other persons to whom he had sold land on this tract, acting by his agents, Thomas Morris and Charles Williamson, extinguished the Indian title to all the land, the pre-emption right of which he had purchased of Massachusetts, except the following Indian Reservations, to wit: The Cannawagus reservation, containing two square miles, lying on the west bank of Genesee river, west of Avon. Little Beard's and Bigtree reservations, containing together four square miles, lying on the west bank of Genesee river opposite Geneseo. Squakie Hill reservation, containing two square miles, lying on the north bank of Genesee river, north of Mount Morris. Gardeau reservation, containing about twenty-eight square miles, lying on both sides of Genesee river, two or three miles south of Mount Morris. The Canadea reservation, containing sixteen square miles, lying each side of, and extending eight miles along the Genesee river, in the county of Allegany. The Oil Spring reservation, containing one square mile, lying on the line between Allegany and Cattaragus counties. The Allegany reservation, containing forty-two square miles, lying on each side of the Allegany river, and extending from the Pennsylvania line northeastwardly about twenty-five miles. The Cattaragus reservation, containing forty-two square miles, lying each side and near the mouth of Cattaragus creek, on lake Erie. The Buffalo reservation, containing one hundred and thirty square miles, lying on both sides of the Buffalo creek, and extending east from lake Erie about seven miles wide. The Tonawanda reservation, containing seventy square miles, lying on both sides of the Tonawanda creek, beginning about twenty-five miles from its mouth, and extending eastwardly about seven miles wide; and the Tuscarora reservation, containing one square mile, lying about three miles east of Lewiston, on the Mountain Ridge.

Theophilus Cazenove, the agent general of the Holland Company, resident at Philadelphia, in July, 1797, had engaged Mr. Joseph Ellicott, as principal surveyor of the company's lands in Western New York, whenever their title should be perfected and possession obtained, and likewise, to attend the before-mentioned council and assist Messrs. W. Bayard and J. Linklaen, who were to attend and act as agents for the company, (*sub rosa*,) for the purpose of promoting the interests of their principals in any treaty which might be made with the Indians. Mr. Ellicott attended the council accordingly, and rendered valuable services to the purchasers. This period was the commencement of upwards of twenty years' regular active service rendered by Mr. Ellicott to the Holland Land Company, in conducting their affairs and executing laborious enterprises for their benefit.

As soon as the favorable result of the proceedings of this council was known, Mr. Ellicott proceeded immediately to prepare for the traverse and survey of the north and northwest bounds of the tract. As soon as the necessary preparatory steps could be taken, Mr. Ellicott, as surveyor for the Holland Company, and Augustus Porter, in the same capacity, for Robert Morris, for the purpose of estimating the quantity of land in the tract, started a survey at the northeast corner of Phelps and Gorham's tract, west of Genesee river, and traversed the south shore of lake Ontario to the mouth of Niagara river; thence up the eastern shore of the Niagara river to lake Erie, thence along the southeast shore of lake Erie to the west bounds of the state of New York, being a meridian line running due south from the west end of lake Ontario, which had been previously established by Andrew Ellicott, Surveyor General of the United States, assisted by said Joseph Ellicott. All which was perfected by the middle of November following.

Before Mr. Ellicott left Western New York for Philadelphia, he contracted with Thomas Morris to deliver on the Genesee river or shore of lake Ontario near the mouth of that river, one hundred barrels of pork, fifteen barrels of beef, and two hundred and seventy barrels of flour, for the supply of the surveyors and their assistants the ensuing season. Mr. Ellicott, at the request of the Agent General, made a list of articles to be provided for the next season's campaign, consisting of a diversity of articles, from pack-horses to horse shoes, nails and gimlets — from tents to towels — from barley and rice to chocolate, coffee and tea, and from camp-kettles to teacups; estimated to amount to $7,213 33. This statement, however, did not include medicine, or "wine, spirits, loaf sugar, &c., for head quarters." Mr. Ellicott likewise calculated the wages of surveyors and other hands for six months of the next season at $19,830.

Although the great divisions of the Holland Purchase was intended to consist of townships six miles square, the division of the tract among the three sets of proprietors, the Indian reservations which were not included in the townships, as well as the offsets and sinuosities existing in most of the boundaries, prevent a large portion of the townships conforming to this standard. The townships are situated in ranges running from south to north. The townships in each *range* of townships beginning to number one at the south, raising regularly in number to the north, and the ranges of townships beginning to number one at the east, and proceeding regularly west, to fifteen.

The first plan of the agent general of the company, relative to the subdivision of the townships, was to divide each township which was six miles square into sixteen portions one and a half miles square, to be called sections, and each section again subdivided into twelve lots, each lot to be three fourths of a mile long (generally north and south,) and one fourth of a mile wide containing about one hundred and twenty acres each; presuming that a wealthy farmer would buy a section, whereon to locate himself and his progeny. Twenty four townships were surveyed or commenced to be surveyed in conformity to that plan, although the uniformity of the size and shape of lots was often departed from, where large streams, such as the Tonawanda running through the townships, were, for convenience, made boundaries of lots. From experience however it was ascertained that, in the purchase of land, each individual whether father, son, or son-in-law, would locate himself according to his own choice or fancy. That this formal and regular division of land into farms, seldom was found to be in conformity to the topography of the country, nor to the different requirements as to quantity, likewise that the addition of sections to townships and lots, rendered the descriptions of farms more complex, and increased the liability to err in defining any particular location; for which reasons, the practice of dividing townships into sections was abandoned, and thereafter, the townships were simply divided into lots of about sixty chains or three fourths of a mile square, which could be divided into farms to suit the topography of the land and quantity required by the purchasers. In those townships in which the surveys had been commenced to divide them into sections, and not completed, the remaining sections were divided into four lots only of three fourths of a mile square each. These lots consequently contained about three hundred and sixty acres each, but could not be laid off exactly uniform in shape and area, for the same reason heretofore given in a note, why the townships could not be laid off exactly uniform.

Early in the spring of 1788, Mr. Ellicott dispatched Adam Hoops, Jr., a nephew of Major Adam Hoops, from Philadelphia, to Western New York, with general powers to prepare for opening the approaching campaign of surveying the Holland Purchase, and to co-operate with Augustus Porter, who had previously been engaged to procure horses, employ hands, and transport stores from the places of their delivery by the contractor, Mr. Morris, to the places where they would be required for consumption.

The principal surveyors engaged during the active season of 1798, in township, meridian line and reservation surveys, and in lake and river traverses, were as follows:—Joseph and Benjamin Ellicott, John Thompson, Richard M. Stoddard, George Burgess, James Dewey, David Ellicott, Aaron Oakford, Jr. Augustus Porter, Seth Pease, James Smedly, William Shepherd, George Eggleston. In addition to these, were two Frenchmen, Messrs. Haudecaur, and Autrechy, who were employed in some surveys of Niagara river and the Falls. The last were rather engineers than surveyors. Mr. James Brisbane, then in his minority, came from Philadelphia, with Mr. Thompson, as clerk and store keeper.

Mr. Ellicott and his assistants having arrived on the territory, his first business was to ascertain and correctly establish the east line of the Purchase. He caused the Pennsylvania line to be accurately measured from the southwest corner of Phelps and Gorham's purchase, or the 82d mile stone, twelve miles west, and there erected a stone monument for the southeast corner of the Holland Purchase. The whole company was then divided into parties, to prosecute the undertaking to advantage. The principal surveyor Joseph Ellicott, assisted by Benjamin Ellicott, one other surveyor and the requisite number of hands, undertook to run the eastern boundary line. The other surveyors, each with his quota of hands were assigned to run different township lines.

A line running due north from the monument established as the southeast corner by Mr. Ellicott, to the boundary line between the United States and the dominions of the King of Great Britain in lake Ontario, according to the deeds of conveyance from Robert Morris to the company, constitutes the east line of their purchase. To run a true meridian by the surveyors compass Mr. Ellicott knew to be impracticle,* he therefore determined to run this line

---

* We make use of this strong asseveration, being as we feel fully authorized by the following statement, which, although not originally written for this work, has been

by an instrument, having for its basis the properties of the "Transit instrument" (an instrument made use of, to observe the transits of the heavenly bodies,) improved for this purpose by a newly invented manner of accurately arriving at the same; to effect this object, an instrument possessing all these qualities, was manufactured in Philadelphia by his brother, Benjamin Ellicott, as no instrument possessing all the qualities desired, was then to be found in the United States.

This instrument has no magnetic needle attached to it, but its peculiar qualities and prominent advantages are, that by means of

---

put in our hands by the writer. For the benefit of persons interested in the process of surveying, we publish the whole statement, although an extract from it would have fully sustained our assertion:—

VARIATION OF THE MAGNETIC NEEDLE.

From divers publications emanating from really scientific writers, but predicated on speculative theory, without any regard to practicability or the real excellencies or defects of the magnetic needle, when applied to practical purposes; many well informed people, on general subjects, have been led to believe that, that instrument really possesses talismanic attributes and unerring precision; that it is always governed by, and true to never failing and well understood laws; that although it varies from indicating the true meridian, that the variation from truth, progresses slowly, constantly and regularly, at a rate clearly conceived and well understood by the scientific surveyor. If this position was correct, the needle could be for all practical purposes, a true and perfect index, whereby to ascertain any point of the compass, for the sights could easily be adjusted to the known variation of the needle. But this fine spun theory, whatever it may amount to in a scientific point of view, is entirely merged and wholly lost in the practical variation of the needle from *itself*, or rather its uncertainty, variability, and mutability.

To support this position, I feel gratified that I have it in my power to produce an authority, which carries with it its own ponderous weight and relieves me from further urging my own views, or stating my own experience to prove the truth of the position. The following is an extract from a semi-official document prepared by the late Joseph Ellicott, who was principal surveyor, and I may say, sole engineer for the Holland Company in locating and surveying their large tract of land in Western New York.

The document referred to, was an explanatory accompaniment of Mr. Ellicott's report to the agent general at Philadelphia, of the survey of the Holland Purchase into townships. The deliberate and unqualified statement of so great a scientific and practical surveyor on such an important occasion, must be admitted as unquestionable authority. It will be seen that what Mr. Ellicott meant by "the variation of the needle," was nothing more nor less than its fickleness and uncertainty.

"The difference that is discernable in the size of the several townships, is occasioned by the variation of the needle, which from certain *occult causes* is found to differ essentially between *any two stations that may be fixed on*, and much more between some stations than others. Hence in taking the magnetic courses of any two townships, it will follow that a disproportion in size of the several townships will necessarily arise, as *the needle is seldom known* to preserve a uniform position, *between places but a few hundred yards from each other*: so that inaccuracies will arise though the greatest circumspection should be observed in correcting courses."

In the foregoing statement (although I confess it adds nothing comparatively to the weight of the original) I fully concur, and feel confident in asserting that if a surveyor, being guided by the magnetic needle only, strikes, or very nearly strikes his intended point, he has more reason to give credit to *good luck*, than to any scientific acquirements, or practical knowledge.

BATAVIA, Sept. 1848.   EBENEZER MIX.

its telescopic tube and accurate manner of reversing, by it, a straight line can be correctly, and, comparatively speaking, expeditiously run. But such an instrument, by reason of its magnifying powers is as illy calculated to run a line through woods and underbrush, as would be a microscope to observe the transits of the satelites of Herschel. Therefore it became necessary to cut a vista through the woods on the highlands and on level ground, sufficiently wide to admit a clear and uninterrupted view.

Mr. Ellicott having provided himself with such an instrument, caused the vista to be cut, some three or four rods wide, ahead of the transit instrument, in a north direction as indicated by the compass, which sometimes led the axemen more than the width of the vista from the meridian sought; therefore the true meridian line, called the transit line, from the name of the instrument with which it was run, being of no width, runs sometimes on one side of the middle of the vista cut in advance, and sometimes on the other.

Thus prepared with a suitable instrument, Mr. Ellicott, assisted by his brother Benjamin Ellicott, together with surveyors and their assistants, established a true meridian line north from the corner monument, by astronomical observations, and pursued it with the transit instrument, taking new astronomical observations at different stations, to guard against accidental variations.

The progress in running this line was slow, as it could not be otherwise expected, considering the great amount of labor necessarily to be performed, in clearing the vista, and taking other preparatory measures, and above all, the vast importance of having it correctly established, which rendered anything like precipitance or haste an experiment too hazardous to be permitted. June 12th, the party on this line had advanced so far north that they established their store house at Williamsburg, (about three miles south of the village of Geneseo,) and soon after Mr. Ellicott made it his head quarters at Hugh M'Nair's in that vicinity. On the 22d day of November following, eighty-one and a half miles of the line was established, which brought them within about thirteen miles of the shore of lake Ontario; the precise date of its completion is unknown.

This line defined the west bounds of Mr. Church's hundred thousand acres, but passed through the Cotringer, Ogden, and Cragie tracts, about two miles from their west boundaries, as described in the deeds of conveyance from Robert Morris to the several grantees; but as their titles were of a later date than the conveyance to the Holland Company, no deviation from the first established meridian was made by Mr. Ellicott.

On arriving at the south line of the hundred thousand acre tract conveyed by Robert Morris to Leroy Bayard and M'Evers, now called the Connecticut tract (the conveyance of which, from Robert Morris, claimed seniority over that to the Holland Company,) Mr. Ellicott found that his meridian intersected the south line of that tract, one hundred sixty-six chains and thirty links east of its south-west corner, on which he moved his position that distance to the west, from which point he ran the transit due north to lake Ontario.

The clashing of the boundary lines of the several tracts, located from the north end of the Reserve, as conveyed by Mr. Morris, and the Holland Company's land which was located from the south, was arranged in the following manner, and taken possession of accordingly. The conveyance of the Connecticut tract by Mr. Morris, to Watson, Cragie and Greenleaf, being anterior to that of the Holland Purchase to Wilhelm Willink and others: that tract retained its full size and location, according to the description in the deed. The Ogden and Cotringer tracts, held their size and shape, but their location was moved about two miles east, and fixed according to the original intention of Mr. Morris, there being land sufficient in that direction, on the Reserve, not otherwise appropriated by him. The conveyance of the Cragie tract being likewise subsequent to that of the Holland Purchase, about two miles of the western part of it was cut off by the location of that tract; and as the triangular tract, Phelps and Gorham's tract, west of Genesee river, and the forty thousand acre tract, with their prior conveyances and locations, bounding it on the east, which prevented its extension in that direction, was consequently reduced in area to between thirty-three and thirty-four thousand acres. The proprietors however not being content to rest quietly sustaining this loss, have since instituted suits in ejectment against the occupants of lands, west on the Holland Purchase and south on the Ogden tract, to try the legal interpretation of their rights, in extending their limits in one way or the other of those directions, but have failed in both.

Although the eastern bank of the Niagara river had been traversed, the east bounds of the New York mile strip had not been ascertained, and the state would participate in it no further than to give the proprietors of the land adjoining, to wit: the Holland

Company, liberty to run the line at their own expense, and if so run as to be approved by the Surveyor General of the state, it should be established as permanently located, and passed a law to that effect. This was, undoubtedly, the most difficult piece of surveying ever performed in the state. Some preliminary matters as to the construction of the terms of the treaty or agreement between New York and Massachusetts had to be first settled. At the north end where the river disembogued itself into the lake, at almost right angles with its shore, there could no doubts arise; but at the south end of the straits or river a different state of things existed; lake Erie narrowed gradually and became a river; where the lake ends and the river begins may be considered a difficult question; but it was finally agreed between the parties interested, the river should be deemed to extend to where the water was one mile wide and there cease; the line of the strip east of this point, extending to the shore of lake Erie on an arc of a circle, of one mile radius, the centre being in the eastern bank at the termination of the lake and head of the river, giving to the mile strip all the land lying within a mile of the river, whether east or south. For this arc of the circle, which could not be practically run, a repetition of short sides, making a section of a regular polygon, was substituted. Seth Pease, a scientific surveyor and astronomer, was engaged, in the fall of 1788, to run this line, who executed the survey in a masterly manner, and to the satisfaction of all the parties concerned.

During the year 1799 and 1800, few events transpired relative to the settlement of the Holland Purchase, which require a circumstantial detail, or would admit of one which would be interesting to the reader. The surveyors and their assistants, under the direction of their principal, Joseph Ellicott, continued the same steady routine of encamping in the woods, pitching their tents, transporting provisions, surveying lines, and striking their tents and removing to new positions; and although at times many individuals, undoubtedly, suffered pain and endured hardships, such incidents must have been caused by accidental occurrences, unforeseen events, or carelessness and imprudence in themselves or their companions, as the well supplied coffers of the Company, accompanied by their liberality, furnished sufficient means, and the provident care of Mr. Ellicott kept their store-houses well supplied with the best kind of provisions for that service, as well as all other necessaries and many of the comforts of life. This might be seen from Mr. Ellicott's catalogue of items, for the outfit of the first campaign, and its cost, heretofore refered to, which was adopted and its contents provided. Of those events, however, the following deserve notice.

The Indian treaty of 1797, in which the Indian title to the Holland Purchase was extinguished, except to certain reservations, as has been before stated, prescribed the quantities contained in, and general shape and location of each reservation, leaving the precise location of the boundary lines to be determined thereafter. The Indians reserved two hundred thousand acres, one indefinite portion of which was to be located on Buffalo creek, at the east end of lake Erie, and the remainder on the Tonawanda creek. As the New York reservation excluded the Holland Company's land from the waters of Niagara river, and from the shore of lake Erie one mile southerly from the river, it became very important to the company to secure a landing place and harbor at the mouth of Buffalo creek, and sufficient ground adjoining whereon to establish a commercial and manufacturing village or city.

Capt. William Johnston, an Indian trader and interpreter, settled himself near the mouth of the Buffalo creek at an early period, under the auspices of the British Government, and remained there until the Holland Company had effected their purchase. His dwelling house stood south of Exchange street and east of Washington street; he had other buildings north of Exchange and east of Washington streets. Capt. Johnson had procured of the Indians by gift or purchase two square miles of land at the mouth of Buffalo creek, including a large portion of the territory on which now stands the city of Buffalo. He had also entered into an agreement with the Indians, which amounted to a life lease, of a certain mill site and the timbered land in its vicinity, on condition of supplying the Indians with all the boards and plank they wanted for building at, and near the creek. This site was about six miles east of the mouth of the creek.

Although Johnston's title to this land was not considered to have the least validity, yet the Indians had the power and the inclination to include it within their reservation, unless a compromise was made with Johnston, and taking into consideration his influence with them, the agents of the company concluded to enter into the following agreement with him, which was afterwards fully complied with and performed by both of the parties:—

Jonhston agreed to surrender his right to the said two square miles, and use his influence with the Indians to have that tract and his mill site left out of their reservation, in consideration of which the Holland Company agreed to convey by deed to said Johnston, six hundred and forty acres, including the said mill site and adjacent timbered land; together with forty-five and a half acres, being part of said two square miles, including the buildings and improvements, then owned by said Johnston, four acres of which was to be on the "point." These lands as afterwards definitely located, were a tract of forty one and a half acres, bounded north by Seneca street, west by Washington street, and south by the little Buffalo creek; the other tract was bounded, east by Main street, south-westerly by the Buffalo creek, and north-westerly by little Buffalo creek, containing about four acres. This matter will again be referred to, in connexion with some farther notice of early events in Buffalo.

Mr. Ellicott, before leaving Philadelphia—in the time that intervened between his appointment, and his departure—was actively engaged in making all the necessary preparations for the campaign. David Rittenhouse, the eminent American philosopher, was then of the firm of "Rittenhouse and Potts," mathematical and astronomical instrument makers, in Philadelphia; orders were given them for compasses, chains, and staffs—all things in their line, necessary to surveyor's outfits. Letters were written to Augustus Porter at Canandaigua, to have ready such provisions, pack-horses, axe-men and chainmen, as he had been ordered to provide; to Thomas Morris at the same place, requesting his prompt performance of some agencies that had been entrusted to him; to different persons at New York, Albany, Fort Schuyler, and Queenston, containing orders to facilitate the transportation of stores, and aid the surveying parties in getting upon the ground, and in supplying themselves with all things necessary for going into the woods. All things requisite were remembered, and provided for. Clark and Street, at Chippewa, were ordered to have ready, two yoke of oxen and a stout lumber wagon; (that was undoubtedly the pioneer ox team upon the Holland Purchase, other than such as had been used upon the portage;) even axe handles and tent poles were not forgotten. To each principal surveyor, or sub-agent, starting from Philadelphia or elsewhere, written orders were issued, what route to pursue, where to first rendezvous, where to draw his supplies, and where to commence operations. Formulas were made out for each surveyor, prescribing definitely the manner of his duties, of marking lines, keeping field notes, and generally embracing all the minutiæ of his operations. It was as if the General of an army was acting as his own commissary, and putting a force into the field, distributing it, and making all things ready for a campaign; and the records of our war department would hardly furnish better examples of systematic and well ordered enterprises. Embraced in these preliminary proceedings, was a correspondence with Mr. Williamson in reference to a road from the west branch of the Susquehannah to the "Genesee country;" and with the Surveyor General of this state in reference to the laying out of towns at Lewiston and Fort Schlosser.

Mr. Ellicott arrived at Canandaigua, 12th June, 1798. The reader will best be enabled to catch glimpses of early events— those that attended the surveys, and preceded land sales and the commencement of settlement—by occasional references to, and extracts from his correspondence,— the only existing records.

A letter from Mr. Thompson to Mr. Ellicott, dated at Buffalo creek, states that the stores had all arrived safely at Schlosser, except what had been left with Mr. Brisbane at the "Chenesee" river; that Mr. Hoops, who had arrived in advance of him, had gone on to "Chetawque" * where he had been joined by Mr. Stoddard; that he himself was engaged in getting "axes ground and handled, and in sundry other things preparatory to going to the woods." Letters follow this very soon, by which it would seem that the camp was erected at "Chautauque creek," and all things prepared for active operations, as early as the 19th of June.

Messrs. Smedley and Egleston, were located at Buffalo creek, with surveying parties. In a letter to Mr. Ellicott, written from there, under date, June 27th, Mr. Egleston says the goods have arrived, and that the "family in the house on the hill" are about to move out, to make room for the surveyors. Mr. Ellicott, it would seem, had arrived at Schlosser. Anticipating his arrival at Buffalo, Mr. Egleston, very providently suggests that he had better bring with him some boards to make a mapping table, as there were none to be had in their new location—"Mr. Winne having carried off those that were in the partition."

---

* These are specimens of the early orthography of names of places; not introduced as errors of the writer, for he was well educated, and scientific in his profession.

The two Frenchmen that have been named, made but poor help in the woods. While the other surveyors dashed off in different directions, located their camps, and soon reported themselves to Mr. Ellicott as actively engaged in their duties; making no complaints of hard fare; the Frenchmen were a constant annoyance, making complaints by letter as often as messengers could be found to carry them. Autrechy took up his quarters at "Fort Schlosser," from which place he reports himself to Mr. Ellicott:

"Fort Schlosser, 4th July, 1798.

"This comes to acquaint you that I arrived here this morning, and find an agreeable place, but nothing here to eat or drink. I should be glad to know how I am to be situated for provisions. I request you will let me know on the receipt of this, how I shall be accommodated for these articles. I would be glad to see you here yourself. Should that not be the case, please write me on the receipt of this. I left my companion Mr. Haudecaur at Fort Schlosser, and determined to go by water to take care of the instruments he brought with him.

I am, sir, yours,
ALEX'R AUTRECHY."

Haudecour, in making some surveys at the Falls, on the Canada side, was arrested and detained as a spy, and afterwards by the American commandant at Niagara, upon suspicion that he was a "French emissary." His release in both instances, cost Mr. Ellicott a good deal of trouble.

It may not be uninteresting to the reader to see some account of the first assault and battery that occurred upon the Holland Purchase—our own race being the participants—of which we have any record. The unfortunate French "engineer and surveyor," seems to have had the especial faculty of disagreeing with his woods associates. Mr. Egleston makes the following candid *report* to Mr. Ellicott, of an affray which happened at his quarters. The reader will conclude that he makes out a good *ex parte* justification; a clear case of self-defence, and that not resorted to until he had complied with a portion of the scriptural injunction:—

Joseph Ellicott, Esquire, "Buffalo Creek, Nov. 22, 1798.

Dear Sir,— Yesterday, the 20th, about noon, Mr. Brown and myself walked out and staid a little longer than common dinner time, when we came back, we found that Haudecour had been swearing to the cooks, for not setting the table before we returned. I then came into the office, took up my pen and began to write an order; Haudecour then began with me, he being a little vexed on account of my having sent on his matrass by the wagon, and other little disputes, and at the time of my writing, he put me out with his talking. I told him to go to ——, and not to be bothering me. With this, he gave me a slap on the side of my face, and I turned the other side to him. He struck it a full stroke with his fist. I then perceived that he was in earnest. I caught up the first thing I could see, which happened to be a long walking stick. I retreated back so that I could get a good chance, and I let slip, which hit him on the head with the but end. He came up to me again. By that time I was fast in the corner of the office, without any kind of a weapon to defend myself with, for Mr. Pease had taken the stick from me, and was trying to part us. Whilst the rascal was kicking me with all his might into my body, Mr. Brown then stepped up and we were soon parted. It happened very well for Haudecour that there were none of our hands in the house at the time that the affray happened. This he was well apprised of, for before he offered to strike me, he looked into the kitchen to see if any of them were there. He afterwards paid for it. The business soon got wind, and the hands that were at work in the neighborhood quickly came up. The old fellow was soon hustled out of the house, and he marched over to Palmer's. There was not one in the party but who wished to get the first stroke at him. I told them not to strike him, but to let him go about his business. The letters you gave me for him, when you went from here, I never have copied, on account of his coming in so quick after you went out. When he saw the letter lying on the desk, he took it up and has since detained it, though I have often asked him for it in the hearing of Mr. Pease, and he has as often promised me that he had no objection to my copying the letter, and would let me have it by and by. But God knows that he has not done any thing since he came from Schlosser, only wasting of paper. He says he will give you the the letter when he gets to your quarters. Mr. Brown was witness to the business.

I am, sir, with the greatest respect, your hbl. servt,
GEORGE EGLESTON.

It would appear that Mr. Ellicott was not long in discovering that he (or their general agent in Philadelphia,) had made a bad selection of men in these two instances, with reference to their adaptation to life in the wilderness, and the surveyors' camp; their stay was short. We hear no more of Haudecour, after the affray at Buffalo, except the allusion to him and his associate, in a letter to Mr. Ellicott from J. G. Van Staphorst, a connection of one of the Dutch proprietors, who had been upon the Purchase at that early day. The letter is dated at "Oldenbarneveldt," (Oneida county,) November 19th, 1798. The extract is as follows:—"Mr. Autrechy took a sketch of Cazenovia, at Mr. Linklaen's, and is now busy at that of Oldenbarneveldt; but is prevented by the badness of the roads from going to the Black river. I think I shall ged rid, however, of his agreeable company; and really I wont be sorry for it. How does the other noble engineer, at Fort Schlosser? has he finished yet his canal? and how did he digest your last letter from Buffalo creek, before we departed from there? I am anxious to hear all that from yourself before I get to Philadelphia."*

---

* The only clue the author can get to the objects of surveys at the Falls, is contained in the above extract. The inference is, that Mr. Cazenove, as an incipient measure upon the Holland Purchase, had employed the French engineers to make some tests of the practicability of a canal around the Falls. In a letter to Mr. Ellicott, Haudecour informs him that he had finished taking the levels upon Gill creek.

Of these Pioneer adventurers one still survives,—JAMES BRISBANE, Esq. of Batavia, long known as an active, enterprising, business man; and even now, vigorous in mind and body, superintending a large estate, incident to which is a leading participation in a rail-road direction. He is the oldest living resident of the Holland Purchase,—or in other words, there is no person now living, who came in at as early a period of survey and settlement.*

To him the author is indebted for some reminiscences of the primitive advent. The party started from Philadelphia in April, 1798, taking different routes; Mr. Thompson, the principal in this expedition, and Mr. Brisbane, coming by the way of New York, with the stores and surveyor's instruments, and camp equipage.† When the batteaux with which they had came from Schenectady, arrived at the mouth of the Genesee river, the stores, &c. were divided, Mr. Thompson proceeding by the way of Niagara river, to Buffalo with a part of them, designed for use in the western portion of the Purchase; and Mr. Brisbane taking charge of the remainder to convey upon the eastern part of the Purchase, took them over the portage at the Genesee falls, and up the Genesee river to Williamsburg, where a surveyor's store house was just established.

It having heretofore been observed that an influence was exerted in Canada, detrimental to the progress of early settlement upon the Holland Purchase, it is but justice here to remark, that Mr. Ellicott upon his arrival here, found in no quarter more cordial coöperation and friendly offices, than he met at the hands of some of the prominent men upon the other side of the river. Among them were Judge Hamilton at Queenston, Clark & Street at Chippewa, Mr. Douglass the merchant, and Col. Warren the commandant at Fort Erie. In all their correspondence with Mr E., they seem to have wished well to the enterprise in which he was engaged, and to have considered rightly that the interest of their locality was to be vastly benefitted by the

---

* The statement is thus qualified, in consideration of the fact, that Judge Cook of Lewiston, whose name has been already introduced, came in the year previous — yet he was attached to the garrison at Niagara, and had at first, no identity with survey or settlement; though, as will be seen in subsequent pages, his father's family and himself, were early pioneer settlers.

† Mr. Brisbane mentions the fact that Mr. Thompson, had, previous to this advent, while connected with Andrew Ellicott in surveys in the neighborhood of Presque Isle, constructed a sail-boat there, with which he and others, had made the journey to Philadelphia, via Niagara Falls, Oswego, Oneida lake, and New York. It was considered so remarkable an adventure, that the boat was put up in Independence Square, and kept as a show until it rotted down.

settlement and improvement of this region. It will have been observed that Capt. Bruff, the commandant at Fort Niagara, had early intimated to the Indians, the necessity of opening a road from Lewiston to Tonawanda village. Judge Hamilton and a Mr. Canby at Queenston, followed up this suggestion by an early coöperation with Mr. Ellicott, in measures to secure the desirable object.

The first principal stations of the surveyors—their head quarters or depots—were at Buffalo creek and Williamsburgh; before the close of 1798, however, the principal establishment was located at the Transit line, (Stafford,) the locality designated as "Transit store house;" Mr. James Brisbane, moving his quarters from Williamsburgh, continued as the principal clerk or agent. While upon the Purchase in 1798, Mr. Ellicott's time was principally spent at Buffalo creek, Williamsburgh, and upon the eastern Transit line.

In the spring of 1798, when the surveys of the Holland Purchase first commenced, all the travel between the Phelps and Gorham tract and Buffalo was on the old Indian trail; the winter previous, however, the legislature of this state passed an act appointing Charles Williamson a commissioner, to lay out and open a state road from Cannewagus on Genesee river to Buffalo creek on lake Erie, and to Lewiston on the Niagara river. To defray the expense of cutting out these roads, the Holland Company subscribed five thousand dollars. Mr. Williamson laid out and established the roads in 1798, generally adhering to the course of old Indian trails; but they were not opened throughout according to contract, under his superintendence. The first wagon track opened upon the Holland Purchase, was by Mr. Ellicott, as a preliminary step in commencing operations, early in the season of '98. He employed a gang of hands to improve the Indian trail, so that wagons could pass upon it, from the east transit to Buffalo creek. In 1801 he opened the road from transit line as far west as Vandeventer's. The whole road was opened to Le Roy before the close of 1802.*

But little reference can be had to the order of time in noting the events of this period; up to the period of the commencement of land sales and settlements, our sketches must necessarily be desultory.

The Hon. NATHANIEL W. HOWELL of Canandaigua, was, as early as this season (1798) Mr. Ellicott's legal adviser, in several

---

* Not wholly upon the present route. The first road opened, was from Batavia, via Dunham's Openings, &c., coming out at Vandeventer's.

matters connected with his primitive duties. Some embarrassment occurring connected with the Indian reservation at Cattaragus, he gave him, by letter, his legal opinion. This circumstance is noted principally, to observe, that the author has before him the paper above referred to, and a recent letter from the same hand, written plainly and legibly, and evincing a memory, and an intellect generally, vigorous and unimpaired. Fifty years intervene between the dates of the two letters. There are but few instances of so extended a period of active participation in the affairs of life; and still fewer instances of a life that has so adorned the profession to which he belongs, and been as eminently useful and exemplary. To him, and to such as him—his early cotemporary, for instance— Gen. VINCENT MATTHEWS, (and others of his cotemporaries that could be named,) is the highly honorable profession of the law, in Western New York, indebted for early and long continued examples of those high aims, dignity, and exalted integrity, which should be its chief and abiding characteristics. They have passed, and are passing away. If days of degeneracy should come upon the profession—renovation become necessary—there are no better precedents and examples to consult, than the lives and practice of the pioneer lawyers.

Mr. Brisbane first saw Buffalo, in October, 1798. There was then the log house of Middaugh and Lane — a double log house — about two squares from Main street, a little north of the present line of Exchange street. Capt Johnston's half log and half framed house, stood a little east of the main building of the present Mansion House, near Washington street. There was a two story hewed log house, owned by Capt. Johnston, about where Exchange street now is, from six to eight rods west of Main street, where a tavern was kept by John Palmer. This was the first tavern in Buffalo. Palmer afterwards moved over to Canada, and kept a tavern there. Asa Ransom lived in a log house west of Western Hotel. Winne had a log house on bank of Little Buffalo, south of Mansion House. A Mr. Maybee, who afterwards went to Cattaragus, kept a little Indian store in a log building on west side of Main street, about twenty rods north of Exchange street. There was also a log house occupied by a man by the name of Robbins. The flats were open ground; a portion of them had been cultivated. Such was Buffalo — and all of Buffalo — in 1798.

Aaron Burr, and Alexander Hamilton, were in '98, both contractors for lands west of the Genesee river; the former for a tract upon the Holland Purchase. The following letter would indicate that Mr. Burr, regarded himself at its date, a land proprietor in this region:—

"Sir— 5 May, '98.
From the copy which you lately sent me of Mr. Ellicott's survey, it appears that the Tonawanta Bay falls within my tract on lake Ontario. If this Bay is as large as hath been represented to me, it ought not to be estimated as land, because it cannot belong to your company, and after any sale, will still be the property of the public. It will be necessary therefore, that Mr. Ellicott ascertain the figure and superficial contents of this Bay, which will enable us to determine the propriety of considering it as land.
I am, respectfully, your obd't serv't,
Th. Cazenove, Esq'r   A. BURR.

Mr. Burr had made the contract for the purchase of the tract, at twelve shillings per acre, at an early period of Holland Company ownership. The transaction was blended with other land speculations, and eventually the purchase was abandoned. Out of it, however, had originated a bond for twenty thousand dollars, which was given up. The surrendering of the bond gave rise to reports that Col. Burr had been bribed by the agents of the Holland Company, to favor the passage of the alien bill in our state legislature; the one allowing foreigners to hold real estate. John B. Church, Esq. had in some way identified himself with this report. He received a challenge from Col. Burr; the parties met at Hoboken, exchanged an ineffectual shot; Mr. Church apologized; and thus ended the land speculation and the duel. *

The project of a town upon the Niagara river was early entertained by the public authorities of this state. The following letter from the Surveyor General had preceded Mr. Ellicott's

---

Note.—The tract must have been located in what is now Orleans county, and the mouth or "Bay" of Oak Orchard creek, must have been called "Tonawanta Bay," from the fact that the stream heads principally in the Tonawanda swamp.

* A good anecdote however, came of it. Judge Burke of South Carolina, was Col. Burr's second. "Previous to leaving the city of New York, Colonel Burr presented to Judge Burke his pistol-case. He explained to the Judge, that the balls were cast intentionally too small; that chamois leather was cut to the proper size, to put round them, but that the leather must be greased (for which purpose, grease was placed in the case,) or that there would be difficulty in getting the ball home. After the parties had taken their stand, Colonel Burr noticed the Judge hammering the ramrod with a stone, and immediately suspected the cause. When the pistol was handed him by his friend, he drew the ramrod, and ascertained that the ball was not home, and so informed the Judge; to which Mr. Burke replied, 'I forgot to grease the leather; but you see he is ready, don't keep him waiting; *just take a crack as it is; and I'll grease the next.*' Colonel Burr bowed courteously, but made no reply, and discharged his pistol in the state it had been given to him. The anecdote for some time after, was the subject of merriment among those who had heard it."— *Davis' Life of Burr.*

arrival. He recommended Lewiston as the site, and complied generally with the requirements of the letter.

Sir—   "Albany, 24th May, 1798.

Being directed by our legislature to make out and report the plan of a town to be erected in the most convenient place along the Niagara river, where the Indian title has been extinguished, I have to request the favor of you, while you are in that country, to examine where such town can be most conveniently placed, and to furnish me with a survey and map thereof, together with your ideas of the most eligible manner of laying it out into streets, lots &c., as directed by the law enacted for that purpose.

The expense of such survey, I shall pay to your order.

I am with respect, Sir, your obd't serv't,

Mr. Joseph Ellicott.   S. DE WITT."

The first crops raised upon the Holland Purchase, were at the Transit Store House. In the spring of '99, Mr. James Dewey was waiting there with a gang of hands, to start upon a surveying expedition as soon as the weather would permit. At the request of Mr. Brisbane, he cleared ten acres upon either side of the present road, twenty rods west of the Transit, which was mainly sowed with oats, though some potatoes and garden vegetables were planted. The early tavern keeper there—Mr. Walthers—reported by letter to Mr. Ellicott, that the yield was a good one, and fully demonstrated the goodness of the soil of the region he was surveying for settlement.

In the summer of 1799, there not being a house erected on the road from the eastern Transit line to Buffalo, Mr. Busti, the Agent General of the company, authorized Mr. Ellicott by a letter dated June 1st, 1799, to contract with six reputable individuals, to locate themselves on the road from the eastern Transit to Buffalo creek, about ten miles asunder, and open houses of entertainment for travelers, at their several locations, in consideration of which, they were to have a quantity of land, from fifty to one hundred and fifty acres each, "at a liberal time for payment, without interest, at the lowest price the Company will sell their lands, when settlements shall be begun."

Three persons accepted of this offer, to wit, Frederick Walthers who was then residing on the land, took one hundred and fifty acres in township number twelve, range one, west of and adjoining the eastern Transit, including the Company's store house, and being where the village of Stafford now stands. Asa Ransom located himself Sept. 1st, 1799, on one hundred and fifty acres, in township number twelve, range six, at what is now known as Ransom's

Grove, or Clarence Hollow. Garritt Davis located himself Sept. 16th, 1799, in township number thirteen, range two, on one hundred and fifty acres on the south line of said township, and east of and adjoining the Tonawanda Indian Reservation, (the Buffalo road then run through the reservation, some distance north of its present location.) These lots were severally laid out and surveyed for the purchasers, before the several townships in which they are located, were surveyed. These three persons erected and 'furnished comfortable houses for the purposes intended, as soon as practicable; which although not as splendid, yet were more eagerly sought, and cheerfully enjoyed by the forest traveler and land explorer, than any of the "Astor Houses," "Americans," or "Eagles" of the present day.

With the exception of those residing at Buffalo, Mrs. Garrett Davis and Mrs. Walthers, were the pioneer women upon the Holland Purchase. In 1800, Asa Ransom and Garrett Davis raised summer crops, which were second to those raised at the Transit Store House the year before.

Next to Messrs. Brisbane and Cook, Gen. TIMOTHY HOPKINS of Amherst, Erie county, has been longest a resident upon the Holland Purchase. He became a settler in March, 1799; his first business was the management of Johnston's saw mill. In company with Otis Ingalls, he cleared land two miles east of Clarence Hollow and raised wheat upon it in 1800—the first raised upon the Holland Purchase. The wheat was ground at Street's mill at the Falls. The General speaks of making an expensive trip to mill, the ferriage for his three yoke of oxen at Black Rock, being twenty shillings each way; O'Neil, an Irishman, kept the ferry, the only resident there. He built a framed house for Elias Ransom, seven miles east of Buffalo, which he thinks was the first framed building west of Batavia. It is now standing, and forms the rear of the dwelling house of a German settler, whose name is Baer. Mr. Ransom built the first framed barn, and set out the first orchard upon Holland Purchase. Douglass' store at Fort Erie furnished the glass and nails used by the first settlers. When the settlement first commenced, Fort Erie was garrisoned by a company of British soldiers.

Gen. Hopkins is now seventy-two years old; a fine specimen of hale, hearty, and contented old age. If one should see him who was not acquainted with the history of the Holland Purchase, and should be told that he had witnessed its entire conversion from a wilderness to what it is now, he would be incredulous, or regard either the country or the man a miracle. He has been the father of ten children, five of whom are married and settled upon the Purchase. Nelson K. Hopkins, Esq., of Buffalo, and T. A. Hopkins, the present sheriff of Erie county, are his sons. Mrs. Hopkins, whom he married in 1805, died in 1848.

The General says that Mr. Thompson, the surveyor, built the first saw mill at Williamsville in 1801; and the first dwelling house there; a block house, which has been clapboarded, and is still standing.

Our old friend, Mountpleasant, speaks of the advent of the Holland Company surveyors—the brisk times it made; he had seen previously but few white people, other than soldiers and emigrants to Canada. As soon as the surveyors had taken possession of "Bill Johnston's house at Buffalo creek," he applied to them for employment, and was axe-man for one of the parties the first season. He says that Mr. Ellicott used to be called the "Surveyor General." Whiskey distilleries in early times were quite sure to follow settlement, but seldom preceded it. There was a distillery at Schlosser, while the country was in possession of the British; so says Mountpleasant; and one of the first applications that Mr. Ellicott had for lands, came from one who dated his letter at Schlosser, and wished to turn out a copper still as the advance payment.

The following vivid description of a tornado, on the Alleghany, is contained in a letter from Benjamin to Joseph Ellicott, dated, "Camp, twenty-one and a half miles north of Pennsylvania line, July 29, 1799."

"While on the south side of the Allegany, we had small showers almost every day, but after crossing the river no rain fell till the 25th. I was at the Vista, in order to see if Mr. Cary was cutting in a right direction at 21½ miles, (the place that my camp is at present,) when the thunder sounded from a distance, the clouds ascended, and I saw through the instrument the trees bend on the mountains, to the north, (distance four miles,) but soon became obscured. I now prepared to receive it,—stripping from the hemlock the bark that had inclosed it for ages, which I placed against an old log, I crept under, when the rain came in torrents, the lightning flashed, thunder roared incessant, wind tearing from the sturdy trees their boughs, and dislocating others that had stood for many years apart, as if war had been declared against the forest; but at last the lightning ceased to glare, the thunder to sound terrific, and rain to fall in such abundance. I now crept out of my obscure but serviceable tenement, and cast my eyes along the avenue to the north, saw the mountain smoke with the late deluge, (the avenue on the south side of Allegany still invisible,) I returned to camp (distance one mile,) the surface of the mountain covered with water foaming down every crevice, in cascades, till it found rest in the valleys below.

No part of the world can boast of a purer air than this place, and but few biting insects. The camp is at present on the top of a high hill or mountain, near a good spring."

Extract from a letter from Joseph Ellicott to Paul Busti, dated, New Amsterdam, July 15th, 1799:—

"Our business regarding surveys, &c., is progressing with all dispatch, although the season is somewhat unfavorable on account of the abundance of wet weather. I expect to have six settlers placed on the road before I leave the woods. I have already had a great number of applications for those situations, and I intend to select such as I conceive the best calculated for the several stands.

"It is with pleasure I can add, that myself and all the people in the Genesee Purchase in the Company's employ, continue in good health, which blessing may you and your family long enjoy."

Extract of a letter from Paul Busti to Joseph Ellicott, dated Philadelphia, 15th August, 1800:—

"The opening of the communication through the country, is a matter deemed of such importance, that it will not escape your attention, that the application of money for that purpose has been appropriated on a much larger scale than you thought necessary. By extending the amount of expenditures on that head, I mean to evince to you how much I am persuaded of the usefulness of having practicable roads cut out. The benefits of them being not only confined to the lands on which the present settlement is to be undertaken, but to those on which the two million acre tracts which afterwards are to be sold. You will have to take care that the roads to be laid out at present, are to be cut in such a direction as to become of general advantage to the whole country. The knowledge you possess of it will teach you where your attention ought to be most particularly directed. As I am speaking of roads, it will not be amiss to add a recommendation to you, that in making choice of the spot on which your office and residence is to be fixed, you will select a situation of an easy and convenient approach, so as to induce the emigrants to visit you."

In Nov. 26th, 1800, Mr. Ellicott was at Albany on his way west, from which place he informs Mr. Busti by letter, that he had issued handbills, offering a part of the Holland Company lands for sale, and that he is informed that many purchasers are awaiting his arrival. On the 17th of Dec. he had arrived at Canandaigua, from which place he writes Mr. Busti that he is informed that land sales in that region were brisk, the sales of the season having amounted to more than in any five seasons preceding.

A portion of the handbill to which Mr. Ellicott alludes is copied. The issuing of it was the important step in the commencement of the settlement of the Purchase:—

HOLLAND LAND COMPANY WEST GENESEO LANDS–INFORMATION.

The Holland Land Company will open a Land Office in the ensuing month of September, for the sale of a portion of their valuable lands in the Genesee country, State of New York, situate in the last purchase made of the Seneca Nation of Indians, on the western side of Genesee river. For the convenience of applicants, the Land Office will be established near the centre of the lands, intended for sale and on the main road, leading from the Eastern and Middle States to Upper Canada, Presque Isle in Pennsylvania, and the Connecticut Reserve. Those lands are situate, adjoining and contiguous, to the lakes Erie, Ontarie, and the streights of Niagara, possessing the advantage of the navigation and trade of all the Upper lakes, as well as the river Saint Lawrence, (from which the British settlements derive great advantage,) also intersected by the Allegany river, navigable for boats of 30 or 40 tons burthen, to Pittsburgh and New Orleans, and contiguous to the navigable waters of the west branch of the Susquehannah river, and almost surrounded by settlements, where provision of every kind is to be had in great abundance and on reasonable terms, renders the situation of the Holland Land Company Geneseo Lands more eligible, desirous, and advantageous for settlers than any other unsettled tract of inland country of equal magnitude in the United States. The greater part of this tract is finely watered (few exceptions) with never failing springs and streams, affording sufficiency of water for gristmills and other water works. The subscriber, during the years 1798 and 1799, surveyed and laid off the whole of these lands into townships, a portion of which, to accommodate purchasers and settlers, is now laying off into lots and tracts from 120 acres and upwards, to the quantity contained in a township.

The lands abound with limestone, and are calculated to suit every description of purchasers and settlers. Those who prefer land timbered with black and white oak, hickory, poplar, chestnut, wild cherry, butternut, and dogwood, or the more luxuriant timbered with basswood or lynn, butternut, sugar-tree, white ash, wild cherry, cucumber tree, (a species of the magnolia,) and black walnut, may be suited. Those who prefer level land, or gradually ascending, affording extensive plains and valleys, will find the country adapted to their choice. In short, such are the varieties of situations in this part of the Geneseo country, every where almost covered with a rich soil, that it is presumed that all purchasers who may be inclined to participate in the advantages of those lands, may select lots from 120 acres to tracts containing 100,000 acres, that would fully please and satisfy their choice. The Holland Land Company, whose liberality is so well known in this country, now offer to all those who may wish to become partakers of the growing value of those lands, such portions and such parts as they may think proper to purchase. Those who may choose to pay cash will find a liberal discount from the credit price.

CHAPTER II.

BIOGRAPHICAL SKETCHES — GENERAL AND LOCAL AGENTS OF THE HOLLAND COMPANY.

THEOPHILUS CAZENOVE.

He was the first General Agent of the Holland Company. Little is known of his personal history. When the Company made their first purchases of lands in the interior of this state, and Pennsylvania,— soon after 1790— he had arrived in this country, and acted as their agent. In all the negotiations, and preliminary proceedings, connected with the large purchase of Mr. Morris, of this region, the interests of the Company were principally confided to him. His name is intimately blended with the whole history of the title. When the purchase was perfected, he was made the General Agent, and under his auspices the surveys commenced. The author can only judge of him from such manuscript records as came from his hands. They exhibit good business qualifications, and great integrity of purpose. In all the embarrassments that attended the perfection of the title, he would seem to have been actuated by honorable and praiseworthy motives; and to have assisted with a good deal of ability, the legal managers of the Company's interests.

He returned to Europe in 1799, ending then his connection with the Company. His residence for a considerable period after this, was in London, after which, it was in Paris, where he died.

PAUL BUSTI.

He was a native of Milan, in Italy; was born on the 17th of October, 1749. After receiving his education in his native country, he entered the counting house of his uncle in Amsterdam, where he afterwards established himself in business, married, and acquired a high reputation for business talents, industry and integrity.

About retiring from commercial life, and connected with one who was interested in the Holland Company Purchase, he was induced to accept the General Agency at Philadelphia, in the place of Mr. Cazenove; aud most faithfully and satisfactorily did he perform its duties, for a period of twenty-four years,—up to the day of his death, July 23, 1824. He left no children.

The author will here make a remark which is applicable not only to the general, but the local agents of the Holland Company. Of all that men leave behind them, after having been actively engaged in the affairs of this life, there is nothing that affords better tests of their characters and motives, than their private correspondence. It is here, that, in all the familiarity and confidence of private friendships — a necessary mutual reliance is indulged in — men are prone to throw off all disguise, and disclose the real motives by which they are governed. If indeed, they even here attempt the practice of concealment, it is seldom successful; what they would conceal will in some form or other, escape their precaution, and demonstrate itself.

Few opportunities could be as ample for applying this test as those the author has enjoyed, connected with the entire agencies of the Holland Company. He has had free access to the great mass of correspondence that passed between general and local agents: much of it was private and confidential. And from such evidences, he is prepared to say, that few enterprises have ever been conducted upon more honorable principles, than was that which embraced the purchase, sale and settlement of the Holland Purchase. In all the instructions of the general to the local agents, the interests of the settlers, the prosperity of the country were made secondary in but a slight degree, to the securing to their principals, a fair and reasonable return for their investments. The general policy adopted, its ultimate results, it will occur to speak of in another place; but here it may be remarked — and it is no greater praise than the historian is fully authorized to bestow—

PAUL BUSTI.

that which should not be withheld,—that in the entire history of settlement and improvement in our widely extended country, large tracts of the wilderness have no where fallen into the hands of individuals—become subject to private or associate cupidity— where the aggregate result has been more favorable, or advantageous to the settlers.

The original proprietors—the eleven who constituted the primitive Holland Company—were merchants in the city of Amsterdam, (then in the Republic of Batavia.) They had little of the spirit of speculation; had acquired wealth by regular approaches to it; by careful investments and fair profits. They had spare capital and wished to invest it; their highest anticipations were perhaps, a realization of something near the per cent. interest which was generally fixed upon money in this country, instead of the then low per cent. that money yielded in Europe. And here it may be remarked, that considering the period of investment—1792 and '93—but ten years after the close of the war of the Revolution— these Dutch merchants were far in advance of the prevailing sentiment in Europe, as to the success and permanency of the experiment of free government. We should respect their memories for such an earnest, at that early period, of confidence in the stability of our system.

Mr. Busti's agency, as it will be observed, commenced before the completion of surveys and the opening of sales; consequently it was under his auspices that settlement began. In his early instructions to Mr. Ellicott, he proposed liberal measures—seems to have started upon the basis that the interests of his principals and the interests of the settlers were mutual. While he guarded strictly and with rigid economy, the one, his views and his munificence were liberal, in reference to the other. Mr. Ellicott acted under general instructions from him, as to the opening of roads, building of mills and public buildings; but when he advised, as he often did, additional measures of improvement, or increased outlays, he was quite sure to be seconded by his principal.

Next to Mr. Ellicott, Mr. Busti was more closely identified with the settlement of the Holland Purchase, than any other individual; his administration of the General Agency, embraced almost the entire period of pioneer settlement. The author knows little of his personal history. Saving the period of his mercantile enterprise in Amsterdam, the active years of his life were spent in the General Agency of the Holland Company; the records of that company, therefore, are his principal history. They furnish conclusive evidence of clear judgement, industry, great integrity of purpose, and a disposition to promote the interest of his principals, and the prosperity of that region of wilderness he was assisting to settle and improve.

The following anecdote, which the author introduces as a note, answers the double purpose of getting a glimpse of the personal character of the General Agent, and of furnishing a succinct history of church benefices upon the Holland Purchase. The reader will bear in mind that Mr. Busti was a Catholic; and a liberal one it will be conceded, in view of his dislike of sectarianism.

NOTE.—In the fall of 1820, Mr. Busti was visiting the land office in Batavia; the Rev. Mr. R. of the Presbyterian sect called on Mr. Busti and insisted on a donation of land for each society of his persuasion, then formed on the Holland Purchase. Mr. Busti treated the Rev. gentleman with due courtesy, but showed no disposition to grant his request. Mr. R. encouraged by Mr. Busti's politeness, persevered in his solicitations, day after day, until Mr. Busti's patience was almost exhausted, and what finally brought that subject to a crisis was, Mr. R's following Mr. Busti out of the land office, when he was going to take tea at Mr. Ellicott's and making a fresh attack on him in the piazza. Mr. Busti was evidently vexed, and in reply said "Yes, Mr. R. I will give a tract of one hundred acres, to a religious society in every town on the Purchase, and this is *finis.*" "But" said Mr. R. "you will give it all to the Presbyterians, will you not; if you do not expressly so decide, the *Sectarians* will be claiming it, and *we* shall receive very little benefit from it." "Sectarians, no" was Mr. Busti's hasty reply, I abhor sectarians, they had not ought to have any of it, and to save contention, I will give it to the first religious society in every town." On which Mr. Busti hastened to his tea, and Mr. R. home (about sixteen miles distant) to start runners during the night or the next morning, to rally the Presbyterians in the several towns in his vicinity to apply first, and thereby secure the land to themselves.

The land office was soon flooded with petitions for land from societies organized according to law and empowered to hold real estate and those who were not, one of which was presented to Mr. Busti before he left, directed to "General Poll Busti," on which he insisted that it could not be from a religious society, for all religious societies read their bibles and know that *P o* double *l,* does not spell Paul. Amidst this chaos of applications, it was thought to be unadvisable to be precipitant, in granting those donations, the whole responsibility now resting on Mr. Ellicott to comply with this vague promise of Mr. Busti; therefore conveyances of the "gospel land" were not executed for some space of time, notwithstanding the clamor of petitioners for "deeds of our land" during which time the matter was taken into consideration and systematized, so far as such an operation could be, pains was taken to ascertain the merits of each application, and finally a tract, or tracts of land, not exceeding one hundred acres in all, was granted, free of expense, to one or more religious societies regularly organized according to law, in each town on the purchase, where the Company had land undisposed of, which embraced every town then organized on the purchase, except Bethany, Genesee county, and Sheldon, Wyoming county, the donees always being allowed to select out of the unsold farming land in each town. In some towns it was all given to one society, in others to two or three societies, separately, and in a few towns to four different societies of different sects, twenty-five acres to each.

In performing this thankless duty, for the land was claimed as an absolute right by most of the applicants, the whole proceedings were so managed, under Mr. Ellicott's judicious directions, that amidst all the clamor and contention which, from its nature such a proceeding must elicit, no complaint of partiality to any particular sect, nor of the undue weight of influence in any individual was ever charged against the agent of the Company or his assistants acting under him.

J. J. VANDERKEMP.

JOHN J. VANDER KEMP.

This gentleman was the successor of Mr. Busti, entering upon the duties of general agent on the day of the death of his predecessor. He is a native of the city of Leyden, in the kingdom of Holland. His parents emigrated to the United States in 1788, and settled upon the Hudson, near Esopus, Kingston, Ulster county, New York. In 1794 the family changed their residence to the shores of Oneida lake, and soon after, to Oldenbarnevelt, in the town of Trenton, now Oneida county, where they enjoyed the society of Col. A. G. Mappa's family who were likewise emigrants from Holland, and of Mr. Gerrit Boon, who had commenced a settlement on the lands of the Company in the then county of Herkimer, simultaneously with the commencement of another settlement about forty-five miles above Utica, by Col. John Linklaen, late of Cazenovia, Madison county. Col. Mappa having succeeded Mr. Boon in the land agency, Mr. Vander Kemp, early in life, entered the office as a clerk, succeeding H. J. Huidekoper, Esq., now of Meadville, Pennsylvania, who was appointed chief clerk in the office of the General Agency in Philadelphia. In 1804 Mr. Huidekoper accepted the agency of the Holland Company's lands in Pennsylvania, went to the Alleghany river, and Mr. Vander Kemp was called to occupy the situation vacated by him. He continued to occupy this position, until the death of Mr. Busti, in 1824, when he succeded him in the General Agency; having been before provisionally appointed as successor in case of resignation or death. Thus, as chief clerk, and General Agent, he has been connected with the affairs of the Holland Purchase of Western New York, from 1804 to the present period; or rather, was, until the final disposal of its interest.

As in the case of his immediate predecessor, he has little personal history beyond the records of the General Agency. In succeeding Mr. Busti, he seems to have adopted his policy, and made him his pattern of strict integrity, and careful and judicious management. All that the author has seen coming from his hands; his correspondence, and business papers generally, are indicative of a high degree of business talents, and a matured and excellent judgment. He is well entitled to a full share of the encomium that has been already awarded, in the abstract, to the conduct of the General and Local Agencies.

Those who have enjoyed a personal acquaintance with Mr. Vander Kemp, give him the praise of great amiability of character, intelligence, and fine social qualities.

The early clerk in the office of the General Agency, and the after General Agent,—one thus identified with almost the entire history of this region, is yet a resident of Philadelphia, in the enjoyment of a competency of wealth, and what is far better, the respect and esteem of his fellow citizens, and a numerous circle of acquaintance, beyond his immediate locality, acquired in the course of an extended and active life.

JOSEPH ELLICOTT.

His history is so intimately blended with our main subject, that little beyond personal biography, is required in a separate form. No man has ever, perhaps, been so closely identified with the history of any region, as he is with the history of the Holland Purchase. He was not only the land agent, superintending from the start, surveys and settlement—exercising locally, a one man power and influence—but for a long period, he was far more than this. In all the early years of settlement, especially—in all things having reference to the organization of towns, counties, erection of public buildings, the laying out of roads, the establishment of Post Offices—in all that related to the convenience and prosperity of the region over which his agency extended—he occupied a prominent position, a close identity, that few, if any Patroons of new settlements have ever attained.

His portrait—appropriately, as will be conceded—is made the frontispiece to our local annals; and the author congratulates himself, that the skill of the artists, has enabled him to present to the pioneers of the Holland Purchase, so correct a likeness of their old intimate acquaintance.

The physiognomist, or the more modern professor of the philosophy of intellect and its developments, will not fail to discover, in the head and face presented, quite enough to attract his attention. There is the ample forehead, the clear and expressive eye, the compressed lip, the whole contour of the face, indicative of no ordinary man. Chance made him the founder of new settlements, the ruling spirit of backwoods enterprise, and high achievements in the work of progress and improvement. Had it cast his lot elsewhere, given to him other pursuits, other fields of action, his career would not have been one of mediocrity.

The ancestors of Mr. Ellicott, were Andrew Ellicott and Ann Bye Ellicott, natives of the town of Cullopton, in Wales. They came to this country in the year 1731. Andrew, who was a member of the society of Friends, had married Ann, who was not of that society; had committed an offence against the discipline of the society, termed "marrying out of Friends' meeting." He was "disowned." Deeming himself unjustly dealt by — alienated from religious and social ties — he resolved on emigration to the new world, the refuge of the persecuted of church and state. Tradition awards to Andrew, the brief but comprehensive eulogy, "He was a man of high character in every respect — one indeed, of nature's noblemen." To Ann, the praise of being a "woman of great goodness — worthy of her husband."* The adventurers, with an infant son, landed in New York with what, in those times, was deemed a "considerable estate," purchased a tract of new land, and settled upon it.

We here lose sight of the family and their history for a long period. Previous to 1760, however, they had become residents of Buck's county in Pennsylvania; and had four sons, the elder of whom, about that period, were starting out upon business enterprizes. From some dates in the author's possession, he is disposed to conclude that the stay in New York was a short one, as it would appear that they were pioneers of Buck's county. The sons of these pioneer adventurers were, Nathaniel, Joseph, Andrew, and John. As early as 1770, they purchased a tract of wild land on the Patapsco, in Maryland, and erecting mills and machinery, became the founders of what was long known as "Ellicott's Mills," now, for the sake of brevity, termed "Ellicotts."

Joseph was the father of the subject of this memoir. He was a man of large scientific attainments, and possessed uncommon genius

---

* And a poetess withal, as the following relic witnesses. It was written on her departure from Wales:—

> "Through rocks and sands,
> And enemies' hands,
> And perils of the deep,
> Father and son
> From Cullopton,
> The Lord preserve and keep.—1731."

in the mechanic arts.* His sons, other than Joseph, were Andrew, Benjamin, and David.

Andrew the eldest son, became an eminent surveyor; surveyed the Spanish boundary line under the administration of Mr. Jefferson; was afterwards Surveyor General of the United States; and died the Professor of Mathematics at West Point, in 1820 or '1. While engaged in the survey of the Spanish boundary, he wrote a "Journal," which was published in a quarto form, and which alone would entitle its author to a high rank among the literary and scientific men of his period. It was an early and successful essay to make the people of the United States acquainted with the climate, soil, topography, and vast resources of the country acquired by the Louisiana treaty. He enjoyed the friendship and intimacy of Mr. Jefferson. His three sons, were Andrew A., John B. and Joseph, who all became residents of the Holland Purchase. Andrew A., the eldest, became a resident at Shelby, Orleans county, where he died, and where his descendants now reside. Joseph, a resident of Batavia, where he died in 1839, leaving a family, who are still residing there. John B., the only surviving son, is a resident at Ellicott's Mills, six miles west of Batavia. One of his daughters married the Hon. Henry Baldwin, Judge of the Supreme Court of the United States; another, Major Bliss of the army, and another, Major Douglass of the army; a third was the wife of Thomas Kennedy Esq., of Meadville, Pennsylvania; a fourth, of Dr. Nathaniel E. Griffith of New York; a fifth, was the wife of the late Dr. Woodruff, of Batavia.

BENJAMIN ELLICOTT, as will have been seen, entered the service of the Holland Company at an early period, as the assistant of his brother Joseph. He was at an early period, one of the Judges of Genesee county, and a Representative in Congress, from the district. He was a bachelor; died a resident at Williamsville, Erie county, in 1827.

The younger brother, David, a somewhat erratic genius, was in

---

*A very decided evidence of his skill and ingenuity, is furnished in a clock of his construction, now in the possession of the Hon. David E. Evans, his grandson. The admirers of mechanical ingenuity — good judges — have pronounced it the climax of that branch of the mechanic arts. It has four faces, each looking towards the cardinal points of the compass. One face tells the time of day — another exhibits an orrery, and on it are displayed the motions of the heavenly bodies in perfect order; a third face exhibits a display of musical bells, formed to play twenty-four distinct tunes, one for each hour; the remaining face exposes to view the whole internal machinery of the instrument.

some of the earliest years, a surveyor upon the Purchase. He went south, and no tidings ever came of him.

There were five sisters, three of whom married three brothers, by the name of Evans. In this circumstance, the reader will find the explanation of the numerous heirs of Joseph Ellicott, bearing that name.

With Ellicott's Mills, Baltimore — Howard county, in fact,— the family of Ellicotts were as much identified, as with the Holland Purchase. In the local annals of that region, they figure as early millers, iron founders, builders of wharves, inventors, and the patrons of inventors. Years before the advent of Joseph and Benjamin to this region, their father and uncles had penetrated the then wild and rugged valley of the Patapsco, founded new settlements — triumphed over no ordinary obstacles. The name has been made synonymous, with enterprise and perseverance.

Their business establishments in Maryland were but just fairly under way, when the war of the Revolution commenced. Though great sufferers in their business, from the effects of the war, and belonging to the peaceful society of Friends, they nevertheless, like Gens. Greene and Mifflin, deemed the resistance of the oppressed colonies justifiable, and warmly espoused the whig side. "In this respect, there was not throughout the whole family, a solitary exception. No tory blood ran in the veins of a single Ellicott."

Joseph Ellicott was but fourteen years of age, when his father removed from Buck's county to Maryland. Up to that period, he had enjoyed no other facilities for an education, than the common schools of a new country afforded. His early lessons in surveying, were given him by his elder brother, Andrew. His first practical surveying, was as an assistant of his brother, in the survey of the city of Washington, soon after that site had been selected for the national capital. In 1791, he was appointed by Timothy Pickering, then Secretary of War, to run the boundary line between Georgia and the Creek Indians. After completing this survey, he was employed by Mr. Cazenove, to survey the Holland Company lands in Pennsylvania.

This completed, he was engaged for a short time in Maryland, in business with his brothers, and then enlisted in the Holland Company's service in this region.

The active years of his life were those, principally, intervening between the years 1790 and 1821 — a period of about thirty years.

At least ten or twelve years were spent in the arduous duties of a surveyor; and when he left the woods and settled down in the discharge of the duties of a local agent, his place was no sinecure, as the records of the office will abundantly testify. He was a man of great industry; careful, systematic in all his business, and required of all under his control a prompt and faithful discharge of their various duties.

His education was strictly a practical one. He was a good mathematician, a scientific surveyor, a careful and able financier. The voluminous correspondence that he has left behind him, with the General Agency at Philadelphia, with the prominent men of this state of his period — in reference to the business of the company, political measures, works of internal improvement, and public policy generally — indicate a good degree of talents as a writer, and enlarged and statesman-like views. His memory is not only identified, as we have observed, with the surveys and settlement of this region, but with the crowning achievement — that which consummated local prosperity — the origin and prosecution of the Erie canal; as will be shown in connection with that branch of our subject. In the day that the vast benefits of that work shall be fully realized and gratefully acknowledged; when an enduring tablet is erected to commemorate the services of all who were conspicuous in its projection and progress, his name will be recorded upon it.

In person, Mr. Ellicott was rather above the middling size — six feet three inches in height. In youth he was of spare habits, but about the age of forty became corpulent. He had a strong constitution, capable of much endurance; and enjoyed for the greater portion of his life uninterrupted health.

He was possessed of fine conversational powers; when in humour he was a great talker and a convincing reasoner; and had a remarkable faculty of influencing the opinions of all with whom he associated.

A life of great usefulness, of extraordinary enterprise; a career of personal success, and the success of the enterprises with which he was connected, was destined to a melancholy close. As early as 1816 or '17, he became subject to depression of spirits, melancholy, which by degrees became a confirmed and inveterate hypocondria. If we were to look for the causes of this infirmity, they would perhaps be found in the peculiar temperament and constitution of the man, and the circumstances under which he found himself as his years increased—youth and middle age were passed—and life was verging to the "sere and yellow leaf." Wise as he may have been in other respects—prudent and far seeing—he had yet strangely neglected himself; been improvident in that which could alone have promised him temporal happiness, and contentment. Enterprise had been rewarded; wealth had come at his bidding, and filled his coffers. Broad acres, the sites of flourishing villages, the favorite grounds of an embryo city, were his. But he had no one to share all this with him. He was wifeless and childless. "Man must love something," is the truthful and beautiful philosophy of Kotzebue in his play—The Stranger. He must have something to hope for and care for, or with him the "pitcher is broken at the fountain," and the "grasshopper has become a burden." Wealth, in view of one who is alone in this cold and cheerless world; who feels that he is approaching old age, and that no destiny is linked with his; that there is no one to inherit from him his name, and be the filial conservator of his memory—is assayed, and turns to dross. It has been accumulated but to palsy the mind, crush the hopes, and embitter the declining age of its possessor. The very largesses he has to bestow, beget jealousy and distrust of even the well-intended offices of friendship. Does disease and pain come upon him, the hand that is held out to alleviate may be a sinister one. Perhaps the real, or it may be, the morbid sense of ingratitude comes, blighting all the buds of hope and promise that disease and despondency have spared!

His agency ceased in October, 1821. It was by his own act, though not in the absence of a state of things that would have rendered a farther connection with the office irksome, if his health had not been unimpaired. Although laboring under the combined mental and physical infirmity that has been named, he had continued to discharge the duties of the office in the absence of any considerable interruption. No mal-administration or neglect of duty was alleged against him. A feeling of discontent had begun to prevail —one that afterwards became rife upon the Purchase. Indebtedness upon land contracts had increased to such magnitude, as to press heavily upon the settlers, and create fearful apprehensions of the ultimate result. A formidable portion of them had conceived that a change of the local agency would be attended with some relief, or favorable modification of the terms and condition of indebtedness, and the General Agent was perhaps not unwilling to listen to the expediency of the measure, in hopes to appease the discontent and gratify the desire of change. Conscious of this state of things, Mr. Ellicott resigned the agency. It cannot justly be deduced from after events, that any anticipated benefits came from the change. The modification of the terms of indebtedness that was sometime afterwards made, was under the direction and instructions of the General Agent.

The close of his agency was the end of the active and busy life of Mr. Ellicott that commenced with his youth, and continued without interruption up to that period. Our country above all others —or in that degree which naturally arises from a prevailing spirit of enterprise—furnishes frequent examples of the effect upon strong minds and business habits, of an attempt to retire from active duties, and live at ease. The experiment is seldom one of favorable issue. In the case we have under consideration it served to increase and confirm a malady.

In November, 1824, under the advice of physicians, he was removed to the city of New York to get the benefit of a council of physicians to be called there. He was accompanied by Dr. John B. Cotes, his nephews, the Hon. David E. Evans, and Joseph Ellicott, 2d, Ebenezer Mix, Esq. and Judge Nixson. A packet boat was chartered at Albion to convey the party to Albany. At this period—as it had been from the first—his aberrations of mind, were decidedly those of monomania; sane upon all other subjects, he was insane when himself and his real and imaginary diseases were his themes. Passing down the canal, he would give his attendants minute and interesting details of its history, the part he had taken in it; and converse upon general topics, in the absence of all indications of impaired intellect. But changing the theme to himself, his mind would wander and conjure up fearful apprehensions of present and approaching disease, and their speedy and fatal termination.*

---

*The author has in his possession, a half dozen sheets of paper, that Mr. Ellicott scribbled over, while in the Asylum. It is a strange medley; as perfect an indication perhaps as could be given of his peculiar malady. In a few lines he would seem to be writing to a friend; then in direct connection occurs soliloquies, the subjects, the pathology and prognosis of disease, and its remedies. Occasionally, his sentences are well connected, and his ideas well expressed; generally it is so, until he begins to talk of himself and his own infirmities; then he becomes wild and incoherent; dwells upon his afflictions, imagines that his digestive organs are all out of tune—his whole system ruined by disease and the injudicious use of medicine. It may truly be said, in the

Arrived in New York, a council of physicians was called, consisting of Drs. Post, Nelson, and Cheetham. The favorite projects of his friends, were, a journey to Pennsylvania and Maryland—a visit to his kindred and the scenes of his youth—or a sea voyage. The council decided upon his entering the Hospital at Bellevue; a decision which was perhaps somewhat influenced by the fact, that the institution was under the superintendence of his old friend and associate upon the board of Canal Commissioners, Thomas Eddy A residence with him seemed not against his inclinations. He had a carriage provided for him, and rode out occasionally, as a part of the sanative discipline recommended.

The anticipated benefits of the Asylum were not realized; neither its curative measures, or the change of residence—the abstraction from the cares and annoyances of his business,—could

"cure a mind diseased."

Mental and physical infirmity increased upon him, until July or August of 1826, when, escaping the vigilance of his attendant, he consummated that which had long been apprehended by those who had known most of the despondency and depression of spirits that had conquered the once strong man, and expelled reason from its throne.

Thus died the Patroon and founder of settlement, upon the Holland Purchase.

A few months after his death, his remains were brought to Batavia, and deposited in the village cemetery.

Although Mr. Ellicott, in all the active years of his life, took a deep interest in public affairs, his time was too much occupied to allow, generally, of the acceptance of office. He was, however, in 1804, one of the Presidential Electors of this state, and a Canal Commissioner, as has been stated. On the primitive organization of Genesee county, he was appointed First Judge, but declined, and Ezra Platt was appointed in his place.

A brief statement of the terms of his engagement with the Holland Company, will account, principally, for the large estate which he left. For his first ten years' service, it was stipulated that he should have five per cent. upon all sales; six thousand acres of farming lands, and five hundred acres of land in the village of

---

language of the physician of the Asylum, that his was a case of "inveterate hypocondria, acting upon a very extraordinary mind."

Batavia. At the close of the ten years, the General Agent proposed that he should receive, instead of a cash commission of five per cent., one twentieth of all the contracts he had made. This arrangement was acceded to, and the land embraced in one twentieth of all the contracts was deeded to him in fee, and the contracts assigned. This was in 1810. The reversion of land embraced in these assigned contracts, explains his ownership of detached farm lots, scattered over that portion of the Purchase first settled; principally in Genesee, Niagara and Erie.

The occupants of these reverted lands, were thus legally made subject to his discretion. The records of the land office, however, bear witness, that he made no discrimination; that the occupants of his lands, were in all cases, as liberally dealt by, as were the occupants under the expired contracts of the Company. There is probably no one of the settlers upon the lands thus situated, or their descendants, who can justly complain of other than fair treatment at his hands. He commenced a renewal of the contracts, and continued to renew them, as long as he had the management of his own affairs. A large number of the contracts, unfulfilled and expired, existed at the period of his death, and became the property of his devisees. Honorable testimony would generally be borne to their liberality; with some few exceptions, in the case of those who did not regard the example set by their liberal benefactor. This variation between the spirit and policy of a donor and inheritor, is not unusual.

The six thousand acres, stipulated in his contract with the Company, was located in what was long known as the "Eleven Mile Woods," on the Ridge Road, near Lockport, Niagara county. He afterwards added by purchase, a strip of twelve hundred acres on the south side of this. The tract was principally unsold at the period of his death. The tract between Lockport and Ridge Road —about two thousand five hundred acres—which has been usually considered a part of the "Ellicott Reserve," was a separate purchase, made jointly by Joseph and Benjamin Ellicott. Joseph Ellicott also purchased a tract on either side of the Tonawanda, at the old "Fishing Ground," or "Rapids," with the intention, at one time, of securing the erection of mills there, by raising a dam, and constructing a race across the land below.

He purchased seven hundred acres upon the Oak Orchard, embracing the water power, and site of the now village of Shelby;

and afterwards the fourteen hundred acres below, which embraces the village of Medina. Joseph and Benjamin also purchased jointly, some detached tracts in Somerset, Niagara county.

In the original survey of Buffalo, he had plotted for himself one hundred acres, which he afterwards purchased of the company. It was called an *out lot*. The reader will regard it now an *in lot*, when told how conspicuous a position it occupies in the now widely extended city. Its front is all the ground opposite the Churches, between Swan and Eagle streets. In the centre of its front, there was originally a curve—a semi-circle—projecting beyond the line of the street. Tradition affirms that Mr. Ellicott intended that ultimately as the site of his residence. It would have commanded an uninterrupted view of Main Street, in each direction, and through Erie, Church, and Niagara Streets—called by Mr. Ellicott in his original map of "New Amsterdam," Stadtnitski, Vollenhoven and Schimmelpenninck Avenues. He thus early identified his interests with that of Buffalo, and through his life entertained high anticipations (though they came far short of what has since been realized,) of its destinies. His careful guardianship of the locality commenced with his agency. The difficulty obviated—his negociations with William Johnston and the Indians having terminated in securing the "mouth of Buffalo creek" as a part of the Holland Purchase—he congratulated Mr. Cazenove upon the great acquisition. In a letter dated June 25, 1798, he says:—

"The building spot is situated about sixty perches from the lake, on a beautiful, elevated bank, about twenty-five feet perpendicular height above the surface of the water in the lake; *from the foot of which, with but little labor, may be made the most beautiful meadows*, extending to the lake, and up Buffalo creek to the Indian line. From the top of the bank, there are few more beautiful prospects. Here the eye wanders over the inland sea to the south west, until the sight is lost in the horizon. On the north west is seen the progressing settlements in Upper Canada; and south westerly, with pruning some trees out of the way, may be seen the Company's lands, for the distance of forty miles; gradually ascending, variegated with valleys and gently rising hills, until the sight passes their summit at the source of the waters of the Mississippi."

It will be new to those even most conversant with the history of the Holland Purchase, the fact that Black Rock was looked upon as a rival to Buffalo as early as 1802. Extract of a letter bearing date in May of that year, from Mr. Ellicott to Mr. Busti:—

"While speaking on the subject of taking things in the proper time, I cannot refrain from mentioning that the Company delaying the opening of their lands for sale in New Amsterdam, and the lands adjoining thereto I fear the nick of time will pass by, at least for making a town of New Amsterdam. The state, last session of the Legislature, passed a law for purchasing the natives' rights of land, the pre-emptive right of which was in the state, (on our map called the New York Reservation.) The southern part of which lands reach near to New Amsterdam, and there is a situation on said lands, intended to be purchased equally or more advantageous for a town than New Amsterdam, so that if the state shall make the intended purchase this summer and offer this spot for sale before New Amsterdam gets in operation, the nick of time will be lost to the future prosperity of that place. It would therefore evidently tend more to the advantage of the Dutch proprietors to give to the Agent General of their concerns in this country full and discretionary powers to act and transact their business as existing circumstances might evince to be most conducive to the interests of the Proprietors."

It only remains to speak of the final disposition of the large estate that had accumulated principally from the ownerships and investments that have been noted. His will was executed in the year 1824. At the period of his death, in 1826, his estate was estimated at about six hundred thousand dollars; though it was difficult then to make any correct estimate of its value; the prices of farming lands were low, and Buffalo village property had not then hardly begun the rapid advance in value that has since been realized. The entire landed estate of which he died seized, would now be estimated by millions, instead of hundreds of thousands.

Over one half of his estate was disposed of by special devises and bequests. These were to his favorite relatives; those mostly with whom he had been closely associated in the latter years of his life. The residuary portion of his estate, was devised to his brothers' and sisters' children, and their children who might be living at his decease; to be divided equally between them, except, that such of his brothers' and sisters' children as should be childless at the time of his decease, should receive a double share. There were eighty seven of these residuary legatees, seven of whom drew double shares, making ninety four shares.

Three commissioners, appointed by the Supreme Court, after an examination of all lands thus bequeathed, fixed a value upon them amounting in the aggregate to ninety-four times fourteen hundred and fifty dollars. This estimate was merely nominal, to fix a basis of division. There was beside this, a large amount of personal property, not included in his special devises and bequests, which remained to the residuary legatees. His interest in various tracts of land in common with his brother Benjamin, was devised to his three sisters.

The residuary legatees drew their portions by lots; some, of course, were more fortunate than others, as after value proved. While some portions drawn, have remained nearly stationary in value,.others have doubled, trebled, quadrupled; and increased even ten fold.

In addition to the purchases of Mr. Ellicott, which have been enumerated, he and his brother Benjamin purchased the peninsula between Buffalo creek and the lake shore, in the city of Buffalo.

JACOB S. OTTO.

This gentleman was the successor of Mr. Ellicott in the local agency. He was previously a resident of Philadelphia; had been engaged in mercantile and commercial pursuits.

The period of his agency was from 1821 to his death, in 1826. Although possessed of many amiable qualities, his previous pursuits and business experience were not well adapted to fit him for the new and peculiar duties of the place he was called to fill; though the period of his incumbency was one of active and extensive sales, and his efforts were not wanting to perpetuate the liberal policy that had so generally characterized the ownership and agencies of the Purchase. The measures adopted during his agency were such as tended to promote the interests and prosperity of the Holland Purchase.

At the great canal celebration, in Lockport, on the 26th of October, 1825, he was one of the delegation from the county of Genesee. From some exposure upon that occasion, he contracted a cold, which terminated in his death, May 2d, 1826.

It was during Mr. Otto's administration, that the plan of receiving cattle and grain from the settlers, that had previously been entertained, was effectually commenced. Depots were designated in different parts of the Purchase, for the delivery of wheat; where the settler could carry it, and have its value endorsed upon his contract. Agents were appointed to receive cattle. They advertised yearly, the times and places, when and where the cattle would be received, fixed upon their price, and endorsed it upon contracts. It was one among the measures of relief, and its operation was highly beneficial. The agencies were, however, expensive to the company, and allowing the market price for the grain and cattle, they were largely the losers by the operations.

DAVID E. EVANS.

During the administration of Mr. Otto, Mr. Evans had been appointed as his associate, to give the incumbent the advantage of his long experience and familiarity with the details of the business. Yet he did not, to any considerable degree, participate in the joint administration proposed; his time being chiefly occupied with his own private affairs, and the duties of a member of the Senate of this state.

Upon the death of Mr. Otto, he entered upon the discharge of the duties of the local agency. Early in life, he had been a clerk in the office, under his uncle, Joseph Ellicott, and had for a long period occupied the desk of the cashier and accountant of the agency. Few, therefore, could have been more familiar with the wants, interests and welfare of the settlers. They were old familiar acquaintances, and his interests were identified with theirs.

It was during the second year of Mr. Evans' administration, (in Sept. 1827,) that a general plan for the modification of land contracts was adopted. It was regarded at the time, as a very decided measure of relief to the settlers, and its operations were highly beneficial to a very large class of the debtors of the Holland Company. The plan of modification was mainly as follows:—

"Any person or persons holding a contract for land, or holding land, which is under a mortgage, whether the contract has expired or not, and whether the whole of the money has become due on the mortgage, or not; where the principal and interest already paid and to be paid, amounts to more per acre than the maximum prices subjoined, may surrender the said contract, and enter into a new contract for the same, according to the following principles, and if under a mortgage, the money shall be reduced in conformity to the same.

"Where partial payments have been made, ascertain how many acres those payments (an original advance of five per cent, excepted) would have paid for at the original contract price, (deducting five per cent.,) had that quantity been in a separate contract; estimate what the residue of the land would amount to at the maximum price, and charge the same on the whole of the land in the original article, or under the original mortgage; at which time all reasonable divisions will be made where several individuals claim parts of the original article; and in case of a mortgage, reasonable divisions will be made, and accounts opened for each proprietor or claimant of such divisions, and those several parts released when paid for. Provided, however, that such claimant of the whole, or any part of the land held under an old contract, or covered by a mortgage, shall pay at least one-eighth part of the new price so found, at the time such deductions shall be made, and such divisions take place, and covenant or agree to pay the residue in six equal annual payments with interest annually. The maximum price is not to be enhanced by adding interest until January 1st, 1828.

Previous to the year 1828, much difficulty and embarrassment had occurred throughout the Holland Purchase, from a provision in the School Act of the state, that sites of school houses should be secured by deeds in fee, or by leases from the possessor of the fee, of the land. In numerous instances there was no deeded lands in the district; or if there was, not conveniently located. In the absence of such title or lease, the trustees of the districts could not legally levy and collect taxes for building or repairing school houses. About the period above named, Mr. Evans adopted the following plan to remedy the evil, and prevent the hindrances that were in the way of a full realization of the benefits of the common school system upon the Holland Purchase. It was entered upon the books of the office, and the benefits of it extended whenever asked:—

"In every legally organized School District on the Holland Purchase, where the most convenient site for a school house shall fall on land not deeded from the Holland Company, a deed for such site. not exceeding half an acre of land, shall be granted, from the Company to such district, gratis. Provided that whenever such site shall fall on lands held under contract, from the Company, by any person or persons, such district shall procure a relinquishment of the right to such piece of land, by virtue of said contract to be endorsed thereon by the person or persons holding the same."

Mr. Evans' agency continued until 1837. It embraced the large sales of the Holland Company's interest; in fact before it closed, the entire business and interests of the Company, had progressed nearly to a termination.

Having served one term as a State Senator, Mr. Evans had been elected a Representative in Congress at the period of Mr. Otto's death. He resigned to take upon himself the duties of the agency.

He became the purchaser of the fine residence of Mr. Ellicott, from the three sisters and the brother's wife, to whom Mr. E. had willed it. Extending and carrying out the plans of his uncle, he has made it one of the most beautiful and tasteful residences in the state; and a seat of hospitality, as will readily be inferred, by those who know the generous and social character of its owner.

CHAPTER III.

COMMENCEMENT OF SETTLEMENT, AND ITS PROGRESS UP TO THE WAR OF 1812.

The chain of narrative in a preceding chapter was interrupted by the introduction of a chapter of personal biographies, just as Mr. Ellicott had so far progressed with the surveys as to admit of the announcement of the commencement of land sales. There were then but three settlers under the auspices of the Holland Company; the three pioneer tavern keepers. Settlement and its progress will now be taken up, and continued with reference to the order of time in which it occurred, and its localities. An attempt will be made to show the reader when and where the bold and enterprising Pioneers dashed into the wilderness in different directions — erected their humble primitive log cabins, and laid here and there, over a wide region, the foundations of the wealth, prosperity and happiness, which he may now witness. He will find that the commencement, and the progress for a long period, was surrounded with formidable difficulties; that they involved privation, suffering, and indomitable perseverance; and in the end will feel to venerate the names of the living, and the memories of the dead, of those who reclaimed the wilderness, and prepared the way for its conversion to the fairest portion of our Empire State.

As soon as Mr. Ransom had built his house at Pine Grove, Mr. Ellicott had made it his head quarters, as has been indicated by the dates of his letters. His appointment as Local Agent, took effect October 1st, 1800, at which time he commenced sales of land — a portion of Mr. Ransom's house being appropriated for his office, and Mr. James W. Stevens, whom he had brought on from Philadelphia for that purpose, acted as his clerk; Mr. Brisbane occasionally acting in that capacity, though his duties were mostly at the Transit Store House.

Before introducing the names of the settlers, we will insert some desultory sketches, which have a bearing upon this primitive period of settlement:—

Extract of a letter of Joseph Ellicott to Paul Busti, Esq., of Philadephia, dated New Amsterdam, January 16th, 1801:—

"I have the satisfaction to inform you (although after a disagreeable journey) that I arrived here in good health the 1st instant, since which period I have been busily employed in making arrangements for the sale of the land placed under my charge. The season of the year being such as to prevent persons from making their establishments, prevents me at present from effecting any *bona fida* sales.

Settlers generally wishing to defer entering into articles before they are enabled to commence their improvements. I have, however, abundant reason to conclude, that at the opening of Spring I shall effect the sale of considerable land."

In a letter to Messrs. Le Roy & Bayard, dated "West Genesee" May 7th, 1801, Mr Ellicott says:—

"In respect to sales of lands, we have not as yet made rapid progress. The best and most eligible situations are only in demand. However, we dispose of more or less almost every day. Settlements form more rapidly on the east side of the Purchase than the west, owing to its contiguity to the *old settlement* in the Genesee, where provisions and necessaries for their beginning is more easily attainable. However, there are some going on on the western side, and I continue to live under the expectation of selling a considerable quantity of lands in the course of the summer and fall, and presume after this season the sales will increase, the ice will then be broken, and conveniences will be had for the settlers on the Purchase."

In May, 1801, Mr. Ellicott acting as the special agent of Messrs. Le Roy and Bayard, employed Mr. Richard M. Stoddard to survey the Triangular tract, giving minute directions, especially as to the laying off of five hundred acres at "Buttermilk Falls."

In a letter to Mr. Munger, at Transit Store House, dated at "Pine Grove," (Ransom's,) May, 1801, he says, he has been informed "that the inhabitants of your neighborhood have undertaken to open the road to Ganson's. You will please consider me a subscriber towards the expense of the undertaking."

In May of this year, Gen. James Wilkenson came upon the western frontiers of this State, commissioned to open a communication by land between lake Erie and Ontario. Making Black Rock his head quarters, with his surveyors and a corps of U. S. soldiers for laborers, soon after his arrival, he addressed Mr. Ellicott for advice in reference to the best route to pursue. The answer pointed out with but little variation the route that was adopted. Mr. Ellicott forwarded to Gen. Wilkenson such maps and field notes as would facilitate the enterprise; in acknowledging the reception of which, the General expresses his apprehensions that "evil disposed persons will labor to excite clamor and discontent among the Indians on this occasion;" but he trusts Mr. Ellicott and Gen. Chapin "will prevent any obstruction from that quarter."

Gen. Wilkenson and his corps, located the road. He directed Major Porter, then in command at Fort Niagara, to open it with the soldiers of the garrison. In the season of 1802 it was opened as far west as the brow of the mountain at Lewiston; and from thence to a mile west of Tonawanda creek, the timber was cut down but not removed. The work of the season included the erection of bridges over the Tonawanda and Cayuga creeks. The road was left in this condition until 1809, when an appropriation was made by the legislature of this State for its farther improvement, of fifteen hundred dollars; the sum to be collected from the debtors to the State for lands purchased upon the "Mile Strip." Joseph Landon, Peter Vandeventer, and Augustus Porter were appointed commissioners to lay out the money. It was used to make a passable wagon road from Black Rock to the Falls. This was the end of government appropriation.

While Gen. Wilkenson was upon the frontier he located the site of a Fort at Black Rock. At the session of the legislature that followed, the general government made application for a cession of land to carry out the project. The cession was refused, unless the general government would pay for the land. The condition was declined, and the project abandoned. This narrow, and strange legislative policy induced the general government to abandon the prosecution of the military road; and to it, is also to be attributed the defenseless condition of the frontier on the breaking out of the war of 1812.

In a letter dated July 14th, Mr. Ellicott informs Mr. Busti generally as to land sales, their amount, and location. In closing the letter he makes the following suggestions:—

"When we reflect that there are lands for sale in every possible direction around us, that every purchaser who comes into this quarter has to pass by almost innumerable land offices, where lands are offered on almost every kind of terms imaginable; and that in Upper Canada, adjoining this Purchase the government grants lands at 6d Halifax currency per acre; we cannot calculate to make very rapid sales, until we have saw and grist mills erected, and roads opened; all of which are going forward.

"If some modes could be devised to grant lands to actual settlers, who cannot pay in advance, and at the same time not destroy that part of the plan which required some advance, I am convinced the most salutary consequences would be the result, which I beg leave to suggest for Mr. Busti's consideration, as three-fourths of the applicants are of that description; and as every acre of land that is cleared, fenced, and sowed on the Purchase, at the labor and expense of others, makes the district at least $25 more valuable, it appears to me some mode might be devised, to grant to such actual settlers lands, without restricting them to pay in advance. Monied men are loath to settle before conveniences can be had, and deprive themselves of the benefits of society, which accounts for the reason why our sales have not been more extensive to that class of purchasers."

Mr. Thompson, who had charge of the building of the house for Mr. Ellicott's office and residence at Batavia, expressed to him in a letter his disapprobation of "log houses," and considers the money expended upon them "thrown away." Mr. Ellicott in his answer thus quiets his scruples upon that point:—"you will please consider the expense solely chargeable to me, and I hope I may never want for a worse house than a good log house. Indeed I should prefer living in such a house, to that of being obliged to board in the best brick house in Canandaigua."

Extract of a letter from Mr. Ellicott to Mr. Busti, dated July 21st, 1821:

"You will permit me to mention to you the propriety of opening a township or two for sale on the lake Ontario shore, as no doubt people will be moving into this purchase by water, and unless we have some establishment on the Lake, and a road effected from the district to said establishment, such persons will be put to considerable inconvenience. I would therefore propose, as there is a good harbor for boats in township No. 16, 2d Range that the said townships should be opened for sale. Indeed an establishment on the Lake cannot, in my opinion, be begun at too early a period, as the farmers in the Purchase will require a place to convey their potash to deposit on the Lake, in order to be sent to Montreal or New York, as may be most likely to produce a market, and also for a place to receive their salt, and without such an establishment many will have to go considerably farther, as well as carry their money into other settlements in which we are not interested.

"Another object of no small moment to our prosperity, would be the setting apart for sale township No. 11, in the 8th Range, including New Amsterdam, which would shortly become the place for the inhabitants of the western tract to receive their supplies, and in a little time would be a place of trade, which would give a spring to the settlement, and of course could not be too soon commenced for the benefit of the interior part opened for sale. All which is respectfully submitted, dear sir, with great respect and esteem."

Among the primitive tavern keepers, there was a backwoods philosopher. It was the Mr. Walthers, that had been sent from Philadelphia to be the landlord at the Transit Store House. Established in his location, he made himself quite officious; his letters came thick and fast upon Mr. Ellicott, whenever he knew where they would reach him. They were an odd mixture of philosophy, and advice and suggestions in reference to the best manner of settling a new country. In one letter he would talk of his domestic troubles; in another, would announce that one, or two, or three landlookers had been his guests, not forgetting to assure Mr. Ellicott how hard he had labored to convince them of the splendid prospects of the new country; in another he would inform him of false reports that had been started as to the title of the land, and how he had put a quietus upon them; in another he would express his regrets that his house was full of strangers, who were passing the Purchase, and going to "swell the numbers of his Brittanic Majesty's subjects in Upper Canada." In Mr. Ellicott's absence, he was wont to consider himself a sub-agent; taking some airs upon himself, from some favors that had been shown him by the General Agent at Philadelphia. He did not last long, as will be observed in an extract of a letter from Mr. Ellicott to Mr. Busti. Mr. Ellicott answers a letter received from "Mrs. Berry and Miss Wemple"—(names familiar to old settlers, as household words.) They were applicants for two town lots, at the "Bend of the Tonewanta." He very courteously informs them, that when he lays out a town there, the lots will contain forty acres each, and their application shall be held in remembrance.

One of the earliest attempts at gardening in Buffalo, is indicated in a letter from Henry Chapin to Mr. Ellicott, dated March, 1801. He asks the privilege of fencing in the ground on Seneca street, from Main to Washington street, opposite the Post office, for the purpose of raising some "garden vegetables."

Extract of a letter from Mr. Ellicott to Gen. Payne:—

"Mr. Ellicott makes a tender of his compliments by Gen'l. Payne to Mr. Kirtland, informs that gentleman, that as yet, the Holland Land Company have made no provision for opening the road through their lands from Buffalo creek to the eastern boundary of the Triangle.

"Mr. Ellicott has recently mentioned that subject to the General Agent, and is waiting his answer. He thinks it probable the Company may unite with the Connecticut Land Company, but this he cannot speak of with certainty."

About this period, a lost horse gave Mr. Ellicott much trouble. He had borrowed the horse at Schlosser, to ride down to Niagara, and from thence to "Howell's," where he strayed away. The owner, presuming he had a good customer, demanded an exorbitant price. In a letter, he orders his friend Robert Lee, Esq., at the garrison to advertise the horse in "Tiffany's paper at Niagara." The horse is not much flattered in the advertisement; is not made to come up to the hundred dollars that the owner demanded; he is neither "shod before nor behind, and is tender footed;" (for which neither the horse nor the owner was probably to blame, for there were as yet no blacksmiths in the country.) After paying for the horse, it was found that the Tonawanda Indians had appropriated him to their use.

Extract of a letter from Mr. Ellicott to Mr. Busti, dated Batavia, 7th November, 1801:—

"Having as yet not removed my office from Mr. Ransom's I am unable to detail particulars of the Agency. It is with regret that I inform you that we lost, three weeks since, another of our most valuable settlers, who fell a victim to the prevailing fever:—Mr. Garrett Davis, whose name you will see on the map of the west bounds of the Tonawanda Reservation, the place of his residence. He has left a wife and two children who will long feel his loss. Since the cold weather has set in the settlers are regaining their health, and I hope another season will be sufficiently healthy to enable me to report more favorably of the salubrity of this part of the Purchase."

Extract of another letter from the same to the same, dated Pine Grove, Dec. 4th, 1801:—

"I have made no actual sales this fall where the stipulated

advance has been paid. I begin to be strongly of the opinion you always expressed to me, (but which, I must confess I rather doubted) that few purchasers will come forward and pay cash for lands in a new country.

The saw mill I have been erecting at Batavia, which has cost a deal of labor, not being a natural seat, but a place where a convenience of this kind is absolutely necessary, will, the mill-wright informs me, be in motion by the 10th instant, at which period we expect to begin to make ourselves and the settlers comfortable with floors, &c. which will be a great acquisition to our present situation."

Then follows a long correspondence, or a long series of letters from Mr. Ellicott to Mr. Busti, proposing some general principles of land sales and settlements; and in reference to taxes, the assessors of Ontario county, having as he thought begun taxation of the Holland Company lands pretty promptly. In a letter dated at "Ransom's Grove," Feb. 14th, he informs Mr. Busti that many settlers are preparing to commence their establishments as soon as the spring opens. He says:—" My present situation, (although the accommodations are as good as could be expected,) is gloomy for the want of society; our nearest neighbors being eighteen miles distant." In the same letter he announces that " Mr. Walthers had sold his possessions and fled the country. It is said, has gone down the Mississippi to the Spanish Settlements."

About this period a venerable relative of Mr. Ellicott in Maryland, expresses his concern for him in his wilderness home, as follows:—

"I observe thou says thou art living without society, that thy nearest neighbor is ten miles. Pray can a person be justifiable in spending the few years he has to live in a way that is not the most agreeable to him? Think on this and retire from that toilsome life thou hast pursued so many years, and enjoy thy few remaining years to the fullest extent."

In a letter from Mr. Ellicott to his brother Benjamin, dated in March, 1801, and directed to him at Davis' Hotel, he mentions that White Seneca is looking out a place for the Buffalo road south of the Reservation; and approves of his brother's selection of the site for the offices "at the Bend," and his general plan of the town plat he is surveying there.

In a letter to Mr. Busti, dated at "Ransom's, West Genesee," August, 1801, Mr. Ellicott states that his quarters had been visited by the Hon. Jonathan Mason, U. S. Senator from Massachusetts, on his way to the Falls. In the same letter he complains that the inhabitants of the town of Northampton off from the Purchase are disposed to tax the company exorbitantly, for roads, bridges, &c. laying out the money beyond the bounds of the Purchase. The evil he thinks will be remedied when that part of the town which embraces the Purchase gets enough inhabitants to insure a fair division of the town offices; and ultimately, when a separate town can be organized. To hasten these events, he states that he is encouraging settlement, by waiving the requirement of advance payments for land, when he can secure a settler. He complains that the county of Ontario have built "an elegant and commodious brick jail, such an one that few of the old counties of Pennsylvania can boast;" with the intention of making the Holland Company, foot a large portion of the expense. In this letter he informs Mr. Busti that many of the settlers are "greviously afflicted with the fever and ague."

In a letter to Mr. Busti, dated May 30th, Mr. Ellicott describes the selection he had made at the "Bend of the Tonewanta" for his head quarters; the reasons generally for the location; the principal one being the intersection of roads at that point. He informs him that one lot was sold, and one house built, in his new town, that he had concluded to call the place "BUSTIA," or "BUSTIVILLE."* He also informs him that land sales were going on encouragingly; that in one place, along the "Great Road," in the space of ten miles, there are "thirteen new improvements," and he confidently expects that before the close of winter, "more than half of the road will be settled." He congratulated Mr. Busti, upon the in-coming of the new administration, (Mr. Jefferson's,) and construes the advent of Gen. Wilkenson as an earnest that some attention would be paid to this frontier.

Dr. Cyrenus Chapin first visited the Purchase in the fall of 1801. In November of that year, he addressed a letter to Mr. Ellicott dated at Sangerfield, Oneida county. He wishes to take a lot in New Amsterdam, about which he had held some conversation with Mr. Ellicott; and this matter disposed of, he is ambitious to con-

---

* The honor was promptly declined. Mr. Busti objected to it from an indisposition to be made thus conspicuous in the new country; and besides the name was not enphonious; it conveyed to the mind something "ferocious." Mr. Ellicott promptly abandoned the name, but he very courteously informs Mr. Busti, that he thinks it no more "ferocious" than "Oldenbarneveldt." The name, BATAVIA, was substituted; it was of the Republic to which the Dutch proprietors belonged.

tract for what would now be considered a pretty large estate. His proposition, if it had been acceded to, would have made him and his friends the patroons of the city of the lakes:—

"And further I would petition you for a township of land there at the Buffalo—the one that will take in the town, for since my return a number of my friends have solicited me to petition you for a township, and for that purpose forty respectable citizens that are men of good property, have signed articles of agreement to take a township, if it can be purchased; and we will pay the ten per cent. when we receive the article."

The proposition was as a matter of courtesy forwarded to the general agent. In a few weeks Mr. Ellicott informed Dr. Chapin that the answer did not favor his application.

The commissioning of the first Justices of the Peace upon the Holland Purchase, is announced in a letter from Dewitt Clinton, (then private secretary to his uncle, Gov. George Clinton,) to Mr. Ellicott, dated, Dec. 1801:—

"Asa Ransom and William Rumsey were this day appointed Justices of the Peace for Ontario county, on your recommendation. Sickness prevented my attendance in October, which was the reason of the delay of the appointment. Their commission will, according to the regular routine, be transmitted to the Clerk of the county."

June 19th, 1801. Mr. Ellicott being absent from "Pine Grove," Mr. Ransom writes to him as follows:—

"We are happy to inform you that Mrs. Ransom has become the mother of a fine boy, and is in comfortable circumstances. We shall be ready to wait on you whenever you think proper to return."

The "fine boy," is now Col. Harry B. Ransom, of Clarence. He is the first born upon the Holland Purchase.*

Asa and Elias Ransom, were from Birkshire, Massachusetts. The early resident at Pine Grove, was a silver smith; his first location was at Geneva, engaged in the manufacture of trinkets for the Indians. From thence he removed to Buffalo and engaged in the same business, and from thence to Pine Grove. He died in

---

* A sister, Mrs. Merrill, (wife of Frederick B. Merrill, Esq. of Cheektowaga,) was born in Buffalo, previous to the removal of the family to Pine Grove. Her birth was before the settlement of Holland Purchase commenced. She was undoubtedly the first white child born in all this region, outside the walls of Fort Niagara.

1837, aged seventy years. His brother Elias, whose early advent is noticed, in connection with some reminiscences of Gen. Hopkins; and who as it will be seen, was an early settler at Buffalo, died seven or eight years since, aged nearly 80 years. He was the father of Elias Ransom, Esq. of Lockport; of Mrs. Street, of Chippewa, and Mrs. Kirby, of Waterloo.

The following letter from the early tavern-keeper at Buffalo, to Mr. Ellicott, indicates the first movement ever made there in reference to a school. The request was granted:—

"BUFFALO, 11th Aug'st. 1801.

SIR,—The inhabitants of this place, would take it as a particular favor if you would grant them the liberty of raising a school house on a lot in any part of the town, as the New York Missionary society have been so good as to furnish them with a school master, clear of any expense, excepting boarding and finding him a school house; if you will be so good as to grant them that favor which they will take as a particular mark of esteem. By the request of the inhabitants.

I am yours, &c.

Jo. ELLICOTT, ESQ.   JAS. R. PALMER.

N. B.—Your answer to this, would be very acceptable, as they have the timber ready to hew out."

The following list embraces the names of all the settlers upon the Holland Purchase from the commencement of land sales, up to Jan. 1st, 1807. They are in the order in which the contracts were taken in each year; their locations designated by Townships and Ranges. The reader who is curious to see in what directions settlement progressed after the commencement of it along the Buffalo road, will only have to become familiar with the plan of survey of the Holland Purchase—the location of Townships and Ranges, with reference to the present territories of towns and counties:—

1 8 0 1.

BATAVIA VILLAGE.	T. 12, R. 1.	T. 12, R. 1.
Abel Rowe,	William Blackman,	Jesee Rumsey,
Stephen Russell,	Hiram Blackman,	John Dewey,
David McCracken.	William Munger,	Zenas Bigelow.
TOWNSHIP 12, RANGE 1.	Eleazer Cantling,	T. 12, R. 2.
Worthy L. Churchill,	Nathaniel Walker,	Gideon Dunham,
William Rumsey,	John A. Thompson,	Isaac Sutherland,
Daniel Curtis,	Peter Stage,	Samuel F. Geer,

NOTE.—In this list the names of settlers upon Hoops' tract at Olean, Phelps and Chipman's purchase in Sheldon, and Loomis' purchase in Bennington, are not included. The settlements of those tracts will be noted separately. ☞Much pains has been taken to include in the list, the names of all settlers, during the years 1801, '2, '3, '4, '5, and '6, but still there may be some names omitted of those who were actual settlers during the period; and there may be names of those who took contracts and never became settlers; though the instances are but few in either case.

HOLLAND PURCHASE.

T. 12, R. 2.
Peter Lewis,
John Forsyth,
John Lamberton,
Russel Noble.

T. 12, R. 5,
Orlando Hopkins,
Otis Ingalls,
David Cully,
Peter Vanderventer.

BATAVIA VILLAGE.
Charles Cooley,
James McKain,
Elisha Gettings,
Joseph Alvord,
Zerah Phelps,
Elijah Tillotson,
James W. Stevens,
Hezekiah Rhoads,
Rufus Hart,
Israel M. Dewey
James Brisbane,
William Wood,
Major Nobles,
Russell Crane,
Oswald Williams,
Rowlen Town,
Silas Chapin,
Ebenezer Cary,
Paul Hinkley,
Timothy Washburn,
Moses Hayse,
James Holden,
Elijah Spencer,

BATAVIA VILLAGE.
John S. Leonard,
James Clement,
Jeremiah Cutler,
Elisha Mann.

T. 5, R. 1.
Job Phillips,
Nehemiah Sayer,
David Sanford,
Ezra Sanford,
Stephen Van Demark,
Samuel Lamb,
Ziber Ruff.

T. 9, R. 1.
Elizur Webster,
Josiah Hovey,
Nehemiah Fargo,
Samuel Chamberlin,
Gideon R. Truesdell.

T. 10, R. 1.
Samuell Ewell,
John Hill,

T. 13, R. 2.
Aaron White,
Peter Rice.

T. 12, R. 6.
Asa Chapman,
Christopher Saddler,
Levi Felton,
Abraham Shope,
John Haines,
John Gardner,

1802.

BATAVIA VILLAGE.
Benjamin Russell,
Paul Hill,
Peter Powers,
Silas Chapin,
Daniel Curtis,
Libbeus Fish,
Henry Wilder,
Jessee Hurlbut.

T. 10, R. 1.
Enos Selleck,
Jabez Warren,
Sterling Stearns,
Thomas Cahoon,
James Fay.

T. 11, R. 2.
Lewis Disbrow.

T. 12, R. 1.
Elisha Adams,
Roswell Graham.

T. 10, R. 2
Benjamin Porter,
Stephen Crow,

1803.

T. 10, R. 1.
Frederick Gilbert,
Reuben Chamberlin,
Elijah Cutting,
David Torrey,
Job Cowen,
John Roberts,
Zophar Evans,
Daniel Vanorman,
Jonathan Curtis,
Samuel Toles.

T. 11, R. 1.
John Torrey,
Charles Culver,
Abner Ashley,
Elisha Wallace,
David Hall,
Sylvester Lincoln,
M. Scott,
Nathaniel Pinney,
Orsamus Kellog,
George Lathrop,
Solomon Kingsley,

T. 12, R. 6.
Frederick Buck,
John Warren,
Timothy Hopkins,
Joseph Roades,
Wm. Updegraff,
Timothy Janes.

T. 10, R. 2.
Nathaniel Sprout, Jr.,
Nathaniel Sprout.

T. 11, R. 2.
Alexander Rea,
John Olney,
George Darrow.

T. 12, R. 2.
Samuel F. Geer,
Benjamin Morgan.

T. 13, R. 2.
Daniel Ayer,
Job Babcock.

T. 12, R. 5.
Samuel Hill,
Samuel Miles,
John Hill.

T. 12, R. 6.
Thomas Stancliff.

T. 14, R. 6.
John Dake,
Jedediah Darling.

T. 11, R. 1.
Jedediah Riggs,
Horace Shepherd,
John Dewey,
Lyman D. Prindle,
Samuel Prindle,
Oliver Fletcher.

T. 12, R. 1.
Lewis Disbrow,
Ebenezer Eggleston,
Peter Powers,
Enos Kellog,
Charles Culver,
John Henry,
Moses Dimmick,
Robert Berry,
Stephen Wickham,
Lemuel T. Pringle.
James Guttridge,
James Fuller,
John Berry,
John Spencer,
Burgess Squire,

HISTORY OF THE

T. 12, R. 1.
Moody Stone,
Asa Osborne,
Elisha A. Eades,
Parley Fairbanks.

T. 13, R. 1.
Archileus Whitten,
David Kingsley,
Thomas Parker.

T. 9, R. 2.
L. Nathan Finch,
James Sayres,
John Place,
Joseph Ethridge,
Christopher Sly,
Benjamin Sly,
Benjamin Spencer.

T. 10 R. 2.
Parmenio Adams,
Isaac Townsend.

T. 11, R. 2.
Ezekiel Churchill,
George Darrow,
Elijah Root,
Joseph Fellows,
Miles Wilkinson,
Benedict Ames.

T. 12, R. 2.
Peleg Douglass,
Alanson Gunn,
Benjamin Tainter,
Henry Lake,
John Lamberton,
Hugh Henry,
Amos Lamberton,
Joshua Sutherland,
William Pierce,
Elisha Cox,
David Bowen,
Abraham Starks,
William Lucus.

T. 13, R. 2.
Hiram Smith,
Silas Pratt,
William McGrath,
George Lathrop,
Darius Ayer,
Philips Adkins,
Lemuel L. Clark,
James Robinson,

T. 16, R. 2.
John Farrin,
James De Graw,
Cornelius De Graw,
James Walworth,
Elijah Brown,
John G. Brown,
James McKenny,
Elisha Hunt,
James Dunham,
David Mussleman,

T. 16, R. 2.
Samuel Utter,
Ray Marsh,
Henry Z. Lovell,
John Parmeter,
William Carter,
Martin Griffin,
Stephen Hoyt,
Eli Griffiith,
William Griffiths.

T. 10, R. 3.
Nathan Tolls,
Gilbert Wright.

T. 12, R. 3.
Jessee Tainter,
Abner Lamberton,
Micajah Brooks.

T. 12, R. 5.
Gilbert Yeomans,
Charles Barney,
Aaron Beard,
William Chapin,
Asahel Powers,
Samuel Hill,
Jacob Durham,
Robert Durham,
Benjamin Smith.
Samuel Estell.

T. 14, R. 5.
Gad Warner,
Lemuell Ashley,
Henry Elsworth,
David Munn,
John Caldwell.

T. 15, R. 5.
John Morrison,
Amason Darling,
James Davidson,
John Dunn.

T. 11, R. 6.
Alanson Egleston,
William Sheldon,
Amos Woodward.

T. 12, R. 6.
Andrew Durmat,
Thomas Cahoon,
Jacob Baum,
George Shumer,
Zera Ensign,
Jacob Shope,
Richard Coffin,
Dennis McNay,
Thomas M'Clintock.

T. 14, R. 6.
Michaga Howe,
Daniel Bachelder,
John Pickard,
Major Slayton,
Henry Swartz,
John Brewer,
Israel Owen,

T. 14, R. 6.
Nathan Powers,
Dennis Mackey,
Ransford White,
Stephen Hoyt,
James Dunn,
Thomas Slayton.

T. 8, R. 7.
Charles Johnson,
Oliver Johnson,
Benjamin Vanorman,
George Heacocks,
James Clemmons,
Bedford Hecocks,
Samuel Eaton,
Cyrus Hopkins.

T. 12, R.
Henry Lake,
Samuel Kelso,
Benjamin Gardner,
Perez Brown,
Abijah Hewit,
William Lewis,
John Sample,
Ezekiel Lane.

T. 14, R. 7.
William Howell,
Isaac Tyler.

T. 11, R. 8.
Elijah Rowan,
James S. Young,
Stephen Welton,
Zadock Butler,
Jonathan Burnett,
Matthias Clute,
Joseph Wells,
Richard Munn,
Abram Round,
Thomas Fourth,
Abraham Bemer,
Nathaniel Titus,
William Keeler.

T. 14, R. 8
Philip Beach,
John O. Prentice,
Chapman Hawley,
Adam Strouse,
Eli Harris,
Jessee Beach.

T. 14, R. 9.
John Beach,
Lemuel Cook,
David Thompson,
Samuel Taylor,
John Gould,
Solomon Gillett.

T. 15, R. 9.
Elijah Doty,
John Waterhouse,
Silas Hopkins,
Peter Hopkins,

HOLLAND PURCHASE. 457

T. 15, R. 9.
Obadiah Hopkins,
Coonrod Zittle,
Ephraim Hopkins,

BUFFALO.
William Robbins,
Henry Chapin,
Sylvanus Maybee,
Asa Ransom,
Thomas Stewart,
Samuel Pratt,
William Johnson,
John Crow,
Joseph Landon,
Erastus Granger,
Jonas Williams,
Robert Kain,
Vincent Grant,
Louis Le Couteulx.

IRVING.
John Mack,
Charles Avery.

T. 4, R. 1.
Benjamin Chamberlin,
Calvin T. Chamberlin,
Jedidiah Nobles,
Elisha Chamberlin,
William Pinkerton,
Marvin Harding,
Isaac Sanford,
Abraham D. Hendern.

T. 9, R. 1.
William Knapp,
Jonas Cutting,
Elijah Cutting,
Josiah Boardman,
Shubael Morris,
Josiah Hovey, Sen.,
Josiah Hewitt,
Josiah Jewitt,
Lyman Morris.

T. 10, R. 1.
Abner Bacon,
Amzi Wright,
Asahel Wright,
Reuben Chamberlin,
Gideon Bardock,
Samuel Ewell,
Jonathan Whitney,
Reuben Hall,
Elihu Hall,
Edmund Curtis,
Samuel Olcutt,
Henry Ewell.

T. 11, R. 1.
Peter Adley,
Isaac Wright,
Elijah Bristol,
Israel Shearer,

T. 15, R. 9.
John Clemons,
Robert Bigger,
James Benedict,

1804.

T. 11, R. 1.
Alanson Jones,
Joseph Hawks,
Joel S. Wilkinson,
Peleg Douglass,
Isaac R. Wright,
Elisha Giddings,
John Smith,
Abner Ashley,
Charles Culver,
William Coggshall,
William B. Coggshall,
John Halstate,
John Grimes,
James Cowdry,
John Roberts,
David Tyrrill.

T. 12, R. 1.
Nathaniel Walker,
Pardon Starks,
Zenos Keyes,
Benjamin Cary,
Alfred Lincoln,
Horace Jerome,
Nathan Miner.

T. 13, R. 1.
John S. Sprague,
Nathaniel Johnson.

T. 16, R. 1.
Nathan Wilson,
Halley Foster,
James Walworth.

T. 9, R. 2.
Solomon West,
John Ames.

T. 10, R. 2.
John Smith,
John Richardson,
Stewart Gardner,
Daniel Gardner,
Daniel Burbank,
Nathaniel Sprout, Jr.,
Eli Hays,
Daniel White,
Zadock Williams,
Zadock Whipple.

T. 11, R. 2.
Elijah Root,
Samuel Russell,
Benham Preston,
Elisha Carver,
Elias Lee,
Jessee Hawkins,
Solomon Blodgett,
Rufus Blodgett.

T. 15, R. 9.
William McBride,

T. 11, R. 2.
John Lee,
Ezekiel T. Lewis,
Elijah Rowe.

T. 12, R. 2.
Elizur Messenger,
Isaac Smith,
Levi Davis,
Azor Marsh,
David Smith.

T. 13, R. 2.
Rufus Hastings,
Roraback Robinson,
Benjamin Chase,
Solomon Baker,
Samuel Jerome, Sen.,
Samuel Jerome, Jr.

T. 16, R. 2.
Samuel M'Kinney,
John Jason,
Henry Lovéwell,
William Carter,
Job Shipman,
Ephraim Waldo.

T. 10, R. 3.
William Webber,
John Jones,
Asa Jones,
Isaac A. Kerman,
Ebenezer Smith,
Almond C. Law,
Elial C. Spencer,
Joseph Browning,
Stephen Smith.

T. 12, R. 3.
David Goss.

T. 12, R. 4.
John Richardson,
Stephen B Tilden,
Jacob Farnham.

T. 13, R. 4.
James Walworth.

T. 9, R. 5.
Thomas Tracy,
Cornelius Annis.

T. 12, R. 5.
Robert Durham,
Silas Hill,
Tobias Cole,
John Felton,
Abraham Voak,
Stephen Tilden, Jr.,
Charles Bennett,
Thomas Hill.

T. 15, R. 5.
Daniel Brown,
John Palmeter.

T. 9, R. 6.
Joel Adams,
John Adams,
Daniel Hascall,
James Merriam,
Henry Godfrey,
Nathaniel Walker,
Walter Paine,
Reuben Hall,
Epaphroditus Nott,
Nathaniel Emerson,
Joseph Sears,
Humphrey Smith,
Peter Wells.

T. 11, R. 6.
Joseph Halks,
Silas Pierce,
Peter Pratt,
David Hamlin,
John Truman,
James Woodward,
Warren Hull,
Joseph Parmelee,
Matthew Wing,
Lawson Egberton,

T, 12, R. 6.
David Bailey,
Gideon Royce,
Riley Munger.
David Hamlin,
Daniel Robinson
Gardner Spooner,
Peter Pratt,
David Bailey, Jr.
Isaac Vanorman,

T. 14, R. 6.
Charles Wilber,
Isaac Clark,

T. 15, R. 6.
Jedediah Riggs,
Joshua Slayton,

T. 8, R. 7.
Noah Smith,
Jesse Norton,

T. 9, R. 7.
Paul Sturdevant,

T. 9, R, 7.
Colton Fletcher, H. L. Co's. Surveyor.
Ezekiel Smith,
Amos Colrin,
David Eddy,

T. 11, R. 7.
William Maltby,

T, 12, R. 7.
Joel Chamberlin,
John Wisner,
Harry White,
Abijah Hewett,
Abiel Gardner,
Jacob B. Vanatter,
Elisha Cox,
Samuel McConnell,
Joseph Draper,
Caleb Rogers,
Stephen Colvin,
Zebulon Ackley,
Isaac Underwood,

T. 14, R. 7.
John Forsyth,

T. 9, R. 8.
Joel Harvey,
Denniston Foster,
William C. Dudley
Nathaniel Titus.

T. 11, R. 8.
Joseph Hewitt,
Ira Allen,
John Starkey,
Samuel Joy,
Daniel Chapin,
John C. Staley,
John Farr,
Peter Getty,
Amasa T. Grant,
Edmund Raymond,
Joseph N. Rood,
Ezra Whipple,
John Aiken,
Rowland Cotton,
Nathan Perry,
Asa Chapman,
Christian Staley.

T. 14, R, 8
Joseph Howell,
Joash Taylor.

T. 13, R. 9.
Nicholas Whittinger

T. 14, R. 9
George Armisted,
Erasmus Enos,
James Powers,
Robert Moore,
Hugh Hewitt,
Amasa Stoughton,
Samuel Stoughton,
James Pue,
Benjamin Pomeroy,
Philip Beach,
Elias Rose,
Daniel Totten,
Henry Totten,
Parley Wallace,
Josiah Benjamin,
Joseph Taylor,
Asahel Taylor,
Asahel Sage.

T. 15, R. 9.
Ephraim Hopkins,
Samuel Hopkins,
Peter Hopkins,
John Freeman,
John Wilson.

T. 6, R. 11.
Zenas Barker,
Francis Webber,
Hasadiah Stebbins,
William Webber,
Alanson Holmes,
Abner Holmes.

T. 2, R. 12.
William Bemus.

T. 6, R. 12.
Thomas McClintock,
Low Munnagan,
Benjamin Barrett,
Zatter Cushing.

T. 5, R. 13.
James Dunn.

T. 3, R. 15.
Alexander Cochrane,
Thomas Robinson.

1805.

BATAVIA VILLAGE.
William Ewing.

BUFFALO.
Cyrenus Chapin,
Thomas Sidwell,
Nathaniel W. Seaver,
Isaac Rhoads,
Samuel Tupper.

T. 5, R. 1.
Loring Francis.

T. 7, R. 1.
Peter Granger,
Isaac Granger,
Eli Griffith,
Philip Fuller.

T. 8, R. 1.
William Bristol,
Benjamin Morse,
Elnathan George,
James Cravath.

T. 9, R. 1.
Nehemiah Fargo,
Josiah Boardman,

HOLLAND PURCHASE. 459

T. 9, R. 1.
Daniel Bates,
Hezekiah Wakefield,
Giles Parker,
Lott Merchant.

T. 10, R. 1.
Elihu Hall,
James Hall,
David Tyrrill,
Israel M. Dewey,
George Harper,
William White,
Ward Davis,
Marshall Davis,
Samuel Bartlett,
James Ward,
Ephraim Cleveland,
Zira Dunbar,
Dudley Nichols,
David Morgan,
Walter Underwood,
Joel Strong,
John White,
Abraham Thomas,
Humphrey Gardner,
Edmund Curtis,
Robert Wilson.

T. 11, R. 1.
Phineas Smith,
Harvey Prindle,
Cyrenus Glass,
William Williams,
David Anderson,
Solomon Lathrop,
Jonathan Bixby,
Jason Bixby,
Ezekiel Fox,
Philo Whitcomb,
John Greenough,
Gersham Orvis,
Heman Brown,
Nathaniel Brown,
Peter Putnam,
Patrick Alvord,
Alford Rose,
Richard Stiles,
John Chambers,
Thomas Halsted,
John Boynton,
Eli Perry,
Abel Buell,
Joseph Bartlett,
David Morgan,
Asher Lamberton,
Israel Buell,
William Bannister,
Amasa Robbins,
Jesse Cowdry,
Isaac Wilson,
Josiah Southard,
John Grimes.

T. 12, R. 1.
Asa Webster,
James Heacocks,
Oliver Sweatwell,
Asa Osborn,
Hiel Chapman,
Abel McKain,
Nathan Graham,
Joseph Bentley.

T. 13, R. 1.
Hiram Smith,
Col. Samuel Hall,
Horace Carr,
Benjamin Chase,
Elisha Kellogg,
Dudley Sawyer,
Samuel Cumings,
Nathan Miner,
Silas Torry,
Edmund Burgess.

T. 9, R. 2.
Seth Sherman, Jr.
Lemuel Chase,
Seth Sherwood,
Adiel Sherwood,
Eebenezer Tyrrell,
James Coates,
Samuel Wilson,
Enos Smith,
John Wilcox,
James Duncan,
Gideon Sly,
Noah Willis,
Elisha Doty,
John Grover.

T. 10, R. 2.
Lemuel Whaley,
Zadock Whipple,
Nehemiah Osborn,
Joseph Munger,
John Kean,
Francis Rogers,
Joel Bradner,
Dan Adams,
Elihu Beckwith,
Elijah Rice,
Joseph Hopkins,
David Beckwith,
Benjamin Moulton,
Simeon Porter,
Luther Stanhope,
Stephen Crawford,
Orator Holcomb,
Benjamin Nelson,
Nathaniel Eastman,
Samuel Smith,
Nancy Wood,
Thomas Whaley,
Patrick Alvord,
Levi Stanhope,
Joseph Munger,
John M. Coffin,

T. 10, R. 2.
Eliphalet Hodges,
Benjamin Powers,
Clark Burlingame.

T. 11, R. 2.
John M'Cormick,
Levi Harris,
William Prout,
Asa Buckley,
Ezra Blodgett,
Noah Brooks,
Asa Frost,
Nathaniel Eastman,
Thomas Lee,
Daniel Rawson,
David Rowland,
Elisha Fox,
Seth Landon,
Stephen Day,
Abijah Warren,
Samuel Reed,
Daniel Davis,
Manna Chase,
Amos Adams,
Joseph Gladden,
Joseph Cady,
John Olney,
Gurdon Williams,
Jonas Marsh,
Charles C. Jackson,
Elisha Sutton,
William Burton,
William King,
Isaac King,
Samual Benedict.

T. 12, R. 2.
Timothy Washburn,
Thomas Godfrey,
Reuben W. Wilder,
Rufus M'Cracken,
Azor Nash,
Lemuel L. Clark,
Joel Tyrrell,
Hugh Duffy,
James Henry,
Richard Godfrey,
John Algur,
John Herring,
Jonathan Wood,
Reuben Lamberton,
Amos Lamberton,
Paul Hill,
Silas Dibble, Jr.

T. 16, R. 2.
Paul Brown,
Job Johnson,
Ephraim Waldo,
David Miller,
Thaddeus Moore.

T. 10, R. 3.
Peter Putnam,
William Adams,

T. 10, R. 3.
Job Matteson,
John Calkins,
William Hudson,
Bartholomew Armstrong,
Charles Armstrong,
Jonathan Wirten,
Jonas P. Tracy,
Samuel Rust,
Charles Imus,
John Culver,
Aaron Whitney,
Eleazer B. Stillwell,
David Hand.

T. 11, R. 3.
Orange Carter,
Israel Doane,
Samuel Russell,
James Jones,
David Clark.

T. 4, R. 4.
Joseph McCluer,
John Kent,
John L. Irwin,
Solomon Curtis,
Henry Conrad,
Daniel Cortrecht.

T. 5, R. 4.
Asaph Butler,
Jeremiah Burroughs,
John McCluer,
William Vinton,
Calvin Chamberlin,
Elijah Johnson.

T. 12, R. 4.
Francis B. Drake,
David Sarles,
Noah Pease,
Ephraim Pease.

T. 9, R. 5.
John Hunter,
Ezekiel Hall,
Solomon Hall,
Asa Hall,
Samuel Hays,
Mons Hays,
Charles McKay,
William Alden,
Amos Clark,
William Hoyt,
John Rolph,
Peleg Witmore.

T. 12, R. 5.
John Beamer,
Eli Hammond,
Isaac Smith,
William Hill,
Mons Fountaine,
Salmon Sparling,
George Sparling,
Henry Russell,
John Henry.

T. 4, R. 5.
David McCluer,
John S. Warner,
Job Pixley,
Thomas Horton,
Willard Humphreys,
John Warner.

T. 13, R. 5.
John Henry.

.... T. 15, R. 5.
Oliver Castle.

T. 14, R. 2.
David Dunn,
Micajah Howe.

T. 9, R. 6.
Abel Adams,
Simeon Lackey,
Christoper Stone,
Luther Hibbard,
Timothy Paine,
Nathaniel Morey,
Amasa Lackey,
Asa Hall,
Humphrey Smith,
Calvin Field.

T. 11, R. 6.
John Barrow,
Jacob Mussleman,
William Rogers,
Dudley Norton,
John Redford.

T. 12, R. 6.
Edmund Thompson,
George Croup.

T. 14, R. 6.
Nathan Clark,
Reuben Lewis.

T. 15, R. 6.
Nathan Toles.

T. 16, R. 6.
William Gordon,
Rimmon Colton,
Stephen Colton,
Isaac B. Tyler,
Burgoyne Kemp,
Ira Potter,
William Wisner,
David Wisner,
Francis Albright.

T. 3, R. 7.
Stephen Hazelton,
John Ricard.

T. 8, R. 7.
Benjamin Whaley,
Jotham Bemus,
Thurston Waters,
Richard Cary,
Aaron Lindsley,
Jonathan Bump,
William Drake,

T. 8, R. 7.
Oliver Johnson,
Samuel Eaton.

T. 9, R. 7.
John Somers,
Thomas Carroll,
George Colvin,
Jotham Bemus,
Jonathan Emerson,
Benjamin Enos,
Henry Arnold,
Jacob Eddy,
Daniel Rooks,
Reuben Newton,
Asa Sprague,
Samuel Knapp,
Joseph Sheldon,
William Coltrin,
Henry Cole,
Thomas Walton,
Jonathan Fish,
John Garrison,
Stephen Kellogg,
Gilbert Palmer,
Oliver Curtis,
Abijah Nichols.

T. 11, R. 7.
James Harmon,
Horatio Kelsey.

T. 12, R. 7.
Alexander Logan,
John King,
John Hersey.

T. 14 R. 7.
Isaac Trowbridge,
Garrett Stoughton.

.... T. 15, R. 7.
Moses Hutchins,
William Chambers,
John Armstrong,
Digby Small.

T. 9, R. 8.
Tyler Sacket,
Jacob Depue,
Russell Goodrich,
Rufus Belden,
Jabez Lewis,
John Reeves,
Abel Buck,
Ezekiel Chapman,
Gideon Dudley,
Nathaniel Titus,
Samuel P. Hibbard,
King Root,
Winslow Perry.

T. 11, R. 8.
Leander Hamlin,
James Harris,
Abijah Hewitt,
Ransom Harmon,
Ezra Beebe,

HOLLAND PURCHASE. 461

T. 11, R. 8.
Samuel Beebe,
William Desha,
Abel Beebe.

T. 12, R. 8.
Abial Walton.

T. 13, R. 8.
Benjamin L Kelso.

T. 14, R. 9.
Benjamin Dickson.

T. 8, R. 9.
Elijah Kenny.

T. 13, R. 9.
Zacharias Warren,
Dennis Morris,
Isaac Swain.

T. 14, R. 9.
Solomon Skinner,
Jacob Bragbill,
Reuben Hurd,
Frederick Bragwell,
Elias Benchard,
Solomon Gould.

T. 15, R. 9.
William Coggswell,
Jonathan Jones,
Samuel Shelly.

T. 6, R. 10.
Jesse Skinner,
John Skinner,
John Tyler,

BUFFALO.
Asa Chapman,
David Mather,
Daniel Lewis,
Oziel Smith,
John White,
Eleazer Hovey.

IRVING.
Aaron Dolph,
William Tuttle,
Elijah Lane,
Henry Johnson.

MAYVILLE.
Judah Chamberlin,
Bartle Laffert,
Lawrence Cary.

T. 3, R. 1.
Simon Gates,
William Burnett,
James Green,
Seth Marvin,
William Higgins,
Levi Couch.

T. 6, R. 1.
Roger Mills,
Frederick Mills,

T. 6, R. 10.
David Marsh.

T. 5, R, 11.
Abiram Orton.

T. 6, R. 11.
Jared Griswold,
Orsamus Holmes,
Thomas Phillips,
John Hollister,
William Gould,
William Waker,
Clark Cleveland,
Joseph Phillips,
Manassah Munn,
Simeon Austin,
Luke Coon,
Abner Holmes,
Thomas Stebbins,
Jonathan Webber.

T. 3, R. 12
William Bemus.

T. 5, R. 12.
Edmund Barber,
Samuel Davis,
Samuel Perry,
Augustus Burnham.

T. 6, R. 12.
Benjamin Burnett,
Seth Roberts,
Amzi Rue,
Asa Hamlin,

1806.

T. 6, R. 1.
Elisha Mills,
Joshua Skiff,
Moses Robinson.

T. 7, R. 1
Azel Lyon,
Asahel Newcomb,
Micah Griffith,
Joshua Powers,
Alanson Landon,
Oliver Stacy,
Arunah Cooley,
Amos Bill,
Abner Bill,
Aaron Fuller, Jr.
Eli Griffith, Jr.
Thomas Warden,
Christopher Olin,
Thomas Dole,
Asahel Trowbridge,
John Stewart,
Eli Stewart,
John Willard,
Alexander Axtell,
David Hoyt,
Roger Mills.

T. 6, R. 12.
Ambrose Dean,
Salah Seymour,
Joel Lee,
Richard Douglass,
Rufus Langdon,
Philip Osborn,
Seth Cole.

T. 3, R. 13.
Calvin Chamberlin,
Elijah Bennett,
Alanson Waite,
Philo Sackett,
Joseph Thayer, Jr.
William Sackett,
Jonathan Smith,
Peter Barnhard,
Andrew Rogers,
John Cochran.
Elias Scofield,
William Webber.

T. 5, R. 13.
Thomas McClintock.

T. 3, R. 15,
Benjamin Avery,
Nathan Wisner,
Israel Warriner,
Ira Tracy,
Daniel Cornwell,
Samuel Harrison,
Israel Goodrich.

T. 8, R. 1.
Elijah Warner,
Barzilla Yeats,
Reuben Orvis,
Nehemiah Parks,
Isaac George,
Wheelock Wood,
Willard Thayer,
Ebenezer West,
Ithurial Flower,
Pearl Flower.

T. 9, R. 1.
Solomon Morris,
Shubael Morris,
Abijah Jacocks,
Daniel Ferguson, Jr.
Daniel Knapp,
Elkanah Day,
Peter W. Harris,
Aaron Bailey,
Nathan Pierce,
Stephen James,
Dwight Nobles,
Stephen Perkins,
Joseph Palmer,
John Utter, Jr.
Ames Keeney,

T. 9, R. 1.
Gideon R. Truesdell,
Jeremiah Truesdell,
Isaac Jacocks,
Gideon Thayer,
Josiah Hovey, Jr.
Alexander Blowers.

T. 10, R. 1.
Willard Chaddock,
Solomon Prindle,
John Smith,
Eliphalet Owen,
David Thompson,
Jonathan Thompson,
Isaac Marsh,
Timothy Mallison,
David Foster,
Elisha Smith,
Joseph White,
Daniel Hoyt.

T. 11, R. 1.
Daniel W. Bannister,
Jerry Cowdry,
Thomas Starkweather,
Mons Goodrich,
Lewis Barney,
David Morgan,
Ebenezer Wilson,
David Filkin,
Peter Davidson,
Chester Davidson,
Franklin Putnam,
David Stewart,
Lyman D. Prindle,
Joseph Shedd,
Henry Miller,
Orsamus Kellogg,
Ebenezer Eggleston,
Henry Rumsey,
Elijah Bristol,
Elisha Andrews,
David Ingersoll,
Joseph Bartlett.

T. 12, R. 1.
Solomon Sylvester,
Daniel B. Brown,
Israel Graham,
Moses Norton,
Peter Putnam,
Amos Jones,
Alvah Jones,
Stephen Powell,
Webster Powers,
Robert Norton,
Benjamin Graham,
Joseph Savacool,
Henry Stringer, Jr,,
Samuel Ranger,
Peter Stage,
Gurden Huntington,
John Gould.

T. 13, R. 1.
Joel Jerome,
James Mills,
Horace Jerome,
Aaron White,
Enos Kellogg,
Ephraim Wortman,
Benjamin Chase,
Sylvester Eldridge,
Silas Terry,
John Roraback.

T. 1, R. 2.
Thomas Lightfoot,
Thomas Smith,
John Watson.

T. 3, R. 2.
Benjamin Riggs,
Enos Silsby,
Andrew Hawley,
Stephen Coles,
George W. Higgins,
Levi Gregory,
Richard Friar,
James Haskins.

T. 4, R. 2.
William Pinkerton,
Jonathan Dodge,
Samuel Crawford,
Alpheus Dodge,
Daniel Dodge,
Ebenezer Horton.

T. 9, R. 2.
Aaron Kinsman,
Silas Beckwith,
Isaac Gardner,
Truman Lewis,
John Grover,
Stephen King,
Seth Sherwood,
Jacob Howe,
Reuben Morse,
Ahaz Allen,
Shubael Atkins,
Lyman Cody,
Levi Atkins.

T. 10, R. 2.
Jacob Wood,
Charles M. Imus,
John Grant,
Levi Nelson,
Dudley Nichols,
Joseph Chaffer,
Samuel Stanhope,
William Osborn,
Joseph Munger,
Jonas Osborn,
John Bailey,
Elihu Beckwith,
David Beckwith,
James Sprout,
Luther Stanhope,

T. 10, R. 2.
Noah Barker,
Joel Maxon.

T. 11. R.2,
Elijah Root, Jr.
Ezra Whipple,
John Humphrey,
James Clisby,
Jacob Thompson,
Amos Thompson,
George Harrick,
Joseph Carpenter,
David S. Clement,
William Wood,
James Clisby,
Jacob Thompson,
Noah Brooks,
Benjamin C. Goodrich,
Joel Munn,
Phineas Munn,
John W. Lawson,
Andrew McLean,
Ebenezer Seeley,
John Olney,
Joseph Van Debogart.

T. 12, R. 2.
Newcomb Godfrey,
Elijah Clark,
Richard Godfrey,
Wm. J. McCracken,
Edmund Badger,
William H. Bush,
Othniel Field,
James Post,
Caleb Blodgett,
Samuel Risey,
Elisha A. Eades,
Joshua Barrett,
Elisha Morehouse,
Thomas Godfrey,
Caleb Blodgett.

T. 13, R. 2.
Micajah Green,
Caleb Blodgett, Jr.
George Hoge,
Eldridge Buntley.
Nicholas Bently,
George Harper,
James Crossett,
John Harper,
David Woodworth,
David Clark,
William Parrish,
Ezra Thomas,
Caleb Blodgett.

T. 1, R. 3.
Jacob Swar,
John Young,
Asahel Atherton,
Rufus Atherton,
William Atherton,
Daniel Edwards,

HOLLAND PURCHASE.

T. 1, R. 3,
John Holdrich,
Simeon Munson,
Samuel Todd,
Richard Frayer,
Isaac Phelps,
Ira Higgins,
Daniel Church,
Daniel McKay,
Reuben Clark,
James Green.

T. 4. R. 3.
Robert Brooks,
Solomon Rawson,
David Markham,
William Markham,
Orrin Upson.

T. 11, R. 3.
Amos Jones,
Joseph Fellows,
Timothy Fay,
Henry Rumsey,
David Carter,
Elnathan Wilcox,
John Chamberlin,
Alexander Little,
Nahum Thompson,
Jonas Blodgett,
Isaac Chaddock,
John M'Collister,
Burnham Lyman,
Henry William,
David Clark,
John Churchill, Jr.
Reuben Nichols,
Joseph Peters,
Aaron Gale.

T. 19, R. 3.
Joseph Burlingham,
Silas Call,
Elial T. Spencer,
Gardner Godfrew,
Henry V. Champlin,
Joseph Flint,
Henry Clark.

T. 2, R. 4.
Asahel Beach,

T. 10, R. 4.
Chauncey Loomis,
Justin Loomis.

T. 12, R. 4.
John Richardson,
Jariel Scott,
Samuel Carr.

T. 5, R. 5.
Gabriel Larkin,
David Jenkins,
Bell Teed,
Ira Pratt,
Ebenezer Reed,
James Jennings.

T. 9, R. 5.
Amos Clark,
Oliver Pattengell,
Enock Lewis,
Luther Adams,
Asa Cook,
James Hampton,
Samuel Green,
Rufus Earl,
Stephen Kellogg,
James Caldwell,
Thomas Wortman,
Johnson Street,
Alexander McKay,
Phinehas Stephens,
Simeon McKay,
Martin Roar,
Abner Edwards.

T. 12, R. 5.
Aaron Beech,
James Cronk,
Elisha Geer,
Jonathan Fisk,
Joel Finch,
Israel Taylor.

T. 13, R. 5.
David Higgins.

T. 1, R. 6.
Rufus Jemison.

T. 9, R. 6
John Conant,
Solomon Hall,
Timothy Fuller,
Josiah Sumner,
Ira Paine,
Walter Paine,
James S. Henshaw,
James Hinds,
Levi Lewis,
Josiah Gale,
Joseph Mallery,
Oliver Pattengill,
David Pattengill,
Humphrey Smith.

T. 11, R. 6.
Stephen Morgan,
Eli Carcutt,
Thomas Mansfield,
Samuel Clark,
Arthur Miller,
Peter Pratt,
John W. Lawson,
Ezekiel Sheldon,
Luther Youngs,
John Lawson,
Jesse Hall,
Stephen Chatfield,
Joel Isbel,
John Dunbar,
Stiles Torrence.

T. 12, R. 6.
Perkins Shay,
Asahel Canfield,
David Nettle,
Levi Felton,
Edward Carney,
David Bailey,
John More,
Jonathan Bennet,
Henry Doney,
Justice Webster.

T. 14, R. 6.
Leander Hamlin.

T. 3, R. 7.
Benjamin Jones,
Adam Johnson,
Barnabus Weekham,
Luther Stewart,
John Wainwright,
Alpheus Bascom,
William Gilmore.

T. 8, R. 7.
Benjamin Whaley,
Job Palmer,
Daniel Smith,
Jonathan Bump.
Zenus Smith,
Jacob Newkirk,
Aldridge Colvin,
Samuel Beebe,
Calvin Doolittle,
Elias Streeter,
Josiah Metcalf,
Joseph Yaw,
Terrill Algur.

T. 9, R. 7.
Richard Smith,
Zenus Smith,
Ezekiel Smith,
Josiah Gale,
Thomas Webb,
Nathan Peters,
Jacob Wright,
John Weaver,
Eliakim Bradley,
William Coltrin,
Nathan Clark,
Joseph Browning,
Almon C. Lair,
William Halladay.

T. 11, R. 7.
Seth Canfield,
Enos A. Armstrong,
James Harris.

T. 12, R. 7.
Emanuel Winter,
Joseph Hayward,
Oliver Standard,
John Cunningham,
Josiah Guthrie,
Ebenezer Cone,

T, 12, R. 7.
Thomas Harman.
Joseph Hersey.

T. 14, R. 7.
John Griffith,
William Molyneux,
John Freeman,
Ephraim Waldo.

T. 8, R. 8.
Joseph Tubbs,
Stephen Baright,
Benjamin Tubbs,
Stephen Clifford,
Benjamin Hodges.

T. 9, R. 8.
Abner Amsdell,
Peter Pilky,
Joseph Barnhart,
Heman Newton,
Henry Cheny,
Frederick Lewis,
Anna Bell,
Sylvanus Rice,
Matthew Blair,
William Dean,
Daniel Smith,
Abel Buck.

T. 13, R. 7.
George VanSlyke,
Eli Bradley.

T. 11 R. 8.
Daniel Ross,
Joseph Wells,
Jasper Parrish,
John Lyon,
Gideon Mosher,
Samuel Haskell,
Daniel Curtis,
Marshall Smith,
Major Nobles,
John Semple,
Benjamin Hodges,
Addison Stewart,
Samuel Sturgeon,

T. 11, R. 8.
Eli Hunt,
Thomas Burger.

T. 14, R. 8.
Jonah Coolidge,
Joseph Howell, Sen.
Aaron Dennis,
Charles Richards,
Lewis Harris,
James Burley.

T. 13, R. 9.
Ezekiel Hill,
Benjamin Hopkins.

T. 14, R. 9.
Daniel Howell.

T. 15, R. 9.
Peter Ripson,
John Brown,
William McBride.

T. 6, R. 10.
Abner Cooley.

T. 6, R. 11.
Ozias Hart,
Justus Hinman,
Thomas Stebbins,
John E. Howard,
John Cass,
John Prior.

T. 2, R. 12.
William Bemus.

T. 5, R. 12.
Philo Orton,
Daniel Redfield,
Elisha Satterlee,
Philip Osborne,
Elijah Ripley,
David Cooley, Jr.,
Reuben Edmunds.

T. 6, R. 12,
Elisha Mann,
George Patterson,
Ephraim Pease,
Daniel S. Cole.

T. 3, R. 13,
Isaac Young,
David Marshall,
Joseph Cowell,
James Prendergast,
Marlen Prendergast,
Jedediah Prendergast,
William Prendergast, Jr.,
Elizabeth Prendergast,
Susannah Whiteside,
Matthew Prendergast,
Philo Taylor,
Amos Huntington,
Paulus Pardee,
Reuben Ellis,
John Putnam,
Robert Tupper,
Jonathan Barnhart,
Asher Moore,
Uriah Scofield,
Elias Scofield,
Jared Goodrich,
Peter Hogeboom,
James Brown,
Jonathan Cheeney,
Harry Ingersoll,
Henry Mott.

T. 5, R. 13.
James Dunn,
Nathan Fay,
Elisha Fay,
Peter Kain,
David Eaton.

T. 3, R. 15.
Daniel Cornwell,
William Monman,
Asa Spear,
Josiah Farnham,
William McBride,
John Ayers
Augustus Skinner,
Benjamin Hutchins,
Thomas Clump,
William Crossgrove.

The survey of the town plat of Batavia village having been made in 1800—or it having been designated as the future site of the land office, and some lots platted—in 1801, the three persons named in the list, took contracts for lots. Rowe was the first tavern-keeper in Batavia; his location was nearly opposite the present land office, but afterwards changed, Mr. Ellicott making his five hundred acre reservation there. He became the founder of the "Keyes' stand." Under the administration, first of Rowe, and afterwards of Wm. Keyes, this stand was well known in all early times. It was the home of the early settler, when he had business at the land office; about its yard used to be seen the huge covered wagons that transported goods from Albany to Buffalo, and in the war of 1812 it was often the head quarters of the officers of the army. It was *the* tavern of early days. How changed! "Eagles," "Genesee Houses," and "Americans," overshadow it; the sign of a worthy mechanic "H. Naramor," swings in front of the venerable pioneer tavern.

Russell was the founder of the site of the present Genesee House; was the next tavern-keeper after Rowe. His wife, the early landlady, now Mrs. Gibbs, is with her husband, among the Mormons, in the gold regions of California! M'Cracken was a physician; the first upon the purchase; enjoyed for a long period an extended practice; he died in Rochester a few years since. Four or five of this name, brothers, were early settlers at Batavia. The names of most of the settlers of 1801 are familiar to early residents. They formed the nucleuses of early settlements; the Buffalo road being at this period the only road, except Indian trails, they were scattered along almost its entire length upon the Purchase. Their log houses — their rude, imperfect accommodations, were luxuries in those primitive times; havens of rest and comfort for the weary emigrant and his family, and the land explorer.

In the month of February, 1802, Mr. Ellicott employed John Lamberton and ——— Mayo, to cut out the road through the village of Batavia. About this period he informed Dudley Saltonstall, Esq., that the Company were prepared to loan money to actual settlers, "who would erect saw-mills, &c."

In the winter of 1802, Mr. Ellicott spent a considerable time in Albany, "lobbying," as such visits to our state capital were afterwards termed; his paramount business being the project of a new county. This was consummated, but not without opposition. Mr. James Wadsworth had a counter project. It contemplated the erection of a county embracing all the territory west of a north and south line, which would cross the main road about midway between the Genesee river and Canandaigua; and the making of Hartford (Avon) the county site. Mr. Ellicott attributed his success to the absence of Mr. Wadsworth from Albany just at the time the subject came up for a final decision. He concluded that if he had been there, his "plausibility and address" would have occasioned him much trouble; and especially as his proposed territory contained enough inhabitants to immediately organize as a county.

In the month of July, 1802, an occurrence took place at New

Amsterdam, which was well calculated to create excitement and alarm among the few scattered and defenceless inhabitants. The inkeeper, Joseph Palmer, was sitting in the evening near his house, in company with William Ward and Joseph Keeler. An Indian from the Seneca village, approached them, and drawing a knife, made an ineffectual attempt to stab Palmer. He then turned upon Ward, and stabbed him in the neck. An alarm spread which soon drew together the few white inhabitants. In the attempt to secure the assassin, he stabbed John Hewitt in the breast, and in two other parts of the body, killing him almost instantly. The Indian was secured, and taken during the night to Fort Niagara, and lodged in safe custody. The next day a band of forty or fifty warriors appeared in the settlement, armed with rifles, tomahawks, and knives, threatening if the Indian was executed, they would put all the white inhabitants to death. Finding where some of the blood of the Indian had been spilled in securing him, the armed warriors howled over it in a manner to create dismay and consternation among the inhabitants, many of whom fled from the settlement.

The circumstance created additional alarm, from the facts, that there was no personal provocation on the part of the three citizens attacked, and the Indian was sober.* The inference drawn by the defenceless inhabitants, was, that the attack was premeditated and concerted, and was the preliminary step to a general war upon the new settlers. Mingled with all this were jealousies that influences in Canada were operating upon the Indians.

The few white inhabitants at New Amsterdam drew up and signed a petition to Gov. George Clinton, soliciting his influence with the general government to secure a small garrison of troops, at the "village of Buffalo creek, alias, New Amsterdam;" Mr. Ellicott interesting himself zealously in the measure; surveyors and settlers throughout the Purchase co-operating. The petition set forth that the Seneca Indians had on other occasions manifested an unfriendly spirit.

The new county obtained, and the site of its public buildings determined upon, Mr. Ellicott soon gave his attention to the securing of a Post Office. Mr. Seth Pease, one of his surveyors, was a brother-in-law of Mr. Granger, the then Post Master General. Taking advantage of a visit he made to Washington, he secured

---

* The Indian was the one named in the biography of Major Barton. The friend who furnished the data of that biography to the author, was mistaken in supposing that the murder occurred in a drunken frolic.

his influence, and made him the bearer of an application. In his letter to the Post Master General, he confesses that but little revenue can be expected from the proposed office, but he gives him an elaborate description of the country, its condition, prospects; and informs him that Avon is the nearest Post-office to the new county site. The application was granted; Mr. James Brisbane being appointed Post Master.

In 1802, Alexander Rhea and Lewis Disbrow, it will be observed, took lands south of the Buffalo road. Mr. Rhea became the founder of the village of Alexander; erected a saw-mill there in 1804; he was an early surveyor of the Company, from Pennsylvania. His wife was a sister of Horatio and John H. Jones. Although Mr. Rhea took the first contract of land there, William Blackman was the pioneer settler of the town. He raised the first corn and the first wheat. A child of his was the first born in the town. Lewis Disbrow was the pioneer settler of Bethany. Rhea, Blackman and Disbrow were the pioneers of all the Holland Purchase south of the Buffalo road. The four settlers noted in T. 10, R. 1, were, the same year, the pioneers farther south, in what is now Middlebury.

Gideon Dunham, the pioneer who gave the name to the beautiful grove on the Batavia and Lockport road, died a few years since, at an advanced age. His son, Col. Shubael Dunham, died last fall, after an illness of several years. He had been a member of the State Legisture and a Presidential Elector. Previous to his decease the author obtained from him some of his recollections of early times. His father, it will be observed, was a settler in 1801. The road was cut out from Batavia to the Openings in that year. The road as first traveled was laid on the banks of the Tonawanda, to a point near the western side of the farm of William H. Bush, where it bore off passing through the back part of the farm of Isaac Sutherland, coming out on the present Lewiston road on the farm of Peter Lewis. Aaron White, who was a settler in 1801, was a Captain of militia in the war of 1812, and was killed at the battle of Black Rock on the morning Buffalo was burned.

Among the early settlers in Elba, was Patrick O'Fling. In 1813 the old gentleman, with three sons and a son-in-law, enlisted in the army. At Fort George, in 1813, Gen. Dearborn had his attention attracted by the soldier-like bearing of the old man, and asked him where he had seen service. He replied, "in the Revolution, under

Captain Dearborn." A recognition followed, and Gen. Dearborn took so much interest in the family of soldiers, that, through him, two sons obtained commissions of Lieutenant in the army, and another was admitted as a cadet at West Point. One of the sons was killed at the sortie of Fort Erie.

Col. Dunham said that in early years the speckled trout were abundant in all the small streams in that region. In 1804, he went with a party of the new settlers to attack a den of rattlesnakes at the Falls of the Tonawanda. It was in the spring—the snakes lay upon the rocks in coils, or bunches, as large in some instances as a bushel basket; there were hundreds of them. The party killed them by scores; it seemed to thin them out; but few were observed in that region afterwards.

For four or five years after settlement commenced, salt was made at a salt spring on the Reservation.

And here in the reminiscences of this primitive period, occurs the name of one who, if he did not follow as useful an employment as the keeping of a house of public entertainment, made himself as well known. Russell Noble! At the bare mention of his name, there are surviving Pioneers, who will be reminded of their younger days, and their enjoyments; and, if there is "music in their souls,"—as there was wont to be with most of them,—they will almost fancy they hear the notes of his old violin! A fiddler was no obscure person in those early days; and Noble had no competitor—for he was the pioneer fiddler;—he and his old violin mark the advent of music upon the Holland Purchase. Compared with his,

———"Italian trills were tame."

In those primitive times, in sleigh, or (ox-sled) rides, at recreations that followed log-house raisings, logging bees, road cuttings; at Christmas and New Years frolics; far and wide, in the early sparse settlements,—Noble and his fiddle, formed an accustomed and necessary part. It was to be hoped that his reputation as a fiddler would have remained unquestioned; but recently, a facetious gatherer up of reminiscences has ventured to slur it, by intimating that he used to have no more "regard for *time* than he had for *eternity*."

The old fiddler still lives; and it was only last winter, that he was an occasional guest at the houses of surviving Pioneers—stripping the same old green bag from the same old fiddle, and reminding his auditors of early days.

HOLLAND PURCHASE. 469

Captain Samuel F. Geer, now of Medina, Orleans county, came to Batavia as early as 1802. Mr. Ellicott had erected the saw mill and got it in operation. Capt. Geer, assisted by Maj. Sutherland, built the Court House at Batavia in 1802, and the grist mill in 1803. Capt. Geer built a saw mill at Medina as early as 1805; and in the same year, a building for the salt works, a mile and a half below Medina. Mr. Ellicott rented the works, and they soon run down.

The author will here introduce some narratives of early settlers, which will enable the reader to get a more distinct view of early events—the commencement and progress of settlement—than could be obtained in any other form. They consist chiefly of notes taken by him in conversations with the early pioneers.

A surviving son of the pioneer Jedediah Darling, has given the author some account of early times in Niagara. His father moved in in August, 1803; and died but a few weeks after, while returning from a visit to the land office; the sons were, therefore, principally identified with pioneer settlement. The Darling family took the first lands in all the region north of the Tonawanda Swamp, but were not the first settlers at the Cold Springs. Adam Strouse, a brother-in-law of the Howells, who had first lived at Lewiston, and had made the first commencement at Howell's Creek, had erected a shanty at the Cold Springs in the winter of 1802. The permission was granted at the instance of Stephen Bates, Esq., of Canandaigua, the then mail contractor from Canandaigua to Fort Niagara. In his application to Mr. Ellicott, Mr. Bates is desirous that a fire should be kept there at least, that his mail carrier could have some place to warm his fingers.

John Young settled on Oak Orchard road near Pine Hill, in 1804. He took the first deed ever given by the Holland Conpany. From his aged widow, now a resident of Batavia, with her son Brannan Young, Esq., the author derived the following narrative:—

My husband having the year before been out and purchased his land upon the' Holland Purchase, in the fall of 1804, we started from our home in Virginia on horseback, for our new location. We came through Maryland, crossing the Susquehanna at Milton; thence via Tioga Point, and the then usual route.

In crossing the Allegany mountains, night came upon us, the horses became frightened by wild beasts and refused to proceed. We wrapped ourselves in our cloaks and horse blankets, and attempted to get some rest, but had a disturbed night of it. Panthers came near us, often giving terrific screams; the frightened horses snorted and stamped upon the rocks. Taking an early start in the morning, we soon came to a settler's house, and were informed that we had stopped in a common resort of the panther.

Arriving at our destination, a family by the name of Clark, had preceded us in the neighborhood. Myself and husband, and the family named, were the first settlers on the Oak Orchard road,— or in fact, north of Batavia. Mr. Clark was kind enough to give us a shelter for a few days until my husband built a shanty. It was about ten feet square, flat roofed, covered with split ash shingles; the floor was made of the halves of split basswood; no chimney; a blanket answered the purpose of a door for a while, until my husband got time to make a door of split plank. We needed no window; the light came in where the smoke went out. So much for the shanty, and now for the furniture:—For chairs, we had benches made by splitting logs, and setting the sections upon legs. A bedstead was made by boring holes in the side of the shanty, inserting pieces of timber, which rested upon two upright posts in front; a side piece completing the structure; pealed basswood bark, answering the place of a cord. We of course had brought no bed with us on horseback, so one had to be procured. We bought a cotton bag of Mr. Brisbane, and stuffing it with cat-tail, it was far better than no bed. Buying a little iron ware, crockery, and a few knives and forks, we were soon under way, house, or shanty keeping.

We got our flour and meal the first year at Caledonia. The second year we were in, I had an attack of the fever and ague, which confined me for nearly a year. That year my husband cleared four acres; besides taking care of me, and doing the cooking. It was no uncommon thing, in the first years of settlement, for women in child birth to be deprived of the aid of a physician, and often, the attendance of their own sex had to be dispensed with. Mr. Young died in 1836.

The old lady is 75 years old; enjoying a contented old age, cheerful, and even humorous in some of her descriptions of early pioneer life.

Mrs. Anna Foster, wife of Eden Foster Esq. of Batavia, was the daughter of Jonah Spencer, who was a resident upon the Genesee river as early as 1791. She has given us an interesting narrative of events in that region at an early period, the preliminary portion of which we are under the necessity of omitting. In 1796 she was the wife of Moody Stone, and resided at Palmyra Wayne county:—

In the year 1796, I went with my husband to visit a brother-in-law, (Zenas Bigelow, Jr.) west of the Genesee river. We went by the way of Irondequoit; Dunbar kept a tavern there; forded the Genesee river above the Falls; there was but one house in Rochester, and that was occupied by Col. Fish. I remember, hearing my sister Mrs. Bigelow, say that she was present at the mouth of the river when the first schooner was launched, in 1798.

In February, 1805, we settled upon a farm near Batavia. There was then inhabitants enough to make an agreeable neighborhood; [Here she enumerates the names of the settlers, most of which are inserted in our preceding list.] We used to have ox-sled rides, occasionally it would be out to uncle Gid Dunham's, where we used to avail ourselves of the services of the left handed fiddler, Russel Noble. Some of our earliest parties, were got up by first designating the log house of some settler, and each one contributing to the entertainment; one would carry some flour, another some sugar, another some eggs, another some butter, and so on; the aggregate making up a rustic feast. These parties would alternate from house to house. Frolics in the evening, would uniformly attend husking bees, raisings, quiltings, and pumpkin pearings. All were social, friendly, obliging—there was little of aristocracy in those primitive days.

The first general training west of the river was in 1706 or '7, it was north of Caledonia; Col. Atchinson was officer of the day; the next was at Alexander, in 1808; Col. Rumsey officer of the day.

Wm. H. Bush, Esq. came from Bloomfield, Ontario county, and settled upon the Tonawanda three miles and a half below Batavia, at the place now called Bushville. His brief narrative well illustrates pioneer settlement and progress:

I moved my family from Bloomfield, in May, 1806. The settlers on Buffalo road, between my location and Batavia village, were Isaac Sutherland, Levi Davis and Timothy Washburn. Rufus M'Cracken, Daniel M'Cracken, Thomas Godfrey, Linus Gunn, Henry Starks, Alanson Gunn, David Bowen, John Lamberton, lived on the road west. There was then less than one hundred acres of land cleared on the Buffalo road in the distance of six miles west of Batavia.

I built a log house, covered it with elm bark—could not spare time to build a chimney; the floor was of slabs and hemlock boards. I immediately commenced building a saw mill and had it completed before the middle of October. That summer my wife did the cooking for family and hired men by an out of door fire, built up against stumps. The first winter, I attended my own saw mill, working in it from day light to dark, cutting my fire wood and foddering my stock by the light of a lantern. Before winter set in, I had built a stick chimney, laid a better floor in my house, plastered the cracks, and hired an acre of land cleared—just enough to prevent the trees falling upon my house. When the mill was built I had it paid for, but to accomplish it, I had sold some pork and grain I had produced by working land upon shares in Bloomfield—in fact, every thing but my scanty household furniture. My saw mill proved a good investment, boards were much in demand at seven dollars and fifty cents per thousand; the new settlers stocked the mill with logs to be sawed on shares.

In 1808 I built a machine shop, a carding and cloth dressing establishment. These were the first upon the Holland Purchase. On the 10th of June of that year, I carded a sack of wool, the first ever carded by a machine on the Holland Purchase. It belonged to George Lathrop of Bethany. In February, 1809, I dressed a piece of full cloth for Theophilus Crocker, the first ever dressed upon the Holland Purchase. There are on my books, the names of customers, from as far south as Warsaw and Sheldon; from the east, as far as Stafford; from the west, to the Niagara river and lake Erie, including Chautauque county; from pretty much all of the settled portion of the Holland Purchase. I carded in the season of 1808, 3,029 lbs. of wool; the largest quantity for any one man, was 70 lbs. the smallest, 4 lbs. The lots averaged 18 lbs. Allowing 3 lbs. to a sheep, the average number of sheep then kept by the new settlers, would be six; though it is presumed that the number was larger, as in those days, much of the wool was carded by hand.

The machinists of the present day, may be glad to learn how I procured my machinery. I bought my hand shears of the Shakers at New Lebanon; my press plate at a furnace in Onondaga; my screw and box at Canaan, Conn.; my dye kettle, press papers, &c. at Albany. My transportation bill, for these things, was over two hundred dollars.

I built a grist mill in 1809; in 1817, a paper mill and distillery. I manufactured the first ream of paper west of the Genesee river.

During all the period of my milling operations, I was clearing up the farm where I now reside. Coming into the woods as I have related, dependent almost wholly upon the labor of my hands, in the first twenty years, success had so far attended my efforts, that I had accumulated some fifteen or sixteen thousand dollars.

The early pioneer miller, carder, cloth dresser, distiller, paper maker and farmer, is now in his 77th year, but little broken with age—his frame erect, his step firm—his whole appearance hardly indicating a life of early toil and hardships, such as is to be inferred from his history. The pioneer wife and mother, who was his helper in early years—she who patiently and courageously took up her abode in the rude cabin in the dense forest—who well fulfilled all the duties of life—died in 1842.

The first settler in all the southern portion of Erie county, was Joel Adams. He, in company with others, whose names will be found under the year 1804, T. 9, R. 6, took up land in what is now Aurora, in April of that year. None of them remained but Adams; he put up a shanty, and lived alone the first summer; his only neighbors, Joseph Sears and Roswell Turner, in Sheldon. In the fall his family joined him. His sons were Enos, Ezekiel, Luther and Erasmus. In the winter of 1805, the two oldest boys brought a barrel of flour from Selleck's mill, at Attica, on a hand sled. Their provisions, the first year, were mostly brought from Genesee river, on their backs. The family raised a few crops in 1805, the first in that region.

The prominent pioneer settler in Aurora, was Jabez Warren. He was, as will have been seen, a settler in Middlebury, in 1802; the first settler there. He built a log house and made a small improvement at what is now called Wright's Corners; raised crops there in 1803, the first in that region. In moving in, he cut his own road from Le Roy to Middlebury. Sterling Stearns and his family came in with him. Stearns was a revolutionary soldier—volunteered in the war of 1812, and was killed at the battle of Queenston. Joseph Selleck, Frederick Gilbert, Israel M. Dewey, and Reuben Chamberlin, settled in Middlebury within the same year.

Gen. William Warren, the son of the early pioneer, gives the author the following reminiscences:—

My father's family, and those who came with them, camped out, while making their own road from Le Roy to Middlebury.

In 1803, I took up land and commenced an improvement, on the little Tonawanda, where the Wilson's afterwards settled. Judge Webster went to Warsaw, in 1803, and built a log house.

In 1804, my father sold out in Middlebury, came to the site of the present village of Aurora, built a log house, and made a small opening in the forest. His hired men got their bread baked at Roswell Turner's in Sheldon. In March 1805, moved family in from Middlebury, on ox sled. There came in with him, Henry Godfrey, and Nathaniel Emerson. My father had cut the road from Transit line to lake Erie, for Holland Company, in 1804. He had also opened a road from Attica, three miles west, and then south, to Godfrey's hill.

NOTE.—Tabor Earl brought his wife in 1804, and, it may be claimed, was a settler cotemporary with old Mr. Adams. He, however, went down to Buffalo and wintered, Mr. Adams being the only one that remained over the first year. Mrs. Earl was the pioneer female of all that region.

I sold out at Middlebury, and came here with my family, in 1805. Our first school was in 1806—kept by Mary Eddy, a sister of David Eddy. In 1808 we erected a framed school house. I opened the first tavern in Aurora, in a log house where upper village now is. The first merchants in town, were Adams and Hascall. The first birth in this region, was of a sister of mine, in 1805; first funeral, that of a daughter of Humphrey Smith. My father raised the first wheat, and built the first frame house.

In 1806, Major Phineas Stephens came in, and bought of my father the 200 acres of land, including the water power at the lower village. In that year he built a saw mill, and a grist mill in 1807; first south of Buffalo road and west of Attica. Major Stevens, in the war of 1812, organized a corps called 'Silver Greys,'—volunteered under Smyth's proclamation, and died at Buffalo of the then prevailing fever.

The author will arrest the narrative of the venerable pioneer ong enough to speak in brief terms, of a son of the early miller and enterprising and valuable settler he has introduced. Who in early days, did not know James Stevens? The wild, the eccentric, the odd, the dare devil—and yet the kind good hearted—"Jim Stevens." He was a wayward youth, and yet he was the general favorite in back woods life; ever present at rustic frolics; where there was fun, glee, hilarity, mischief, he was sure to be one of them, and a pretty prominent one too. The boys of the early pioneers generally had to work, as we all recollect—but work, and "Jim" had an early falling out and they never became reconciled. Was he set to a task in the field, he would bare headed and bare footed, wander away and find a congenial home among the Indians upon the Reservation, for weeks. There was a free and easy sort of life there that he liked; and he was a favorite with the Indians. He would be set to tend the mill, and the old gentleman's back turned, down went the gate, and the young miller would likely enough be found entertaining the boys who were waiting for their grists, with his fun and drollery. Approaching his majority, he submitted to the inconveniences of a hat and pair of shoes, and pushed out into the world, an adventurer. Just about the breaking out of the war of 1812, he was the teacher of a singing school on the Canada side of the Niagara river, head over heels in love with the daughter of a good loyalist. He was too much of a patriot to stay upon that side of the lines, and too good a lover to leave, without an arrangement for a Gretna Green affair. Coming upon this side, in a cold winter's night, accompanied by a friend, he crossed the Niagara in a canoe, and approaching the dwelling of his betrothed, managed to smuggle her aboard of his boat. Pushing out into the rapid water a little above Chippewa, in a violent snow storm, in the more than usual darkness it occasioned, the party were carried down with the strong current on the Canada side of Navy Island, and with all their exertions at the oars, were just enabled to strike the head of Porter's mill race. It was a narrow escape; marriage followed; and she, the object of his daring adventure, well repaid him for the risk of life. He had a military turn withal—took some little part in the war of 1812; and he may be remembered within the last twenty five years, as the sometimes bare headed, bustling, clever and jovial Inspector of the —— Brigade of N. Y. state militia.

Timothy Paine, an early settler in Aurora, was a brother of Gen. Edward Paine, the founder of Painsville, on the Reserve. Ephraim Woodruff was the early blacksmith in Aurora.

Humphrey Smith, built the mills before the war, in 1809 or '10. Settlement was rapid in this region, for a few years previous to the war; but was pretty much suspended during its continuance.

My father died in 1810, at the age of 47 years. My mother is living in Chautaque, with my brother Enos, aged 84 years.

Gen. Warren, whose age the author neglected to ascertain, is yet vigorous — was during the last summer a constant laborer upon his farm. He is the father-in-law of A. M. Clapp, Esq., editor of the Buffalo Express.

The venerable David Eddy, who yet survives — a resident at Potter's Corners, in Hamburgh — was in all that region a pioneer, second only to Didimus Kinney, who settled on the Eighteen Mile creek in the now town of Boston, a few months previous. He has obligingly given to the author his distinct recollections of early events:—

I made a beginning in the woods in 1804 — came in with my brother Aaron, and brother-in-law Nathan Peters, and my sister Mary Eddy, to keep house for us, in September; built a log house. I brought along some cows, the wood's feed was abundant. The same fall, Amos Colvin and Ezekiel Smith came in with their families. In 1805 a number of settlers came in — among them, Asa Sprague and Nathaniel Titus.

I think my old pioneer friend William Warren is mistaken as to Phineas Stevens' saw-mill being the first one. In 1805 I was employed by Erastus Granger to build a saw-mill for the Indians on the reservation, on south branch of Buffalo creek. That mill furnished the first boards in all this region; before it was built our log houses were built without boards. In 1807 I built a saw-mill on Smoke's creek. In building both these mills I had to send to Albany for cranks, saws, &c., the transportation costing four and five dollars per hundred. David Reese, the Indian blacksmith in Buffalo did our first work in that line. Our first resources for bread, after exhausting the little stock we brought in, was to buy strings of corn of the Indians, burn out a hollow place in a stump, suspend a pounder by a spring pole, and thus make of the corn a coarse meal. One stump, pounder and spring pole, would answer for several families.

Before Phineas Stevens got his mill going, Daniel Smith, who lived on a small stream two miles south-west of Potter's Corners, built a rude mill. He put up a log building about eighteen feet square — had an over shot wheel — wood gearing throughout — no bolt, for there was no wheat to grind. The rock stones weighed about sixty pounds each. With this rude structure, he could grind five or six bushels of corn per day. He would run the corn through once, then separate the hulls with a sieve, then grind it again, and in this way make pretty good meal.

In 1805, an old bear made her appearance in the neighborhood and made sad havoc with the pigs. We caught her by first securing her cubs, and by that means enticing her into a steel trap. She was uncommonly large. We were not so much troubled here with wolves and bears, in an early day, as they were in other portions of the Purchase, on account of our proximity to the Indian hunters. Deer was very plenty, all this region was a *reserve.* The young Indian hunters were prohibited by an edict of a council from hunting deer within a given number of miles from their village, in order to give the old men a chance. Trout used to be abundant in the small streams.

The Indians were always friendly, good neighbors; our first seeds were obtained from them; they seemed pleased to have white neighbors, and there used to be much traffick between them and the new settlers. When I first came to this region, Farmers Brother, Young King, Big Kettle, Jack Berry, Stephenson, Pollard, (who was half French,) were the influential ones among them. Red Jacket, so far as I have observed, was not generally popular with his own people; with all his talent, he had some bad traits of character, and was too intemperate to be a safe counsellor.

The Wm. Johnston, who was the British interpreter, when the settlement of the Holland Purchase commenced, had a son whose mother was a Seneca Squaw. He was educated; for many years a chief and interpreter. He married a daughter of Judge Barker on the lake shore; died a short time previous to the war.

Nathaniel Titus was the first tavern keeper on the lake shore; commenced there as early as 1805; Elisha Enos succeeded him; ———Smith succeeded Enos. Zenas Barker bought the property and commenced keeping the tavern, I think during the war.

At the mouth of the Eighteen, Joel Harvey commenced keeping a tavern in 1806.

Friends' meeting was first organized in 1806; built a meeting house in 1807; had monthly meetings in 1808; quarterly, in 1816. The first settlers here were mostly Friends.

A Presbyterian church was built at Abbott's Corners, after the war; that place took its name from Seth Abbott, who built a large tavern house there after the war. White's Corners, took its name from an early settler there who kept a public house.

We had a school in this neighborhood as early as 1806, in a log school house, where Friends' meeting house now stands; Henry Hibbard was the first teacher. Ezekiel Smith built the first framed house, and I built the first framed barn. I set out the first orchard, in 1808. The first season I came in, I broke into heavy timbered land, commenced by first building fires to burn the dry leaves, and clearing away the underbrush. I then chopped down the trees, cut, piled, and burned the tops, leaving the bodies upon the ground; planted corn and pumpkins and had a crop of near 1000 bushels of corn, which proved very useful to the new settlers.

In some of the earliest years, a young man by the name of John Sumner, took up a lot in this neighborhood; built a house; was enterprising and industrious; kept bachelor's hall. After he had been here two or three years, doing well, apparently, he was missed, search was made for him for a long time, and finally abandoned. Some time afterwards, his body was found on the banks of Rush creek, in a secluded place, where he had committed suicide. He was buried by his log cabin. This was the first death in this region, except that of a small child of Daniel Smith. We afterwards got information that the young man had left Massachusetts in consequence of a disappointment in a love affair.

In early times there was an Indian living upon the reservation, who I think was 115 years old. He was a christian in all his sentiments; had been a peace-maker through life. I will give you the benefit of a tradition he related to me. He said that a nation called the Eries once inhabited all this region; that they were a powerful, warlike nation, dreaded and feared by all other nations. They were finally warred upon, and their country conquered by the Senecas.

Fish, caught in the lake, was a great help to the new settlers. In the absence of that resource for food, many must have abandoned their new homes in the woods.

Samuel and Benjamin Tubbs, were the pioneer settlers in Eden at the place called Tubb's Hollow, at first, now Eden Valley. There followed soon after, Joseph Thorn, ——— Hill, David Pound.

Jacob Taylor was first settler of Collins; he was agent of Friends' Indian Mission.

Town of Boston was first settled by Didimus Kinney, as has been observed, in 1805, Charles and Oliver Johnson followed soon after, settling on the plains. There was an open spot, pretty much clear of timber; there was an ancient fort there; many relics of ancient occupancy in the neighborhood. There was found in 1807, in a ravine, 500 lbs. of old French axes; the iron was excellent, and was much needed by the new settlers. Axes and brass kettles were found all over this region. A brass kettle was found that would hold sixteen quarts, in a situation where it had kept dry; it was in a good state of preservation.

Mr. Eddy is now 70 years of age, his health and constitution tolerably good, though laboring under the effects of a fractured limb; his wife died in 1844. He was in an early day, an agent of Mr. Ellicott; assisted in locating settlers, and from time to time reported to him how the settlers were getting on with their improvements. There is now living in Hamburg, beside him, of the earliest settlers, Asa Sprague.

The following reminiscences of the primitive settlement of Warsaw, and its neighborhood, were derived from Messrs. Daniel Knapp and Josiah Hovey:—

The Pioneer settler of Warsaw, as has been mentioned by Gen. Warren, was Elizur Webster, Esq. [For names of early settlers, see T. 9, R. 1.]

Judge Webster opened a tavern soon after he came in, and soon after Nehemiah Fargo opened a house of public entertainment. Judge Webster built a saw mill in 1804, and Joseph Manley built a grist mill in 1806, with one run of stones, which he soon after sold to Solomon Morris. Previous to the erection of Webster's saw mill, the log dwellings of the settlers were built without boards.

Judge Webster raised the first crops. He set out a large orchard in an early day. It is presumed that he erected the first cider mill upon the purchase; his first cider was sold for $7 per barrel.* The early settlers were supplied with apple trees from the nursery planted by Josiah Hovey.

Seymour Ensign erected the first carding and cloth dressing establishment at Warsaw. He was succeeded by Simeon R. Glazier, and David Seymour. Col. Elkanah Day, father of Judge Day of Olean, was the first blacksmith.

In 1806, there was no settler on road from Warsaw to Leicester. The road was opened in that year. The first settlers on the road were———Woodward, at Perry Centre. He opened a tavern, was

---

* Judge Webster's orchard was early and widely known. In all the earliest years, before that began to bear, apples and cider were brought from over the river. The arrival of a barrel of cider and a few bushels of apples, at the primitive log taverns, was no ordinary event; it would generally be the occasion of a sleigh ride and a frolic. Apples were often sold at two shillings per dozen, and cider at the same price per quart. A basket of champaign, is not now enjoyed with the zest and relish that a barrel of cider was in those days.

succeeded by ——— Beebe. Elisha and Amos Smith, on inlet of Silver Lake; Elisha opened a tavern. The Atwoods came in as early as 1807 or '8.

A Presbyterian church was organized at Warsaw in 1807—a fine church, the best then upon the Purchase, was erected in 1817. Father Spencer officiated at the formation of the church.

Dr. Chauncey L. Sheldon, was the first physician. Previous to his coming in Dr. Eastman of Attica, and Dr. Sill of Geneseo, were occasionally sent for. In many cases of child birth, the attendance of a physician had to be dispensed with; old Mrs. Palmer used to be toated about on an ox-sled to supply the place of a physician.

The first stock of goods brought to Warsaw, was by Gen. Almond Stevens. The goods were furnished by Dixon, the early merchant in Richmond, Ontario Co.

The surviving early residents of Warsaw and its neighborhood, are Josiah Hovey and wife, Simeon Hovey and wife, Lyman Morris, Shubel Morris, David Fargo, Silas C. Fargo and wife, Amos Kinney and wife, Ezra Walker, Mrs. Young, wife of A. W. Young, (author of Science of Government, and other school books.) Mrs. Young is a daughter of Judge Webster, and was the first born in town. John Munger and wife, Daniel Knapp, Mrs. Norton, (wife of Col. E. Norton, and daughter of Judge Webster.) Harry, a son of Simeon Hovey, the first male child born in town. A son of Deacon Walker, an early and prominent settler, is a Presbyterian clergyman, and another son is a resident and ex-mayor of Baton Rouge.

Judge Webster the early pioneer of Warsaw, sold out his fine farm during the era of speculation, (1837 or '8,) for a high price, and emigrated to Ripley, Chautaque Co. where he now resides. He is 80 years old, but yet vigorous in mind, and physical constitution.

John Wilder, Esq. of Warsaw, was an early pioneer, locating at Attica, in 1806. The author, as in other instances, will principally give his narrative as he related it:—

I came in with another young man, Asa Johnson. We were both millwrights. Our first work was the putting in of the running geers to a saw mill that Zera Phelps was building. Phelps then owned the land now occupied by Attica village, principally. A grist mill had been put up a year before, by John Munger, and purchased by Phelps. We overhauled it and put in new running geers. In 1806, Wm. Vary, who was himself a millwright, had put up a saw mill at what is now called Varysburgh. Johnson and myself put him up a small grist mill—one run of rock stones.*

---

* This was the first mill, in all the region south of Attica. Well does the author remember the mill, the miller, the miller's wife, and the miller's boys. The old gentle-

In July 1807, myself and Johnson, and my brother Joseph Wilder, bought out Zera Phelps at Attica. The grist mill was burned in 1809 with 1000 bushels of grain. In that year we built a new grist mill and saw mill.

The first clothing and carding establishment was erected at Attica by two brothers, named Fuller. Hoisington and Esquire Wright were the early blacksmiths at Attica.

The first merchant establishment in Attica was a stock of goods sent from Batavia by Trumbull Cary, Esq., in 1809; they were put up in a part of my dwelling house. Gaius B. Rich, Esq., now of Buffalo, established himself in Attica as a merchant, in 1811. Myself and my brother Joseph, retained the mills in Attica until 1818, when we sold out to Parmenio Adams and John Peabody. Peabody was an early tavern keeper in Attica, commencing there as early as 1811. His widow is now a resident of the city of Buffalo. I erected a distillery in Attica in 1811.

In 1809, my brother Joseph built a grist mill in Hume for Elisha Mills, the first in all that region; a saw mill had been erected a year or two before. In 1810 I built a grist mill for Judge Griffin in Pike. In 1811, myself and brother built a grist mill in Wales for Isaac Hall. In 1810 we built a grist mill for Judge Wilson, where Linden village now is, in Bethany. In the same year, a grist mill for Elder Brown, on the little Tonewanda, three miles from Alexander, in the town of Bethany.

We held our first singing schools in Attica, in a hollow buttonwood tree. It was felled and a section about thirty feet long cut off. The hollow was large enough for a man of ordinary height to walk upright through it. Benches were made in it; holes cut to admit the light, and it answered a good purpose; the voices of the young folks would sound in it as they would in an arched room.

The narrator of these early events, who has witnessed almost the entire progress of settlement upon the Holland Purchase, is now but sixty-one years of age—young enough and vigorous enough to assist in the settlement of another new country. He has been deputy sheriff and sheriff of Genesee county; in the war of 1812, he was first sergeant in Capt. Seth Gates' company of Grenadiers. He was made a prisoner at the battle of Queenston. His brother

---

man was enterprising, persevering, as any one that ever penetrated that rough, wild region; droll and eccentric. Who of the early mill boys of all that region, does not remember the old man, his "by Gosh," and "by Golden," the rusty horse shoes nailed upon his mill wheel to keep off the witches? He was an early magistrate; many are the anecdotes told of the early marriages he performed. In 1807, he got injured by the fall of a tree; a splinter striking him in the forehead. When the wound was healed, there was a depression large enough to admit the half of an ordinary hen's egg. Although it was attended with a partial loss of faculties, he survived many years. With all of his eccentricities, he was in early times, a good helper in the work of settlement and improvement; possessed of many excellent qualities.

Joseph, was an early magistrate in Attica; held various military offices up to the grade of colonel. He died in 1836.

The town of Sheldon, Townships 9, Ranges 3 and 4, was purchased of Holland Company, in 1803, by Oliver Phelps and Lemuel Chipman. Judge Chipman, with his brother Silas, it will have been seen, were settlers in Pittstown, Ontario county, as early as 1794. They were both physicians from Vermont; brothers of the Hon. Nathaniel Chipman of Middlebury. Lemuel Chipman had been a surgeon in the army of the Revolution. The two brothers were some of the best of the early pioneer stock. Lemuel was for a long period one of the prominent men of Western New York; was a member of the legislature, and one of the Judges of Ontario county. He died in Sheldon, ten or twelve years since. His sons were, Fitch, Lemuel, and Samuel; the last of whom is well known as an early laborer in the temperance cause. Mrs. Guy H. Salisbury of Buffalo, is a daughter of Lemuel. Fitch Chipman, formerly a member of the Legislature from Genesee, whose wife was of the widely known family of Spaffords of Vermont, is still a resident of Sheldon. Dr. Silas Chipman emigrated to Michigan; was one of the earliest settlers at Pontiac.

The purchase of Phelps and Chipman having been perfected, in the summer of 1803, Elijah Warner, a surveyor, was employed to survey the land into farm lots. His assistants were, Roswell Turner, (father of the author,) Joseph Sears, and Tabor Earl. While out, a supply of provisions failed to reach them, and the party were five days without food, except the fish that they caught, wild berries, and roots. Attempting to make their way out of the woods, when nearly exhausted — some of them in fact unable to proceed any farther — they were met by Judge Chipman with a plentiful supply of provisions.

Roswell Turner, having been appointed the agent of Phelps and Chipman, moved upon their land in the month of March, 1804; thus becoming the pioneer settler in all the region now constituting the northwestern portion of Wyoming and southern portion of Erie counties. The first winter was one of severe trials and hardships; the snow was deep, and he had sixteen head of cattle to winter, principally upon browse. At times the deep snow would prevent cattle getting into the woods, and the browse would have to be cut and carried to them in bags. Provisions, and some grain for cattle, had to be brought in from Honeoye and the Genesee river. Upon one occasion, during the winter, he started from the Genesee river with a load upon an ox sled, and *went back to stay the first and second nights.* Progressing as far as he could through the deep snow, breaking his road as he went along, when night came he would go back with his oxen, leaving his load, and return in the morning and renew his slow journey. The snow was two and a half and three feet deep, and no track before him. He was five days making the journey from Genesee river to Sheldon—distance about twenty-five miles. In the winter previous to this, he was preceding his family with a load of provisions, and in fording Allan's creek below the present village of Warsaw, had his feet badly frozen. He found his way to the shanty of the early pioneer Morris, and eventually had to be taken back to Honeoye on his ox sled.

There came in, the first winter, Joseph Sears and family; they did not, however, become actual settlers. Robert Carr and David Hoard were the next settlers, or rather the first named; Hoard died while he was out looking at the country; his was the first death and funeral upon Phelps and Chipman's Purchase. His family came in and occupied the land he had selected. In 1806, the settlers in Sheldon, beside those named, were Deacon Seth Gates, Lemuel Castle, Levi Street, Marvin Brace, Stephen Welton, and Orange Brace. In 1805 and '6, emigration was brisk in that quarter; settlers were pushing on to Willink, Hamburgh and Eighteen Mile Creek. Roswell Turner soon opened a log cabin house of entertainment for the emigrants. It is remembered that, in addition to the stock of provisions he carried in with him, he brought from over the river, the first two winters after, twenty loads of provisions, principally for the supply of new settlers. His house was the home of the earliest class of pioneers. Young men would push on beyond him, build shanties, keep bachelors' hall, and when they were tired of the woods, make a visit to "the settlement;" get their clothes mended, perhaps, or their bread baked. The humble log house that he erected upon the four corners—now called North Sheldon—is a land-mark in the recollections of the early settlers of Wyoming, south part of Erie, and a part of Cattaragus and Chautauque. With the exception of a child of Joseph Sears, who is mentioned as having remained but a short time in Sheldon; a son of Roswell Turner, (Chipman Phelps Turner, of Black Rock, Erie county,) was the first born in all the western portion of Wyoming county. His name was derived from the land owners. Another son of his — the late Judge Horace S. Turner, of Aurora, Erie County, — had been, at the period of his death, longer a resident of that portion of the Purchase named in connection with the advent of his father, than any male survivor. Mrs. Farnum, of Bennington, a daughter of Roswell Turner, is now the oldest resident of the territory named.

The early pioneer settler died in 1809.

Marked, as were hundreds of the Pioneer advents upon the Holland Purchase, with extraordinary privations and endurances, perhaps there were none more so than his. It is a wild, rough region, even now. The reader who may have passed over it, can realize in some degree what it must have been when penetrated by the first settlers.

The first school in Sheldon, was in a log house, erected by Roswell Turner, where Elihu Parson's tavern now stands; the first religious meetings were held at the house of Roswell Turner; the first ministers who were in that region, were Elders Butler and Throop, and father Spencer. The first physician in Sheldon, was John Rolph, after him Benjamin Potter (father of Dr. Potter of Colesville, and Dr. Potter of Varysburgh.) Dr. Ziba Hamilton came in, in 1809. He is now nearly 80 years old, and practising yet, occasionally. He is presumed to be the oldest living resident physician upon the Holland Purchase; his has been a long life, and one of more than ordinary usefulness. For forty years, he has been in one location, the kind and skilful physician, and the useful citizen.

Who of the early residents, does not remember Levi Street ! Commencing at an early period, he carried the mail on the route from Canandaigua through Geneseo, Warsaw and Sheldon, to lake Erie. He was the carrier through all that region, for many years, of the Ontario Repository, Ontario Messenger, and Moscow Advertiser. He removed to Cincinnati, Ohio, where he met the singular fate of death from hydrophobia, caused by the bite of a horse.

Deacon Seth Gates, (father of Hon. Seth M. Gates of Warsaw,) it will be observed, was an early settler. He assisted prominently in the organization of the first church in Sheldon, and was an exemplary and useful citizen. He died a few years since in Warsaw, where his aged widow resides with her children. Some notice of the family of Orange Brace, will be found in connection with the war of 1812. The early physician, Dr. Rolph, was a highly educated man, but singular and eccentric. He chose a residence where he and his family were in a great measure excluded from the little society there was in early times. His wife was the sister of the poet Selleck Osborn.

In addition to the early pioneer settlers of Sheldon, already named, there were Joshua Gates, Lodowick Thomas, Benjamin Joslyn, the Godfreys, Grinnel, Uriah Persons and his sons, Uriah, David, Joseph, John, William, Robert, Charles, Hiram, Henry, Elihu, and two younger ones—twelve, all told; Hubbard Fitch, Simeon Hoard, the Weltons, Joel Harris, Edward Brace, ——— Feagles, ——— Woodruff, Robert Waters, ——— Frink, Shermans, Jared and Roswell Barber, John Sutherland, and a few others whose names are not recollected.

But few of the old inhabitants of Sheldon are left there. Emigration and death, have perhaps thinned their ranks in a greater degree, than in any other early settlement upon the Purchase. Over one half of the whole town, has been purchased within a few years by foreign emigrants; principally Germans.

At an early period, bears, wolves, wild-cats and foxes, preyed upon the sheep, hogs and fowls of the new settlers. Sheep in all cases, had to be folded nights. There used to be a large bounty for wolves: some of the new settlers made a profitable business of trapping them. In cold winters, when snow was deep, the wolves would get hungry and ravenous. There were several instances of their obliging men to climb trees to avoid them. Bears would come and take hogs within a few rods of the dwellings. Deer were abundant. The hills and valleys of Wyoming, were favorite camping and hunting grounds for the Indians long after white settlement commenced. In periods of deep snows and crusts, the deer were easily taken; hundreds were knocked in head,—for several winters, for their pelts alone, the meat being too poor to eat; or if not too poor, the meat would be so flavored with hemlock, (the principal food of the deer in times of deep snow,) as to be unpalatable. In early times, there would once in a while, an elk stray into the neighborhood, from the regions of the Allegany. The trapping of martin, was very common with the young men in winters. Trout were plenty in all the streams.

Chauncey Loomis was the founder of settlement in Bennington. In 1805, he purchased for himself, his mother, his brother-in-law P. Case, his brother Justin, and Jonah Barber, T. 10, Ranges 3 and 4. Bennington was previous to 1818, included in Sheldon; the family name of old Mrs. Loomis, was Sheldon. Chauncey Loomis came on with his mother in July, 1806. There came with him beside, Pelatiah Case, Ezra Ludden, Aaron and Adolphus Clapp, with their families; Joseph Farnum, George Loomis, Nathan Clapp. Justin Loomis had come in the winter previous, built a log house and kept bachelor's hall. This was the first tenement erected in Bennington. Several log houses were erected in the summer of 1807. In that year, Chauncey Loomis erected a saw mill. It was built by Ezekiel Hall, the afterwards widely known landlord—now the keeper of the Eagle tavern, Batavia. In raising a barn for Chauncey Loomis, the first summer, Mr. Hall remembers that it took all the able men in a circuit of ten miles, which included of course, the then considerable settlement in what is now Sheldon. In 1808 and '9, Roger Rowley, George Hoskins, Joab Rockwell, Joseph and Walter Burnham, came into Loomis' settlement. Jonah Barber, who was interested in the land purchase, came on and prepared to erect a log house; returned to Connecticut, and in coming again into the country, was taken sick and died in Bloomfield.

Chauncey Loomis, for Holland Company, in 1808, cut out the road from Bennington through Indian Reservation, coming out upon Willink road a half mile above Red Jacket's wigwam. The first team that passed through on that road was a wagon and three yoke of oxen, going to Buffalo for salt. It was three days in getting to Buffalo. The teamsters were Lester Brace, (late sheriff of Erie county,) Joseph Farnum and Levi Street. The Allegany road from Bennington to Sheldon was cut out in 1807; next year, was continued north to South Buffalo road. In 1808 a road was opened from Bennington to Attica.

The first physician in Bennington was Salmon King; the next, Ira Cross. The first school was organized in 1810; Webster Parsons, Griswold Palmer, George Loomis, Avis Stickney, Seth Pomeroy, Rhodema Durgee and Affa Case, were early teachers. The Baptist church in Bennington was the second church organized upon the Purchase; old Mrs. Loomis made it a donation of one thousand dollars. Elder Herrick was the first settled minister in Bennington. The first born in town was a daughter of Adolphus

Clapp; the first death, that of an infant daughter of Joseph Farnum. The first religious meeting held in Bennington was in the fall of 1807—Elder Peter B. Root officiating. The first merchants in town, were Joseph Farnum and Roswell King. Joseph Farnum opened the first tavern.

In 1810, Chauncey Loomis married Rachel Evans, a niece of Joseph Ellicott. He was elected a State Senator, and died in Albany in 1817, leaving no children. Mrs. Loomis became a resident of Buffalo, where she died a few years since, lamented at least by her old backwoods neighbors, who remembered her many amiable qualities. Justin Loomis, who married a daughter of Dr. Rolph, of Sheldon, is still living, but has been partially insane for many years.

THE LOST BOY.

Among the early events, which will long be remembered, in the region of which we have been speaking, was that of the Lost Boy. David Tolles was a settler on the road between Loomis' settlement and Attica as early as 1806. In July of that year, he had a small patch cleared and sowed to oats, not fenced; the cattle would come out of the woods, and get upon the oat field. A boy, eight or nine years old, a son of Mr. Tolles, was set to watch and keep them off. Just before sun set, he drove the cattle back into the woods, and did not return. That night some few of the immediate neighbors searched for him, and the next day the alarm was spread throughout the whole country. None but those who have witnessed the lively sympathies that exist among backwoods pioneers, can imagine the prompt gathering and faithful search that commenced. The new settlers came in from all directions, organized in companies, and scoured the wilderness. The third day, a party of Indians came from the Buffalo Reservation, and joined in the search. The force collected had to be supplied with provisions; the settlers furnished them to the extent of their means; Mr. Ellicott sent a load from Batavia; and Jabez Warren, who had provisions stored at Roswell Turner's, in Sheldon, ordered them to be served out in rations. The search was continued for a week by the whites; the Indians were hired to continue it longer. But it was all unavailing; the fate of the Lost Boy is unknown to this day.

The second day of the search one party found his tracks; the third day, another party found where he had gathered hemlock bows, and slept; on the fourth day, a party discovered where he had been in a creek, washing some roots. His foot prints upon the rocks were so recent that the water was not dried off; the water of the running stream was yet riled. He had probably fled at the approach of the party. This was the last trace of him discovered.

How much greater the affliction to the parents, than if they could have known the fate of their child! Long years followed of hopes revived from time to time, only to be crushed. The father became a wanderer in search of the Lost Boy. Rumors, cruel to him, would get afloat, that a wild boy had been found in Pennsylvania, or perhaps Ohio; and he would start out on foot, on a pilgrimage of paternal affection. Returning, while attempting to be reconciled to the bereavement, a rumor would reach him, perhaps that his child was among some of the Western Indians; and another long journey would be made.

There are few old settlers who do not remember the Lost Boy, and the intense excitement it created throughout the then thinly settled region.

James M'Kain, the father of James M'Kain, Jr. of Lockport, was a resident of Batavia as early as 1802. In 1804 he opened the first tavern upon the present site of the American. The old gentleman died in Lockport a few years since. The son relates many adventures of early days; especially descriptive of the woods road he used to travel between Ganson's and Batavia, bringing in provisions from Canandaigua on horse back. In the early years the woods road could only be traveled on foot and horse back, when there was no snow upon the ground; the transportation was mostly done by sleighing.

Capt. John Ganson came from Bennington, Vermont, and settled on the Genesee river in the year 1790 or '91. He had accompanied Sullivan's expedition. His first location was on the river, two miles below Avon; his title there proving bad, he purchased land on the Canandaigua road, four miles east of Avon. In the year 1798, he pushed on into the wilderness, and located a little east of Allan's creek, (LeRoy,) becoming the well known pioneer tavern-keeper west of the Genesee river. Charles Wilbur had preceded him, and built a small framed house. He bought him out.

Mrs. Warren, (formerly Mrs. Forsyth,) now residing on Ridge road, in Cambria, is a daughter of Capt. Ganson. Few have seen more of pioneer life — and that, principally, upon the Holland Purchase. She has obligingly given the author some interesting reminiscences of early times:—

Soon after my father had come on west of the river, and opened a public house, other settlers began to come in. There was nothing on the road to Batavia, until Mr. Ellicott's surveyors made their head quarters at Stafford. The Indians were frequent visitors at my fathers. I used to see them often, the chiefs, Hot Bread, Jack Berry, Red Jacket, and Little Beard. Sometimes the Indians were turbulent; they would become a terror to the new settlers. My father was a stout athletic man; had great influence over them; would quell them in their worst drunken frolics.

In 1802, having become the wife of John Forsyth, (a brother of Wm. Forsyth, the well known landlord of the Pavilion, at Niagara Falls,) we settled five miles west of Batavia, near Dunham's grove. Remaining there until 1807, we moved upon the spot where I now reside. When we came here, there were but three or four settlers between Dunham's grove and Lockport. East, there was no settler till we passed the Eleven Mile woods. Our nearest neighbor west, was Joseph Hewett, at Howell's creek.

In 1808, the Ridge road was laid out by General Rhea, Elias Ransom, and Charles Harford. I remember well the arrival of the surveyors; their delight at finding a bed to sleep in, and something to eat that was cooked by a female. Previous to this there had been nothing but an Indian path through the low grounds, west of Wright's Corners.

We brought in a few sheep with us, I think they were the only ones in the neighborhood; they became the especial object of the wolves. Coming out of the Wilson swamp nights, their howling would be terrific. Two years after we came in, I was alone with my then small children one day, when I heard the sheep bleating and running, and went out to see what the matter was. A large wolf had badly wounded a sheep. As I approached him he left the sheep and walked off snarling at me as if reluctant to quit his prey. I went for my nearest neighbor, Mr. Stoughton to get him to come and dress the sheep. It was three fourths of a mile through the woods. On my way a large grey fox crossed the road ahead of me. Returning with my neighbor, a large bear slowly crossed the road in sight of us. I could tell many stories of wild beasts in this region; but I think I never saw as much of them in any one day, before or since. We had no way to keep fowls, but to secure them well in their roosting places. The first settlers found it very difficult to keep hogs; the bears would even come out of the woods and take them by daylight.

Asahel Sage, Esq. of Lewiston, a surviving early settler, gave the author the benefit of his recollections of early times:—

I moved upon the farm in Lewiston, where I now reside in 1807. John Gould, ——— Bragbill, ——— Smith, were then settled on first tier of lots back of mile strip; no other settler farther east upon the mountain. Sanders, Doty, Goodwin, Webster, Hawley, were the pioneer settlers in Sander's settlement. Jarius Rose, ——— De Foe, Springsteen, the Carneys, went in west of Pekin after the war. The Reynolds and Carneys were the first settlers at Pekin. Beamer, Wilson, Bridge, Dr. Orton, Bliss, Earls, were among the earliest settlers between ridge and mountain, west of Scott's.

From some old store bills, that Col. Sage has preserved, the author has extracted some prices. In 1811, trading at a store in Lewiston, he is charged 5s. 6d. for cotton shirting; for "Hum Hum," 3s. 9d. per yard; In 1813, he is charged for muslin, 5s. per yard; for a pound of tea, 12s.; for coffee, 3s. per lb.; for sugar, the same; for a hat $8,00; for a plug of tobacco, 2s.; for nails, 2s. per lb.; for powder, 8s. per lb.

The reader will have observed that the narrative of Judge Porter was arrested about the period of his becoming a resident of the Holland Purchase, in 1806. He gave the author many reminiscences of early times in this region; many of them have already been included in portions of the work derived from other sources. From memorandums taken in conversation with him the following reminiscences are principally derived:—

The Judge moved from Canandaigua to the Falls, in June of the year already named. After the fashion of emigrants in those days, he was his own teamster; coming to his new home with whip and reins in hand, his family, consisting then of his wife and three sons, constituting his freight. He was four days making the journey; and that in favorable weather. The Portage company, consisting of himself, his brother Peter B. Porter, Benjamin Barton, Jr. and Joseph Annin, had in February, of the year previous, leased of the State, the Portage and Stedman Farm at Schlosser;* and at the same time, the company had bought of the State, lots 1, 2, 3, and 4, of Mile Strip, which included the Falls on the American side, extending three fourths of a mile below

---

* The lease was for the term of twelve years; on its expiration in 1816, it was extended four years, in consideration of the interruption that had been occasioned by the war.

them, and half a mile above. They had erected a saw mill the same year of the purchase.

Judge Porter took possession of the Stedman house, for his residence. It was a substantial framed building; besides this, there were at Schlosser, several dilapidated log buildings. All that was left of the old English fort, were the entrenchments; several pickets, and the ruins of some framed and log buildings that had been used as barracks. During English occupancy, Stedman had built a saw mill on the rapids, where a woolen factory now stands.* At Schlosser there was an old apple orchard, a hundred trees or more, and several peach, pear, and plum trees.

In 1806, and up to the period of the war, water fowl were abundant at the Falls. Large flocks of geese and swans would make their appearance generally in September, and remain until the fore part of winter. But few came during or after the war. It is supposed that the firing of cannon and muskets, scared them away. The eagle used to nest about the Falls in early years of settlement. The Judge accounts for the fact that ducks often go over the Falls, (which has had so many different versions,) in this way:—In still dark nights, sitting upon the water in the wake of Grass Island, they fall asleep, and float into the rapid water, where they cannot rise upon the wing. Sometimes they have encountered this fate in large numbers. After being disabled by the descent over the Falls, they are easily taken below.

The rattle snake existed in great numbers at the Falls in an early day. At the whirlpool was a large den of them; they were of uncommon size. Above the Falls, between Sclosser and Gill creek, there used to be large colonies of an entire different species; they were small, not exceeding twelve or sixteen inches in length. It is a singular fact, that the rattle snake was never known to approach Niagara Falls, within a distance of from a half to three-fourths of a mile.† They were so numerous at one time, at their principal den below the Falls, that the Tuscarora Indians could not safely

---

* There was a year or two since, if there is not now, a stick of oak timber, that was taken from the ruins of this mill perfectly sound. The mill it is supposed, was built previous to 1763. When Judge Porter went to Schlosser, there were in a fence some chestnut rails that then appeared very old. The same rails are now in his fences there, perfectly sound.

† The Judge attributes this to the trembling of the earth for that distance. Open a penknife, stick the point into a tree near the Falls, and a tremulous motion of the handle will be observed.

occupy a favorite fishing ground there. They extirpated them in great numbers, by setting fire to the dry leaves—burning over the steep bank, about the time they were crawling out for their summer excursions. On another occasion, as related by Messrs. Fairbanks and Gould, the white inhabitants collected and made war upon them; over five hundred were destoyed in one day. In this way, with the help of the hogs, that would hunt and devour them, they were gradually extirpated.

Judge Porter names some facts in connexion with the rattle snake that may be interesting to naturalists:—They never strike except in self-defence; they will always first endeavor to retreat. He has taken the head off of one, opened the jaws with a stick, and observed a drop of fluid, resembling milk and water, exuding from each fang. It seemed to be the effort of the head to do its work of mischief after it was separated from the body. The body, after the head is off, when touched, will coil and make an impotent attempt to strike.

In the first few years after Judge Porter went to the Falls, the visitors were but few; there was no tavern upon this side. Upon the opposite side, William Forsyth had opened a house. The visiting upon this side, to any considerable extent, commenced with the completion of the bridge to Goat Island.

In the spring of 1807—all Niagara being in the town of Buffalo—Judge Porter and Robert Lee, Esq. attended town meeting at Buffalo, to get some path masters elected.

In 1806, the inhabitants along the frontier, in Niagara, were, besides Judge Porter at Schlosser, Jesse Ware, Wm. Miller, Stephen Hopkins, William Howell, Joshua Fairbanks, Philemon Baldwin, Joseph Howell, Isaac Colt, Erastus Parks, James Murray, between Falls and Lewiston; Isaac Swain lived on military road. At Lewiston there were, Capt. Lemuel Cook, Thomas Hustler, John Beach, Solomon Gillett. Between Falls and Black Rock, there was only "Big Smith," at Cayuga creek.

In 1806, the Portage Company built a mill of two run of stones, at the Falls. To raise the mill, it took all the able bodied citizens of the neighborhood, and a party of forty soldiers, from the fort who were accompanied by Lieut. (now General,) Armisted.

The first time that Judge Porter succeeded in getting upon Goat Island, (previous to 1810,) there were old dates there upon trees; there had been a tree cut there, and a canoe built. The remains of five or six human skeletons, were found there in early years. There were three or four acres that had been cleared by Captain Stedman to make a pasture for *goats* that he had once kept there;—hence the name.

In 1811, Judge Porter and his brother General Porter made an attempt to buy Goat Island of the state; but could not succeed in getting the consent of the Legislature. In 1814, they had the good fortune to secure it. Samuel Sherwood, a lawyer of considerable eminence in his day, had a *float*, as it is now called in our western states. It was an instrument given him by the state of New York, (such as are often issued from the General Land Office of the United States,) allowing the bearer to locate two hundred acres of any of the unsold or unappropriated lands of the state. It was given Mr. Sherwood as a consideration for some failure of title to lands he had purchased of the state. The brothers (Porters,) bought the instrument of him, and during the next year selected Goat Island, and the small islands about it, as a part of the two hundred acres; in all, about seventy acres. In 1816, they received their "patent," or deed. The boundaries, as stated in the deed, are as follows:—"A certain island, commonly called Goat Island, being in the Niagara river, immediately above and adjoining the Great Falls;—together with several tracts, or masses of rock, surrounding and appendant to the said principal Island;—according to a plan or survey of Parkhurst Whitney." The deed is signed by Daniel D. Tompkins, then Governor of the State; by Archibald Campbell, Deputy Secretary of State; and Martin Van Buren, as Attorney General, certified as usual in such cases.

In 1817, Judge Porter threw a bridge across in the smooth, strong current, some distance above the present site. The bridge was completed in that year. During the next March, lake Erie was broken up suddenly by a violent wind; large masses of ice came down with such violence as to carry away the central and greater portion of it. In 1818, he erected another bridge, on the present site. He chose a location where the rapids were still stronger than at the previous one. There was this advantage in it, however—it is low enough down to have the masses of ice principally broken before they reach it, and consequently not striking with as much force. A decided advantage, too, is gained in the location of the piers. There are, in the rapids a succession of eddies

The piers are in each instance located in one of them. The main structure erected in 1818, is now standing, though it has required frequently, new planking, and other repairs.*

Judge Porter is of the opinion, that Goat Island was formed by a gradual deposit, commencing at a period when there was not a very strong current. He thinks in the progress of the Falls from Lewiston to their present location, they were arrested a long time at the Whirlpool; thence the deep pit, or chasm, that has been excavated there.

The Stedman family left Schlosser in 1795, the British portage having been transferred to the other side of the river, in anticipation of the surrender of this frontier. They left Jesse Ware in possession of their home and farm. He in fact not only claimed the Schlosser property, but some four thousand five hundred acres of land beside, including the Falls. He claimed as the successor of the Stedmans, their claim having been founded upon an assumed grant of the Seneca Indians of all the land that lay between the Niagara river, and the circuit he made in his flight from the massacre at the Devil's Hole. The state having put Judge Porter and his associates in possession, no attempt was made to enforce the Stedman claim until 1823. In that year, Samuel Street, and Thomas Clark, of Chippewa, commenced a suit in ejectment in the Supreme Court of this state, in the name of the heirs of Philip Stedman. It was assumed that the Indians had once deeded the land to Stedman, and that the deed had been lost. The trial resulted in a nonsuit.†

The Stedman family were in possession at Schlosser, from the period of British conquest in 1759, to 1795. Philip Stedman died in New York, in 1797, where he had gone for medical advice.

---

* Great skill and ingenuity were required in the erection of these bridges. The process by which the piers were located was as follows:—An abutment was first laid a short distance out in the water; sticks of timber eighty feet long were hewed tapering; the light ends were carried out and the heavy ends secured upon the abutment. A man would then walk out upon each of these sticks, and the two would throw a girth across, secure it, and then manage to thrust posts into the swift water for the structure to rest upon. From this commencement, the cribs or piers were constructed; the process being repeated upon each extension. Soon after the bridge was completed, Red Jacket was at the Falls, and was invited by Judge Porter to go and view it. After he had surveyed it attentively, with less than his usual stoical indifference, he muttered, "*Tamn the Yankees,*" as much as to say, it took them to a difficult thing.

† If the Indians did anything more than to promise such a grant to Stedman, they were unmindful of it the next year after the affair at the Devil's Hole. In that year (1764,) they made no reservation of land about the Falls, in their cession of the carrying place to the King of Great Britain.

The transportation for all the region west of Cayuga lake, was by water, (the portages excepted,) until the completion of the Turnpike in 1803. After that it was mostly done with the "big wagons." When staging commenced, the time was usually two days from Albany to Utica, three days from Utica to the Genesee river, and two days from the river to Buffalo. Judge Porter has been seven days in coming from Albany to Canandaigua by stage; in 1802, he had the contract for carrying the mail from Utica to Fort Niagara. The route was the usual one to Buffalo; from thence, down on Canada side to Fort Niagara. Luther Cole was the first mail carrier west of Utica.

Judge Porter was the first Post Master in Niagara county; he held the office until 1837, and was succeeded by Judge De Veaux.

Major John Morrison, now residing upon lake shore, a mile and a half below Fort Niagara, was one of the first to make an opening in the woods of Niagara, in all the region north of Batavia and Lewiston road and east of Howell's creek. In the fall of 1803, he erected a log cabin in what was afterwards called Slayton's settlement, on Eighteen Mile creek, a mile below Maybee's mill. Keeping bachelor's hall, he chopped five acres, and in the spring brought his wife and children there from Niagara, U. C. His cabin not being large enough to accommodate the new comers, he put up in one day, with the help of Mrs. Morrison, a very considerable addition; covering it with peeled elm bark. Raised that season, among the logs, patches of corn and potatoes. Gad Warner, Thomas Slayton, Loudon Andrews, Samuel Capen, were his neighbors in 1804. Mrs. Morrison, who yet survives, gives a relation of the events of a night, which will interest the reader:—In the summer of 1804, her husband had gone out to Batavia to get some provisions; leaving her alone with her children over night. A pack of wolves came near the cabin and set up a terrible howl — such as is usual with them when scenting prey. Mrs. M. got up from her bed, and heard them for a long time, apprehending no danger until she found they had approached within a few feet of the door place. There was no door, a blanket supplied the place of one; this, as she was aware, afforded but a poor protection. Careful not to wake her sleeping children, lest the sound of their voices might excite the wolves to a bolder siege, she took her husband's axe and stood sentry, for hours and hours, until, day light approaching, the wolves retired into the depths of the forest.

The author will here observe, that a necessary brevity of narrative, obliges him to omit many relations of events like the above, and others that were attendant upon primitive forest life.

The Ridge road, through all the eastern portion of Niagara, was *discovered* in 1805. Some of the new settlers in Slayton's settlement in 1805, were hunting cattle, and observed that there was continuous elevated ground, and changed their location, settling upon it east of Hartland Corners. It was not however known in its full extent through that region, until some years after. Jedediah Riggs, John Palmeter, and Daniel Brown, were the first settlers upon the Ridge, east of Howell's creek, in Niagara and Orleans counties.

The pioneer in all the region named in connexion with the advent of Major Morrison, was Thomas Slayton. He was on his way to Canada, with his family; broke his wagon down, about two miles east of the Cold Springs, stopped in consequence, liked the country, took up land and chopped an acre or two. His horses having strayed away from his log cabin, he went into the woods in pursuit of them, and in his rambles saw the fine soil and black walnut groves below the mountain, and soon changed his location, becoming the founder of Slayton's settlement. Those who pass now through that beautiful, highly cultivated region, will conclude that the early pioneer made a good selection, when he had a wide field before him.

Stephen Bugbee, who went to Slayton's settlement in 1805, still survives. Joshua Slayton, one of the earliest residents, is still living, his residence, at Jackson, Michigan. The first religious meeting held in the pioneer neighborhood, (now town of Royalton,) was in 1808; Elder Joel Doubleday, of the Christian denomination, officiated. The church formed by him there, is supposed to be one of the first upon the Holland Purchase. Dr. David Dunn, was the first physician in town; Ezra Harwood, the first merchant; Thomas, or Joshua Slayton, raised the first crops; Stephen Bugbee built the first framed house and barn; William Curtiss planted the first orchard; Daniel Vaughn, who is still a resident of the town, was the first born. The church edifice erected by the Christian denomination in Slayton's settlement, is the first house built for public worship on the Holland Purchase; if we except the log church, built by Brant at Lewiston, before white settlement commenced.

Gladly would the author, from memory, in the absence of dates, if space permitted, bestow especial notice upon more ot the pioneer settlers of Niagara. There was one of the pioneer landlords upon the Ridge Road, William Molyneux, widely known in early times, and especially in the war of 1812; one of the best specimens of the "green isle of the ocean;" jovial, kind hearted and benevolent. The old landlord, and she, the companion in his early advent, who served up for long years, welcome repasts for the weary traveller—one of the best of pioneer wives and mothers—both, side by side, rest in a quiet rural spot, that will arrest the attention of the traveller as he passes along the Ridge Road, near their once residence; and near by, under the same green shade, rest the remains of a son who closed an early life of promise at West Point, a tasteful monument, erected by his brother cadets, indicating the high respect they entertained for his memory. The surviving sons of William Molyneux, now residents of Niagara, are Charles, (the landlord at the old stand,) William and Robert. An only daughter, is the wife of ex-sheriff, Hiram M'Niel.

Capt. Lemuel Cooke was a first sergeant in the U. S. army, and came to Fort Niagara at an early period of American occupancy; remaining in the army but about one year, he opened a tavern near the fort at the ferry landing. In 1802 he removed to Lewiston. The sons of this early pioneer were Bates, Lothrop, and Isaac. Bates Cook, Esq. was the early P. M. at Lewiston, for a long period a practicing Attorney in Niagara, and ultimately filled the office of Comptroller of the State. He died at Lewiston a few years since. Judge Lothrop Cooke and his brother Isaac are yet residents of Lewiston. The family will again be referred to in connection with some events at Lewiston in the war of 1812; no family has been longer, and few more conspicuously identified with the history of the Holland Purchase.

Judge Cooke mentions the fact that in the year 1799, he was sent to school to East Bloomfield, the then nearest one to the residence of his father's family. The first school at Lewiston was in 1806, kept by a Scotchman named Watson.

And there is another reminiscence of his that should have been in an earlier connection:—In the summer of 1799, the garrison at Niagara was kept in readiness for action, in anticipation of a renewal of Indian wars. At one period a large body of Indians came down and camped on the Canada side.

Few were better known all along during the period of the war of 1812, than the early landlord and landlady at Lewiston, Mr. and Mrs. Hustler. He is said to have been the model Sergeant Hollister, of Cooper's Spy, and his wife the model Betty Flannagan. Both were taken prisoners at St. Clair's defeat, and were afterwards with Wayne's army.

The Loyds, Browns, Dotys, Zittles, Swains, Hopkins were among the earliest settlers in Porter, and that, it will be observed, was one of the earliest settled towns upon the Purchase.

Jacob Christman was the pioneer settler on Tonawanda creek, between Indian village and the Niagara river, settling at Christman's Rapids, as early as 1804. He was for several years the only settler in the distance named; George Van Slyck was the next settler.

Reuben Hurd, a surviving pioneer, settled on Ridge Road in Cambria, in 1805. He says:—The early settlers used to go to Canada for their supplies of provisions; sometimes they would have no supplies there and then they would have to manage the best way they could. The Tuscarora Indians generally had corn to sell. Billious fevers and fever and ague, in early years, along the Ridge Road, were very prevalent, discouraged settlement. I have known, at several periods, more than half of the population sick. Before there was any mill at the Falls, we used generally to pound our corn out in stump mortars. The first school on Ridge Road was in a small log house, a mile west of Howell's. Mrs. Neal, the mother of George Neal was the teacher. Our earliest meetings were at the mission house, in Tuscarora; Methodist preachers soon came along, holding their meetings in the log houses of the settlers. At the breaking out of the war of 1812, I think there was not over one hundred acres of cleared land between Hardscrabble and the Cold Springs.

Jeptha Dunn was one of the earliest settlers on Ridge Road, in Hartland; now in his old age, the owner of a large and valuable farm; an anecdote of his early advent, may serve to illustrate how beneficial to settlers and the prosperity of the country was the policy of admitting settlers without requiring more than nominal advance payments. He applied to Mr. Ellicott for the land upon which he now resides. It was required that he should pay the usual per cent; this he was unable to do, for four dollars was all the money he possessed. Eventually, the land was "booked" to him, he advancing the four dollars, half of which, was handed back to him, upon Mr. Ellicott's understanding that he had a journey to make a considerable distance to the east on foot. A good settler was thus secured, and he paid for his land. It is not exaggeration to say, that there were a thousand of instances, that would as well illustrate the benefits that have flowed from giving men possession of soil, and trusting to their industry and energy for payment of the purchase money. To be sure, the poor man obtains a few hundred dollars now, easier than he could then, but how many Jeptha Dunns have there been since the sales of public lands commenced at the west, who would have gone there and become free holders and useful citizens, if they could have got possession of lands as easy as he did? If they went there and located under pre-emption laws, sale days would come about, long before they could meet them.

And here, through the aid of a venerable surviving pioneer, Mr. David Mather, of Lockport, we get another early glimpse of Buffalo:—

I settled in Buffalo in April, 1806; there was then sixteen dwelling houses, principally framed ones; eight of them were scattered along on Main street, three of them were on the terrace, three of them on Seneca, and two on Cayuga streets. There were two stores; one the "contractor's" on corner of Main and Seneca streets, (east side of Main,) Vincent Grant, kept it. The other was the store of Samuel Pratt, adjoining Crow's tavern. Mr. Le Couteulx kept a drug store in a part of his house on Crow street. David Reese's Indian blacksmith shop was on Seneca street, and William Robbins had a blacksmith shop on Main street. John Crow kept a tavern where Mansion House now stands, and Judge Barker kept one on the site of the market.

I remember very well the arrival of the first public mail that ever reached Buffalo. It was brought on horse-back by Ezra Metcalf, he came to my blacksmith's shop and got his horse shod. He told me he could carry the contents of his bag in his two hands.

William Johnston died in 1807, aged 65 years. He was a good neighbor, a man of a good deal of intelligence; was much respected by the Indians. I was with him a good deal during his last illness, and from what escaped him then, I judged that he had been familiar with some of the most barbarous scenes of the border wars.

From 1809 to the commencement of the war, a good many settlers came into Buffalo, and a good many buildings were put up.

In early times, I have on several occasions seen the water less than knee deep across the mouth of Buffalo creek. The few vessels then on the Lake, would lay off from a half to three fourths of a mile, or go down to Black Rock, anchoring below the rapids.

Mrs. Mather, the wife of David Mather, also survives. She came to Batavia in 1802, was then the wife of Joseph Hawks, and a sister of the earliest physician there, Dr. Alvord. Mrs. Mather moved with her first husband to Williamsville, in 1805. Jonas Williams, a brother-in-law of Andrew A. Ellicott, from whom the village of Williamsville took its name, was then a young man just commencing a farm there—had purchased the old saw mill and water power, and was rebuilding the mill. For two years Mrs. M. was the only female at Williamsville; kept house for Mr. Williams. The nearest family was a half mile on the road east. She remembers that a Mr. Lewis opened the first tavern in the neighborhood, a mile and a half west of Williamsville, at the Henshaw stand, and that the settlers came in pretty fast upon the openings, in 1805. Mrs. M. says that she and her husband were three days getting from Batavia to Williamsville, with a yoke of oxen and wagon.

Mrs. Mather became a resident of Buffalo in January, 1807. She participated in the formation of the first religious society; a union of Presbyterians and Congregationalists. The Rev. Thaddeus Osgood was the officiating minister. The first meetings were held in the court house. The primitive members of the church were: —Mrs. Landon, Nathaniel Sill and wife, Mrs. Mather, Mrs. Pratt, and a young man whose name is not recollected. If Deacon Callender was not a member of the church on its first organization, he was soon after; except when missionaries came along, he took the lead in the meetings. Mrs. M. thinks that the Rev. Miles P. Squires, was the first settled minister in Buffalo.

In the disposal of lots in Buffalo Mr. Ellicott was even more careful to confine the sales to actual settlers, and to require a certain stipulated amount of improvements, in a given time, than in the sale of farming lands. He often refused to sell lots for the whole purchase money in advance, without buildings were first erected upon them, or some earnest given that there would be. This accounts for the slow sale of lots there. The whole original village plat, would have sold in the absence of such conditions, at the low prices asked, before 1820. As in the rest of the Purchase, there was a resident in the confidence of the local agent, who would report to him from time to time the progress of improvements. Mr. Le Couteulx, at "New Amsterdam," would inform Mr. Ellicott that such an one had a "framed house up and covered;" that another "had the frame out for a house;" that another "had a cellar dug;" that another had an inner lot "cleared and fenced in;" that another on an outer lot, had one two or three acres, "cleared and enclosed." Upon the contract books, there are numerous instances of entries stipulating the improvements that were to be made in a given time. These conditions it should be observed, were not for the usual purpose of increasing the value of the premises, and keeping the lien for the purchase money good; but were intended to make every purchaser an actual settler. It would amuse the reader to see with what care Mr. Le Couteulx would inform Mr. Ellicott that cellars were dug, frames up and partly covered, or the timber cleared away and enclosures made, where the land is now worth from two to three hundred dollars per foot, and covered with four and five story brick blocks.

It may interest the reader to see some of the early prices of lots in New Amsterdam. No sales were made until 1804; such settlers as had made locations and improvements had done so with the promise of a pre-emptive right. In that year, lot 1, site of Mansion House, was sold for $140, (deeded afterwards to Joseph Landon at that price.) Prices of lots in this year, generally corresponded with this example of prices. In 1805, Thomas Sidwell paid $35 and $45 for lots 75 and 76 on Pearl Street. In 1806, Asa Chapman paid for lot 36 opposite Farmer's Hotel, $120; Eleazer Hovey, paid for out lots 146 and 147, (near barracks,) 11 and $12 per acre; David Mather, for lot 38 on Main Street, $120,25 in advance. In 1807, Abraham Hershey, paid for lots 150, 151, 156, 157, $20 per lot. In 1808, Alpheus Hitchcock paid $4 per acre for out lots 88 and 89. One of the first sales after the war, in 1816, was to Smith H. Salisbury; lot 183 on Washington Street; price $480,80; was to erect a "house 20 feet square." Next sale in that year, was of lots 85 and 86, to Miles P. Squier; purchase money, $550. There were but three sales in this year. In 1817, Frederick B. Merrill paid for lots 87 and 88, $580; was to "erect a house 20 by 24." Barent B. Staats, for E. pt. inner lot 90, $300; was to erect a house "24 feet square, 2 stories high." There were but two sales in this year. In 1818 no sales. In 1819, F. B. Merrill paid for outer lot 115,

LOUIS LE COUTEULX.

$20 per acre; and for parts of inner lots 87 and 88, (35 feet,) $175. No other sale in that year. In 1820, J. D. Hoyt, paid for outer lot 69, $30 per acre; Ralph M. Pomeroy, for outer lot 70, $35 per acre. There were but four sales in this year. In 1821, M. A. Andrews paid for inner lots 202 and 203, $200; for outer lots 120, 121, 127, 128, 129, 130, 131, 132—in all 79 acres—$25 per acre. Roswell Chapin for inner lot 133, $250. Sally Haddock, for 3½ acres, outer lot 28, $150. Ebenezer Johnson, for lots 100 and 102,—one acre —$200. Moses Baker, for lots 23 and 24, $400. Gilman Folsom for lot 198, $150; under a stipulation, to have "a framed house built in one year." Avery C. Tiffany, for lot 201, $180; was to erect a "brick house." John Rickard and Isaac Hampton for lot 199, $150; were to build "a framed or brick house, immediately."

About the middle of September, 1821, under the new agency of Mr. Otto, and a policy differing from Mr. Ellicott's with reference to conditions of sales, occupation, improvements, &c.; and with the prospect that the Erie Canal would terminate at Buffalo; a new impetus commenced; sales of lots were brisk. Before the close of the year, 91 lots were sold; the prices of inner lots ranging from $80 to $250; outer lots from $12 to $17 per acre. In 1822 there were 64 sales made; in fact, all that remained of the original plat of New Amsterdam; the prices not varying materially from those cited of 1821. A large portion of the original plat of New Amsterdam was sold in the nine months, ending June 1st, 1822.

LOUIS STEPHEN LE COUTEULX.

Louis Stephen Le Couteulx de Chaumont, was born at Rouen, in France, on the 24th of August, 1756. He was the only son of Anthony Le Couteulx, a counsellor at law, and delegate to the Parliament of Normandy. He was the head of the eldest branch of the Le Couteulx family.

This family, which originated in Normandy, was ennobled in 1505, on account of some service rendered the government, with the privilege, usually denied to the nobility, of engaging in commerce. It always enjoyed high distinction and formed many

---

NOTE.—All that part of the city lying east of Ellicott Street, (which runs northerly and southerly about ten rods east of the Court House,) and all north of Chippewa Street and south of Terrace, were denominated outer lots by the Holland Company, and sold, by the acre.

alliances with distinguished families in France, particularly with that of La Fayette.

He was destined for the magistracy; having no taste for that occupation, entered the commercial house of his relations, who had establishments in France and many other parts of Europe.

Understanding the English and Spanish languages, he was sent to London and Cadiz, where he passed several years.

In September, 1786, he married, in Paris, Miss Clonet, whose father held an honorable office in that city. She was a niece of General Touzard, who came to America with General La Fayette, during the Revolutionary war, and lost an arm in our service. This did not prevent him from remaining in the employ of our government until his death, which occurred in 1811.

Immediately after his marriage, Mr. Le Couteulx was sent to the United States to negotiate a settlement of accounts with the house of Robert Morris. He arrived with his wife at New York on the 15th of December, 1786, and repaired to Philadelphia, whither his business called him. Having arranged the accounts with Mr. Morris, and being pleased with this country, he rented a house in Trenton, New Jersey, where he remained until the July following. He then purchased an estate in Bucks county, near Philadelphia, of about two hundred acres, called "La Petite France."

Wishing to become a citizen of the United States, he made his first declaration on the 7th day of July, 1787, and eventually obtained his certificate of naturalization.

The climate of this country not agreeing with his wife, he accompanied her to France the 17th of October, 1789, with his two sons, and returned alone to Philadelphia, the 17th of February following.

He was among the first who introduced merino sheep into the United States, having imported a pair from Spain, in 1789, which he presented to Robert Morris. They were sent from Cadiz by the house of Le Couteulx, not without great difficulty and risk, as the Spanish government had forbidden their exportation under severe penalties.

Having arranged his business with Mr. Morris, and being fond of traveling, he set out on horseback, accompanied with a servant, and visited the greater part of the United States. This occupied him two years, a part of which time he spent among various tribes of Indians for the purpose of studying their manners and customs

During this sojourn among the Indians, he was adopted by the Senecas. He wrote an interesting journal of his travels which unfortunately has been lost.

After finishing his travels, he established himself in business at Albany in the spring of 1795, where he continued to reside for many years.

He set out in the month of September, 1800, with a large quantity of merchandize destined for Detroit, where he had determined to reside, in case he found it a good market for his goods.

The usual route of travel to Detroit at that early period, was by way of Fort Niagara, Fort George, and Queenston to Chippewa, and Fort Erie, where shipping could be obtained direct to Detroit.

On landing at Fort George on the 7th day of October, 1800, he was arrested by the English, on suspicion of being a French spy, and sent prisoner to Quebec, where he endured a rigorous captivity from the 4th day of November, 1800, until the 29th day of July, 1802, when he was released in consequence of the ratification of peace between Great Britain and France.

During his detention, strenuous exertions were made by his friends to procure his release, and the Government of the United States in vain claimed his discharge as an American citizen.

His affairs experienced sad derangement during his long captivity, but with what he could save from the wreck of his fortune, he soon after purchased from the Holland Company several lots in the then village of New Amsterdam—(now Buffalo.)

Mr. Le Couteulx came to reside in Buffalo in the year 1804, soon after employed some Canadians to construct him a frame house opposite Mr. Crows, on the site of the building now known as the "LE COUTEULX BLOCK," and in which he lived until the burning of Buffalo, with his second wife, whom he married a short time after his release from his captivity.

He was soon after employed by the Holland Company as an agent for the sale of their lands in Buffalo and its vicinity, and was appointed first Clerk of Niagara county, the 26th of March, 1808, which office he continued to hold until the war of 1812.

He then removed to Albany, where he had still a small property, and re-established himself in business in that city.

He received the appointment of Forage Master in the service of the United States towards the close of the late war, which he held until June, 1815.

He was elected Sergeant at Arms by the Constitutional Convention of 1821, and also by the New York Senate.

He soon after returned to Buffalo, where he resided until his death, which occurred October 16th, 1839, at the age of 84 years. His wife had died the year previous.

Thus have we sketched the prominent events of the life of Louis Stephen Le Couteulx, one of the earliest pioneers of Buffalo. He died regretted by all who were capable of appreciating his good qualities. As a private citizen, no one was more worthy of the general esteem and consideration in which he was held.

He was a kind father, affectionate husband, and firm friend. He was honest beyond suspicion; as a Catholic, he strictly observed all the requirements of his religion, and especially those of the Gospel, which induced him to regard all the unfortunate as his brethren, and to afford them assistance without reference to their religion.

In the discharge of his public duties he was distinguished for his integrity, his zeal, and his affability.

Although a foreigner by birth, no one excelled him in love of his adopted country, or more highly appreciated its institutions, and he was ever ready to sacrifice his personal interest for the general good. Some proofs of this may be found in the donations he has made to the city of Buffalo and other corporations, for benevolent purposes. He was the founder of St. Louis Church, erected by the Catholics on a large lot fronting on Main Street, in the City of Buffalo, which he presented to the Bishop of New York, and his successors in office, for that purpose, and for the construction of which he contributed a large share of the funds. He also gave another lot to the Irish Catholic congregation, on which they have recently erected a church.

In acknowledgement of these benevolent acts, and to perpetuate his memory, the Common Council of the City of Buffalo procured his portrait to be painted a short time before his death, and have placed it among those of the mayors of the city, in the Common Council chamber.

In 1804, Major Adam Hoops, whose name has occurred in connection with the earliest movements of the Holland Company in this region, purchased about ten thousand acres of land at Olean Point, and commenced founding a settlement there. Ebenezer F.

Norton was interested with him in the purchase. At that early period, and in fact, until the completion of the Erie Canal, Olean Point, the head of navigation on the Alleghany river, was deemed to possess important advantages, as will be seen in connection with other accounts of early movements in that quarter. Anticipations were entertained, the fulfilment of which has been postponed, but which are in a fair way to be yet realized. It is here that the Genesee Valley Canal enters the Alleghany river; it is where the Erie rail road comes upon its banks; and it is the point up to which the river will in all probability, in the course of a few years, be made navigable for steamboats.

Major Hoops, and his brother Robert, settled there, and built a small log house, in the same year the purchase was made. Previous to the commencement of the settlement of the Holland Purchase, there was a small isolated settlement on the Osway, in Pennsylvania, adjoining the line of this state. Although a little beyond our bounds, it is quite too remarkable to be passed over:— Francis King, a member of the Society of Friends, came from London to Philadelphia, an adventurer in the new world, in 1795. In '97, at the suggestion of some capitalists of Philadelphia, he set out as a land explorer; after journeying over the wild regions of western Pennsylvania, for weeks in the forest, camping out; losing his way, and coming near famishing for food, he found his way out of the woods, and returning to Philadelphia, his representations induced Keating & Co. of that city, to purchase of Wm. Brigham Esq. (who had purchased of the state,) 300,000 acres of land in what is now Potter and M'Kean counties. The explorer became the resident agent of the owners. In the summer of '98, he came upon the purchase, with a few hired hands, and put up a log building on the Osway, near the present village of Ceres, or Cerestown. His son and three daughters, joined him in his wilderness home in '98. There are few instances of pioneer life, so isolated, and that too, of a family who had been transferred from the largest city of Europe. Their nearest neighbors for two years, were in Dyke's settlement, at what is now Andover, in Allegany county, N. Y. The nearest neighbor in Pennsylvania was at the distance of fifty-six miles; no supplies could be obtained short of a journey of one hundred and forty miles, to a settlement on the Susquehannah. The pioneer settler used to send his son once a month, on a pack horse road to the nearest P. O. (Williamsport,) for his letters.

The journey used to be made on foot, and in all cases, involved the necessity of camping out one night going and coming. In 1800, several families came in.

Francis King died in 1814. He was succeeded in the land agency, by his son John King, whom the author found last summer, a resident near Ceres, in a quiet and romantic spot, his hospitable mansion surrounded by shrubbery, and a display of fine floral and horticultural taste. It is a wild spot even now. The road to it from the Allegany river, is most of the way through a dense pine forest, along the base and sides of a mountain, and the settlement, with a pleasing rural aspect, reminds one of the descriptions of secluded retreats among the mountains of Switzerland. If any of our readers should take a summer ramble in that direction, to breathe pure air, angle for trout in the streams, or indulge in the chase; they should not fail to visit Ceres, and make the acquaintance of John King, or "Quaker John" as he is sometimes called.

His residence for a half century, having been in close proximity to the Holland Purchase, he was enabled to give the author many reminiscences of early events.

Soon after the Hoops settled at Olean, they were joined by the Russell and Read families. There followed soon after, settling on village plat, and upon Oil creek, Elisha Johnson, Ebenezer Reed, James Brooks, Zacharia Orsterhout, James Green. The early tavern keepers were Sylvanus Russell, and Jehiel Boardman; the early merchants were Levi Gregory, and Ebenezer Lockwood; the early physicians were Norman Smith, A. C. Bennett, and Andrew Mead, the last of whom still survives.

The first saw mill built on the upper waters of the Allegany, was on the Osway, a mile and a half above the mouth, by Atherton and Horton; or rather this was the first built to make lumber as an article of commerce. Francis King had built a saw mill at Ceres in '99, to accommodate the settlers. He built a grist mill at Ceres in 1801; before that, all the corn of the settlers was pounded in mortars; no mill within one hundred miles. Lumber was first taken down the river from above Olean in 1807. It was sawed in King's mill.

In 1809 or '10 Olean Point began to become the place of embarkation for emigrants, and for a long period, in portions of each year, great numbers assembled there, built arks, and embarked on their way down the Allegany and the Ohio. For a few years pending the completion of the Erie Canal, every spring, the emigrants awaiting the opening of navigation on the river counted to the number of thousands; are said to have amounted to over three thousand in 1818. On that as well as other occasions, the great numbers accumulating there, created great scarcity of food. The river would remain closed longer than they had anticipated, supplies of provisions would be exhausted; and that too, at seasons of the year when the state of the roads made it extremely difficult to get provisions in. The families of emigrants, far exceeding the capacity of public and private houses, were obliged to erect tents and shantees to live in. Flour has sold at Olean upon such occasions, as high as $25 dollars per barrel, and pork, for $50. In numerous instances emigrants would become penniless, before they could get down the river. Sometimes large numbers of emigrants would commence their journeys towards the last of sleighing, intending to reach Olean just before the breaking up of ice in the river; the snow would go off before their journey was accomplished; sleighs would be left and wagons substituted; and then followed long days and weeks of slow progress; (the roads almost impassable;) deprivation and suffering. This affords the reader a glimpse of what it was to emigrate to the western states, before the facilities were afforded that now exist. How slow must have been the progress of settlement at the west, in the absence of the Erie Canal, and the facilities to transportation upon the Lakes which it promoted! Vast as have been the benefits of the Erie Canal at home, it has speeded the founding of a new empire at the west.

Although it is going some years beyond the period we have generally so far embraced, in tracing the progress of settlement, we will add in this connection some account of the early advent of Friend's missions upon the Allegany Reservation, obtained from John King. The mission was first established in the year 1798, by the Yearly Meeting of Philadelphia. Joel Swayne, Halliday Jackson, Chester Simmons, three young Friends from Chester county, Pa. became residents upon the Reservation, locating about five miles below the Cold Springs. They became teachers of agriculture and other arts of civilized life; and school teachers. The Yearly Meeting soon after purchased three hundred acres of land of the Holland Company, and built a saw mill and grist mill. The mills did work for the white settlers, upon the usual terms, and furnished lumber, and ground corn for the Indians, free. Robert

Clendenon, from Chester county, Pa. with his wife and two daughters, occupied the mission station as early as 1812. Under his supervision the mills were rebuilt that had been first built by Jacob Taylor and Jonathan Thomas. The Clendenon family remained there four years; the daughters were school teachers, and taught the squaws to sew, knit, spin and the duties generally of house keeping, as practiced in civilized life. One of them is now the wife of John King, and the other resides with him. They are familiar with the character and habits of the Indians, and manifest a deep interest in their welfare. One of them informed the author that there were descendants of Sir William Johnson now residing upon the Allegany Reservation.

The author was amused, and it is presumed the reader will be, with the reason that John King gave for the slow progress of settlement and improvement on the Allegany. He said it was owing to the easy facilities of getting away from there; that the new settlers would get dissatisfied, discouraged, and had only to get together a few slabs, form a raft, and be carried with the current of the river to a new home. He inferred that there were periods with most of those who attempt the settlement of new countries, when they would back out, or go further on, if they could do it as easily; and he added, what many a pioneer settler will sanction, that there are many prosperous citizens of the whole region of Western New York who have reason to be thankful that there were formidable obstacles to getting away in early days of privation and endurance.

A brief abstract of memorandums made in conversation with John Green, the son of the early pioneer, James Green, will embrace some of the earliest events in that region:—

I came with my father to Olean in 1806. He was the first supervisor of Olean; used to go to Batavia to attend the sitting of Board of Supervisors; the town of Olean was all Cattaragus. He built a saw mill on Haskell's creek in 1808, the first mill built for the lumber business on the Allegany.

I am now the oldest resident of Cattaragus county. The first death and funeral in Cattaragus were those of ——— Husten. He was killed by the springing of a tree, while getting out spars on the river, in 1807. There was no one to take the lead of any religious service; it was as much as we could do to get together enough to bury him. Marius Johnson, Esq. son of Elisha Johnson, was the first born male child in Cattaragus, and a sister of mine, the first female.

I remember the execution of a squaw on the Allegany, in 1807. She was convicted of witchery. The principal proof against her was that she had foretold that some of the Indians would die, who were very sick at the time. Cornplanter was absent; when he returned he disapproved of it; the Prophet, who had been the principal means of condemning her, was obliged to go to Canada to get rid of the vengeance of the surviving relatives. The execution was a horrid one; the executioner, an Indian by the name of Sun Fish, struck her on the head with a hatchet; she came to and groaned, when he cut her throat with a knife.

I had a long and familiar acquaintance with Cornplanter. I have no doubts as to his parentage. He was the son of O'Bail, an Irishman, who was an Indian trader; his mother was a Seneca squaw. His Indian name was Ki-en-twa-ka, which means a large cornfield; it came in consequence of his cultivating large cornfields, when he resided down the river, near Pittsburgh. He died in 1837 or '38, aged 100 years. He was a strong minded man, always temperate: he had a great veneration for Washington. He had no education, has often brought papers to me to read and explain to him. He was a confirmed pagan; he once favored a Methodist Missionary upon the Reservation—was rather disposed to favor religion—but relapsed into paganism. He was for a long time opposed to schools, for the reason that learning had so bad an effect upon his son Henry.

Mr. Green located on the Allegany, at Great Valley, where he now resides, in 1813. He has consequently, for a long period, been a neighbor of the Indians on the Allegany Reservation. He is familiar with much of their history, and speaks their language. When he settled at Great Valley, there was no other white inhabitant on the Allegany below Olean.

In these brief sketches appertaining to the neighborhood of the Allegany, one who may well be considered the "oldest settler," should not be overlooked:—Governor Blacksnake, head chief of the Allegany Reservation, still survives. His residence is in a small framed house, on the river, a mile and a half above Cold Springs. He has passed his hundredth year, but yet walks erect, travels a good deal, spends most of his time visiting his numerous descendants, and giving his people the benefit of his counsels. Although a pagan, he is yet tolerant, and makes no serious opposition to missionary efforts. It was during last summer, that he gave to an intelligent informant of the author, a pretty distinct declaration of his religious views. He said he was an old man, familiar with the ancient rites and customs of his people; that the mission of the Saviour was to the white and not to the red man; that with the Indians, the christian religion is an innovation. In his speeches in councils, he urges the Indians to habits of temperance; advises them to cultivate their lands and build comfortable houses. His memory of events, is retentive, and it embraces a period of ninety years; the wars of his own people, their wars with the English, and the border wars of the Revolution. His descendants are to the fifth generation. He is one of the few who have survived, and realized what the familiar language illustrates:—"Arise daughter, and go to your daughter, for your daughter's daughter, has got a young daughter."

Peter R. Crouse, an educated, intelligent half blood, is a resident at the Cold Springs; his wife is a grand daughter of Mary Jemison. His father, then a boy fifteen years old, was taken prisoner during the border wars of Pennsylvania, conformed himself to Indian habits, married a squaw, and spent his life, as a matter of choice, among his captors. There are fifty of his descendants living. From the son who has been named, the author gathered some interesting facts, in reference to the Indians upon the Allegany Reservation:—They now number about nine hundred. They chiefly consist of two tribes, the Senecas and Onondagas; the Oneidas, a few in number, have recently been adopted by the Senecas. Jacob Blacksnake, a son of the Governor, generally presides in council. The early Friend's mission establishment is still kept up. The Presbyterians have besides, two mission establishments upon the Reservation. There are four schools. The general tendencies upon the Reservation, are to agricultural and general improvement.

By a reference to the preceding list of settlers, and the townships settled, it will be observed that up to Jan. 1st, 1807, the pioneers of Chautauque were along and near Lake road, from Cattaragus creek to Pennsylvania line, and in the vicinity of Mayville and Jamestown.

Mrs. Marshall, the relict of the late Dr. Marshall, of Buffalo, who still survives and resides in the city with her son, Orsamus H. Marshall, Esq., is a daughter of the early pioneer in Chautauque, Orsamus Holmes. She remembers distinctly the events attending the advent of her father, with his family, in June, 1805. Arriving at Buffalo, after spending a night in the humble travelers' home of John Crow. There was but the beach road upon the lake, for them to travel to their new home in the wilderness. Crossing Buffalo creek at its mouth, on the bar, their progress was a slow and tedious one. All the inhabitants then on the route were the family that preceded Judge Barker, eight miles up the lake, a family at Eighteen Mile creek, Capt. Sydnor, at Cattaragus creek, and a family by the name of Dickinson, at Silver creek. Mr. Holmes' location was three miles east of Fredonia, on the main road. Mrs. Marshall names all the settlers along on the road, in 1805 and '6; the reader will find them by referring to list of names, and the townships along the lake shore, in Chautauque. Mr. Holmes died in Ohio, where he had gone to reside with a son, in 1835. Dr. Marshall, who was the first physician in Mayville, and the first County Clerk of Chautauque, died in Buffalo, in 1838.

Col. James M'Mahan, from Northumberland county, Pennsylvania, was the pioneer settler of Chautauque. He had commenced negotiations for the purchase of a township, in a personal visit to this region soon after the surveying commenced. In September, 1802, he contracted for the purchase of T. 4, R. 14, which included the mouth of Chautauque creek, and site of the village of Westfield. Although he first settled there, and built a mill, it would seem that the land was never conveyed. His location was transferred to T. 3. R. 15, now town of Ripley, where he purchased a tract of eight or nine thoussnd acres, and became the founder of what was long after known as M'Mahan's Settlement.

In some published accounts, which are noticed in the preface, it

---

NOTE.—Hon. Daniel G. Garnsey, a former Representative in Congress from the district composed of Chautauque, Erie and Niagara, has related to the author some passages in the life of Mr. Holmes which furnish extraordinary instances of suffering and perseverance. He gathered them from a memorial he presented to Congress, in his behalf, asking a pension, which was granted. In the year 1775, when he was but seventeen years old, he accompanied the expedition of General Montgomery, against Quebec. Returning, he re-enlisted in the army, and was enrolled in the Green Mountain crops, under Col, Herrick. About the period of the evacuation of Ticonderoga by the British, he was upon a scouting party, and himself and a companion were taken prisoners and carried to Quebec. While confined on board a prison ship, he and three others made their escape, and in a ship's boat crossed the St. Lawrence and struck into the wilderness without compass or guide. The four traveled seventeen days in a dreary region, subsisting the first seven days on four hard biscuits and eight ounces of pork a day; and the remaining ten days on the inner bark of the white pine and a few fish they caught with their hands. At the expiration of this period they were re-taken by a party of Indians and taken back to Quebec. Three of them escaped again, by leaping from the second story window of the provo prison, evading a guard of eighteeen men. They crossed the river, and, striking again into the wilderness, after many days of suffering reached the frontier settlement of Vermont. The reader will conclude that such an adventurer was well fitted to be a pioneer of a new settlement.

is stated that Edward M'Henry, was the next settler on "an adjoining tract." The author is disposed to conclude that M'Henry settled under the auspices of Gen. M'Mahan, inasmuch as there is no record of any contract of his with the Holland Company. John M'Henry, born in 1802, was the first white child born in Chautauque. In 1803 M'Henry was drowned while attempting to make a trip from the mouth of Chautauque creek to Erie, in a small boat, after provisions.

The first white resident of Chautauque, was Amos Sottle. He had resided near the mouth of the Cattaragus creek for three years before the sale of the Holland Company lands commenced.

The present village of Irving, or that portion of it which embraces the mouth of the Cattaragus creek, was at an early period of the surveys of the Purchase, platted as a village site, and called "Cattaragus;" village lots were sold there, as in Mayville and other of the original Holland Company villages, cotemporary with the sale of farming lands in the neighborhood. In addition to the Amos Sottle, that civilization found there, those who took contracts in early years, (not included in the list,) were Sylvester Maybee, Sylvester Mark, Nathan Cole, Benjamin Kenyon, Joseph Hadsell.

Settlements were commenced in the neighborhood of Fredonia in 1804; David Eason was the pioneer. In the same year, Dr. Kennedy, from Meadville, Pa., who is mentioned in a preceding chapter as having married one of the daughters of Andrew Ellicott, erected a saw mill on the Conewango — the first structure of the kind in Chautauque, and the first step in the way of improvement taken south of the Ridge.

The mill of Gen. M'Mahan, on Chautauque creek, was erected in 1804, though the author is disposed to conclude, was not in operation that year, for in some reminiscences furnished by an early settler, it is mentioned that Judge Cushing, and some of his neighbors, the first year after they went into the woods, made trips to Street's mill, at Niagara Falls, on foot, carrying flour and meal home on their backs. And in fact, it is difficult to conclude what a mill would have found to do in Chautauque, until the fall of 1805, as previous to that, there could have been no crops raised of any consequence. In 1805, Mr. Dickinson, the pioneer at Silver Creek, erected a saw mill, to which he attached a pestle and mortar, for pounding corn. Mr. Moore erected a grist mill at Forestville in 1806. Along in 1805 and '6, flour was worth in that part of the Purchase, from $12 to $15, and pork from $18 to $30 per barrel.

In April, 1806, the town of Chautauque, (including all of what is now Chautauque county,) having been set off from Batavia, a town meeting was held, Gen. M'Mahan elected supervisor, and James Montgomery, town clerk. Previous to this, as will be seen by some account we shall give of the organization of Genesee county, the early settlers had to go to Vandeventer's, on Buffalo road, for the transaction of their town business.

John M'Mahan, David Eason and Perry G. Ellsworth, were the first justices of the peace commissioned for Chautauque county.

William Wilson, in 1806, was the pioneer settler of the town of Ellicott; Joseph Aikin, of the town of Carrol; Messrs. Griffith, Bemus and Barnhart, were the pioneers on the eastern shores of Chautauque lake. ☞ For names of settlers up to Jan. 1st, 1807, see townships 6, ranges 10 and 11, townships 2, 5 and 6, range 12, townships 3 and 5, range 13, township 3, range 15, Irving and Mayville.

The settlement of the county of Chautauque was rapid, almost from the commencement up to the war of 1812. It had at an early period, a high reputation, which has been so abundantly justified since; or rather demonstrated, in the almost universal and substantial prosperity that exists there. The author can well remember, when (along in 1809, '10 and 11,) the early emigrants, with their covered wagons, or sleighs, were to be seen almost daily, upon either the Buffalo road, or the south road that terminates on the lake, eight miles above Buffalo. It was a land of promise with them then, and such it has proved; but the full fruition, as in all other portions of the Holland Purchase, was only to be realized after long years of privation and endurance, such as the settlement of the wilderness involves. With what stout hearts they would move along in their emigrant journeys; the pioneer himself, driving his team, with ruddy and cheerful countenance, undismayed by all the difficulties that were ahead of him; behind him, his boys, driving a cow, a few sheep and hogs; and often his wife and daughters, trudging along on foot. There are many of the now prosperous farmers of Chautauque, whose journeys into the wilderness were after the manner described. Their advents are mingled with the earliest recollections of the author; he has seen them making their slow progress over the rough, muddy, primitive roads; them, and their glorious pioneer wives, worn down, almost overcome with the toils and fatigues of a long journey; at nights sheltered in the humble log cabin tavern, their scanty stores of provisions spread out; and yet cheerful and happy;—and well pleased has he been in long after years, to hear that a deserved success had crowned their efforts; that peace and plenty smiled around their once forest homes.

Hundreds of anecdotes could be told of the early settlers of Chautauque, that would illustrate that there, as well as upon all the rest of the Purchase, the pioneers were as poor a class of men, generally, as ever became founders of new settlements. Many of them got possession of their lands by paying mere nominal sums in advance; in some instances not over twenty-five cents. There are now in Chautauque and south part of Erie, (and the remark may be applied to the whole Holland Purchase,) many families, now the most prosperous, whose last dollar was spent when they had arrived at their locations in the forest, erected their log cabins, and supplied themselves with some scanty stores of provisions; and far the more credit is due to them, in consideration that such was their humble, hard beginnings. It may seem incredible; none but those who have seen the hardest features of pioneer life, can realize the truth of it; but the author has seen those who are yet surviving, surrounded with all the blessings that wealth can bestow, and those who have died after laying foundations of wealth for their descendants; making long journeys on foot, through wilderness paths, and primitive roads; returning with a peck of meal, perhaps a bag of flour, and sometimes with but a few potatoes, for the sustenance of themselves and families.

One of the earliest pioneers of Chautauque; afterwards a prosperous farmer; for a long period occupying a seat upon the bench of the county, obtained possession of his lands by depositing in the land office at Batavia, his watch, to secure a part of the small advance payment. The transaction is minuted upon the books, and entry was afterwards appended that he had redeemed his watch.

The circumstance of Mr. Ellicott's getting frequent reports through Mr. Le Couteulx, of what the purchasers of lots in Buffalo were doing in the way of improvement has been noticed. All over the Purchase there were the same reports made. Below the entries in all the early contract books, there are memorandums, generally in Mr. Ellicott's hand writing, after this manner:—"D.

E. reports that ——— has gone on to the lot, and put up the body of a log house." "J. F. reports that ——— has chopped two acres." "G. H. reports that ——— has cut logs for a house, and intends bringing his family in this fall." "H. K. called at the office to-day and reports that ——— has never yet been upon his lot, and doubts whether he ever will." "H. P. reports that ——— has three acres cleared, which he is intending to sow to wheat this fall." And in this way an eye was kept on the progress of improvement, and a general knowledge obtained of who were becoming actual settlers, and who were not. Appended to the leaves of the contract books are frequent short notes, addressed to Mr. Ellicott, recommending the bearers as worthy, industrious men, who are disposed to become settlers, signed by residents of the neighborhoods where the locations were intended to be made.

It will be observed that the Chamberlin family were the first to take contracts in that portion of the county of Allegany which is on the Holland Purchase. The patriarch of that family, so numerous and so closely blended with the settlement and progress of the counties of Allegany and Cattaragus, was Benjamin Chamberlin. He was the pioneer settler of Angelica, locating there in 1802. Few had more actively participated in the war of the Revolution. He was in the battles of Lexington, Bunker Hill, with Arnold at Quebec, (where he was made a prisoner and confined through the winter,) at Saratoga and Stillwater, White Plains, Stony Point, and Valentine's Hill. At Bunker Hill he had his left arm broken; at White Plains he was shot through one of his thighs; at Stony Point he was thrust with a bayonet; was shot in one of his feet at Valentine's Hill. In addition to all this he lost the use of an eye. He carried to his grave the marks of the heavy irons that were put upon his wrists, while a prisoner at Quebec.

The old veteran, whose eventful life should be the subject of a volume, rather than of a sketch so brief, was a native of Cheshire, Massachusetts. He died at Angelica, in 1847, aged 90 years. He was the father of Hon. Calvin T. Chamberlin of Cuba, and Judge Benjamin Chamberlin of Ellicottville. There are over one hundred of his descendants now residents of Western New York.

There is little in the way of settlement to notice, in Allegany, previous to the close of 1806. The condition of the whole of the south-eastern part of the Purchase at that period, will be realized from a statement of an old gentleman by the name of Metcalf, a resident at Ellicottville. His father, John Metcalf, came to Bath with Mr. Williamson, and was the keeper of the public house he erected there. Mr. Metcalf says:—"In January 1806, I came through from Bath to Angelica, and then on to Olean Point. The road from Angelica to Olean was then only underbrushed; the logs were not cut out; I had to lift my sleigh over them. There was then no inhabitants between Genesee river and Olean. I found large hunting parties of Indians encamped about the small settlement that the Hoops had commenced, with whom I bartered goods for furs. I then started for Buffalo, taking an Indian trail that crossed the Cattaragus creek a short distance below Arcade. In all this route, I saw no white man, except at Olean, and after I had reached a few pioneer settlers in the south part of Erie."

Pike was one of the earliest settled portions of Allegany. Phineas Harvey was the pioneer. He settled there in May, 1806. Eli Griffith settled there the same year, and in that year, or the next, opened a road for Holland Company, from Leicester to Castile. Griffith built a saw mill in 1808, and a grist mill in 1809. Michael Griffith, the father of Eli Griffith, and the Mr. Harvey that has been named, settled three miles east of village. Peter Granger and Asahel Newcomb settled same year. The settlers that followed soon after, were:—Christopher Olin, Salmon Simonds, Alanson Langdon, Payne Turner, Josiah Metcalf, Rufus Metcalf, Thomas Dole, Asa Lyon, Robert Boggs. Settlement in that quarter was brisk until the breaking out of the war. The early pioneer, Eli Griffith, went out under Smyth's proclamation and died on his way home; his neighbors, Jonathan Couch and Charles Benton, met the same fate. Mr. Caleb Powers, from whom we derive some local reminiscences of Pike, says, that in 1816 and '17, there was much suffering for food among the new settlers in all that region. The first born in Pike were twins, children of Mrs. Harvey; did not survive. The first death of an adult was that of Phineas Harvey. It was in 1807; there was no one to take the lead in any funeral ceremonies. The earliest ministers who visited that region, were Elder Smith, from Caneadea, and Elder Goodale, from Pittstown, Ontario Co. The first settled minister was Elder Gillett. A Baptist church was formed in 1812; a Presbyterian soon after. The first merchant was Tilly Parker. In the earliest years of merchandizing there, common tea cups and saucers were two dollars a sett; factory shirting, four shillings per yard. Andrew Dutton was the first physician. Eli Griffith kept the first tavern. The first clothing and cloth dressing establishment was at "Bloody Corners;"* Miles Rood was the proprietor.

The Thomas Dole, named above, was the afterwards Judge Dole, a conspicuous pioneer of Allegany, and deserving a more extended notice. In this instance however, as well as numerous others, the author relying upon the promise of those who could furnish the necessary data, has been disappointed.

James Cravath, William Bristol, Benjamin Morse, Elnathan George, were the pioneer settlers south of Warsaw, in all of the present county of Wyoming; their locations, Gainsville and Weathersfield. During the war, Mr. Cravath built a grist and saw mill on the Wiscoy, between Hermitage and Springs.

The first settlers at Hermitage, were Eugene F. Stowe, Sidney Stowe, Augustus Hurlburt, Wm. R. Groger, Daniel Granger, and James Weeks.

It will be observed by list of settlers, that there is little to be said of settlement in Orleans, previous to Jan. 1st, 1807. It would seem that Mr. Ellicott had at an early period, selected the mouth of Oak Orchard creek as the site of a village. It was platted in 1803, and called "Manilla." Looking to the lake route, as the course that trade from a large portion of the Holland Purchase would take; Lewiston and Manilla were the anticipated depots. At that period, such vessels as were upon the lake, could enter the mouth of the Oak Orchard; the barrier there, was progressive, up to the period of commencing the recent harbor improvement. The Oak Orchard road from Batavia north, so early projected and opened, had reference to Manilla as the commercial depot for the middle and eastern portions of the Purchase. It will be seen that a few lots were sold there, previous to 1807, though but little was done in the way of founding a village. Sickness alone would have prevented it in all the early years; and in later years—the projection of the Erie Canal, arrested the projects of commercial depots upon the Lakes.

James Walsworth, known in all early years, as the tavern keeper on Lockport and Batavia road, upon the borders of the Tonawanda swamp, was the pioneer settler of Manilla, and in fact, of all Orleans county. In May, 1803, he landed at mouth of Oak

---

* There was an early tavern keeper there, who made his house celebrated for broils and fights; thence the name

Orchard in an open boat, with his family, and built a solitary hut, the first and only one, between Fort Niagara and Braddock's Bay; his nearest neighbor west, at Cold Springs, near Lockport, his nearest south, Pine Hill, (Elba;) his nearest east, Braddock's Bay. After they landed, he and his wife cut and barked poles for their cabin, covering with bark. The early adventurer was very poor; all the provision he had when he landed, was a few bushels of potatoes; fish had to supply the rest for the sustenance of his family, save a little barter with the crews of bateaux, as they were passing few and far between, up and down the lake; and the author observes by the old books kept at the Irondequoit pioneer store, that he used to take some furs and peltries down there, and exchange them for some of the necessaries of life. Among some reminiscences of this early pioneer, it is mentioned, that either while living at Oak Orchard, or after he moved up on to the Lewiston road, in 1806, his wife gave birth to a pair of twins. The parturition was in the absence of either her own sex or a physician.

After clearing up the large farm on the Lockport and Batavia road, Mr. Walsworth, many years since, again became a pioneer; emigrated to the west.

Walsworth, and the few others that located at Oak Orchard, were all the settlers in Orleans, before 1809, except Whitfield Rathbun, who was the pioneer upon all that part of the Ridge Road, in Orleans county, embraced in Holland Purchase.

It will be noticed, by reference to tabular list of settlers, that settlement had just begun at the mouth of Eighteen Mile creek, in Niagara, and at Johnson's creek, in Orleans, in 1806. Burgoyne Kemp settled at the Eighteen Mile creek in 1808. There was then settled there William Chambers and ——— Colton; and there was one family at Johnson's creek, on lake. At that period there was no settler between lake and Ridge, in Niagara or Orleans.

Richard M. Stoddard, it will have been observed, was early in the employ of Mr. Ellicott as a surveyor; and was afterwards employed by him to survey the Triangular Tract for Messrs. Le Roy and Bayard. He became the agent for the sale of the tract. He had married in 1799, Miss Saltonstall, of Canandaigua, a sister of Dudley Saltonstall, Esq. Messrs. Stoddard and Saltonstall purchased of the proprietors the five hundred acres which is now the site of Le Roy village. The interest of Mr. Saltonstall was soon after sold to Judge Ezra Platt. Stoddard and Platt became the pioneer settlers upon the Triangular Tract, in 1801, opening a land office at Le Roy, and soon commencing the building of mills.

The aged widow of Mr. Stoddard is now residing with her son, Thomas B. Stoddard, Esq., near Irving, in Chautauque county. She relates some interesting reminiscences of early times; few are more familiar with the early history of all Western New York.

The primitive residence at Le Roy, was a log house on the bank of Allan's creek. During the first winter of their residence there, Mr. Stoddard was engaged in tending the saw mill during a night. A party of intoxicated Indians came into the kitchen, built up a large fire and commenced making a pow wow, as if they were masters of the premises. Mrs. Stoddard, who was abed in another room, managed to get a little girl out of the window, who went to the mill and alarmed Mr. Stoddard. As he came into the house the Indians attacked him and a severe fight ensued; Mr. S. was, however, the victor, and succeeded in expelling the intruders. There are many traditions of his adventures. related by the earliest class of settlers in that region; especially such as occurred when he was sheriff of Genesee county. He was fearless and determined; had seen much of backwoods life; and few were better adapted to the work of settling a new country, and becoming its chief executive officer. Anecdotes are told of his many acts of kindness to the new settlers, especially in the discharge of his official duties. He was much esteemed by the Indians; and was often consulted by their chiefs, in reference to the interests of their people. Mrs. Stoddard redeems the Indian character from the disgrace of the drunken frolic, by stating that upon one occasion, when the whole family were sick with a prevailing influenza, a party of Indians and squaws greatly mitigated the disease by coming to their house, and giving the invalids an "Indian sweat." They dug holes in the earth, put in hot stones, poured water over them, and placed the patients under the influence of the steam, covering them over with blankets, and giving them warm drinks.

"Sheriff Stoddard," as he is familiarly called by the earlier class of pioneers, died in 1810. His only daughter, was the first wife of the Hon. John B. Skinner of Wyoming. The family circle, in its various branches, are conspicuously blended with the history of Western New York.

On the 1st of March, 1803, the town of Batavia having been set off from Northampton, the first town meeting ever held west of Genesee river was convened at the "house of Peter Vandeventer." The following town officers were chosen:—

Supervisor—Peter Vandeventer.
Town Clerk—David Culley.
Assessors—Enos Kellogg, Asa Ransom, Alexander Rea.
Commissioners of Highways—Alexander Rea, Isaac Sutherland, Suffrenus Maybee.
Overseers of the Poor—David Culley, Benjamin Porter.
Collector—Abel Rowe.
Constables—John Mudge, Levi Felton, Rufus Hart, Abel Rowe, Seymour Kellogg, Hugh Howell.
Overseers of Highways—Martin Middaugh, Timothy Hopkins, Orlando Hopkins, Benjamin Morgan, Rufus Hart, Lovell Churchill, Jabez Warren, Wm. Blackman, Samuel Clark, Gideon Dunham, Jonathan Willard, Thomas Layton, Hugh Howell, Benjamin Porter, Wm. Walsworth.

Among the few ordinances passed at this primitive town meeting—this first gathering of the scattered pioneers—was, that "a bounty of $5 should be paid for wolf scalps; half price for whelps; and 50 cts. for foxes and wild cats.

A special town meeting was held at Vandeventers, in Sept., 1803, at which it was resolved to petition the legislature for the division of the town of Batavia into five towns.

The next town meeting (in 1804,) was held at the same place. Alexander Rea was chosen supervisor, and Isaiah Babcock, town clerk.

An ordinance was passed, imposing a fine of $5 upon any person "living in any other county or town, who should drive cattle into the town of Batavia to be kept." * It was also ordained that no person should be licensed to keep a tavern, who had not a securely enclosed yard, sufficiently large to contain all the "sleds, sleighs, wagons, carts and other carriages, that he or she may have at his or her tavern, at any one time, for entertainment or refreshment." A bounty of $5 was voted for "panther's scalps."

The first election held in the town of Batavia, was at Vandeventers, in April, 1803. The inspectors certified to the following votes.—

---

* This was intended to preserve the fine feed upon the openings, on the Lockport and Batavia road, for the use of the settlers upon the Purchase. The settlers upon tracts adjoining the Purchase on the east, had been in the habit of driving cattle there for pasture.

For Senators—Caleb Hyde, 146; Vincent Matthews, 5.
For Members of Assembly—Daniel Chapin, 182; Ezra Patterson, 155; John Swift, 160; Polydore B. Wisner, 4; Nathaniel W. Howell, 28; Amos Hall, 9.

At the second election, held in April, 1804, the vote was as follows:—

For Governor—Morgan Lewis, 111; Aaron Burr, 11.
For Lieutenant Governor—John Broome, 115; Oliver Phelps, 7.
For Senators—Jedediah Peck, 113; Henry Huntington, 113; Jedediah Sanger, 7; Moses Kent, 7.
For Members of Assembly—Alexander Rea, 140; Ezra Patterson, 133; Elisha Granger, 133; Daniel W. Lewis, 13; Amos Platt, 9.
For Congress—Silas Halsey, 132; N. W. Howell, 15.

In June, 1803, the Holland Company having so far completed the Court House at Batavia, as to admit of holding the Courts in it, the courts of the county were first organized. The Judges were Ezra Platt, John H. Jones, and Benjamin Ellicott; Nathan Perry, was an assistant Justice. Timothy Burt, and Governeur Ogden, "being Attorneys of the Supreme Court; and John Greig, Richard Smith, and George Hosmer having been Attorneys of the Court of Ontario county," were admitted to practice in the new Court as Attorneys and Counsellors.

The first Grand Jury west of Genesee river, was organized at this term of the Courts. As it was the Pioneer Grand Jury, the author gives the names:—

Alexander Rea, Asa Ransom, Peter Vandeventer, Daniel Henry, Samuel F. Geer, Lovell Churchill, Jabez Warren, Zera Phelps, Jotham Bemus, Seymour Kellogg, John A. Thompson, John Ganson, Jr., Isaac Smith, Elisha Farwell, Peter Shaeffer, Hugh M'Dermott, John M'Naughton, Luther Coe.

No indictment was found at this term of the Court.

The Courts convened again in November, 1803; same Judges present. Ebenezer F. Norton, Robert W. Stoddard, Jonathan T. Haight, John Collins, Daniel B. Brown, Jeremiah R. Munson, were admitted to practice as Attorneys.

The first issue joined in a court of record, west of Genesee river, was at this term. The parties were Rufus Hart, vs. Erasmus Enos.

An entry made upon the court records at this term, is as follows:—"Nathan Perry, assistant justice having withdrawn from the bench, a petition was presented from him for license to keep a ferry across the Niagara river, at a place called Black Rock."

At this term the jail limits for bailed debtors were prescribed. They consisted of the side walks of Batavia, "fifteen links wide," and several dwellings and yards, to allow the debtors access to boarding houses; in all only about three acres of ground. The unfortunate debtor had to study a chart to avoid stepping over his bounds.

The next term of the Courts, was in June, 1804. Nearly half of the Grand Jury, were the same persons that served at the previous term; as it required freeholders; for such only could serve at that early period. At this term an indictment was tried against three persons for misdemeanor. The jury was the first traverse jury drawn and organized in the new court of record. The names were as follows:—

William Rumsey, Joseph Selleck, Abel Rowe, John Forsyth, Benjamin Morgan, Alexander M'Donald, Peter Campbell, James Woods, Benjamin Gardner, Lovell Churchill, John Anderson, John M'Vean.

The first jury empannelled in a civil suit, were as follows:—

Job Pierce, Andrew Wortman, Gilbert Hall, John M'Naughton, Isaac Smith, Archileas Whitten, Isaac Sutherland, Samuel Davis, Ransom Harmon, Peter Vandeventer, Hugh M'Dermott, Jabez Fox.

At this term a license was given to Robert Lee, to keep a ferry over the Niagara river, at the "north end of the portage or carrying place." Daniel Curtiss, to keep a ferry on Genesee river, on road from Leicester to Geneseo. William G. Sydnor, to keep a ferry at the mouth of Cattaragus creek.

At a Court of Oyer and Terminer, held in June 1804. Hon. Ambrose Spencer presided. The first indictment for an offence in which the loss of life had been involved was at this term. The indictment was for manslaughter:—The People vs. Joseph Rhineberger. The offence was committed in what is now Allegany; occured in a drunken frolic. The prisoner was found guilty, and sentenced to "States Prison at New York, for 10 years." He was defended by Judge Howell, Daniel B. Brown acting as assistant counsel. The jurors were:—

John Forsyth, Alexander M'Donald, Daniel M'Pherson, John M'Vean, James Woods, John Anderson, Alexander Thompson, Benjamin Morgan, John M'Clanan, Orlando Hopkins, Benjamin Gardner.

NOTE.—Name of twelfth Juror not preserved.

At the November term of the Courts, in 1805, Samuel Tupper, took his seat upon the bench. Josiah Robinson, and James T. Johnson, were admitted as Attorneys. Zenos Barker, was licensed to keep a ferry across Buffalo creek. This was upon the new road that had then just been opened up the Lake; the Pratt ferry as it was afterwards called. At the same time, John Crow, was licensed to keep a ferry below, to accommodate the travellers upon the beach of the Lake. James Barnes, was licensed to keep a ferry over the Genesee river, "near the house of Maria Berry." Benjamin Barton, Jr. was licensed to keep a ferry "between the towns of Northampton in the county of Genesee, and Northfield in the county of Ontario."

The first trial in a case of murder, was in June, 1807. Daniel D. Tompkins was the presiding Judge. James M'Lean stood indicted for the murder of William Orr. Judge Howell was prisoner's counsel. He "challenged the array," upon the ground that prisoner being an alien, he was entitled to be tried by a jury, one half of whom were aliens.* The challenge was allowed. The jury were as follows:—

Citizens.—Benjamin Morgan, Ebenezer Cary, Samuel Geer, Worthy L. Churchill, John Oney, Daniel Fairbanks.

Aliens.—Duncan M'Lelland, James M'Lelland, John M'Pherson, John M'Vane, Daniel M'Kinney, Patrick Powers.

The prisoner was found guilty, and sentenced to be hung in August, following.

The murder was committed near Caledonia Springs. M'Lean, Orr, and M'Laughlin were squatters on the forty thousand acre tract. The three had been together to the Springs, had drank each a glass of beer, but M'Lean was not intoxicated. A dispute arose about a whitewood tree that Orr had cut on land that M'Lean claimed. M'Lean struck Orr down with an axe, killing him at two blows; M'Laughlin interfering, met with a fate quite as summary and horrid. M'Lean staid that night in a hollow log near his house, and the next morning, took to the woods. The alarm was immediately spread through all the new settlements west of Genesee river; Judge Platt called out the militia, who were distributed in squads and scoured the woods in all directions. After several days the fugitive ventured out of the forest, was endeavoring to make his

---

* A right then existing by common law, now abolished by statute.

escape eastward, when he was recognized at a public house a few miles east of Canandaigua, and arrested.

The circumstance created an intense excitement, in the new country, and at the execution of M'Lean the citizens collected at Batavia from all the settlements upon the Purchase. Such was the curiosity to witness an execution in those early days, that surviving pioneers remember that some settlements were almost entirely deserted; men women and children, on foot and on horseback, wending their way through forest paths, and woods roads, to Batavia.

As the village of Batavia enlarged, new houses were built where debtors wished to board, or mechanic shops where they could obtain employment, the jail limits were altered. Where a boarding house was included, a narrow walk was prescribed to get across to it, and access even to privies was prescribed by law and the surveyor's compass and chain. Such things once were, strange as they may now seem, in these days of a better appreciation of the relations and rights of debtor and creditor.

In all the early years there was considerable litigation, the sums involved generally small; seldom exceeding one hundred dollars. A large proportion of the indictments were for misdemeanors.

Once in every year, one of the Judges of the Supreme Court would hold a Circuit Court and Court of Oyer and Terminer. Revered names occur upon the records from time to time:—Livingston, Van Ness, Spencer, Platt, Yates, Tompkins. And attending upon their courts, mostly guests at the old "Keyes House," would be the early lawyers:—Howell, Porter, Hosmer, Matthews, Haight, Root, Marvin, Brown, Greig, Spencer, Walden; young men then, or but in the prime of life. How much of gay repartee, the ready joke, the keen encounter of wit, of joyous hilarity has the walls of that old primitive tavern witnessed! There is a long catalogue of rich anecdotes of early times, the venues of which are laid there, the names of the early lawyers involved. "Lawyer Root;"—"Alas poor Yorick!" When he would enjoy his joke, or display his wit, it mattered not at whose expense; even the high dignitaries of the Supreme Court were not always exempt. He ventured upon one occasion to tell one of them that a decision he had made was only equalled by a memorable one made by "Pontius Pilate;" and upon another occasion, when the presiding judge of a County Court had decided that his conduct was "contemptuous;" he complimented the judge by saying, that "it was a very correct decision, — the only correct one he had made in the whole term."

Robert M. Stoddard was the first Sheriff of Genesee county; and David M' Cracken the first Under Sheriff and jailor. James W. Stevens was the first county Clerk; James Brisbane was his deputy.

The first six settlers on Holland Purchase who had deeds recorded were: — John Youngs, John Lamberton, William Rumsey, Isaac Sutherland, Samuel Geer, Benjamin Morgan. The first public library established upon the Holland Purchase, was in November 1804. A meeting for the purpose was convened at "the house of Abel Rowe;" Joseph Ellicott was the chairman of the meeting. The trustees were Richard Smith, William Rumsey, John Branan, Reuben Town, Nathaniel Coleman.

Ebenezer Mix was appointed deputy clerk of the county, in March, 1811.

Asher Bates succeeded Benjamin Barton, as sheriff, in 1808; Aaron Van Cleve succeeded Asher Bates in 1811.

From a book of miscellaneous records in Genesee county clerk's office, the author gathers some reminiscences:—

In 1811 a public library was established in Alexander. Alexander Rea, Harvey Hawkins, Seba Brainard, Samuel Latham, Henry Hawkins, Noah North, Ezra W. Osborn, were the trustees.

A Protestant Episcopal church was established in Sheldon, in 1811. The first church wardens were Joshua Mitchell and Fitch Chipman; the vestrymen were:—John Rolph, John W. Coleman, Seneca Reed, James Case, Philo Welton, James Ward. This was the first Episcopal church organized upon the Purchase. Bishop Hobart has visited this church when there was no other west of Allen's Hill, Ontario county, in his diocess.

In 1812, the "Union Religious Society," was established in Warsaw. At the preliminary meeting, Chauncey L. Sheldon acted as moderator, and Ezra Walker, as clerk. The trustees appointed were:—Isaac Phelps, Abraham Reed, John Munger, William Bristol, Zera Tanner, Shubael Goodspeed.

In 1812, a Baptist church was organized in Sheldon, (now Bennington.) Pelatiah Case, Darius Cross, Justin Loomis, Solomon King, William W. Parsons, Ezra Ludden, were appointed trustees.

In 1814, "The Trustees of the Society of Corinth," in Orangeville, was organized. The trustees were Simeon Morse, Putnam Cowden, Jonathan Coburn, Zoar Blackmor, Noah Merrill.

The Episcopal church at Batavia was organized in 1815. Rev. Alanson Welton officiated. John Hickox and Samuel Benedict, were first trustees; the first vestrymen were Richard Smith, Isaac Sutherland, Isaac Spencer, John Z. Ross, Chauncey Keyes, David C. Miller, Aaron Van Cleve, Oswald Williams; Simeon Cummings and Trumbul Cary were secretaries of the meeting.

In 1817, the "First Congregational Society" of the town of Batavia, was organized. The first trustees were Lemuel Foster, Wm. H. Bush, Horace Gibbs. The Rev. Calvin C. Colton, the since well known author, was one of the earliest ministers of this church.

The following list embraces the names, generally of the first six, (sometimes more and sometimes less,) of the persons who took contracts, and in most instances, became pioneer settlers, in all the townships upon the Holland Purchase, in which no contracts were taken previous to Jan. 1st., 1807. *

ELLICOTTVILLE.
1818.
Baker Leonard,
Stephen Webb, Jr.
Alvin Leavenworth,
James Reynolds,
Moses Chamberlin,
Abel P. Wightman,
David Goodwin,
Lathrop Vinton,
John A. Bryan.

BARCELONA.
Lyman Middington,
James Ray,
Silas Spencer,
M. M'Clintock,
James B. Longhead,
Dyer Carver,
James Farnsworth,
George M. Fowl,
James Post.

T. 1, R. 1.
1821.
Hiram Lowell,
Austin Cowles,
Christopher Tyler.
Asa Cowles,
Zephaniah Smith,
Levi Appleby.

T. 2, R. 1.
1810.
Chauncy Axtell,

T. 2, R. 1.
1810.
Azel Buckley,
John Hopkins,
Hyra Axtell,
Daniel Willard.

T. 14, R. 1.
1812.
Oliver Benton,
Stephen Paine,
Philip Bonesteel,
Nathan Angel,
Asa Billings,
James Healey.

T. 15, R. 1.
1808.
John Barrett,
Elliott Barrett,
Isaac Bennett,
Samuel Crippen,
Henry Drake,
Moses Bacon,
Clarkson F. Brooks,
John Proctor.

T. 2, R. 2.
1821.
James Reed,
Hiram Hill,
Abraham VanNess,
Clark Lewis,
Elijah Seaver,
Daniel Seaver

T. 5, R. 2.
1808.
Charles Swift,
Eneas Garey,
Othniel Perry,
William Vaughan,
Andre Bennett,
Joshua Wilson.

T. 6, R. 2.
1808.
Joseph Maxson.
Russell Thrall,
Thomas Clute,
Strong Warner,
David Gelatt,
Samuel Webster.

T. 7, R. 2.
1808.
John J. Drake,
Silas Hodges,
Sylvanus Eldridge,
Alpheus Bascom,
William Adams,
James Waldron,
Dan Beach.

T. 8, R. 2.
1809.
Erastus Richards,
Jason Smith,
Joel S. Smith,
Peter Lott,

---

* With the exception of lands that were donated by the Holland Company to the Canal fund, and such townships as were sold at wholesale.

NOTE.—The year indicates the period when first contract was taken in the township.

HOLLAND PURCHASE. 527

T. 8, R. 2.
1809.
Ebenezer Tyrrill,
Gideon Bently.

T. 14, R. 2.
1813.
Gregory Storm,
Selah Belden,
Christopher Paine,
Bela Benton,
Abraham Matteson,
John Doak.

T. 15, R. 2.
1809.
Andrew Jacox,
Whitfield Rathbun,
William Sibley,
Cotton M. Leach.
Noah Burgess,
James Mather
Henry Luce.

T. 2, R. 3.
1813.
James Haskins,
Israel Curtis
Joel Wakefield,
Rodolphus Scott,
Joseph Smith,
Alfred Dodge.

T. 3, R. 3.
1807.
Jotham Blakesley,
Barnabas Strong,
John Brooks,
Samuel Kimball,
Asa Folsom,
Simeon Hicks.

T. 5, R. 3.
1811.
Gideon Lewis,
Ezekiel Runals,
Samuel Blancher,
Benjamin Jenks, Jr.
William Parks.
Peter Ten Broek,
George Park.

T. 6, R. 3.
1810.
Warren Stanley,
Enoch Howlett,
Ezekiel D. Runals,
Rufus Metcalf,
Earl Sawyer,
Jonas Irish.

T. 7, R. 3.
1808
John Nichols,
Silas Meech,
Amasa Kilbourn,
Samuel Nichols,
Abraham Jackson,
Porter Belknap.

T. 8, R. 3.
1809.
Samuel Coleman,
Joshua Gates,
David Woolcott,
Erastus Wells,
Guy Morgan,
Abraham C. Hollenbeck.

T. 13, R. 3.
1810.
Jesse Lund,
David Gary,
Charles Bliss,
Levi Smith,
John S. Wolcott,
Nathan M'Cumber.

T. 14, R. 3.
1810.
Andrew A Ellicott,
Orange Wells,
Leonard Dresser,
Zeno Ross,
Champion Wells,
Abel P. Sheldon,
Joel Briggs.

T. 15, R. 3.
1810.
Israel Douglass,
Eli Moore,
Ezra D. Barnes,
Cyrus Daniels,
Elijah Hawley,
Thomas Hawley.

T. 16, R. 3.
Preserved Greenman,
John Eaton,
George Housman,
Darius Knickerbocker.
Giles Slater.
John Wallis,
Elisha Sawyer.

T. 7, R. 4.
1813.
Silas Knight,
Cornelius Van Orsdal,
Guy C. Irving,
Rufus Wetherbee,
Rollin Pratt.

T. 3, R. 4.
1813.
Lewis Wood,
Seymour Bouton,
Julius Underwood,
Emery Wood.

T. 6, R 4.
1809.
Aquilla Robbins,
Joseph Edminster Jr.,
Seth Pratt,
Elisha Daggett,
Joseph Franklin.

T. 7, R. 4.
1809.
Abner Bump,
Abraham Jackson,
Leonard Parker,
Silas Parker,
Jacob Jackson,
Simeon Wells,
Walter Hinckly,
Abraham Smith.

T. 8, R. 4.
1811.
Timothy Kirby,
Daniel H. Wooster,
Amasa Joslyn,
James Hall,
Leonard J. Paul,
Orrin Waters.

T. 11, R. 4.
1807.
William Humphrey,
Emery Blodgett,
Joshua Bailey,
Josiah Lee.
Rufus Kidder,
Amos Humphrey,
David Long.

T. 13, R. 4.
1822.
Benjamin Patterson,
Solomon Force,
Augustus L. Barton,
Joseph Barber,
Ezra N. Russell.

T. 14, R. 4.
1809.
Alexander Coon,
Samuel C. Wells,
Joseph Hagaman,
Elijah Bent,
Ezekiel Bentley,
Joshua Park,
Eleazer Frary,
David Demaray.

T. 15, R. 4.
1810.
Boaz Lambson,
Seymour Murdock,
Jonathan Cobb,
Bostion Weatherwax,
Amos Barritt,
John F. Hunt,
Israel Murdock.

T. 16, R. 4.
1815.
Zebediah Heath,
Jemison Henry,
William Weaver,
Thomas Stafford,
Reuben Peck,
Zenas Conger.

T 1, R. 5.
1823.
Bareck Clark,
James Townsend Jr,
Calvin Pratt.

T. 2, R. 5.
1820.
Andrew B. Northrop,
David Orton,
James Green,
Andrew Allen,
Isaac Eggleston.

T. 3, R. 5.
1815.
Russell Chapell,
Henry Willsy,
Thomas Barber,
William Baxter,
Oliver Marsh.

T. 6, R. 5.
1810.
Major Evans,
Morton Crosby,
Betheul Bishop,
John Johnson,
Dennis Riley,
Benjamin Felch.

T. 7, R. 5.
1809.
Sumner Warren,
William L. Warren,
Ira P. Paine,
Ebenezer Warren,
Ezra Nott.

T. 8, R. 5.
1807.
Abner Carrier,
Arthur Humphrey,
Ezekiel Colby,
Jared Scott,
Timothy Fuller,
Asa Jones.

T. 11, R. 5.
1808.
Jonas Varney,
Zopher Beach,
Samuel Huntington,
Ephraim Salmon,
James Harvey.

T. 13, R. 5.
1810.
Clark Beach,
William B. Smith,
Semar Sinclear,
Nathan Bradley,
Silas Pratt,
Lawrence M'Mullen,
Patrick Grace.

T. 16, R. 5.
1809.
Daniel Kemp,
Jacob Fitts,
John Landers,
Henry Palmer,
Hezekiah Brace,
Dorastus Chapman.

T. 3, R. 6.
1811.
Daniel M'Kay,
Laurin Norton,
Orlando C. Fuller,
Elijah Gibbs,
Abraham Searle,
Alexander Wood.

T. 4, R. 6.
1813.
Ricketson Burlingam,
Harvey B. Hays,
Archalaus Brown,
Orrin Brown,
Amos Ingalls,
Grove Hurlbut.

T. 5, R. 6.
1816.
William Shultz,
George Shultz,
Andrew Frank,
Daniel Oyer,
Benjamin Rhoads,
Marsena Rhoads.

T. 6, R. 6.
1807.
Christopher Stone,
George Richmond,
Calvin Doolittle,
Samuel Cockran,
Joseph Yaw, Jr.
Benjamin Douglas.

T. 7, R. 6.
1808.
John Albro,
Stephen Pratt.
Luther Hibbard,
James Vaughan,
Lemuel Cooper,
Luther Curtis.

T. 8, R. 6.
1819,
Richard Buffum,
Stephen Southwick,
Lodowick Owen,
Sylvester Owen,
Richard Bowen,
Martin Sprague.

T. 13, R. 6.
1810.
Aaron Crego,
John Stranahan,
Abraham Flagg.

T. 13, R. 6
1810.
Palmer Utley,
Daniel Hamlin,
John M. Cole.

T. 4, R. 7.
1818.
Benjamin Chamberlin,
Nathaniel Fish,
Lathrop Vinton,
Edmund Kemp,
Zina Finton,
Timothy Morgan.

T. 4, R. 7.
1816
Elisha Hicks,
Daniel Kelly,
Philip Bonesteel,
Hiram Wells,
Ephraim Rolph.
Jabez Hull.

T. 6, R. 7.
1809.
William Smith,
Ephraim Hall,
Samuel Hill,
Peter Pratt,
Stephen Peters,
Isaac Belot,
Samuel Nichols.

T. 7, R. 7
1809.
John Stewart,
Amasa Ashman,
Solomon Field,
Thomas M'Gee,
Lyman Drake,
Smith Russell.

T. 13, R. 7
1808.
George Van Slyke,
Peter Taylor,
Peter Conley,
Silas Pratt,
David Sprague,
Abraham Miller,

T. 2, R. 8.
1819.
Artemas Houghton,
Philip Tome,
Jesse Hotchkiss,
Isaac Dow,
Milton Holmes.

T. 3, R. 8.
1819.
Harlow Butler,
Gurdon Cheesbrough
Timothy Boardman,
Asa Watson,
Sargeant Morrill,
William Foy.

HOLLAND PURCHASE.

T. 4, R. 8.
1816.
Samuel Blanchard,
James Godard,
A. Smith Waterman,
David Hammond, Jr.
Jonathan Kennecutt,
Paul Harvey.

T. 5, R. 8.
1820.
Abel M. Butler,
John Beverly,
Isaac W. Skinner,
Job Mick,
Barnard Cook,
Chester Cook.

T. 6, R. 8.
1816.
Jacob Taylor,
Abraham Gifford,
Nathaniel Rawson,
Peter Boss,
Luke Crandall,
Charles M. Barden.

T. 7, R. 8.
1809.
Sylvester Hussey,
Isaac Hathaway,
Thomas Bills,
Moses Eddy,
George Southwick,
Nathaniel Sisson,
Abram Tucker.

T 13, R. 8
1807.
Edward Smith,
Marvin Judd,
Daniel Judd,
Ozias Judd,
Solomon Wolcott,
Thomas Whiles,
Benjamin Graham.

T. 15, R. 8.
1810.
Benjamin Burgess,
Abner Baley,
Stephen Sheldon,
Cyrus Coats,
David Wood,
Martin Sparbeck,
George G. Scrafford.
Garritt Gray.

T. 1. R. 9.
1821.
Alexander Van Horn,
George Fenton,
Joseph Russell,
Reuben Owens,
Mathias Bovee,
William Sprague.

T. 2, R. 9.
1821.
Howard Fuller,
James Powell,
Samuel J. York,
William Eames,
Howard Chapman,
Thomas Hovey,
Edmund Fuller.

T. 3, R. 9.
1815.
William Sears,
Edmund Mullett,
Daniel Philips,
Harry Davidson,
Peter Blanchard,
Rufus Wyllys.

T. 4, R. 9.
1818.
Edmund Dudley,
James Franklin,
James Franklin, Jr.
John Dye, ...
Nathaniel Cooper,
Nathan Skinner,
Asher Glover,
Harlow Beach.

T. 5, R. 9.
1810.
Sherebiah Lee,
Moses Morgan,
William Read,
Simeon Bunce,
Reuben Pitcher,
Ambrose C. Ford.

T. 6, R. 9.
1815.
John Clark,
Benjamin Waterman,
Joseph Brownley,
Joseph Weeks,
Elder Moses,
John Thatcher,
Frederick Bentley.

T. 8, R. 9.
1809.
Adoniram Eldridge,
Anderson Taylor,
Aaron Salisbury,
Martin Sprague,
Gideon Dudley,
Sylvester Maybee.

T. 1, R. 10.
1809.
Abiel Walton,
Robert Russell,
Thomas Russell,
John True,
George Sloan,
Charles Bills.

T. 2, R. 10
1807.
Thomas R. Kennedy,
Stephen Radley,
John Owen,
James Culverson,
Gideon Gilson,
John Brown,
Abraham Tupper.

T. 3, R. 10
1815.
John Love Jr.,
James Battles,
Frederick Love,
James Bates,
Moses White,
Roswell Kenney.

T. 4, R. 10.
1815
Isaac Curtis,
James Marks,
Joshua Bentley,
Gurdon Crandell,
Elisha Wilcox,
Jonathan Andrews,
Barber Babcock.

T. 5, R. 10.
1809.
Ezra Puffer,
John Kent,
Daniel Whipple,
Samuel Hoppin,
Nathaniel Bown,
Calvin Collins,
Sylvester Morris.

T. 1, R. 11.
1808
Robert Russell,
Benjamin Dyer,
James Akin,
Joseph Akin,
Ebenezer Cheeney,
Nathan Lazell.

T. 2, R. 11.
1807.
Eleazer Crocker,
Edward Shillitto,
William Wilson,
Thomas Bemis,
Jonas Seman,
Dyer Nichols.

T. 3, R. 11.
1809.
Amos Aikin,
Seth Cole Jr.,
Stephen Jones Jr.,
William Gilmore,
Orrin Adkins,
Samuel Sinclear.

T. 4, R. 11
1809.
Daniel Picket,

T. 4, R. 11.
1809.
Asa Duran,
Seth Richardson,
Barnabas Cole, Jr.
Arva O. Austin,
John Picket,
Joseph Arnold.

T. 5, R. 11.
1809.
Othello Church,
Urial Johnson,
Augustus Burnham,
Abiram Orton,
Chauncey Roberts,
Horace Clough.

T. 1, R. 12.
1810.
Josiah Carpenter,
Heman Williams,
John J. Gibb,
William Harris,
Nathaniel Fenner,
Jonas Lamphear.

T. 3, R. 12.
1809.
John Thompson,
Darius Sumner,
Joshua Woodward,
John Hemot,
William Armstrong,
Orrin Strong,
Robert Dodge,
Thomas Bemis.

T. 4, R. 12.
1809.
Jonathan Alverson,

T. 4, R. 12.
1809.
Samuel Newell,
Samuel Berry,
Benjamin Miller,
Silas Gates,
Shadrack Scofield,
Peleg Redfield.

T. 1, R. 13.
1811.
Israel Carpenter,
Joseph S. Pember,
Joseph Wall,
Robert Chappell,
Stephen Grover,
Ezekiel Griswold,
Isaac Carpenter.

T. 2, R. 13.
1807
Elisha Phillips,
Josiah Carpenter,
Willian Forbes,
John Thompson,
Mathew Nealy,
Joseph Prendergast
Josiah Phelps.

T. 4, R. 13.
1809.
John Pratt,
Jonathan Frost,
Rufus Frost,
Russel Morgan,
John Dexter,
Philo Hopson,
Ira W. Couch.

T. 3, R. 14.
1810.
Amos Thomas, Jr.
Robert Dickson,
Artemas Herrick,
Anselm Potter,—
Samuel Jemison,
John Daggett,
Caleb Hamilton.

T. 4, R. 14.
1810.
John M'Mahan,
John Dull,
Nathan S. Roberts,
Hugh Whitehall,
Jonn Allen,
Robert Sweet,
William Thurstan.

T. 1, R. 15
1812.
Roswell Coe,
Amos Beebe,
Alanson Root,
Abraham Pier,
Ande Nobles,
Aaron Barney,
Daniel Frisbee,
George Hascall.

T. 2, R. 15.
1811.
Alexander Findley,
Artemas Stowell,
Francis Smith,
Benjamin E. Spear,
Nathan Thompson,
Elijah Drury.

[The reminiscences of pioneer settlement have so far in the main, been applicable to the first six years after land sales commenced. Those that will follow, will generally embrace the period from Jan 1, 1807, to the war of 1812; though in some instances, be extended along through the war, and up to 1820.]

Settlement upon the Purchase was rapid after the expiration of the first six years, and up to the commencement of the war. Generally, when a pioneer had entered a new township, others soon followed, though there were many instances, where one, two and three families, were for several years isolated, their wilderness neighborhoods long and dreary miles away from any considerable settlements. In early years the geographical designations almost throughout the entire Purchase were made by the use of the term, "Settlements;" the name of the settlement, that of the first or most prominent pioneer settler. When there was but one, and afterwards, when there were but four and five towns upon the entire Purchase, the detached neighborhoods, were necessarily thus distinguished.

The progress of settlement in the first nine years, will be very distinctly indicated by the number of land sales made in each year: — In 1801, they were 40; in 1802, 56: in 1803, 230; in 1804, 300; in 1805, 415; in 1806, 524; in 1807, 607; in 1808, 612; in 1809, 1160.

A brief reference has already been made to the early settlements in Genesee and Wyoming. The narrative of Mr. Wilder and others, embraces some of the earliest advents in that quarter.

The pioneer settlers of Alexander have been noticed. The first framed house in town was erected by John and Samuel Latham, in 1810. A grist mill was erected by William Adams in 1807; the first death was of a man by the name of Whitting, in 1804; the first religious meeting was held in 1805, Elder Burton presiding. Two of the early citizens of the town, Jacob Seymour, and ———— Seward, were killed in the war of 1812. Henry Hawkins was the first merchant; Charles Chaffee, the first physician; the first marriage, was of Benjamin Moulton and Eunice Olney. The first school was organized in 1807; the first church, built in 1828. Among the early settlers of the town, there were: — Rodolphus Hawkins, Harvey Hawkins, Henry Hawkins, Rensselaer Hawkins, Elijah Root, Jr., Lillie Fisher, Royal Moulton, Ezekiel Lewis, Seba Brainard, Timothy Hawkins, Stephen Day, John Riddle, Caleb Blodgett, Emory Bloodgett, William Parish, Ezekiel Churchill.

The Hawkins family came in along in 1804 and up to 1808; were enterprising and successful; known in long years as prosperous farmers and merchants. They were generally of strong, robust constitutions; but disease and death entered the family circle, and in the short space of two years, five of the prominent members of it, died. Henry Hawkins, (formerly a State Senator,) died Oct. 1845; and Harvey but two weeks after; both, of the small pox. It is worthy of remark, that both when young had the small pox by inoculation. The father, (Rodolphus,) died in June, 1847, his wife in October following, and about the same time, Van Rensselaer. Among the bequests made by Henry Hawkins, was the endowment of the Genesee and Wyoming Seminary, located at Alexander, with the sum of $5000, in addition to the donation of the building, grounds and furniture.

In reference to early times in Attica and its neighborhood, the author adds to what has already been given, some reminiscences obtained from Roswell Gardner, Esq. who settled there in 1809. The oldest resident is Eliphalet Hodges. He was a settler in 1805; is now 86 years old. When he built his log house it took all the able bodied men in the neighborhood, and there then were not enough to finish raising in one day. The first born in town, was Harriet, daughter of Zera Phelps. The early name of Attica was "Phelp's Settlement." Parmenio and Dan Adams were among the early settlers. Parmenio was Sheriff of Genesee county for two terms; twice elected to Congress. He died in 1822 or '23. Dan who was a Lieutenant in the company of grenadiers commanded by Capt. Seth Gates of Sheldon, was killed at the battle of Queenston Heights.

The pioneer settlers along up the creek between Attica and Varysburg, were, Joseph Munger, Joel Maxon, Benjamin Nelson, John Bogart.

The earliest physicians in the neighborhood were Dr. Nathaniel Eastman and his son, Dr. Hezekiah Eastman; the first settled minister was Elder Cheeny.

Paul Richards, Esq. of Orangeville, was a settler in that town as early as 1811. He says there were then from forty to fifty families in the town.

In few towns upon the Purchase, have the pioneer settlers had to contend with more formidable difficulties. Well does the author remember, when there, as in Sheldon and Bennington, they were dotted around in the forest, miles of impassable roads intervening, (or in many instances none but woods paths,)—with a few acres cleared around them, the dense and towering forests, of hemlock, beech and maple, reminding them of how much there was yet for their hands to do—enough, in prospective to appal even stout hearted men;—and it was a source of no unaffected gratification, to see after an absense of long years, that there too, as well as in all the rest of this favored region, the substantial comforts of life, were rewarding the toils of the pioneer adventurers. An early pioneer of Orangeville; one who has swung his axe among its sturdy hemlocks; ended his life in Buffalo, a few years since, at the head of a banking institution he had founded.*

---

*Oliver Lee, Esq.

It will be new perhaps to most readers, to learn that there was one attempt upon the Holland Purchase, to subdue the forest with slave labor. Two of the early settlers of Orangeville, Joshua Mitchell and Adiel Sherwood,* married the daughter of a Mrs. Wood, from Maryland, who came into the country with them, bringing ten slaves. Involuntary servitude proved a difficult anomaly in the backwoods of the Holland Purchase. The moral sense of the new settlers was manifested, as was alledged, by encouraging the negroes to escape from time to time; prosecutions were instituted against one or two of the neighbors. In the end most of the slaves liberated themselves. It was no difficult matter for them to walk over to Canada, or in fact, in almost any direction they chose to go. One of the last of the lot was sold to Mr. Keyes of Batavia, and will be remembered as the only dark feature in the history of that very respectable pioneer tavern, to which allusion has before been made.

Alba Williams, an early settler of Orangeville, was chopping in the woods; his wife started out to make an afternoon's visit at a neighbor's house, taking her child in her arms. Toward evening the husband went to accompany her home, and in crossing a log bridge over a small stream, discovered his wife and child lying upon their faces in the water, both dead. It was supposed that Mrs. W. had gone to the edge of the stream to wash the face of her child, and while in the act of doing so, was attacked with a fit, fell forward, her face becoming sufficiently immersed in the water to produce suffocation; the child sharing her fate.

Ormus and Reuben Doolittle, though not settlers upon the Holland Purchase, until 1820, were prominent, enterprising and early residents at Weathersfield Springs. John W. Perry, David Rood, Daniel Wolcott, were previous residents there. The names of the two brothers, and their various well directed enterprises, involves a seeming paradox. They have been farmers, merchants, lumbermen, and woolen manufacturers. A neat Episcopal church, and parsonage—cost $5000—was built at their expense; as was a school house, which they kept in repair ten years, and sold to the district. Reuben Doolittle died while on a visit to Illinois in 1846; he was the father of James R. Doolittle, Esq. of Warsaw. Ormus Doolittle is still carrying on various branches of business, in the

---

*Afterwards, the founder of the Sherwood tavern stand, five miles east of Buffalo.

pleasant rural village, which the two brothers have done so much to build up.

Benjamin Bancroft, was the first, and is still the resident physician at the Springs.

Joel S. Smith, an early tavern keeper, drover, merchant and farmer—an enterprising and valuable citizen, is still a resident in the south part of Weathersfield.

Wheelock Wood, after having been a pioneer east of the river—settling where the Lima Seminary stands, in 1795—became a resident at Gainsville, in 1807; from his son, Lewis Wood, the author derived some reminiscences of that region. In 1807, all the dwellings of the pioneers there, were built of logs and covered with bark; floors and doors of split plank; there was but a wood's road from Warsaw to Gainsville. A saw mill was built by the Woods, in 1809, on Allan's creek. Mr. Wood mentions the fact that he was collector of the town of Gainsville in 1812; the whole tax was but $350.

In an early day (the year not recollected,) Wheelock Wood, erected a saw mill on Deep Gulley creek, (within the limits of Rochester, or near the north line of the city.) The mill was abandoned for the reason that it was so sickly in that region that no one would reside there to tend it.

While Mr. Wood resided east of the river, he carried hay and sold it to new settlers upon the Holland Purchase, as far west as Vandeventer's.

Roger Mills was the prominent pioneer settler of Hume; built saw mill and grist mill on the Wiscoy. The village of Cold Creek grew up on lands included in his purchase. C. G. Ingham, Charles Mather, Sylvanus Harmon, Ira Higby, Joseph Balcom, were early settlers at Cold Creek. The first school there, was in 1823; the first physician, Joseph Balcom; first settled minister, Rev. Oliver Reed. C. G. Ingham, kept the first tavern at Cold Creek; commencing in 1823, and still continuing at the same stand. He was the first P. M. The mail route from Angelica to Warsaw, was established in 1826: first mail contained one letter and no newspaper.

Joseph Maxson, was the pioneer of the town of Centreville, and his advent into the wilderness is well worthy of notice. Leaving his native place, (Hartwick, Otsego Co.) when but eighteen years old, he arrived at Pike in April, 1808. Two cents in money, a few articles of provisions, and a scanty wardrobe, constituted the worldly wealth of our young adventurer. Taking a new pair of shoes from his feet, he bartered them for an axe, and pushed into the wilderness, miles away from any habitation. Selecting his land, he erected a rude shanty, and to supply bed and bedding, pealed basswood bark, using one piece to separate himself from the cold ground, and another for covering. The snow fell to the depth of six inches, after he fixed himself in his new home. He spent eight months solitary and alone. It is noted on the books of the land office that he had five acres cleared, July 22, 1808; at which date, he had his land "booked" to him, paying nothing down. It is presumed that he had only chopped down the timber and burned the brush. He raised the first season, a few bushels of corn and potatoes, and in the fall sowed two acres of wheat.

Success rewarded the extraordinary efforts of the young pioneer. He became an early tavern keeper, the owner of a large, well improved farm; and selling out, was a short time since, building mills in Wisconsin. He has preserved as relics of his early advent upon the Holland Purchase, the axe that he got in exchange for his shoes; one of the cents that has been named; one kernel of the seed corn he procured to plant in 1808; and an old wooden fan with which he cleaned the first wheat raised in the town of Centreville.

Mr. ——— Carpenter built the first framed house in Centreville; James Ward the first framed barn, and planted the first orchard. John Griffith officiated at the first religious meeting; Sparrow Smith was the first merchant; Calvin Cass the first physician.

The town of Rushford was set off from Canadea in the year 1816. [*For early settlers, see T. 5, R. 2.*] William Gordon and Sampson Hardy, were early pioneers in addition to those named in the list. The first saw mill was built by M. P. Cady and others, in 1816; the first grist mill, by ——— Warren in 1813.* The early miller was drowned in 1815, while in the act of mending his mill dam. James M'Call was the first merchant; commencing the business in 1816; his store was the first framed building in town. D. J. Board established the first blacksmith shop. The first church organization was that of the Baptists and Methodists, in 1817. The Baptists built a meeting house in 1817, the Methodists, in 1819.

---

* It was a small concern; the bolting cloths were made of book muslin. The upper stone was upon a spindle which was at the end of the shaft of a tub wheel; no intermediate gearing.

It is a fact that tells much for the moral character of the citizens of Rushford, that, for the space of fifteen years, no indictable offence was committed in the town. The mail route was established from Perry to Olean, in 1816; Levi Benjamin was the first P. M. at Rushford.

The venerable Judge James M'Call, the early merchant, who has been for a considerable period, a state senator, and filled many other important public offices, may perhaps be regarded as the patroon of the village of Rushford; conspicuous in the various enterprises that have contributed to its prosperity; his life has been an exemplary and useful one. He still survives; having reached his 74th year. He has reared a family of thirteen children, twelve of whom are married and settled; and has in all, over forty living descendants.

From some reminiscences the author has in his possession, he is enabled to glean a fact highly creditable to the subject of the above brief notice:—After the almost entire loss of the small crops of the new settlers, in the cold season of 1816, there, as in most of the new settlements upon the Purchase, extreme scarcity of provisions prevailed. The Judge owning a mill, controlled all the grain in the neighborhood, except a little corn that the Indians had upon the Canadea reservation; and his monopoly was kindly exercised.— He gave his miller orders to sell to no one man over forty pounds of flour or meal; and not to sell any to those who had teams, and the means of procuring bread stuff by going out to the older settlements after it. And when his supplies became reduced, he restricted the amount to be sold to any one man, to twenty pounds. In this way, the poorest and most destitute of the new settlers were carried along until the harvest of 1817.

The Erie Canal has been a work diffusive in its benefits, and yet its opening had the effect, temporarily, to create depression, and retard the settlement of the southern portion of the Holland Purchase. As has been before observed, the current of emigration to the west, was transferred from the main roads that led to the navigable waters of the Allegany river, to the canal and the lakes. A brisk travel and transportation suddenly ceased; Olean ceased to be a market for produce; in fact, all the local advantages that are derived from great thoroughfares, were lost. This, added to the financial crisis of 1818 and '19, and cold untoward seasons, almost brought settlement to a stand; there were times when farms in the western portion of Allegany, and southern portion of Cattaraugus, with fifty acres of improvements, would not bring two hundred dollars over and above the original purchase money. A large proportion of the settlers abandoned the idea of paying for their lands, and stopped improvements; many left the country, and more would have done, so, could they have realized enough for their improvements, to pay the expenses of emigration.

In 1822 and '23 the gloomy prospect began to change; the Holland Company reduced the price of lands, began to pay liberal prices for cattle; and it was not long before the southern portion of the Purchase, in various ways, began to feel the effects of the prosperity, to which the Erie Canal had given so powerful an impetus, in its more immediate neighborhood.

The wolves made it difficult to keep sheep in all early days, in Allegany and Cattaraugus. In these as well as many other counties of the state, large bounties were paid for wolf scalps. It was with reference to those counties and several others in the northern portion of the state, that Gen. Root, in proposing a large increase of bounty, said, that "the British and the wolves had entered into a combination against American manufactures, and for one, I wish to break it up."

Elder Nathan Peck, was an early missionary in Allegany and Cattaraugus; and the indefatigable "Father Spencer" found his way to the log cabins of the early settlers about as soon as they were dotted, here and there, in the dense forest; partaking with the pioneers their humble fare, and reminding them that their wilderness homes were not beyond the pale of civilization, or the wanderings of the faithful and searching missionary.

It will surprise those who are not already acquainted with the curious fact, to learn that there is a spot upon the Holland Purchase, where the speckled trout, passes from the waters of the Gulf of St. Lawrence, to those of the Gulf of Mexico, and *vice versa.* About six miles from Rushford, on the Olean road, in the town of New Hudson, the head waters of the Canadea and Oil creeks approach each other, and in freshets, mingle; affording the facility for the trout to pass over the dividing ridge.

Deacon Solomon Rawson, was the pioneer settler in Linden. An emigrant from Pennsylvania, he came in from the south, and settled on the Olean road, seven miles south-west of Rushford. He opened a woods road to Rushford. His house was often thrown open to accomodate the emigrants when they began to pass on that road to Olean. He raised the first crops; a daughter of his was the first born in town. The first preacher in the neighborhood was the Rev. Mr. Hubbard. The first church organized in Linden, was of the order of Free-will Baptists; the first physician, was Dr. Hotchkiss. Deacon Rawson says there was much suffering for food among the new settlers in 1817 and '18; flour was from $11 to $16 pr. barrel; pork, 25 cts. pr. lb.; many of the poorer class of new settlers subsisted on milk, boiled greens, and leeks.

The traveler who passes over the road from Rushford to Cuba, will have his attention arrested soon after he first strikes the head waters of Oil Creek, by a cluster of neat farm buildings, in the centre of a highly cultivated farm; the whole nestling rurally and quietly amid the surrounding hills. It is where the venerable pioneer we have introduced, first broke into the wilderness, and where he still lives to enjoy the rewards of his early toils and privations.

Four miles from Deacon Rawson's, toward Cuba, on Oil creek, two settlers located soon after 1808, but the prominent settler in that vicinity, was Col. Samuel Morgan, who located there in 1811, and became the founder of a public house, that was widely known in all early years. He was an enterprising, useful pioneer. He died in 1845.

The land which embraces the site of Cuba village, was originally purchased by James Strong, in 1817. Gen. Calvin T. Chamberlin settled two miles from the village, in 1816; he built the first saw mill in town in 1817. Stephen Cady and Jacob Baldwin, built saw mill and grist mill in 1822, two miles above the village.

Judge John Griffin was an early and prominent citizen of Cuba, locating there in 1820, and becoming the purchaser of the village site. There are few who have not heard anecdotes of the eccentric Judge. He was a man of unusual muscular power; tall, fearless, generous, with more than ordinary native intellect; enterprising and public spirited. In the war of 1812, (then a citizen of Ontario county,) he organized a corps of troops, and went out under Smyth's proclamation. He was a senator from the 8th district, previous to 1836, and for several years, one of the Judges of Allegany. He died in Cuba, in 1845, where his family now reside.

The founding of Cuba village commenced in 1835. In that year, Stephen Smith purchased out the property of Judge Griffin; and

Gen. Chamberlin erected a public house, and opened a mercantile establishment.

The subject of the Genesee Valley Canal was first agitated at a public meeting in Cuba. The participators in the proceedings of the meeting, were John Griffin, Calvin T. Chamberlin, Daniel Raymond, Samuel Morgan, Simeon C. Moore, and other citizens of Allegany and Cattaraugus.

The celebrated Oil spring, is two miles from the village of Cuba, on Oil creek. Most readers are familiar with its peculiar character. It is a curious fact; and demonstrates how wide was the range of the French Jesuits and traders, over the region of Western New York; that Joncaire knew of the existence of this spring, and described it to Charlevoix, in 1721. The mile square of land embracing it, was one of the reservations of the Seneca Indians, in their treaty with Robert Morris. The Indians regarded it of great value; attributed important medicinal qualities to the oil; in early years, after settlement commenced, it was a place, with them, of frequent resort. They used to spread their blankets upon the water, wring them, collecting the oil in their brass kettles.

Soon after the settlement of the country, the oil was collected and sold; and has been in use more or less, for nearly fifty years, though it is not certain that it possesses much virtue. The waters of the spring are pure and cold, not tainted with the oil. When the oil is skimmed off it will accumulate again, over the surface of the water, in one hour. It has a strong bituminous smell; in appearance, not unlike the British oil.

The venerable Samuel S. Haight, an early lawyer of Western New York, prominent in its annals, is a resident upon a farm near Cuba; now over 70 years of age.

The early settler on Allegany road between Cuba and Olean, was Simeon Hicks. He settled there in 1813. "Hick's tavern," was widely known, after emigration commenced via Olean, to the west. As many as two hundred emigrants have been sheltered under his roof at one time. When he went into the woods, his nearest neighbor east, was Elisha Strong, where the village of Friendship is now located; his nearest west, was James Brooks, who lived two miles from Olean. Andrew Hull, who settled on a branch of Oil creek, in 1814, raised the first crops in that region.

Judge Moses Van Campen surveyed road from Angelica to Olean, in 1815.

The author has no reminiscences of Hindsdale, except a list of its first town officers, and the names of the first who took articles of land in the town. [*See T.* 2, *R.* 3, *and T.* 3, *R.* 3.] The first town meeting was in 1821. The officers chosen, were Israel Curtiss, Supervisor; Robert Hinds, Town Clerk; Thomas Warren, Samuel Boughton, Jedediah Strong, Assessors; H. Gross, Collector, Charles Price, Harvey Parker, Emory Yates, Com. of highways; Henry Gross, Lambert Fay, Com. of common schools.

Major Adam Hoops, the founder of settlement at Olean, died in Westchester county, Pennsylvania in 1845; was in indigent circumstances; subsisted in the last years of his life, upon his revolutionary pension; having at one period during that struggle, been one of the aids of Gen. Washington.

Joseph M'Clure, was the early settler at Franklinville, and the founder of the village. He surveyed many of the early roads of Cattaraugus and Allegany, and was somewhat noted for his faculty of making them terminate at the settlement he had commenced; was an active and enterprising pioneer.

A sketch, drawn from some reminiscences of primitive settlement in Farmersville, Cattaraugus county, will furnish the reader with a pretty distinct view of pioneer life. In 1816 and '17, Richard Tozer, Peleg Robbins, Peter Ten Broek, and Cornelius Ten Broek, began the settlement which they called Farmersville. They were all unmarried men except Richard Tozer. Isolated as they were, in their wilderness home, they found it necessary to make some local laws for the government of their small colony. They drew up a code, signed it themselves, and induced other settlers to sign it as they came in. One section of their mutual statute, was as follows:—"If any single woman who is over fourteen years of age, shall come to reside in our *village*, and no one of this confederacy shall offer her his company, within a fortnight thereafter, then and in such case, our board shall be called together, and some one shall be appointed to make her a visit; whose duty it shall be to perform the same, or forfeit the disapprobation of the company, and pay a fine sufficiently large to buy the lady thus neglected, a new dress." Few towns upon the Purchase have been more prosperous; and it is quite likely that this early regulation aided essentially in the work of founding a new settlement and speeding its progress.

These pioneer adventurers carried their provisions ten and even twenty miles upon their backs, through the woods; and as a contrast between the past and the present; as an example of what industry and enterprise will accomplish, it may be remarked, that one of them (Judge Peter Ten Broek,) is now the owner of three thousand acres of land, and in the raising of stock and grain is not excelled by any farmer west of the Genesee river.

Richard Tozer built the first framed house in Farmersville; Levi Peet the first framed barn, and planted the first orchard; Joseph A. Tozer was the first born in town. Rev. Eliab Going preached the first sermon. Richard Tozer was elected supervisor, on the first organization of the town, in 1822, and Elijah Price, town clerk.

It will be noticed, by reference to the map of Cattaraugus, that Farmersville is upon the summit, embracing within its limits, the tributaries of the Allegany and Genesee rivers, and Cattaraugus creek, which is a tributary of lake Erie. There are two small streams that rise in the town, one running due east, and the other, nearly due north. They *cross each other at right angles;* flowing on as if undisturbed, though their waters must be supposed to have lost their identity, in the singular blending. There is one spot in the town, where a man can stand still and spit in the waters of the Gulf of St. Lawrence, and the waters of the Gulf of Mexico. These things do not belong to the subject of pioneer settlement, but their extraordinary character has invited a brief notice.

The author has a distinct recollection of some events attending the primitive breaking into the woods, in the south-west part of Wyoming county, upon the Cattaraugus creek; to which he is enabled to add some reminiscences obtained from Abraham Smith, Esq. (the present sheriff of Wyoming,) whose father was a settler there as early as 1811.

The pioneers in that region, were Abraham Jackson, and his sons, Capt. Amasa Kilbourn, Alfred Kilbourn, John Johnson, Samuel Nichols, Abner Bump, and his sons, and Silas Meach; these, with Moses Smith, comprised all the settlers in the town of China, previous to 1812. The settlement commenced in 1809; Roswell Turner, the pioneer of Sheldon, had for the Holland Company, partly opened a road from his residence south to Cattaraugus creek; and in that year, he took up a lot upon the creek, made a small improvement, and a son-in-law of his, Ichabod R. Sanders, went on to the land, but did not become a permanent settler there.* In 1812

---

* It was in an attempt to reach the residence of her daughter, through a woods path, on horseback, accompanied by a small boy, that the mother of the author was overtaken

and '13, there was added to the neighborhood, Col. Dewell Rowley, Walter Hinkley, Israel Kibby, John Nichols, Porter Belknap, James Steel, Thomas Root, David Barrows. Col. Rowley built a grist mill in 1812 or '13; Moses Smith, a saw mill about the same time. The only boards used in the settlement previous to this, were obtained from saw mills in Sheldon and Hume. When the wife of one of the pioneers died, (Mrs. Kilbourn,) her coffin was constructed of hewed plank. Deacon Hinkley held the first religious meetings, and officiated in religious exercises at the primitive log school house. Dr. Benjamin Potter, and Dr. Ziba Hamilton, of Sheldon, often visited the settlement in early years, as physicians.

A pioneer in this neighborhood, mentions the circumstance, (a very common one, as most pioneers will recollect) — that the early visiting, ball, and quilting parties, went upon ox-sleds, in the principal season of back woods festivities; that he has himself been one of the parties that have gone from the settlement, over into Sardinia, (eight miles,) on ox-sleds, for an evening's visit.

A Congregational church was organized in China in 1815 or '16, the Rev. Mr. Ingalls was the first settled clergyman. The first merchant in town, was Silas Parker. The first school was kept by Joel Dutton, in 1813. The early pioneer, Capt. Amasa Kilbourn, was killed at the capture and burning of Buffalo.

The early settlers upon the Cattaraugus creek felt severely, the general scarcity of provisions in 1816 and '17. Many families were weeks without bread, subsisting principally upon milk; a settler who could go out to the older settlements, do a day's work, and get half a bushel of grain for his family, even felt himself highly favored. In 1817, wheat in some instances was sold as high as $3,00 per bushel, and corn for $2,00. The author was knowing to this price having been paid for wheat, in Attica, and for corn, at Squakie Hill and Gardeau.

There are few of the surviving early settlers in south part of Wyoming and Erie, who will not remember the alarm that was spread through the new settlements, about the period of the great eclipse, in 1806. It caused much commotion and alarm with the

---

by a storm, lost her way, and spent a dreary night in the wilderness; the hooting of the owl, the snarling of the wild-cat, and the howling of the wolf assailing her ears, and helping to make
 "Night hideous."

Indians; and just about that time large numbers of them were passing and repassing between their Reservation at Buffalo, and the Reservations on the Genesee river. The mischievous rumor followed that there was to be an incursion of Indians from Canada, under Brant and Butler, that the Senecas were to become their allies, and the scenes of the Border Wars were to be re-enacted. It is not strange, that even an absurd rumor should have created apprehensions of danger in detached and defenceless pioneer settlements. All was alarm; work was suspended; some left their houses and sought refuge in the woods; and others prepared retreats, in case the necessity of flight should occur. In Hamburg, the settlers, at considerable labor, made a barn the centre of a fortress, ditching and picketing in the ground around it, and erecting block houses; the men chopping and digging, and the women cooking for them; there was mutual effort, for mutual self defence. It is scarcely necessary to add, that the alarm died away, and the back-woodsmen were soon again swinging the axe, and making openings in the forest.

The opening of the old road, from Sheldon to Aurora, has been noticed. The first wagon that ever went over that road, was in July, 1806. Ichabod R. Sanders, a house carpenter, was moving his family to Black Rock, where he had contracted to build a house for Capt. Robert Lee. There were but a few acres cleared at Black Rock; and but three or four families.

As an instance of the improvident waste of valuable timber, which is quite too common in new countries, it may be mentioned, that the town of Bennington was once pre-eminent for its fine groves of cherry. It was used as freely as hemlock, and even logged and burned, in some instances. There are now fences in the town, the rails of which were split from the finest cherry trees that grew upon the Holland Purchase.

Quartus Clapp commenced settlement at Cowlesville, building a saw mill in 1816, and a grist mill in 1818. Joseph Fitch built a saw mill at Scottsville in 1822 or '23. David Scott, Esq bought the property in 1825, and commenced the mercantile business there, Benjamin Folsom, going there as his clerk, became a partner and ultimately the proprietor; and has been, for many years, an enterprising merchant and miller.

As in other instances, the list of settlers in Wales only embraces those who took contracts previous to Jan. 1, 1807. Along in the next few years, those who were conspicuous, (and may be deemed early settlers,) located there. Jacob Turner and sons were there as early as 1808, and built the first mills. The old gentleman was an enterprising and useful pioneer settler. The Allens, Blackmans, Coles and Burts, were early settlers.

The author has no reminiscences of early settlement in most of the south towns of Erie county, aside from the brief sketches he has already given, and the names of the first settlers of each township. Settlement that commenced on the main east and west road, in 1804 and '5, soon extended south of that road, and previous to the war of 1812, there were scattered pioneer settlements in what now constitutes nearly all of the south towns of Erie county.

The author is indebted to James Clark, Esq., of Lancaster, for reminiscences of early events in that region. The first two settlers of the territory now included in the town of Lancaster, were James and Asa Woodward, who made a beginning there as early as 1803. Alanson Eggleston and David Hamlin became settlers in 1804; Joel Parmelee, in 1805; Warren Hull, in 1806; William Blackman, Peter Pratt, ——— Kearney, Elisha Cox, in 1807; Elias Bissell, Pardon Peckham, Benjamin Clark, in 1808.

In 1808, the main road from Lancaster to Buffalo was underbushed, and made passable for sleighs in winter. Previous to this there had been a woods road opened by the Holland Company, from Alexander to Alden; and from thence it was continued along the Cayuga creek, to the Indian village; and from thence to Buffalo. It was called the "Lawson road."

The first saw mill in town was erected by ——— Robinson, in 1808 or '9, upon the present site of Bowman's mills. Benjamin Bowman built a grist mill there soon after the war. The first school house was built in 1810 or '11, and answered the double purpose of a school and meeting house; Henry Johnson and Asa Field took the lead in the primitive religious meetings. "Father Spencer" made his appearance soon after settlement commenced the Rev. Mr. Alexander was one of the earliest missionaries.

Mr. Clark mentions a circumstance of a singular character transpiring in Lancaster, in 1812 or '13, which will at least interest the ornithologist. Early in the spring, a species of bird unknown in this region before or since, made their appearance. They were red, except a little black at the tip of the wings. Soon after they made their appearance, there was a change of weather; it became cold; and the strange visitors perished in great numbers.

In 1804, the town of Batavia was divided into four towns. Batavia retained all the territory upon Holland Purchase, east of a line running north from the Pennsylvania line between the present towns of Portville and Olean, through the middle of the towns of Hillsdale, Franklinville, Farmersville, Freedom, China, Java, Sheldon, Bennington, Darien, Pembroke, Alabama, Shelby, Ridgeway, and Yates, to lake Ontario. The town of Willink was bounded east by the above described boundaries, and west by the west Transit, which starts from the Pennsylvania line on the west bounds of the present town of Carrolton, and running due north, terminates a little east of the village of Olcott, on lake Ontario. The town of Erie was bounded on the east by the west Transit, and west by the division line between the 10th and 11th ranges of townships, which terminates on lake Erie, a short distance west of the mouth of Silver creek. The three towns named, as will be seen, stretched north and south, from the Pennsylvania line to lake Ontario. The fourth town (Chautauque,) embraced all the present county of Chautauque, except the townships east of the last mentioned boundary. ☞ For county divisions that followed, see some statistics that precede maps.

The town of Willink organized in 1805, as did Erie and Chautauque. The first town officers of Willink, elected at a town meeting held at the house of Peter Vandeventer, were as follows:

Supervisor—Peter Vandeventer.
Town Clerk—Zerah Ensign.
Assessors—Asa Ransom, Aaron Beard, John J. Brown.
Collector—Levi Felton.
Commissioners of Highways—Gad Warner, Charles Wilber, Samuel Hill, Jr.
Constables—John Dunn, and Julius Keyes.
Overseers of the Poor—Henry Ellsworth, and Otis Ingalls.
Pathmasters—Augustus Curtiss, Alexander Hopkins, Jedediah Riggs, James Degraw.
Pound Keepers and Fence Viewers—John Beemer, Asa Ransom, Peter Pratt, Lawson Eggleston.

The aggregate vote of the town of Willink at the annual election, in 1807, on the assembly ticket, was but 115.

Asa Ransom, Daniel Chapin, Aaron Beard, Commissioners of excise of the town of Willink in 1807, certify that John Richardson, Samuel Carr, Francis B. Drake, Peter Vandeventer, Thomas Clark, Charles Wilber, Ephraim Waldo, James Walsworth, William Warren, and Levi Felton, were qualified "to keep an inn or a tavern."

The author has some reminiscences of early pioneer events derived from Samuel Slade, Esq. of Alden, which are made to apply to the town of Alden as at present organized, but which, on comparison with some cotemporary records, would seem rather to belong to that neighborhood, or region. Mr. Slade settled there in 1811. The pioneer of the region, the first settler, the one who raised the first wheat and set out the first orchard, was Moses Fenno, who was killed at Black Rock, on the morning of the burning of Buffalo. Joseph Freeman, Arunah Hibbard, James Crocker, Samuel Huntington, Joseph Stickney, and William Dayton, were settlers previous to the war.

The first religious meetings were held at the house of Joseph Freeman. Elder Troup, was the first minister to conduct them. The Presbyterian church was founded by Father Spencer in 1813 or '14. The Methodists had a class in town previous to 1820. The first school was in 1815—kept by Mehetabel Esterbrooks, in a log school house, on the present site of Alden village. The first born, was a daughter of Arunah Hibbard. The first saw mill was built by John Rodgers, on the Eleven Mile creek, in 1813 or '14; he built a grist mill in 1817.

As late as 1811, the Cayuga creek road was impassable with teams, except in winter.

Mr. Slade says:—"The greatest difficulty the early settlers had to contend with, was bad roads. It used to take two days to go to Lancaster, (eight miles,) to mill; in times of drought, we used to have to go to Niagara Falls for our grinding. In the summer of 1817, this neighborhood suffered severely for the want of food; many families subsisted on milk and roots, for days and weeks."*

The Rev. Gleason Fillmore, of Clarence, was the first Methodist minister licensed upon the Holland Purchase. He located at Clarence in 1809, then in his 19th year, and soon after received

---

* In that year of scarcity, which has so frequently been alluded to, it was very common to shell out the berry of the wheat as soon as it was formed, boil, and eat it with milk.

his license. From that period to the present, he has been engaged in the able and faithful discharge of duties that he took upon himself in his early wilderness advent. It is said of him, that he "labored for years, generally preaching two sermons every Sunday, alternating between the detached and scattered neighborhoods, attended the funerals of a wide region, and scarcely received as many dollars as he labored years."

The first Methodist missionaries that came upon the Holland Purchase, were the Revs. Peter Van Nest and Amos Jenks, in 1807, under the auspices of the Philadelphia conference. The first Methodist society, or church, was formed by Mr. Van Nest, in July, 1807, at the house of Jedediah Felton, Sen. at Clarence Hollow; it consisted of twelve members; Charles Knight was the first class leader. Of those twelve members, three yet survive, as does their founder, who is now a resident of the state of New Jersey. In 1807, there were forty-five members of the Methodist church west of Genesee river; in 1808, ninety-five.

A Methodist church was founded in Buffalo in 1809, by the Rev. James Mitchell, but it had no permanent organization. Elder Fillmore re-organized a church there in 1818, his primitive materials being only eight persons, who "called themselves Methodists, mostly transient and poor." In the month of January, 1818, however, the society had erected a small church, twenty-five by thirty-five, on Pearl street, nearly opposite where the First Presbyterian church now stands. This was the first church erected in Buffalo. It was erected in forty-eight days. It is yet standing, and is used as a joiner's shop, on the east side of Franklin, between Niagara and Church streets.

Theodore C. Peters, of Darien, is the son of an early pioneer of that region — Joseph Peters, Esq. A short sketch he has obligingly furnished the author, affords a distinct glimpse of early times:—

"My father came to this town in 1808, and purchased the farm we now occupy near the village, or as I observe it is correctly designated on your map, 'the city.' I can well remember, though young at the time, the long journey the family made in their advent to the Purchase, from Litchfield county, Conn., on an ox sled, in the winter of 1810. There was a small colony of some eight or ten families, who came together. Arriving upon the Purchase, our new home was a log house, with a bark roof, its crevices chinked and mudded; no jambs, but a stone back against which the fire was made. The door was hung with wooden hinges; the floor was of hewed plank, and the hearth was the primitive mother earth. Around the house was a little opening in the forest of about five acres, and a log shed for the cattle.

"Of the hardships and privations of the early settlers, you can, and I hope have, spoken feelingly; for none of us who came upon the Purchase in that early day, can ever forget them, though surrounded by all the comforts and luxuries of the present time. I can well remember when an apple was an unfrequent luxury.

"The 'city' was named by an eccentric individual, when a tavern, blacksmith's shop and store was all it contained. 'Murder creek' took its name from the circumstance of my father and some of his neighbors finding a grave upon its banks. It was in a lonely place, and had been sometime made, as the body upon exhumation, was found much decomposed. The inference was, that some traveler had been decoyed and murdered."

The territory now comprising the county of Niagara, it will be seen by some sketches already given, was mostly a wilderness in the beginning of 1807; the few settlers in it were principally upon the Ridge road, on the Lewiston road, in Slayton's settlement, and on and near the Niagara river. During the five years preceding the war of 1812, settlers broke into the woods, all along upon the fine grade of land under the Mountain Ridge, along on the Lake shore, upon the Eighteen Mile creek, and in a few other localities.

The venerable Reuben Wilson, of the town of Wilson, is one of the few survivors of the early pioneers of Niagara. Identified with almost the entire history of the county; taking for a long series of years an active part in its concerns; his memory of events distinct and retentive; the author has derived from him a narrative which he prefers to give the reader pretty much in the language and manner of the narrator:—

"Emigrating from Massachusetts, I first settled in Canada, near Toronto, but remained there but three years. In April, 1810, I embarked with my family, consisting of a wife and five children, in company with John Eastman and his family, in a batteau, crossed the lake, and landed at the mouth of the Twelve Mile creek. Making a short stop at Niagara, I bought a few necessary articles, in all amounting to fifty cents; but small as was the outlay, it was my entire cash capital. Two cows that had been driven around the head of the lake, a few articles of household furniture, and a few farming tools, constituted the bulk of my worldly wealth. I took up one hundred and seventy acres of land, at $2,50 per acre, paying nothing down, but agreeing to pay five per cent. in a few months.* There had come into this neighborhood a short time previous, (in what is now Wilson,) Stephen Sheldon, Robert Edmonds, and Dexter P. Sprague, (who afterwards went to Hartland,) and Robert Waterhouse. Several families of the Mays and Finches, were in before the war. [Mr. Wilson mentions the names of the settlers along on lake shore, some of whom, have already been noticed. Those that have not, who were settlers previous to the war, were the families of the Wisners and Albrights, since widely known as enterprising and successful farmers; James M'Kenney, Zebulon Coates, Benjamin Halsted, Joseph Pease, Samuel Crossman, John Brewer, Geo. Ash, Jr. Peter Hopkins, David Porter.]

When I came in, there was scarcely an acre of ground cleared in what is now Wilson. There was no road up and down the lake. In the fall of 1811, there was a road opened from fort Niagara to Somerset; it was generally along the lake shore, though deviating at the streams; at its termination, a foot path continued on to Johnson's creek on Ridge Road.

In 1811, I was honored with the office of Constable, of the town of Cambria. It was a very easy station, no precept being put into my hands during the year. The first year after I came in, I had my provisions to procure from Canada; the second year, I raised my own; at the end of two years, had fifteen acres of improvement. When I first began to raise grain, I had to go across to Port Hope and Hamilton for my grinding. Even after mills were built upon the Purchase, it was easier to go across the lake, than to travel the new roads. My first seventy acres of improvement was made pretty much with my own hands; after that, my sons were old enough to assist me.

Previous to the war, myself and neighbors did our trading at Niagara. Dr. Alvord, and Dr. Smith, of Lewiston, were our early physicians. We had no meetings or schools previous to the war; after it, and up to 1820, we had but occasional preaching in the neighborhood, by missionaries. We organized a school in 1815; built a log school house; Dr. Warner was our first teacher. He was both school teacher and physician. Our school commenced with only 12 or 15 scholars. A saw mill was built in 1815, at the mouth of the Twelve, by Daniel Sheldon and Joshua Williams. I purchased the property in 1816, and built a grist mill in 1825. The first saw mill north of the Ridge, in Niagara, was built by Judge Van Horn, in 1811, and he built the first grist mill in the same year.

The war created a demand for any produce we had to sell, while it continued. In 1816 and '17, the seasons were unpropitious. In

---

* This condition, it is presumed, was waived, as in numerous other instances. There is an entry upon the contract book, dated Jan. 10th, 1811, in which it is noted that Mr. Wilson had a house built and ten acres cleared. Such an earnest of permanent settlement as this was, usually obviated any failure to meet payments.

1818 we had good crops, and the courage of the new settlers was revived, after a long period of gloom and depression, of struggling against formidable difficulties. When we began to have surplus produce, it was mostly needed by the new settlers that came in. For any thing we had to send off, Montreal was our market until the Erie Canal was finished. There was in all this region, a stop put to settlement and improvement during the war; more left the country, by far, than came in."

The remainder of the narrative that Mr. Wilson has furnished the author, has reference principally to the events of the war of 1812, and will be used in that connection. The town, (as will be inferred,) takes its name from the early and enterprising pioneer. He was its Supervisor, on its first organization, and continued to be, for eighteen years. He is now 71 years old, but so little broken with age and a life of toil, that he is often in his fields, laboring at whatever his hands find to do. He has been the father of fourteen children, but five of whom survive; they are sons, and heads of families; all residing in Wilson. His son Luther Wilson, Esq. is the patroon of the rural and flourishing village of Wilson, has been for many years, prominently connected with lake commerce; a miller and a merchant; and one of the principal founders of a successful and flourishing literary institution—the Wilson Collegiate Institute.

The Holland Purchase has been a region of successful enterprise; affording every where, examples of the triumphs of industry and perseverance, over obstacles formidable as any that were ever encountered in a new country; but nowhere is the contrast between the past and the present, more striking, than in the town of Wilson. Less than forty years since, the prominent founder of settlement there, made his advent into the wilderness, built his log cabin, and commenced making an opening in the forest; poor, as will have been seen; his last shilling expended; a wife and young children dependent upon the labor of his hands; a rugged soil to be subdued and paid for. Disease was encountered, at times, converting his humble primitive cabin into a hospital in the wilderness; his scattered neighbors perhaps equally afflicted. Soon there was added to the sufferings and privations of pioneer life, war, with all its horrors, in near proximity; and ultimately its scourges laid waste almost his entire neighborhood. Then followed cold and unpropitious seasons. There was ten long years of patient endurance before any "good time" came, or even partial prosperity was realized:—So much for the past. The present is the reverse of all this. The early pioneer is drawing toward the close of a life of industry and usefulness, surrounded by all the comforts and many of the luxuries of life; all is prosperous with him and about him; a succession of finely cultivated fields, of orchards, and more than comfortable farm houses, have taken the place of the dense forest, where there was but "half an acre cleared" when he first entered it; a smiling rural village—with dwellings, stores, and public edifices that would grace a place of more pretensions—has grown up on his early possessions. All this has necessarily partaken much of individual relation; but it is a sketch of life upon the Holland Purchase—its early difficulties and endurances, and its triumphs.

Judge Van Horn, whose name has been introduced in connection with the first mills north of the Ridge, still survives. He was not only one of the founders of settlement, but has been, for a long series of years, a prominent and useful citizen; the frequent incumbent of town and county offices. In his old age, he is surrounded by the fruits of his early toils; has a numerous circle of descendants; and enjoys in an eminent degree the respect and esteem of his fellow citizens.

In the neighborhood of Lockport, the prominent pioneer settlers were Daniel Pomeroy, the Weavers, Daniel Alvord, the Wakemans, Webster Thorn, Daniel Smith, Stephen Hoag, Jacob Loucks, Lyman Liscomb, Messrs. Norton and Williams, the Harringtons, John Smith and brother, James Conkey, Nathan B. Rodgers, Jonathan Rummery, Joseph Otis, Eseck Brown, John Comstock, Isaac Titus, Isaac Mace, Christopher Freeborn, Nathan Comstock, John Ingalls, Alexander Freeman, David Carlton, Coonrod Keyser, Francis Brown, Deacon Crocker, Zeno Comstock, Asahel Smith, Reuben Haines, Jesse P. Haines. These constituted nearly all the settlers in that region, (except the few families that have been named in an earlier connection,) before the canal was located and Lockport village commenced. There was not six hundred acres of land cleared in the four square miles of which Lockport is the centre, before the canal was located; not one hundred on what is now embraced in the village corporation. In 1820, there was no framed house or barn within five miles of Lockport.

Lawrence M'Mullen, was the first settler upon the Tonawanda creek, between the Reservation and the rapids, and for eight years was the only one. He went there in 1815. In 1823, Elias Safford, Esq. moved from Batavia with his large family, and became the first settler upon the north side of the creek, in T. 13, R. 5. Although his pioneer advent was at a late period, he encountered all the difficulties of a life in the wilderness. He persevered, and lives to enjoy the comforts of a fine farm, and to see the wild region he had the fortitude to enter as a pioneer, mostly settled and rapidly progressing in improvement. He has been not only the founder of settlement, but he has reared in his log cabin, upon the banks of the Tonawanda, an excellent family, that have gone out into the world, richly endowed with paternal precepts and examples.

Daniel Benedict was a settler upon the creek in 1824.

The first settlers of all Royalton, south of the Lockport and Batavia road, have been migratory to an extraordinary degree. There are not more than five or six families there, who were residents in 1824. In one school district, sixty families have moved in and out, yet there is permanent settlement there now, as any one will conclude who has witnessed the earnest that the inhabitants are giving of their intention to remain.

The author is indebted to Alexander Coon, Esq. of Shelby, who was one of the first, (if not the first,) settler in that town, for some early reminiscences of pioneer life in that portion of Orleans county:—

"My father and his family came into the woods two miles west of Shelby village, in 1810. The whole family, with a hired man, left the Lewiston road at Walsworth, and arriving upon our land, four crotches were inserted in the ground, sticks laid across, and the bark of an elm tree used for roof and sides. The hut was only intended for a sleeping place; the cooking was done in the open air. So much accomplished, my father and mother went out to Walsworth's for a few nights to get lodging, the hired man and boys lodging in the hut. A log house was the next thing in order. A very comfortable one was built in five days, and that too, without the use of boards, nails or shingles. Our cattle were carried through the first winter entirely on browse; the next winter we had a little corn fodder to mix with it.

"Our nearest neighbor south, was Walsworth, there was one family north, on the Ridge Road; west, there was no settler nearer than Hartland. Eleazer Tracy, came in next after my father; John Zimmerman, Nicholas Smith, Henry Garter, Robert Garter, the same year; William Bennett, James Carpenter, Samuel

Carpenter, William Older, David Hagerman, David Demaray, Elijah Bent, soon after. When the British were in possession of the frontier, many of the early settlers left the country; some of them did not return. It was hard times during the war; provisions were scarce and high. I have been from Shelby, over the Genesee river for two bushels of wheat; getting it ground at the mill on the Conesus. In the cold season of 1816, I paid $11 for a barrel of flour, in Rochester, and $3 for its transportation. A circumstance I well remember in 1818, will shew how new settlers had to manage to get along. I was the collector of taxes; had a small tax, less than a dollar I think, against one man, who to raise the money, made black salts, and conveyed them to Gaines on a hand sled. The first boards we had in all this region, was from the saw-mill built by Andrew Ellicott."

The early settlers of Shelby, locating there generally after the period embraced by Mr. Coon, were David Burroughs, Esq. the Gregorys, Freemans, Sherwoods, Snells, Servoss, Squires, Potters; and others, of whose names the author has no record.

David Burroughs, Esq. (the father of S. M. Burroughs, Esq.) was the first supervisor of the town; for a number of years, and until his death, a magistrate; and was one of the representatives from Genesee in the state convention of 1821. In each station, he was distinguished as an efficient and faithful public servant.

Col. Andrew Ellicott, was the patroon of Shelby village. He is remembered for his many acts of kindness to the new settlers; and especially for the interest he took in the welfare of the Indians at Tonawanda. He was adopted into their nation under the Indian name of "Kiawana," which means, a "good man." He has often helped them to bread in seasons of scarcity with them.

Rev. James Carpenter, was the early and faithful minister in that region; and well deserves a passing notice in these necessarily brief pioneer annals. One who knew him well, says of him: — "He was truly a good man, possessed a bold and vigorous mind; and a deep seated love of his Master. He used to make the forest reverberate the "glad tidings," in echo to his stentorian voice. His sermons seldom occupied less than two hours; and often began at noon and were not finished until sunset. "The Elder," as he was familiarly called, when there was no other preacher in town, was fond of hunting as well as preaching; and wo! to deer or bear, that became the object of his unerring aim. A bear of large size, made a nocturnal visit to the Elder's pig pen, which stood close to his log cabin; one of the pigs gave pretty distinct indications that he was within the fatal grasp, or hug. Its Reverend owner, sprang from his bed, and taking an axe, approached the bear, and with one blow, directed to the brain, saved the pig and secured a bear skin of uncommon size.

The office of Christian ministers was no sinecure upon the Holland Purchase, in early years; as the reader must have already inferred. They encountered the roughest features of pioneer life; penetrated the forests by woods roads, and paths that were only indicated by blazed trees; preaching a sermon in a log school or dwelling house in one settlement, attending a funeral in another, performing the marriage ceremony in another; and returning to their homes after thus itinerating, labored with their hands, that they might not "be chargeable upon the brethren." It is remembered of one faithful pioneer settler and minister in Niagara, that he has often spent the day in meeting some appointment,—perhaps officiating at a funeral—and, returning to his home, split rails, burned log heaps, planted patches of corn and potatoes, or hoed them, by moonlight. Instances, numerous ones, could be cited, which would illustrate the early endurances, and the faithful, disinterested and devoted services of those who founded the first churches upon the Holland Purchase. The churches to which they severally belonged, should gather up their names, and cherish their memories.

Joseph Hart was a pioneer in that portion of Orleans county, contiguous to the village of Albion. He settled on the Oak Orchard road, a little south of the village, in 1811; and is yet residing there, having reached his 77th year. From a son of his, Mr. E. Hart, of Albion, the author received a few brief reminiscences of early events:—

"William M'Allister was the pioneer of Barre; his farm embraced the eastern portion of the village of Albion. Oliver Benton, Esq. settled in the town in 1811.* John Holsenburg and Jesse Bumpus

---

* This early pioneer of Orleans county died in 1848. In an obituary notice in the Orleans Republican, it is said:—

"The life of Mr. Benton is identified with the history of this country. In early manhood he emigrated to the place of his late residence, then a waste wilderness, which, by his industry and perseverance, he subdued, and converted into fruitful fields. His life has ever been one of activity. He was Sheriff of this county at an early period after its organization, and, for a number of years, Post Master; and filled other stations of usefulness and responsibility among his fellow citizens. Up to the period of his last confinement, he was a prominent citizen, and an active, influential man in the business relations of community—esteemed by his neighbors, and his acquaintances generally. By his industry and frugality, under the smiles of Providence, he had accumulated a goodly substance—and he had lived to see a thrifty neighborhood and a respectable and promising family grow up around him."

were early settlers; their farms were lands that are now embraced within the village corporation.

"The only road passable for teams when settlement commenced here, was the Oak Orchard road. The first milling that my father had done, was at Irondequoit. A fact that I have often heard my father mention, will convey some idea of the condition of things here in an early day:—The pioneer, M'Allister, brought in with him a hired man, who was accompanied by his wife; the first female that resided in Barre. She died soon after coming here. At the funeral, there was no one of her sex present; nor any one to conduct religious services; there was no boards to be had to make her coffin; hewed plank, pinned together, was used as a substitute.

"In all the early years, the inhabitants of this region, had few resources that would command money or store trade. Soon after the war, Van Rensselaer Hawkins and James Mathers, and the firm of E. & D. Nichols, commenced the manufacture of pot and pearl ash, at Gaines, and the purchase of black salts. This afforded the new settlers the first facilities they had to command a little money, and it was such a help to them as few can realize in these days of plenty. All of them who could raise a five pail kettle, or club with their neighbors and get a cauldron, commenced the manufacture of the new article of commerce. It not only brought money into the country, but it promoted the clearing of land. The fine crop of wheat in 1818 helped but little. My father sold his wheat that year for twenty-five cents per bushel; it was worth but *thirty-one cents* in Rochester. The avails of black salts, furnished provisions at a period when settlement must in a great measure have been abandoned for the want of them; this is especially applicable to the seasons of 1816 and '17.

"Our first religious meetings used to be held upon the Ridge road, by itinerating Methodist ministers; we used to go through the woods, generally on foot, whenever we heard of one of their appointments. The first school in the town of Barre, was kept by the wife of Silas Benton; she attended to her domestic affairs, kept boarders, and managed a school."

James Mathers, Esq. was the first settler in Gaines, in 1810. He says:—

"When I made my location, the settlers between Gaines and Clarkson were, Elijah Downer, John Proctor, Samuel Crippen, the

---

NOTE.—The remarks of Mr. Hart, with reference to the timely aid that came from a market being opened for black salts, are applicable almost to the entire Purchase. It helped in all the new settlements; enabled the settlers to pay taxes, and purchase necessary articles of domestic use, the want of which had added much to the privations of pioneer life. It is a fact, the making of a record of which is due to the memory of the late Hon. Ephraim Hart, of Utica, that being a merchant at Batavia, at the period spoken of, he transported from Utica one hundred potash kettles, and sold them to the new settlers, mostly on credit, to enable them to embrace the opportunity of converting their ashes into a marketable commodity.

Farwells, ———— Mattison, and a family at Sandy creek. West, in what is now Orleans, there was Noah Burgess, Cotton M. Leach, Isaac Leach, Messrs. Sibley, Jacobs, Wilcox, Joseph Adams, Daniel Pratt, Daniel Gates.

"Previous to the war there was but a few scattered settlers north of the Ridge.

"I built the first framed barn in Orleans county, procuring my boards at Turner's mill on the Oak Orchard, and at Dunham's mill at Johnson's creek. Noah Burgess set out the first orchard. William Perry was the first merchant in Gaines. The Nichols were next after him, commencing in 1816. Guernsey and Bushnell started a mercantile establishment here in 1817, Van Rensselaer Hawkins was connected with it.

"The first mail was carried through on Ridge Road, on horseback, by James Brown. Daily stages were put on in 1816. Stage traveling increased rapidly and became very large before the opening of the Canal. I have often known eight and ten loaded coaches pass in a day.

"About half of all the residents upon the Ridge Road, left during the war; most of them, however, returned. In all the early years, we had much sickness upon the Ridge Road; ague and fever, and bilious fever, principally. I have known half, and even two-thirds of the inhabitants sick at the same time. In the years 1816 and '17, there would have been suffering for food, if the inhabitants had not been kind to each other; dividing as long as they had anything to divide. When I came here in 1811, there was but little bread to be had; our living was principally potatoes, corn and fish.

"The first school was established in Gaines in 1815; in a log school house, of course."

Mr. Mathers speaks of the commencement of the manufacture of pot and pearl ashes, and attributes to it all the good effects that have been stated; and adds that the next article of commerce of Orleans, was staves, which found a market at Montreal. He dates the commencement of lumbering upon the lake, in 1816. In 1817 and '18, it was extended along the lake, to the Niagara river; the mouths of Oak Orchard, the Eighteen, the Twelve, Youngston and Lewiston, were the principal depots. The trade was at first in butt staves; ship timber followed, and continued until the fine groves of oak, between ridge and lake, have pretty much disappeared. As soon as the Canal was completed as far west as Lockport, the commerce in staves and ship timber commenced upon it. Daniel Washburn and Otis Hathaway, first engaged in the business at Lockport, under a large contract with the eminent ship builder in New York, Henry Eckford. The fine oak that grew in the immediate vicinity of Lockport, was used to fill their contract. Since that, the business of shipping staves and timber from Lockport, and other points on the canal and Tonawanda creek, has continued, employing in the earliest years of canal navigation, a large amount of capital and labor; and even now the commerce has not ceased; but is of course much diminished; for although no other district of country in the United States, even bore as much oak, it was not exhaustless. Lake and canal, have conveyed the great bulk of it to Montreal and New York.*

In the history of pioneer settlement in Orleans, there is the well remembered attempt to form a "Bachelor settlement;"—a kind of Fourierite community of joint, yet "single blessedness." They commenced the settlement in 1811; their location being about a mile below still water, on the Oak Orchard creek, in T. 16, R. 2. It was a failure, as the reader has probably already anticipated. As in the primeval locality of the progenitor of mankind:—

> "In vain the viewless seraph lingering there,
> At starry midnight charmed the silent air;
> In vain the wild bird caroll'd on the steep,
> To hail the sun slow wheeling from the deep;
> In vain, to soothe the solitary shade,
> Aerial notes in mingling measures play'd;
> The summer wind that shook the spangled tree,
> The wispering wave, the murmur of the bee;—
> Still slowly passed the melancholy day,
> And still the stranger wist not where to stray.
> The world was sad;—the garden was a wild;
> And man, the hermit, sighed — till WOMAN smiled."

An old Pioneer, quaintly observed to the author: "they began to go east and get wives in a year or two." The introduction of wives and the coming on of the war broke up the "Bachelor settlement," though most of its founders became permanent settlers, and heads of families. Like Benedict in the play, when they said they should "die bachelors," they did not think they "should live to be married."

Judge Otis Turner, recently of Medina, now residing at Niagara

---

*As specimens of the native timber growth of Niagara, the author cites the fact, that a black walnut tree was cut down, while clearing the ground to build the locks, in Lockport, a saw log from which, fourteen feet in length, made 1643 feet of inch boards. An Englishman, who had a nursery of forest trees in England, in an early day, procured in the neighborhood of Lockport, a black walnut, an oak and a whitewood plank, all eighty feet in length, and measuring at their butts, over five feet in breadth, clear of the wane. He took them to London for exhibition, to promote the sale of his young trees. While at the wharf in New York, Major Noah called public attention to them, by a notice in his paper, and they were visited by thousands.

Falls, came upon the Holland Purchase in 1811. Starting from Palmyra, Wayne county, with an ox team to transport his family and household goods, he forded the Genesee river at the rapids, above the Falls. It was in November and there was not a little of peril and danger attending the fording at that inclement season. Taking his near ox by the horns, he was the pioneer, or pilot of his team, stemming the strong current himself, and selecting the best track, though at times there was iminent danger of his oxen loosing their foothold upon the slippery rocks, a ship, or rather a wagon wreck, and an aquatic excursion over the Falls. The intrepid adventurer however, arrived upon the western shore in safety. Proceeding west upon the Ridge Road, there was no stream bridged that crossed it.

Judge Turner located at Oak Orchard. From some minutes taken in conversation with him, the author selects a few brief sketches of early events in that region, in addition to those furnished by others.

Dr. William White of Palmyra, became the neighbor of Judge Turner, soon after he located. The two pioneers built a saw-mill, on the Oak Orchard between Medina and Ridge. This was the first saw-mill in all the region, except the one that had been erected by the Holland Company.

The salt works at Oak Orchard were first worked by Israel Bennett, in 1818. He bored about 150 feet, and obtained water tolerably strong. At one period he had seventy pot ash and caldron kettles set, and furnished most of the salt consumed in all the northern portion of the Purchase. Henry Boardman became the proprietor in 1823. The gradual completion of the Erie canal, induced the abandonment of the works.

The earliest prominent settlers west of Oak Orchard, on Ridge, in Orleans, were:—Ezra D. Barnes, Israel Douglass, (the latter was the first magistrate north of Batavia;) Seymour B. Murdock and sons, Eli Moore. The milling of the first settlers was obtained at Niagara Falls and the Genesee river.

The salmon in their seasons, were abundant, in the Oak Orchard, at the early period of settlement, and in fact, up to 1816 and '18. These and other fish, were a great help to the pioneer settlers; not only a substitute for food which it was difficult to obtain, but enabled them often to drive a brisk trade, an exchange or barter, with the new settlers who were farther removed from fishing grounds. In the months of June and September, the salmon would ascend the main stream and its small tributaries, in great numbers, and were easily taken; sometimes they would ascend in high water, and when it receded, would be left upon the banks. They have been picked up in the cultivated fields along the streams, after a freshet.

The transportation of the early settlers in the region of the Oak Orchard, used to be both upon the Ridge Road and the lake. In 1812, and for some years after, vessels could enter the Oak Orchard that drew less than five feet of water. When settlement first commenced, there were indications that the mouth of the Oak Orchard had been a favorite stopping place for lake navigators, from the earliest period of French occupancy in this region.

The reader has already, in the course of the narrative, had occasional glimpses of early events at Niagara Falls. It remains to speak of one, who for nearly forty years, has been closely identified with that world-renowned locality. Gen. Parkhurst Whitney, has not only been a pioneer upon the Holland Purchase, but he is the son of one of the earliest pioneers of Western New York. His father came as far west as Seneca lake, in the summer of 1789, and erected a small log house upon the "old castle" farm, ploughed five acres of land and sowed it to wheat, made a few tons of hay and stacked it, returned, and in the following February brought his family to his new home. Arriving at Rome, he found the road so bad, and his team so jaded, that he was obliged to leave most of his stock of provisions, and even after that his eldest son and hired man were obliged to lend the team frequent assistance, putting themselves upon the lead whenever they arrived at hard spots, and that was pretty often. The journey was one of peril and hardship; the pioneer mother, wading through mud and water on foot, and camping with the rest in the woods, three nights during the journey.

Gen. Whitney settled at the Falls in 1810; in 1814 he opened a small tavern in a house belonging to Judge Porter. and in 1815 he bought the Fairchild stand, the site being the same now occupied by the Eagle. Joshua Fairchilds had been the pioneer landlord at the Falls. When Gen. Whitney took possession of the premises, the house was of logs, two stories, with a small framed addition. After taking possession, he continued to make additions and improvments, to tear down and build up, until 1831, when he bought the Cataract House, of which he became the occupant in 1835. Then the house was of very respectable dimensions, but not of a size adequate to the increase of visitors at the Falls. He added to it in 1835, one addition, forty feet by fifty-six feet, four stories high; in 1842 and '43, another addition of nearly the same dimensions; in 1845 and '46, another addition, forty-two by one hundred and thirty-three feet, five stories, beside basement and attic. Beside all this, there has been added a two story kitchen, twenty-five by thirty feet; a stone factory, fifty by sixty feet, has been purchased and connected by a gallery, for sleeping rooms; and many out buildings have been put up. The reader has concluded by this time, that the establishment, taken altogether, is of mammoth size, as it really is; vieing in magnitude and management, with the first class of hotels in the United States. The whole, its humble beginning, and what has been consummated, furnish a striking instance of progress, in a region of rapid change and improvement.

The veteran landlord and founder of most of this large establishment, who used to be his own hostler, bar tender, and table waiter, (while his excellent wife was no less tasked in her departments,) has retired from an immediate supervision of it; and a son and son-in-laws, are his successors. With a constitution but slightly impaired by age, the model landlord has become a model farmer, as all may see who will visit his fine farm near the Falls, or who attend our county and state agricultural Fairs.

The following brief notices of pioneer settlement in four separate localities, were omitted in the connection to which they belong:—

The village of Lodi, which is located on either side of the Cattaraugus creek, in Cattaraugus and Erie counties, had its commencement in 1822. It has grown up on lands that were a part of a tract of seven hundred acres, belonging to Turner Aldridge, an enterprising member of the Society of Friends, who emigrated there from Farmington, Ontario county, in 1814 or '15. He built the first grist and saw mill. Judge Amasa L. Chaffee, Dr. Crumb, Alvin Bugbee, Enoch Palmer, L. H. Pitcher, were the first settlers in the village. Ralph Plumb, Esq. was the first merchant, and soon after him, Phineas Spencer and Norton Davison commenced the business. Chaffee and Bugbee, started the first cloth dressing establishment. The Post Office was established in 1823, Benjamin Waterman becoming the first P. M. A Methodist church was organized in 1824; a Presbyterian, in 1832.

Charles and Oliver Johnson were the pioneers of the town of Boston, Erie county,* locating there at the early period of 1804.

---

* So says one informant of the author. It will be observed that David Eddy makes Didimus Kinney the pioneer, and the Johnsons the next settlers.

It is mentioned in some memorandums that the author has of their early advent in the wilderness, that during the first winter, Colonel Charles Johnson, bought a bushel of corn of the Indians, and conveyed it upon a hand sled and upon his back, a distance of fifteen miles through the woods, the snow being at the time, two feet deep; and that he also, during the same winter, backed another bushel from Batavia. The two brothers raised the first crops, and planted the first orchard. The first town meeting was held in Boston, in 1818; Samuel Abbott was elected Supervisor, and Sylvester Clark, Town Clerk. The first merchant in town, was Zadock Stevens; the first physician, Sylvester Clark; the first born in town, was Pliny Johnson, a son of Oliver Johnson. Two citizens of the town, Calvin Cary and ―――― Hoofman, were killed at the capture and burning of Buffalo.

The road from Buffalo to Olean, through Springville and Ellicottville, was opened in 1810; the commissioners to locate it, were David Eddy, Timothy Hopkins, and Peter Vandeventer. It was opened by the state, and the county of Niagara, each paying one-half of the expense.

The family of Prendergasts were among the early pioneers of Chautauque. It consisted of six brothers and a sister, Mrs. Whiteside. Martin and Jedeiah were the founders of the village of Mayville, and were the primitive merchants there, commencing in 1806 or '7, in a log store, on the bank of Chautauque lake. James was the founder of Jamestown. Matthew settled on Chautauque lake, a few miles from Mayville; William and Thomas, in the town of Ripley. In an early period, few families were more prominent upon the Holland Purchase, or more identified with settlement and its progress. As in numerous other instances, the author has to regret the absence of data for a more extended notice. The only surviving one of the six brothers, is Col. William Prendergast, of Mayville. Mrs. Whiteside, the sister, who settled at Mayville with her brothers, was the mother of the first wife of the Hon. John Birdsall.

James M'Clerg, an Irishman by birth, was the patroon of the village of Westfield; was an early merchant there, and the founder of the large public house, that at the period of its erection, was not surpassed in magnitude and cost, by any similar establishment in Western New York.

THE PIONEER SETTLER UPON THE HOLLAND PURCHASE, AND HIS PROGRESS.

> "Through the deep wilderness, where scarce the sun
> Can cast his darts, along the winding path
> The Pioneer is treading. In his grasp
> Is his keen axe, that wondrous instrument,
> That like the talisman, transforms
> Deserts to fields and cities. He has left
> The home in which his early years were past,
> And, led by hope, and full of restless strength,
> Has plunged within the forest, there to plant
> His destiny. Beside some rapid stream
> He rears his log-built cabin. When the chains
> Of winter fetter Nature, and no sound
> Disturbs the echoes of the dreary woods,
> Save when some stem cracks sharply with the frost;
> Then merrily rings his axe, and tree on tree
> Crashes to earth; and when the long keen night
> Mantles the wilderness in solemn gloom,
> He sits beside his ruddy hearth, and hears
> The fierce wolf snarling at the cabin door,
> Or through the lowly casement sees his eye
> Gleam like a burning coal." *

The engraved view, No. 1, introduces the pioneer. It is Winter. He has, the fall preceding, obtained his "article," or had his land "booked" to him, and built a rude log house; cold weather came upon him before its completion, and froze the ground, so that he could not mix the straw mortar for his stick chimney, and that is dispensed with. He has taken possession of his new home. The oxen that are browsing, with the cow and three sheep; the two pigs and three fowls that his young wife is feeding from her folded apron; these, with a bed, two chairs, a pot and kettle, and a few other indispensable articles for house keeping, few and scanty altogether, as may be supposed, for all were brought in upon that ox sled, through an underbrushed woods road; these constitute the bulk of his worldly wealth. The opening in the woods is that only, which has been made to get logs for his house, and browse his cattle for the few days he has been the occupant of his new home. He has a rousing fire; logs are piled up against his rude chimney back; his fire wood is convenient and plenty, as will be

---

* Alfred B. Street.

observed. There is a little hay piled on a hovel off to the right; the cattle and the sheep well understand that to be a luxury, only to be dealt out to them occasionally. The roof of his house is of peeled elm bark; his scanty window is of oiled paper; glass is a luxury that has not reached the settlement of which he forms a part. The floor of his house is of the halves of split logs; the door is made of three hewed plank—no boards to be had—a saw mill has been talked of in the neighborhood, but it has not been put in operation. Miles and miles off, through the dense forest, is his nearest neighbor. Those trees are to be felled and cleared away, fences are to be made; here, in this rugged spot, he is to carve out his fortunes, and against what odds! The land is not only to be cleared, but it is to be paid for; all the privations of a wilderness home are to be encountered. The task before him is a formidable one, but he has a strong arm and a stout heart, and the reader has only to look at him as he stands in the foreground, to be convinced that he will conquer all obstacles; that rugged spot will yet "blossom like the rose;" he will yet sit down there with his companion in long years of toil and endurance—age will have come upon them, but success and competence will have crowned their efforts. They are destined to be the founders of a settlement and of a family; to look out upon broad smiling fields where now is the dense forest, and congratulate themselves that they have been helpers in a work of progress and improvement, such as has few parallels, in an age and in a country distinguished for enterprise and perseverance.

SECOND SKETCH OF THE PIONEER.

No 2.—It is Summer. The pioneer has chopped down a few acres, enclosed them with a rail fence in front, and a brush fence on the sides and in the rear. Around the house he has a small spot cleared of the timber sufficient for a garden; but upon most of the opening he has made, he has only burned the brush, and corn, potatoes, beans, pumpkins, are growing among the logs. He has got a stick chimney added to his house. In the back ground of the picture, a logging bee is in progress; his scattered pioneer neighbors, that have been locating about him during the winter and spring, have come to join hands with him for a day, and in their turns, each of them will enjoy a similar benefit. His wife has become a mother, and with her first born in her arms, she is out, looking to the plants she has been rearing upon some rude mounds raised with her own hands. She has a few marygolds, pinks, sweet williams, daffodills, sun flowers, hollyhocks; upon one side of the door, a hop vine, and upon the other a morning glory. Knowing that when the cow came from the woods there would come along with her a swarm of musquitoes, she has prepared a smudge for their reception. A log bridge has been thrown across the stream. It is a rugged home in the wilderness as yet, but we have already the earnest of progress and improvement.

THIRD SKETCH OF THE PIONEER.

No 3.—It is Summer. Ten years have passed; our pioneer adventurer, it will be seen at the first glance, has not been idle; thirty or forty acres are cleared and enclosed. Various crops are growing, and the whole premises begin to have the appearance of careful mangement, of thrift, comfort, and even plenty. The pioneer has made a small payment upon his land, and got his "article" renewed. He has put up a comfortable block house, but has had too much reverence for his primitive dwelling to remove it. He has a neat framed barn, a well dug, a curb and sweep; a garden surrounded with a picket fence. His stock is increased as may be seen, by a look off into the fields. The improvements of his neighbors have reached him, and he can look out, without looking up. A school district has been organized, and the comfortable log school house appears in the distance. A framed bridge upon the stream, has taken the place of the one of logs. The pioneer, we may venture to assume, is either Colonel of militia, a Captain, a Supervisor of the town, or a Justice of the peace; however it may be, he is busy in his haying. And she, the better part of his household, must not be lost sight of; and she need not be, for the artist has been mindful of her. She is busy with her domestic affairs; there is quiet and even loneliness about her; but, depend upon it, there are in yonder log school house, some half a dozen that she cares for and hopes for.

FOURTH SKETCH OF THE PIONEER.

No. 4.—It is Winter. Forty-five years are supposed to have passed since the artist introduced the pioneer and his wife to us, just commencing in their wilderness home. The scene has progressed to a consummation! The pioneer is an independent Farmer of the Holland Purchase. His old "article" has long ago been exchanged for a deed in fee. He has added to his primitive possessions; and ten to one that he has secured lands for his sons in some of the western states, to make pioneers and founders of settlements of them. He has flocks and herds; large surplus of produce in his granaries, which he may sell or keep as he chooses. He is the founder, and worker out, of his own fortunes; one who in his old age should be honored and venerated, for his are the peaceful triumphs of early, bold enterprise, as we have seen; and long years of patient, persevering industry. He has more than comfortable farm buildings, orchards, and fruit yards; the forest has receded in all directions; he is prosperous in the midst of prosperity. There is the distant view of a rural country village that has sprung up in his neighborhood; a meeting house, a tavern, a few stores and mechanic shops, and a substantial school house. The stream that was forded, when the pioneer entered the forest with his oxen and sled, has now a stone arched bridge thrown over it. The artist has given us a rural landscape, in which is mingled all the evidences of substantial, well-earned prosperity; there is an air of comfort and quiet pervading the whole scene; the old pioneer, true to the instincts and habits of his youth and middle age, is not idle, as we can see. He has yet an eye upon his affairs, and a hand in them; and could we look within doors, we should see the young wife that bravely penetrated the forest with him; she who has lightened his burthens, and solaced him in such hours of despondency as will come upon the stoutest hearts; transformed into the staid, aged matron; yet looking to the affairs of the household; and blending precept with example, fitting her daughters for the vicissitudes, the trials, and the duties of life.

Such has been pioneer life and progress upon the Holland Purchase. A fancy sketch it may be called; but yet it is a faithful illustration of such realities as will be recognised by all who are familiar with the events that have attended the conversion of Western New York, from a wilderness, to a theatre of wealth, enterprise, and prosperity, such as it is now.

EBENEZER MIX.

EBENEZER MIX.

The artist, it will be conceded, has been successful. The features he has presented will be recognised in every school district upon the Holland Purchase. To have rendered the portrait more familiar the old land office clerk should have been represented holding in his hands an "article," (tattered and torn, upon its reverse side, endorsements, assignments, and re-assignments,) peering over it with a mathematical eye, determining metes and boundaries, adjusting conflicting claims, "modifying" or reviewing, or perhaps cancelling it preparatory to a deed in fee. Then the picture would have been true to life and reality; but these are associations that all the "old settlers" will readily supply.

Mr. Mix is a native of New Haven, Conn. He became a resident at Batavia in 1809; working first at his trade, that of a mason, he became a school teacher, then a student at law in the office of Daniel B. Brown, Esq., and in March, 1811, entered into the service of the Holland Company, as a clerk in their land office, where he continued for twenty-seven years. He had been in the office but a few months, when he took the place of contracting clerk. His duties were, to make contracts, calculate quantities of land, renew and modify contracts, make subdivisions of lands, and generally, to do all things appertaining to the place of salesman. In this way, he participated in the sale of all the lands of the Holland Company made after 1811, which were not within the boundaries of the several branch offices. Beside this, the author observes by the records, that he took a prominent part in arranging the details of measures appertaining to the whole Purchase; the fixing of the basis for the modification of contracts; the disposition of church donations; the plan for vesting school house sites, that were upon articled lands, in trustees, in fee; and in other measures that necessarily devolved upon the main office at Batavia. No one in the service of the Company, has been brought into so direct a contact with the settlers, or has had a more intimate acquaintance with them, and all the relations that have existed between them and the original proprietors. Few men could have better filled the place he so long occupied. Possessed of extraordinary talents, as a practical mathematician; a memory of localities, boundaries, topography, which mapped the Holland Purchase upon his mind; he was for a long series of years, eminently useful, not only to his principals, but to the settlers upon the Purchase;—and yet survives, answering the purposes of a book of reference, or an encyclopedia, whenever conflicting questions arise, touching land boundaries, highway locations, or any of the primitive surveys or allotments. Irritable — a little rough and stubborn — he may have seemed at times, when hard pressed with the importunities of a crowd of settlers at the land office; but beneath the rugged exterior, there was a good heart, an inherent love of justice and right, that invested him with the confidence and esteem of the settlers generally, and constituted him the frequent and safe arbiter of their interests and welfare.

For twenty consecutive years, the subject of this sketch of artist and author, filled the office of Surrogate of the county of Genesee. In the war of 1812, in a crisis of danger with the frontier settlers upon the Holland Purchase, he transferred himself from the land office to the camp and the post of danger. He was the volunteer aid of Gen. P. B. Porter, at the memorable and successful sortie, at Fort Erie, September 17th, 1814. He has within a few years, been the author of a work entitled "Practical Mathematics," which needs only to be better known, to become a standard work in that branch of education. His age is now 61 years.

Judge JAMES W. STEVENS, entered the service of the Holland Company at the earliest period of land sales; was the clerk of Mr. Ellicott when an office was opened at the house of Mr. Ransom, at "Pine Grove," in 1799, and remained a clerk in the land office until his death, in 1841. He was a native of New Jersey, a graduate of Princeton college; a man of quiet, unobtrusive habits; possessed of a fine literary taste; in early life, was the contributor to a literary periodical in Philadelphia. In business, he was careful and methodical; all that came from his hands, is remarkable for its neatness and perspicuity, as volumes of manuscripts in the land office, will testify. To habits of industry, he added the character of scrupulous integrity. His public and private life were blameless. He was respected in his life time, for his many excellent qualities; and no where among his old associates, and the pioneers of the Holland Purchase, is his memory revived, but in terms of esteem.

EBENEZER CARY was in the employ of Mr. Ellicott as early as 1795, in the survey of lands in Pennsylvania; and came with him upon the Holland Purchase; acting sometimes in the capacity of surveyor; at others, as clerk or agent, at the store house in Stafford, and in superintending the purchase and transfer of provisions. He was an early merchant at Batavia; was the founder of the mercantile establishment, afterwards so long and widely known upon the Holland Purchase, in the hands of his brother, the Hon. Trumbull Cary. His early correspondence with Mr. Ellicott, would alone justify the conclusion, that he was a man of no ordinary mould; enterprising, faithful and persevering.

He had been thoroughly inured to back-woods life. In a letter to Mr. Ellicott, written toward the close of a winter of inactivity, he says: — "The approach of another surveying season, increases my anxiety to be off; like the savage, I am sighing for the wilderness." In another letter, proposing to be employed, he is in a philosophic, or reflecting mood; he says: — "I wish to go with you, but I am not willing to wear out this old carcase for nothing. I must be preparing for the winter of life; for, generally speaking, he that has no money, has no friends." He died at Batavia, in 1825.

WILLIAM PEACOCK, Esq. of Mayville, is one of the few survivors of the early surveyors of the Holland Company; at one period he was a clerk in the office at Batavia. He surveyed most of the townships of Chautauque into farm lots, and in 1810 was appointed local agent at Mayville, which office he continued to fill until the sale of lands in Chautauque, to Messrs. Cary and Lay, of Batavia. He surveyed the city of Buffalo; there are few, in fact, who have had a larger participation in the events connected with the surveys, sale and settlement of the Holland Purchase. He has reached the age of 69 years. Among the old Pioneers who were drawn together at the last State Agricultural Fair at Buffalo, was the old surveyor and land agent, wondering with others, in view of the evidences of wealth, prosperity and improvement which came from the region they had traversed when it was a wilderness. Mr. Peacock married a niece of Joseph Ellicott.

DAVID GOODWIN, Esq. was also an early surveyor, and clerk in the land office. When the branch office was established at Ellicottville, he took charge of it, and continued to be the local agent there until succeeded by Stahley N. Clark, Esq. Mr. Goodwin married a niece of Joseph Ellicott. His widow survives; is a resident of Lewiston, with her son-in-law, S. B. Piper, Esq.

Our brief sketches of Pioneer advents upon the Holland Purchase, which have been intended to embrace detached localities, in all parts of it, must now be brought to a close; and not in the absence of regrets that they could not have been more full, and included all who took a prominent part in the founding of settlements, in our now so highly favored and prosperous region; a consummation, which, however desirable, the intelligent reader will readily see, would have swelled that branch of the main design of the work to an extent that must have excluded that which the author hopes will prove quite as acceptable. There was a sameness every where in Pioneer life; more of detail, of individual or local relation, would not better inform the reader of its privations and vicissitudes. Wherever the wilderness was penetrated, the same difficulties were to be encountered; the same years of hardship and endurances were to intervene between the primitive settlement, and the attainment of the comforts and conveniences of life.

THE TOPOGRAPHY OF THE HOLLAND PURCHASE.

The topography of the Holland Purchase admits of the following natural divisions, each possessing a similarity in soil, climate and productions through its several parts, and varying from each other in a greater or less degree, in those points. The most prominent division is made by an elevated dividing ridge, commencing west of Genesee river, in township number six, in the first range, and running thence westerly through or near township number six in the second range, five in the third, fourth, fifth, sixth, seventh, eighth, ninth, tenth, eleventh, and twelfth ranges, to within about six miles of lake Erie; thence south-westerly, through township number four, in the thirteenth range, and southerly through township number three, in the thirteenth range; thence west near the line between townships number two and three, in the fourteenth and fifteenth ranges to the Pennsylvania line. The extent of this ridge in width, is from three to six miles, the descent of its sides, however, is nowhere abrupt, nor is its extent defined with precision. Although the summit of the ridge is from one thousand to one thousand five hundred feet above the level of lake Ontario, it nowhere receives or deserves the name of a mountain. It is watered by springs and streamlets, and timbered with beech, red and black oak, white ash, ironwood, and hemlock; the soil is mostly gravel and yellow loam, tolerably free from stone; a great portion of it, if not the whole, is arable land, when cleared and prepared for cultivation. It is better adapted to grass than to grain, although good crops of oats, barley and other coarse grain have been raised on it; like other high ground, it is subject to late and early frosts, and in winter, to heavy falls of snow; the climate is healthy, and the water and air pure. The waters from the summit of this ridge flow to the north-west and north into lake Erie, Niagara river, and Genesee river, and to the south and south-east into the Allegany river, although a few small streams at its eastern extremity, fall into Genesee river, yet the whole territory, south and south-east of the dividing ridge may well be termed the valley of the Allegany.

That part of this valley lying north of the Allegany river, is hilly and rolling, but not mountainous; it is well watered by crystal springs and purling streams; the timber is beech, sugar maple, pine, cherry, elm, black oak, hemlock, basswood, white ash, and cucumber: the soil in general, is gravelly or sandy loam, containing no limestone, and very few stone of any kind; stone quarries, however, are to be found scattered through the whole territory: it is well adapted to the growth of barley, oats, peas, flax, potatoes, and various other esculent roots; and has produced tolerable crops of spring wheat, rye and corn; and the hardier kinds of fruit, such as apples, pears, and cherries are cultivated with success in this district. The climate is rather mild, and the snows seldom fall over one or two feet deep; but the summer season is usually from two to three weeks shorter than it is in the vicinity of the lakes, north of the dividing ridge; the water and air of this district are pure and salubrious.

The territory south of the Allegany river, is mostly rough, covered by precipitous, rocky hills of considerable height, some portions of it, such as the flats on the streams and less rugged borders, are, or rather were covered with excellent pine timber; much of the land thus timbered, is arable and fertile, after being brought to a state of cultivation, although in a cold climate; but by far the greater portion of the whole, is sterile, waste land or rocks covered at the interstices with mountain laurel, dwarf pines and other evergreen shrubs.

The narrow glade of land between the dividing ridge and lake Erie, from Cattaraugus creek to the Pennsylvania line, gradually descends from the termination of the ridge to the lake shore; the soil is gravelly or sandy loam, timbered with beach, sugar maple, whitewood, basswood, hemlock, and some pine; yielding abundant crops of grass, wheat, rye, corn, oats, barley and the several kinds of esculent roots and vines produced in this region. It is well watered with springs and numerous streams descending from the dividing ridge; although the earth is calcarious, there is no lime stone in this region, and very few stone of any kind, except in quarries. The climate is not severe, although subject to sudden changes, being in a great degree controlled by the vacillating lake winds. Apples, peaches, pears, plums and similar fruits are produced in great abundance on this territory. The lake shore furnishes several small harbors, as Silver Creek, Dunkirk, Van Buren and Barcelona.

The country north of the dividing ridge, including the head waters of Cattaraugus, Eighteen Mile of Lake Erie, Buffalo, Tonawanda and Allan's Creeks, forms another district, possessing great uniformity of character. This is a rolling country, well watered with pure water: the timber is beech, sugar maple, elm, basswood, cherry, white ash and hemlock; the soil is gravelly loam, with clay in some sections, containing no lime stone, nor a surplus of any kind of stone. It produces good grass, and at least middling crops of most kinds of grain and esculent roots raised on the Purchase; winter wheat is probably the only exception, for which spring wheat is substituted; of fruits, apples, pears, cherries and a variety of plums are grown in this district. The climate is generally mild and salubrious, the snow is seldom deep, and the summer season, usually is long enough to bring crops to maturity: this may be called the central district.

The territory north of the central district and south of the steep which causes the falls of Niagara, including the vallies or plains of the Buffalo and Tonawanda creeks, and the head waters of the Oak Orchard, forms another district the face of which although somewhat rolling, is comparatively level, and as a whole, forms a glade of upland heavily timbered with beech, sugar maple, white oak, elm, whitewood, basswood, chestnut, cherry, white ash and hemlock, although it contains some districts of openings, thinly occupied by shrubby oaks and some of swamps and swales, timbered with black ash, white cedar and other lowland timber, of which the chief is Tonawanda swamp stretching itself in a kind of broken chain from near the Niagara river, two or three miles north of the mouth of Tonawanda creek in an eastern direction to the Genesee river, south of Rochester, where it is called "black creek swamp." This territory is not as well watered as the other districts described: the prevailing winds are from the south-west or rather south of west from the surface of lake Erie, which renders the air pure and salubrious. This is a limestone district: the soil in general, is a calcarious gravelly or sandy loam, covered generally with rich vegetable mould, and easily cultivated; it produces in great abundance, grains of the various kinds, wheat, rye, corn, oats, barley, &c. including all the different kinds of grain, esculent roots, melons and other vegetable productions of Western New York. The climate is milder, and the summer season continues longer, exempt from frosts than in the more southern districts of the Purchase, on account of its less elevated situation, and its contiguity to the lakes. The soil and climate combined renders this district very productive in almost all the fruits raised in the temperate zone, among which, are apples, pears, cherries, peaches, apricots, plums and grapes of various kinds; perhaps the productions of the soil in no country on earth yield a greater variety and at the same time so great an abundance of the substantials, delicacies and luxuries for food and refreshment as this territory.

The territory lying north of the Niagara steep, forms the lower plateau of the Purchase. This district is poorly watered, when compared with the southern and middle districts, although it has many fine streams passing through it, emptying into lake Ontario. These are the main bodies of the Eighteen, of Lake Ontario, and Oak Orchard creeks, the Four Mile, Twelve Mile, Golden Hill, Johnson's, Otter, and Marsh creeks, and the head waters of a branch of Sandy creek. This district is divided near its centre by the Ridge Road running through it in an eastern and western direction. The face of the country is apparently level, although it gradually descends to the north towards lake Ontario. South of the Ridge Road the soil is gravelly loam, interspersed with considerable tracts of alluvion near the Niagara steep. The soil on the north side of the Ridge Road is of a lighter loam than on the south. The timber on this tract, is beech, sugar maple, white oak, black walnut, elm, whitewood, basswood, white ash, and hemlock; black walnut abounds the most on the south side of the Ridge Road, and white oak the most on the north. Although there is no limestone north of the Niagara steep, or mountain ridge, that the soil is calcarious, that is, impregnated with lime, is fully proved by the large crops of plump and perfect wheat produced on this plateau. The productions of the soil, and the climate, are so similar to those of the second or upper plateau, that an enumeration of their items, and statement of their qualities would be a mere repetition. If any distinction was to be made, it might be alledged that the productions of the soil on the lower plateau are not quite so diversified, and that the climate is more mild and uniform than on the upper. For the productions of the several portions or districts of the territory, as experimentally ascertained, both as to kind and quantity, see statistics of the several counties accompanying the maps.

GENESEE COUNTY

This having been the Pioneer county, or rather the old hive from which counties have swarmed, a sketch of its organization has occurred in the course of our narrative. It remains but to add some statistics — such as it is intended shall accompany the map of each county—which taken collectively, will in a distinct form, enable the reader to ascertain the population and vast resources of the Holland Purchase in 1845; and to estimate them, by a ratio of increase, in 1849. The district of country embraced in the Holland Purchase, may date the commencement of its settlement, in 1799. Upon a comparison of the statistics that will be given, with those of other portions of the United States, it will be found, that no where, has there been as much consummated in a half century, in population, resources, wealth and improvement; and that too, as will have been seen, under early disadvantages, such as have no where been exceeded:—

That part of the county of Genesee included within the Holland Purchase, lies principally on the second terrace, although the south part occupies a portion of the central district as described in the topography of the Purchase. It contains about 219,520 acres of land, 127,508 acres of which were under cultivation in 1845, according to the state census of that year. It then contained a population of 9,660 males, of whom 4,221 were entitled to vote; and 9,100 females; 5,155 were children between 5 and 16 years of age, and 49 were persons of color. The year preceding, (1844,) the territory produced 416,000 bushels of wheat, 53,623 of barley,

135,344 of corn, 908 of rye, 285,131 of oats, 14,696 of buckwheat, 3,063 of beans, 46,550 of peas, 226,946 of potatoes and 4,627 pounds of flax. It then contained 17,306 head of neat cattle, 7,929 cows, from which 687,582 pounds of butter and 216,613 pounds of cheese were made the preceding year; 6,510 horses, 98,024 sheep, 16 churches, 3 academies, 1 female seminary, 120 common schools, 18 grist-mills, 40 saw-mills, 36 clergymen, 18 attornies and 31 physicians.

[For soil, climate, timber &c. of each county, ☞ see topography of the Holland Purchase.]

ERIE COUNTY.

The old county of Niagara, of which Buffalo was the county site and from which Erie county was erected in 1821, was organized in 1808. The first courts were held at the public house of Joseph Landon, in Buffalo, in June of that year. Augustus Porter was the first Judge, Erastus Granger, Zattu Cushing, James Brooks, Martin Pendergast, Judges.* Asa Ransom was the first Sheriff, Louis Le Couteulx the first Clerk. The Court House and Jail, were completed in 1810 by the Holland Company. The Court House was burned in the year 1813 when Buffalo was captured and burned, and rebuilt soon after the war. The Jail was fired, but not materially injured.

The attornies of Niagara, (Erie,) at the period of its first organization, were:—Ebenezer Walden, Jonas Harrison, Truman Smith, John Root, Heman B. Potter, Alvin Sharpe, Bates Cooke, Philo Andrus.

These are all that are recollected as practicing attornies before the war; in the first few years after the war there was added to the list, William Hotchkiss, Albert H. Tracy, Thomas C. Love, Ebenezer F. Norton, Joseph W. Moulton, James Sheldon, Samuel Caldwell Benjamin C. Chaplin, W. A. Moseley.—Messrs. Potter and Walden are the only survivors of the earliest Attornies. Judge Walden is now 69 years of age; retired from practice, but yet active, exhibiting less of mental and physical infirmity, than usual, at his advanced age; superintending as yet, the business appertaining to

---

* The author failing to avail himself of the records of the primitive organization of Niagara, (Erie,) has been obliged to rely upon the memory of those who had cognizance of early events. Silas Hopkins, and Archibald S. Clarke, were early Judges, and may have been when the courts were first organized.

a large estate. Gen. Potter, though his early cotemporary, is by some years his junior; his personal appearance would hardly indicate that he was one of the pioneer lawyers of the Holland Purchase.

Erie county lies about one half, the north, on the second plateau, and the other, on the central district as designated in the topography of the Purchase. It contains about 610,600 acres of land, 224,196 acres of which were under cultivation in 1845 according to the state census of that year. It then contained a population of 41,208 males, of whom 14,631 were entitled to vote, and 37,427 females; 20,240 were children between 5 and 16 years of age, and 847 persons of color. The year preceding (1845,) the territory produced 251,781 bushels of wheat, 40,485 of barley, 238,293 of corn, 11,007 of rye, 637,513 of oats, 31,592 of buckwheat, 4,636 of beans, 51.401 of peas, 552,091 of potatoes, 17,899 of turnips, and 36,819 pounds of flax. It then contained 57,506 neat cattle, 26,809 milch cows, from which 1,728,021 pounds of butter and 1,288,780 pounds of cheese were made the preceding year; 148,732 sheep, 93 churches, 3 academies, 1 female seminary, 285 common schools, 45 grist-mills, 209 saw-mills, 125 Clergymen, 103 attornies, and 139 physicians.

CHAUTAUQUE COUNTY.*

Chautauque county was taken from Genesee in 1808. At that period, the population not being sufficient to entitle it to a separate organization, it remained a part of Genesee until 1811; though the location of the county buildings at Mayville, was made soon after the division of counties occurred. The commissioners for fixing upon the county site, were, Jonas Williams, Isaac Sutherland, and Asa Ransom. The record they made of the manner they had discharged their duties, describes in general terms the spot they had designated, and that there should be no mistake in identifying it, they add that they have "erected a large hemlock post."

In the final organization of the county, in 1811, Zattu Cushing was appointed first Judge, Matthew Pendergast, Philo Orton, Jonathan Thompson, and William Alexander, associate Judges; David Eason, Sheriff, and John E. Marshall, Clerk. The first Court

---

*Or, "Ja-da-queh;" as the author entertains the hope that the empire agricultural county of the Holland Purchase, in the course of its rapid improvements, will improve its name, by adopting the preferable one, which would better correspond with Indian tradition.

of Common Pleas was held at Mayville, in June, 1811. The Attornies then residing in the county and admitted to practice, were, Messrs. Patton and Brackett, Jacob Houghton, Daniel G. Garnsey, Caspar Rouse, and Anselm Potter. Rouse emigrated to Missouri where he was killed in an affray; Brackett was killed at the capture of Buffalo, in the war of 1812. Messrs. Houghton and Garnsey are the only survivors, of the earliest members of the bar of Chatauque. James Mullett was a resident of the county in 1811; a clerk in the pioneer store of Gen. Risley. He afterwards studied law in the office of J. Houghton, Esq. was admitted to practice; is now one of the Judges of the Supreme Court.

Gen. Leverett Barker, was foreman of the first Grand Jury. He was also the first tanner and currier in the county; and at a later period the founder of the flourishing village of Versailles, on the Cattaraugus creek. He died in 1847.

Chautauque county lies between the dividing ridge and lake Erie, on the dividing ridge and in the valley of Allegany. It contains about 668,200 acres of land, 252,784 acres of which were under cultivation in 1845, according to the state census of that year. It then contained a population of 23,453 males, of whom 10,159 were entitled to vote, and 23,095 females; 129 persons of color, and 9,552 children between 5 and 16 years of age. The year preceding (1844) the territory produced 268,261 bushels of wheat, 32,833 of barley, 313,121 of corn, 3,158 of rye, 448,835 of oats, 20,000 of buckwheat, 3,183 of beans, 28,746 of peas, 6,816,869 of potatoes, 22,143 of turnips and 129,749 pounds of flax. It then contained 66,885 neat cattle, 25,024 cows, from which 2,130,303 pounds of butter, and 974,474 pounds of cheese were made the preceding year; 10,506 horses, 235,403 sheep, 73 churches, 4 academies, 307 common schools, 43 grist mills, 206 saw mills, 106 clergymen, 61 attornies and 90 physicians.

CATTARAUGUS COUNTY.

The county of Cattaraugus, although set off as a separate county in the act of 1808, had no separate organization until 1817. Up to this period, it was merged with the old county of Niagara.

The first term of the courts was held at Hamilton, (Olean,) in July, 1817. The bench, at that period, consisted of Timothy H. Porter, first Judge; James Brooks, Ashbel Freeman, Francis Green, Judges. Israel Curtiss was the first Sheriff of the county; Daniel Cruger the first District Attorney; Sands Boughton the first Clerk.

The same commissioners who located the county site of Chautauque, in 1808, located the county site of Cattaraugus the same year, at Ellicottville. It would seem that, as in the first instance, they were obliged to erect a land mark. They certify in reference to Ellicottville, that they "erected a large iron-wood post" to designate the spot. A Court House and Jail were erected soon after the organization of the county, which were burned in 1829; but immediately rebuilt. The Court House is of brick, two stories high, forty feet square; there is a stone Jail, and brick Clerk's office. An ample Public Square was donated by the Holland Company.

Mr. Schoolcraft, in reference to the constant succession of hills and dales in Cattaraugus, says, they resemble "a piece of rumpled calico." The reader may imagine Ellicottville as occupying one of the deepest indentations, or "rumples." The location is picturesque in the extreme; and the scenery of the village and its neighborhood, would be a fine subject for the pencil of the artist. An interval of about half a mile in width, upon the Great Valley creek, furnishes a beautiful village site; but it is hemmed in with hills whose altitudes would well entitle them to be called mountains. It is a village hid away in one of the deep gorges of that region; and yet a happy and contented population have found it, and are making it a pleasant abiding place; in the way of business, a brisk and large participator in the progress and improvement of the southern portion of the Holland Purchase. The sojourner there, who sees high elevations upon either hand, is astonished when told that he is over fifteen hundred feet above tide-water; though he feels that he is breathing pure air, and that he is in a bracing and healthy atmosphere.

Cattaraugus county lies principally in the valley of the Allegany

and on the dividing ridge; it includes the whole of the sterile tract south of the Allegany river, described in the topography of the Purchase. It contains about 852,500 acres of land, 157,442 acres of which were under cultivation in 1845, according to the state census of that year. It then contained a population of 15,447 males, of whom 6,588 were entitled to vote; 14,692 females; 69 persons of color; 8,945 children between five and sixteen years of age. The year preceding, (1844,) the territory produced 177,927 bushels of wheat, 13,671 of barley, 96,540 of corn, 934 of rye, 459,770 of oats, 24,026 of buckwheat, 1,830 of beans, 18,370 of peas, 506,919 of potatoes, 20,813 of turnips, and 42,886 pounds of flax. It then contained 45,256 neat cattle, 15,582 cows, from which 1,284,635 pounds of butter and 567,867 pounds of cheese were made the preceeding year; 6,908 horses, 103,780 sheep, 30 churches, 220 common schools, 24 grist mills, 144 saw mills, 67 clergymen, 28 attornies, and 46 physicians.

ALLEGANY COUNTY.

Allegany county was taken from Genesee in 1806. That part of the county included within the Holland Purchase, lies in that district called the Valley of the Allegany, although some of its waters pass into Genesee river. It contains about 276,500 acres of land, 75,457 acres of which were under cultivation in 1845, according to the state census of that year. It then contained a population of 7,560 males, of whom 3,347 were entitled to vote, 7,429 females; 4,410 were children between 5 and 16 years of age, and 56 persons of color. The year preceding, (1844) the territory produced 251,781 bushels of wheat, (mostly spring wheat,) 7,008 of barley, 42,103 of corn, 629 of rye, 173,473 of oats, 16,936 of buckwheat, 591 of beans, 16,799 of peas, 212,206 of potatoes, 6,574 of turneps, and 38,820 pounds of flax. It then contained 19,859 head of neat cattle, 8,111 milch cows, from which 584,204 pounds of butter and 310,935 pounds of cheese were made the preceding year; 3,793 horses, 56,878 sheep, 22 churches, 113 common schools; 15 grist mills, 118 saw mills, 45 clergymen, 15 attornies, and 32 physicians.

WYOMING COUNTY.

Wyoming county was erected from Genesee in 1841. The courts were organized at a public house at East Orangeville, in June, of the same year. The commissioners named in the act of division, for locating the county site, were, Davis Hurd, John Thompson, and Peter R. Reed. They decided in favor of Warsaw; East Orangeville and Weathersfield springs were both competitors for the location. The act organizing the county, authorised the comptroller to loan to it ten thousand dollars for the erection of public buildings. The building commissioners, were, John A. M'Elwaine, Paul Richards, Jonathan Perry. Trumbull Cary, Esq. of Batavia, gave to the county an ample public square, upon which were erected a neat and commodious brick Court House, Jail and Clerk's office. The Court House was completed in 1842; previous to that however, the courts had been removed from Orangeville, and held in the Masonic Hall in the village of Warsaw. The primitive Judges of the county were as follows:—Paul Richards, First Judge, James Sprague, Peter Patterson, Joseph Johnson. W. Riley Smith was the first District Attorney; N. Wolcott, the first clerk; W. R. Groger, the first Sheriff. Upon motion of Isaac N. Stoddard, at the opening of the first Court in Orangeville, the following attornies, most of whom, if not all, were residents of the county, were admitted to practice:—John B. Skinner, James J. Petit, Harvey Putnam, Lewis W. Pray, Moulton Farnham, F. C. D. M'Kay, William Mitchell, Linus W. Thayer, Leverett Spring, James R. Doolittle, Levi Gibbs, Miles Moffitt, Harley F. Smith, W. Riley Smith, Isaac N. Stoddard.

Some sketches of the pioneer settlement of Warsaw, have already been given. An early and for a long period, a prominent citizen of the Holland Purchase—Judge Simeon Cummings of Batavia—became identified with the village soon after the war of 1812. He became proprietor, by purchase from Judge Webster, of forty acres of what constitutes the north-west portion of the village, including the principal water power. He built a grist mill and an oil mill in 1817. In 1819, the Hon. Trumbull Cary, of Batavia, became the proprietor of the property. Descriptions of things as they now are, are not within the province of pioneer history; but, lest the reader should have never wandered from the main east and west thoroughfares of the Holland Purchase, and witnessed the progress

and improvement in the southern portion of it, he may be assured that he will seldom see a more pleasant rural village, than is the county site of Wyoming; or one which gives better indications of the thrift and prosperity of the country that surrounds it. The public edifices are neat and substantial; the private dwellings have about them the indication of comfort, convenience, economy and good taste. Gen. M' Elwaine, long identified with the prosperity of the place, is the landlord of a public house there, of which he was the founder, which well deserves a rank with the first class hotels of Western New York.

That part of the county of Wyoming included within the Holland Purchase, lies principally in the central district, as described in the topography of the Purchase. It contains about 311,040 acres of land, 156,246 acres of which were under cultivation in 1845, according to the state census of that year. It then contained a population of 11,925 males, of whom 4,331 were entitled to vote, 11,761 females; 6,941 were children between 5 and 16 years of age, and 40 persons of color. The year preceding, (1844) the territory produced 164,131 bushels of wheat, 33,096 of barley, 65,808 of corn, 778 of rye, 471,688 of oats, 21,067 of buckwheat, 2,387 of beans, 30,950 of peas, 381,064 of potatoes, 12,458 of turnips and 123,218 pounds of flax. It then contained 32,003 head of neat cattle, 12,706 milch cows, from which 571,588 pounds of butter and 732,004 pounds of cheese were made the preceding year; 6,330 horses, 140,342 sheep, 46 churches, 2 academies, 154 common schools, 29 grist mills, 64 saw mills, 57 clergymen, 33 attornies and 42 physicians.

ORLEANS COUNTY.

The county of Orleans was erected from Genesee, in 1824. The first courts were organized in June, 1825, at the house of Selah Bronson, in the village of Gaines. The bench of the county at that period, consisted of Elijah Foot, First Judge; S. M. Moody, Cyrus Harwood, Eldridge Farwell, William Penniman, Judges. The early attornies of the county, were Henry R. Curtiss, Alexis Ward, George W. Flemming, Seymour Tracy, Orange Butler, A. Hyde Cole, W. W. Ruggles, Cyrus Harwood, W. S. Moody. William Lewis was the first Sheriff of the county, Orson Nichoson the first Clerk, and Orange Butler the first District Attorney.

The aggregate vote of the county, at the first election, in 1825, was 1,702.

The site was located at Albion in 1825, upon lands conveyed for that purpose, by Nehemiah Ingersoll. The village of Gaines was the only competitor for the location.

That part of the county of Orleans included within the Holland Purchase, lies principally on the first or lower plateau, the south part—being nearly one-third—lying on the second or upper plateau, as described in the topography of the Purchase. It contains about 195,840 acres of land, 102,924 acres of which were under cultivation in 1845, according to the state census of that year. It then contained a population of 9,858 males, of whom 4,341 were entitled to vote, and 9,714 females; 5,569 were children between 5 and 16 years of age, and 63 were persons of color. The year preceding, (1844) the territory produced 528,961 bushels of wheat, 14,593 of barley, 16,060 of corn, 40 of rye, 183,656 of oats, 6,062 of buckwheat, 2,560 of beans, 37,885 of peas, 215,626 of potatoes, 8,682 of turneps, and 12,330 pounds of flax. It then contained 14,992 head of neat cattle, 8,273 cows, from which 571,588 pounds of butter and 174,721 pounds of cheese were made the preceding year; 6,897 horses, 68,358 sheep, 33 churches, 3 academies, 1 female seminary, 100 common schools, 17 grist mills, 43 saw mills, 47 clergyman, 26 attornies, and 43 physicians.

NIAGARA COUNTY.

When the division of the old county of Niagara took place, in 1821, although Niagara retained the name, the county buildings, and of course, the old county organization, belonged to Erie. The separate organization of the Courts of the present county of Niagara took place in May, 1821. The first Courts were held at the school house, in the village of Lewiston. The act making the division of the old county of Niagara, appointed Lothrop Cooke, Sheriff, and Oliver Grace, Clerk, of the new county. Silas Hopkins was first Judge; James Van Horn, and Robert Flemming, were the two additional Judges. The first Circuit Court held in the county, was at Lewiston, Judge Platt presiding.

The first Commissioners to locate county buildings, were, Erastus Root, Jesse Hawley, William Britton. Mr. Britton died soon

HOLLAND PURCHASE.

after his appointment. Messrs. Root and Hawley, upon visiting the county in 1821, disagreed; the former taking ground in favor of Lewiston as the county site, but expressing a willingness to compromise and make the site at Molyneux's; the latter adhering to Lockport. At the next session of the Legislature, a new Commission was instituted, consisting of James M'Kown, Abraham Keyser and Julius H. Hatch. In July, 1822, they fixed upon Lockport as the county site; locating the buildings upon two acres of land, deeded to the county for that purpose, by William M. Bond. The Courts were held at Lewiston until July, 1823, at which time the Circuit Court was held in an upper room of the old Mansion House, in Lockport, Judge Rochester presiding. The Court House was completed, and the first court held in it, in January, 1825. At this period, Samuel DeVeaux had been added to the bench of Judges, before named.

At the first annual election, after the organization of the county —in Nov. 1822—Almon H. Millard was elected Sheriff; Asahel Johnson, Clerk; Benjamin Barlow, Member of Assembly. The duties of Clerk, principally devolved upon James F. Mason, Esq. during the term of Mr. Johnson, and he was elected as his successor. The aggregate vote of the county, at the first election, was 1,324.

The members of the bar of the county, in '23, were, John Birdsall, W. Hotchkiss, Z. H. Colvin, Bates Cooke, J. F. Mason, Elias Ransom, Hiram Gardner, Theodore Chapin, Sebride Dodge, Harvey Leonard.

Niagara county lies about one half, (the north,) on the first or lower plateau, and the other on the second or upper plateau, as designated in the topography of the Purchase. It contains about 329,500 acres of land, 148,108 acres of which, were under cultivation in 1845, according to the state census of that year. It then contained a population of 17,827 males, of whom 6,784 were entitled to vote, and 16,724 females; 9,552 were children between 5 and 16 years of age and 243 persons of color. The year preceding (1844,) the territory produced 713,318 bushels of wheat, 58,340 of barley, 188,166 of corn, 498 of rye, 292,099 of oats, 20,101 of buckwheat, 2,185 of beans, 84,626 of peas, 333,658 of potatoes, and 170 pounds of flax. It then contained 27,836 head of neat cattle, 11,924 of cows, from which 861,300 pounds of butter and 154,976 pounds of cheese were made the preceding year; 8,614 horses, 80,549 sheep, 49 churches, 1 academy, 1 female seminary, 156 common schools, 14 grist mills, 58 saw mills, 59 clergymen, 37 attornies and 51 physicians.

PART SIXTH.

CHAPTER I.

BRIEF REMINISCENCES OF THE WAR OF 1812.

[General histories of the war have been multiplied to an extent that brings them within the reach of all classes of readers; it was the original intention of the author, however, to embody in this work a brief account of most of the events upon the Niagara frontier, and for that purpose he prepared himself with materials. When collected, their magnitude, the extent to which it would be necessary to go to preserve an unbroken chain of events, with any degree of minuteness, soon convinced him of the impracticability of the original design. The subject upon which he could bestow but a few pages, required three hundred; and that without going but incidentally beyond local events. He is, therefore, under the necessity of disposing of the subject, at present, with a few brief reminiscences, that will serve to illustrate the condition of the Holland Purchase when the war commenced; its effects upon settlement and progress; and an account, somewhat in detail, of events, the effect and bearing of which, had a direct relation with the main subjects of his history. The materials in his hands, and which can now be obtained, are ample for a separate volume, confined to local reminiscences of the war; so full of interest, throughout, as to render it difficult to discriminate, in the selection of a few pages. At a period of more leisure, it is his present intention to prepare and publish in a cheap form, a separate volume of some three hundred pages, devoted to the local events of the war of 1812, and such portions of its general history as are necessary to a connected and intelligent narrative.]

There are no statistics from which the precise amount of the population of the Holland Purchase, at the commencement of the war of 1812, can be ascertained. In 1811, it was, in the estimation of Mr. Ellicott, a little over 23,000; in 1812, probably not far from 25,000; distributed as has been indicated in our account of the progress of settlement. The only portion of the entire Purchase where there was anything like compact settlement, was in the few small villages, and upon the Buffalo road. Mr. Mellish, who was in this country in 1811, in an account of his journey from Buffalo to Batavia, says, that "the houses were so thick along the road" that he "was seldom out of sight of one." This was far more than could have been said of any other road upon the Purchase at that period. Aside from the villages, there were more framed tenements upon this road, than upon all the rest of the Purchase;

indeed, elsewhere, there was not one settler in an hundred that had dispensed with his primitive log house, and not one in fifty that had even a framed barn. Away from the main thoroughfare, the population existed in detached neighborhoods and isolated families; it was in but few instances that settlers had fifty acres under improvement; the average extent of improvements upon the entire Purchase did not exceed fifteen acres. The Buffalo road — bad enough, as all will recollect — was by far the best road at the period of which we are speaking; all else, even those most traveled, were but the primitive roads of a new country; but few of the streams were bridged, and but the deepest mud holes crosswayed. A framed bridge over a stream was a novelty; and a chinked or covered crossway was a luxury that marked a neighborhood that was getting ahead of the country generally in the march of improvement. Away from the villages, and off the Buffalo road, not over one in ten, of all the public houses, were other than log tenements. Such, briefly, was the condition of the Holland Purchase in 1812. Add to this, the consideration that nine-tenths of the population were poor; struggling for a scanty subsistence upon small patches of openings in the forest; the soil as yet but partially subdued; and it will be seen that the frontier region was but illy prepared to encounter the shock of war in its midst; to adapt itself to its exigencies, and participate in its burthens and dangers, as its local position rendered necessary.

It was as illy provided for war, in its military, as in its civil condition. Military organization under our then imperfect militia system, had been but partially consummated. Here and there, were those who had participated in the war of the Revolution; but those few were legally exempt from military duty; the local militia consisted of those whose military experience and discipline, had been acquired in no better school than the semi-annual backwood's muster; an enrolment, an answering to names; an imperfect "inspection and review;" and, generally, an easy compliance with requirements, far from being either stringent or effective. But, as in other similar cases, the exigencies of war converted the peaceable pioneer settlers, from raw and inexperienced soldiers, into brave and effective ones, as the local annals of the war often evince. There were no better soldiers upon the lines, in the war of 1812, than those who were called out, or came out as volunteers from the backwoods of the Holland Purchase;

and upon the other hand, justice, perhaps, requires us to say, that there were no worse ones.

There had been forebodings of the event of war in the proceedings of Congress, and in some preliminary military preparations; and yet the arrival of the news of its actual existence, created consternation and alarm. The proclamation of President Madison was carried through the country by expresses, which reached Fort Niagara on the 26th of June, 1812, and Col. Swift at Black Rock, the same day. The express riders spread the news as they passed upon the main roads, the Buffalo road and the Batavia and Lewiston road, and thence it spread in every direction, from settlement to settlement. The usual avocations of life were suspended; here and there, in all the detached neighborhoods, were small collections of citizens, deliberating and consulting upon measures of safety, defence or flight. The more timid resolved upon the latter alternative, while the more resolute determined to remain and abide the consequences. There was a general feeling of insecurity, induced by a knowledge of the fact, that the enemy upon the Canadian frontiers were prepared even for a war of invasion, while upon this side, the preparations for defence were inadequate. Many, over-estimating the immediate danger, made hasty preparations, and were soon on their way, seeking asylums beyond the Genesee river. The singular spectacle was presented upon most of the main thoroughfares, leading east from the Holland Purchase, of families fleeing from supposed danger, meeting emigrants, who were undismayed by the terrors of a frontier residence. Many families who left, returned after a few weeks' absence.

The news of the declaration of war had reached Canada twelve hours before it was received upon our frontier. John Jacob Astor, had sent an express from New York, announcing it to Thomas Clark, Esq., of Queenston. This was a measure of precaution, having reference to the fur trade at the west, and the safety of the cargoes of fur that might be coming down the lakes. In consequence, preparations for hostilities and overt acts of hostility, had actually preceded the reception of the news upon this side. As soon as the news was received by the British authorities, all Americans in Canada were arrested and detained; among whom was Lieut. Gansevoort, of Fort Niagara, who happened to be at the time, on the wrong side of the lines. At Buffalo, the citizens were first apprised of the existence of war, by the capture of a small vessel, which had just started from Black Rock with a load of salt, bound up the lake. The vessel, cargo and crew, were taken to Fort Erie. The tidings of all this, did not fail to reach the greater portion of Western New York simultaneously with the news of the declaration of war. All was bustle and confusion; then followed days and weeks of musters, and drafting of militia, marching to the lines in small squads from the back settlements, and in consolidated ones, along the main Buffalo road. Batavia was soon converted from a quiet country village, into a military rendezvous. Then was heard there, the constant rolling of the drum, the shrill tones of the fife, the din of weapons of war, the rattling of the wheels of baggage wagons; troops were arriving and departing in constant succession.

On the 21st of May, 1812, there were but six hundred men under arms upon the Niagara frontier, beside those attached to the garrison at Niagara. These had been called out in pursuance of an act of Congress, and the requisition of the Governor of the State. The requisition ordered a draft of miltia, but generally, the force was composed of volunteers. They were placed under the command of Col. Swift; several volunteer companies were added previous to the declaration of war; on the 4th of July, eight days after the news of the declaration of war had been received, the aggregate militia force upon the frontier, was about three thousand. Soon after the declaration of war, Gen. William Wadsworth assumed command. On the 28th of July, the command devolved upon Gen. Amos Hall, and on the 11th August, upon Major General Van Rensselaer, who established his head quarters at Lewiston.

Such was the state of alarm upon the Holland Purchase, that Mr. Ellicott deemed it necessary to quiet it, by an address to the settlers dated on the 4th of July, in which he assures them of the effectual guarding of the lines, and of the safety of the whole region from invasion.

War preparations were as active in Canada as upon this side of the lines. When the declaration of war came, the state of defence there was by far the best; there were from six to seven hundred regular troops stationed between the lakes, along the Niagara river. The militia of the Upper Province were ordered out *en masse*. While there was no artillery upon this side, until some weeks after the declaration of war, upon the other were over one hundred pieces. Fort Erie was put in repair, a redoubt was thrown up opposite Black Rock; a battery erected at Chippewa, and another below the Falls. Defences were also erected on Queenston Heights directly opposite Lewiston village, on the river opposite Youngston, and Fort George was strengthened. One of the incipient steps in Canada, was to secure the services of the Indians in the Province. This had been too long a favorite policy of England, to be abandoned. Gen. Brock, the acting Governor of the Province, assumed the immediate command of the troops.

The prompt assembling of troops upon our frontier had the effect to quiet alarm, and many families who had left returned to their homes. After the first turmoil and bustle were over, there succeeded comparative quiet; weeks and months of inactivity upon the lines; the usual avocations were partially resumed in the settlements, though frequently disturbed by militia drafts and harrassing, unfounded rumors of actual or contemplated incursions of the British and Indians. There was little real cause for anticipating danger of this nature, for the preparations upon the other side were wholly defensive ones, and the state of alarm among the inhabitants there, was even greater than here. So far as the respective inhabitants upon each side of the lines were concerned, there was the singular spectacle presented of mutual fear of invasion. There was even a greater fleeing from the lines in Canada than upon this side.

One of the most fruitful sources of apprehension and alarm in the earlier stages of the war, was the fear that the Seneca Indians would revive their ancient predilections, and be found allies of the British and Canadian Indians. Their position was at first enigmatical—undefined. Their chiefs, prominent among whom was Red Jacket, at that period, counseled and maintained neutrality; and neutrality was unfavorably construed by the border settlers. Their position of neutrality was, however, early secured by a talk in council. But when these apprehensions were partially quieted, every breeze that came from Canada, or from the west, brought with it to the scattered border settlements of the Holland Purchase, rumors rife with accounts of contemplated Indian leagues, and banded descents with the tomahawk and scalping knife. Judge Erastus Granger, the then Government Agent of the Senecas, took an early opportunity to hold a council with them and get assurances of neutrality. In a letter from Mr. Ellicott to Mr. Busti, dated July 7, 1812, he assures him of the entire safety of the country from invasion—of comparative quiet, and adds:—"I send by the mail that carries this letter, our last newspaper, which contains a speech made by an Indian chief to the inhabitants of this village, and our reply, by which it will be seen that our Indians are disposed to be on good terms with us—and that they have declared the Mohawk Indians, residing in Canada, out of the confederation of the Six Nations, and of course, 'enemies in war, in peace, friends.'" This position of neutrality, partially preserved in the first stages of the war, was not long maintained. The Senecas, rightly determining their true position and interests, soon became fast friends to the United States,—useful armed allies, in several contests.

Having thus given a brief *pioneer* sketch of war preparations; the condition of this region when the trying and eventful crisis arrived; and arrayed the combatants, ready to commence a long series of engagements, to encounter the vicissitudes and the varying fortunes of war; we proceed to occupy an allotted and stinted space, with two prominent events, selected for their more immediate bearing upon the frontier settlers of the Holland Purchase, and their prominent participation in them; and for the additional reason that, while a faithful relation of the one is humiliating to pride of country, and sullies the reputation of our citizen soldiery, that of the other elevates the former, and redeems the latter.

The calamities with which the Niagara frontiers were visited, in the winter of 1813 and '14, had their origin, as it is well known, in the injudicious (not to say wanton,) destruction of Newark, now Niagara village. After nearly two years' duration of a war, which, upon this frontier at least, had been wretchedly conducted; a vascillating policy prevailing that, even now, after the lapse of thirty-six years, is a mystery yet unraveled; the whole sum of the triumphs of our arms, was the military possession of this small town, and its garrison, Fort George. This constituted our only foothold in Canada, and that, as it will be seen, was to be most shamefully abandoned.

The withdrawal of the entire regular force from this frontier, had left Gen. M'Clure, of the New York State militia, in command of the conquered territory. After an unprofitable occupancy of a few weeks, he ordered the evacuation of Fort George, and applied the torch to the village of Newark, destroying every house in the village, and leaving its population houseless, exposed to the inclemency of the season.

M'Clure and his army took shelter in Fort Niagara, and the abandoned ground was soon occupied by Col. Murray with a force of five hundred British soldiers and Indians. The news of this rash and improvident act, met with unqualified disapprobation every where; and especially upon the frontier, where the blow of retribution was soon to fall; among those who justly appreciated the penalty they must pay for the act of folly. If, as was alleged, by the few apologists of Gen. M'Clure, it was an act of retaliation for British spoilations elsewhere, it was an untimely one, taking place under circumstances that insured a heavy penalty. The weak defences then upon our frontier, to encounter the retaliation that but a little foresight would have anticipated, should have counseled prudence, if not a warfare more in consonance with humanity. But we drop a fruitful source of comment and reflection, that belongs to a general history of the war, and proceed to sketch briefly the consequences that followed; and they were not slow in coming.

Gen. M'Clure remaining but a short time at Niagara, took up his head-quarters at Buffalo, from which place he, in a short time, had occasion to address a dispatch to the Secretary of War, containing, in his own language, and what must have been, the "mortifying intelligence of the loss of Fort Niagara." With that disgraceful surrender, even the partial reader of war history is familiar.

The force that landed at the Five Mile Meadows, under Col. Murray, was about 500 — they completed the landing before daybreak.

A party of Indians, leaving the main body, came up to Lewiston, — arriving about sunrise. There was stationed there but a small force under the command of Major Bennett, that retreated with the loss of six or seven men; among whom were two sons of Horatio Jones. The attack upon the village, was after the Indian fashion, a sudden surprise. There was little of warning; the Indians preceding for a few minutes, a detachment of British soldiers, swarmed out of the woods, and commenced an indiscriminate shooting down of flying citizens, plundering and burning. Among the slain in the attack on Lewiston, was Dr. Alvord, who has been mentioned as the early physician at Batavia. He was shot from his horse while endeavoring to make his retreat. Miles Gillitt and a younger brother, sons of the early pioneer, Solomon

Gillitt; Thomas Marsh, William Gardner, Tiffany and Finch. That day, December 19th, the Ridge Road presented some of the harshest features of war and invasion. The inhabitants upon the frontier, *en masse*, were retreating eastward; men, women and children; the Tuscarora Indians having a prominent position in the flight. The residents upon the Ridge that had not got the start of the main body, fell in with it as it approached them. There was a small arsenal at the first four corners, west of Howell's creek, a log building, containing a number of barrels of powder, several hundred stand of arms, and a quantity of fixed ammunition. Making a stand there, the more timid were for firing the magazine and continuing the retreat. The braver councils prevailed to a small extent. They made sufficient demonstrations to turn back a few Indian scouts that had followed up the retreat to plunder such as fell in the rear. The mass made no halt at the arsenal, but pushed on in an almost unbroken column, until they arrived at Forsyth's, where they divided, a part taking the Lewiston road, and seeking asylums in Genesee county, and over the river; and a part along the Ridge Road, and off from it in the new settlements of what is now Orleans and Monroe counties, and in what is now Wayne, and the north part of Ontario counties. All kinds of vehicles were put in requisition. It was a motley throng, flying from the torch and the tomahawk of an invading foe, without hardly the show of a military organization to cover their retreat.

Almost the only resistance that the invaders encountered, was an attack upon Lewiston Heights, in their attempted advance to Niagara Falls, by Maj. Mallory, and his small corps of Canadian volunteers, who were stationed at Schlosser. They compelled them to retreat below the mountain, and afterwards contested the ground to Tonawanda, with a bravery that was the more creditable, as it was a rare article at that unfortunate period. And it should be mentioned to the credit of a small band of Tuscarora Indians, that they effectually aided the flight of the citizens of Lewiston, by firing upon the Indian scouts that were following them up, from an ambush, upon the side of the mountain, near where the road from their village comes upon the Ridge. It helped to turn back the pursuers.

There are many interesting reminiscences connected with the attack upon Lewiston and the flight of its citizens, but a small portion of which can be given in this brief notice of the events of the war.

At the period of the invasion, Judge Lothrop Cooke, was an invalid, having had, but a short time previous, one of his legs amputated. He was laid upon an ox-sled, and accompanied by his brother, the late Hon. Bates Cooke. When they had proceeded but a few miles upon the Ridge, a scout of five Indians overtook them, and ordered a halt. Bates Cooke seized a gun that was lying upon a sled directly behind them, fired, and shot one of the Indians through the neck. He fell from his horse, jumped upon his feet, and after running about fifteen rods, fell and died. Mr. C. having no farther means of defence, ran, the Indians making two ineffectual shots at him in his retreat. The firing of the guns brought some Tuscarora Indians to the spot, who fired upon the British Indians that remained, and compelled them to turn back; the sled with the invalid passing on in safety. In the pocket of the dead Indian, was found a paper addressed to the Indian Agent at Niagara, saying that the bearer was an "Ottawa brave, worthy of being entrusted with any daring expedition."

During the succeeding summer, the British being in possession of Fort Niagara, small marauding parties, generally Indians, occasionally visited the settlers who had ventured back to their homes in the neighborhood. Upon one occasion, an Indian strolled from the Fort alone, and passing through the woods, came out upon the Ridge at the house of Sparrow Sage, three miles east of Lewiston. Entering the house, he found Mrs. Sage and a female companion unprotected, and made them his prisoners. Ordering them into the woods, and directing their course toward the Fort, the companion of Mrs. Sage made her escape, and hastily apprised Mr. Sage of his wife's captivity. He pursued — overtook the captor and captive, and inflicting a severe wound upon the Indian with an axe, caused him to release Mrs. Sage, and save himself by flight. It was an exploit of heroism, chivalrous, in view of the relation that existed between the rescuer and the rescued, worthy of a rank with the best and bravest deeds that are recorded in the history of the border wars of the Revolution.

There is a solitary grave upon the Ridge road, near the eastern extremity of Hopkins' Marsh. It is that of a teamster whose name was Mead. He was conveying some household furniture from Lewiston, in the morning of the invasion. An Indian overtook and shot him. This was the farthest advance that either the British or Indians made upon the Ridge road.

Three or four days after the British obtained possession of Fort Niagara, a scouting party sallied out with orders to proceed down the lake as far as the Eighteen Mile creek, and burn every tenement. The leading object of the expedition was the destruction of the mills of Judge Van Horn, where some flour destined for our army was stored. The order was pretty thoroughly executed; in twenty-four hours the scattered settlers along the lake road, and at the mouth of the Eighteen, were as houseless as were those of the frontier, from Fort Niagara to Tonawanda; save a few dwellings that were saved by the commanding officer, against orders. Seldom has there been a more peaceable and humane march of invaders through a conquered territory. The orders of the officer, from his superior, were stringent, and even sanguinary; but he managed to discharge his duty according to the dictates of humanity. In several instances he ordered his own men to assist in removing some of the most necessary articles of household furniture, before firing houses; and when the mill of Judge Van Horn was fired, he ordered several barrels of flour to be rolled out for the use of the families he had reluctantly made destitute. The author regrets that he cannot fix upon his name with certainty, and record it with this tribute of praise so well deserved; one informant says it was Captain Sherwood, and another, that it was Lieutenant Williams.

The invaders returned to Fort Niagara, taking back with them fifteen or sixteen men as prisoners, and leaving such women and children as had not fled before them, unharmed. Among the prisoners was Reuben Wilson, Esq. The old gentleman, in relating these events to the author, closed by saying:—"Myself and neighbors were retained eight days at the fort, and then paroled. Returning, we gathered up what was left of our effects, and went east, scattering along the Ridge Road principally, some going over the Genesee river. In a few days there was no family upon the lake, west of Gen. Wisner's;" [two miles below Olcott,] "except Messrs. Crossman's, Brewer's, and Chalmers', at the mouth of the Eighteen; all else was desertion and desolation. I returned in about three weeks, and several of my neighbors returned during the winter and spring; some of them, not until after the close of the war; and some of them never returned, having seen enough of the hardships of a new country, and of harassing frontier life."

The news of all that had occurred spread terror and consternation throughout Western New York. A farther march of the invaders was anticipated; an immediate attack upon Buffalo, and at least an advance into the interior as far as Batavia, where there were an arsenal and military stores. Gen. Hall, on hearing of the invasion, at his residence in Bloomfield, soon collected a considerable force from General Wadsworth's Brigade, in Ontario, and volunteers from Genesee county, establishing his head-quarters at Batavia. An arming and organization was perfected by the 25th of December, and the troops marched to Buffalo. General Hall, in his official dispatch, says:—"I arrived at Buffalo on the morning of the 26th, and there found a considerable body of irregular troops, of various descriptions, disorganized and confused;—every thing wore the appearance of consternation and dismay." He reports the entire number of men at Buffalo, on the 26th, at a little over two thousand, to which was added, before the 30th, three hundred from Chautauque. Organization, from the short time that was allowed to perfect it, was necessarily imperfect.

On the night of the 29th of December, between eleven and twelve o'clock, it was announced at Buffalo, that a patrol of mounted men, under the command of Lieut. Boughton, had been fired upon by a British force, that had crossed near the head of Grand Island, advanced, and taken possession of a battery which stood upon the site of the present lower village of Black Rock. The troops at Buffalo were immediately paraded, but not ordered to march upon the invaders, Gen. Hall concluding that the attack below was intended to draw off his force preparatory to an attack upon Buffalo. General Hopkins being absent at the time, the command at Black Rock devolved upon Colonels Warren and Churchill. They were ordered by Gen. Hall to attack the enemy in the battery where they had taken position, dislodge and drive them from their boats. The attack, made under all the disadvantages of hasty preparation, in a dark night, failed to accomplish its purpose. The entire force was dispersed. Orders were immediatly given for the main force at Buffalo to march in the direction of Black Rock. A second attack upon the British force in the battery, by a small corps headed by Col. Chapin and Maj. Adams, ended like the first, in failure and dispersion. All that succeeded, was but a chapter of disasters and failures, which are principally comprised in the following extract from an official dispatch of Gen. Hall to Gov. Tompkins:—

"As the day dawned, I discovered a detachment of the enemy's boats crossing to our shore, and bending their course towards the rear of Gen. Porter's house. I immediately ordered Col. Blakeslee to attack the enemy's force at the water's edge. I became satisfied as to the disposition and object of the enemy. Their left wing, composed of about one thousand regulars, militia, and Indians, had been landed below the creek, under the cover of the night. With their centre, consisting of four hundred royal Scots, commanded by Col. Gordon, the battle was commenced. The right, which was purposely weak, was landed near the main battery, merely to divert our force; the whole under the immediate command of Lieut. Col. Drummond, and led on by Maj. Gen. Riall. They were attacked by four field pieces in the battery at the water's edge, at the same time the battery from the other side of the river opened a heavy fire upon us, of shells, hot shot, and ball. The whole force now opposed to the enemy was, at most, not over six hundred men, the remainder having fled, in spite of the exertions of their officers. These few but brave men, disputed every inch of ground, with the steady coolness of veterans, at the expense of many valuable lives. The defection of the militia, by reason of the ground on which they must act, left the forces engaged, exposed to the enemy's fire in front and flank. After standing their ground for half an hour, opposed by an overwhelming force and nearly surrounded, a retreat became necessary to their safety, and was accordingly ordered. I then made every effort to rally the troops, with a view to attack their columns as they entered the village of Buffalo, but all in vain. Deserted by my principal force, I fell back that night to Eleven Mile creek, and was forced to leave the flourishing villages of Black Rock and Buffalo a prey to the enemy, which they have pillaged and laid in ashes. They have gained but little plunder from the stores; the chief loss has fallen upon individuals."

Such is the official account of the memorable and disastrous events of the morning of the 30th of December. A long catalogue of cotemporary accounts, of personal recollections, might be added, which would furnish pages that belong upon the dark side of American war history. It was the consummation of a series of untoward events, which had their origin in the general bad management of the campaign of 1813; promoted, its climax of folly added, by an act of wanton aggression, such as was the destruction of Newark, at a period when retribution was sure to follow, and be disastrously successful as it was; at a crisis when the efficient defences upon our frontiers were withdrawn, and the inadequate protection of a militia force, suddenly drawn from their homes at an inclement season, without opportunity for efficient organization, substituted. The British force that landed at Black Rock was inferior in point of numbers, to the opposing American force, according to the estimates of Gen. Hall. The British official accounts make the whole invading force under Gen. Riall but little over one thousand. Upon the one hand, however, there were all the advantages of efficient organization, tolerable discipline, and of attack under cover of the darkness of night; upon the other, the disadvantages that have already been enumerated, to which may be added, cowardice and flight, disgraceful to the American arms. And yet the battle of Black Rock, the generally inefficient defences that were made against an invading foe, were not without some redeeming features. There were creditable and honorable acts of bravery, but they were isolated ones. There were those who stood firm in the midst of flight, until resistance seemed no longer of any avail. But after a few ineffectual attempts to beat back the invaders, it was a general rout and flight, through every avenue of escape from danger; and squads of armed soldiers, in many instances, preceded even women and children in the hasty retreat. It was odd enough, and disgraceful enough, but it was nevertheless a fact, that retreating soldiers, and even some officers, as they arrived in the back settlements, added to the panic and dismay, that the cooler headed and less timorous were endeavoring to allay. The local history of the war of 1812, in the aggregate, is creditable, highly so, to the frontier settlers upon the Holland Purchase. Never in the history of this or any other country has there been a more prompt compliance with military requisitions, attended with greater sacrifices, than in that crisis, throughout the whole region of Western New York. In the settlements upon the Holland Purchase, during more than one campaign, there might have been seen the small harvest fields of the new settlers, ripening for the scythe and the sickle, maturing and going to waste; while the owners, whose toil had cleared, planted, and sowed, were away, enrolled and under arms, in the service of their country. Improvements, as has been before said, were in their infancy; there would have been no surplus produce, with seasonable harvests; the reader will readily infer in what degree, late and often neglected harvests added to the distress and suffering of the inhabitants. There was in the whole trying and eventful crisis, on the part of the men of Western New York, in the main, no absence of a devotion to country, or willingness to defend its soil; but the events of the

30th of December, 1813, are seldom now recurred to in the presence of those who witnessed them, and participated in their consequences, without bringing to their minds lively and painful recollections of imperfect and abortive measures of defence; the rout, the hasty, panic stricken retreat, the unnecessary surrendering of a frontier, and its then largest village, to the arms and the torch of an invading foe, not formidable either in numbers or military prowess.

And it here may be added, in reference to the whole history of the war upon this frontier, that it furnished a distinct, and ever to be remembered demonstration of the inutility of a drafted militia. Where ever such troops were relied upon, there were failure and disaster. While the volunteer militia that came out at different periods, and in different corps, during the whole war, seldom failed to render efficient service; often competed successfully with regular troops, for preference in good conduct and achievements, upon the battle field.

Arresting this slight digression, we will return to Buffalo, and detail events of easy conquest, retreat, flight, pillage and devastation, which General Hall, in his official despatch, has so summarily disposed of. Before daylight, the citizens of Buffalo were fully apprised of the feeble and ill managed defence at Black Rock; of its prospect of failure. Tidings that all was hopeless, had reached them, and were confirmed by the hasty retreat of squads of militia, who were making palpable demonstrations of their innate love of life, in their eagerness to outstrip each other in the race that was taking them beyond the reach of danger. Those of the citizens who had teams of oxen or horses, put them in requisition, hastily snatching but a small portion of the personal effects of themselves and families—in most instances, but a scanty wardrobe —and seeking, in terror and dismay, the most convenient avenues of retreat. In numerous instances, women and children, inadeqately provided with the means of protecting them against the inclemency of the season, started out on foot, to wade through the snow many weary miles, before they could expect to find shelter and rest. The British army advanced from Black Rock, or rather from the last point at which they had met with any considerable resistance, annoyed only by a few discharges from a twelve pound cannon, manned by a small corps that had taken position at the junction of the Black Rock and the main road. When it had advanced to within a few rods of the old burying ground, many of the families of the citizens were but just leaving their dwellings, and others had not got far beyond the bounds of the village. At this critical juncture, when the Indians were leaving the main army, in scouts, and were about to enter the village, commence the work of plunder, and fall upon such of the inhabitants as were late in the retreat, with the tomahawk and scalping knife, Col. Cyrenius Chapin, in the absence of any one who had authority to treat with the invaders, and agree upon terms of capitulation, mounted a horse, and with a white handkerchief raised upon the end of his cane, approached the enemy and sought an interview with Gen. Riall. Terms of capitulation were hastily arranged. It was agreed that all public property should be given up, and private property respected; that the invading force should not be attacked while it remained in possession of the village. While this negotiation was going on, time was given for the lagging citizens to make their escape. The main body of the invaders soon entered the village. Among the few citizens who had remained, to endeavor to save their property, beside Col. Chapin, were Judge Walden, Messrs. Cook, Pomeroy and Kane, and Mrs. St. John and Lovejoy. At the suggestion of the British officers, all the intoxicating liquors that could be found in the village, were destroyed, to prevent the Indians getting access to them, and becoming uncontrollable.

In this position of affairs, a building was discovered on fire. Judge Walden enquired of Col. Chapin, the meaning of this infraction of the terms of capitulation; the Colonel, surprised himself, requested the Judge to have an immediate interview with Gen. Riall. Failing to meet with him, he found Colonel Elliott, who had command of the Indians. He justified the commencement of burning, upon the ground that an American force was marching to attack them. Looking up main street, Judge Walden saw a small force approaching, and immediately started out to meet it. It proved to be a detachment of forty regular soldiers, who had been exempts at the hospital in Williamsville, under the command of Lieut. Riddle, marching in to save the village! Judge Walden remonstrated against the rash and hair brained enterprise, and persuaded the Lieutenant to secure a retreat, but not without a few discharges of a cannon he had brought along with him, and vehement protestations against the capitulation, and the authority that had sanctioned it.

The firing of buildings had now progressed to a considerable extent, under the direction of a Lieutenant, who moved from house to house, with a small corps, that applied the torch under his direction. A simultaneous plundering was commenced by the Indians. All the buildings were burned during the first day, except Mrs. St. John's house, Mrs. Lovejoy's, Dr. Chapin's, Judge Walden's and Reece's blacksmith shop. Mrs. St. John remained in her house, and claimed protection for herself and property, which was granted. Mrs. Lovejoy, less fortunate, and less prudent, had some altercation with the Indians, who entered her house for plunder, was stabbed, and her lifeless body thrown into the street. Judge Walden carried the body back into the house, where it was consumed the next day, with the house.

About 3 o'clock P. M., the village was evacuated by the invaders, the main force moving down to Black Rock, and crossing the river with the public property they had captured, and their plunder. On the second day, all was quiet; there were no British nor Indians in the village, or rather where the village had been; but there were plunderers of a different character, those who claimed, but were unworthy of, the name of American citizens—marauders and land pirates—hanging around the scene of desolation, stealing and carrying off the little the enemy had left; and this domestic rapine was continued as long as there was anything left to steal. Revolting it is, to be obliged to record the shameful truth in the annals of the Holland Purchase. We must place it to the account of war and its demoralizing tendencies.

In the forenoon of the third day, a small party of British and Indians returned, burnt all the buildings that had before been spared, except Mrs. St. John's house and Reece's blacksmith shop; after which they passed down the Niagara river to Fort Niagara.

The reader will have observed that Col. Chapin exercised an influence somewhat extraordinary, for one who had been conspicuous in a previous invasion of Canada. This may be attributed to the stand he had taken at Newark, against Gen. M'Clure, and the rash measures there, which were so promptly retaliated. Judge Walden and the few other citizens that remained, probably owed their exemption from harm, to his influence. The Judge was at one time, with others that remained, formally made prisoner, but by walking off unobserved, and dodging from point to point, while the enemy were engrossed with the business of plundering and burning, he escaped. Col. Chapin was made a prisoner, taken to Montreal, and retained several months.

The few citizens that had remained in Buffalo, went back into the country. Days and weeks of desertion, stillness and desolation, succeeded. The villages of Buffalo, Black Rock, Niagara Falls, Lewiston and Youngstown, and the farm houses and other tenements that intervened, presented but one extended scene of ruin and devastation. Mr. James Sloan, a resident of Black Rock, an active participator in many of the stirring scenes of the war of 1812, says, that a few days after the evacuation of Buffalo, himself and Judge Wilkeson, passed down the lake from the Barker stand, and through the main street of the site of Buffalo, to the Cold Springs. That, between the Pratt ferry and the Cold Springs, a cat that was wandering about its former home, was all that they saw of any living thing!

The Buffalo road was the main avenue of retreat and flight for the citizens, though large numbers of them went up the lake, and through the Seneca Indian village, Willink, (Aurora,) Sheldon and Warsaw. During the whole day, (the 30th,) the Buffalo road was crowded with squads of retreating soldiers—the retiring "bulwarks of their country's defence;" families upon sleighs, ox sleds, and on foot; in many instances half clad children, the wounded, the aged and infirm, were wading through snow, bands of able bodied armed men often passing them, pitiless and unobserving, absorbed in deep concern for their own individual and especial safety. Here and there, along the road, were feeble attempts to rally and stand; some resolute individuals would propose it, and partially succeed; but on would come the idle rumor that the invaders were pushing their conquests, and the feeble barriers would give way, as does the momentary deposits in flood tide, and on, on, would sweep the strong current of dismay, rout and flight! Idle rumors we have said, and so they were. Timidity, fear, marked every movement of the invaders, from the landing at Black Rock, to the final evacuation. They had no idea of extending their march. They were astonished themselves, in view of their easy conquests, and during their short stay in Buffalo, their eyes were strained to catch the first glimpses of a force they expected would soon be rallied to drive them from our soil. Alas! for the honor of our country and its arms, such a force never came. Even the approach of a small band of invalids from Williamsville, made them shake in their shoes; and occupation of the whole conquered frontier, was brief, stealthy, and full of apprehension, save at the strong fortress of Niagara, and within the limits where it furnished an easy refuge. There was but little of glory, or high military achievements upon either hand. The taking of Fort Niagara, was but a well managed surprise, a rout, almost in the absence of any resistance; all else, from there to Buffalo, was brief, desolating occupation, and marauding; scarcely entitled to the dignity of a military campaign, and ordinary conquests.

Batavia became the head quarters, the final rallying point of small remnants of an army; a halting place, for the fleeing, homeless and houseless citizens of the frontier; to the extent of the capacity of all the tenements in the village and neighborhood. The most valuable effects of the land office were taken beyond the Genesee river; the house of Mr. Ellicott converted into quarters for army officers, and his office into an hospital; private houses were thrown open, barns and sheds occupied; families that were separated in the hasty departure from Buffalo, became united there; their scattered members, male and female, dropping in one after the other, and giving by their presence the first assurance of escape from danger. All along the Buffalo road, as far as the Genesee river, there were deserted houses, which did not fail to have new occupants, soon after the flight from the frontiers commenced. The owners sojourning in some hospitable neighborhood over the river, would hear that their deserted homes had tenants, of whom they had never before heard, who had entered without the formality of a lease.

And here, in these necessarily brief and imperfect reminiscences, the author must not omit to name his old friend and fellow craftsman, Smith H. Salisbury. The Buffalo Gazette, published by himself and his brother, Hezekiah A. Salisbury, during the earliest years of its existence, and by himself, after May 1813, was the only local chronicler of events upon the immediate frontier, during

---

NOTE. — Mrs. Mathers, who has already been named as one of the earliest residents of Buffalo, says that she and her daughters started from the village on foot a little before daylight:—"It was very dark, we could hear from Black Rock the incessant roar of musketry, and see flashes of light rising above the intervening forest. When day-light came, the Buffalo road presented a sad spectacle of sudden flight, misery and destitution."

the war of 1812. Its weekly arrival in the back settlements, was always anxiously looked for, and seldom has a public journal been more useful and reliable. Frequently, did it serve to allay unnecessary excitement and alarm throughout Western New York; and it preserved, throughout the eventful crisis, a high character for truth, and careful and judicious management. There was an hiatus in its publication, a few weeks, which embraced the invasion of the frontier, but when the disturbed elements began to settle down into comparative quiet,—as early as the 24th of January, after the invasion, the public were again served with the "Buffalo Gazette, printed at Harris' Hill, near Williamsville—Smith H. Salisbury, Editor."

Of the stirring and diversified scenes of flight and refuge, presented upon the south route, via Willink and the old "Big Tree" road on the 30th of December, the author is enabled to give some account from personal observation and recollection. Detached members of many of the families of Buffalo, took that route. During the latter part of the 30th, and forenoon of the 31st, the road from Willink to Turner's Corners in Sheldon, presented one continuous column of retreating soldiers, men, women and children from Buffalo, families from the settlements in all the southern portion of what is now Erie county, and the Indians *en masse*, from the Buffalo Reservation. An ox sled would come along bearing wounded soldiers, whose companions had perhaps pressed the slow team into their service; another, with the family of a settler, a few household goods that had been hustled upon it, and one, two or three, wearied females from Buffalo, who had begged the privilege of a ride and the rest that it afforded; then a litter, borne upon men's shoulders, upon which was reclined, a wounded soldier, or an infirm citizen; then squads of women and children on foot; then a remnant of some dispersed corps of militia, hugging as booty, "as spoils of the vanquished," the arms they had neglected to use; then squads and families of Indians, on foot and on ponies, the squaw with her pappoos upon her back, and a bevy of juvenile Senecas in her train; and all this is but a stinted programm of the scene that was presented. Bread, meats and drinks, soon vanished from the log taverns on the routes, and the stationary and fleeing settlers divided their scanty stores with the almost famished that came from the frontiers.

It was a crisis of suffering and privation; a winter of gloom and despondency. Language, at this distant day, is inadequate to enable the reader fully to realize the then condition of the Holland Purchase. Throughout all the back settlements, there were the half deserted neighborhoods; the solitary log house, no smoke rising from its stick chimney; cattle, sheep, and swine, hovering around, and looking in vain for some one to deal out their accustomed food. Upon the immediate frontier, stretching out in a long continuous line, from a strong fortress, where the invaders were entrenched, were the blackened remains of once happy homes, scathed and desolated; a gloomy stillness brooding over the scene, so profound, that the gaunt wolf, usually stealthy and prowling, came out of his forest haunts at mid day, and lapped the clotted snow, or snatched the dismembered limb of a human corse that in haste and flight had been denied the right of sepulture!

Thus ended the disastrous campaign of 1813. To give the reader, in a concise form, that which will furnish a vivid and truthful description of the condition of the Holland Purchase, after the invasion, the author selects some cotemporary accounts. The first is a circular letter, the nature and objects of which are sufficiently explained by its contents:—

CANANDAIGUA, 8th Jan. 1814.

GENTLEMEN —

Niagara county and that part of Genesee which lies west of Batavia are completely depopulated. All the settlements in a section of country forty miles square, and which contained more than twelve thousand souls, are effectually broken up. These facts you are undoubtedly acquainted with; but the distresses they have produced, none but an eye witness can thoroughly appreciate. Our roads are filled with people, many of whom have been reduced from a state of competency and good prospects to the last degree of want and sorrow. So sudden was the blow by which they have been crushed, that no provisions could be made either to elude or to meet it. The fugitives from Niagara county especially were dispersed under circumstances of so much terror that in some cases, mothers find themselves wandering with strange children, and children are seen accompanied by such as have no other sympathies with them than those of common sufferings. Of the families thus separated, all the members can never again meet in this life; for the same violence which has made them beggars, has forever deprived them of their heads, and others of their branches. Afflictions of the mind so deep as have been allotted to these unhappy people, we cannot cure. They can probably be subdued only by His power who can wipe away all tears. But shall we not endeavor to assuage them! To their bodily wants we can certainly administer. The inhabitants of this village have made large contributions for their relief, in provisions, clothing and money. And we have been appointed, among other things, to solicit further relief for them, from our wealthy and liberal minded fellow citizens. In pursuance of this appointment, may we ask you, gentlemen, to interest yourselves particularly in their behalf. We believe that no occasion has ever occured in our country which presented stronger claims upon individual benevolence, and we humbly trust that whoever is willing to answer these claims will always entitle himself to the precious reward of active charity. We are gentlemen, with great respect.

> WM. SHEPARD,
> THAD'S CHAPIN,
> MOSES ATWATER,
> N. GORHAM,
> MYRON HOLLEY,
> THOMAS BEALS,
> PHINEAS P. BATES.
> *Com. of safety and relief at Canandaigua.*

To the Hon. PHILIP S. VAN RENSSELAER,
  Hon. JAMES KENT,
  Hon. AMBROSE SPENCER,
  STEPHEN VAN RENSSELAER, ESQ.
  ELISHA JENKINS, ESQ.
  REV. TIMOTHY CLOWES,
  REV. WILLIAM NEILL,
  REV. JOHN M. BRADFORD.

In answer to this stirring and timely appeal for aid, the Legislature of the State made an immediate appropriation of fifty thousand dollars; the Common Council of Albany, one thousand; that of New York, three thousand; and liberal subscriptions were made by the citizens of Albany, New York, Canandaigua and in other localities; to which, among other donations were added, a donation of two thousand dollars by the Holland Company, and one of two hundred dollars, by Joseph Ellicott. In the forepart of March, the Committee at Canandaigua, reported that they had received from different sources, over thirteen thousand dollars; making, with the Legislative appropriation, over sixty three thousand dollars. It was a much needed and timely aid, and did much to relieve the immediate necessities of the sufferers.

As soon as the news of the invasion reached Washington, President Madison despatched Gen. Cass to the Niagara frontier, to enquire into the causes of the disasters, and recommend such measures of relief and defence as should seem necessary. The following letter was addressed by him to the Secretary of War:—

WILLIAMSVILLE, January 12th, 1814.

I passed this day the ruins of Buffalo. It exhibits a scene of distress and destruction, such as I have never before witnessed. The events which have recently transpired in this quarter, have been so astonishing and unexpected, that I have been induced to make some inquiry into their causes and progress; and doubting whether you have received any correct information upon the subject, I now trouble you with the detail.

The fall of Niagara has been owing to the most criminal negligence. The force in it was fully competent to its defence. The commanding officer, Captain Leonard, it is confidently said, was at his own house, three miles from the fort, and all the other officers appear to have rested in as much security as though no enemy was near them. Captains Rogers and Hampton, both of the 24th, had companies in the fort. Both of them were absent from it. Their conduct ought to be strictly investigated. I am also told that Major Wallace of the 5th, was in the fort. He escaped and is now at Erie. The circumstances attending the destruction of Buffalo, you will have learned before this reaches you. But the force of the enemy has been greatly magnified. From the most careful examination, I am satisfied that not more than six hundred and fifty men, of regulars, militia and Indians, landed at Black Rock. To oppose these we had from two thousand five hundred to three thousand militia. All except a very few of them, behaved in the most cowardly manner. They fled without discharging a musket. The enemy continued on this side of the river until Saturday. All their movements betrayed symptoms of apprehension. A vast quantity of property was left in the town uninjured, and the Ariel, which lies four miles above, is safe. Since the first inst., they have made no movement. They continue to possess Niagara, and will probably retain it until a force competent to its reduction arrives in its vicinity.

LEWIS CASS.

Extract of a letter from a gentleman in Niagara county, to his friend in Oneida county, copied from the Buffalo Gazette of Feb. 1st. 1814:—

"I have visited the smoking ruins of the once pleasant, delightful and flourishing village of Buffalo. Black Rock, Manchester, Lewiston, and the whole frontier, which were, not long since, enjoyed by hundreds of families, now present a scene of desolation; all swept by the besom of destruction. The wretched tenants of this whole frontier have been driven from their homes in the severity of winter; many, in their haste to snatch their wives and children from the tomahawk and scalping knife, were enabled to preserve but little of their effects from the flames; and many, whose houses were not burned by the enemy, after having abandoned their dwellings, to escape the ravages of their foe, returning after the alarm was over, found that their effects were plundered, by the villians who prowl about the deserted country, too cowardly to face an enemy of inferior force, and base enough to rob their neighbors of the property the enemy had spared.

"It would make your heart ache to see the women and children of the county fleeing from their homes and fire sides, to encounter the wintry blast, and all the miseries of a deprivation of all the necessaries and comforts of life. Many poor families have lost all — many persons in trade have been ruined — and many, whose circumstances were affluent, have been brought almost to beggary. I cannot, for a moment, suppose that the general government, will turn a deaf ear to the legal demands of the sufferers. Should Congress not act promptly on this occasion an application should be made to our State Legislature; and in order that immediate relief should be extended to the sufferers, a subscription ought to be circulated in our principal cities; and from their liberality on occasions less operative on the public sympathy, we have every hope of something very efficient being done, by the exertions of individuals."

During the last winter, Major Douglass, an officer in the U. S. army, serving upon the Niagara frontier in the war of 1812, efficiently and bravely, as the records of that period testify, delivered a course of lectures before the Young Men's Association in Buffalo, replete with interesting personal recollections, of war events.

The following was his graphic description of Buffalo, as he first saw it:-

"On the 9th of July, at noon, we arrived at Buffalo — not the enterprising and busy metropolis of Western New York, that it now is, spreading its noble avenues miles in length on every side, and rearing aloft its stately edifices and glittering domes — but a wide and desolate expanse — with only two small houses visible — a few rude sheds and shanties — a soiled tent here and there — and in one or two places, a row of marquees, of the better sort — apparently giving shelter to some wounded men. They were all the habitations, or substitutes for habitations, that the place afforded. Half a dozen isolated sentinels were seen on post keeping guard over as many irregular piles of loose stone and camp equipage; and the grounds recently occupied by the camp, thick set with rows of measured squares, worn smooth on the surface, and scattered here and there with fragments of soldiers' clothes, old belts and accoutrements of various kinds, gave an air of desolation to the whole scene only rendered more striking by these details; — and in fact, Buffalo, just deserted by the busy groups which had a few days before occupied it — was desert and comfortless beyond any power of mine to describe. The two buildings were, above and below, filled with wounded officers from the battle of Chippewa; — and here during an hour's halt, under no very pleasing auspices, commenced our intercourse with the realities of war."

As promised in some remarks made at the commencement of this chapter, the author adds to these brief glimpses of the war of 1812, a passage of its history, of a far different character than the one that precedes it. The gallant conduct of the volunteers of the Holland Purchase, and all Western New York, at the Sortie of Fort Erie, goes far to redeem the character of our local militia, so tarnished and forfeited, by cowardice and flight— by the unnecessary surrender of the whole frontier to a weak invasion; — as a finale to a campaign of failures and disasters.

About the first of September, 1814, the militia in all the counties west of the Genesee river, were called out *en masse*, and ordered to march to Buffalo; the object of this extraordinary movement was well known and fully appreciated by most of the pioneers on the Holland Purchase. The whole body of our regular troops on the Niagara frontier, being about one thousand effective men, were closely beseiged in Fort Erie, a position of no considerable strength being little better than an open encampment, by an army of about four thousand well disciplined British troops and a body of Canadian militia: under this state of things, our little army could not be expected, long to retain their position, neither could they safely evacuate the fort and retreat. These considerations fired the breast of every patriot; if the prescribed regulations of the militia law were in many instances disregarded, they were in most instances over-leaped on the side of patriotism: the enquiry was not "am I subject to perform militia duty," but "how and when can I be of most service to my country." The land office was shut; the merchants' stores were closed; the mechanics' shops ceased to produce their wonted din of industry, and the husbandman's working cattle enjoyed a long sabbath; rich and poor, youth and old age, were impelled more forcibly by the voice of patriotism, than by the warning summons of the officiating sergeant: they were all wending their way to Buffalo to assist our brave soldiers who had then so lately crowned themselves with glory at Chippewa and Lundy's Lane.

Buffalo, at that period, exhibited nothing but the ruins of a sacked and burnt village. Some twelve or fifteen roofs only had been raised over those ruins, and a portion of these were erected on the ground, over the old cellars. After the militia had chiefly congregated, they were paraded two successive days, where now stand the lofty edifices of the city, and volunteers solicited to cross the Niagara and repair to Fort Erie. The call was generally responded to with alacrity, although there were some who had left their homes under charge of officers, merely to save their fines; men who availed themselves of their constitutional privilege of refusing to cross the lines. These scrupulous heroes were not suffered to return to their homes, but were retained and organized into a separate corps, called "Buffalo Guards."

Fort Erie, or rather the encampment called by that name, lying at the outlet of lake Erie into the Niagara river, on the Canada side, was, at that time, composed of "Old Fort Erie," consisting of two large stone mess-houses and one bastion, mounted with cannon, situated near the margin of Niagara river, and a high, artificial mound, transformed from Snake Hill, about one hundred and fifty rods southerly of the old fort. This mound was surmounted by breast-works and planted with cannon, and was called Towson's battery. This redoubt was connected with the old fort by a parapet of earth thrown up between them with a western angle; from this parapet traverses extended into the encampment. The open esplanade on the west and north of our works was but from sixty to eighty rods wide, where it terminated in a dense forest; standing on a marshy or swamp bottom between this lengthy parapet and the shores of the Niagara river and lake Erie, was the encampment of our regular soldiers.

The British invested this encampment or fort, the latter part of

July. In the first place, they erected a battery at the water's edge on the Niagara river below the fort, to annoy the navigation between the fort and Buffalo, and proceeded to approach the fort regularly by erecting batteries in the edge of the woods farther and farther south, and unmasking them in the night by chopping out a vista towards our works.* Thus was Fort Erie circumstanced when our volunteers were conveyed in boats, from Buffalo to Fort Erie, which was effected principally in the night, to guard against the British fire from their water battery. The ground designated for the encampment of the volunteers, about fifteen hundred in number, was on the lake shore, above Towson's battery, extending some fifty rods westward to near the corner of the woods; on the summit of the bank thrown up by the surges of the lake in boisterous weather, there was a sod breast-work, hastily erected by the volunteers, between which and the lake shore they encamped on the 8th, 9th and 10th of September, and were placed under the immediate command of Gen. Peter B. Porter, who bivouaced in their midst.

Maj. Gen. Brown, commander-in-chief of our forces on the Niagara frontier, having his head quarters in the regular encampment, was well informed of the situation and proceedings of the British army. The main encampment of the British was on a farm about one and a half miles west of the fort. The British force was divided into three divisions or brigades, of fourteen or fifteen hundred men each, one of which was kept on duty at the batteries, four and twenty hours, every three days, and quartered in the main encampment the rest of the time. They had unmasked two swamp batteries and had nearly completed another which was nearer our works and was placed in a better position for raking our encampment than either of the others. One of the British brigades was composed chiefly of Germans, called the De Waterville brigade, and Gen. Brown knew that this brigade would be on duty at the batteries on the 17th of the month, and determined on a sortie from the fort on that day, as it would precede the time of unmasking the third battery. On the 16th, Majors Frazer and Riddle, volunteer aids to Gen. Porter, with a party of one hundred men each, half having axes and the other half carrying their arms, proceeded in a circuitous route through the woods to within a few

---

* On the night of the 15th of August they attempted to carry it by storm, but being repulsed, they continued the siege, pushing their advances nearer the fort.

yards of their third battery, which was on the south of the others, from whence each party underbrushed a track back, curving and diverging, to escape the most miry swamps; this they effected in good order without even exciting the suspicion of the enemy.

On the morning of the 17th, although the sky was lowery, the faces of the volunteers were bright and cheerful, they had learned that something was to be done that day to bring the siege to a close, many knew and most of the others suspected the manner in which it was intended to be effected; during the forenoon the several companies were paraded, the object of the intended movement explained, and excuses for not participating therein received. During this time, one of the "Batavia volunteers," (a kind of independent partizan corps,) while on Towson's battery, heard read a hand-bill announcing the victory obtained by our sailors and militia at Plattsburg six days before; the volunteer solicited the handbill of Col. Towson, to be read to the volunteers on parade, which was granted. The effect the reading of this handbill before the several companies had on the volunteers, can be easier imagined than described, although an almost unanimous assent had been cheerfully given to participate in the fortunes of the enterprise; headaches, colds, and lameness, which had been mentioned, were instantly dispensed with for the time being; a new impetus was given to the valor of the whole; all were anxious to march.* Each volunteer, officers as well as privates, was required to dispense with his hat or cap, and substitute a pocket handkerchief or a strip of red glazed cloth, of which large rolls were furnished; not a hat or cap was worn except by Gen. Porter.

At noon, the whole of the volunteers were formed in two columns, each headed by a detachment of regular riflemen and dismounted dragoons as vanguards, the whole under the immediate command of Gen. Porter. They were marched a short distance up the lake shore to the two paths, traced by Majors Frazer and Riddle, when they merged into the dense miry forest. At the commencement of the march, the two columns were flanked by about twenty Seneca Indians and the Batavia volunteers under

---

*Several years after this campaign, while General Miller and another gentleman were reviewing this ground, the General pointed out to the gentleman the ravine in which the regular troops lay awaiting the attack, and observed that the handbill abovementioned was brought into the ravine and read to his men while there, to which circumstance he attributed their spirited conducted and undaunted bravery at the time of the attack, which followed immediately

Capt. Robert Fleming. The Indians, however, finding that their position would become the most hazardous of any, huddled together and refused to proceed; on which the two columns were halted, a portion of the regulars were detached to carry the left wing, and the Batavia volunteers and Indians ordered between the two columns. About this time it began to rain, which continued the residue of the day. After a slow and silent march of upwards of two hours, having halted several times to regulate disorders occasioned by the rough and mazy paths pursued, the heads of the columns arrived, unperceived by the enemy, within pistol shot of the new battery, No. 3. A musket was hardly discharged by the sentinel on duty, when the whole assailing party brought into requisition the full strength of their lungs. In giving their shouts or whoops, which literally "made the welkin ring," they were distinctly heard at Buffalo and Black Rock. The German troops posted at this battery and blockhouse, being taken by entire surprise, at mid-day, at once surrendered. The volunteers pursued their victory to battery No. 2, and were taking possession of that at the point of the bayonet, when the regulars appeared in front, issuing from the ravine in which they had lain concealed. The volunteers and regular soldiers now joined, attacked and carried battery No. 1, although large reinforcements were constantly arriving from the main encampment of the British army. The object of the sortie, being to drive away the besiegers, spike their guns, and blow up their magazines, being effected, a retreat was ordered, and the American troops returned to the fort, the rear arriving about sunset.

In this battle the rules of discipline were, from necessity, entirely waived by the regular soldiers as well as by the militia; the surface of the ground was covered with mud and mire; strewed with logs and brush, interspersed with ditches and ridges. The rain had wet the priming in many of the muskets, and rendered them useless as firearms, therefore it was in a great measure fought man to man and hand to hand, so much so that Gen. Porter was once made a prisoner, he having his hand cut with the sword of his antagonist in the scuffle, but was soon rescued by a small party of his own men.

In this action, the loss suffered by the volunteers, in killed, wounded, and prisoners, in point of numbers, was not great, although they lost their local commander, Maj. Gen. Daniel Davis of Le Roy, Genesee county, who fell while bravely mounting a

PETER B. PORTER.

parapet between batteries Nos. 2 and 1, and urging his volunteers to "press forward," at which time a musket ball pierced his neck and caused instant death. Some twenty or thirty valuable citizens shared a similar fate; others were wounded, and Colonel W. L. Churchill and Maj. O. Wilson, together with several other patriotic officers and privates were taken prisoners, while bravely meeting and opposing the British reinforcements as they approached from their main encampment. On the other hand the British loss in killed, wounded, and prisoners, was at least one thousand men and as many stand of small arms. They were compelled to raise the siege, and four days thereafter broke up their main encampment and retired down the Niagara river. On which the volunteers were discharged and returned to their respective homes, with a consciousness of having "rendered to their country some service."

PETER B. PORTER.

So identified with, and merged in, the events of the war of 1812, was this early and prominent pioneer of Western New York and the Holland Purchase, that a portrait and brief biography of him, is an appropriate and fitting appendage to this portion of our local annals. Any history, or even historical sketch of the war upon this frontier, would be incomplete, if it did not embrace some notice of one, who so largely, bravely and honorably, participated in it. Locally, to borrow a dramatic illustration, he was the "Hamlet of the play."

Gen. Peter B. Porter, was a younger brother of the Hon. Augustus Porter. He was born in Salisbury, Litchfield Co., Conn., in 1773; graduated at Yale College, and studied the profession of law in the office of Judge Reeve, at Litchfield. His first advent to Western New York, was in 1793. The event is thus noticed, in an address that he prepared* for delivery before the Euglossian Society of Geneva College, in 1831:—"It is now, if I do not mistake, thirty-eight years since I first traversed the shores of the beautiful lake on whose banks we are assembled, and set my feet upon the ground which had been marked out as the

---

* A severe domestic affliction, the illness and death of Mrs. Porter, prevented the attendance at Geneva and the delivery of the address. The author has been permitted to copy from the manuscript.

site of this rich and flourishing town. I was then a youth, with a mind filled, as I hope and believe yours now are, with visions of future enterprise and exploit and usefulness to my country, whenever I should be released from the restraints of a scholastic education. I had heard of the far famed 'Genesee Country'—of its fertile soil, its genial climate, of its beautiful lakes and rivers—and resolved to visit it; with an intention, which was a few years afterwards realized, of making it the place of my future residence. Accordingly, accompanied by a friend, whose views and feelings accorded with my own, we entered the interminable forests of the west, at the German Flatts, on the Mohawk, which was then the extreme verge of civilized improvements, and plodded our weary way, day after day, to the Genesee river. The only evidences of civilization, at that time, consisted of some half a dozen log huts at Utica, as many more at this place, and the same again at Canandaigua. Beside these, there were a few miserable cabins, sprinkled along the road, at a distance of five to fifteen miles apart, where the traveler might look, not as now, for comfort or for rest, but for the sheer necessaries for continuing his journey."

As intimated in the above extract, he did not then determine upon a location in the region, the primitive condition of which, he so well portrayed. In 1794, he went to Plattsburg, in this state, was admitted to practice, remained there but a brief period, and returned to Connecticut. In 1795, he accompanied his brother Augustus, on his return to Canandaigua, and became a resident of Western New York, where he was destined to have a long and brilliant career, at the bar, in the social and conventional relations of the new country; and subsequently, in the councils of the state, in the defence of the frontiers, and in the councils and cabinet of the nation.

He was engaged as counsel, in 1795, at Canandaigua, in the first trial in a court of record in Western New York. He was appointed Clerk of Ontario county in 1797, elected a member of the Legislature in 1802. In 1810, he became a resident at Black Rock, then in Niagara county. He was twice elected to Congress; the first time, in 1810, and the second time, in 1814. In 1815, he filled the office of Secretary of State, of this state; in 1816, he was appointed by President Madison, one of the Commissioners to run the boundary line between the United States and the British Possessions; and in 1828 was appointed Secretary of War, by

John Quincy Adams. These data indicate mainly, his varied and extended public services in military capacities.

He was an active and influential member of Congress, pending the war of 1812, and filled the important post of Chairman of the Committee of Foreign Relations. Had he consulted his own interests instead of the rights and honor of his country, he would have inclined to the peace party in Congress in that memorable crisis. His home, and his large property were upon the immediate frontier to be endangered in the event of a war with Great Britain; he could well have counted the cost to himself, of a war that was to array hostile forces upon the Niagara frontier; and well could he foresee the calamities it would inflict upon a large portion of his constituents. But, with a devotion to his country that could not yield to selfish or local considerations, he took a firm and decided stand in favor of the war. In the latter part of November, 1811, he reported a set of resolutions authorizing immediate and active preparations for war; and on the 11th of December, justified their propriety and necessity by a speech of great ability, firm and energetic in its tone, and yet temperate and judicious. He assumed that further negotiation was useless, and must be abandoned; recounted the wrongs that Great Britain had inflicted upon our country, its dogged refusal to make reparations; and announced that the committee of which he was chairman, only awaited the consummation of the measures they had recommended; and that then, if reparation continued to be withheld, the committee would recommend "open and decided war — a war as vigorous and effective, as the resources of the country and the relative situation of ourselves and our enemies would enable us to prosecute." He said that "he was aware there were many gentlemen in the House who were dissatisfied that the committee had not gone further and recommended an immediate declaration of war, or the adoption of some measure which would instantly have precipitated us into it. But he confessed such was not his opinion. He had no idea of plunging ourselves headlong into a war with a powerful nation, or even a respectable province, when we had not three regiments of men to spare for that service. He hoped that he should not be influenced by the howlings of the newspapers, nor by a fear that the spirit of the Twelfth Congress would be questioned, to abandon the plainest dictates of common sense and common discretion. He was sensible that there were many good men out of Congress, as well as many of his best friends in it, whose appetites were prepared for a war feast. He was not surprised at it, for he knew the provocation had been sufficiently great. But he hoped they would not insist on calling in the guests, at least, until the table had been spread. When this was done, he pledged himself on behalf of the Committee of Foreign Relations, that the gentlemen should not be disappointed of the entertainment for want of bidding; and he believed he might also pledge himself for many of the members of the committee, that they would not be among the last to partake personally, not only in the pleasures, if any there should be, but in all the dangers of the revelry."

And well did he redeem the pledge thus given. His duties discharged at the seat of government, he participated in the "dangers of the revelry," often with a bravery that commanded admiration, and an efficiency that helped to turn the tide of war in this quarter, and shed lustre upon arms that had been dimmed by a series of defeats and untoward events. To trace his military career from battle field to battle field; from his first unfurling of his country's standard upon this frontier, and appealing in glowing language of patriotism and deep concern for his country's welfare, to his fellow citizens to range under it, would be to write a history of a large portion of the war upon the Niagara frontier. Locally, his name was a tower of strength; when confidence in other men flagged— when a seemingly vascillating policy governed in our national councils—when the weight of war pressed heavily upon all the region of the Holland Purchase—hope revived, reliance was strengthened, by his voice, his pen, and his sword. No chieftain in the Highlands of Scotland, with bugle blast, ever drew clansmen from glen or heath, that came more readily and joyously to the foray, than did the ardent volunteers from the back-woods and log cabins of the Holland Purchase, when he appealed to their patriotism and invited them to his standard. With those not familiar with the events of that period of peril—with the local exigencies that existed—this may be regarded as eulogy too highly colored; but its fidelity and truthfulness will not fail to be recognized by those who remember how universal was cotemporary public sentiment in Western New York, in yielding praise and warm commendation to the military services of Peter B. Porter. It is but a transcript of the distinct recollections of the author, of those times, and the men who bore a conspicuous part in them; and he only regrets that the circumscribed limits of this portion of his work forbids a recognition of the names and brilliant services of other of the men of the Holland Purchase, and Western New York.

Gen. Napier, in his "Peninsular War," makes the sortie of Fort Erie a brilliant achievement; the only instance in history, where a besieging army was entirely broken up and routed by a single sortie. The conspicuous position that all historians of the war have assigned to Gen. Porter, upon that memorable occasion, would alone entitle him to a high rank as a military commander.

He was appointed Brigadier General of volunteers, by Governor Tompkins, in 1814, and brevet Major General soon after the battle of Lundy's Lane. In 1815, he was appointed by President Madison, Major General in the United States service, and was to have had command of the northern division of the army, had another campaign been necessary. Indeed, he had left Washington, and arrived as far as Albany on his way west to prepare for the campaign, when the news of peace overtook him.

The active years of his life were mostly spent in the councils of his country, and in the field; had his destiny been differently shaped — had he been left to pursue the quiet walks of his profession, of literature, of arts and science, he would have no less excelled; if less conspicuous, would no less have demonstrated extraordinary mental endowments. His, in the progress of literature in our country, was an early school; yet in the records of legislation in state and nation, there are few better specimens of eloquence than he uttered, or of compositions, than those that came from his pen.

He was a statesman of enlarged mind, one of the most far-sighted and right-judging of his day. This is attested by all his views and services connected with the boundary commission, the War and Indian departments of our government, and the system of internal improvements of our state.

This early pioneer of Western New York, the early lawyer, legislator and prominent citizen; the leader of our volunteer citizen soldiery, in the war of 1812; the able defender of his country's rights and honor in our national councils; closed a long, useful and honorable career, at his residence at Niagara Falls, on the 20th day of March, 1844, aged 72 years. His funeral was at an inclement season, and yet there was assembled a large concourse of citizens of Niagara and Erie counties. Among them, was an aged chief of the Tuscaroras, the stoicism of his race yielding the tribute of tears, that coursed down his furrowed cheek, when he gazed upon the remains of one who had been his friend, and the early and constant guardian of the welfare and interests of his people. Gen. Porter married late in life, Mrs. Lætitia Grayson of Kentucky, the daughter of the late John Breckenridge, formerly Attorney General of the United States. She died at Black Rock, in July, 1831, aged 41 years. He left, as the inheritors of his good name, and a large estate, accumulated by early and judicious investments, a daughter and son; the latter of whom, has just reached his majority, and is entering upon the career of life with an ample fortune, and what is far better, if he justly appreciates it, he is endowed with a rich legacy of parental example.

NOTE.—In a notice of the death of Mrs. Porter, which appeared in the columns of the Buffalo Journal, the author of it renders a deserved tribute to her more than ordinary mental endowments, and thus speaks of her excellent example in the domestic and social sphere:—" Much of her time, her labor, and her solicitude were always her free-will offering at the command of those who desired the assistance of her ready hand. The poor and the distressed had their anguish and their wants mitigated by her alleviating attentions; but all that she affected was performed so much in the simplicity of her heart, and such were her lofty conceptions of the awful responsibilities of the Christian, that she shrunk from the thought of calling them acts of religion. In the spirit of the reply which the blessed shall make to the Almighty Judge, she would say in reference to her rewards, ' when saw I thee an hungered and fed thee; or thirsty and gave thee drink; naked and clothed thee; sick and in prison and came unto thee?' There was concealed in the recesses of her soul a richer fund, both of principle and feeling, than its owner estimated."

CHAPTER II.

THE ERIE CANAL.

A long, uninterrupted enjoyment of individual as well as public blessings, their full fruition, a familiarity with their use, tends to make us unmindful of their magnitude. Especially is it so in the progressive age in which we live. Scarcely have we done wondering at some new achievement, calculating its results, before another is projected and consummated to divert the attention. Now that canals and rail roads have been multiplied—steam has had its new and wonderful triumphs on land and water—the lightnings of Heaven, like the wild steed of the prairie, has been lassoed, tamed and fitted to the practical, familiar use of man—it is difficult to enable the younger portion of our readers to go back beyond all the important events that have been crowded into the last quarter of a century, and realize to its full extent, the magnitude of the projection of the Erie Canal, how great was the triumph achieved in its construction, and how vast and diffusive were the local and general benefits that flowed from it. To enable them to judge of its local influences, the change for the better that followed its completion, upon the Holland Purchase, we must go back to the years pending its final consummation.

Here at the western extremity of the state, upon the Holland Purchase especially, new settlers had for several years failed to create a sufficient demand for the surplus produce that began to be realized. The early settlers had passed through all the vicissitudes that have been enumerated in the progress of our narrative; the privations of their forest advents; the diseases of a new country, its chills and agues; the war and its scourges; the cold seasons and their attendants, frosts and stinted crops. They had subdued a rugged soil, and it had given good earnests of productiveness and plenty; but the difficulty of reaching a market had begun seriously to be felt; its consequences were a low range of prices for all they had to dispose of, stagnation of business, and the slow progress of improvement. It will be remembered that the son of a pioneer settler of Orleans county, relates that his father sold his wheat for twenty-five cents per bushel, in 1818; in 1823, it was sold in most of the village markets upon the Holland Purchase, as low as thirty-seven and a half cents. The bulk of the original debt to the Holland Company remained unpaid, and interest was adding to principal. There were no remunerating prices for anything the settlers had to dispose of, save, perhaps, the lumber that was in near proximity to lake Ontario, and the articles of black salts and potash; the gloomy prospect before them was the holding on to their decaying log tenements, after they had hoped to supply their places with better ones, an increasing indebtedness for their lands and the liability of ultimate dispossession.

Such was the general condition of the Holland Purchase in the years immediately preceding the completion of the Erie canal, up to those points, where it began to be reached by the surplus produce of this region.

All that relates to this great work — its projection and consummation — has a direct and important bearing upon progress and improvement upon the Holland Purchase; and yet it is a subject mainly belonging to the province of the general history of our state. In these local annals it can only form an incidental chapter; a brief chronological account of events that preceded it, are allied to its history, its advance westward, and its final completion.

The great "mother of invention" as well as founder of schemes of public utility — necessity — was the projector of the Erie canal. The progress of settlement in the western portion of the state; the absence of facilities for the transportation of the products of field and forest, and merchants' goods; the danger that the trade and commerce of a vast region bordering upon our western lakes, would find other avenues to a market upon the Atlantic, would be diverted from our own commercial emporium; were existing, stimulating exigencies. Let us briefly consider who were foremost — what events occurred to supply these existing exigencies — to consummate what necessity so imperatively demanded.

By a reference to page 176 of this work, it will be seen that in a remote period of English colonization upon the Hudson, the Mohawk river, Wood creek, Oneida lake, and Oswego (Onondaga) river, furnished an internal water communication for commerce with the Iroquois. With the exception of occasional allusions in the messages of the colonial Governors to some measures for the improvement of the navigation of some stream, the subject of internal improvement does not appear to have received much attention until after the Revolution.

Christopher Colles, as early as 1772, delivered a course of public lectures in Philadelphia, on the subject of lock navigation. In 1785, he made proposals to the Legislature of New York, for improving the navigation of the Mohawk, but the Legislature did not give him sufficient encouragement to enable him to carry out his views. He renewed his application again in 1786 with little better practical effect. Discouraged and embarrassed, he gave up his plans, and relinquished all attempts to accomplish them. In 1791, his scheme for "connecting the northern and southern, and eastern and western waters, was revived," but he is not known to have had any agency in it. In 1786, Jeffrey Smith, a member of the Legislature of this State, asked leave to introduce a bill for the improvement of this navigation, and "for extending the same, if practicable, to lake Erie;" a measure which must have been premature at the time, in view of the fact that the English had not yet surrendered the posts at Oswego and Niagara.

Before the Revolution, Washington had turned his attention to the subject of internal improvement, but that event suspended the prosecution of whatever plans he might have contemplated. But no sooner had he fought the last great battle of freedom, and secured to his country the inestimable blessings of peace, than he again renewed his favorite projects. He visited New England in 1784, and extended his journey in New York as far west as Fort Stanwix. In a letter addressed to the Marquis of Chastellux, a French nobleman, distinguished as a traveler, writer, and soldier, he thus enthusiastically sketches the impressions which were made on his mind.

"I have lately made a tour through the lakes George and Champlain, as far as Crown point; then returning to Schenectady, I proceeded up the Mohawk river to Fort Schuyler, crossed over to Wood creek, which empties into the Oneida lake, and affords the water communications with Ontario. I then traversed the country to the head of the eastern branch of the Susquehanna, and viewed lake Otsego, and the portage between that lake and the Mohawk river, at Canajoharie. Prompted by these actual observations, I could not help taking a more contemplative and extensive view of the vast inland navigation of these United States, and could not but be struck with the immense diffusion and importance of it; and with the goodness of that Providence, which has dealt his favors to us with so profuse a hand. Would to God we may have wisdom enough to improve them. I shall not rest contented until I have explored the western country, and traversed those lines, (or a great part of them) which have since given bounds to a new empire."

George Clinton accompanied Gen. Bradstreet, in his expedition against Fort Frontenac, on lake Ontario, in 1756, as a Lieutenant in a company commanded by his brother, the afterwards Gen. James Clinton. The opportunity that was thus afforded to the young and aspiring soldier, to obtain information of his country, and its first commercial wants, seems to have been well improved in an after period, when the English Lieutenant had become Governor of the finest province that he had helped wrest from English dominion. In his message to the legislature, in 1791, he says: — "Our frontier settlements, freed from apprehensions of danger, are rapidly increasing, and must yield extensive resources for profitable commerce. This consideration forcibly recommends the policy of continuing to facilitate the means of communication with them, as well to strengthen the bonds of society, as to prevent the produce of those fertile districts from being diverted to other objects." Then followed this, in the same year, an act, authorizing a survey of the grounds between the Mohawk river and Wood creek. The survey was made and reported to the legislature.

Elkanah Watson was among the first to appreciate the importance of a safe, easy, and expeditious channel of communication between the Hudson and the lakes. In 1788 he made a tour to the extreme settlements on the western frontiers of New York. In his journal of that tour he says:—"I left Fort Stanwix on my way down Wood creek to lake Ontario, and perhaps to Detroit, having a strong presentiment that a canal communication will be opened sooner or later, from the great lakes to the Hudson." Mr. Watson is justly ranked as one of the foremost to call public attention to works of internal improvement; his propositions were bold, far-seeing, and marked with great ability and energy of purpose. When, however, in after years he claimed that to which he was well entitled, a large share in the primitive movements having reference to the internal commerce of this state, he conceded that his views were only "to follow the track of Nature's canal, and to remove natural and artificial obstructions;" but that he never entertained the most distant conceptions of a canal from lake Erie to the Hudson. We should not have considered it much more extravagant to have suggested the policy of a canal to the moon."

To Mr. Watson it may justly be conceded, that if he was not absolutely among the first, he was one of those who early entertained favorable views of the importance of such a work; but not only by his own admission, but by his generously attributing the conception of the overland route of the Erie Canal, having its western termination at the foot of lake Erie, to another, he cannot be named as one of its very earliest promulgators and friends, however favorable he may have been to its prosecution when its success became more apparent.

It will not be our intention to canvass all the conflicting and "disputed claims," to the honor of first suggesting the overland route of the Erie Canal. Whether Gouverneur Morris expressed the idea of "tapping lake Erie," in 1777, or not; whether Joshua Forman had conceived it practicable without consulting any one before he introduced his celebrated resolutions, in the Assembly, in 1808, or not, there is every reason to conclude that the views contained in the essays written by Jesse Hawley, over the signature of Hercules, were entirely original with their author, who had, even before he commenced those celebrated canal papers, expressed the same opinions in his private correspondence. Mr. Hawley was the first to present this great subject seriously and intelligibly before the public, and urge its adoption as a work not only within the means of man to accomplish, but as of the greatest public importance and utility—a work which would not only pay for the original cost of its construction, but be a reliable and unfailing source of future revenue.

De Witt Clinton, to whom is attributed a pamphlet written under the name of Tacitus, on the subject of the canals, speaks of Mr. Hawley in the following terms:—

"The first hint on this subject, which I have seen in print, was suggested by Jesse Hawley, Esq. of Ontario county—a gentleman of an ingenious and reflecting mind. On the 27th of October, 1807, he commenced a series of essays on internal navigation, under the signature of Hercules, in the Ontario Messenger, printed at Canandaigua, which extended to fourteen numbers."

Mr. Watson, whose impartiality and candor on this subject should not be questioned, awards to Jesse Hawley full and merited praise and credit for the early part he took in this great and difficult enterprise. Mr. Watson, in his "History of the Rise and Progress of the Western Canals," written in 1819, speaks as follows of Mr. Hawley:—

"I have not been able to trace any measure, public or private, tending towards this great enterprise, till the 27th of October, 1807, when an anonymous publication, under the signature of Hercules, appeared in the Genesee Messenger, which is attributed to Jesse Hawley, Esq. now collector of the port of Rochester. These invaluable essays continued through a course of fourteen weekly numbers, to the 2d of March, 1808. They are evidently original, and display deep research—views vastly extended—indeed, they may be pronounced prophetic in striking out, as will be seen by a comparison with the annexed map, nearly the track of the northern route of the canal, which has been since adopted, at least to the Seneca river. His point of commencement was Buffalo; thence to the outlet of the Tonnewanda creek, to be crossed by an aqueduct; thence easterly crossing the Genesee river by another aqueduct, above the Falls; thence running near Mud creek; thence near the outlet of the Cayuga lake; and terminating about Utica;—a distance of two hundred miles,—which he estimated would cost five millions of dollars. And then improving the bed of the Mohawk, with occasional canals to Schenectady; and ultimately into the Hudson river."

The resolutions introduced by Joshua Forman in the House of Assembly, February 4th, 1808, are the first legislative action ever had on the subject. Judge Forman claims that the idea of a direct canal was original with him, whoever else might have thought of it before, and that he did not derive it either from Gouverneur Morris or Jesse Hawley. In a letter to David Hosack, which is published in his appendix to the Memoir of De Witt Clinton, Judge Forman says:—"I never claimed that I first thought of such a plan, nor is that the issue; but I do claim to have been the first man who, having conceived the idea, appreciated its importance, set about carrying it into effect, and by the happy expedient of turning the eyes of the Legislature to the general government for its accomplishment, induced them to take the first steps in a project too gigantic for them to have looked at for a moment as an object to be accomplished by the means of the state."

On the 21st of February, a joint resolution was offered by Mr. Gould of the Senate, in which the Assembly concurred, directing the Surveyor General to have made the survey contemplated in Mr. Forman's resolution, and appropriating six hundred dollars for that purpose. This survey was made by James Geddes, who in January, 1809, made a report favorable to the enterprise, as entirely practicable and within the means of the state.

In 1810, Jonas Platt, at the suggestion of Thomas Eddy, who was an early, active, and efficient friend of the enterprise, offered a joint resolution in the Senate, which was concurred in by the Assembly on the 12th of March, appointing Gouverneur Morris, Stephen Van Rensselaer, De Witt Clinton, Simeon De Witt, Wm. North, Thomas Eddy, and Peter B. Porter, to explore the whole route for inland navigation from the Hudson river to lakes Ontario and Erie.

About this time, several memorials were presented to the Legislature, "representing that Canada was attracting the greatest portion of our internal commerce, in consequence of the facilities which were afforded by water communications to transport commodities to her markets." De Witt Clinton, who was then a member of the Senate, and about this time warmly associated himself with this movement, strongly advocated Mr. Platt's resolution, and became a zealous and able champion of the measure.

The commissioners made the exploration, and submitted the results of their labors in the form of a report, drawn by Mr. Morris, to the Legislature, in the winter of 1811. In the same year, a bill was introduced into the Senate by De Witt Clinton, then Lieut. Governor, providing for the appointment of two commissioners to solicit the aid of the General Government in constructing this great work. De Witt Clinton and Gouverneur Morris were appointed the commissioners. They went to Washington and presented the subject to the President, the Secretaries of the Departments, and prominent and influential members of Congress, but they failed to secure either aid or encouragement. Having been refused help by the General Government, in March, 1812, the commissioners made a report to the Legislature, in which they stated that "sound policy imperatively demanded that the canal should be made by the state of New York alone, as soon as circumstances would permit; that it would be a want of wisdom not to employ for public advantage those means which Providence had placed so completely in their power;" that it would be "a testimony to the genius, the learning, the industry, and intelligence of the present age."

In June, 1812, the Legislature passed a law authorizing the commissioners to borrow five millions of dollars in Europe, on the credit of the state of New York, for the construction of the canal. But the United States soon after becoming involved in war with Great Britain, this law, in 1814, was repealed, and nothing more was done in relation to the canal, until the restoration of peace.

After peace between the United States and Great Britain had been restored, the subject of inland navigation was again revived and engaged public attention. Thomas Eddy, James Platt, and De Witt Clinton, promoted the calling of a public meeting in the city of New York, which was large and enthusiastic, attended by the most prominent and influential citizens. Resolutions were passed in favor of the construction of the canal, and a committee, consisting of De Witt Clinton, Thomas Eddy, Cadwallader D. Colden, and John Swartout, were appointed to prepare a memorial to be presented to the Legislature. A memorial, written by Mr. Clinton, was prepared, widely circulated throughout the state, and produced a most decided and beneficial influence. The advantages and the necessity of a canal were forcibly demonstrated, and it had the effect to produce a strong impression upon the public mind. This meeting was followed by a succession of meetings on the subject, held in different cities and villages in various parts of the State, all in favor of the project. Petitions were forwarded to the capital which were laid before the Legislature. The newspapers of the day were soon filled with communications, written by distinguished men, showing the great need there was of such a channel of communication, and the wealth and honor it would confer on the State and people that provided it. The public mind being thus informed, awakened, and prepared, it would not do for the representatives of the people either to oppose their wishes or refuse their requests. Gov. Tompkins, in his message to the Legislature in 1816, presented the subject for their consideration, and alluded to the propriety of making appropriations for that purpose. This portion of the message was referred, by a concurrent resolution, to a joint committee of both Houses. On the 21st of February, Mr. Clinton's memorial was presented, and soon after another memorial from the mayor, aldermen, and commonalty of the city of New York. On the 8th March the canal commissioners presented their Report, recommending the adoption of such preliminary measures as might be necessary for the accomplishment of this important object. On the 21st of March, Col. Rutzen Van Rensselear, chairman of the joint committee on Canals, presented his report, urging the immediate commencement of the Erie and Champlain Canals, and brought in a bill providing for these works. On the 5th of April, the house resolved itself into a committee of the whole, and took up the bill. The consideration of the bill was resumed from time to time, in committee of the whole. Animated and interesting debates took place. Various amendments were proposed, which were favored or opposed, as the friends or enemies of the Canal supposed they would aid or retard the enterprise. During the sitting, on the 13th, a proposition was made to put a local tax on lands lying within twenty-five miles, along the sides of the canals. After some other amendments and modifications, it finally passed the Assembly by a vote of 83 to 16.

On the 16th, the Senate took the bill as it came from the house. Mr. Van Buren moved to strike out those parts which authorized the commencement of the work, and moved an amendment, directing the commissioners to make further estimates and surveys. This amendment was adopted. When the consideration of the bill was again resumed, a motion was made to reject it, but it was lost. The number of the Canal Commissioners was reduced to five, viz., Stephen Van Rensselaer, De Witt Clinton, Samuel Young, Joseph Ellicott and Myron Holley. In this form, it passed the Senate.

It was sent back to the Assembly, for concurrence in the amendments. The house refusing to concur, it went back to the Senate. The Senate refused to recede. It was the last day of the session—time and business pressed—the friends of the canal thought it was better to have the bill as it was, than none, and succeeded in inducing the House to recede and concur in the bill as it came from the Senate. It accordingly become a law. By this law, the Canal Commisioners were generally empowered to make surveys, estimates of expense, and to ascertain the practicability of making loans upon the credit of the State.

In November, 1816, an extra session of the Legislature was held for the purpose of appointing Presidential electors. The Governor sent a message, in which he alluded to the subject of the contemplated canals, in such a manner and connection, that gave evidence of no very friendly feelings for them, if it did not indicate settled hostility to them. January 14th, 1817, the Legislature again met, but the Governor made no communication. On the 17th of February, the report of the Canal Commissioners respecting the Erie Canal was presented, and that on the Champlain Canal, on the 19th. These reports were written in the ablest manner— they contained a large amount of interesting and valuable information on every subject relating to the Canals, clearly showing "the physical facility of this great internal communication, and that a little attention to the resources of the state, would demonstrate its financial practicability." The first of these reports was referred to a joint committee of both houses.

Without attempting to trace minutely the history of the bill, with all the different amendments that were offered and rejected, it will be sufficient to state, that on the 10th of April, 1817, it passed the house of Assembly, by a vote of 64 for, and 26 against it.

On the 12th of the same month, it was taken up by the Senate. A long and able discussion took place. Several amendments to it were made by the Senate, in some of which the Assembly concurred, and from others the Senate receded. And, on the 15th day of April, 1817, it became a law. Col. Young and Myron Holley, were the acting commissioners on the middle section of the Canal, which it was determined should be first commenced. Ground was first broken near Rome on the 4th of July, 1817. A large concourse of citizens assembled with the commissioners and engineers. An address on behalf of the citizens was made by the Hon. Joshua Hathaway, at the conclusion of which he handed a spade to the commissioners. On receiving it, Col. Young replied to the speech and eloquently portrayed the vast magnitude of the enterprise, and the vast benefits that would be realized by its consummation. Inspired, as it would now seem, with the gift of prophesy, he said: "It will diffuse the benefits of internal navigation over a surface of vast extent, blest with a salubrious climate and luxuriant soil, embracing a tract of country capable of sustaining more human beings than were ever accommodated by any work of the kind. By this highway, unborn millions will easily transport their surplus production to the shores of the Atlantic, procure their supplies, and hold a useful and profitable intercourse with all the maritime nations of the earth. The expense and the labor of this great undertaking bear no proportion to its utility. Nature has kindly afforded every facility;—we have all the moral and physical means within our reach and control. Let us then proceed to the work, animated by a prospect of its speedy accomplishment, and cheered by the anticipated benedictions of a grateful posterity."

Col. Young then handed the spade to Judge Richardson, the first contractor on the work, who broke ground for the construction of the Erie Canal, amid the roar of cannon, and the enthusiastic cheers of a large assemblage of citizens.

In 1819, the middle section of the canal was completed. On the 23d of October in that year it was navigated from Utica to Rome. Parts of the eastern and western sections of the Erie canal were so far completed that boats passed from the east side of the Genesee river in Rochester, as far east as Little Falls, in 1821. The eastern section was completed and boats entered the Hudson on the 8th day of October, 1823. The whole work was completed from the Hudson to lake Erie, and opened for navigation on the 26th of October, 1825.

The discussion of the relative merits of those who projected and were foremost in aiding the consummation of the great work is a hackneyed theme, and for the most part has been an unprofitable one. Dr. Hosack, in his memoirs of DeWitt Clinton, arranges the names of the projectors, or those who made suggestions, in reference to internal improvements in this state, and those who earliest and most prominently participated in forwarding the construction of the Erie canal, chronologically, as follows:—

C. Colden,	1724	E. Watson,	1791	T. Eddy,	1810
G. Morris,	1777	P. Schuyler,	1792	J. Platt,	1810
G. Washington,	1787	G. Clinton,	1729	S. Van Rensselaer,	1810
C. Colles,	1784	J. Hawley,	1807	C. D. Colden,	1818
J. Smith,	1786	J. Forman,	1808	DeWitt Clinton.	

The biographer and friend of Mr. Clinton, it will be observed, attaches no date to his identity with our works of internal improvement, but makes his the base of his pyramid of names. It has never been assumed that Mr. Clinton was a projector of the Erie canal, but it has passed into an adage, is a fact that may now be written down in history as conceded, and no longer to be questioned, that he was the Father of our canal system. Whatever others may have done before him in the way of suggestion, projection, or incipient movements, it was he, who, more than others, by an early and zealous espousal of the project of the Erie canal, at a period when a strong opposition was arrayed against it—in a dark and unpromising hour—threw the whole weight of his extraordinary talents and influence in favor of the measure, and by continued and unremitted labor in its behalf, taking the lead in winning for it popular favor and legislative co-operation, insured its commencement and prosecution up to a period when the great enterprize began to take care of itself. Such is the feeble but truthful tribute of history to the memory of a great Public Benefactor; a more enduring tribute will soon evince the gratitude of a state he so much aided in its rapid and unparalleled advances to the high position it now occupies.

We, of Western New York, have some reason to complain of omissions in Mr. Hosack's list. Cotemporary with the names he enumerates, as belonging to the canal period of 1810, he should have included the names of Peter B. Porter and Joseph Ellicott. The former was one of the primitive board of Canal Commissioners, and in Congress, an able and zealous advocate for a system of internal improvements by the general government, which would have included aid to this state, in prosecuting its works. The latter was the early correspondent of Mr. Clinton, in reference to the canal, gave efficient aid to the project, by his sound practical judgement, and intimate topographical knowledge of the country, and was a member of the board of Canal Commissioners, as early as 1816.

And in these, the local annals of the Holland Purchase, and incidentally, of Western New York, the claims of Jesse Hawley may well be re-asserted, and insisted upon, as the plain and undeniable deduction from cotemporary history. He was the projector of the Erie canal. By this the author would be understood to mean that the essays he wrote and published in the Ontario Messenger, in 1807 and '8, contained the first proposition that contemplated such a work of internal improvement as the Erie canal now is; that all the projects that preceded his, had reference to works of another character, contemplated improvements of existing internal navigation of the state, and the use of lake Ontario, as a western extension; works far inferior in magnitude to the one he projected; such as would have come far short of accomplishing the mighty results we have witnessed; especially, in reference to its influences upon the prosperity of the western portion of the state.

The story may be made a brief one—the main points are conceded in citations that have already been made.

Jesse Hawley was a native of Newfield, (now Bridgeport,) Conn.; was born in 1773. He was engaged in the mercantile business at Geneva, Ontario county, as early as 1805, in which business he was unfortunate. He spent the winter of 1806 and '7 in Pittsburgh. He published his first essay on the subject of the Erie canal, in the Pittsburgh "Commonwealth" of Jan. 14, 1807. He returned to Ontario county in the same year, and during the summer, re-published his first essay in the Ontario Messenger, and followed it up with a series of essays which were continued at intervals, up to March, 1808. These essays contain the first suggestions, ever made for connecting the Hudson river with lake Erie, by a continuous overland water communication. They were written with much ability, and no one can read them now, without a feeling of surprise, excited by their boldness of design, at a period so primitive in reference to internal improvements; their vast foresight, in anticipating so much that has become reality. On a slip of paper, in the author's possession, is the following reminiscence, in the handwriting of this prominent public benefactor:—"I first conceived the idea of the over land route of the canal, from Buffalo to Utica, in Col. Wilhelmus Mynderse's office, at Seneca Falls, in 1805." In his mercantile operations at Geneva, during that year, he purchased wheat which he had floured at Col. Mynderse's mill, and shipped to Schenectady and Albany. Upon the occasion alluded to, he was engaged in superintending the shipping of flour, and while in the office of Col. Mynderse, the subject of a better navigation came up. Mr. Hawley, stepping to a map of the state, drew his finger over the country from Utica to lake Erie, and said:—"There is the head of water." This may be regarded as the first intimation having reference to such a work as the Erie canal.

The efforts of Mr. Hawley in behalf of internal improvements, did not end with his early essays. He continued up to the period of his death to devote a large portion of his time in that behalf. He aided the project of canal enlargement, materially in its early stages; and subsequently, when that measure was threatened with suspension, or reduction, he brought before the Legislature a mass of useful statistical information, facts and figures, well calculated to aid in a right understanding of the subject. In this as in other instances, it was his fate to see another profit by his suggestions and indefatigable labors. The Senator, to whom he entrusted his manuscripts, incorporated them in a report of which he claimed the paternity, using the thunder as if he was the Jove that made it.

That his public services, his early and continual devotion to the cause of internal improvements, have never been sufficiently appreciated, will be generally conceded. That he entertained a deep sense of this neglect, and that it weighed heavily upon a sensitive mind — is well known to those who enjoyed his intimacy; and is it to be wondered at, that one who had so eminently contributed to public prosperity, should have manifested a laudable ambition to receive at the hands of that public some suitable recognition of the debt of gratitude, that was due to him?

Mr. Hawley was a resident of Lockport, Niagara county, at the period of his death — Jan. 1842. He was spending an evening at the house of a friend in the adjoining town of Cambria, when he was suddenly attacked with hemorrhage of the lungs, and expired in a few minutes.

The remains of one so conspicuously identified with the history of the Erie canal, occupy a spot of elevated ground in the rural Cold Spring cemetery, near Lockport, overlooking the great work he projected. Now that justice has been done to the memory of DeWitt Clinton, by provisions for a suitable monument, next to his services, are there any that better deserve a similar public acknowledgment, than those of Jesse Hawley?

Resuming the brief sketch of the progress of the canal westward, we can only allude to the prominent events. In 1816 the route of the canal west of Genesee river had not been determined. In that year, Mr. Ellicott employed Mr. Peacock to explore a route from Buffalo to the site of the present village of Pendleton, and thence eastwardly, south of the Mountain Ridge, to the Genesee river. The summit of this route, proved to be 75 feet above lake Erie, which of course prevented its adoption. At the same time, James Geddes surveyed a route from Pendleton northwardly to the Mountain Ridge; and thence eastwardly to the Genesee river. This route was afterwards, in the main, adopted, the principal variation being at Lockport. The attention of the commissioners being engrossed with the middle section, nothing farther was done west of the Genesee river, until near the close of 1819, and then no more than the adoption of Mr. Geddes' northern route. In 1820, David

Thomas was appointed principal engineer west of the Genesee river. In that year he carefully examined Geddes' line from Rochester to Pendleton, and made examinations of the Tonawanda creek. He varied the line from Pendleton to Lockport, from the survey of Mr. Geddes' which had proposed descending the Mountain Ridge, in the gorge, a mile and a quarter west of the present locks; a variation which has been fully approved by time, and upon the score of practical utility; and another important and judicious variation east of the Oak Orchard creek. David Thomas' survey and report was adopted in the spring of 1821, and the rock sections at Lockport, immediately put under contract. During the summer, the principal engineer, revised the line from Rochester westward, and extended it up the Niagara river to Buffalo. The whole was put under contract before the close of 1821, and prosecuted with a vigor that public anxiety and expectation demanded, as the great work approached nearer and nearer to a consummation.

A detached history of the western section of the canal, would involve a long and bitter controversy, touching its termination at the foot of lake Erie—a rivalship between Buffalo and Black Rock, if indeed, even then it could not well be dispensed with. Ere the record of that controversy, which should be made now had lost its freshness, PROGRESS, the vastly increasing commercial operations at the foot of lake Erie, will have so far outstripped the sectional views of the men of that period, that even the land marks of their controversy will be obliterated.

Never in any age or country, has a public work, of any kind, been carried on by agents more faithful and persevering, than were the men who had charge of the construction of the Erie Canal from the Genesee river, to lake Erie; and this local designation is not made for the sake of any invidous comparison with other portions of the great work. The earliest commissioner identified with construction, was Myron Holley; so eminently able and faithful were his services that the recollection and acknowledgment of them, outlive and palliate the mixed offence of fault and misfortune, with which they were destined to close. His successor was William C. Bouck. Who, at the west, who had cognizance of those times and their local events, does not remember how faithful and indefatigable, he was in the discharge of his duties? Or, almost imagine that they can see him now as they saw him in those primitive canal times, traversing the forest on horseback and on foot, from the log shanties of one contractor to those of another; sleeping and eating where emergency made it necessary, in quarters no matter how rude or humble; or in his room at the old "Cottage" in Lockport, coolly and good naturedly resisting the fierce importunities of the dissatisfied contractor; yielding to exigencies here and there, when public interest demanded it, or strenuous and unyielding when it did not; pressing on the difficult work upon the Mountain Ridge, amid great difficulties and embarrassments; persevering to the end, until he had seen the last barrier removed that prevented the flow of the waters of lake Erie through their long artificial channel.

There was the early principal engineer, David Thomas; in the public service, in all his extended conventional and social relations — amiable, unassuming; when wronged, not reviling; the pattern of a man; endowed with intellectual powers, and high scientific attainments, that well entitles him to a high rank among the men of New York. His sudden removal from a sphere of great usefulness, in which no blemish or wrong doing was shown, with another memorable instance, must always be passed over by the historian, with the conclusion that the times, and not the men, were at fault. He yet survives, with faculties unimpaired, to make voluntary, liberal offerings, to the common stock of scientific knowledge. The other early engineers employed west of the river, as principals, were David S. Bates, and Nathan S. Roberts, to both of whom, the work was largely indebted for successful management. Of the resident and assistant early engineeers, there were, Davis Hurd, Charles T. Whippo, ——— Price, Alfred Barrett, Porteus Root, and John Hopkins; all of whom, in the discharge of their duties, abundantly justified the early expressed opinion of Mr. Ellicott, that the genius and enterprize of the young men of our country would obviate the necessity of going to Europe for engineers.

A jubilee, such as has never, upon any other occasion, been witnessed in our country, awaited the completion of the Erie Canal. All else consummated, a signal from the Mountain Ridge was anxiously looked for, to commence the work of preparation for the great event. It was given as follows:—

"*To the Hon. Stephen Van Rensselaer, President of the Board of Canal Commissioners:*

Sir — The unfinished parts of the Erie Canal will be completed and in a condition to admit the passage of boats, on Wednesday, the 26th day of October next.

It would have been gratifying to have accomplished this result as early as the first of September, but embarrassments which I could not control, have delayed it.

On this grand event, so auspicious to the character and wealth of the citizens of the state of New York, permit me to congratulate you.

WM. C. BOUCK, *Canal Com.*

Lockport, Sept. 29, 1825."

On the promulgation of this gratifying intelligence, active preparations commenced. Committees of conference on the part of New York and Albany, taking the lead, a general plan of celebration was agreed upon, which was concurred in by a conference of committees of Rochester, Lockport and Buffalo.

In all the space that intervened from the announcement of Commissioner Bouck, up to the appointed day, the celebration was the engrosing topic of conversation, preparation for it the paramount business. There was the active correspondence of committees and sub-committees, processions and dinners projected, speeches and toasts prepared; artillery and other military companies were brushing up their ordnance and arms; fire companies, mechanics' and other associations, in cities and villages, preparing their appropriate banners; bands of music, were practicing enlivening strains; managers of dancing assemblies were issuing their cards of invitation. In short the "busy note of preparation" was sounding from lake Erie to Sandy Hook. All were looking forward to a gala-day—a period of joy and hilarity—the celebration upon a scale of grandeur and magnificence, of the peaceful triumphs of state energy, enterprise and perseverance.

An important feature in the general arrangements for the celebration, was the stationing of cannon of a large calibre, (generally 32s,) from Buffalo to Sandy Hook, to announce the departure of the first boat from lake Erie to tide water, and answer the purposes of a continuous salute.

As the appointed day drew near the forces of the contractors upon the Mountain Ridge were largely increased, and every means put in requisition to be in readiness. On the evening of the 24th of October, the work was completed, the guard gates were raised, and the filling of the lake Erie level commenced. On the evening of the 25th, the entire canal from Buffalo to Albany was in a navigable condition.

Buffalo, then a village of only twenty-five hundred inhabitants, but making up in public spirit and enthusiasm any now seeming want of numbers, from its position at the head of navigation, was of course to lead off in the ceremonies. And well did the germ of a now great city, acquit itself.* The New York Committee that arrived there on the evening of the 25th, in their after report, say that they "found every thing in readiness for the commencement of the celebration."

At 9 o'clock on the morning of the 26th, a procession was formed in front of the Court House. It consisted of the Governor and Lieutenant Governor of the state, the New York delegation, delegations from villages along the whole line of the canal, various societies of mechanics with appropriate banners, and citizens generally; the whole escorted by the Buffalo band, and Capt. Rathbun's Rifle Company. The procession moved down Main Street to the head of the canal, where the pioneer boat, the "Seneca Chief," was in waiting. The Governor and Lieut. Governor, and the Committees, including that of Buffalo, were received on board. The whole standing upon the deck, there were mutual introductions and congratulations. Jesse Hawley, Esq. in behalf of the Rochester Committee, made a short address, which was replied to by Judge Forward.

All things being in readiness, the signal gun was fired, and continuing along from gun to gun, in rapid succession, in one hour and twenty minutes the citzens of New York were apprized that a boat was departing from the foot of lake Erie, and was on its way, "traversing a new path to the Atlantic ocean."

The Seneca Chief, led off in fine style, drawn by four grey horses fancifully caparisoned. Three boats, the Perry, Superior, and Buffalo, followed. The fleet moved from the dock under a salute from the Rifle Company, accompanied by music from the band. The procession marched to the Court House, where an address was delivered by Sheldon Smith, Esq. after which an original ode written for the occasion, was sung to the tune of "Hail Columbia." A public dinner succeeded, and the festivities of the day were closed by a splendid ball at the Eagle Tavern.

At Lockport, a salute of thirteen guns was fired at sunrise. At nine o'clock a procession was formed in front of the Washington House, under the direction of Gen. Parkhurst Whitney, as marshal of the day, assisted by Col. Samuel Barton and Maj. M. H. Tucker. The procession moved to the foot of the locks, when the President

---

*It is questionable whether the same thing could be better done now. A vast increase of numbers, would hardly supply the spirit and joyous feeling that then existed. Surfeited with prosperity, communities as well as individuals, became stolid and indifferent.

and Vice President of the day, the Canal Commissioners and Engineers, the Committee of Arrangements, Visiting Committees and many citizens of distinction from abroad, embarked on board the packet boat William C. Bouck, that had been selected as the first to pass the locks. Over two hundred ladies were escorted upon the boat Albany, of the Pilot Line. The remainder of the procession embarked on other boats lying in the basin. Immediately after the grand salute had passed from Buffalo east, the lock gates were opened, and the fleet commenced ascending to the lake Erie level. As it ascended the stupendous flights of locks, its decks covered with a joyous multitude, it was greeted with the constant and rapid discharge of heavy artillery, thousands of rock blasts or explosions prepared for the occasion, and the shouts of spectators, that swarmed upon the canal and lock bridges, and upon the precipices around the locks and basin. As soon as the two forward boats had passed out of the upper locks, they were drawn up side by side, and after a prayer by the Rev. Mr. Winchell, an address was delivered by Judge Birdsall. Stepping upon an elevated platform upon the deck of one of the boats, in the stillness that had succeeded the earthquake sounds, and the shouts of human voices, he exclaimed: "The last barrier is passed! We have now risen to the level of lake Erie, and have before us a perfect navigation open to its waters." The address was one of marked ability, replete with stirring eloquence and the spirit of the occasion. At the close of the address, under a discharge of artillery, the explosions of rocks, the fleet of boats started for the west. At Pendleton it halted, and the fleet of boats from the west, that had been joined by a boat from Black Rock with a local committee on board, soon came up. The boats that had passed the locks acting as an escort, the combined fleet passed down to Lockport, where it was received under a discharge of artillery. A supper was served up at the Washington House, after which the pioneer fleet from Buffalo and Black Rock continued upon its voyage to the ocean.

Night setting in, no farther prominent demonstrations marked the progress of the fleet until it arrived the next morning at Holley. At that village and at Brockport, its arrival was welcomed by the firing of cannon and other joyous demonstrations. The spirited citizens of the then just rising village of Newport (Albion) determined not to forego a participation in the jubilee. They had a celebration on the 26th; a procession, an address by G. W.

Fleming, Esq. firing of cannon, a dinner and toasts; prolonging the ceremonies of the day even to the "small hours of the night," not to let the procession of boats pass in the absence of such demonstrations as the darkness allowed.

At Rochester, the demonstrations were upon a scale, and of a character, corresponding with the local position and the immense advantages that its citizens anticipated, from the completion of the great enterprize. The Seneca Chief, with the boats in her train, arriving there about 2 o'clock P. M. on the 27th, were received with eight uniform companies under arms, and an immense concourse of people. Upon the wharf under an arch, were the Rochester and Canandaigua Committees. Short congratulatory addresses were made by Jesse Hawley and John C. Spencer, Esqs. which were replied to by Gov. Clinton. A procession moved to the Presbyterian church, where a prayer was offered by the Rev. Mr. Penny, and an address delivered by Timothy Childs, Esq. A dinner followed at the Mansion House, Gen. Matthews presiding assisted by Johnathan Childs and Jesse Hawley, Esqs. and in the evening there was a ball and a general illumination. At 7 o'clock in the evening the fleet took its departure for the east, the "Young Lion of the West," having on board a Rochester Committee, being added to the flotilla. From Rochester to Albany, during its transit there was at all the canal villages, a succession of celebrations. It was in the language of one who witnessed the demonstrations, "a protracted 4th of July celebration." The fleet arrived at Albany on the 2d of November, at 1 o'clock P. M. The celebration there was upon a scale of magnificence never upon any other occasion attempted at our state capital. But it was reserved for the Empire City of the Empire State, to add the grand finale, to terminate the great Jubilee, by putting in requisition her immense facilities upon land and water. It was said by a gentleman present, who had witnessed the naval fete given by the Prince Regent of England, upon the Thames, during the visit of the allied sovereigns to London after the dethronement of Napoleon, that the spectacle upon the waters of New York, far transcended that in the metropolis of England. The crowning ceremonial, was the sailing of an immense fleet down the bay to Sandy Hook, when from the deck of a vessel Gov. Clinton poured a keg of water that had been carried down from lake Erie on the Seneca Chief, into the Ocean, accompanying the act with suitable explanatory remarks. The vessel upon which this ceremony was performed, was surrounded by a fleet three miles in circumference. Upon the return of the Seneca Chief to Buffalo, there was brought on board of her a keg of the water of the ocean which was poured into lake Erie by Judge Wilkeson, chairman of the Buffalo Committee, who made a short address, which included a brief account of the splendid pageantries the Buffalo Committee had witnessed in their tour. Thus ended the protracted Jubilee! A long successions of demonstrations, of public rejoicings, such as in the aggregate have never attended any other peaceful triumph of the wisdom, foresight and energy of any people, in any age.

There are readers of the present day, who, perhaps, will be likely to look back upon the events we have narrated, and deem the demonstrations extravagant; unable, as they will be, to form a just estimate of all that stimulated and promoted them. They will, at least, not fail to acknowledge, how more than realized, have been the seemingly extravagant anticipations of that period. The half was not seen, even in those days of anticipations and rejoicings. Even then, had some bold anticipator of coming events, more confident than the mass, ventured to predict the results that have flowed from the construction of the Erie Canal, he would have been called a dreaming enthusiast! Who, then, would have ventured to foretell what is now reality? Who would have been bold enough in his imaginings, to have pointed forward to the end of twenty-three years; to the great cities that have been doubled in population; to the new ones it has created; to the large and prosperous villages that are dotted along its banks; to the new Empire it has helped to create around the borders of our western Lakes, and the fleets of steam and sail vessels it has put afloat upon their waters?

CHAPTER III.

COMMERCE OF THE UPPER LAKES.

The vast internal commerce upon the chain of Upper Lakes, has a distinct identity with our local region, and a brief sketch of its progress, will be looked for, as a part of our pioneer annals. The foot of lake Erie is its eastern termination. The "mouth of Buffalo creek," as Mr. Ellicott used to designate the locality, in dating his earliest letters from the Holland Purchase; the "New Amsterdam," as he was disposed to call it, after he had determined to make it the site of a village, and platted it for that purpose'— has become the MART of the commerce of states, of a vast and fertile region. Buffalo creek, that sluggishly flowed into lake Erie, a sand bar at its mouth, over which, even the bateaux of the early French traders, had to be dragged, is now crowded with a long line of shipping; at times, having the appearance of some of our chief harbors upon the Atlantic. Upon its bank, a long, continuous wharf, and capacious store houses, filled with the produce of the west, and merchandize from the east, meeting here in their transit of exchange. Where, at one period, and that within the memory of living witnesses, the sum total of other than native residents, was Black Joe, William Johnstone, Benjamin Middaugh, Winne, and Ezekiel Lane; and even these, assimilated in habits and inclinations, to the wild sons of the forest, by whom they were surrounded, and whose tenants they were; now are the principal operations of a commerce, equal to the export trade of the whole Union with foreign nations. Where stood the primitive log cabin, which afforded the only resting place for the surveyors, after their long pilgrimages in the wilderness, are now magnificent hotels, brick blocks, piled up four and five stories high, to economize in the matter of room; the value of the ground having gone up from five dollars per acre, to three, and even four hundred dollars per foot. The grounds between, below the "beautiful elevated bank," "extending to the lake, and up Buffalo creek," which Mr. Ellicott congratulated Mr. Cazenove upon having kept out of the Indian Reservation, inasmuch, as with "little trouble it could be converted into beautiful meadows," is now traversed by the Erie Canal, and its arm or extension, the Hamburgh Canal; in almost the centre of it, the state is now constructing an immense artificial basin, or harbor, to accommodate the vastly increasing commerce of the Canal; and throughout its greatest extent, is a compact, built-up portion of the embryo "New Amsterdam," now appropriately called the "CITY OF THE LAKES."

Even in an age, a country, and a local region of Progress, all this is wonderful; a prominent, marked feature. It is almost wholly, the joint offspring of lake and canal commerce.

An account of the pioneer advent of La Salle, in the navigation of the lakes, has been given. It marked a new era with the French missionaries and traders. Up to that period, their route from the St. Lawrence, to their stations at the west, had been through Canada, to lake Huron. Other vessels must have soon supplied the place of the wrecked Griffin, for the new lake route of La Salle, became the avenue for reaching the forts, missionary and trading stations, that were soon multiplied, and embraced the straits of Detroit and St. Clair, the northern shore of lake Michigan, and the vallies of the Maumee and Wabash. Many years previous to the English conquest, the French commerce, it seems, required the construction of a railway up the mountain at Lewiston, a portage road, and a landing place at Schlosser. Two vessels were probably quite sufficient for the trade, however, and that number—the two fired and sunk at Burnt Ship Bay, in the Niagara river—is all we hear of, at the termination of French dominion.

The history of English commerce upon the lakes, previous to the surrendering of these posts in 1796, is a brief one. It was carried on with one or two vessels, and consisted only of the transportation of men and supplies, to the western posts and trading stations, and furs and peltries, on their way to Montreal. It had undergone but little progress in all the long periods of French and English occupancy. Mr. Fairbanks, who resided at

Chippewa, in 1795, says that an armed brig, a few gun boats, and one merchant vessel, was all the English had on the lakes at that period.*

There were a long series of years, following after the close of English dominion, that the commerce of the lakes had little, if any progress. For a long period after the settlement of this region commenced, there was only added to the carrying trade that has already been named, the downward freight of a small, yearly supply of white fish, and fruit from the orchards on the Detroit river. The completion of the Erie Canal had not the immediate effect to materially increase lake commerce. It awaited the new impetus, the commencement of rapid emigration to the western states and territories. "The breaking out of the Black Hawk war, in 1832, first brought out a knowledge of the richness of the soil, and salubrity of the climate of northern Illinois and Indiana, and the territory of Wisconsin, and exhibited the commanding position of Chicago, for commercial business. This war being closed that same season, and peace being re-established in all those parts, a strong current of emigration set in that direction, the next year, and the rich prairies of that country began to fill with a vigorous, hardy and enterprising population; and from that time, only the short space of eight years, may it in truth be said, that there has been any commerce west of Detroit." †

The first steam vessel on the upper lakes was the "Walk-in-the-water," built at Black Rock, and launched in August, 1818. In 1819, she made a trip to Mackinaw, to carry up goods for the American Fur Company. This boat was wrecked on the beach near Buffalo, in 1821. In 1822, her place was supplied by the steam boat Superior.

The building of this second steam boat not only marks a period in the history of lake commerce generally, but, connected with it,

---

* The following reminiscence of English lake commerce, is taken from a number of the "New York Gazette and Weekly Post Boy," of February, 1770: — "By letters from Detroit, we are informed that several boats with goods, have been seventy days in crossing lake Erie; the distress of the people was very great; they were obliged to keep two human bodies, found unburied upon the shore, in order to collect and kill the ravens and eagles that came to feed on them, for their preservation. Many other boats are frozen up, within forty miles of Detroit. A great many trader's small boats have been lost."

† Letter of James L. Barton, Esq. to Capt. W. G. Williams, of the topographical engineer department, dated December, 1841. To that letter, and other productions of this able and indefatigable, early and persevering friend and historian of lake commerce, the author is farther indebted for materials for his brief sketch.

were some pioneer movements in the construction of Buffalo harbor. Previous to 1820, no lake craft larger than a canoe or French batteau, had entered the mouth of Buffalo creek. The stinted commerce of the Lakes had no harbor at the foot of lake Erie, except Black Rock; vessels discharging freight destined for Buffalo, or taking freight from there, either did it at Black Rock, or, laying off the mouth of Buffalo creek, received and discharged freight by means of small boats. In 1818, the legislature authorized the survey of Buffalo creek, at the expense of the county of Niagara. This survey was made by William Peacock, gratuitously. In 1819, the legislature authorized a loan of $12,000 for the construction of a harbor. It was secured by bond and mortgage upon real estate, executed by Oliver Forward, Charles Townsend, Samuel Wilkeson, and George Coit. Under the superintendence of Judge Wilkeson, the money was expended, and a pier extended into the lake about eighty rods, reaching twelve feet water. In 1821, obstructions were so far removed as to admit small vessels into Buffalo creek. When an agent came on from New York, to build the steam boat Superior, however, in January, 1822, he did not regard the harbor improvements sufficiently advanced to insure the passage of the boat out of the creek, if constructed upon its banks, and at first determined upon building at Black Rock. To divert him from this purpose, a few prominent citizens of Buffalo, —Charles Townsend, Samuel Wilkeson, George Coit, Ebenezer Johnson, E. D. Efner, and Ebenezer Walden, executed a bond agreeing to pay the steam boat company one hundred and fifty dollars for every day the boat should be detained in Buffalo creek, after the first of May. This induced the agent to build the boat at Buffalo. During the season of 1822, the harbor improvements were prosecuted with great vigilance, and before the setting in of winter, enough had been accomplished, as was supposed, to ensure against the penalty of the bond. The spring freshet, unfortunately, filled up the channel, reducing the depth of water for a considerable distance, to three feet and a half. The completion of the steam boat, and the first of May, were events near at hand. With extraordinary public spirit, the citizens of Buffalo raised a subscription, the able-bodied among them, without distinction of occupation or profession, becoming laborers upon the work, cleared out the recent deposit, the Superior passed out as soon as she was ready for the lake, and the bond was thus canceled. This is the brief *pioneer* history of the Buffalo harbor; to which may be added the mention of the first appropriation made to the work by the general government. This was in 1826—the sum $15,000—procured through the influence of the Hon. Daniel G. Garnsey, then Representative in Congress, from Niagara and Chautauque.*

The waters of lake Michigan were first visited by a steam vessel in 1827, a boat having that year made an excursion with a pleasure party to Green Bay. The first steamboats that reached Chicago, were those employed by the Government to transport troops and supplies for the Black Hawk war.

The commerce of the Lakes, originating in the pioneer advent of La Salle in 1668, may be said to have had almost a sameness — a few vessels answering all the purposes of a small carrying trade, connected with the western military and trading stations—until the commencement of the navigation of the Erie Canal, in the season of 1826; with the exception perhaps of a small increase that had kept pace with settlement in the lake region of Ohio and in a small portion of Michigan. This embraces a period of one hundred and forty-eight years. The commerce that embraces the entire chain of the upper lakes, as connected with the ordinary business of life, settlement and improvement, has in fact existed but a little over twenty years. Its progress is one among the wonders of the age. To make a full exhibit of its rapid increase, would require the insertion of a series of statistical tables, and a larger space than the author has now at his disposal. The reader, however, can well estimate the immense magnitude of the commerce of the upper lakes, from the following aggregates, selected from the commercial statistics of the Buffalo Commercial Advertiser for 1847:—

In that year there were in commission upon the lakes, ninety-eight steamers, thirty-five propellers, four barques, eighty-two brigs, four hundred and ninety-five schooners, twenty-three sloops and scows; total tonnage, 131,460 tons. Selecting only the prom-

---

* This early and prominent Pioneer of the Holland Purchase was named in connection with early events in Chautauque. His life has been one of enterprise and public usefulness. He was the projector of the scheme of lighting the lighthouse at Barcelona with natural gas, the only successful instance of the kind in the world. He has been one of the founders of two or three now flourishing towns at the West; and yet survives, zealous and ardent in whatever concerns the progress of his race and age; one of the few specimens left of the excellent materials of which the early Pioneers of the Holland Purchase were composed.

SAMUEL WILKESON.

inent articles of produce arriving at Buffalo in that year, they were as follows:—

Flour, bbls	1,857,000	Oats, bu.	446,000
Pork "	42,000	Butter, kgs	101,584
Beef "	38,900	Lard, lbs.	3,436,000
Staves, ps.	8,800,000	Cheese, bxs.	30,840
Wheat, bu.	6,489,100	" casks,	6,450
Corn, "	2,862,000	Lumber, M. ft.	17,313

There were exported from Black Rock and Buffalo, by canal, in 1847, 710,943 tons, principally the products of field and forest, of the regions bordering upon the western lakes. The total value of imports of Buffalo from the lakes, in 1846, was ascertained and estimated to amount to nearly $20,000,000. In the same year, there arrived at Buffalo, via the Erie Canal, the great bulk of which was shipped to the west, 153,761 tons of merchandise and other property, valued at $23,199,665. The monied value of the business of Buffalo and Black Rock, done on the Erie Canal, and which came from and went on to the lakes, was $40,000,000. The amount of capital invested in all descriptions of vessels upon the upper lakes in 1846, was not far from $6,000,000. The number of men employed in lake commerce, about 6,000. The number of passengers arriving and departing from Buffalo, in 1846, was not far from 250,000.

SAMUEL WILKESON.

The excellent portrait of Judge Wilkeson, which the artist has furnished for this work, accompanied by a brief biographical sketch, has been appropriately reserved as an appendage to a branch of our narrative, with which, it has been seen, he was closely identified. When the period arrives in which the gratitude of those who are enjoying in so eminent a degree the fruits of the labors, the indomitable enterprise and perseverance, of the early pioneers and fathers of the City of the Lakes, shall assume the active form of some enduring testimonial, conspicuous upon the tablet they erect, will be the name of Samuel Wilkeson.

Judge Wilkeson was born at Carlisle, Pa. in 1781. To say that he was cradled and nurtured amid the hardships of pioneer border life, would not be merely a figure of speech. When but an infant, his father's family was one of twenty families that penetrated the forests of Western Pennsylvania, and encountered not only the usual privations of the wilderness, but the long series of Indian border wars that ensued.

He became a resident upon the Holland Purchase in 1807, at Portland, Chautauque county, where he engaged in the salt trade; transporting his salt over a portage to Chautauque lake, and down the Allegany and Ohio rivers. This early enterprise probably ended in loss, as the opening of the Kanawa salt works occurred while he had upon his hands salt that had cost him $16 per barrel. He continued at Portland until towards the close of the war of 1812, when he became a citizen of Buffalo, commencing trade in a small way upon the present site of the Kremlin Block on Main street.

Becoming thus identified by residence and interest, with the locality, he was, for thirty-four years, during the progress of village and city, an active and prominent helper in all that concerned their welfare. In long seasons of severe controversy, during the rivalship of localities, he was prominently a champion of Buffalo and its interests. There were "giants in the land," even in those early days; with some of whom it was his province to contend; and with what success, many of that day will well remember. The triumphs in which he bore a conspicuous part, are prominent features in the history of a prosperous city, whose early cause he espoused with all the ardent zeal and native strength of mind which formed the distinguished characteristics of the man. The prominent early Pioneers of the Holland Purchase were, with few exceptions, all self-made men; it has been a region where strong men have wrestled with adversity from early life, been the founders of their own fortunes from humble beginnings, and signally triumphed. Distinguished even among such men, his early cotemporaries, was the subject of this sketch.

The various offices he filled during a long and active life, were those of Justice of the Peace, Member of Assembly, Judge, Senator, and Mayor of the city of his residence. Retiring, in a great measure, from an active political life, with an ample fortune, he engaged early in the great scheme of benevolence embraced in the organization of the American Colonization Society. That, and the interests of a religion and a church he had zealously espoused at a late period in life, engrossed a large share of his time and his mind, during his latter years.

This early Pioneer of the Holland Purchase, conspicuous among the founders of the prosperous city that marks its rapid progress — the uneducated boy from the back-woods of Pennsylvania, that lived to identify his name, not only with the history of this entire local region, but with the legislation of the state, and a scheme of benevolence which deeply concerned the interests of his country, and an unfortunate race — died in Kingston, Tennesee, in July, 1848, while on his way to visit a daughter who resided in that state. He left a large estate, and a richer legacy, in the following extract of a letter, the last that he wrote to his sons:—"I may never see you again; whether I do or not, be kind to each other, be liberal and generous — forgiving all injuries, whether real or imaginary."

APPENDIX.

DEDUCTION OF TITLE FROM ROBERT MORRIS TO THE HOLLAND COMPANY.

Having, in the body of this work, traced the title of the Holland Purchase from James II, William and Mary, and Charles II, Sovereigns of England, to Robert Morris, we here append a succinct deduction of title from Robert Morris to the last proprietors, who held the property under the appellation of the Holland Company. In the first place, however, we will trace the title of three portions of the tract, containing, by estimation, three millions, three hundred thousand acres, from Robert Morris to Wilhem Willink, Nicholas Van Staphorst, Pieter Van Eeghen, Hendrick Vollenhoven, and Rutger Schemmelpenninck; in whom the title to those three portions was vested on the 31st day of December, 1798, and the title to the remaining portion, estimated at three hundred thousand acres, to the last Dutch proprietors. These estimated quantities, it will be understood, are mere assumptions, predicated on no known data, except the million and a half acre tract described in the first mentioned deed.

Ist. Deed from Robert Morris and Mary, his wife, to Herman Le Roy and John Linklaen, by deed dated December 24, 1792, conveying one and a half millions acres, in two tracts, as described in said deed: the west tract as described, containing one million acres, and the east tract, containing half a million acres. The two collectively, forming one tract, comprising four hundred and twenty-two chains, and fifty-six links, off the western parts of each of the townships in the seventh range, and the whole of the townships in the eighth, ninth, tenth, eleventh, twelfth, thirteenth, fourteenth, and fifteenth ranges of townships.—*See Secretary of State's Office, Albany, Lib. M. R. No. 24, fol. 510, and Clerk's Office, Ontario, Lib. 1, fol. 327.*

Deed from Herman Le Roy and John Linklaen to William Bayard, conveying the same land, dated May 30th, 1795.—*See Secretary of State's Office, Albany, Lib. M. R. No. 33, fol. 514, and Clerk's Office, Ontario, Lib. 6, fol. 38.*

Deed from William Bayard and wife to Herman Le Roy, John Linklaen and Gerrit Boon, dated June 1st, 1795.—*See Secretary of State's Office, Albany, Lib. M. R. No. 33, fol. 518, and Clerk's Office, Ontario, Lib. 6, fol. 36.*

Deed from Herman Le Roy and Hannah, his wife; John Linklaen and Helen, his wife; and Gerrit Boon to Paul Busti, dated July 9th, 1798.—*See Secretary of State's Office, Albany, Lib. M. R. No. 31, fol. 212, and Clerk's Office, Ontario, Lib. 5, fol. 300.*

Deed from Paul Busti and wife to Herman Le Roy, William Bayard, James Mc Evers, John Linklaen, and Gerrit Boon, (in trust for the benefit of Wilhem Willink and others, citizens of the United Netherlands, and with covenant to convey the same according to their directions and appointment,) dated July 10th, 1798.—*See Secretary of State's Office, Albany. Lib. M. R. No. 32, fol.* 115, *and Clerk's Office, Ontario, Lib.* 5, *fol.* 315.

Deed from Herman Le Roy, William Bayard, James McEvers, John Linklaen, and Gerrit Boon to Wilhem Willink, Nicholas Van Staphorst, Pieter Van Eeghen, Hendrick Vollenhoven, and Rutger Jan Schimmelpenninck, dated December 31st, 1798.—*See Secretary of State's Office, Albany, Lib. M. R. No.* 32, *fol.* 40, *and Clerk's Office, Ontario, Lib.* 6, *fol.* 33.

The title to the last named grantees was confirmed to them by Thomas L. Ogden and Gouverneur Morris, by deed, dated February 18th, 1801.—*See Secretary of State's Office, Albany, Lib. M. R. No.* 34, *fol.* 246, *and Clerk's Office, Ontario, Lib* 8, *fol.* 340.

2d. Deed from Robert Morris and wife to Herman Le Roy, John Linklaen and Gerrit Boon, conveying one million acres, comprising townships Nos. 5, 6, 7, 8, 9, 10, 11, 12, 13, 14, 15, and 16, in the first range of townships; townships Nos. 4, 5, 6, 7, 8, 9, 10, 11, 12, 13, 14, 15 and 16, in the second and third ranges; and townships Nos. 1, 2, 3 and 4, in the fourth, fifth and sixth ranges of townships, dated February 27th, 1793.—*See Secretary of State's Office, Albany, Lib. M. R. No.* 25, *fol.* 38, *and Clerk's Office, Ontario, Lib.* 1, *fol.* 324.

The preceding conveyance confirmed by deed between the same parties, dated June 1st, 1798.—*See Secretary of State's Office, Albaay, Lib. M. R. No.* 31, *fol.* 149, *and Clerk's Office, Ontario, Lib.* 5, *fol.* 294.

Deed from Herman Le Roy and Hannah, his wife, John Linklaen and Helen, his wife, and Gerrit Boon, to Paul Busti, dated July 9th, 1798.—*See Secretary of State's Office, Albany, Lib. M. R. No.* 31, *fol.* 218, *and Clerk's Office, Ontario, Lib.* 5, *fol.* 305.

Deed from Paul Busti and wife to Herman Le Roy, William Bayard, James Mc Evers, John Linklaen and Gerrit Boon, in trust for the benefit of Wilhem Willink and others, with covenant to convey the same according to their directions and appointment, dated July 10th, 1798.—*Secretary of State's Office, Albany, Lib. M. R. No.* 31, *fol.* 358, *and Clerk's Office, Ontario, Lib.* 5, *fol.* 307.

Deed from Herman Le Roy, William Bayard, James McEvers, John Linklaen and Gerrit Boon to Wilhem Willink, Nicholaas Van Staphorst, Pieter Van Eeghen, Hendrick Vollenhoven, and Rutger Jan Schimmelpenninck, dated December 31st, 1798.—*See Secretary of State's Office, Albany, Lib. M. R. No.* 31, *fol.* 247, *and Clerk's Office, Ontario, Lib.* 6, *fol.* 27.

The title to the last mentioned grantees was confirmed to them by Thomas L. Ogden, by deed dated February 13th, 1801.—*See Secretary of State's Office, Albany, Lib. M. R. No.* 33, *fol.* 241, *and Clerk's Office, Ontario, Lib.* 8, *fol.* 412.

3d. Deed from Robert Morris and wife to Herman Le Roy, John Linklaen and Gerrit Boon, conveying eight hundred thousand acres, consisting of townships Nos. 5, 6, 7, 8, 9, 10, 11, 12, 13, 14, 15 and 16, in the fourth, fifth and sixth ranges of townships, dated July 20th, 1793.—*See Secretary of State's Office, Albany, Lib. M. R. No.* 25, *fol.* 147, *and Clerk's Office, Ontario, Lib.* 2, *fol.* 158.

The last mentioned conveyance was confirmed by deed between the same parties, dated June 1st, 1798.—*See Secretary of State's Office, Albany, Lib. M. R. No.* 31, *fol.* 153, *and Clerk's Office, Ontario, Lib.* 5, *fol.* 288.

Deed from Herman Le Roy and Hannah his wife, John Linklaen and Helen his wife, and Gerrit Boon, to Paul Busti, dated July 9th, 1798.—*See Secretary of State's Office, Albany, Lib. M. R. No.* 31, *fol.* 205, *and Clerk's Office, Ontario, Lib.* 5. *fol.* 303.

Deed from Paul Busti and wife to Herman Le Roy, Wm. Bayard, James McEvers, John Linklaen, and Gerrit Boon, in trust, for the benefit of Wilhem Willink and others, with covenant to convey according to their directions and appointment, dated July 10th, 1798.—*See Secretary of State's Office, Albany, Lib. M. R. No.* 32, *fol.* 127, *and Clerk's Office, Ontario, Lib.* 5. *fol.* 311.

Deed from Herman Le Roy, William Bayard, James McEvers, John Linklaen, and Gerrit Boon, to Wilhem Willink, Nicholaas Van Staphorst, Pieter Van Eeghen, Hendrich Vollenhoven and Rutger Jan Schimmelpennink, as joint tenants, dated Dec. 31, 1798.—*See Secretary of State's Office, Albany, Lib. M. R. No.* 31, *fol.* 243, *and Clerk's Office, Ontario, Lib.* 6, *fol.* 29.

The title to the last mentioned grantees was confirmed to them by Thomas L. Ogden, by deed, dated Feb. 13th, 1801.—*See Seeretary of State's Office, Albany, Lib. M. R. No.* 34, *fol.* 251, *and Clerk's Office, Ontario, Lib.* 8, *fol.* 408.

4th. Deed from Robert Morris and wife to Herman Le Roy, William Bayard, and Matthew Clarkson, conveying three hundred thousand acres, consisting of townships Nos. 1, 2, 3 and 4, in the first range of townships, and townships Nos. 1, 2, and 3, in the second and third ranges of townships, and also one hundred and thirteen chains and sixty eight links off the east part of all the townships in the seventh range, dated July 20th, 1793.—*See Secretary of State's Office, Albany, Lib. M. R. No.* 25, *fol.* 131, *and Clerk's Office, Ontario, Lib.* 6, *fol.* 58.

The title of the last named grantees was confirmed to them by deed between the same parties, dated June 1st, 1798.—*See Secretary of State's Office, Albany, Lib. M. R. No.* 31, *fol.* 144, *and Clerk's Office, Ontario, Lib.* 5, *fol.* 284.

Deed from Herman Le Roy and Hannah his wife, William Bayard and Elizabeth his wife, and Matthew Clarkson, to Paul Busti, dated July 9th, 1798.—*See Secretary of State's Office, Albany, Lib. M. R. No.* 31, *fol.* 207, *and Clerk's Office, Ontario, Lib.* 5, *fol.* 297.

Deed from Paul Busti and wife to Herman Le Roy, William Bayard, and Matthew Clarkson, in trust for Wilhem Willink and Jan Willink, with covenant to convey according to their directions and appointment, dated July 10th, 1798.—*See Secretary of State's Office, Albany, Lib. M. R. No.* 32, *fol.* 122, *and Clerk's Office, Ontario, Lib.* 5, *fol.* 320.

Deed from Herman Le Roy, William Bayard, and Matthew Clarkson, to Wilhem Willink, Jan Willink, Wilhem Willink, Jr. and Jan Willink, Jr. as joint tenants, dated January 31st, 1799.—*See Secretary of State's Office, Albany, Lib. M. R. No.* 31, *fol.* 257, *and Clerk's Office, Ontario, Lib.* 6, *fol.* 31.

The title of the last mentioned grantees was confirmed to them by Thomas L. Ogden, by deed, dated Feb. 27th, 1801.—*See Secretary of State's Office, Albany, Lib. M. R. No.* 33, *fol.* 277, *and Clerk's Office, Ontario, Lib.* 8, *fol.* 420.

The several re-leases by Thomas L. Ogden were for the purpose of re-instating the title from the effects of sheriff's sales, made by virtue of judgments against Robert Morris.

The individuals forming the Holland Company being aliens, were not authorised to hold and convey real estate within this state, therefore they held these lands, in the first place, by trustees. Fearing that some flaw might be found in the regularity of their title, according to the common law of Great Britain, which decided such matters in the absence of statutory provisions; two statutes were passed by the Legislature of the State of New York, for their especial benefit, as well as two other statutes relative to aliens holding lands generally. By these four statutes, the titles of which follow, the conveyances herein before named, and those which follow, are fully authorised and indisputable titles, preserved in the last grantees.

"An act for the relief of Wilhem Willink, Nicholaas Van Staphorst, Christiaan Van Eeghen, Hendrick Vollenhoven, Rutger Jan Schimmelpenninck, and Pieter Stadnitski, being aliens; passed 11th April, 1796."

"An act supplementary to the act entitled, 'an act for the relief of Wilhem Willink, Nicholaas Van Staphorst, Christiaan Van Eeghen, Hendrick Vollenhoven, Rutger Jan Schimmelpenninck, and Pieter Stadnitski, being aliens,' passed 24th February 1797."

"An act to enable aliens to purchase and hold real estate, within this state, under certain restrictions therein mentioned, passed 2d April, 1798."

"An act declaratory of the construction and intent of the act entitled 'an act to enable aliens to purchase and hold real estate within this state under certain restrictions therein mentioned,' and to amend the same, passed 5th March, 1819."

Statement deducing the title of the land included in the three first mentioned chains of title, from Wilhem Willink, Nicholaas Van Staphorst, Pieter Van Eeghen, Hendrick Vollenhoven, and Rutger Jan Schimmelpenninck, in whom the title to the whole of the Holland Purchase was vested, on the 31st day of December, 1798, except the three hundred thousand acres owned by Wilhem Willink, Jan Willink and others.

Deed from Wilhem Willink, Nicholaas Van Staphorst, Pieter Van Eeghen, Hendrick Vollenhoven, and Rutger Jan Schimmelpenninck, by their attorney, Paul Busti, to James McEvers, dated March 24th, 1801, conveying nine hundred eighty-three thousand, nine hundred and ninety-seven acres, consisting of seven thousand, two hundred and eighty-six acres of the west part of township fourteen, and the whole of townships Nos. 15 and 16, in the fourth range of townships; the west four hundred twenty-two chains and fifty-six links of townships Nos. 6, 7, 8, 9, 11, 12, 13, 14 and 15, in the seventh range of townships; the whole of townships Nos. 6, 7, 8, 9, 11, 12, 13, 14 and 15, in the eighth range; townships Nos. 8, 13, 14 and 15, in the ninth range; townships Nos. 1, 2, 3, 4, 5 and 6, in the eleventh and twelfth ranges; townships Nos. 1, 2, 3, 4 and 5, in the thirteenth range; townships Nos. 1, 2, 3 and 4, in the fourteenth range; and townships Nos. 1, 2 and 3, in the fifteenth range of townships.—*See Secretary of State's Office, Albany, Lib. M. R. No. 33, fol. 210, and Clerk's Office, Ontario, Lib. 8, fol. 370.*

Deed from James McEvers to Wilhem Willink, Nicholaas Van Staphorst, Pieter Van Eeghen, Hendrick Vollenhoven, Rutger Jan Schimmelpenninck, Wilhem Willink the younger, Jan Willink the younger, Jan Gabriel Van Staphorst, Roelif Van Staphorst the younger, Cornelis Vollenhoven, and Hendrick Seye, as joint tenants, dated April 1st, 1801.—*See Secretary of State's Office, Albany, Lib. M. R. No. 34, fol. 226, and Clerk's Office, Ontario, Lib. 8, fol. 330.*

Deed from Wilhem Willink, Wilhem Willink, Junior, and Cornelis Vollenhoven, (survivors of the above joint tenants,) to Egbert Jean Koch, dated February 9th, 1829. —*See Secretary of State's Office, Albany, Lib. 42, fol. 51; Niagara County Clerk's Office, Lib. 4, fol. 401; Chautauque County Clerk's Office, Lib. 8, fol. 20; Cattaraugus County Clerk's Office, Lib. 2, fol. 292; Erie County Clerk's Office, Lib. 12, fol. 113; Orleans County Clerk's Office, Lib. 2, fol. 364.*

Deed from Egbert Jean Koch to Wilhem Willink, Walrave Van Heukelom, Jan Eeghen, Cornelis Isaac Van Der Vliet, Wilhem Willink, Junior, and Pieter Van Eeghen, as joint tenants, dated February 10th, 1829.—*See Secretary of State's Office, Albany, Lib. 42, fol. 56; Niagara County Clerk's Office, Lib. 4, fol. 405; Chautauque County Clerk's Office, Lib. 8, fol. 23; Cattaraugus County Clerk's Office, Lib. 2, fol. 295; Erie County Clerk's Office, Lib. 12, fol. 113; Orleans County Clerk's Office, Lib. 2, fol. 264.*

APPENDIX.

Deed from Wilhem Willink, Walrave Van Heukelom, Jan Van Eeghen, Cornelis Isaac Van Der Vliet, Wilhem Willink, Junior, and Pieter Van Eeghen, together with Nicholaas Van Beeftingh and Gerrit Schimmelpenninck, (son of Rutger Jan,) to Egbert Jean Koch, dated February 11th, 1829, conveying township No. 14, in the fourth range of townships, containing 13,950 acres.—*See Secretary of State's Office, Albany, Lib. 42, fol. 61; Orleans County Clerk's Office, Lib. 2, fol. 369.*

Deed from Egbert Jean Koch to Wilhem Willink, Walrave Van Heukelom, Jan Van Eeghen, Cornelis Isaac Van Der Vliet, Wilhem Willink, Junior, and Pieter Van Eeghen, as joint tenants, dated February 12th, 1829, conveying seven thousand, two hundred and eighty-six acres of the west part of township No. 14, in the fourth range of townships.—*See Secretary of State's Office, Albany, Lib. 42, fol. 64, and Orleans County Clerk's Office, Lib. 2, fol. 373.*

Deed from Wilhem Willink, Hendrick Vollenhoven, Rutger Jan Schimmelpenninck, survivors of Nicholaas Van Staphorst and Pieter Van Eeghen, to Hendrick Seye, dated April 18th, 1821; conveying townships Nos. 5, to 16, in the first range of townships, both inclusive; townships 4, to 16, in the second and third ranges, all inclusive; townships Nos. 1, to 13, in the fourth range, both inclusive; townships Nos. 1, to 16, in the fifth and sixth ranges, all inclusive; the west four hundred twenty-two chains and fifty-six links of townships Nos. 1, to 5, in the seventh range, both inclusive; townships Nos. 1, to 5, in the eighth range, both inclusive; and townships Nos. 1, to 6, in the ninth and tenth ranges, all inclusive; containing, by estimation, two millions acres. —*See Secretary of State's Office, Albany, Lib. 40, fol. 400; Genesee County Clerk's Office, Lib. 15, fol. 492; Niagara County Clerk's Office, Lib. 1, fol. 110; Erie County Clerk's Office, Lib. 6, fol. 519; Cattaraugus County Clerk's Office, Lib. 1, fol. 128; Allegany County Clerk's Office, Lib. C. fol. 196; Chautauque County Clerk's Office, Lib. 4, fol. 62.*

Deed from Hendrick Seye to Wilhem Willink, Hendrick Vollenhoven, Rutger Jan Schimmelpenninck, Walrave Van Heukelom, Nicholaas Van Beeftingh, Jan Van Eeghen, Wilhem Willink, Junior, and Gerrit Schimmelpenninck, (son of Rutger Jan) as joint tenants, dated April 19th, 1821; conveying the same premises as the last.—*See Secretary of State's Office, Albany, Lib. 40, fol. 403; Genesee County Clerk's Office, Lib. 15, fol. 490; Niagara County Clerk's Office, Lib. 1, fol. 114; Erie County Clerk's Office, Lib. 6, fol. 522; Cattaraugus County Clerk's Office, Lib. 1, fol. 131; Allegany County Clerk's Office, Lib. C. fol. 192; Chautauque County Clerk's Office, Lib. 4, fol. 65.*

Deed from Wilhem Willink, Walrave Van Heukelom, Nicholaas Van Beeftingh, Jan Van Eeghen, Wilhem Willink, Junior, Gerrit Schimmelpenninck, (survivors of Hendrick Vollenhoven and Rutger Jan Schimmelpenninck,) together with Cornelis Isaac Van Der Vliet and Pieter Van Eeghen, to Egbert Jean Koch, dated February 11th, 1829; conveying township No. 14, in the fourth range of townships, containing thirteen thousand, nine hundred and fifty acres.—*See Secretary of State's Office, Albany, Lib. 42, fol. 61; Orleans County Clerk's Office, Lib. 2, fol. 369.*

Deed from Egbert Jean Koch to Wilhem Willink, Walrave Van Heukelom, Nicholaas Van Beeftingh, Jan Van Eeghen, Wilhem Willink, Junior, and Gerrit Schimmelpenninck; dated February 12th, 1829, conveying six thousand, six hundred and seventy-four acres of the east part of township No. 14, in the fourth range of townships. —*See Secretary of State's Office, Albany, Lib. 42, fol. 66; Orleans County Clerk's Office, Lib. 2, fol. 375.*

APPENDIX.

THE TOWNSHIPS OF THE HOLLAND PURCHASE, WITH REFERENCE TO TOWNS AS NOW ORGANIZED.

ALLEGANY.

T. 1, R. 1, Bolivar.
T. 2, R. 1, Wirt.
T. 3, R. 1, Friendship.
T. 4, R. 1, Belfast.
T. 5, R. 1, Caneadea.
T. 6, R. 1, Hume.
T. 1, R. 2, Genesee.

T. 2, R. 2, Clarkesville.
T. 3, R. 2, Cuba.
E. pt........T. 4, R. 2, Belfast,
W. pt........T. 4, R. 2, New Hudson.
T. 5, R. 2, Rushford.
T. 6, R. 2, Centreville.

WYOMING.

T. 7, R. 1, Pike.
T. 8, R. 1, Gainesville.
T. 9, R. 1, Warsaw.
T. 10, R. 1, Middlebury.
T. 7, R. 2, Eagle.
T. 8, R. 2, Weathersfield.
T. 9, R. 2, Orangeville.
T. 10, R. 2, Attica.

T. 7, R. 3, China.
T. 8, R. 3, Java.
T. 9, R. 3, Sheldon.
T. 10, R. 3, Bennington.
T. 7, R. 4, China.
T. 8, R. 4, Java.
T. 9, R. 4, Sheldon.
T. 10, R. 4, Bennington.

GENESEE.

T. 11, R. 1, Bethany.
E. pt..........T. 12, R. 1, Stafford.
W. pt..........T. 12, R. 1, Batavia.
T. 13, R. 1, Elba.
T. 11, R. 2, Alexander.
T. 12, R. 2, Batavia.
E. pt..........T. 13, R. 2, Elba.

W. pt........T. 13, R. 2, Oakfield.
T. 11, R. 3, Darien.
T. 12, R. 3, Pembroke.
T. 13, R. 3, Alabama.
T. 11, R. 4, Darien.
T. 12, R. 4, Pembroke.
T. 13, R. 4, Alabama.

ORLEANS.

T. 14, R. 1, Barre.
S. pt..........T. 15, R. 1, Barre.
N. pt..........T. 15, R. 1, Gaines.
T. 16, R. 1, Carlton.
T. 14, R. 2, Barre.
W. tier lots....T. 15, R. 2, Ridgeway.
S. E. pt.......T. 15, R. 2, Barre.
N. E. pt......T. 15. R. 2, Gaines.

T. 16, R. 2, Carlton.
T. 14, R. 3, Shelby.
T. 15, R. 3, Ridgeway.
T. 16, R. 3, Yates.
T. 14, R. 4, Shelby.
T. 15, R. 4, Ridgeway.
T. 16, R. 4, Yates.

CATTARAUGUS.

T. 1, R. 3, Portville.
S. pt..........T. 2, R. 3, Portville.
N. pt..........T. 2, R. 3, Hinsdale.
S. pt..........T. 3, R. 3, Hinsdale,
N. pt..........T. 3, R. 3, Rice.
T. 4, R. 3, Lyndon.
T. 5, R. 3, Farmersville.
T. 6, R. 3, Freedom.
T. 1, R. 4, Olean.
S. pt..........T. 2, R. 4, Olean.
N. pt..........T. 2, R. 4, Hinsdale.
S. pt..........T. 3, R. 4, Hinsdale.
N. pt..........T. 3, R. 4, Rice.
E. pt..........T. 4, R. 4, Lyndon.

W. pt........T. 4, R. 4, Franklinville.
T. 5, R. 4, Farmersville.
S. W. cor. lot,.T. 6, R. 4, Machias.
Residue......T. 6, R. 4, Freedom.
T. 1, R. 5, Burton.
T. 2, R. 5, Burton.
T. 3, R. 5, Humphrey.
T. 4, R. 5, Franklinville.
T. 5, R. 5, Machias.
S. tier lots.....T. 6, R. 5, Machias.
Part..........T. 6, R. 5, Yorkshire.
S. E. pt......T. 7, R. 5, Yorkshire.
T. 1, R. 6, Carrolton.
S. pt..........T. 2 R. 6, Carrolton.

APPENDIX.

CATTARAUGUS, Continued.

N pt........	T. 2, R. 6, Great Valley.	T. 2, R. 8, Cold Spring.
	T. 3, R. 6, Great Valley.	T. 3, R. 8, Napoli.
	T. 4, R. 6, Ellicottville.	T. 4, R. 8, New Albion.
S. pt	T. 5, R. 6, Ellicottville.	E. pt........T. 5, R. 8, Otto.
N. pt.........	T. 5, R. 6, Ashford.	W. pt........T. 5, R. 8, Persia.
S. pt.........	T. 6, R. 6, Ashford.	S. E. pt......T. 6, R. 8, Otto.
	T. 1, R. 7, Little Valley.	S. W. pt......T. 6, R. 8, Persia.
	T. 2, R. 7, Little Valley.	T. 1, R. 9, South Valley.
	T. 3, R. 7, Little Valley.	T. 2, R. 9, Randolph.
	T. 4, R. 7, Mansfield.	T. 3, R. 9, Connewango.
	T. 5, R. 7, Otto.	T. 4, R. 9, Leon.
S. pt.........	T. 6, R. 7, Otto.	T. 5, R. 9, Dayton.
Part..........	T. 6, R. 7, Ashford.	T. 6, R. 9, Perrysburg.
	T. 1, R, 8, South Valley.	

ERIE.

N. W. pt......	T. 6, R. 5, Sardinia.	W. tier lots,.. T. 8, R. 7, Eden.
N. & W. pts...	T. 7, R. 5, Sardinia.	E. pt........T. 8, R. 7, Boston.
	T. 8, R. 5, Holland.	T. 9, R. 7, Hamburg.
	T. 9, R. 5, Wales.	W. 2 tier lots, T. 11, R. 7, Black Rock.
	T. 11, R. 5, Alden.	N. tier lots,... T. 11, R. 7, Amherst.
	T. 12, R. 5, Newstead.	Residue, ...T. 11, R. 7, Cheektowaga.
S. pt.........	T. 13, R. 5, Newstead.	S. E. 2 lots,... T. 12, R. 7, Tonawanda.
N. E. pt......	T. 6, R. 6, Sardinia.	Residue, ...T. 12, R. 7, Amherst.
N. W. pt......	T. 6, R. 6, Concord.	S. pt.........T. 13, R. 7, Amherst.
E. pt.........	T. 7, R. 6, Sardinia.	N. pt.........T. 6, R. 8, Collins.
W. pt.........	T. 7, R. 6, Concord.	T. 7, R. 8, Collins.
	T. 8, R. 6, Colden.	T. 8, R. 8, Eden.
	T. 9, R. 6, Aurora.	S. W. pt.....T. 9, R. 8, Evans.
	T. 11, R. 6, Lancaster.	Residue, ...T. 9, R. 8, Hamburg.
	T. 12, R. 6, Clarence.	S. W. pt......T. 11, R. 8, Buffalo City.
S. pt.........	T. 13, R. 6, Clarence.	Residue, ...T. 11, R. 8, Black Rock.
N. E. pt......	T. 6, R. 7, Concord.	S. & E. pt...T. 12, R. 8, Tonawanda.
N. W. pt......	T. 6, R. 7, Collins.	S. pt.........T. 8, R. 9, Brandt.
E. pt,........	T. 7, R. 7, Concord.	N. pt........T. 8, R. 9, Evans.
W. pt.........	T. 7, R. 7, Collins.	

NIAGARA.

N. pt.........	T. 13, R. 5, Royalton.	E. pt.........T. 14, R. 7, Lockport.
	T. 14, R. 5, Royalton.	W. pt........T. 14, R. 7, Cambria.
	T. 15, R. 5, Hartland.	E. pt.........T. 15, R. 7, Newfane.
	T. 16, R. 5, Somerset.	W. pt........T. 15, R. 7, Wilson.
N. E. pt......	T. 13, R. 6, Royalton.	N. W. pt.....T. 12, R. 8, Wheatfield.
N. W. pt......	T. 13, R. 6, Lockport.	T. 13, R. 8, Wheatfield.
E. pt.........	T. 14, R. 6, Royalton.	E. pt.........T. 14, R. 8, Cambria.
W. pt.........	T. 14, R. 6, Lockport.	W. pt........T. 14, R. 8, Lewiston.
E. pt.........	T. 15, R. 6, Hartland.	E. pt.........T. 15, R. 8, Wilson.
W. pt.........	T. 15, R. 6, Newfane.	W. pt........T. 15, R. 8, Porter.
E. pt.........	T. 16, R. 6, Somerset.	T. 13, R. 9, Niagara.
W. pt.........	T. 16, R. 6, Newfane.	T. 14, R. 9, Lewiston.
N. pt.........	T. 13, R. 7, Pendleton.	T. 15, R. 9, Porter.

CHAUTAUQUE.

	T. 1, R. 10, Carrol.	T. 6, R. 10, Hanover.
	T. 2, R. 10, Poland.	N. tier lots,... T. 1, R. 11, Ellicott.
	T. 3, R. 10, Ellington.	S. E. pt......T. 1, R. 11, Carrol.
	T. 4, R. 10, Cherry Creek.	S. W. pt.....T. 1, R 11, Busti.
	T. 5, R. 10, Villanovia.	T. 2, R 11, Ellicott

CHAUTAUQUE, Continued.

T. 3, R. 11, Gerry.	N. E. lot,....T. 3, R. 13, Stockton.
T. 4, R. 11, Charlotte.	Res. E. tier,..T. 3, R. 13, Ellery.
T. 5, R. 11, Arkwright. ..	W. pt........T. 3, R. 13, Chautauque.
S. E. pt. 4 lots, .T. 6, R. 11, Hanover.	E. tier lots,..T. 4, R. 13, Stockton.
Residue, ...T. 6, R. 11, Sheridan.	N. W. pt.....T. 4, R. 13, Portland.
E. pt..........T. 1, R. 12, Busti.	Residue, ...T. 4, R. 13, Chautauque.
W. pt.........T. 1, R. 12, Harmony.	T. 5, R. 13, Portland.
S. E. pt.......T. 2, R. 12, Busti.	T. 1, R. 14, Clymer.
S. W. pt......T. 2, R. 12, Harmony.	T. 2, R. 14, Sherman.
N. pt..........T. 2, R. 12, Ellery.	E. pt........T. 3, R. 14, Chautauque.
N. tier lots,....T. 3, R. 12, Stockton.	W. pt........T. 3, R. 14, Westfield.
Residue, ...T. 3, R. 12, Ellery.	S. E. pt......T. 4, R. 14, Chautauque.
T. 4, R. 12, Stockton.	Residue, ...T. 4, R. 14, Westfield.
T. 5, R. 12, Pomfret.	T. 1, R. 15, French Creek.
T. 6, R. 12, Pomfret.	T. 2, R. 16, Mina.
T. 1, R. 13, Harmony.	T. 3, R. 15, Ripley.
T. 2, R. 13, Harmony.	

CANAL VILLAGES.

Although advancing somewhat beyond the Pioneer History of the Holland Purchase, as the construction of the Erie Canal has been included, some pioneer sketches of the villages it has created, are suggested:—

BLACK ROCK.—At an early period, as will have been observed, this was a place of some note, a prominent point of ferriage over the Niagara river, and until 1823, the principal depot of lake commerce, at the foot of lake Erie. With its store house, tavern and ferry house, a few scattered dwellings, and soldiers' barracks and batteries, it was a busy, stirring place in the war of 1812; a battle ground upon two or three occasions. It recovered slowly after the burning and pillaging during the war. In the construction of the capacious harbor for lake and canal commerce, it seemed to have acquired advantages to ensure its rapid progress and permanent prosperity. During the progress of the construction of the harbor, and for several years after the completion of the entire Canal, population increased rapidly, building was brisk, and business establishments followed one after another, in rapid succession. At one period there was no locality upon the Erie Canal that seemed to have acquired a better start.

The securing, however, of a harbor at Buffalo, and its gradual improvement, diverted the commerce of the lakes, and whereever that went, canal commerce was sure to follow. At a critical period of village rivalry, Buffalo was fortunate in the possession of men in her interests of extraordinary enterprise and perseverance; capital and ownership of lake craft began to centre there; and the scale turned in its favor. For a long period the village of Black Rock declined, or remained but stationary, in the lee or shadow of its successful and powerful rival; the traveler never failing to wonder, while passing up its capacious harbor, and witnessing the hydraulic power it created, why such advantages were so little improved.

In the mean time, its successful and over-shadowing rival, growing generous in its career of prosperity— forgetful of old controversies — has been expanding, and extending a right arm to embrace and merge it in one continuous and consolidated CITY OF THE LAKES. And who that has witnessed the mighty influences of lake and canal commerce; that sees new states and territories becoming tributary to this most fortunate locality; the fertile regions of the west that are calling for more room at the foot of lake Erie; doubts the speedy consummation of the event that we have indicated?

TONAWANDA.—Previous to the construction of the Canal, there had been, upon the site of Tonawanda village, but a small beginning in the way of farming, and a log tavern which was, in an early day, kept by Garrett Van Slyke, who afterwards moved up the creek. A toll bridge was erected in 1825.

In 1823, William Williams, Latham A. Burrows, Samuel Wilkeson, Townsend & Coit, and Albert H. Tracy purchased five or six hundred acres of land, which embraced the site of the village, on the Erie side of the creek. Mr. Williams erected a saw mill upon the dam, in 1825. In 1824, John Sweeny and George Goundry purchased the land which embraces that part of the village which lies on the Niagara side of the creek; Mr. Sweeny erected a saw mill in 1825. The proprietors platted the village soon after their purchases.

With many business advantages, connected with lake, river, and canal commerce, the growth of the place was, in early years, seriously effected by the flooding of lands, consequent upon the raising of the water of the Tonawanda and Eleven Mile creeks, to perfect canal navigation. In 1840, the state constructed ditches, the effects of which have been to reclaim drowned lands, improve the health of the place, and give a start to improvements. The agricultural interests of the neighborhood, as in all similar cases, have suffered from the attention of a large portion of the population being diverted to the business of lumbering. That hindrance being gradually obviated, as the fine oak of the region has been exhausted, there are few portions of the Holland Purchase, which, for the last few years, have given more evident signs of improvement and progress, than the neighborhood of Tonawanda.

A new impetus has been given to the place within the present year. A company of capitalists from Cleveland, invited by the facilities that exist there for transhipments from lake craft to canal boats, have purchased thirteen or fourteen hundred acres of land on the Erie side of the creek, erected a capacious storehouse and elevator, a storehouse for rolling freight, and have other improvements projected. A new era may be said to have commenced at Tonawanda.

LOCKPORT.—This large flourishing village, now numbering its eight thousand inhabitants, its five extensive flouring mills, and as many lumbering establishments, aside from a large cotton factory, and various other branches of manufactories; its Union School, liberally endowed, with its five and six hundred pupils; its fifty or sixty mercantile establishments; is the offspring wholly of the Erie Canal. The site was a wilderness, dotted with but two or three log houses, and stinted improvements, when the canal was located. Its *pioneer* history is all that is embraced in our present object.

The original proprietors of the village site, or those who purchased the lands from the Holland Company, were, Zeno Comstock, Nathan Comstock, Webster Thorn, Daniel Smith, Eseck Brown, Almon H. Millard, Reuben Haines, David Frink, John Comstock, Nathan B. Rogers, Joseph Otis, Daniel Washburn, Asahel Smith, and James Conkey. ☞ *See page* 551. The first saw mill (or machinery of any kind erected upon the village site) stood in the gulf just above the cotton factory. It was erected by Zeno Comstock, in 1819. David Frink built the first saw mill down the stream; Warren Saddler the next, and Otis Hathaway the next.

The author cannot give, in any form, a more graphic account of primitive things, of the early pioneer period, in the history of Lockport, than is contained in the following sketch, furnished with reference to this work, by Morris H. Tucker, Esq. the pioneer merchant:—

"When I came to Lockport in the summer of 1821, there were some half dozen families residing in unfinished log houses, and a number of men were building small houses, expecting to bring their families as soon as they could finish the tenements.

" Eseck Brown kept the only tavern, in a log house, on the rise of ground a little west of the Lutheran Church. Here the canal contractors all boarded, and a happier set of fellows I never saw collected together. John M'Kay and Claudius V. Boughton had the contract for a considerable distance of the rock cutting, were clearing and grubbing from the Main street bridge, westwardly, and soon commenced excavating at the head of the locks.

"Jared Comstock and Eseck Brown were selling village lots on Main street. Brown's land was cleared from Genesee street to a little north of Caledonia street, and extended from Prospect street to the Transit. Jared Comstock's land was cleared from his south bounds to the north side of Niagara street. From the north side of Niagara street the land of Comstock was uncleared, and the land from the head of the locks, around the ravine, embracing all the Lower Town, and extending as far east as the residence of Judge Dayton, was a dense forest. Here Nathan Comstock's improvements commenced.

"In the summer or fall of 1821, Col. William M. Bond came on from New Hampshire and purchased several acres of Brown's land and laid it out into village lots. He united with John M'Kay, Henry Wright, (an engineer, son of Benjamin Wright, one of the early Principal Engineers,) and myself, in persuading Brown to lay out a good part of his farm into village lots; and he was induced to add Niagara, Ontario, Caledonia, Genesee, Bond, and Prospect Streets, to his village plat. Jared Comstock also added, east of the Transit, Walnut, Genesee, Cottage, Pine, Locust, Elm, and Canal Streets, representing a large city on paper, causing much merriment to our elder neighbors of Buffalo, Lewiston, and the Falls; and they were not sparing of their jokes at our village, with its log taverns, including the noted log 'cottage.'

"I brought with me from Batavia an old stock of goods, which I stored at Eseck Brown's until I could build a store. There was no store nearer than Hartland Corners. When it became known to the women that I had good tea stored at Brown's, no excuse would answer, have it they would, and I was obliged to open shop. In two or three weeks I moved my goods into a new framed store, an imposing building at that time, twenty-two feet square, a story and a half high. Here for several weeks I had no opposition in trade. Soon, however, House & Boughton got their new store finished, and Libbeus Fish brought on goods from Batavia, and Lockport began to be a place of no little importance. Sheperd & Towner's shoe shop, George Rogers' blacksmith shop, Seaman & Batty's shoe shop, John Jackson's bakery, with several small groceries, were often named and counted over, when recommending our village to some new adventurer, to induce him to buy a village lot. That summer the rattle snakes were so numerous that they occasioned much alarm to the villagers."

The proprietors who had an interest in the village plat east of the Transit with Jared Comstock, (of whom Mr. Tucker speaks,) were his brothers, Darius and Joseph, and Seymour Scovell, and Otis Hathaway. Joseph Comstock died in 1822. Jared Comstock, however, had the largest interest, and the titles to the largest share of that portion of the village have come from him. Elias Ransom, Esq. becoming his agent at an early period, and generally perfecting the sales. The purchase that the above named proprietors made, was principally of Zeno Comstock, who had bought of Holland Company. In possession of the most valuable portion of what now constitutes the Upper Town, he sold, and bought at the head of the gulf, a mile and a quarter west, at a time when there was a prospect of the canal taking that route.

Jesse Hawley early became interested with Wm. M. Bond, (of whom Mr. Tucker speaks,) with whom was associated John G. Bond, an early and prominent pioneer of Rochester, who became a resident of Lockport in 1822. They purchased most (if not all) of the original farm lot of Eseck Brown. They may be regarded as the founders and patroons of the village west of the Transit; while the Comstocks, Scovell, and Hathaway, bore that relation to the portion of the Upper·Village east of that line.

There had been a newspaper printed at Lewiston, for a short time previous to 1822, the first in the country, by Bartemus Ferguson. Some of the prominent citizens of Lockport purchased the printing materials and transferred them and its publisher to Lockport, early in that year. A paper was started, entitled the "Lockport Observatory." The author purchased the establishment, and became the editor and publisher of the paper, in August, of that year. And a rough and primitive village it then was, as any, perhaps, that ever gloried in an old fashioned Ramage press, and a few fonts of worn-out type! The village had advanced considerably in one year, from the condition described by Mr. Tucker, and yet there were log heaps and huge piles of rocks in the principal streets. There were not over a dozen or fifteen frame buildings, and but one of stone, a store that had been erected by Sydney and Thomas Smith; the rest were of logs. The old Mansion House had first been erected by James M'Kain, and Samuel Jennings had built the framed tavern house, now standing, near the Eagle Tavern. The author well recollects that, on the evening of his arrival in the village, there was a dancing party at this last named "Lockport Hotel," highly pleased with the idea that they had got a matched and planed floor to dance on. It marked a new era. With the exception of Nathan Comstock's improvements, it was a dense forest from the present site of the American to Wright's Corners, on the Ridge Road. Culver and Maynard were clearing the timber from the slopes of the mountain, around the ravine, and excavating the first rock section; Childs and Hamlin were excavating the second section; Darius Comstock, the third; John Gilbert, the fourth; Norton, Bates, House, and Boughton, the fifth and last rock section. The dense forest between Lockport and Tonawanda creek looked as if a hurricane had passed through it, leaving a narrow belt of fallen timber, excavated stone and earth; and that, to complete the ragged scene, log boarding houses and Irish shanties had been strung along the whole distance. The blasting of rocks was going on briskly, on that part of the canal located upon the village site; rocks were flying in all directions; framed buildings, and the roofs of log buildings were battered by them, and huge piles of stone lay upon both banks of the canal, with a narrow opening to admit the passage of teams over a log bridge, on Main Street. Joseph Landon was grubbing the timber, preparatory to the construction of the first section, east of the locks. The first stone of the old locks was laid in the spring of 1823.

Two circumstances attending the construction of the canal through the Mountain Ridge are worthy of note:—As the rock excavation deepened, it baffled the ingenuity of commissioners and contractors, became expensive beyond all estimate; no greater facilities existed for raising the rock, than wheelbarrows and long runs. In this exigency, Orange Dibble, since widely known as a canal contractor on various public works of the United States, and as Post Master at Buffalo, with a brother-in-law of his, by the name of Olmsted, invented and introduced a simple crane, that revolutionized the work, vastly cheapened it, and in the end, was the means of completing the canal one year before it could have been done in the absence of it. In the original construction of the locks, the contractors, at great expense, opened a road through the woods, to Williamsville, to procure their water lime. At the same time, in excavating the lock-pits and a portion of their rock section, they were removing immense quantities of stone capable of making an hydraulic cement equal in quality to the best that has been discovered in the United States. It was used in the construction of the new locks, and has become an article of commerce upon the canal and lakes, for use in public structures, or whereever such a material is required. The credit of demonstrating its superior quality, and introducing it into extensive use, belongs to Mr. Seth Pierce, of Lockport.

The early merchants of Lockport, not named by Mr. Tucker, were Sidney and Thomas Smith, Jonathan Childs, Joel M'Collum, Lyman A. Spaulding, Harvey W. Campbell, Price & Rounds, Joel M. Parks, William and Seth Parsons, George W. Rogers, Hall & Barber, (W. Barron Williams, as agent for Van Rensselaer, of Utica,) Jacob Gould, Daniel O. Davis, and Cummings & M'Whorter. Among the early mechanics not before named, were Allen Skinner, Hull & Story, John Galt, Charles Belden, Levi Taylor, —— Lozier, —— Long, John Moore. The early physicians were Isaac W. Smith, —— Webb, Stephen M. Potter, Lloyd Smith, Marlin Johnson,

George W. Palmer, Henry Maxwell. The early attornies have been named in another connection.

The pioneer movements in Lower Town commenced in March, 1827. Joel M'Collum, Seymour Scovell, Otis Hathaway, and Sylvester R. Hathaway, purchased three hundred acres of land of Nathan Comstock, which extended from Main Street, through to the old Lewiston road, and embraced nearly all of what is now designated as the Lower Town. These proprietors, after making considerable improvements, constructing roads, building saw mills, &c. sold an interest in their purchase, of seven-tenths, to Charles E. Dudley, Benjamin Knower, Thomas W. Olcott, William L. Marcy, and Lott Clark. These last named proprietors were what was termed the "Albany Company." They had, previous to this, by purchase from the Holland Company, become the owners of all the unsold lands in Niagara, Orleans, and the north parts of Genesee and Erie; tracts comprising, in the aggregate, about eighty thousand acres. The agency was established in the Lower Town, Mr. Clark becoming the agent. In 1830, the bank, the Episcopal church, the large brick block, several fine dwellings were built, and other improvements made; Seymour Scovell making large additions to the old Lockport House that had been erected by ———— Van Velzer. The Albany Company continued to retail these wild lands, until 1834 or '35; Washington Hunt entering the office of Mr. Clark, previous to his majority, and transacting most of the business appertaining to land sales. At the period above named, Judge Hunt, in company with Henry Walbridge, purchased the unsold lands of the Albany Company, and under their auspices the lands have been sold and settled, upon terms of liberality and indulgence, that have materially aided the prosperity of the region in which they were located.

The early merchants in Lower Town were Tucker & Bissell, Otis Hathaway, John & Isaac Henning, Frederick Bissell, Stephen Gooding, Eaton & Brown, Stafford & Humphrey, G. W. Merchant, Scovell & Saxe. The earliest physician was J. K. Skinner. Among the earliest mechanics were Horace Birdsall, Daniel W. Ballou, Willis Peck, Asher Torrance, Stephen Brizee, William Olney, Harvey Norton, ———— Stimpson, William Shepherd, Enos Steel, William Hewitt, Samuel Works, Warren Grant, Peter Besancon.

John Gooding was the patroon of what is known as "Pioneer Hill," and Samuel Allen and Otis Hathaway, of that portion of the village in the neighborhood of the Union School and the Catholic church.

In the process of canal enlargement, the old double tier of locks have been removed, and new ones erected, that surpass, in magnitude, and in the manner of construction, any work of the kind in the world. The contract for rebuilding was at first taken by Smith, Parmelee & Co. who, after getting the first tier in a considerable state of forwardness, sold their contract to Judge Buel, of Rochester, by whom the work has been nearly completed. The magnificent structure has been made under the superintendence of the following engineers, who have, at different periods, had the superintendence of it:—Alfred Barrett, J. D. Fay, Thomas Evershed, Stephen F. Gooding. The cost of the work has been over $575,000.

MIDDLEPORT.—This flourishing, rural village, pleasant in its aspect, as any that are dotted along the Erie Canal, grew up on lands, and in the immediate neighborhood, of Pioneers that had preceded canal location; they were James Lyman, James Williams, Jr. Asher Freeman, Asa Sawtell, Philarius Williams, Russell Ewings, Arunah Bennett, William Taylor, Thomas T. Smith. Levi Cole became a resident there about the period of the canal letting, became a contractor and the pioneer tavern keeper. Benjamin Barlow, Jr. an early member of Assembly from Niagara, was a resident there as early as 1820 or '21. Dr. Packard was the early physician. Dunlap & Craig, Francis B. Lane, Alden S. Baker, —— Northam were early merchants. Lane & Baker had been contractors on the canal at the Sulphur Springs, west of Lockport, settled at Middleport about the period of the completion of the canal, and have been conspicuously identified with its history and progress. Mr. Lane died during the last winter. Dr. Hurd settled there as a physician in an early day. Elijah Mathers and Thomas N. Lee were among the earliest mechanics. The village commands the principal trade of a fine region of country, and has kept pace with its rapid improvements.

MEDINA.— The site of the village was an unbroken wilderness when the canal was located. The village was laid out in 1823, by Ebenezer Mix, and named by him. Its site occupied nearly the center of a tract of fourteen hundred acres, owned by David E. Evans and John B. Ellicott. The large mill now owned by Wm. R. Gwinn, was going up in 1823, when the village was projected. Mr. Gwinn, who married a niece of Joseph Ellicott and a sister of D. E. Evans, became a resident at Medina in 1828, and has been prominently connected with the settlement and progress of the village. The improvements at Medina have been gradual and permanent. There is a valuable water power created by a fall in the Oak Orchard creek, and the Tonawanda feeder. Like the whole region around them, Medina and Shelby villages furnish evidences of progress and improvement; they are going ahead, as all villages upon the Holland Purchase are. [The author has to regret the absence of memorandums which would enable him to name the earliest citizens of Medina.]

ALBION.— [For some notice of the pioneer settlers upon and near the village site *see page* 554.] The fine lands in the immediate neighborhood of Albion had attracted settlers at a pretty early period in the settlement of the country, and previous to the location of the canal a considerable advance had been made in improvements. The village, however, was one of the creations of that great founder of villages and cities; commencing gradually, as the work progressed, and was brought into use. In 1823 it had sufficiently advanced to indicate the necessity of a press and newspaper, and Oliver Cowdery, (who has been the pioneer printer in at least a half dozen localities,) took a part of the old battered "small pica" that had been used in printing the Lockport Observatory, and adding to it indifferent materials from other sources, commenced the publication of the "Newport Patriot."

Wm. Bradner, Harvey Goodrich, R. S. & L. Burrows were early merchants. The early physicians were Orson Nichoson, A. B. Mills, William White, Stephen M. Potter. Philetus Bumpus was an early tavern keeper, if not the pioneer in that line. The author, as in reference to Medina, has to regret the absence of minutes which would enable him to name the early mechanics and other village Pioneers.

The first Methodist society was organized in 1830; the first Baptist society, the same year; the first Presbyterian society, in 1822; the first Episcopal organization was in 1844. Albion Academy was incorporated in 1837; Phipp's Union Seminary, in 1840.

The first Board of Trustees of the village were as follows:—Alexis Ward, *President;* Orson Nichoson, William Bradner, Freeman Clark, Franklin Fenton.

The progress of Albion has been gradual and uniform, keeping pace with agricultural improvements in its fertile neighborhood. In the midst of universal prosperity, such as every where exists upon the Holland Purchase, it is difficult to discriminate; but no where are the evidences of increasing, substantial wealth exhibited in a greater degree, than in Orleans and its smiling and flourishing villages, Albion, Gaines, Medina, Shelby, Knowlesville, Eagle Harbor, and Gaines' Basin.

APPENDIX.

THE ELLICOTT MONUMENT.

The monument to Joseph Ellicott, the plan of which is annexed, is now in the course of erection, the materials of which were principally carried upon the ground during the last winter. It is to be erected at the expense of a portion of the heirs, under the general supervision of the Hon. David E. Evans. The elevation is to be thirty-two feet; the main shaft, sixteen and one-half feet. The inscription not being prepared, is omitted upon the drawing.

NOTE.—The architects are Messrs. B. & J. Carpenter, of Lockport; the materials are from their valuable quarry of limestone. The shaft is a fine specimen of what the quarries of the Mountain Ridge are capable of producing, except as to length. At either of the three quarries of the Messrs. Carpenters, Jerome B. Ransom's, (formerly Buell's,) or that of J. D. Shuler, at the Cold Springs, shafts of solid limestone may be procured, up to eighty feet in length. The superior quality of the stone, its extraordinary durability, and capability of resisting the action of dampness and frost, have been abundantly tested, especially upon our public works.

EXPEDITIONS OF GENERAL SULLIVAN AND COLONEL BRODHEAD COTEMPORARY RECORDS.

These two expeditions, together with that of Col. Van Schaick, had for their end the punishment and conquest of the hostile Indian nations that had, with assimilated Tories, so long and often desolated the frontier settlements of Western New York and Pennsylvania. Of Gen. Sullivan and Col. Schaick's expeditions accounts will be found in the text. Of Col. Brodhead's, nothing has been related, though it was organized about the same time, formed an important part of the general plan, which originally contemplated the union of both armies, and a combined attack on Fort Niagara. Both were successful so far as their separate objects were concerned, but their ultimate destination was never reached;—the large bodies of Tories and Indians collected around the fortress at Niagara, furnishing a safe retreat and shelter for fhe finally broken and defeated bands of Johnson, Butler, and Brant—were left undisturbed.

Since that part of the volume relative to the Border Wars of the Revolution was written, some original, authentic and entirely trustworthy documents—now in possession of Mr. Daniel W. Ballou, Jr., of Lockport—have been kindly furnished the author, and are here inserted. It is not known that they have ever before been published, or even alluded to, by historians of the Revolution. They are copied directly from an old manuscript journal of the year 1779, in which are recorded daily orders issued by Gen. Washington to the army, proceedings of Court Martials, with the names of officers forming the boards, the names of those tried, their acquittal or conviction, beside other transactions connected with affairs of the camp. These extracts may, therefore, be regarded as copies of official announcements made by the Commander-in-Chief to the troops under his immediate command, at West Point. The victory of General Sullivan is thus communicated by General Washington, October 17th:—

"*Extract from His Excellency, Gen. Washington's Orders.*

"HEAD QUARTERS, MORE'S HOUSE, Oct. 17, 1779.

" The Commander-in-Chief has now the pleasure of congratulating the army on the complete and full success of Maj. Gen. Sullivan, and the troops under his command, against the Seneca and other tribes of the Six Nations, as a just and necessary punishment for their wanton depredations, their unparalleled and innumerable cruelties, their deafness to all remonstrances and entreaty, and their perseverance in the most horrid acts of barbarity. Forty of their towns have been reduced to ashes, some of them large and commodious; that of the Genesee alone containing one hundred and twenty-eight houses. Their crops of corn have been entirely destroyed,—which, by estimation, it is said, would have provided 160,000 bushels, besides large quantities of vegetables of various kinds. Their whole country has been overrun and laid waste; and they themselves compelled to place their security in a precipitate flight to the British fortress at Niagara;—and the whole of this has been done with the loss of less than forty men on our part, including the killed, wounded, captured, and those who died natural deaths. The troops employed in this expedition, both officers and men, throughout the whole of it, and in the action they had with the enemy, manifested a patience, perseverance, and valor that do them the highest honor. In the course of it, when there still remained a large extent of the enemy's country to be prostrated, it became necessary to lessen the issues of provisions to half the usual allowance. In this the troops acquiesced with a most general and cheerful concurrence, being fully determined to surmount every obstacle, and to prosecute the enterprise to a complete and successful issue. Maj. Gen. Sullivan, for his great perseverance and activity; for his order of march and attack, and the whole of his dispositions; the Brigadiers and officers of all ranks, and the whole of the soldiers engaged in the expedition, merit, and have the Commander-in-Chief's warmest acknowledgements, for their important services upon this occasion."

As nothing has been said of Col. Brodhead's campaign, it may be proper to state that on the 22d of March, 1779, Washington ordered him to make the necessary preparations for an expedition against Detroit, to throw a detachment forward to Kittaning, and another beyond to Venango, at the same time preserving the strictest secrecy as to his ultimate object. Though this expedition was soon found impracticable and abandoned, preparations were immediately made for the one which was actually undertaken against the Indians at the head of the Allegany river, French creek, and other tributaries of the Ohio. On the 11th of August, 1779, with about six hundred men, including militia and volunteers, and one month's provisions, Col. Daniel Brodhead left Fort Pitt and began his march to the Indian country. The result was announced by Gen. Washington to his army at West Point:—

"*Extract from General Orders.*

"HEAD QUARTERS, MORE'S HOUSE, Oct. 18th, 1779.

" The Commander-in-Chief is happy in the opportunity of congratulating the army on our further success, by advices just arrived. Col. Brodhead, with the Continental troops under his command, and a body of militia and volunteers, has penetrated about one hundred and eighty miles into the Indian country, on the Allegany river, burnt ten of the Muncey and Seneca towns in that quarter, containing one hundred and sixty-five houses; destroyed all their fields of corn, computed to comprehend five hundred acres, besides large quantities of vegetables; obliging the Savages to flee before him with the greatest precipitation, and to leave behind them many skins and other articles of value. The only opposition the Savages ventured to give our troops, on this occasion, was near Cuskusking. About forty of their warriors, on their way to commit barbarity on our frontier settlers, were met here. Lieut. Harden, of the 8th Pennsylvania regiment, at the head of one of our advance parties, composed of thirteen men, of whom eight were of our friends the Delaware nation, who immediately attacked the savages and put them to the rout, with the loss of five killed on the spot, and of all their canoes, blankets, shirts, and provisions, of which, as is usual for them when going into action, they had divested themselves; and also of several arms. Two of our men and one of our Indian friends were very slightly wounded in the action, which was all the damage we sustained in the whole enterprise.

" The activity, perseverance, and firmness, which marked the conduct of Col. Brodhead, and that of all the officers and men, of every description, in this expedition, do them great honor, and their services justly entitle them to the thanks, and to this testimonial of the General's acknowledgment."

In a letter dated " West Point, 20th October, 1779," addressed to the Marquis de Lafayette, Gen. Washington incidentally alludes to these two campaigns, and their probable effects upon the Indians. He informs Gen. Lafayette as news that may be interesting to him, that —

" Gen. Sullivan has completed the entire destruction of the country of the Six Nations; driven all their inhabitants, men, women, and children, out of it; and is at Easton on his return to join this army, with the troops under his command. He performed this service without losing forty men, either by the enemy or by sickness. While the Six Nations were under this rod of correction, the Mingo and Muncey tribes, living on the Allegany, French creek, and other waters of the Ohio, above Fort Pitt, met with similar chastisement from Col. Brodhead, who, with six hundred men, advanced upon them at the same instant, and laid waste their country. These unexpected and severe strokes have disconcerted, humbled, and distressed the Indians exceedingly; and will, I am persuaded, be productive of great good, as they are undeniable proofs to them, that Great Britain cannot protect them, and that it is in our power to chastise them whenever their hostile conduct deserves it."—*Spark's Writings of Washington*, Vol. VI, p. 384.

THE SEQUEL OF HOLLAND COMPANY INVESTMENT.

The author has no data to determine what was the final result, so far as profits are concerned, of the Holland Company's investment. Some indication of it is perhaps afforded by the fact, that in 1821, the Dutch proprietors offered to make an assignment of their entire interest, for a consideration which would cover the original amount of purchase money, and an interest of four per cent. In 1822, they offered to Messrs. Tibbets & Huntington, well known capitalists of that period, all the unsold lands, for four shillings per acre. Nearly half of the entire Purchase was then unsold. These offers, however, may have been somewhat induced by a disposition to close up a protracted business, and to avoid the perplexities and litigations which were then in prospect. The final result was probably better than would be inferred from these offers.

THE OGDEN PRE-EMPTION.

In 1810, the Holland Company sold all their pre-emptive right to the Indian Reservations, to David A. Ogden, for fifty cents per acre. What is known as the Ogden Company, have extinguished the Indian title to all the Reservations, except the Cattaraugus, Allegany, and the largest portion of the Tonawanda. They assume to have, by treaty, extinguished the title of the Indians to the whole of the Tonawanda Reservation; but possession is resisted by the Indians, and proceedings are now pending in our courts in reference to it; from which controversy may this remnant of the Iroquois, whose history has been mingled in our narrative, have a good deliverance. There has been quite enough of attainted Indian treaties in Western New York, under this Ogden claim, and removal and possession in pursuance of them.

GERMAN EMIGRANTS.

The location of German emigrants upon the Holland Purchase, forms a prominent feature of recent events. In Buffalo, they already compose nearly one-third of the entire population, and are mingled in almost all of its branches of business. They have spread out from there, into the towns of Cheektowaga, Lancaster, Black Rock, Tonawanda, Newstead, Amherst, Clarence, Hamburg, Eden, Boston, Wales, Sheldon, Bennington, Orangeville, and Attica; in some of the towns named, making a large proportion of the aggregate population.

In Niagara county, there are three villages or colonies of Prussians; the first came into the county in 1843, purchased and located upon 4000 acres of land in the northern and central parts of Wheatfield, in which is located the village of Bergholtz. During the same year, another village was founded on the Tonawanda creek, at the mouth of Cayuga creek, called Martinsville; and a third has been added, on the Shawnee road leading from Lockport to Niagara Falls, called Wallmow. The three villages are all in the town of Wheatfield; their aggregate population, is nearly 2000. They are refugees from religious persecution; their religious faith is purely Lutheran, with the Augsburg confession as their standard. They are not communists, or Fourierites, their lands being held in severalty, and yet there is among them a system of mutual aid and common interests, that grows out of their position and religious organization. The poor among them have small tracts of land set apart for their use, and have the privilege of purchasing upon long credits. They brought with them their ministers, school masters, and mechanics; the excellent indications, meeting and school houses, marked their advent; industry and thrift are the general aspects of their settlements.

RICHARD SMITH.

The name of this Pioneer lawyer upon the Holland Purchase, occurs in the body of the work but incidentally. He was a native of Sharon, Connecticut, a relative of Gov. John Cotton Smith; and is a lineal descendant of Dr. Cotton Mather. He became a resident at Batavia on the first organization of Genesee county, and is now the oldest

APPENDIX.

resident lawyer west of the Genesee river. He has held the office of Surrogate of Genesee county for sixteen years, and has been one of the judges of the county courts. He has lived a uniform life of usefulness; has been the exemplary lawyer and honest citizen; enjoying, at all times, the confidence and esteem of a wide circle of social and business acquaintances.

THE ISLANDS OF THE NIAGARA RIVER.

The Senecas ceded to the State of New York all the islands in the Niagara river, within the jurisdiction of the United States, at a treaty held at Buffalo, September 12th, 1815; the consideration was one thousand dollars down, and five hundred dollars per annum, in perpetuity.

ANCIENT REMAINS.

Since this portion of the work was prepared, many additional interesting localities have been suggested to the author; especially a series of ancient fortifications that exist north of Aurora village, in Erie County, on the banks of Buffalo creek. Mr. E. G. Squier, an industrious and highly intelligent antiquarian, made a partial survey of Western New York, during the last winter, and intends to revisit the region during the approaching summer. His preliminary observations and drawings are already published in the second volume of the American Ethnological Society, and in a separate pamphlet form.

CLERKS IN LAND OFFICE.

In addition to the clerks in the principal office at Batavia, that have been named in the body of the work, there have been the following, nearly in the order in which their names occur:—

John Branon,
Andrew A. Ellicott,
David Goodwin,
Pieter Huidekooper,
Stahley N. Clark,
James Milnor,
John Lowber,
Oliver G. Adams.

William Wood,
Walter M. Seymour,
Abram Van Tuyl,
Lewis D. Stevens,
William Green,
Robert W. Lowber,
Moses Beecher,

Ira A. Blossom was Principal in the branch office at Buffalo, during its whole continuance.

PIONEER PRINTERS UPON THE HOLLAND PURCHASE.

A history of the press in Western New York has been prepared and published by Frederick Follett, Esq. a worthy member of the craft, under the direction of a committee appointed at the Franklin Festival, held at Rochester, in Jan. 1847. The pioneer printers upon the Holland Purchase, not heretofore named in this work, were as follows: —

Olean.—Benjamin F. Smead, 1818.
Ellicottsville.—Richard Hill, 1826.
Lodi.—G. N. Starr, 1829.
Fredonia.—James Percival, 1817.
Mayville.—R. H. Curtiss, 1819.
Panama.—Dean & Hurlbut, 1846.
Warsaw.—L. W. Walker, 1828.
Attica.—David Scott, 1834.

Perry.—G. M. Shipper, 1834.
Pike.—Thomas Carrier, 1838.
Forestville.—W. Snow, 1824.
Jamestown.—Adolphus Fletcher, 1826
Westfield.—H. Newcomb, 1829.
Dunkirk.—Thompson & Carpenter, 1834
Batavia.—Elias Williams, 1807.
Alexander.—P. Lawrence, 1837.

APPENDIX.

MIDDLEBURY ACADEMY.

This institution pioneered the way on the Holland Purchase, beyond the institution of the ordinary district schools. It was the first Academy. It was founded in 1818. At that early day, several of the early settlers there, prominent among whom was Silas Newell, appreciating the value of education, moved in the matter, and in 1819 had built a permanent brick building, and obtained an act of incorporation. The enterprise involved even the mortgaging of the farms of some of the public spirited founders. The Rev. Joshua Bradley was its first Principal; the Rev. Eliphalet M. Spencer was his successor. There are many, now prominent men in Western New York and the Western States, who were educated at this Pioneer Academy.

NOTES.

Page 85.—During the last winter, O. H. Marshall, Esq. of Buffalo, communicated to the New York Historical Society the new fact in the history of this state, that four years after the expedition of Champlain to lake Champlain, he was in another expedition, which embraced the present site of the county of Onondaga. To the same industrious researcher of the early history of our local region, the Historical Society were indebted for the fact that the celebrated Archbishop Fenelon was once a missionary on the northern shore of lake Ontario.

Page 102.—Their "Sainted Seneca maiden." Mohawk should probably be substituted for Seneca, though her abiding place was sometimes with the Senecas. She was called by the Jesuits, "Catharine, the Iroquois Saint." In a letter from Father Choloner, written to one of his superiors in France, dated in 1715, she is described as a remarkable instance of superior piety and devotion; making in early life, vows of chastity, and setting herself apart from her people and the world for devotional exercises and a life of holiness. She died at one of the mission stations upon the St. Lawrence, at the age of twenty-four years. Her tomb became a shrine of prayer, where supplications were offered in her name; pilgrimages were made to it by devotees, for the cure of their diseases. The Grand Vicar of the diocess of Quebec certified that "a diarrhœa which even ipecacuana could not cure," was assuaged by a vow that he would visit the tomb of Catharine. The Commandant at Fort Frontenac certified that his prayers, offered for nine days in succession, in the name of "Catharine Tegakouita," together with a vow to visit her tomb, had cured him of a gout that afflicted him twenty-three years.

Page 187.—Joncaire was made a prisoner by the Senecas when quite young, adopted, grew in high favor with them, and exercised, for a long period, a powerful influence against the English in favor of the French. In 1750, Kalm, the German traveler, found a son of his residing at Lewiston. There were two of his sons, officers, among the French Seneca allies, at the English siege of Fort Niagara. Washington met a son of his at the mouth of French creek, while on a mission to the French, in 1753; and mentions the fact, that he asserted the French claim to the Ohio by virtue of its discovery by La Salle. There are probably descendants of Joncaire among the Senecas.

Page 231.—Some years since, there were exhumed a number of Indian skeletons, in the garden of Col. Bird, at Black Rock, having about them all the accompaniments of Indian war burial. Were not these the killed in the attack upon the English troops?

Page 260.—Judge Thomas Butler, of Niagara, who was intimately acquainted with

APPENDIX.

Joseph Brant and his personal history, confirms the position of Mr. Draper, in reference to his birth place.

Page 330.—The author supposed he had derived his account of the death of Mr. Williamson from a reliable source, and yet it would seem to be erroneous. In the address which Gen. Porter prepared to deliver at Geneva, he states that Mr. Williamson had embarked from England at the first "dawnings of liberty and symptoms of revolution," in South America, with an intention to take a conspicuous part in the contest; and that he died on his passage.

Page 357.—In compiling the biographical sketch of Robert Morris, the author has availed himself of information derived directly from his son, the late Thomas Morris, Esq. of New York, from an article in the American Review, to the writer of which he contributed some information, and from original manuscripts obtained from other sources.

Page 431.—In the preparation of the brief biography of the family of Ellicotts, the author relied upon some sketches prepared for a newspaper at Ellicott's Mills, Md. they seeming the most authentic data within his reach. From some reminiscences that have since been furnished him, it would seem that the ancestors, Andrew Ellicott and Ann Bye, came from "Collumpton," in Devonshire, south part of England, instead of "Cullopton, in Wales;" that they settled, originally, in Pennsylvania, and not New York; and that their marriage took place in Bucks county, in 1731. This may be the truer history, and yet it is strangely at variance with the fragment of verse and the date attached to it, which is attributed to the maternal ancestor, "Ann Bye."

Page 475.—It should have been added, that Gen. Warren passed through the several grades of militia offices, up to that of Major General, and that he served in the war of 1812, and participated in several engagements.

Page 484.—The details of the war of 1812 have not taken a range wide enough to embrace such reminiscences as the one promised upon this page. There was a singular and mournful fatality attending the family of the early pioneer mentioned by Judge Porter, in connection with one of his early advents, and by the author, in connection with some sketches of early settlement in Wyoming,—Orange Brace. At the commencement of the war, the family consisted of the parents, three sons, and three daughters. The old gentleman and one of the sons went upon the lines under Smyth's proclamation, and both died at Buffalo, of the prevailing epidemic; and a daughter died at Canandaigua, where she was attending school, about the same time. A son-in-law, Ardin Merril, was afterwards killed on board of a ferry boat, near the Canada shore, opposite Black Rock. The neighborhood of their residence, in Sheldon, was more than ordinarily afflicted; almost every family in it mourned the death of one or more of its members.

Page 597.—The names of those, as far as recollected, who had resolved not to let Buffalo be captured without some show of defence, were Seth Grosvenor, the early Buffalo merchant, now a resident of the city of New York; Elijah D. Efner, who became a citizen of Buffalo, in 1808; after serving as a United States soldier, in some of the early north-western campaigns, under Gen. Harrison, during which he was engaged in the battle of the Thames, he returned, and has since remained, an enterprising and useful citizen; his fine residence, on the high grounds between the city and Black Rock, furnishing evidence of the success that has attended a life of activity and industry; James Sweeny, his early partner in business, a brother of Col. John Sweeny, of Tonawanda; Robert Kaene, an early citizen of Buffalo, whose name, in other instances, is honorably associated with the war of 1812; Elisha Foster, now of Fredonia, and

Messrs. Hull & Johnson, of whom the author has no recollections or memorandums They had taken the cannon from an old beached vessel, mounted it upon truck wheels, and were contesting British conquest bravely, when one of the wheels broke, just as Col. Chapin went to meet the invaders with a flag of truce.

Page 539.—Joncaire told Charlevoix that at a place the Iroquois called "Ganos," (the present Seneca name of Oil Spring Reservation is "Ganohs," differing, as will be seen, but slightly,) there was a spring, the waters of which were like oil, and their taste like iron; and he also told him that at a little distance from it there was another of the same character, the waters of which were used by the savages to cure all manner of diseases. The spring is also described minutely in the Jesuit Relations for 1656 and '57. It is there said that the oil is used by the Indians to "anoint themselves, and to grease their heads and bodies;" and in the same connection we recognise the fact that the Jesuits had a knowledge of the Sulphur Springs at Avon.

Page 616.—A deserved tribute to the memory of Gen. Porter has been rendered by the late Secretary of War, Gov. Marcy, in bestowing the name "FORT PORTER," upon the U. S. fortification recently erected at Black Rock.

BRIEF APPENDIX TO SECOND EDITION.

PROJECTION OF THE ERIE CANAL. — The first suggestion of an overland navigable canal, such as the Erie Canal now is, connecting the waters of the Hudson and Lake Erie, was undoubtedly that made to Col. Mynderse, by Jesse Hawley, as noted on page 629. The first public essay upon the subject, was that published in the "Pittsburgh Commonwealth" of date, Jan. 14, 1807, which was written by Jesse Hawley. The following letter was writted by him in the July following, previous, as will be observed, to the first essay of "Hercules" in the Ontario Messenger. It has never before been published, as the author infers from observation and enquiry. It was found among the papers of Mr. Granger, and as it would seem, has hitherto been overlooked in the searches that have been made for the early historical reminiscences of the Erie Canal. Mr. Hawley, having zealously espoused the over land canal, was jealous of the proposed survey of the Oswego River, and the taking of the "elevation of the waters of Lake Erie, above those of Ontario," and interposed his letter to divert the attention of his friend Mr. Granger from the Lake route. — The author inserts the letter as one intimately connected with the history of our internal improvments, and deserving of preservation in an enduring form: —

"Greensburg, Pa., 12th July, 1807.

Erastus Granger, Esq.

Sir. — Gideon Granger, Esq. in passing through this place, on his late tour to New Connecticut, observed in a conversation with some gentlemen of this place, that the United States government were turning their attention to the subject of Canals — and that their first object was to open a course of inland navigation, which would most extensively communicate with the Atlantic and its ports, and the great western waters and territory of the United States, and by extending the commercial connections of the eastern and western sections of the American Empire, would cultivate and strengthen that of the social also, which would aid in preventing a dismemberment of them.

He observed that the government considered the route through the State of New York as best calculated for the purpose, and had employed engineers to examine the Mohawk, Wood Creek, Oswego River, &c. — and that you were to be employed to take the elovation of the waters of Lake Erie above those of Ontario, &c.

Sir, — Although I have no individual interest in the subject, yet I feel even a forwardness to communicate the superficial information which I possess on the subject, and which I have acquired by a very partial attachment to it.

APPENDIX.

The favorite idea of mine is to *tap Lake Erie about your place, and Canal it to the Mohawk at or about Utica.*

Ellicott's map of the Holland Purchase lays down the elevation of Erie above that of Ontario, 450 feet. Say, Utica is 50 feet above Ontario also, (and I think it large enough,) leaves Erie 400 feet above Utica; — is equal to about 2 feet fall per mile, averaged on the whole distance. I think it is allowed that one foot fall in the mile gives a current of six miles per hour. If so, the 400 feet fall would require some Locks, and through that almost level country they could be thrown on almost any part of the route, to the best advantage. After pursuing a northerly course from its departure at your place, for the purpose of obtaining a fall to give it current, it could wind easterly, and probably have to cross the Tonewanta; thence directly east, and cross the Genesee, probably below the junction of Allen's Creek. Thence fall near to, and probably into the bed of Mud Creek, and pursue its channel, with improvements, into and thence down the Seneca River, to about the head of Jack's Rifts. Thence leaving that to the left, run along the foot of the hills and high grounds of Onondaga county, &c. &c., on to Utica.

This Canal would command the two grand *desideratum* of nature, viz. an inexhaustable fountain of water, capable of being gauged to any dimensions required to preserve the navigation for ever in good order, except the interruptions of port, and absolute head and fall which could be pitched by the ingenuity of man almost to his wishes It would also improve the navigation of the Mohawk by the discharge of its surplus water — and could be made productive of some revenue by renting or selling the mill sites made at the places where it would be necessary to raise its bed, or channels, by banking; which would be very valuable through the most of that country, natural ones being scarce; and still more for their convenience of navigation.

To pursue the present water route, while it could, indeed, be much improved by art, still would be subject to *insurmountable* impediments, The upper streams of the Mohawk and Wood Creek afford to the Canal at Rome, and the passages west to Oneida Lake, and east to Utica in the drought of mid-summer, but a stinted supply of water, and a very tedious and laborious passage to boats even of seven and five tons burthen. The Mohawk even below Utica is embarrassed with stinted waters during a large part, (say several months of the season.) This is fully demonstrated by the charges of water transport being as dear as those of the land. To these add the tedious delay of the numerous Locks additional — the 450 feet fall from Erie to Ontario — say 50 feet descent of water without Locks — leaves 400 feet to be locked — say 10 feet to each Lock — (about the average of those at Little Falls) — are 40 Locks; — to these add one at Oswego Falls, with one already at Rome, with its Canal — are 42 Locks.

The proposed Canal would not require, more than, say from 5 to 10 Locks — with its distance abridged, say 50 miles, and the sometimes dangerous navigation of the Ontario rendered safe. Say the difference of number of Locks to be 30 — the expense of which would Canal almost as many miles of good level ground.

To obviate the objection of "incalculable expense," I will extract from Pinkerton's Geography, some partial data; — vol. 1, p. 199, speaking of the Canal of Languedoc, in France, says, this noble Canal begins in the bay of Languedoc.— At St. Ferrol is a reservoir of 595 acres of water," (on the highest ground to supply it.) "It enters the Garronne ¼ mile below Tolouse; its breadth including the towing path is 144 feet; the depth, 6 feet; length 64 French leagues, or about 180 English miles; 15 years labor were employed, the expense more than £ 500,000 Sterling" — say equal to $ 2,500,000. Also, speaking of Denmark, vol. 1, p. 388. "The Canal of Keil is intended to unite the Baltic with the Eydor River, which flows into the German Sea. Its length is 20½ English miles; breadth, 100 feet at top and 54 at bottom; the least depth about 10 feet, so as to admit vessels of about 120 tons; finished in about twelve years."

Say the Reservoir of 595 acres is equal to expense, (which is very conjectural) of 20 miles Canal. This would make the Canal of Languedoc equal to 200 miles — about the distance from Buffalo to Utica, and to cost of $2,500,000. Say from the difference in the price of labor between this country and France, it should cost $5,000,000; or to average, $25,000 per mile or nearly $80 per rod. But the Canal of Languedoc must have passed over some very uneven ground and have required many more Locks than this would do; and Locks are the vortex of expense.

To point out all the advantages — the connections of interest and of Empire — the vast extension of internal commerce — a new and common channel of the Trade of Upper Canada — its aid in regulating the excess of markets between old and new settlements — the rapid settlement of a new country by its facility to emigration — its facility and consequent familier intercourse — its enhancement of the value of property, probably, to once, twice, thrice, and eventually, four times the amount of its first cost; — and its deriving from these generative powers for other Canals, yet untold and unconceived — are themes which might fill a volume. But the details of these items numerous items yet unknown, I must leave to the suggestions of your superior genius.

I presume the magnitude of the subject will form a sufficient apology for my intrusion of it upon your attention. While most of the subjects hinted at *cannot but be imperfect;* yet, sufficiently correct to establish the *main question of* POSSIBILITY.

I am Respectfully,
Yours &c.
JESSE HAWLEY

P. S. — While with a letter in my hand, I will observe on the several letters I have written you on business, under the firm of "Hawley & Corl," of Geneva. If you have received any letters from Detroit, I hope you have been so obliging as to have forwarded them according to my last advice, viz., to Mr. Samuel Colt, of Geneva. If you should yet receive any I have to request the same attention.

The business of that firm has been unfortunate for me. I have been in exile for some months past, in consequence of its difficulties; but now expect to deposit myself in Canandaigua jail in a few weeks. That has caused some delay to this letter.

Yours,   "J. H."

ANCIENT FORTIFICATION ON BUFFALO CREEK. — The author was aware, when the first edition of this work went to press, that he had omitted notices of many localities within the limits of the Holland Purchase, where Ancient Remains were distinctly to be traced; but it was not until further examinations had been made, and more full information had been acquired, that he was aware of the great extent of these interesting subjects of investigation and speculation. The whole field has as yet been but partially explored, but it is hoped that enough has been done to elicit further inquiry, and induce a survey of the whole region of Western New York, with reference to supplying that which should have been provided for in the munificent historical and scientific enterprise now prosecuting by our State.

Upon the middle branch of Buffalo Creek, three and a half miles from the village of Aurora, on the Seneca Indian Reservation, there are the remains of one of the largest class of ancient fortifications. A raised work, or mound of earth, enclosed an area of two acres. It occupied a bluff point, overlooking a bend of the stream, its location evincing much of modern military science. In an early period of the settlement of the country the whole work could be distinctly traced. Upon the spot and in the immediate vicinity, almost as often as the plough or the spade is put into the ground, relics, clearly distinguishable from those that mark the later occupancy of the Indian race, are found.

As in other instances, the spot had attractions for the successive Indian Nations that possessed this region of the Lakes — the Eries, the Neuter Nation, and the Iroquois; for there are palpable evidences of a continued occupancy, extending down to our own period. Second, and even third timber growths were apparent over a space of fifty or sixty acres. When the French Franciscan and Jesuit Missionaries, and Fur traders, came to this region, they undoubtedly found there a considerable settlement of the Iroquois, and made it one of their principal stations. The author found in the posssssion of Mr. John T. King, the present owner of the land, numerous relics he had ploughed up in his fields, and among them two large French *padlocks;* one of them, especially, in its rude construction, marking an early period of the science of lock making. It is of a size unparalelled in locks of modern construction, unique in shape, resembling the padlocks that we see in pictures, upon the doors of ancient castles, prisons, and monasteries. Intelligent foreigners say that such locks are found now in France and Germany, but are regarded there as those of primitive construction. The padlocks were both locked; from which circumstance we may well infer that the French made a hurried evacuation of the locality, during one of the periods of hostile demonstrations on the part of the Iroquois; and it is not likely that such articles would have been left behind in a peaceful or premeditated departure

ANCIENT RECORD, OR TABLET. — In the year 1809, a COPPER PLATE was ploughed up in a field belonging to Mr. Ephriam Woodruff, the early pioneer blacksmith, in Willink, now Aurora.) Those who saw it differ in reference to its size; the average of their recollections would make it twelve by sixteen inches; in thickness not far from the 8th of an inch. It had engraved upon one side of it, in regular lines, extending the whole width of the plate, what would appear to have been some record, or as we may well imagine some brief code of laws, in manner and form, like the tablets of the early nations to which allusions are made in both sacred and profane history. The letters, hyroglyphics, or characters, are described as having a close resemblance to the "old fashioned printed music notes." Upon the reverse side of the plate at each corner, there was an engraved image, resembling, (in the language of one of the author's informants,) some of the pictures in Stevens' work on the ruins of Central America.

Unfortunately for those who take a deep interest in this branch of American history — who are eager to catch even glimpses of that which is involved in so much obscurity, the mysterious plate was a sacrifice to the exigencies of that early period of settlement:— After being looked upon with wonder, (as it would be now,) those who possessed it, and were somewhat unmindful of its value, allowed it to be worked up — converted into kitchen utensils — a dipper and a skimmer. They were not Antiquarians, as must be inferred, and a sheet of copper in those primitive times, was a rarity that must have strongly inclined them to utilitarianism. A surviving son of the early blacksmith, who worked up the plate, is quite confident that he did not hammer out the whole of the engraved lines, All traces of the dipper are lost, but it is confidently believed that the skimmer has been preserved in a branch of the Woodruff family, now residing at the west. If so, and there are any portion of the engraved lines yet legible, it will be put into the hands of some one competent to the task of interpretation. But a partial understanding of the character of the mysterious relic, can, however, be anticipated. But we may well infer, that the plate, had, it been preserved entire, would have furnished something more decisive than any thing that has yet been discovered; and perhaps, have determined what race or people it was that history, and even tradition has lost sight of; but of whose occupancy of this region, there are so numerous and palpable evidences.

Though it is travelling somewhat beyond his bounds, the author is constrained to notice two extraordinary relics that came under his observation during the last summer. A section of an oak tree is now in the possession of Gen. O. G. Barney of Newark, Wayne county, which contains an incision resembling the box made in the maple trees of our forest in the process of tapping, and of about the same dimensions. There is little to distinguish it from cuts made in trees, by our woodsmen, with the common modern axe, The impressions made at each successive blow are about the same as made by the axemen of the present day. *Over this incision there were four hundred and sixty concentric circles, or grains.* Counting a year for each circle, as observation and the conclusions of naturalists enable us to do, and we are forced to the conclusion that this chopping was done with a sharp axe, about the year 1375: one hundred and twenty-two years before Cabot discovered the northern continent of America; and 159 years before Cartier entered and sailed up the St. Lawrence.

During the last summer, in extracting a pine stump upon the farm of Judge Ellsworth, on the banks of Crooked Lake, in Yates county, a small *copper hatchet* was taken out of the pit made by extracting the tap root. The tree was nearly *five hundred years old.*

HUMAN, AND ANIMAL SKELETONS. — In the the village of Pekin, Niagara county, during the last summer, in the process of road making, a large number of human skeletons were excavated from a depth of about 18 inches. There was a striking peculiarity In the position in which they were found. A large number of skulls dislocated from the under jaws were placed in a row, and over them, the under jaws, and the other bones of the human frame were promiscuously mingled.

A few rods from this deposit of human bones, on the slope of the Mountain Ridge, a large niche in the rock was filled with the bones of animals; most of which, especially the jaws and bones of the fore legs, resembled those of bears, of a large size.

PAGE 143. — Although is is to be inferred from notes that follow, it should have been directly stated, that the translation from which the account of De Nonville's expedition was derived, was made by O. H. Marshall, Esq. from the Paris documents, and communicated to the New York Historical Society, by whom it was published in a pamphlet form. — Mr. M. accompanied his translation with a drawing of the battle ground between De Nonville and the Senecas, and numerous proofs of the identity of the location.

PAGE 192. — In a lecture delivered before the Young Men's Association of Buffalo last winter, Mr. Marshall assumes that the earliest notice of Niagara Falls on record, is that of Father Ragueneau, in 1648. He says: — " South of the Neuter Nation is a great Lake, called Erie, almost 200 leagues in circumference, into which is discharged the Fresh Sea; or Lake Huron. This Lake Erie, is precipitated by a *cataract* of frightful hoight into a third Lake, called Ontario, and by us St. Louis."

PAGE 311. — The name of the early drover who was murdered on the Ridge Road, was Nehemiah Street.

PAGE 381. — At the suggestion of George Hosmer, Esq. of Avon, the author corrects an error which does great injustice to a worthy and reputable man. Peterson, the early tavern keeper, at Caledonia Springs, was never implicated as is stated. He was preceded by two foreigners, Moffat and Kane, who, under pretence of keeping a house of entertainment, were undoubtedly robbers. — They were possessed of much valuable property, unsuited to their condition in life, such as watches, jewelry, fine linen, and such articles of furniture as could only be expected in the houses of the wealthy. They left the country to escape the consequences of the probably just suspicions of the early settlers of that region.

PAGE 555. — In our necessarily brief notices of pioneer settlers in Orleans county, the name of Judge John Lee, should not have been overlooked. He settled in the town of Barre, in 1816, becoming the founder of what was called "Lee's Settlement." The town was named at his suggestion, after his native town, Barre, in Massachusetts. He was one of that numerous class of early settlers upon the Holland Purchase — (all of whom the author would have been glad to have noticed in these pages,) — whose memories are entitled to tributes of gratitude from those who are now enjoying the eminent blessings to which their exertions have so largely contributed. His house was open to those who were exploring the new country with reference to settlement; and when located in their wilderness homes, he was ever ready to render them those offices of kindness which none but those who have been settlers in a new country, know how to appreciate. He was the first P. M. in Barre, and filled the office of a county Judge under the old county organization. He died in 1825, aged 60 years. He left a large family of sons and daughters, most of whom are now heads of families, and residents of Orleans county

www.ingramcontent.com/pod-product-compliance
Lightning Source LLC
Chambersburg PA
CBHW030257080526
44584CB00012B/344